P

"The proof of goodness is us[...] ear right off the bat that Dickson has wr[...]

ngeles Times

"Among the few great biographies set in sports. Beyond that it is the story of a singular fellow whose energy, determination, wit, and powerful commitment to fairness spiced with an unquenchable sense of the absurd enabled him to live an exceptionally full and passionate life."
—Bill Littlefield, *The Boston Globe*

"Dickson . . . has done more than write the best baseball biography so far this decade. He's written an important piece of baseball history."
—Allen Barra, *Chicago Tribune*

"*Bill Veeck*, in the language of the subject, is a homerun—a bases clearer. The story of the remarkable full life of this pioneering baseball character is told with the steadiness, detail and flare that we have come to expect from Paul Dickson, the premier all-star writer and reporter. The book is great fun—much like being in the bleachers during a day game."
—Jim Lehrer

"Paul Dickson meticulously chronicles Veeck's engaging story . . . Dickson's exhaustive research not only allows readers to feel as though they're walking through Veeck's daily routines with him, but expertly provides context to his life with comprehensive narratives of baseball's story lines and the social issues of the day . . . Dickson does it artfully and thoroughly in a compelling biography of one of the game's legendary figures."
—Thom Henninger, *Baseball Digest*

"Bill Veeck has finally met his match. Paul Dickson, consummate baseball historian, has given Veeck the biography he deserves. Meticulously reported and exhaustively researched, *Bill Veeck: Baseball's Greatest Maverick* is, like its subject, a show-stopper."
—Jane Leavy, author of *The Last Boy: Mickey Mantle and the End of America's Childhood* and *Sandy Koufax*

"Veeck was a one of a kind whose impact reached beyond the ballpark, into the very fiber of 20th-century America. Dickson has captured it all in entertaining fashion."   —James Bailey, *Baseball America*

"Paul Dickson has written the comprehensive biography."
                    —Dave Hoekstra, *Chicago Sun-Times*

"Bill Veeck didn't want to break rules, he insisted, just 'test their elasticity.' He wasn't talking only about baseball. The master showman, who famously sent a three-foot-seven-inch batter to the plate, also desegregated the American League and proudly marched in the funeral procession for Dr. Martin Luther King—on his peg leg and without crutches. *Bill Veeck* revisits a golden age for baseball, a pivotal time for America and some hilarious moments in the life of a man who helped to change both."   —Clarence Page

"Paul Dickson has written a definitive biography."
                    —Vick Mickunas, *Dayton Daily News*

"Bill Veeck was inventive, courageous, principled, and hugely influential—the Thomas Paine of a revolutionary time in baseball . . . He has awaited a clear-eyed admiring chronicler, and in Paul Dickson he has found him. This amazingly detailed, delicious biography is, as its subject might have titled it, VEECK—AS IN SPEC-tacular!"
                    —John Thorn, Official Historian, Major League Baseball,
                    and author of *Baseball in the Garden of Eden*

"We knew Bill Veeck was the baron of ballyhoo. We didn't know (or at least I didn't) that he was a patriot as high-flying as Ted Williams, a racial barrier-buster as fearless as Branch Rickey, a gadfly who set the mold for Charlie Finley, and a one-of-a-kind iconoclast who was irresistible. So don't resist. Buy Paul Dickson's new book and have a blast."
                    —Larry Tye, author of *Satchel:*
                    The Life and Times of an American Legend

"Any man who wanted to be included on Richard Nixon's enemies list is worthy of a searching biography—and Paul Dickson has been kind enough to do that for us with his compelling portrait of the unregenerate Bill Veeck."
                    —Ray Robinson, author of *Iron Horse: Lou Gehrig in His Time*

"A definitive look at one of baseball's greatest innovators and ambassadors. A must-read."   —Claire Smith, ESPN

"Thorough, entertaining, and superb."
                                        —Bill Littlefield, NPR's *Only A Game*

"Dickson is a master with words . . . He's got a voice that works with this subject, thankfully, and keeps it on track when all craziness could be breaking out . . . In fact, it's about time, and there has to be a way for someone to use this as a launching point for a movie about Veeck's life on the big screen."   —Tom Hoffarth, *Los Angeles Daily News*

"*Bill Veeck: Baseball's Greatest Maverick* is a very fine baseball biography that compares with the best work that has been published on the leaders of the sport over the years. Paul Dickson's breezy style illuminates not only the Bill Veeck of legend, but also the real Bill Veeck who worked hard at his craft even as he honed to a fine art the persona of a maverick and a 'hustler,' the term Veeck liked best in characterizing himself . . . Lost in all of the showmanship, publicity and stunts, Dickson concludes, was a tremendously sound baseball and business mind."
                                                        —Roger Launius,
                        The Washington Independent Review of Books

"I was vastly entertained by Paul Dickson's biography of Bill Veeck, the wild man baseball impresario from Chicago. In addition to being an authoritative chronicle of how the game used to be in that halcyon fifty years between 1930 and 1980, it also gives off a reminiscent aura of grass outfields, the comforting feel of a hard bleacher seat, and airmade redolent of popcorn and tobacco . . . One of the strong points of this book is the easy-reading, yet knowledgeable voice of the author."
                        —James Srodes, *The American Spectator*

"[S]ure to entertain is Paul Dickson's latest: *Bill Veeck: Baseball's Greatest Maverick*. As you'd expect, Veeck's trials, tribulations and experiments with the great game as its greatest promoter may well hold center stage, but Dickson has done something with this biography that I particularly loved . . . which is to write a book that also covers this man's life outside of the game"
                                    —Christina Kahrl, ESPN, *SweetSpot*

"In this crisply written, admiring but never fawning chronicle, Dickson makes a strong case for Veeck as the most influential baseball executive who ever lived. He was certainly the most entertaining."

—**Marc Mohan**, *The Oregonian*

"In his lively (and occasionally beatific) biography, baseball and cultural historian Paul Dickson brings Veeck to life, relentlessly digging into his career and times to create a portrait of the kind of guy you'd like to have in your corner—or at your table for a drink."

—**Chris Foran**, *Milwaukee Journal Sentinel*

"Paul Dickson has knocked another one out of the park with *Bill Veeck: Baseball's Greatest Maverick* a skillfully written biography, scrupulously researched, brimming with revealing anecdotes and historical detail . . . So if you're planning your summer reading list, I recommend you place Dickson's enlightening and highly entertaining biography on one of baseball's most combative if influential owners at the very top of your list."

—**Bill Lucey**, *The Morning Delivery*

"Dickson brings the larger-than-life presence of Veeck into sharper focus, and re-introduces his innovative baseball mind in a fresh light. It's a smart, detailed and precise read, showing the same delightful candor that Veeck displayed during his heyday."   —**Bob D'Angelo**, *The Tampa Tribune*

"[Veeck] never truly got the recognition he deserved. Now he has."

—*Harvey Frommer's Sports Book Reviews*

"*Bill Veeck* is as good as it gets when it comes to describing an American original. FIVE STARS."   —*Sports Book Review Center*

BILL VEECK

Baseball's Greatest Maverick

PAUL DICKSON

WALKER & COMPANY
New York

To Nancy: always and forever.

With an additional dedicatory nod to Dave Kelly for decades of help as the "go to" sports expert at the Library of Congress.

Published by Walker Publishing Company, Inc., New York
A Division of Bloomsbury Publishing

Frontispiece: Jim Hansen photograph of Bill Veeck in 1959 shortly after having taken over the Chicago White Sox. Hansen was a staff photographer for *LOOK*. The image is from the *LOOK* Magazine Collection, Library of Congress Prints and Photographs Division, and appears with the permission of Mrs. James T. Hansen.

All papers used by Walker & Company are natural, recyclable products made from wood grown in well-managed forests. The manufacturing processes conform to the environmental regulations of the country of origin.

LIBRARY OF CONGRESS CATALOGING-IN-PUBLICATION DATA HAS BEEN APPLIED FOR.

ISBN: 978-0-8027-1778-8 (hardcover)

Visit Walker & Company's website at www.walkerbooks.com

First published by Walker & Company in 2012
This paperback edition published in 2013

Paperback ISBN: 978-0-8027-7830-7

1 3 5 7 9 10 8 6 4 2

Typeset by Westchester Book Group
Printed in the U.S.A.

Bill Veeck . . . my choice for the most colorful baseball guy of all time. It's more than that. Give me a last supper with half a dozen people of my choosing, living or dead, and Veeck is at the table.

—DOUG MOE, *CAPITAL TIMES* AND *WISCONSIN STATE JOURNAL*, OCTOBER 20, 2005

Contents

Prologue

The tendency today is to remember Bill Veeck as the guy who would do anything for a laugh or publicity—an irascible showman. Many think of him simply as the eccentric baseball owner who sent a midget, a man named Eddie Gaedel, to the plate for the St. Louis Browns in a 1951 game against the Detroit Tigers, or as the man responsible for one of baseball's most ill-advised promotions, the infamous 1979 Disco Demolition Night, when a stoned mob wrought havoc on Comiskey Park. Former *Chicago Tribune* columnist David Israel called it "Veeckstock"; others called it a disgrace.

But Bill Veeck was much, much more. As a four-time major-league team owner, he was a transformational figure in the history of baseball. Nonconformist, visionary, and showman extraordinaire, he spent a lifetime challenging baseball's staid establishment, cultivating powerful enemies the way others cultivate powerful friends. Today, the game reflects much of what he fought for, and his influence is still much in evidence. "Bill Veeck delighted in being everyman's owner," remembered Andy MacPhail, president of Baseball Operations for the Baltimore Orioles, in a 2009 interview. "His influence is everywhere—all those activities going on at the modern ballpark outside the white lines can in some way be traced back to Veeck."[1]

Physically, Bill Veeck was a larger-than-life figure—a tall, chain-smoking, charismatic, photogenic redhead with a big open face and a voice so deep and compelling that writer Dave Kindred said it "came as a train in the night." He drank prodigious amounts of beer and was known to consume the reddest of red meat. "A group of us went out with him after a World Series game in New York in the early 1960s," Cliff Kachline, then with *The Sporting News*, recalled, "and Veeck orders a steak extra rare. What we found out was that he really meant to bring it from the kitchen meat locker absolutely raw."[2]

If there were excesses, there were also strict limits. Veeck never, ever swore, nor would he let anyone else do his dirty work for him if he could help it. Decades later, those who played for him recall his simple courtesies, which then were rare and today are nonexistent. Virgil Trucks, who started the 1953 season with the St. Louis Browns, was summoned by Veeck one day in 1953 and informed that he had been traded to the Chicago White Sox. "He was the only man to call me into his office to tell me I was traded, and I was traded five times. All the other times I heard it on radio or TV, or read it in the newspapers. So that speaks for what kind of man Bill Veeck was."[3]

Veeck had great relations with the press, yet refused to share confidential information, a fact attested to by Ray Grebey, chief negotiator for the twenty-six owners in baseball's labor wars leading up to the 1981 baseball strike and a friend of Veeck's for more than forty years: "Bill was incapable of leaking anything given to him in confidence."[4]

By nature, he was quick-witted, uninhibited, irreverent, quick to anger, stubborn, and prone to hyperbole. He was also funny and able to coax laughter out of the darkest situations. "Bill Veeck is obviously a dangerous man—he knows how to laugh and how to think," sportswriter Dick Schaap once wrote on a jacket blurb for one of Veeck's three memoirs.[5]

During World War II, he chose not to accept a deferment from military service and instead enlisted in the Marine Corps. He then demanded to be sent to a war zone, where he suffered an injury that would lead to a series of amputations and create unfathomable pain. This would, as his friend Bert Randolph Sugar, the boxing writer, expressed it, "put him on the edge of the volcano between good health and bad health for the rest of his life."[6] "I saw him with welts and sores that would have brought a mere mortal down. I can tell you that except for a wince or trouble getting up and down our stairs in Maryland, he never complained," said his son Mike Veeck, adding that he behaved the same way around his family as he did in the outside world.[7]

"Suffering is overrated—it doesn't teach you anything" was Veeck's mantra, and he turned his missing leg into a sight gag. He took great glee in lighting a cigarette, pulling up his pant leg, and using the ashtray he had carved into the wood. When he took a bad fall at the Baltimore airport, an attendant asked, "Can I call you a doctor?" "No," he shot back, "it's the wooden leg—get me a carpenter."

Bill Veeck brought change to both the business and conscience of baseball. He was a prime mover in the racial integration of the game, both on the field and in the front office. He was the first to integrate the American League when he signed Larry Doby eleven weeks after Jackie Robinson debuted in the National League. In his drive to win the 1948 pennant, he signed the legendary Satchel Paige despite knowing he would be criticized for doing so. By the beginning of the 1949 season, he had fourteen black players under contract, including future stars Orestes "Minnie" Miñoso and Luke Easter. He brought in the second black manager, again Larry Doby. He also brought the African American John H. Johnson, the founder of *Ebony* magazine, into an ownership position as part of a syndicate that bought the Chicago White Sox in 1975.

Veeck loved the game of baseball, both on the field and outside the lines. He would do anything to accomplish what he believed would make it better, no matter how outrageous. Increasing the fans' happiness and having fun were his sacraments.

Alternately playing the role of innovator, catalyst, and gadfly, Veeck pushed for many of the major changes in the game that took place during the last two-thirds of the twentieth century, and he pioneered new ways to treat baseball as a successful business. His wildly innovative marketing techniques drew in so many new fans that he set records for ballpark attendance.

Elements of the game we take for granted today—the designated hitter, interleague play, the playoff system, free agency, an expanded league—were all things that Veeck advocated many years before they went into effect. In 1986, the great slugger Hank Greenberg, his close friend and sometime business partner, told the *New York Times*: "Bill brought baseball into the 20th century. Before Bill, baseball was just winning or losing. But he made it fun to be at the ballpark." Veeck's combination of financial creativity and marketing genius was unlike anything else in the history of sports. Today he is seen as a man decades ahead of his time. In 2004, *Business Week* picked him as one of the great business innovators of the previous seventy-five years. He accomplished this as the last owner to purchase a Major League Baseball franchise without his own personal fortune.[8]

Veeck successively owned three major-league teams—the Cleveland Indians (1946–49), the St. Louis Browns (1951–53), and the Chicago White Sox (twice: 1959–61 and 1975–81). The highlight of his baseball career came in 1948, when his Indians won both the American League pennant and the World Series. It was one of the most exciting—if not *the* most exciting—single season of the postwar golden age of baseball. His revival of the Go-Go White Sox in 1959, and then again in 1977 with his South Side Hit Men, are two of the great comeback stories in baseball history.

Veeck had a long-running feud with the New York Yankees, whose stodginess and refusal to integrate he hated as much as they hated his flamboyance. He relished the irony that his player Satchel Paige gave the Yankees an attendance boost whenever he pitched in Yankee Stadium. "Hating the Yankees isn't part of my act," Veeck said. "It is one of those exquisite times when life and art are in perfect conjunction." He played David to the Yankees Goliath and did everything he could to get under their skin. He also had an uncanny ability to beat them at their own game. From 1947 to 1964, the Yankees were denied the American League pennant only three times—twice by a Veeck-owned team and once by a team that he had built more or less from scratch and that was deeply dependent on men of color.[9]

His life entwined with those of many well-known figures of the twentieth century, both inside and outside of baseball: Hank Greenberg, Satchel Paige, Larry Doby, Lou Boudreau, Casey Stengel, Studs Terkel, Jimmy Breslin, Bob Hope, Bing Crosby, George Steinbrenner, John F. Kennedy, Connie Mack, Paul Newman, Minnie Miñoso, Abe Saperstein, Thurgood Marshall, Gene Autry, Al Capone, Orson Welles, Frank Sinatra, Ty Cobb, Jesse Jackson, Elston Howard, Ray Kroc, Salvador Dalí, and Jack Ruby, to name a few. They too are part of this story, even if they played only cameo roles.

Although he probably did as much or more than any other individual to change the game in the decades following World War II, Veeck did it as a self-anointed outcast. He baited and berated those in power, including umpires. Most owners despised him in return and at critical junctures tried and sometimes succeeded in keeping him out of the game, but he kept coming back.

Ed Linn, who co-wrote three books with Veeck, asked rhetorically in an article in *Sport* magazine why the other owners disliked Veeck. "Apparently they hate Veeck because he has always looked upon baseball as a form of entertainment rather than a religious experience," Linn answered himself, adding that Veeck would do anything to get fans to the ballpark and keep them coming back. William Barry Furlong, a writer who had a special affinity for Veeck, wrote that the real reason for his alienation from the other owners was that Veeck was a person of "greater dimensions and grander vision than his contemporaries." He added: "All this would be tolerable if Veeck fitted the baseball men's image of such an individual—i.e., a failure. But his success offers a suggestion of their own inadequacy and threatens some of the longtime institutions of baseball, such as the domination of the American League by the Yankees."[10]

Marty Appel, who knew Veeck when he served as head of public relations for the New York Yankees, saw it in the starker terms of an upstart confronting an old-boy network: "They were wealthy Republicans and he wasn't."[11]

If most of his fellow owners hated him, writers and sportscasters loved him. Veeck owned the writers because he was so accessible. He would be there game after game telling stories and answering questions. To the late Jim Murray of the Los Angeles Times, Veeck was "America's gadfly." To Robert W. Creamer, who wrote Veeck's Sports Illustrated obituary, he was "more than anything else . . . a fresh breeze blowing through baseball." The late William Barry Furlong wrote of him: "To the public, Bill Veeck . . . is a brashly clamorous individual who has fashioned a brilliant career out of defying the customs, conventions and crustaceans of baseball. It is an authentic yet one-dimensional view. For Veeck is also an intelligent, impetuous, whimsical, stubborn, tough-fibered, tireless individual with a vast capacity for living and a deep appreciation for humanity." As Furlong's prose attests, Bill Veeck attracted adjectives the way others attract mosquitoes—he was also called imaginative, uninhibited, innovative, and fiercely independent, and, on the negative side, confrontational and contentious.[12] "Veeck is a genius, as rare as fragrant cheese," wrote Wells Twombly of the San Francisco Examiner. Dick Victory, writing for the Evening Star in 1970, said that Veeck had at that point "probably been called a 'maverick' more times than any other man associated with any sport." Veeck loved the role of gadfly to the point where he felt snubbed when not singled out as an enemy of the establishment. "One of the most disappointing moments of his life," his widow, Mary Frances Veeck, said, "was the moment he learned he was not on President's Nixon's famous enem[ies] list."[13]

Veeck was an everyman who believed his common touch was the secret of his success. Born into a life of privilege, he attended and quickly departed the finest schools and always chose to take the path that veered away from comfort. Mary Frances Veeck's favorite way of putting it was that Bill "was born on the right side of the tracks, and dragged himself to the other side—and then lived comfortably on both."[14]

Even as a team owner, he insisted on sitting in the bleachers, in part because of his belief that one's knowledge of baseball is in inverse proportion to the price of one's seat. His approach to management was to have the doors removed from his office because he believed that custodians and groundskeepers had as much right to his time as his coaches and players.

Bill Veeck's singular American life story is a multifaceted one, reflecting the changing face of America's favorite sport, the ability of the individual to effect change, and the transformative power of sports in a postwar America just beginning to struggle with the next phase of its historical burden of racial prejudice and injustice. Many knew Veeck as the "Barnum of Baseball," the guy who sent a midget to the plate in 1951, but few knew that he walked—on one leg—in Martin Luther King Jr.'s funeral march in Atlanta or that he became a fervent antiwar and gun control advocate in the final years of his life. At the heart of Veeck's story is the conflict between a stubborn, iconoclastic individual and the entrenched status quo. He once said: "The athlete who catches the imagination is the individualist, the free soul who challenges not only the opposition but the generally accepted rules of behavior. Essentially, he should be uncivilized. Untamed." He was alluding to such men as Babe Ruth and Ty Cobb, but he was also, of course, describing himself.[15]

CHAPTER 1

Senior

THE FIRST BILL VEECK—William L. Veeck Sr.—was born in Boonville, Indiana, a small village near Evansville, on January 20, 1876, the son of Dutch parents. The original family name had been Vander Veeck but later was shortened to Veeck. William became a telegraph messenger boy at age ten and then worked in a drugstore while briefly apprenticed to his father, who made wagons and cabinets. He was minimally educated, having to drop out of school after only three years because of the death of his father in 1886. Like most small-town boys of the time, he played baseball, but not as well as his older brother Ed, who caught for the semipro Evansville team.

At the age of fourteen, William became a printer's apprentice and then a pressroom helper at the *Boonville Standard*, where he worked for six years. He also sold the paper on the streets. Despite his lack of a formal education, Veeck read and wrote constantly, and he had a brief but failed career as a traveling photographer with a friend named Frank Snyder. Veeck moved to Louisville, eventually finding a job at the *Louisville Courier-Journal*, where he spent most of his four years at the paper as a police reporter. While working at the paper, he returned home on October 17, 1900, to marry Grace DeForest, his childhood sweetheart. Her father was the area's only doctor and one of its largest landowners, and he was outraged that his daughter was marrying an itinerant journalist not only younger than she but also poorly educated. However, Gracie, as she was called, was a woman of strong will and determination.[1]

The couple might have stayed in Louisville had it not been for a record-setting heat wave in July 1901.[2] The ordeal was so trying that Veeck determined to embark on a bold plan he had been turning over in his mind for many months: to move to Chicago. In 1902, he took a job with the Chicago *Inter-Ocean* and then shifted to the hotel beat at the Chicago *Chronicle*, covering in particular the Congress Hotel and its many celebrity guests.

Editor Ed W. Smith discovered Veeck's interest in baseball and assigned him a new beat. "He broke in at a fine time, in the days of the Tinker-to-Evers-to-Chance dynasty, the 1906 days of the White Sox Hitless Wonders, days of murderous N.Y. Giants, poisonous Pirates, deadly Athletics—what days!" Smith recalled at the time of Veeck's death.[3]

With the sudden collapse of the *Chronicle* in 1907, Smith and Veeck moved to William Randolph Hearst's *Chicago Evening American*, where Veeck worked as a reporter and rewrite man. He was soon given a regular column on sports, which he wrote under the alliterative pseudonym Bill Bailey. Known as the "madhouse on Madison," the Hearst paper feasted on scandal and violence, fueled by tobacco and whiskey. Veeck worked at the *American* for the next dozen years covering both the Cubs and the White Sox.[4]

The Veecks lived on Lexington Avenue in the Woodlawn section of Chicago, where their first child, Maurice Forest Veeck, had been born shortly after their arrival in 1902. On September 30, 1909, at the age of seven, Maurice was killed while playing "warrior" after school with a friend named Preston Lavin. The boys had been close since they could walk, and they had always gone to and from school together. On the evening of the accident, their teacher had walked the boys home to pay a call on the Lavins, and shortly after she left, the boys went to the Lavins' library to play with wooden guns. However, Lavin picked up a loaded Colt .38 revolver that his father had left on the table. The gun was usually unloaded, but a few nights earlier, the elder Lavin had been awakened by a noise in the basement and had loaded the gun and gone downstairs to investigate. Upon finding nothing, he returned to the library, where he carelessly left the loaded gun on the table. The boys had played with the unloaded gun before. Preston told his mother that he was showing Maurice how the gun worked when it discharged, hitting the Veeck boy under the eye.[5]

The death was ruled accidental, and the body was taken to Boonville for the funeral and burial. The account in Veeck's newspaper contained a picture of Maurice and a paragraph that could only have been informed by his father: "The little Veeck was an only child, and his parents built their lives around him. He was a particularly handsome and manly little fellow, sturdy and strong and more quiet than most children and greatly beloved by a great many people."[6]

Maurice's mother never really got over the tragedy, becoming much less social and given to long, solitary walks. For his part, William Veeck threw himself even more deeply into his work as a sportswriter, becoming one of Chicago's best-known and most popular baseball writers and part of a corps that included Ring Lardner, Hugh Fullerton, and Gus Axelson. Veeck was respected enough to be invited with Lardner and a select group by White Sox owner Charles Comiskey to spend time with him at his wooded retreat in Eagle River, Wisconsin, and to drink with him at the stadium in a small group known as the Woodland Bards Association. Their clubhouse at the ballpark was known as the Bards Room.[7]

ANONYMITY BECAME a dilemma for Veeck, since few people knew that he was Bill Bailey. Even when Maurice was killed, the names were not linked in any of the newspapers reporting the death. Veeck asked repeatedly and with increasing frustration to be able to write under his own name, but he was denied by a managing editor who felt the public might think the great Bill Bailey had left the paper and been replaced by a new man.[8]

On April 27, 1911, Margaret Ann Veeck was born in Chicago, followed by a brother, William Louis Veeck Jr., on February 9, 1914. "After the death of Maurice," says Fred Krehbiel, Margaret's son, "my grandmother really didn't want to have children—or at least that's the impression she gave—but my grandfather prevailed." When young Bill was a year old, the family moved to Hinsdale, west of Chicago, an eighteen-mile train ride from the Loop.[9]

Shortly after Bill's birth in 1914, Smith, still sports editor of the *American*, and the elder Veeck sought to buy the Denver Bears of the Western League. As Smith recalled later, they "would have done so but for the outburst of the Federal League," whose teams were signing key players from Denver and top minor-league clubs. Smith observed that Veeck had long aspired to be a baseball executive, an urge that seemed to get stronger as his family got larger and the newspaper business became more precarious.

YOUNG BILL VEECK made his debut in print as an infant when his father wrote a column for the *Evening American* on the sad state of the Chicago

Cubs as an offensive unit: "My new son can throw his bottle farther than the team can hit!" During the 1918 season, when his son was four, Veeck wrote a series of especially pointed columns about how badly the Cubs were managed both financially and on the field.[10]

The White Sox had been the dominant force in Chicago baseball, but despite their deficiencies, the Cubs won the 1918 National League pennant in a war-shortened season. When the Boston Red Sox beat the Cubs four games to two in the World Series, Veeck's criticism was renewed, suggesting that an outside force had prevented them from winning.*

Information obtained and made public by the Chicago History Museum in 2008 suggests that gamblers may have gotten to the 1918 Cubs. Eddie Cicotte, a pitcher and one of the eight White Sox outcasts from the 1919 World Series, which in fact was fixed, said in an affidavit he gave to the 1920 Cook County, Illinois, grand jury that the Cubs influenced the Black Sox. Cicotte said the notion of throwing a World Series first came up when the White Sox were on a train to New York with the Cubs, presumably in May 1919, when both teams were playing on the East Coast. The team was discussing the previous year's World Series, which had been fixed, according to players Ciccote did not identify in his statement. A few members of the White Sox then tried to figure out how many players it would take to throw a Series. From that conversation, Cicotte testified, the most famous sports scandal in American history was born.

Cicotte's sworn testimony was reinforced by another piece of information unearthed in 1963. Fred Krehbiel, then a White Sox employee at Comiskey Park, stumbled upon a long-lost ledger book and legal pad with two dozen pages of handwritten notes, including allegations of game fixing from four decades earlier. The documents were remnants of a diary kept by Harry Grabiner, a longtime deputy to White Sox owner Charles Comiskey and a confidant of Commissioner of Baseball Kenesaw Mountain Landis.[†] After the game had been hit by a series of gambling allegations in the late

---

* Because the United States had just entered World War I, the Series was played a month early, with the last month of the regular season lopped off and the teams in first place at the end of August being awarded the pennant. On December 26, 1919, the Red Sox sold their star pitcher Babe Ruth to the New York Yankees, who recognized that his bat was even better than his arm and put him in right field.

† Bill Veeck Jr. wrote about this discovery in his 1965 book, *The Hustler's Handbook*. Harry Grabiner would later work for Bill Veeck when he was principal owner of the Cleveland Indians.

teens and early 1920s, Grabiner provided Landis with a list of twenty-seven "dirty" players. The complete diary and list have never been recovered and remain the subject of much speculation. But the papers unearthed in 1963 included a scribbled notation next to the name of former Cubs pitcher Gene Packard: "1918 Series fixer." Packard had not pitched for the Cubs since 1917, but he knew most of the team's personnel.[11]

Baseball columnist Hugh Fullerton—a close friend of Veeck's and the man who eventually blew the whistle on baseball's gambling problem— also suggested that something was afoul in 1918.* Fullerton's accounts of the 1918 World Series repeatedly point out bizarre baserunning mistakes and defensive flubs.[12]

THE 1918 SERIES was played under the dark cloud of World War I, the United States having recently entered the conflict. The national "Work or Fight" order, decreeing that anyone of draft age who was not employed in war-related work—shipbuilding, farming, manufacturing—would be sub- ject to immediate conscription, deemed baseball to be nonessential and forced the premature end of the regular season on September 1. The World Series that year remains the only one played entirely in September, and owners worried that there might not be a 1919 season.

The Cubs announced they would play the Series at Comiskey Park rather than their own, much smaller Weeghman Park. They had an impressive 84–45 record and a dominant pitching staff: Jim "Hippo" Vaughn had led the National League with 22 victories, Claude Hendrix had won 20, and George Tyler 19. The Red Sox, with an elite pitching staff of their own that included Carl Mays, Sam Jones, Joe Bush, and the multitalented Babe Ruth, had won the shortened American League pennant race with a 75–51 record. The young Ruth split time between the outfield and the mound, winning 13 games, batting .300, and hitting a league-leading 11 home runs.

On the eve of the World Series, Veeck—who covered both the Cubs and White Sox and had seen the Red Sox often during his reporting on White

---

* The box scores support this. The Cubs were picked off three times, including twice in the decisive game 6. That game was lost 2–1 on a two-run error by Cubs right fielder Max Flack. Game 4 had been tied 2–2 in the eighth inning, when Cubs pitcher Phil Douglas gave up a single, followed by a passed ball, followed by his errant throw on a bunt attempt that allowed the winning run to score.

Sox games—wrote that Boston could "murder speed, but they certainly do have their troubles with the soft stuff," observing as well the difficulties the Red Sox had against left-handers and that the Cubs had two excellent lefties in Vaughn and Tyler. To Veeck, the margin of victory was Cubs catcher Bill Killefer, the "smartest catcher in the National League," and he predicted that the combination of Killefer and Tyler would be unbeatable.[13]

So confident was Cubs manager Fred J. Mitchell that he predicted, "We will win for sure. I think the Cubs form the better, stronger ball club. The pitchers are in great form, the men have been hitting, are chock full of confidence, and I don't see a chance for them to lose . . . we will be victorious in the end."

With Babe Ruth on the mound for the first of three games at Comiskey Park, the Red Sox took the first game of the Series with a 1–0 shutout over Vaughn. Tyler evened the Series the next day, allowing six hits and driving in two runs in a 3–1 win. Vaughn returned in game 3 but lost a 2–1 heartbreaker to Carl Mays. Ruth led the Sox to a 3–2 game 4 win in Fenway Park, driving in two runs with a booming triple in the fourth, his only hit of the Series.* His consecutive scoreless innings streak in the World Series, dating back to his 1916 appearance, was stopped at 29⅔, when the Cubs scored two runs in the eighth inning.

The next morning in Boston, players from both sides, concerned about the poor attendance in both cities, threatened to strike unless the winners were each guaranteed $2,500 and the losers $1,000. They finally backed off, but no World Series rings or mementos were given out. On the field, Vaughn came back for his third start with two days of rest and blanked the Red Sox 3–0 on five hits in game 5.

Game 6 would be the Cubs' last stand, as Carl Mays won his second game with a three-hit 2–1 triumph that ended the Series and crowned his franchise as five-time World Champions. With two on and two out in the third, Red Sox outfielder George Whiteman lined a hard drive to right field. Max Flack dropped it, allowing the only runs off Tyler, who also was pitching his third game of the series. Righty Claude Hendrix, 20–7 during the year, finally made his first appearance, tossing a final inning for the Cubs.

---

* Ruth batted sixth and remains the only starting pitcher in World Series history to bat other than ninth in the batting order.

In his post-Series analysis, Veeck identified game 4 in Boston as the turning point in what he termed "a disastrous series." In a column entitled "Tyler's Lapse of Memory Fatal," he accused Tyler of violating Cubs manager Fred Mitchell's directive to pitch around Ruth in key situations. With runners on first and second and two outs in the fourth, he appeared to be following Mitchell's instructions, with three pitches off the plate. Ruth clearly expected the walk, taking two perfect strikes. Killefer then called for a curve, but Tyler shook him off. "Killefer," wrote Veeck, "certain that Tyler would never get the ball anywhere near the plate, let him have his way. The pitch was squarely across the heart, there was the swish of the bat and the game was gone."[14]

In the eighth, the Cubs having rallied to tie with two runs, George "Lefty" Tyler was relieved by Phil Douglas, who took the loss when he allowed an unearned run on a single, a passed ball, and his own throwing error to first base.*

At the very least, Veeck was decrying the lack of discipline of a key pitcher compounded by the ineptitude of his reliever, but from the tone of his writing, it would seem he was implying something more sinister, namely, a fix. Veeck was as savvy as any other reporter, and it is all but certain he was aware of the fact that games were sometimes fixed. "A lot of people have the idea that the Black Sox scandal was the only fix of that era," acknowledged Jacob Pomrenke, the chairman of the Society for American Baseball Research's Black Sox Scandal Research Committee. "To tell the truth, there were so many games that were either fixed or had players easing off. It was kind of the culture of that time." Gamblers rode on the trains with the players and bet openly at games. "At Fenway Park they even had their own section."[15]

WILLIAM WRIGLEY JR., a man who had made a fortune manufacturing and selling baking soda and chewing gum, became interested in baseball during a smoking-car discussion with a group of Cincinnati fans on a train in 1913. They took him to task for the fact that the Cubs were owned not by a

---

* Douglas was banned from baseball in 1922 after he offered in writing to a friend on the Cardinals to skip out on the New York Giants (and presumably cost them the pennant) if someone would pay him to head home on the next train.

native but rather by a Cincinnati man named Charles P. Taft. In January 1916, Taft—the half brother of President William Howard Taft and an increasingly unpopular figure in Chicago because of his absenteeism—sold the Cubs to fast-food impresario Charles Weeghman, who had owned a team in the upstart Federal League, which had folded after the 1915 season. Weeghman had built a stadium for that team and moved the Cubs from their run-down West Side Park to the new facility in 1916. Wrigley took an increasing interest in the game and became a dedicated fan in the spring of 1918 when the Cubs were training in Pasadena, California; he invited the players and baseball writers, Bill Veeck included, to his home on Catalina Island for dinner. Having covered the two Chicago teams for nearly a decade and a half, Veeck outlined what he saw as the strengths and weaknesses of the Cubs, and he also opined on such matters as building a large fan base while creating a strong team. Veeck hated the growing influence of gambling on the game and in his columns pioneered the effort to prevent its further spread.[16]

Following the 1918 World Series, Wrigley, A. D. Lasker, and J. Ogden Armour purchased a controlling interest in the Cubs from Weeghman, who needed money to keep his chain of restaurants and bakeries afloat. The business had suffered a double hit, from carrying a German name during a war with Germany and from the effects of the great influenza epidemic of 1918, during which public health officials cautioned people to stay out of public places, especially restaurants. Weeghman was also a gambler who was increasingly over his head in debt.

On November 19 at a club board meeting, Wrigley took control of the team. He invited Veeck in for a second talk in early December. At one point in the conversation, Wrigley asked about the group that had run the Cubs up until this point. "Could you do any better?" he challenged Veeck.

"I certainly couldn't do any worse," replied Veeck.[17]

Veeck was hired on the spot as vice president and treasurer and given stock ownership in the club. Fred Mitchell became club president, and for the moment also doubled as team manager. Whether Veeck was brought aboard to manage as well as tend to any corruption on the club is not known, though all the evidence suggests that Veeck knew something was not right with the Cubs and that Wrigley was a man of scrupulous honesty.[18]

Harry Neily of the *Chicago American* noted that while the appointment came as a surprise, Wrigley could not have made a better choice, because

Veeck possessed a "keen knowledge of the politics of the game and the peculiar code that governs it." Harry Hochstadter of the *Evening Post* called Veeck an "ardent booster" of the game who was known for being fair and impartial and who was now in a position to implement some of the ideas on running a club he had for years shared with fellow members of the press box. Veeck's mission was to turn a second-rate business property into a profitable first-rate baseball operation.[19]

Wrigley and Veeck's first task was to make the ballpark more attractive to patrons of both sexes, with a high priority given to the women's restrooms. Believing players were more attractive clean than dirty, Veeck issued each player six changes of uniform instead of the customary two.

Veeck's first Opening Day in 1919 was a crowd-pleaser. Instead of having a politician throw out the opening pitch, Veeck opted for a battery of two men just back from the service: Sgt. Grover Cleveland Alexander, recently returned from duty in Germany, pitching to Sgt. Bill Killefer, who had served his time at a base in Michigan. In their honor and in honor of the fact that the Great War had ended with an armistice the previous November 11, a new American flag was to be raised over the park. Yet the war debts were immense. Victory loan drives were still ongoing, and the Cubs, like other American businesses, remained under a federal allotment for the sale of war bonds.

Veeck came up with the novel idea that the Cubs would play the New York Giants by telegraph following a set of unique rules: a virtual game in which the players moved around the bases as money was raised to retire the nation's war debt. The Cubs' "home field" was the dining room of the Blackstone Hotel. Fans were admitted to the hotel suite for free, with no limit on how much they might spend to win the game.

The rules were simple. Max Flack, the Cubs' leadoff hitter, would be announced, and his "at-bat" would last two minutes. If $5,000 was raised in that time, Flack would be credited with a base hit and go to first base. If the money was not raised, he was out. Should double that amount be raised, he would get a double, and for three times that amount a home run. Each batter would "hit" under the same rules.

While this was going on in Chicago, the Giants played a similar game in New York, with the results going back and forth by telegraph. The Giants "walked off the field" when the first million-dollar pledge was made by Albert Loeb, the executive in charge of Sears, Roebuck, and Company's prosperous mail-order business.* This was followed by a flurry of Chicago pledges, including another million from the International Harvester Company. Wrigley himself wired in $70,000 from Pasadena. The total pledged for war bonds was $4 million.[20]

Veeck quickly showed himself to be one of the most innovative front-office men in baseball. On July 7, 1919, his mandate grew: Fred Mitchell, challenged by being both club manager and president, resigned the executive position to concentrate his energies on the field. Veeck became president of the Cubs, an appointment he would hold for the rest of his life.

He rapidly became the voice of the Chicago Cubs. In his own articles, syndicated in newspapers around the country, he explained trades, discussed the pennant races, and exhorted readers to believe in the Cubs. As he told readers of the *Fort Worth Star-Telegram* and other newspapers, "We're not quitters; [we're] not going to be counted out of that race until someone throws us out of it."[21]

Veeck, with Wrigley's blessing, was doing with his baseball team what Wrigley had done with his chewing gum: advertise, promote, and create goodwill. An open date at the ballpark was a vacuum Veeck felt he had to fill with something newsworthy, so, for a Saturday late in August when the team was on the road, he staged an Army-Navy baseball game The game benefitted the Chicago Babies' Free Milk Fund and featured enlisted men who had played baseball overseas during the war.[22]

Off the field, the biggest issue facing Veeck, and indeed all of baseball, was the persistance of gambling and the specter corruption cast over the sport. In September of Veeck's first year with the Cubs, what became known as the infamous "Black Sox" episode was played out across town during the 1919 World Series between the Chicago White Sox and Cincinnati Reds. A few influential journalists, including Veeck's friend Hugh Fullerton, suspected wrongdoing. The story finally broke almost a year later, and baseball faced the worst scandal in the history of the game. Eight members of the 1919 White Sox were eventually banished from baseball for taking money from gamblers to throw games in the World Series, handing the championship to Cincinnati.

---

* Loeb was also the father of Richard Loeb, who in 1924 co-conspired with Nathan Leopold to commit the "perfect crime" in the murder of Bobby Frank. The Leopold-Loeb trial, dubbed "the trial of the century," resulted in both men getting life imprisonment.

How and when Veeck learned about what transpired is unknown, but he was acutely sensitive to the issue of gambling in baseball, and even more so after hearing a confession by a utility infielder named Lee Magee. On February 22, 1920, Veeck announced that the Cubs would not offer Magee a contract for the upcoming season. No reason was given at the time, but Magee, who joined the Cubs in 1919, told Veeck and the National League president, John Heydler, on June 10, 1919, that he "wanted to make a clean breast of things" and admitted to trying to fix a game in 1918 while playing for Cincinnati. Unable to land a job with another team, Magee claimed that he was being unfairly blacklisted and took his case to the press, which eagerly fanned the flames of a public argument between Magee and his lawyers and the league president. He finally recanted his confession, sued the Cubs for $9,500, and lost. The Cubs organization was lauded for dealing firmly and decisively with a clear case of game-tossing, even though Magee's team had won the game in question. It was termed "an everlasting warning to other intending wrong-doers."[23]

At the beginning of the 1920 season, Veeck spearheaded an effort to prevent betting on baseball games by banning the practice at his ballpark and by instituting a policy of not naming the Cubs' starting pitcher until the last minute, because many bets were wagered on the strength of that day's pitchers.[24] This had limited success, as most teams, including his own, had a regular and predictable rotation of pitchers.

Determined to purge Cubs Park of gamblers, on May 24, 1920, police officers dressed as sailors, ice wagon drivers, soldiers, bootblacks, and farmers broke up a gambling ring in the bleachers, arresting forty-seven bettors. Each of those arrested was held on $25 bond, and though they were acquitted for lack of evidence, the point was made.

Three months later, prior to the August 31 game between the Cubs and the Philadelphia Phillies, Veeck received a warning telegram from Detroit: "UNLIMITED AMOUNTS OF MONEY TODAY BY CHICAGO SHARPS TO BE WAGERED ON PHILADELPHIA WINNING TODAY'S GAME. SOMETHING PECULIAR." It was signed by one W. H. Brown, a name unknown to Veeck, and was followed by five more telegrams and phone calls from Detroit, Cleveland, and Chicago warning that the fix was in and informing Veeck that thousands of dollars were being wagered against the Cubs in several cities. Veeck immediately yanked the pitcher who was next in the rotation, Claude Hendrix, and in his place put the incorruptible Grover Cleveland Alexander, promising him a $500 bonus if he won the game. Veeck positioned detectives around the ballpark, but nothing suspicious occurred even though Alexander lost the game 3–1.[25]

After the game, Veeck employed the Burns Detective Agency to investigate the telegrams and phone calls. Its operatives were unable to locate any of the senders, and Veeck began to suspect the communications might have been part of a reverse plot to have the Cubs switch to Alexander in the expectation he would win. Two days later, the Chicago *Herald and Examiner* broke the story that the game had been fixed and more than $50,000 had been bet on Philadelphia to win. Veeck called for an immediate investigation by a committee of three Chicago baseball writers, who would be given money to hire private detectives.* "If the charges are proved, we will drive the guilty players out of baseball, even though it shatters the Cubs team," he vowed.[26]

Because interstate commerce was involved, one of the wire services suggested that federal authorities might soon concern themselves with the issue of baseball corruption. That did not happen, but on September 7, a Cook County grand jury convened to investigate gambling in baseball. In addition to investigating the Phillies-Cubs game eight days earlier, presiding judge Charles McDonell recommended that the jury review the 1919 White Sox–Reds World Series. Evidence had suddenly come to light that Sox owner Charles Comiskey had held up the World Series bonus checks of eight White Sox players before finally mailing them out.

The closed hearings commenced on September 22, limiting the public to secondhand information.[27] The curious Cubs-Phillies game was the first order of business, and Veeck testified as to what was at stake: "This scandal—whether true or untrue—is more than the mere business of the Chicago baseball club. Baseball belongs to the American people. For baseball to be unclean would not only be, in American life, a sporting calamity, but a moral calamity." Suspicion fell on pitcher Hendrix and on Cubs first baseman Fred Merkle, infielder Buck Herzog, and pitcher Paul Carter.† No

---

* The fact that Veeck called on journalists to pursue this rather than owners and club officials is telling, according to Black Sox expert Jacob Pomrenke: "He trusted the writers above all other elements in baseball."

† Hendrix denied any knowledge of a fix, but he never played in organized baseball again after the 1920 season. The Cubs released him in February 1921, with the explanation that they were rebuilding their pitching staff, and no other club signed him.

conclusive proof was uncovered against any of them, so the matter was dropped."[28] More significant, Veeck had sparked the investigation into the 1919 World Series, and later in the year eight members of the White Sox were indicted for their roles in the fix.*

More allegations were made of fixed games during the 1920 season. In September an apparent attempt was made to influence the betting odds in an upcoming series when a bogus report was circulated that Babe Ruth and other members of the New York Yankees had been killed or seriously injured in a car wreck. One of the private investigators working for Veeck helped disprove the report.[29]

Veeck made further news in January 1921 when he led a group of fellow executives in banning all clubhouse gambling, which was rampant, pledging to get rid of stars unwilling to follow the rule. In July 1922, Veeck had forty gamblers arrested who he claimed were betting openly and badgering the players to perform in a way that would favorably affect their wagers. A judge threw out the charges, but Veeck had underscored his determination to rid the sport of its persistent gambling problem.[30]

FOLLOWING HIS PROMOTIONAL and business instincts, in late 1920 Veeck rented Cubs Park to George Halas, the player-coach of the Decatur Staleys, and A. E. Staley, the team's owner, to stage a professional football game on December 12, 1920. The Staleys, champions of the Western Division, played the Akron Steel, victors in the East, for the championship of the American Professional Football Association. Akron was led by its star halfback and co-coach, Fritz Pollard, the first African American to play in a professional sporting event at Cubs Park. The match was played before 12,000 fans and ended in a scoreless tie. Afterward, George Halas proposed a rematch, promising a crowd of at least 15,000, but Akron declined.

Encouraged by Staley, Halas sought a city larger than Decatur as home for the Staleys, and Staley agreed to support the club in a new location for one year. Halas then made a deal with Veeck for the 1921 football season, under which the Cubs got 15 percent of the gate (20 percent when the receipts

---

* The eight: pitcher Ed Cicotte, first baseman Arnold "Chick" Gandil, pitcher Lefty Williams, center fielder Happy Felsch, shortstop Swede Risberg, third baseman Buck Weaver, utilityman Fred McMullin, and one of most popular stars of his time, left fielder "Shoeless" Joe Jackson.

exceeded $10,000) and the concession receipts, while the Staleys retained all rights to the game programs. Halas took control of the Staleys after one year and in 1922 renamed them the Chicago Bears in deference to the Cubs. Halas loved baseball, having played in a dozen games as an outfielder for the 1919 New York Yankees, and felt the linking of the two names to be appropriate.[31]

Under Veeck as president, the Cubs came in a respectable third in 1919 (with a record of 75–65), then dropped to fifth in 1920 (75–79) and seventh in 1921 (64–89), and finished in the middle of the pack between 1922 and 1924. Nonetheless, attendance grew steadily, reaching the half-million mark for the first time in 1922. Veeck's improvements to the stadium were doubtless a big factor. Over the winter of 1922, seating was added to raise the capacity from 17,000 to 32,000, the foul lines were extended, and three feet of earth was scraped from the surface of the field. Veeck would add a second deck in 1927.[32]

At the 1924 league meetings in New York, Veeck made an unexpected announcement. "I haven't signed any players recently," he said, "but I'll tell you what I have done that means much to our club. I have, or rather our board of directors has elected a new club secretary, a woman, the only woman secretary in organized ball. Her name is Miss Margaret Donahue and she has been in the club offices for seven years. John Seyes, the former secretary, will have charge of the clubs' concessions hereafter. We feel that in Miss Donahue we have added a real asset to our club organization." Then, as though he thought the title might be underappreciated, he pointed out that the secretary was one of five jobs at the club that required annual reelection by the board of directors.[33] Donahue—who had been the team's bookkeeper and had handled season tickets, press passes, cash receipts, and transfers for the Cubs and for all other Wrigley Field events—was the first female baseball executive who rose from the ranks.*

Donahue was present when Veeck taught his young son, then age eleven, a lesson that would guide him the rest of his life. Following a game in 1925, he took Bill junior over to Donahue's desk, which was covered with that day's gate receipts.

"You know, Bill," Veeck said, "it's a very interesting thing. You can look at that money and it all looks exactly the same, doesn't it? You can't tell who

---

* Helene Britton had earlier inherited the St. Louis Cardinals, which she owned from 1911 to 1918.

put it into your box office. It's all exactly the same color, the same size and the same shape. You remember that." This story became the younger Veeck's answer for decades to come when he was asked why he seemed to be totally without racial or religious bias.[34]

Donahue inaugurated the practice of selling season tickets prior to the 1929 season, which was an immediate success. On February 25, Veeck announced that demand for tickets had broken all Cubs records, with thousands of "pasteboards" sold more than a month before the season began. "It's the greatest pre-season rush in Cub history," he said.[35] Donahue had arranged for tickets to be available at any Western Union telegraph office, rather than only at the box office, and after a three-year battle she succeeded in instituting a reduced price for children under twelve.*

Ever open-minded, Veeck understood that the presence of women at the ballpark meant that whole families were more likely to attend, increasing the club's profits. One of Veeck's early notions was to revive a momentary innovation of the 1890s, Ladies' Day, and bring it into the twentieth century. Beginning with the 1919 season, a few Fridays were announced as Ladies' Days.† Full-page newspaper advertisements offered free tickets for women, many of whom decided to pay an additional fee to upgrade to the box seats, of which Wrigley Field had proportionally more than any other ballpark in the major leagues.[36]

The number of women at games increased gradually until on Friday, July 6, 1930, 30,476 women jammed Wrigley Field, causing late-arriving patrons with tickets to be turned away at the gate. On that day, 51,556 people packed themselves into a ballpark that normally accommodated some 40,000. "I'll never forget it," Veeck recalled. "The biggest mob of women I ever saw in one place in my life. We got in all we could: thousands were left outside. Regular patrons couldn't get to their seats. There was no room for the men who paid. The streets were blocked all around the park: traffic was at a standstill."[37]

---

* Years later, in 1954, when Donahue was still with the Cubs as a full vice president, Bill Veeck Jr.—by then an owner himself—called her "as astute a baseball operator as ever came down the pike." He added, "She has forgotten more baseball in her forty years with the Cubs than most of the so-called magnates will ever know."

† According to the manual given to ushers at Wrigley Field today, Weeghman had earlier introduced a discount on Friday games for women on general admission tickets. Ladies' Day was not an entirely new idea, but the National League had, inexplicably, placed a ban on this promotion in 1909.

A new plan was initiated the next day and announced in the newspapers: beginning with the next Ladies' Day, the following Friday, women could send a self-addressed stamped envelope with a request for no more than two tickets, with the number of such tickets limited to the first 17,503 requests. Those who did not get in received a note wishing them better luck next time. Veeck hired a staff of six to handle these tickets, and 40,000 requests were received for the August 1 game. When two weeks later there were 50,000 requests for the August 15 game, Veeck limited the mail-in requests to one ticket rather than two. The day after the game on the fifteenth, the *Chicago American* carried this notice: "The demand for ladies' day tickets for next Friday has been as heavy as heretofore. There just aren't any."[38]

The elder Veeck publicly played the onslaught for all it was worth, terming it a hand-wringer and a "nightmare" of logistics, but then admitted: "However, every time I get sick of it all I go to the game and see the women—schoolgirls, grandmothers, working women and society matrons—enjoying themselves. That makes up for everything and makes it all seem worth while." He also wondered aloud—and within the earshot of reporters—why the women of other cities did not share the sophistication of their Chicago counterparts, a comment that gained him and the Cubs national attention. Veeck proclaimed that female Cubs fans were not satisfied with only free games but insisted their husbands and sweethearts bring them to other games, "and as a result Chicago leads the league in paid attendance figures."[39] The attraction held even into the Great Depression. In 1930, Veeck estimated that 25 percent of all paying fans on Sundays were women.

Cubs games also offered fans the vicarious opportunity to see some of the most notorious criminals of the twentieth century. The Eighteenth Amendment, which established Prohibition in the United States, was ratified on January 16, 1919, and went into effect a year later, creating a new criminal class. The Cubs' faithful fans included Al Capone and Bugsy Moran, who frequented the boxes along the first base line. First baseman Charlie Grimm would later observe, "They used to come out and watch us practice and used to sit right behind us. There was never a peep out of them. Ted Newberry, Bugsy Moran and Capone." John Dillinger was known to slip into the left-field bleachers for a couple of innings.[40] Even after Capone's imprisonment in 1932, his North Side gang continued to attend. Bill

Veeck Jr. remembered, "Whenever I saw a $100 bill (in the box office till), I knew Ralph Capone (Al's brother) and his boys were at the game."[41] (He would later maintain with a wink that for years he thought "C-note" stood for "Capone-note.")*

---

* Al Capone would arrive with several bodyguards and occasionally a young teen named Sam Pontarelli, one in the extended surrogate family Capone cultivated. On September 9, 1931, Chicago's crime boss got the Cubs' Gabby Hartnett to autograph a baseball before the Cubs defeated the White Sox 3–0. The moment was immortalized by an Associated Press photographer. When the photo appeared in newspapers across the country, an edict came down from Commissioner Landis's office forbidding fraternization between players and fans. Hartnett's reply to Landis's admonishments became legendary: "If you don't want anybody to talk to the Big Guy, Judge, you tell him." At the time, the boy shown in the photo with Capone was identified as Capone's son, Albert Francis ("Sonny"), but Capone never appeared in public with his immediate family. Even today the boy is incorrectly identified, even on the Associated Press Web site.

CHAPTER 2

Veeck on Deck

O NLY FOUR YEARS OLD WHEN his father took control of the Cubs, young Bill Veeck grew up immersed in baseball. Among many others, the legendary New York Giants manager John McGraw visited the house for dinner several times each season when Bill was a schoolboy. These evenings were filled with good-natured banter as well as serious talk on such topics as maintaining a strong fan base even while losing ballgames. One night after the Cubs had emerged from a five-year slump that had begun in 1919, during which period the Giants had dominated the league, McGraw said to the elder Veeck after dinner, "We could have beaten you even with our batboy in the lineup."[1]

In his youth, Bill junior was as pugnacious as he was small. "Whenever he got into a fight, he'd always end up on the bottom, but he'd never give up to the guy on top," his childhood friend Marsh Samuel remembered. "The big guy would get up, but Bill would go right back after him and keep it going. The only way the fight would end was if the big guy just got bored or tired of fighting and walked away." Bill was fearless and carefree to the point of recklessness. "One day," Samuel recalled, "we attached a bobsled to the back of a car. Bill got at the front of the sled as the car was going down a snowy country road at about 40 mph. Then Bill lifted the front end of the sled up off the ground to put on a show. He could have been killed, but Bill never thought of that."[2]

Scott Jones lived on the same street in Hinsdale and quickly discovered that Bill was "very smart" and "absolutely afraid of nothing." Almost nine decades later, Jones clearly remembered an incident that typified Bill's fearlessness. The two third-graders were walking home from school when Bill spotted three older boys across the street and started insulting them, making fun of their names and nicknames.

"I was horrified," Jones recalled. "We ran for our lives for four or five blocks and into my house and slammed the door. My mother was coming down the stairs just then, and when we told her we had been chased by bullies, she figured out what was going on and made us go outside with her. She lined up the three older boys and said we had to face the biggest one—for the two of us to stand up against him and fight. It was over in seconds. Bill went for his legs and tackled him and I hit him high and sat on him."

Veeck would also torment his friends. One Halloween, he painted the curb and much of the road in front of Jones's house bright red, hoping Jones would be blamed, which he was.[3]

In school, Veeck was, in Jones's words, "the devil incarnate." In stark contrast, Bill was also an avid reader. The elder Veeck read to his son and daughter every night he was home, and young Bill acquired an early and intense love of books. "At 8, Veeck was reading three books a week, a rate that he doubled as an adult. He had finished the entire Tom Swift series before I even knew it existed," recalled Jones.[4] At Christmas, his father gave him complete sets of authors such as James Fenimore Cooper, Robert Louis Stevenson, and Alexandre Dumas. By fifteen, he had read most of the books then considered to be classics. "My father had only a third grade education," Bill later observed. "But he was so well read and he wanted me to be that way too."[5]

The perks that accrued to the son of a top baseball executive were shared with Bill's pals. These included season passes to Cubs Park for all football and basketball letter winners at Hinsdale High. Scott Jones recalled: "One of my greatest thrills as a boy was being invited by Mr. Veeck to join him and son Bill at the team's offices in the Wrigley Building, then driving in his big open Packard with the manager of the team, Bill Killefer, to the ballpark for lunch with some of the players.* And finally we'd watch the game from the president's box with Judge Kenesaw Mountain Landis, the distinguished commissioner of baseball. I was on Cloud 9 for a year."[6]

---

* According to Scott Jones, it was rumored that Veeck senior also distributed season passes to all the policemen who patrolled the roads from Hinsdale to the ballpark on the north side of Chicago, which presumably allowed him a little extra latitude in driving to and from Wrigley Field.

Bill idolized the players on his father's team, but none more than Lewis Robert "Hack" Wilson, a stumpy, rectangular man with tiny feet (he wore a 5½ shoe), a barrel chest, and an eighteen-inch neck who joined the Cubs in 1926, when Bill was twelve. In batting practice, he would pick up a handful of dirt and wipe the sides of his pants and the sleeves of his jersey. "By the time the game started," Veeck later wrote, "Hack would always look as if he had just delivered a ton of coal." Wilson also had a big drinking problem. Veeck would tell of Wilson being sobered up in the clubhouse before a game by being doused in a tub of ice water. Despite his addiction, Wilson's batting exploits were legendary, and he led the Cubs back to prominence and the 1929 pennant.[7]

His daily exposure to baseball had an inevitable effect. "By the time I was 12," Veeck remembered, "I decided that I was going to own a baseball team. Oh, I had other plans, too, that I figured could be sandwiched in because for me each day seemed to have at least 30 hours. But my life was going to be centered on baseball. It was inevitable."[8]

After grammar school, Veeck was sent away to Phillips Exeter Academy, an elite private schoool in Andover, Massachusetts. But he became so homesick that he returned home after only a semester.

He entered Hinsdale High, where he played football on the lightweight team, being well under the 135-pound limit. Scott Jones recalled that Veeck chose to play football without a helmet, a practice that was frowned upon but allowed if a player was adamant about it. "Veeck was the only one to do so. With a carrottop mat of kinky curly hair (one of his nicknames was Steel Wool), he could easily be spotted at the bottom of every pile. He loved football." In baseball, he was an excellent sandlot player, but there was no official team in high school.[9]

After two years of public high school, Veeck was sent to the Ranch School in New Mexico, which emphasized rigorous outdoor living and a classical education. It was also very expensive—$5,000 a year—and catered to the sons of the nation's corporate elite. Veeck was a square peg in a round hole: "I was known as 'that public school rowdy,' a description that put me just one rung above the loinclothed savage. I got into a lot of fights. Someone would make a wisecrack and I'd pop him."[10] Veeck grew dramatically during this period, adding eight inches and fifty pounds. He stayed at the Ranch school until Easter of his senior year, as Scott Jones recalled, "with the understanding that he would not return—a genteel way, he later described it, of being kicked out."[11]

Veeck, who never graduated from high school, was nonetheless admitted in the fall of 1932 to Kenyon College in Ohio after passing the era's standardized College Board examinations, including one in history, which he had never taken in school.* This he accomplished by virtually memorizing the textbook.[12]

In January 1932, William Wrigley died in his sleep of a heart attack. He had acquired the club fourteen years earlier with the dream of a World Championship and little concern about profitability. Veeck had brought him profits, a pennant in 1929, and a solid fan base—but no championship. At the time of Wrigley's death, Veeck prophetically told his old boss, Ed Smith: "Just a couple more years and I'll let go. We've got to win the big series you know."[13]

Wrigley, a strong advocate of advertising and promotion, had been the perfect owner for the elder Veeck to work with, and Bill junior could not have failed to learn from them. One of the combined legacies of the two men was the radio coverage of Cubs games that Veeck had arranged, believing that the broadcasts would educate new fans. Late in the 1923 season, Judith Waller, managing director of Chicago's WMAQ, had asked Wrigley and Veeck for a thirty-day trial to air the Cubs games live. At the end of the trial, listeners were asked to write in to give their opinion. Letters came in bundles from all over the Midwest. A Wisconsin dentist wrote: "I have had no trouble with my patients since I installed the radio for the Cubs games. They sit and listen and let me work." An Indiana farmer wrote that he had a radio rigged in his field and caught the score as he finished each turn of the plow.

The experimenting continued, and on June 1, 1925, WMAQ became the first station in the United States to broadcast a team's every home game. Surprisingly, the deal with WMAQ was not exclusive, and through the late 1920s as many as five radio stations carried the games live. But the key was WMAQ, a 50,000-watt clear-channel station that could be heard over much of the Midwest. "The middle as well as the country at large was becoming Cub-conscious," newsman John Carmichael later wrote of the WMAQ deal. "The team was on its way to fame and fortune."[14]

The statistics bore out Veeck's belief in what radio could do for the team. For the seven-year period from 1918 to 1924, the Cubs averaged fourth place

---

* These were given by the College Board Examination Board of New York City and were precursors to the modern Scholastic Aptitude Tests (SATs).

in the National League standings and drew 3,585,439 patrons. From 1925 to 1931, with a club that also averaged fourth place, 7,845,700 fans watched a Cubs game, a gain of 119 percent in a time when the other seven National League clubs increased home attendance by only 27 percent.[15]

But the majority of other teams were increasingly fearful that radio would cut down on ticket sales by allowing the lukewarm fan to stay home and get a word picture of the game for nothing. In December 1931, eleven of sixteen major league teams came to the Winter Meetings in Chicago planning to establish a ban on all radio coverage, but the measure had to be tabled—the night before the ban was to be discussed, Veeck had signed a new radio contract for the 1932 season, infuriating those who were against the broadcasts. President William Harridge of the American League intimated that if radio became an issue of competition with newspapers, he would recommend that broadcasts be eliminated. "Newspaper publicity made baseball," said Harridge.[16] He had the support of the Baseball Writers' Association of America, which had expressed the belief that radio was cutting into the sale of "extra" editions of their newspapers.*

If Veeck was an owner's ideal executive, he was also a player's dream come true. Jim Gallagher, a sportswriter who became the Chicago Cubs' general manager in 1941, wrote of Veeck at the time of his death that his greatest accomplishment was creating the "one happy family" spirit so noticeable on the Cubs and so lacking elsewhere. Each winter, Veeck made trips to sign each of his players in person. He paid what was believed to be the highest salaries in the major leagues, and even in 1929 and 1932, when the Cubs won the pennant, he never had a holdout. "In the spring when awestruck, frightened rookies reported to the Cubs' training camp, it was Bill Veeck who looked them up, introduced himself and endeavored to make them feel at home."[17]

Veeck senior's confidence in matters of promotion was matched by his on-field instincts. When he hired Joe McCarthy to manage the Cubs for the 1926 season, he ignored the credo that former major-league players made the best managers. McCarthy had been, at best, a so-so minor leaguer. Chicago had gone through three managers in 1925 and finished in last place.

---

* Normally reserved for a crisis—but often extended to baseball—these were special editions hastily printed and hawked by street vendors. During a World Series, there would be at least one newsboy on every corner.

Veeck needed someone dynamic, and his former Louisville contacts vouched for McCarthy, who was successfully managing the minor-league Colonels, leading the team to American Association pennants in 1921 and 1925. With the Cubs, McCarthy immediately asserted himself by running a tightly disciplined spring training camp, and then urged Veeck to acquire Hack Wilson from the Giants and trade Grover Cleveland Alexander, an aging alcoholic, to the Cardinals. By 1929 Veeck and McCarthy had turned the Cubs into a powerhouse that finished well ahead of the rest of the National League and played before 1,485,000 home customers, setting a new major-league attendance record. Though it lost the World Series 4–1 to Connie Mack's Philadelphia Athletics, interest in the team was at an all-time high.

Yet when the Cubs fell back to second place in 1930, Veeck unceremoniously fired McCarthy with four days left in the season. Infielder Rogers Hornsby was made player-manager with the expectation he would be a stronger leader than McCarthy. Less than two years later, in the middle of a pennant race the Cubs would ultimately win, Veeck fired Hornsby on August 2, 1932. "I removed him because I came to the conclusion that the only trouble with the Cubs in 1932 was the atmosphere of the club," Veeck declared. He felt the team had peaked in midseason and was falling back, and that Hornsby was overmanaging, holding "too-tight on the reins."[18] Given his position on gambling, Veeck was no doubt also displeased by Hornsby's horsetrack betting losses and his propensity to borrow from his own players, who we were almost universal in their dislike of the man.*

"Rogers Hornsby was all business," Billy Herman, the stellar second baseman, later revealed. "You couldn't smoke or even drink a soda in the clubhouse or read a paper or anything like that. Sort of an odd guy, too. If you were a rookie, he wouldn't talk to you. Never say hello. You might get a grunt out of him, but that was about all. The only time you'd hear his voice with your name in it was when you did something wrong, and then you heard it loud and clear. If he ignored you, then you knew you were doing all right."[19]

---

* An Associated Press report ten days after the Hornsby firing said that Landis was about to open an investigation into the allegation that several Cubs players had joined Hornsby in his racetrack betting (*New York Times*, August 12, 1932).

Veeck replaced Hornsby with Charlie Grimm, the Cubs first baseman, who was as popular with the players as Hornsby had been unpopular. Grimm led the club to its second pennant in Veeck's tenure and a World Series showdown with the Yankees, who since 1931 had been managed by McCarthy.[20]

The Cubs lost four straight games to the Yankees, unable to withstand the onslaught of hits by Babe Ruth, Lou Gehrig, and others. But the Series was most notable for a gesture allegedly made by Ruth in Wrigley Field on October 1, 1932, in the fifth inning of the third game, before hitting a long home run off Charlie Root to break a 4–4 tie. Participants in the game gave varying accounts of whether Ruth had called his shot by pointing at pitcher Root, at the Cubs dugout (which had been riding him mercilessly), or toward center field. Ruth himself gave conflicting accounts, thereby fueling the legend as it grew over the years.[21]

THAT FALL BILL VEECK JR. began his sophomore year at Kenyon College and pledged Beta Theta Pi fraternity, undergoing the hazing that accompanied initiation. His college friend Howard Preston recalled the night: "The final part was a joy ride—for the brothers, not for the fellow being initiated. The boys would remove everything from the guy's pockets, leaving him just his shoes and socks and pants and shirt. Then they'd drive him twenty or twenty-five miles out in the country and dump him out in the dark of night. He had to be back at the house by eight o'clock in the morning, or else. The Betas did that with Bill. They took his wallet, keys, papers, and drove him out in the country. They took him so far out—he was a pretty hot-shot kid— that they got lost themselves a couple of times going and coming. They pushed him out of the car on a dark, lonely country road and left him. Then they went home, losing their way a few times in the backwoods and stopping for a snack at a roadhouse. When they got home, what do you think they found? Veeck had beaten them back."

After being abandoned, Bill delighted in admitting, he had noticed a horse grazing in a field nearby. The horse carried him to a farmhouse; waking the farmer, Bill used his telephone to call a cab company, which picked him up and drove him to the fraternity house. As for the money to pay for the cab, before he left his room Bill had folded a ten-dollar bill into a tiny wedge and concealed it in his tight, curly hair, where his fraternity brothers had never thought to look.[22]

In June, Bill made news of his own. A short Associated Press report, also noted in *The Sporting News,* informed the world that he was in the hospital after falling out of a dormitory window.[23] Veeck had been standing on the ledge of a fourth-floor recreation room window surveying the females who were coming to attend a dance, with one hand firmly clutching a bottle of beer and the other holding on to the inside wall. A friend waved to him from across campus. "I waved back. Being in a somewhat befuddled state, I used the wrong hand, waved myself right off the ledge, and toppled like a sack of wheat to the ground. A sober man would probably have been killed." Veeck got away with two broken legs.[24]

BY 1932 THE FULL force of the Great Depression had affected Major League Baseball; that year had been particularly bad. Foreclosures had become so routine and feared that in many locations local bands of citizens set up armed roadblocks to prevent outsiders from coming in and buying up farms and homes. By the end of the year, the unemployed numbered upward of 13 million, and one family out of every four was without a breadwinner. Perhaps as many as 2 million people, including family farmers turned into homeless migrants, were wandering the country in a random and futile quest for work.[25]

Americans were more likely to be in a breadline than a bleacher seat: overall attendance at major-league games had dropped from more than 10 million in 1930 to just under 7 million in 1932. In anticipation of even worse turnstile numbers, salaries were cut widely for the 1933 season, with Commissioner Landis taking a 40 percent pay cut, from $65,000 to $39,000. Ruth took a $23,000 salary cut; Gehrig, who was paid a lot less, lost $5,000; and some managers took 50 percent cuts.*

In early February, Fred Lieb of *The Sporting News* addressed the problems of baseball in a series syndicated to newspapers throughout the country. Lieb outlined a range of concerns, including the threat posed by the growing interest in golf as both a participation and spectator sport. He was legitimately concerned with the growing aloofness of players toward fans. Though the National League had ceased imposing fines on players who

---

* Attendance was 10,132,262 in 1930, dropping to 8,467,107 in 1931 and 6,974,566 in 1932. The next year, 1933, the numbers hit rock bottom at 6,089,031, the worst since the war-shortened season of 1918, when only 3,080,126 went through the turnstiles.

spoke with the public during the season—a practice that had begun because of the fear that gamblers would get inside information—the American League held on to the ban on fraternization with fans; a White Sox player had even been fined $5 for talking to his father. Lieb felt this rule was deeply offensive to the fans.[26] But nowhere did Lieb suggest that the color line was one of the game's problems.

On February 5, 1933, while Lieb's "What's Wrong with Baseball" series was running in newspapers, the grand ballroom of New York City's Commodore Hotel hosted more than 600 of the game's leaders—including Veeck senior and all the National League officials in town for their annual meeting— at the tenth annual New York Baseball Writers' Association of America dinner. It was a night of fun, frolic, and frivolity. Sportswriters took turns spoofing everyone from the guest of honor, retired New York Giants manager John McGraw, to the New York Yankees, who had won the World Series in October. In addition, the scribes performed their annual blackface minstrel show in front of the predominantly white crowd. *New York Times* sportswriter John Drebinger in his column the next day called the minstrel show the most entertaining part of the evening, but never mentioned its most dramatic moment. Heywood Broun, a talented and outspoken Scripps-Howard columnist who was syndicated in dozens of newspapers and admired by his fellow writers, offered a full-blown proposal for racially integrating baseball, arguing that the game's falling gate receipts could be reversed by dropping its invisible "color line." Branding baseball's segregation as "silly," Broun asked rhetorically: "Why, in the name of fair play and gate receipts, should professional baseball be so exclusive?"[27]

Invoking the name of a man who was one of the leading actors, singers, and activists of his time, Broun continued: "If Paul Robeson is good enough to play football for Rutgers and win a place on the mythical All-America eleven, I can't be convinced that no Negro is fit to be a utility outfielder for the Boston Red Sox. There were a number of superb Negro athletes on the American Olympic track team. Indeed, Eddie Tolan, the sprint champion, was almost a team in himself. . . . If Negroes are called upon to bear the brunt of competition when America meets the world in an international meet, it seems a little silly to say that they cannot participate in a game between the Chicago White Sox and the St. Louis Browns."

Broun addressed head-on the concern that some players would object to racial integration, but then dismissed it by pointing out that ballplayers objected to many things that still took place with a high degree of regularity, such as fines, supensions, and the widespread salary cuts being imposed for the upcoming season.[28]

Bill Gibson, a writer for the *Baltimore Afro-American* and one of a handful of writers from the Negro press at the dinner, found a number of people who expressed an open mind on the subject, including Branch Rickey of the St. Louis Cardinals, Yankees slugger Lou Gehrig, and John Heydler, president of the National League.[29]

Jimmy Powers, a reporter for the New York *Daily News*, was amazed at the sentiment in favor of Broun's proposal. In a column two days later entitled "Colored B.B. Players—OK," he argued the point even more forcefully than Broun, pointing out that blacks were well integrated into college sports, including football, basketball, boxing at all levels, and track and field. "There are only three popular sports today in which the dark skinned athletes are snubbed—tennis, golf, and baseball." Powers became, in the words of Lester Rodney of the Communist *Daily Worker*, "the most articulate and consistent supporter of the Negro stars since the campaign to end Jim Crow baseball began to catch hold."[30]

A few weeks later, the popular Dan Parker, sports editor of the New York *Daily Mirror*, wrote a letter to the *Pittsburgh Courier* fully endorsing an end to the color bar, insisting that club owners who welcomed the patronage of black fans had no right to bar black athletes. "In my career as a sports writer," Parker added, "I've never encountered a colored athlete who didn't conduct himself in a gentlemanly manner and who didn't have a better idea of sportsmanship than many of his white brethren. By all means, let the colored ballplayer start playing organized baseball."[31]

The issue raised by Broun, Powers, and Parker dated back to the period immediately following the Civil War when baseball flourished among both blacks and whites, especially in northern cities, and most notably in Philadelphia, where the Pythians and other all-black professional teams regularly played against white squads.* At the National Association of Base Ball Players national convention in Philadelphia in December 1867, a proposal was introduced from the floor to ban "persons of color" from playing both with and against whites. The proposal was in response to the

---

* The Pythians disbanded after their leader, Octavius Catto, a baseball and cricket player, was murdered in 1871.

Pythians' petition for membership in the Pennsylvania Association of Amateur Base Ball Players, and it was passed by vote, with the Pythians and other blacks jeering from the balcony seats where they were required to sit.[32]

The ban held into 1871, when the National Association of Professional Base Ball Players was created to replace the earlier group. The formal ban was replaced by an informal one under which several Negroes were allowed to play professional ball. At the end of the 1884 season, with the release of Fleet Walker, no person who was obviously black was allowed to play. In 1901 John McGraw, managing the Baltimore Orioles, signed a new second baseman, who, according to the *Cincinnati Inquirer*, was a full-blooded American Indian named Chief Tokohoma. In fact he was a Cincinnati Negro named Charley Grant, and the subterfuge fell apart when the team reached Chicago for an exhibition game against the White Sox. Many of Grant's friends recognized him and showed up at his hotel with a floral tribute and staged an impromptu parade in his honor. The White Sox, owned by Charles Comiskey and managed by Clark Griffith, refused to take the field against the Orioles, and Comiskey told the *Chicago Tribune*: "If McGraw really keeps this 'Indian,' I will put a Chinaman on third base."[33] He was ignoring the irony that all racial minorities except American Indians were part of the unwritten rule, including Asians.*

Since 1885, when the first professional black team, the Cuban Giants, was formed as a product of racial segregation, the Negro leagues had become the solution for black baseball players. The first true Negro league, the Negro National League, was formed in 1920, with teams from the Midwest filling out its ranks. The Negro leagues were loosely organized; seasons varied from forty to ninety games, supplemented by barnstorming tours. The Negro leagues played annual All-Star Games beginning in 1933 and periodically (1924–27 and 1942–48) conducted their own World Series.

Bill Veeck Jr. inherited a sense of tolerance from his father.[34] "I grew up in the ballpark. I liked to see good ball players, and I wasn't really interested in their color because there were some ball players, many ball players, as a matter of fact, in the Negro leagues that were certainly as good, or better than anybody that I would watch in the National League or in the American

---

* In 1916 Walter McCredie, manager of Portland in the Pacific Coast League, signed Lang Akena, a player of Chinese-Hawaiian origin, who was quickly released because of "strenuous objections from prospective team mates." *Chicago Defender*, January 16, 1916.

League," young Veeck would later say. He often told stories of watching the greats, including Josh Gibson, whom he watched drive balls deep into the center-field bleachers at Comiskey Park and of whom he would later say, "If they ever let him play in a small place like Ebbets Field or old Fenway Park, Josh Gibson would have forced baseball to rewrite the rules."[35]

ON FEBRUARY 20, 1933, Veeck senior accompanied the Cubs to spring training for the first time in many years and exuded a rare level of optimism about his pennant-winning team, which he saw as the perfect blend of "pitching, punch, and speed."[36]

As the season began, Arch Ward of the *Chicago Tribune* proposed an idea to be incorporated into the Century of Progress Exposition, the great World's Fair that would open in Chicago at the end of May. He wanted to stage a baseball game made up of the best players of the two major leagues. To be called the All-Star Game, it would be run by the *Chicago Tribune*, with all profits going to a charity, the Association of Professional Ball Players of America, which helped old and dependent ballplayers. The idea was universally supported in the American League but ran into stiff opposition from four of the National League owners.

Ward, who was a close friend of Veeck's, watched with delight as Veeck got the owners to agree. Veeck's first line of resistance was Cubs heir Phil Wrigley himself, who saw the game as an intrusion on the excitement of the World Series but relented after Veeck pointed out how dependent the Cubs were on the goodwill of the *Tribune*. Deep resistance by the owners of the St. Louis Cardinals and New York Giants was overcome with an assist from the persuasive and popular Veeck. The last to relent were the Boston Braves, following an unconfirmed report that Ward threatened to publicly expose owner Emil Fuchs as having personally blocked the game. One of the objections posed by the National League owners was their fear that the contest would be dominated by the American League and by Babe Ruth in particular. The first contest was held on July 6, 1933, at Comiskey Park, the location determined over Wrigley Field by a coin flip. It attracted 49,000 paying fans and yielded a net profit of some $46,000 for the charity. The game was indeed won by the American League—as would be twelve of the next sixteen games—by a score of 4–2, with the aid of a two-run homer by the Babe in the third inning.[37]

Veeck senior was in New York City on August 22 for the Cubs-Giants game, but it was rained out. Gotham scribes were "looking for a rainy day story," which Veeck gave them. With an eye to Cubs attendance, which had shrunk by about 400,000 during the season, he proposed a series of mid-season games between American and National League teams as a means of stimulating interest in the game. He maintained that the game was in "critical condition" and that aggressive action had to be taken to revive interest before the 1934 season. "There is no use kidding ourselves any longer," Veeck told Alan Gould of the Associated Press. "Only one big league club of 16 made money last year." He pointed out that anyone who looked at the attendance figures from July 5 until the middle of August saw that the game was in the doldrums.[38]

Calling these weeks the game's "dog days," Veeck urged their monotony be broken up with interleague games that counted in the standings. Veeck's plan was quite specific: thirty-two interleague games for each club, with four against each team of other league—two home and two away.[39]

Gould's story appeared in every major city. The reaction to what the *Chicago Daily News* called a "radical prescription" was immediate. Cleveland Indians president Alva Bradley and Brooklyn Dodgers president Stephen W. McKeever had declared themselves definitely in favor of the idea, and the Cardinals' Sam Breadon and the Pirates' William Benswanger felt it was worth considering.[40]

Soon, though, the "Veeck Plan," as it was known, was attracting serious American League opposition. Opined Clark Griffith, the gray-haired president of the Washington Senators, "Nobody thinks of that sort of stuff unless he's deaf, dumb, and blind." Col. Jacob Ruppert, the owner of the Yankees, dismissed the notion, saying he had not given it "a single thought."[41] The American League believed itself the superior circuit and did not want to share the box office draw of Ruth, Gehrig, and others.

The day after Veeck's interview with Alan Gould was published, a letter dated August 23, 1933, was sent to Veeck's office from Syd Pollock, owner of the Cuban Stars, a semipro team playing in the Negro leagues. Addressing Veeck's statement that only one major-league club was profitable, Pollock urged that the ban on Negro teams be lifted, which would boost gate revenue throughout baseball. He proposed "placing an entire Colored club to represent a city like Cincinnati in the National League and Boston in the American League. "My solution is simple," he wrote, "yet would meet with plenty of opposition from league moguls, but only because of social pride.

Social pride and prejudice must be overlooked where business enterprise is at stake, and no one can dispute Major League ball is a business."

Pollock based his argument on having sent his Cuban Stars to play in thirty-two states during the previous season, in the process beating every white minor-league team they faced. He wrote about one of his stars, Tetelo Vargas, who he predicted would steal more bases during the season than any two current major-league players combined. Vargas had also hit seven consecutive home runs in two days against top semipro competition in 1931, but this feat was entirely ignored by the white press. "With a colored club in either or both circuits, these feats, common among colored ballplayers, would not go unnoticed and bring greater interest in baseball, with the necessary publicity to go with it."

To bolster his argument, Pollock quoted Babe Ruth's comment that "the colorfulness of Negroes in baseball and their sparkling brilliancy on the field would have a tendency to increase attendance at games," Pirates coach Honus Wagner's assertion that "the good colored clubs played just as good as seen anywhere," and the opinion of former major league catcher and then Yankee coach Cy Perkins, who had played exhibition ball against the Homestead Grays and said that Vic Harris and Oscar Charleston of the Grays would "grace the roster of any big league club." Perkins also thought that Johnny Beckwith, a 230-pound right-handed slugger who hit some of the longest and most memorable home runs in Negro league baseball during the 1920s and early 1930s, could hit a baseball harder than any man he had ever seen.

The letter ended with an assurance that Pollock was in a position to assemble such a team or teams for the 1934 season. Within a week, Margaret Donahue acknowledged receipt of the letter, writing Pollock that the elder Veeck was on the road with the team and said it would be given to him for his personal attention when he returned.[42]

A resident of North Tarrytown, New York, Pollock sent a copy of the letter to the local *North Tarrytown Daily News*, which published it the day after it was mailed to Veeck. In due course, it was picked up by the *Chicago Defender, Pittsburgh Courier, Amsterdam News*, and other Negro newspapers.[43]

Whether Veeck had any thoughts of acting on the idea of a black team or teams in the majors is unknown. No surviving record exsists of a response by Veeck to Pollock, which is most likely explained by the fact that Veeck was suffering the early stages of the illness that would take his life.[44]

Bill junior may well have seen the letter or heard about it from Margaret

Donahue, as the two were close, and it is hard to imagine that the idea was not at least discussed casually with him. The extroverted Pollock and the outgoing Veeck almost certainly crossed paths. As Pollock's son Alan pointed out in his biography of his father, the idea of a black team in the majors was not dropped after the letter was sent: "Dad worked verbally thereafter through all his major league contacts, trying to secure integration of baseball through an all-black team, and, while he hoped his club would break the racial barrier . . . he would have been delighted at any team selected so long as the racial barrier crumbled."[45]

On September 16, the *Defender* published a column by Al Munro complaining that too little had been made of the fact that 20,000 had paid to see a Negro All-Star game played at Comiskey Park the previous Sunday while fewer than 12,000 people showed up to watch the Cubs at Wrigley Field for a doubleheader. Munro jabbed at Veeck senior on the matter of race, though his claim appeared without any supporting evidence: "'Twas Veeck, you know, who laughed loudly when asked about the chances of race players performing in the National League." Munro was also frustrated with Veeck on another count because of Veeck's habit of changing the numbers on players' uniforms to thwart newspapers, such as the *Defender*, from publishing scorecards that were given away gratis with the paper.[46]

Less than a week after the *Defender* article, Veeck came down with what appeared to be influenza, originally believed to have been caused by watching the Cubs play the Giants in Chicago on September 14, a cold, drizzly afternoon. On September 26, he announced from his sickbed in Hinsdale that Charlie Grimm would be retained as Cubs manager for the 1934 season, and Grimm spent a short time with him discussing changes for the 1934 team.[47]

As the elder Veeck's condition worsened, he asked for high-quality champagne—then illegal under Prohibition—to mitigate his suffering. The next day, two cases of the finest French champagne arrived at the house with a note: "Compliments of Al Capone." After almost two weeks in bed, his conditioned worsened to the point that his doctor had him admitted to St. Luke's Hospital on the thirtieth for observation. There his illness was finally diagnosed as leukemia, and he soon drifted into a coma and died in his sleep on October 5, 1933.[48]

Testimonials and telegrams came from everywhere and everyone. Babe Ruth told the *Chicago American*: "If Bill Veeck would have been in the Cub lineup in 1932, I don't think we'd have won in four straight games. He was a fighter and a great guy." Judge Landis, reached at his hotel in Washington, where he was attending the World Series, read through part of a prepared statement, and after calling Veeck one of the fairest men the game had ever known, he broke down in tears.[49]

As per Veeck's final wishes, the funeral was to be at home on the corner lot at 640 South Park Avenue in Hinsdale. Gracie Veeck had declared that the funeral would be simple and asked that members of the Cubs not wear mourning bands at the postseason exhibition game between the Cubs and White Sox on the eve of the funeral. The family received more than 500 telegrams of condolence at the house and 400 floral pieces.[50]

All but a handful of Cubs and White Sox players, as well as a galaxy of baseball executives, were among the hundreds of mourners at the funeral. The house filled quickly, and many people were forced to pay their respects while standing outside on the lawn.[51]

Charlie Grimm and many of his players found it difficult to suppress their tears for a man some of them regarded as a father figure rather than an employer. Pallbearers, all neighbors, carried his coffin through the streets to the nearby cemetery, passing through two columns of Cubs ushers standing at attention in their neat blue uniforms. Immediately following the casket was the Veeck family and Margaret Donahue, who at least one sports editor had already suggested might be an appropriate replacement for Veeck given her remarkable knowledge of the game.[52]

Within two weeks of Veeck's death, an informal poll of owners by the Associated Press made it clear that the idea of interleague play was not going to be seriously considered, opposed as it was by the majority of American League owners, who felt not only that it would compromise the pennant race but also that it was merely an expedient measure that would be unnecessary when fans started coming back to the ballparks. Their National League counterparts argued for it on economic grounds, but the issue was dead.[53]

When National League officials met on December 13 in Chicago, league president John Heydler presented a resolution honoring Veeck for his fourteen years of service to the game, during which he had proved himself to be "a man of powerful intellect, of fine qualities of leadership, clear judgment, and keen logic" and "a forcible advocate of fair play, impressive in speech and convincing in argument. Always sincere and candid in his business relations and honorable in his every act, he was likewise a lovable associate and trustworthy adviser and friend."[54]

Gracie Veeck, then in her fifties, was left with two teenagers in what was emerging as the worst year of the Depression thus far. Many of the family assets had been wiped out in the crash, but her husband had left two life insurance policies, which would pay her an annuity. Several weeks after the funeral Phil Wrigley asked her if she wanted to sell her interest in the Cubs. She agreed, and the team and her lawyer worked out an equitable offer. When the settlement arrived, it was three times the agreed-upon amount, guaranteeing her a secure future.*

---

* As the Depression wore on, two of her sisters got into financial trouble and asked for her help. She agreed under the proviso that they write each month asking for the money and acknowledging their indebtedness to her late husband, the man who had outraged her family with his lack of education and poor professional prospects.

CHAPTER 3

A Rambunctious Cub

IMMEDIATELY FOLLOWING HIS FATHER's funeral, young Bill returned to Gambier to finish out the Kenyon football season. The team had lost its first four games by a combined 84–0 score, suggesting a singular level of commitment by Veeck to a lost cause. On October 28, Veeck started at right halfback in the team's only victory of the season—20–6 over the University of Rochester—which was significant enough to be reported by the Associated Press and the *New York Times*. It would be the first and last time that Veeck's name appeared in the national press as a football player. After the season, Veeck headed home to move back in with his mother and sister and go work for the Cubs, who hired him as an office boy and jack-of-all-trades.[1]

In the wake of Veeck's death, Phil Wrigley assumed the role of president and brought in Charles "Boots" Weber from the West Coast as his new treasurer. Weber had served the Pacific Coast League's Los Angeles Angels in several capacities since 1906. The younger Veeck and Weber arrived within days of each other and formed an immediate friendship. Weber would become young Bill's mentor in the years to come, assigning him more responsibility and serving as his ally in dealing with Phil Wrigley.

Bill's relationship with his boss was strained and, from his standpoint, ever frustrating. He saw Wrigley as a shy man who felt more comfortable with the taciturn gum company men he brought in rather than with the outspoken and gregarious baseball people always promoting the game. "And so while he kept all my father's employees, he also surrounded himself with a kitchen cabinet of gum executives who were always undercutting

41

Boots and me," he recalled later. "The one point on which we clashed, perennially, was promotion. I wanted it. He didn't. He was the boss. He won every argument."[2]

Another ongoing argument, which began almost as soon as Veeck arrived, revolved around his desire to add lights to Wrigley Field. Veeck began plumping for them in early 1934, a year before Larry MacPhail installed the first lights in the major leagues, in Cincinnati. MacPhail had proven in the minors that night baseball could radically improve attendance. In 1930, MacPhail became president of the Columbus, Ohio, franchise in the minor-league American Association and introduced night baseball. The following year Columbus outdrew its parent St. Louis Cardinals by 30,000 fans for the season, largely due to night games.[3]

Veeck would periodically bring the issue of lights to Wrigley's attention as a means of increasing attendance, but Wrigley always rejected the idea, on aesthetic grounds and out of respect for the sanctity of baseball before dusk. Decades after the fact, Veeck recalled: "Old men, playing dominoes across the hearth, like to say that Phil Wrigley is the last of the true baseball men because he is the only owner who still holds, in the simple faith of his ancestors, that baseball was meant to be played under God's own sunlight. I know better. Having blown the chance to be first with lights, Mr. Wrigley just wasn't going to do it at all."[4]

Although he often expressed polite contempt for the trappings of higher education, and he was ever impatient to take on more responsibility, Veeck nonetheless attended night school at Northwestern University for five years after joining the Cubs, taking courses in accounting and business law. He also attended Lewis Institute—now the Illinois Institute of Technology—where he took night courses in mechanical drawing and other practical skills.

Early in his Cubs tenure, Boots Weber entrusted Bill with Wrigley Field's concessions, and Veeck hired a motley crew of vendors to hawk programs, scorecards, hot dogs, and peanuts. One of the first was a young hustler named Jack Ruby, who would become notorious three decades later for shooting Lee Harvey Oswald. Ruby was known as a great "duker," a slick scorecard hustler who would bump into a mark, place the program in his hand, and then demand his quarter in payment. Ruby also hustled paper birds tied to a stick (which chirped madly when twirled) outside the park, taking advantage of unsuspecting boys or girls whose parents would have to intervene to avoid paying Ruby. Veeck later admitted the Cubs had to assign someone with binoculars to monitor Ruby and make sure they were getting their cut of his nefarious sales. Veeck, along with Harry Grabiner of the White Sox, organized a vendors union in Chicago "so the vendors would be guaranteed a living wage and the clubs would be guaranteed a professional working force," as he put it.[5]

Veeck also dealt with a number of small-volume suppliers, including an ardent Cubs fan named Ray Kroc, who sold paper cups and was always putting pressure on Veeck to lay in a larger supply than Veeck needed. Like others he met during this period, Kroc would remain a lifelong friend, and he would go on to build a lone McDonald's hamburger restaurant into the most successful fast-food operation in history and become owner of the San Diego Padres in 1974.[6]

Besides his duties with the Cubs, Veeck worked part time from 1934 to 1941 as a receptionist in the offices of the Chicago Bears, where he came to know, work with, and respect his father's friend George Halas. Veeck represented the Cubs' interest in handling Bears' tickets, checking ticket sellers, and being responsible for ballpark operations.[7]

AT THE SAME time as he embarked on his career with the Cubs, Bill's personal life hit the headlines. One of his Hinsdale school classmates had been Eleanor Raymond. When Bill went west to the Ranch School, she had gone east to St. Mary's on the Hudson, a finishing school in Peekskill, New York. The two had kept in touch and reunited in Hinsdale, and they became informally engaged in December 1934. Both Bill and his sister, Peg, who had married less than a year after Bill senior's passing, were, her son Fred Krehbiel recalled later, eager to get out from under a grieving mother with whom neither child had ever been close. Grace Veeck "disapproved of much of what Bill did and the two fought over many things and would for the rest of their lives. Bill and his mother actually looked alike and were similar in that both of them were feisty."[8]

Eleanor's father was a friend of circus man John Ringling North, and she took a position as an equestrienne and elephant trainer for the Ringling Brothers and Barnum & Bailey Circus. She made her circus debut at Chicago's Soldier Field on August 4, 1935. At the beginning of the nine-day circus run, Veeck sat in the box seats watching her every move. According to a breathless report on page two of the next morning's *Chicago Tribune*, "at the end of the show he gave her a square-cut diamond." The *Tribune* account included a picture of the two arm in arm, slugged "Big Top Romance." When Bill's mother was asked why Eleanor had joined the circus, she presciently replied, "Because she can't stay away from horses."[9]

Mary Margaret McBride, the syndicated and popular women's page editor, featured Eleanor in an article about well-educated girls who went on to do the unexpected. Eleanor went on tour with the circus, and when it came to Newark, New Jersey, in the fall of 1935, Veeck's childhood friend Scott Jones, by then a student at Princeton, made the trek to watch her perform. He visited with Eleanor before the show, watching the matinee in the wings while sitting with the clowns, then saw the evening show as a paying customer in the audience. "She was a real star, a real headliner," Jones recalled years later, noting that she first soloed as a horseback rider and then led a separate act with the elephants.[10]

She stayed with the circus through its sweep into Texas, returning to Chicago to marry Bill on December 18, 1935. The wedding announcement in the papers noted that Eleanor had concluded her contract with the circus before the marriage. The wedding was a private affair performed by a local Episcopal minister. Stories in the papers announced that the couple were taking a honeymoon at an undisclosed location and that they would move into an apartment in Hinsdale, which was actually a room over the Veeck family garage where the servants' quarters had been.[11]

As if he really needed it, Veeck now had a textbook example of how to put himself in the news. Another man might have courted a high-profile socialite who was working in the circus, but only Bill would have the aplomb to show up at ringside with a big diamond and a reporter from the *Trib* in tow. Eleanor was a willing participant. Scott Jones recalled that the two were very much alike in their love of the limelight—"maybe too much alike." On December 14, 1936, almost a year to the day after their marriage, their first child was born, a boy named William L. Veeck III.[12]

VEECK HAD BEEN a fan of the Negro leagues from his early teens and through his days with the Cubs, and he once recalled that in 1926 and 1927 he "watched all the good Negro league clubs come into Chicago and play the Chicago American Giants." He added, "I, of course, later saw—worked, as a matter of fact—most of their East-West All-Star games." The Negro East-West game was a major event on the Chicago calendar, drawing large numbers of black and white fans alike.[13]

In early 1934, in California for spring training, Veeck saw Satchel Paige and Dizzy Dean trade scoreless innings in Hollywood in an exhibition game that lasted thirteen innings, with Satchel's Negro league squad eking out a 1–0 win. "The greatest pitchers' battle I have ever seen," Veeck recalled in his autobiography. "Even in those early days, Satch had all kinds of different deliveries. He'd hesitate before he'd throw. He'd wiggle the fingers of his glove. He'd wind up three times. He'd get the hitters overanxious, then he'd get them mad, and by the time the ball was there at the plate to be swung at, he'd have them way off balance."[14]

The Dean-Paige exhibitions were popular around the country, with a postseason Midwest tour in October 1935, including games in Kansas City and St. Joseph, Missouri, gaining a great deal of media attention. References were continually made to Paige's big-league qualifications. "If Paige were white," Ray Doan, manager of the Dean All-Stars, told the *St. Joseph Gazette*, "he would be worth $200,000."[15]

Besides the Negro leagues and their star attraction, Veeck became increasingly interested in an all-black basketball team, the Harlem Globe Trotters, and their owner, Abraham Michael Saperstein. In background and physical presence, Saperstein was Veeck's opposite. The London-born Saperstein was five feet tall, Jewish, and roly-poly enough that he was sometimes described as resembling a baseball. But the two thought alike to the point that in later years they would be constantly compared.[16]

The team was Chicago-based, but Saperstein chose "Harlem" to indicate that the players were African American, even though they were actually from Chicago. The "Globe Trotters" moniker made it seem as though the team had traveled all around the world, even though in the early years they seldom traveled beyond Illinois and Wisconsin. Veeck admired Saperstein's promotional skills; his freewheeling team attracted large, racially mixed crowds in small venues all through the Midwest—150,000 paying customers, for example, in 1934.*

Through the 1930s, they played straight basketball and gradually developed into a superior team. But almost from their inception, the Globe Trotters were performing showy extras, such as a ball-handling circle that was part of their pre-game warm-up—an exhibition of fancy behind-the-back and between-the-legs passes and of bouncing the balls off knees, elbows,

---

* David Spenard, Saperstein's nephew, said that he always understood that the first time the team appeared in Harlem was in 1968.

and heads, to the fans' delight. Their ability to have fun while competing appealed greatly to Veeck.

Given the level of competition to be found in the small midwestern towns where they played in the early days, the team won more than 90 percent of the 150 or so games they played each year.[17] When the first-ever national professional basketball tournament was held, in 1939 in Chicago, the Globe Trotters placed third, with second place going to the all-white Oshkosh team, which was beaten 34–24 by the New York Renaissance, a black team that, unlike the Chicago-based Trotters, was actually based in Harlem.[18] But the Globe Trotters won the tournament in 1940 by beating the Chicago Bruins of the National Basketball League 31–29, and they became the bona fide champions of professional basketball. This was, as Saperstein put it, the apex of the Trotters as a "straight" basketball team.[19]

As for Saperstein, he had an uncanny ability to attract attention with his relentless promotion: "In four or five years, basketball will be recognized as the national game," he said in 1935. Saperstein was a promoter of the first order, and Veeck saw much to admire in him.

ONE OF BILL VEECK's early tasks with the Cubs was to roam the stands and talk with fans to determine their wishes, bringing back suggestions that would make a day at the ballpark more enjoyable. *The Sporting News* noted this role in a small feature in early 1935: "Contacting the public is the duty of every official of every club, but Veeck is the first to have such a full-time assignment," the article observed.[20]

Using Veeck as a roaming ombudsman fit into Phil Wrigley's plan to merchandise and promote the Cubs year-round to ensure good attendance whether the team was in contention or not. During the winter of 1934–35, advertisements ran in all the Chicago newspapers three times a week exhorting fans to "look ahead to sunshine—recreation—happy hours with the Cubs at Wrigley Field next summer." "You will note that the theme of the campaign is sunshine, recreation and pleasure," observed Wrigley to assistant Charles Drake. "Mr. Wrigley is applying merchandising methods to baseball. It is his belief that, in the past, too much stress has been laid upon the team through newspaper publicity and not enough attention given in offering baseball as a great outdoor game, offering many healthful benefits and many hours of pleasure to the fans."[21]

Wrigley intended to merchandise the Cubs and the experience of going to the ballpark as he had merchandised chewing gum. Heavy advertising and attractive packaging were important to his scheme, and the main package was Wrigley Field.

Young Veeck was increasingly involved in the process. By the end of the 1936 season, he had worked his way up to his biggest assignment, one that would have a long-lasting impact on him and on the "friendly confines" where the Cubs played. He was appointed, at age twenty-two, to take charge of a series of major renovations that would create a beautified and expanded Wrigley Field in time for the 1937 World Series, which the Cubs hoped to be part of. Wrigley envisioned a larger, more comfortable bleacher section and new reserved and box seat sections along the left-field line. The new sections would be adorned with foliage and other artistic features.

"Above all," Veeck said later, "Mr. Wrigley wanted an outdoor, woodsy motif."[22]

By comparison with other stadiums, Wrigley Field had always stood out. Charles Weeghman's aim had been to build a park that would outshine any other in the National or American League, to show that he was serious about his team. Thanks to the strict Chicago building code, the ballpark was built to be fireproof, which was no small thing in an era of claptrap wooden ballparks.

Veeck's job was to make this fan-friendly venue even more so. He settled on a design for the new seating from the firm of Holabird & Root, which had already designed Soldier Field and the Chicago Board of Trade building on LaSalle Street.

Work began after the winter thaw and moved quickly, progressing even when games were in progress The new bleachers were to be the best available, with bleacher seating configured like box seats Offices of glass, brick, and stainless steel were added behind center field. New concession storage was built under the new bleachers, as was storage for the groundskeeping equipment, including head groundskeeper Bobby Dorr's new 30 mph lawn mower.*

The new bleacher seats were made of cypress and elevated twelve feet above the ground, ensuring a much finer view of the playing field. They

---

* Dorr had lived with his family in a bungalow built beneath the left-field grandstand—a unique and whimsical idea that had come to William Wrigley in 1923. According to the Cubs' director of event operations and security, who was interviewed for this book by Brad Beechen, the new groundskeeper's apartment was located in a separate building across Waveland Avenue, which is used now for storage and for staff training sessions.

were built on a reinforced concrete structure, arranged in a series of curves around the corners and stepped up to provide the best sight lines—yet still allowing fans on the rooftops along Sheffield and Waveland Avenues to be able to watch the games for free as they always had.

The new outfield walls were built with distinctive red brick and had six red gates. Veeck had intended to plant ivy along the walls in the off-season. However, one day in early September, Phil Wrigley told Veeck that he had invited some business associates to see a game the next day and wanted to show off his refreshed and increasingly verdant park. Veeck grabbed Dorr and his assistant and hurriedly decided to plant ivy against the red brick that night. The trio strung five strands of copper wire a foot and a half apart across the 1,003-foot curved wall to support the vines. They planted ivy at the base of the wall and intermixed 350 Japanese bittersweet plants that covered the wall entirely.*

Wrigley, an ardent arborist, had also wanted trees in the ballpark, so on his orders, Veeck had earlier planted eight Chinese elms on the steps leading to the scoreboard. Unfortunately, the trees were not meant for such harsh exposure and their fragile leaves were repeatedly blown off by the gusts coming off Lake Michigan. After five unsuccessful plantings, Veeck convinced Wrigley to give up on the idea.

Wrigley added bleacher ticket booths with glass and concrete cupolas, and Veeck redesigned food concession stands, which stood for close to forty years before they were replaced. Using designs based on ideas he had developed in classes at Lewis Institute, new tile and brick dispensaries were erected, as were storerooms housing the latest in food service equipment. Veeck himself worked the concession stands, which led him to a new understanding of the most efficient use of space: "I found out that when I was able to get from the red hots to the beer and coffee without having to move, I would sell both the red hot and a drink. If I had to take but one step, the beverage sales would begin to drop."[23]

---

* They also later added some Baltic ivy, with shiny, leathery leaves that stay green all winter, and Virginia creeper, whose five-leaflet clusters turn reddish brown in the fall. "There are two stories as to the inspiration of the ivy-covered walls," according to Cubs historian Bill Hartig. One is that Bill Veeck was impressed with the ivy-covered walls of Bush Stadium, a minor-league park, in Indianapolis. Another had the White Sox' ivy-covered outfield walls in their spring-training venue in Pasadena as the inspiration. Today's ivy is a Boston ivy–bittersweet blend but still contains elements of the original Veeck-Dorr plantings.

The final phase of the restoration was the construction of a new scoreboard. On September 7, 1937, 150 men under Veeck's supervision began installing it above the new bleachers. The ball-strike-out portion used magnetic principles never before employed, and atop the scoreboard sat a flagpole on the summit of which was a crossbar with a blue light on one side and a white light on the other—blue for a win, white for a loss—to tell elevated-railroad passengers passing by the field on their way home whether the Cubs had won or lost. A colored flag flying from the board during daylight hours also indicated that day's result.[24]

When the renovated Wrigley Field opened on October 1 for the team's last home series, fans saw a vastly expanded bleachers and the new $100,000 scoreboard. An additional 32 feet at the right-field foul line and the loss of 6 feet on the left had altered the dimensions of the park to those that remain today: 355 feet 7 inches to left, 400 feet to center, and 353 feet to right. Throughout, the stadium seats were widened from 18 inches to 22 inches, and many were turned at a thirty-degree angle to improve viewing. The 1937 restoration left fewer than a dozen aisles of the original ballpark unchanged.

Edward Burns of the *Chicago Tribune* declared the renovated Wrigley Field to be nothing less than "the most artistic ballpark in the majors," though the *Herald-Examiner* complained that the scoreboard "proved a disappointment, because the score-by-inning figures are too small." But when the season ended, it could be said that two father-son combinations, the Veecks and the Wrigleys, had given the Cubs the best ballpark in the majors in terms of amenities for fans and ballplayers alike.[25]

Veeck again tackled the concessions department in 1938. State-of-the art hot dog cookers, popcorn poppers, and peanut warmers were added. In 1939, he replaced the old concession stand opposite the pass gate, replacing it with a new stand with 85 feet of counter space, two and a half times larger than the previous counter, at a cost of $25,000. The front of the stand was done in Formica, and the new fixtures were stainless steel, with fluorescent lighting and Tiffany brick above the back bar. Veeck's work on the stadium had gained him invaluable experience in the art of putting people in the seats and keeping them there.

IN THE MIDST of the 1938 season, what became known as the Jake Powell affair inflamed baseball's position on segregation. During a pregame dugout interview at Comiskey Park on July 29, 1938, WGN radio announcer Bob Elson asked Powell, a Yankees outfielder, what he did during the off-season to keep in shape. Powell replied that he was a policeman in Dayton, Ohio, where he kept in shape "beating up niggers and then throwing them in jail."

Outraged listeners besieged the station with phone calls. Others called the Chicago office of baseball commissioner Kenesaw Mountain Landis. Local residents and community organizations representing the heavily black neighborhoods of the South Side demanded Powell be removed from the game permanently. Landis ultimately suspended Powell for ten games, the first known penalty in the history of American sports for a racially intolerant remark. But Landis then stirred up the situation again by stating that Powell's remark was due more to carelessness than to intent. The Yankees asked for police protection, and rumor had it that Powell—who had been sent to a secret location—would never appear in a Yankee uniform again, presumably because of the proximity of Yankee Stadium to Harlem.[26]

Baseball's unwritten but rigidly followed policy of Jim Crow was suddenly back in the forefront. Perhaps the most remarkable commentary came from conservative columnist Westbrook Pegler of the Scripps-Howard syndicate, who suggested that Powell might have gotten his cue from the racial attitudes of the very men whose hired disciplinarian had just benched him. Pegler then made a stunning suggestion: "The Yankees or one of the Chicago teams easily could try the experiment of using a star Negro player from one of the semipro clubs. Customers would suffer no shock, and the Southern white boys would find after a few games that it didn't hurt them much at all."[27]*

Baseball's black eye healed rather too quickly. Powell was soon back in pinstripes, and the Yankees were free to move about the country, but Veeck had witnessed an event that, among many, would lead to the increased testing of the color bar.†

AT AGE TWENTY-FOUR, Veeck was promoted to assistant secretary of the Cubs, which made him a member of the club's executive staff and entitled

---

* Powell was actually not a police officer but simply a resident of Dayton who claimed to be one. Ironically, Powell died in a police station in 1948—while he was being questioned for passing bad checks, he shot himself to death.

† Westbook Pegler drifted further and further to the right until eventually he was banned from writing for the magazine of the John Birch Society because his views became too extreme.

him to go to New York for the National League Winter Meetings in late 1938. There the Brooklyn Dodgers and New York Giants disclosed that they were going to allow sponsors to buy the rights to broadcast their games on the radio during the 1939 season, thereby realizing the elder Veeck's desire to see baseball sold and promoted on the airwaves. At the end of the Winter Meetings, the only radio holdout in either league was the New York Yankees, and they succumbed shortly thereafter.[28]

As Veeck rose through the ranks and his regard for Boots Weber grew, his feelings for Wrigley diminished. At the heart of his frustration with his boss was the way in which Wrigley dealt with people, including his own players. While Bill's father was running the Cubs, members of the roster were regarded as the most content in baseball, their contracts among the quickest to be signed. Under Veeck senior, married players were encouraged to take their wives with them on the road. He reasoned correctly that the more rambunctious, trouble-prone players would fare better with their wives keeping an eye on them. Phil Wrigley had inexplicably ended the practice with Bill's father's passing.

The issue smoldered for several years and flared up when Wrigley acquired Dizzy Dean from the Cardinals before the 1938 season. Dean had hurt his arm by altering his delivery after his toe was broken by a line drive in the 1937 All-Star Game, but Wrigley had insisted the Cubs acquire Dean despite his arm injury. A distracted Dean drove everyone crazy with his poor performance and with what Ed Burns of the *Chicago Tribune* euphemistically termed his "bunk," which had become a "menace to team morale." He missed trains and team meetings and groused about his low pay, arguing that he could make a lot more barnstorming. Burns noted that in Dean's great years with the Cardinals, his wife had always traveled with him and kept him under control. "Dizzy did nothing but mind his pitching when Mrs. Dean was on hand to quell and direct him."[29]

Phil Wrigley projected an image that was not always popular with fans, which he said "mystified him." In contrast with his father's affection for the sport, he had come into baseball admitting that he didn't care for the game, and he had become a self-described "rabid, superstitious" fan who claimed baseball was the only business he knew in which "an outsider seems to know more about it than the men trying to run it." He bragged that he had spent two weeks in total isolation before deciding to change managers, and then said that he had fired popular manager

Charlie Grimm because Grimm would relay his ideas to the team by say-ing "This is Mr. Wrigley's idea, not mine." He also claimed that Grimm was "too swell a fellow" to run a ballclub and appointed Gabby Hartnett, in his opinion tougher and gruffer, to replace him. Wrigley also admitted that technically he knew practically nothing of baseball.[30] Restless and fueled with the same creative spirit and affinity for attracting fans that had characterized his father's career, Bill Veeck wanted a shot at the Cubs presidency; for the moment, however, he would have to settle for less.

Following mediocre seasons in 1939 and 1940, on November 12, 1940, a press conference was called to announce the firing of manager Gabby Hartnett, the resignation of Charles Weber as treasurer, and the appoint-ment of the twenty-six-year-old Veeck to the treasurer's position. Two days later, Wrigley followed his own father's example by hiring a sports reporter as the new head of the team's operations—renaming the posi-tion general manager instead of president. Jim Gallagher of the *Herald-American*, like the elder Veeck, had been critical of the team in print—especially the $185,000 signing in 1938 of pitcher Dizzy Dean, whose sore arm had gotten no better. Weber decided to stay on with the team in an advisory position, realizing he could be a help to Gallagher and to his pro-tégé, Veeck.

Wrigley said that Gallagher had been brought in to end "the confusion" in the Cubs front office and "improve the team's relations with the public."[31] Gallagher seemed as surprised by the appointment as the rest of the Chi-cago press corps and underscored this when he admitted he had not thought much about what he was going to do, including the appointment of a new manager to replace Gabby Hartnett. "First, I've got to cover the Notre Dame–Iowa football game for the *Herald-American* Saturday and wind up my job on the paper. From then on, I'll start learning my job . . . and help straighten out the confusion of the Cubs."[32]

At least one of his fellow writers, Steve Snider of the United Press, recog-nized Gallagher's shortcomings: "He has neither the color of Brooklyn's Larry MacPhail nor the business experience of Cincinnati's Warren Giles."[33] Indeed, Gallagher was everything that the two Veecks were not, starting with the fact that he was, by his own admission, not an outgoing man and not really interested in promotion or dealing with the public. Unlike Veeck senior, who was at ease with the fraternity of sportswriters when he became an executive, Gallagher became an easy target for his former fellow scribes, especially after a series of bad decisions and trades, in particular that of Billy Herman.

The Cubs second baseman, Herman had had a substandard defensive year in 1940, and after getting off to a slow start in the 1941 season, he was traded by the Cubs to Brooklyn for outfielder Charlie Gilbert, infielder Johnny Hudson, and $65,000. On May 7, in his first game as a Dodger, Herman had four hits, and by midseason Larry MacPhail of the Dodgers could brag that without Herman, his club would be as far out of first place as they were in front. Getting rid of Herman was a highly unpopular move with Cubs fans, especially as they watched him help pace the Dodgers to the NL pennant. Gallagher had led off with what would prove the worst trade of his career.[34]

If Veeck felt slighted or let down by being passed over for the president's job, he did not show it. Warren Brown of the *Chicago Herald-Examiner* wrote in his 1945 history of the Cubs that at the time of Gallagher's appointment, there were many who thought Veeck was the best candidate. Veeck, when asked in a 1947 interview if he had wanted the job, replied, "Let's put it this way, I was ambitious."[35] Perhaps an opinion expressed early in 1941 had hindered his chances. While taking night school law courses at Northwestern University, Veeck had written a letter to Commissioner Landis in which he assailed baseball's reserve clause as both "morally and legally indefensible." Landis, who had known Bill from the time he was a child, retorted, "Somebody once said a little knowledge is a dangerous thing, and your letter proves him to be a wizard"[36]

On July 12, 1941, Harry Grayson, sports editor of the Newspaper Enterprise Association, reported that Wrigley had become so disgusted with baseball that he was ready to sell the Cubs. Grayson opined that Wrigley had tried to run the team like the chewing gum business and cared nothing about baseball, which he proved by staying away from Wrigley Field for "months at a stretch."[37]

But by the time Grayson's nationally syndicated column appeared, Bill Veeck had gotten away from Chicago and Phil Wrigley and his chewing gum executives, leaving it to others to speculate then and for many years what would have happened if he had gotten the job rather than Gallagher. In his history of the Cubs, *Wrigleyville*, Peter Golenbock interviewed Cubs from the first half of the twentieth century and concluded, "Not hiring

Veeck to run the Cubs was the single worst personnel move in the entire history of Phil Wrigley's reign as owner of the team. There were other egregious gaffes, to be sure, but this one had the greatest impact on the future of his team."[38]

CHAPTER 4

Brewers Gold

THE 1941 SEASON WAS HARDLY under way when Bill Veeck started talking about taking off," recalled Charlie Grimm, who had befriended the much younger Veeck. In 1932, after playing first base for the club, Grimm had been hired by Veeck's father to manage the Cubs, which he did until he was relieved partway through the 1938 season. Veeck was eager to make a name for himself and get out from under Phil Wrigley. "In adjacent Milwaukee, the Brewers were dying," Grimm recounted years later. "They were last in the American Association. He had been through the mill all these years with the Cubs, he had been inspired by his father's great success with them, and he was anxious to strike out on his own. He sounded me out and I was receptive."[1]

The floundering minor-league franchise had been without an actual owner for the first weeks of the 1941 season. On June 16, league president George Trautman took over management of the club with a power of attorney and a mandate to attract new ownership. The fear was that if the weakest-link Brewers failed, the league might somehow follow or at least be diminished in status.[2]

The banjo-strumming Grimm was a perfect complement to Veeck. Older, wiser, and beloved by many, Grimm could sing and also play the piano, snare drum, harmonica, cello, and xylophone, and he carried a card in the magician's union. And Milwaukee was a perfect city for Veeck in many respects, not least because it was the nation's thirteenth-largest—between San Francisco and Buffalo in population—with a half million potential fans within the city limits alone. Milwaukee was the largest city in the American Association, with a long baseball history and a tradition of strong fan support, though that enthusiasm had been allowed to dissipate.*

For the rest of his life, Veeck would remind listeners that he was dead broke and without personal resources when he took over the Brewers. However, in a matter of a few days he put together a syndicate of Chicago and Milwaukee businessmen who had come up with $50,000 for the club and were willing to assume $50,000 of the club's debt of $118,000. Veeck got help from Philip Clarke of City National Bank of Chicago and Lester Armour of the meatpacking family, both old friends of his father's, along with a sprinkling of Milwaukee investors.

Veeck needed a manager and asked Phil Wrigley to release Charlie Grimm from his first-base coaching duties.† Wrigley agreed and Veeck offered Grimm 25 percent ownership in the club and a salary 25 percent higher than he had gotten from the Cubs.[3] Wrigley not only gave Veeck his blessing but also loaned him some of the more expendable Cubs. Among them was Lou "The Mad Russian" Novikoff, the immensely popular but consistently inept slugger and subpar outfielder who had come from the Pacific Coast League's Los Angeles Angels. The most highly publicized rookie in National League history to that point, he been built up as the next Babe Ruth. Wrigley had paid $65,000 for him, but he was sitting on the bench, having failed at the plate and been a disaster in the outfield, which at least in part appeared to be caused by a fear of Veeck's ivy. He would stop well short of the wall, watching hits fly over his head. Trainer Bob Lewis first thought The Mad Russian feared spiders, then concluded that Novikoff believed the foliage was poison ivy. He walked Novikoff out to the wall and pulled down some vines, rubbed them on his face and hands, and even put some of the leaves in his mouth and chewed on them. Novikoff smiled politely and asked "what kind of smoke would they make," but would not go near them to find out.[4]

Veeck and Grimm now had their star in Novikoff—and their own clown prince to boot. Grimm believed the affable Russian American needed some freedom to be himself and vowed to give him a microphone so that he could

---

* The American Association was the highest level in the minors at the time, so it was the equivalent of the modern AAA, which began in 1946.
† Grimm was replaced as first base coach by Dizzy Dean a few days later.

sing for the fans in Milwaukee as he had done when he was ripping up the Pacific Coast League.[5]

Their prospects improved further when Wrigley also sent them Billy Myers, a shortstop with tremendous potential but almost no playing time in Chicago, followed a few days later by catcher Al Todd, who was under contract with the Cubs and playing for Montreal in the International League.[6]

Although Wrigley maintained that the Brewers were not a farm team of the Cubs, both parties had some of the advantages of such an arrangement. Columnist Edward W. Cochrane wrote that the working arrangement between the two clubs was a "splendid thing for both—the Brewers will get valuable players that the Cubs cannot use. The Cubs will get the pick of Milwaukee players."[7]

On June 21, Veeck and Grimm arrived at the Milwaukee railroad station with a few dollars in cash between them. After taking a break at a tavern with some locals to toast the future of the club—then eighteen and a half games out of first place—they headed over to examine Borchert Field, a dilapidated, old-fashioned wooden stadium built in 1902 with seating for 8,000. Warren Brown of the *Chicago Herald-American* observed that it looked like the home field of the Skid Row Tigers; "if anybody were to come out to see what was going on, it, it would be necessary to go through a fumigating plant after the visit."[8] Bob French of the *Toledo Blade*, who had seen many games at the park, noted in a column following the Veeck purchase that the park was "the only one in the world perhaps where no spectator, no matter where he sits, can see the entire field"—a problem, he argued, that was keeping fans away in droves.[9]

Money needed to be pumped into the facility immediately, and Veeck negotiated a $50,000 loan for that purpose with City National Bank. Many of the changes would be pedestrian but essential, such as painting the stadium and refurbishing the restrooms, especially a nice new one for the female patrons Veeck was determined to attract. Other moves were more inspired. To cut down on graffiti on the freshly painted men's rooms, Veeck installed blackboards, imploring those with anonymous messages to pick up a piece of chalk and "write it here."

Veeck and Grimm inherited Rudie Schaffer, the Brewers secretary, who was also a certified public accountant. A small, vivacious man—Grimm described him as "pixyish"—he had worked for the Brewers for six years for little compensation, but he was motivated by what Veeck called "his boundless love of baseball." As formal personally as Veeck was not, Schaffer agreed to stay on and help bring about the rebirth of baseball in Milwaukee.[10]

Veeck immediately established himself as a new kind of owner, and created a template for his early days in ownership situations to come. He was in the stands and bleachers for almost every game, talking to fans about the club and what they liked and disliked about the stadium. Grimm watched as Veeck worked the crowd for that first half season: "When it was over, I'm sure that Bill, who roamed the stands during every game, had mitted every fan who came to the park. He stood at the main exit as they left the park, in the manner of a preacher at the church door. He invited suggestions and complaints. He and the fans congratulated each other on victory and exchanged sympathies after defeat."[11]

To keep the sportswriters happy, Veeck built a new press box stocked with an unlimited supply of beer and cold meat and made himself available for interviews at all times of the day or night. When he wasn't at the ballpark, he was out speaking to any group—no matter how small—about his team and how it would soon be in contention.[12]

Yet despite early tinkering by Veeck and Grimm, the team continued to slip in the standings. On July 21, Bob French, a columnist for the *Toledo Blade*, noted that the Brewers were now deeper in the cellar than they had been when the Veeck-Grimm team had taken over four weeks earlier. They had won only a third of their games in that time and found themselves thirteen games behind the seventh-place St. Paul Saints, with a won-lost record of 24–66. French noted that attendance at Brewers games had peaked with the advent of new ownership but was dwindling again."[13]

Veeck realized that if he could not yet give the fans a winning team, he could give them entertainment, so he began adding music and other sideshows to the proceedings. Promotional efforts in baseball were rare and often limited to Ladies' Day and doubleheaders. There were no mascots in the modern sense, and music at the ballpark was uncommon, save for opening day and the World Series. Veeck and the ever-playful Charlie Grimm were thus working with a blank canvas.

On August 13 some 5,000 fans paid to watch Satchel Paige and his Monarchs in action in an official Negro American League game. The Monarchs dropped the game 1–0 to the Birmingham Black Barons, but the real attraction was Paige, an established star who in the month of August alone packed stadiums from Massachusetts to California. The long friendship between Veeck and Paige began when they met that night.[14]

A "family party" night in late August drew more than 4,000, which seemed to be the turning point for attendance in terms of a regular league game. In town for a game a few days later, league president Trautman said: "Two months ago, I wouldn't give you a quarter for Milwaukee's baseball future. Look at it today. Why, this town is the talk of baseball."[15]

Meanwhile, Veeck shuttled players in and out on almost a daily basis. In fewer than three months, he bought, sold, or exchanged a record fifty-one players, allowing him to boast of running "three teams—the one that left yesterday, the one playing today, the one coming in tomorrow." Even if only for a few days, the players for the 1941 Brewers were treated well by Veeck, who, for example, provided them with unlimited soft drinks and beer between games of a doubleheader.

Veeck also established an emotional attachment to the team that made him euphoric after a win and gloomy after a defeat. "Bill was a hard loser," Grimm testified. "Often, after we lost, he'd be in bed when I arrived back at our hotel." Others observed that after a defeat he would go to bed without eating. The Brewers cost Veeck a lot of dinners, because they remained in last place to the end of the 1941 season.

The bright spot was Novikoff, who claimed the American Association batting title with a .397 average for the 90 games he played for the Brewers, ensuring that the Cubs would reclaim him for the following season. Veeck and Grimm had catered to his every whim, including allowing him to sing and play the harmonica as part of a pre-game ritual. Recognizing his slugger's inability to field grounders, Veeck kept the grass in left field so long that a ball hit there would quickly slow to a dead stop, allowing Novikoff to easily pick it up.[16]

Veeck's improvements prompted Sam Levy, a young sports reporter for the *Milwaukee Journal* who covered the team as his beat, to describe the Brewers as the best-looking eighth-place team in the history of the American Association. Levy concluded after the Brewers last game of 1941, "The experts will be cautious in making their 1942 guesses—ours is ready: no lower than fourth place."[17]

The 1941 season also netted Veeck a partner in Rudie Schaffer, who immediately assumed the role of Veeck's right-hand man and would remain essential to him for decades to come. "Rudie and I complement each other perfectly," Veeck later observed. "I'm the one who takes the bows, and he's the one who does the work."

As the season drew to a close, Veeck and Schaffer looked for an additional source of revenue to keep themselves and the team afloat during the winter of 1941–42. The answer came from his old Chicago acquaintance Abe Saperstein. In the fall of 1941 Saperstein gave Veeck and Schaffer the right to promote the Chicago-based Harlem Globe Trotters in the upper Midwest.[18]

Wendell Smith, sports editor of the *Pittsburgh Courier* (then regarded as the most popular black newspaper in the country), who would become a close friend to Veeck and Saperstein, later wrote that Veeck was in a financial hole when Saperstein stepped in and "probably saved Veeck's baseball career, as well as the Milwaukee franchise." Veeck added: "We made money on those Globe Trotter promotions, and as a result, Abe and I have been the best of friends ever since." On another occasion almost twenty years later, Veeck claimed that the Globe Trotter bookings had allowed him to make enough money to keep the Brewers going.[19]

Although best known for his basketball promotions, Saperstein was also a major promoter of Negro baseball during the summer months. He was perhaps best known for his handling of the second Negro league's East-West All-Star Game in 1935, which drew more than 50,000 to Comiskey Park.

The other bond to come out of the 1941 season was Veeck's strong relationship with a cohort of writers—Sam Levy, R. G. Lynch, and Ray Grody in Milwaukee, and in Chicago the likes of Warren Brown at the *Chicago Herald-Examiner* and Arch Ward of the *Chicago Tribune*, who seemed to mention Veeck in his "Wake of the News" column at least once a week. Sam Levy nicknamed Veeck "Sport Shirt Bill," which fit his determinedly nonconformist appearance. Veeck was rarely seen in anything other than a white sport shirt, never wore a hat, eschewed overcoats save on the coldest of days, and wore moccasins, which he tended to slip off, allowing him to walk around in his stocking feet. He turned being tieless into an article of faith in a day when male working-class patrons showed up to watch the game in neckties, hats, and lace-up shoes.*

Veeck in essence created himself as a brand, allowing him to get easy

---

* This was a later development, as photographs taken at the time of his marriage to Eleanor show him with a tie.

publicity. Even in the off-season, he attracted ink on the thinnest of premises. On November 5, for instance, he revealed that Grimm had been offered the managership of a major-league team but had turned it down. He also noted that he himself had turned down a major-league offer for Brewers catcher Charlie "The Greek" George. Whether these were bona fide offers or simply rumors, Veeck clearly could get wire service reporters and editors to carry a story with few specifics.[20]

At the end of the 1941 season, with Saperstein's payments in hand, Veeck prepared for his next round of transactions during the Winter Meetings in Jacksonville, Florida, in December. Veeck obtained a few new faces for his club before the meetings ended on Friday the fifth. Two days later, the United States was attacked at Pearl Harbor, and America's involvement in World War II commenced.

The military draft had been instituted earlier in anticipation of war, and a few major leaguers had already served. Hank Greenberg, the Detroit Tigers slugger, had been drafted the previous May, having hit two home runs the eve of his induction. He had served his required time in an Army antitank unit, where he was promoted to the rank of sergeant and was released two days before Pearl Harbor. He wrote to Jack Cuddy of the United Press at the beginning of January 1942 to report that he had, at age thirty-one, reenlisted in the Army a few days after his discharge.[21] The son of Orthodox Jewish immigrants, Greenberg maintained throughout the late 1930s that he was hitting home runs in defiance of Hitler.* Greenberg was not the only star player to serve. Bob Feller of the Cleveland Indians, the leading pitcher in the American League, enlisted in the Naval Reserve and was sworn in by Lieut. Cmdr. Gene Tunney, former world heavyweight boxing champion.

Closer to home, Jim Gallagher had finally persuaded Phil Wrigley to add lights to Wrigley Field for the 1942 season. The Cubs had had a disastrous 70–84 1941 season, with a precipitous drop in attendance to half the 1920 level. Gallagher had long met with the same objections Veeck had earlier, but financial necessity opened the door.[22] Wrigley, who trusted his old treasurer in such matters, had asked Veeck the previous summer to investigate a Milwaukee company that offered a new lighting technique— a hydraulic system where the lights could appear and disappear in a

---

* He was known far and wide as the man who on Yom Kippur in 1934 went to the synagogue rather than the stadium. The Tigers lost that day, but the team beat the Yankees for the pennant.

"telescopic fashion," thereby preserving the daytime look of the stadium. The cost of the equipment was far more than what Wrigley had intended to pay, but he nonetheless purchased the lights for $185,000, storing them beneath the grandstand at the end of the devastating 1941 season. Construction was scheduled to begin the week of December 8, but Wrigley changed his mind after Pearl Harbor and ultimately turned over 165 tons of steel and 35,000 feet of copper wire to the government without taking a nickel in return. He figured it could be better used to build lighting for an airfield or munitions depot, and his lights ended up at the Great Lakes Naval Air Station. Like many others in baseball, Wrigley thought that the games might be cancelled or curtailed for the rest of the war, as had happened during World War I.[23]

When the American and National Leagues held their annual meetings in Chicago on December 9, discussion centered on the war and its impact on the game. Much was made of the fact that baseball was also Japan's national pastime. Indeed, right after Pearl Harbor the *Hollywood Reporter* had related that on the day of the attack "the first American victory over the Japanese was won by the Paramount baseball team when it defeated the LA Nippons, all-Jap team, 6-to-3. No one was aware of the war until the third inning. . . . F.B.I, men allowed the game to finish . . . then rounded up the Jap contingent."[24]

For a minor-league owner such as Bill Veeck, the threat of cancellation or curtailment was a real fear. Relief came from two unlikely figures. Although a friend of baseball, Franklin D. Roosevelt bore no goodwill toward baseball commissioner Kenesaw Mountain Landis, a severe conservative who openly loathed Roosevelt's liberal politics. Nonetheless, the president and commissioner exchanged letters in January 1942, Landis asking about baseball's role in wartime and Roosevelt replying with his famous "Green Light Letter," which argued that the nation needed more baseball, not less. "I honestly feel that it would be best for the country to keep baseball going. There will be fewer people unemployed and everybody will work longer hours and harder than ever before. Baseball provides a recreation which does not last over two hours or two hours and a half, and which can be got for very little cost."[25]

Baseball responded gleefully. "If the shot that was fired at Lexington in 1775 was 'heard around the world,' it is equally true that the 'Play Ball' of President Roosevelt in his letter to Commissioner Landis recently was heard and applauded around the baseball universe," said *Baseball* magazine. In a note to the president, the sports editor of the *Chicago Sun* called it "the most notable contribution to baseball in our time," and *The Sporting News* deemed him to be "Player of the Year."

Roosevelt also lobbied for night games to be extended "because it gives an opportunity to the day shift to see a game occasionally." Each team had been limited to seven home night games per year, and Landis, among others, disapproved of night baseball. But night games improved attendance, and teams in smaller markets wanted more of them. This included Veeck, who immediately began scheduling night contests for the upcoming 1942 season. Phil Wrigley, having given away his lights, now talked about playing at night in Comiskey Park.

Veeck, who had entertained thoughts of building a new park, used the Green Light Letter to help him get zoning approvals to move light stanchions that were blocking spectator views, add restrooms, and strengthen his sagging bleachers, which were unsafe and a potential liability. Veeck had a plan to fill them with kids and others for an admission fee of 44 cents. Veeck also understood that the war would keep Milwaukee factories working at full tilt for the duration, and he was prepared to offer entertainment for war workers after the factory whistle blew.

Unlike most owners, who had adopted austerity measures, Veeck invested in the 1942 baseball season, betting that the war would not hurt his attendance. "We don't believe that this is a time to retrench," he said as he announced that the Brewers had spent $80,000 to $90,000 for new players, including three purchases from the Texas League, and $10,000 sprucing up Borchert Field.[26]

Veeck also adopted a combative stance in his dealings with the other owners in 1942. It was unlike anything that the American Association had ever experienced and perhaps unlike anything organized baseball had ever witnessed at any level. Veeck started riling up his rivals when he complained that Milwaukee was not awarded the Opening-Day attendance trophy. His stadium was overloaded with 15,599 paying customers, but the trophy was awarded to Indianapolis, which had drawn only 11,546. The league, it seemed, gauged the attendance winner on a ratio of fans to their city's total population.

Veeck was steaming mad and struck back at the next home game with a four-foot-tall trophy of his own design, which he presented to himself in a ceremony at home plate, proclaiming the Brewers as winner of the opening day award. Delivered in an armored car complete with a pair of armed guards the trophy was engraved:

PRESENTED TO MILWAUKEE BY THE MILWAUKEE BASEBALL CLUB
BECAUSE OF A TECHNICAL ERROR ON THE PART OF THE LEAGUE
MANAGEMENT

Veeck had laid out $300 for the trophy, an extraordinary sum in 1942. "When you buy something for yourself, you're certainly going to buy the best, aren't you?" he explained.[27] The trophy became a dominant feature in Veeck's Milwaukee office, appearing in a *Look* magazine photograph of the young owner with his feet on the desk and a portrait of Judge Landis on his wall along with a caption that read in part: "Cost of the cup: $300. Value of the publicity: $3,000."[28]

Continuing his performance on that night, Bill sarcastically presented George Trautman, president of the Columbus Blue Birds as well as president of the American Association, which had denied Veeck the attendance trophy, a striped cane and "seeing-eye dog," in reality Veeck's own English bulldog. He topped off the show by giving bouquets of vegetables to the umpires while the loudspeakers blared "Three Blind Mice."* Instantly Veeck had established his two primary adversaries, publicly challenging the authority of his league and its owners and firing an opening salvo in what would become a lingering and genuine distrust and disrespect of umpires. He had begun complaining about the quality of the umpiring in the association shortly after he arrived in Milwaukee, and the easygoing Grimm was quickly convinced that Veeck looked upon umpires as "mortal enemies"—he barked at them from the stands and chewed them out after the game.[29]

Veeck took on the quality of ballpark lighting across the association, which he insisted was inadequate, especially as the Brewers took batting practice. The first place he targeted was Trautman's Columbus stadium. To illuminate his point, Bill and Schaffer arrived early and took seats down front. When the lights came on, Veeck and Schaffer jumped up waving lanterns, solemnly peering out toward the diamond like two shipwrecked sailors.

Veeck seemed to take special pleasure in ribbing Donie Bush, the well-liked president-manager of the Indianapolis Indians. Then in his fifties, Bush had played sixteen years in the majors as one of the leading short-

---

* Almost seventy years after this event, American League umpire Jim Evans was asked about Veeck, and his terse answer was, "He didn't think much of umpires."

stops in the so-called dead ball era. The star of the World Series in 1909, he went on to manage the Senators, Pirates, White Sox, and Reds before returning to Indianapolis to lead the Indians. The Veeck-Schaffer lantern act was restaged for Bush, who ordered his groundskeeper to confiscate the lanterns and actually chased Veeck and Schaffer on foot. Bush swore that Veeck would have to pay to get into his park after that.* "I wonder," Bush asked Sam Levy of the *Milwaukee Journal* at one point in the 1942 season, "how that boy could be so repulsive. His daddy was a fine man, I knew him well. He never feuded with anyone. He was one of the best men the Major Leagues ever had."[30]

But Veeck reserved his most provocative and melodramatic behavior for the St. Paul Saints and owner Lou McKenna. At some point early in the 1942 season, for reasons he never made clear, Veeck ordered his gate man to stop McKenna and ask for his ticket. McKenna bought his way in but vowed he would even the score when Veeck came to his ballpark. This response was all Veeck needed to pull out the stops in needling McKenna, his team, and the city of St. Paul. He would show up in the St. Paul stadium as early as five-thirty for a night game and take a seat in the grandstand next to a pay phone. The phone would ring, and he would answer, listen, and then repeat the caller's question: "Are the Saints playing tonight?" He would reply with a grin, "I don't know if the Saints will have the nerve to show up because the Brewers are in town. In fact, the Brewers already are on the field. They've sent a scouting expedition out to find the Saints."

These calls, which came from a confederate—almost certainly Rudie Schaffer—and Veeck's response were staged for one or more newspaper reporters. When the game began, Veeck would typically relocate to a box seat directly behind the Brewers dugout and cheer loudly and provocatively for his team—all of this designed to anger the home fans. One afternoon when the Brewers were crushing the Saints, a bottle flew out of a box behind him and just missed Veeck's head. The bottle thrower was pointed out to Veeck, who leapt to his feet and confronted the man.

"My little boy who is only four years old has more nerve than you," Bill shouted inches from the man's face. "He's smarter than you—he wouldn't throw a bottle at a person whose back was turned." When a group of fans confronted Veeck, a policeman then suggested that he take refuge in a

---

* Bush remained active in baseball until 1972, when he died at age eighty-four. He was still working as a scout for the Chicago White Sox.

deserted part of the grandstand. McKenna appealed to Sam Levy to get Veeck to join him in the press box before some fan beat him up. Veeck refused to budge, insisting that the press box belonged to the press and he had every right to stay in his seat until the last out of the second game of the doubleheader. When he got up to leave, the crowd cheered.*

Thereafter when the Brewers played in St. Paul, Veeck saw to it that they stayed only in Minneapolis hotels. He explained to a local writer that he did not want his team living "in a very dreary village where the sidewalks were pulled out every night at nine." The wisecrack caused St. Paul fans to threaten to boycott the Brewers. Adding insult to injury, Veeck proclaimed that threats didn't bother him any more than the small receipts he got when the team played in St. Paul. "All I am interested in here is to beat your brains out."

Veeck's pyrotechnics aside, the team had improved vastly on the field, and by midseason in 1942 it was ranked first in the division. Like other teams, Veeck had the added challenge of replacing players who had been called into military service. *The Sporting News* reported on June 4, for example, that Veeck was looking for a pitcher to fill the gap left by the departure of lefty Russ Meers for the Navy.

Veeck employed every trick he could think of to win the 1942 pennant, which added to his growing reputation as someone who believed in bending the rules—even to the breaking point. A Saturday night game in August against the Indianapolis Indians was threatened by imminent rain. The Brewers were batting in the fifth inning with two out and trailed the Indians by one run. If that third out were made, the game would become official, resulting in a loss. As Grimm recalled: "Bill couldn't wait for the rain to come and plunged Borchert Field into darkness." Before the electric failure was solved, the belated downpour arrived. The game was washed out, and a Brewers defeat was averted. Gabby Hartnett, the Indianapolis manager and an old friend of Grimm's from his Cubs days, was furious, openly accusing Veeck or one of his minions of pulling the plug. Hartnett demanded that the game be finished from the point the lights went out, but Trautman ruled that the game be replayed in its entirety. The Indians won the replay, but Harnett was still angry, and Grimm admitted that he did not blame him.

---

* In another report of the incident, he slapped the bottle thrower and ended the game in a seat on the roof of the stadium. This version was secondhand, while the Levy version was presented as an eyewitness account.

The season went into its last weeks with the Brewers in and out of the lead, thanks to some outstanding performances, including that of Eddie Stanky, who hit .452 to win the batting title and was named the Association's Most Valuable Player.*

On the last day of the season, the Kansas City Blues were in Milwaukee for a daylight doubleheader that would decide the championship. The Brewers were a half game out and could take the lead by winning the first game, but the Brewers pitching staff was overused and ailing. "Even if there were a second game, the Blues were almost a cinch to win it, our pitching was in such a sad state," Charlie Grimm later reported. The start of the first game was delayed by rain for more than two hours, and then for an additional half hour after the downpour ended. Roy Harney of the Blues then realized that Veeck had something devious in mind.

Veeck didn't want to play that second game, so the longer he delayed, the less chance there would be that a second one could be played before darkness. Harney appealed to the venerable Tom Hickey, president emeritus of the association, who was representing the absent Trautman. Hickey told Veeck that the lights would have to be turned on to complete the doubleheader. "I wouldn't put the lights on for Franklin D. Roosevelt!" Veeck told the old gent. The Blues were a farm team of the New York Yankees and a call was made to New York for advice, but to no avail: nothing in the rules stipulated that a scheduled day game had to be completed under lights.[31]

The ruse was staged in vain, however, as the Blues won the first game to clinch the pennant, and the second game was called off by mutual consent. Milwaukee finished with an 81–69 record. A few weeks later, at the annual winter meeting, Veeck's wary fellow magnates reworked the rules to foil him. His attempted "larceny" of the pennant resulted in a rule that lights had to be turned on to finish any game whose conclusion was threatened by darkness. Next, the owners agreed that if the lights went out for any reason, that game had to be resumed later at the same point and with identical lineups, as early as possible.

Fueled by his team's improved performance, attendance at Borchert Field had risen from 98,000 in 1941 to 280,000 in 1942. Veeck's clever promotions also played their part, among them a new tradition of giving away odd prizes that became more bizarre as the season progressed. Veeck and Schaffer would haul a gate man's box out in front of the stands to

---

* He was sold to the Cubs at the end of the season and began his major-league career in 1943.

draw tickets, inviting spectators holding the lucky stubs to report for their prizes. In one of the early lotteries, the first fan was presented with a fifty-pound block of ice thrust into his arms by Veeck himself. The next received a keg of nails and the third a stepladder. The crowd squealed with delight as they watched hapless patrons return to their seats to deal with their gifts.

Fruit and vegetable nights followed. A lady fan who won a basket of peaches returned several nights later with an oversized peach pie, which she presented to Veeck, who spoke about it for months to come. During livestock nights the prizes included turkeys, geese, rabbits, and pigs that often "escaped" onto the field, with the winners expected to chase them. The pigs, needless to say, were greased. One night, the fans were surprised to see an old, swaybacked draft horse on the field awaiting presentation to a lucky fan. The perplexed winner had no idea what to do with the animal, so he was advised to sell it back to the farm from which Veeck had purchased it, allowing the fan to pocket $15.[32]

At one game Veeck awarded a man two pigeons. "I can see that poor guy yet," Veeck recalled later, "sitting there during the game, a pigeon in each hand. He couldn't let go and nobody would help him. And you know pigeons!"

Other promotions—free lunches, vaudeville acts, swing bands—helped keep the turnstiles turning during the season. On June 2, Veeck assembled a band made up of players and Milwaukee front office personnel, which included Veeck playing a cheap whistle, Grimm on banjo, and Rudie Schaffer playing a bass created from a three-gallon paint can, a broomstick, and a well-rosined cord. That an owner would be part of a serenade to his fans was big news: "Café de Veeck Wows 'Em in Milwaukee" was the headline in the *Chicago Tribune*.[33]

Veeck created even more publicity when he placed a chicken-wire screen above the right-field fence to turn opponents' home runs into singles. It was then rolled out of the way when the home team came up. The practice was immediately banned.

Decades later when Veeck was serving as a friendly witness in Curt Flood's 1970 lawsuit against major-league baseball, its lawyers used the moveable fence to question Veeck's character. "May I say about the fences, as a prelude, that at that time there were no rules forbidding the motion of fences because . . . I have tried always not to break any rules, but to test highly their elasticity, and I did put into Milwaukee a moveable fence that was on top of our normal 25-foot right field fence. Since I had more right-hand hitters, I put it in right field, made out of chicken wire and connected to a cable that was operated by a steam winch, and I did pull it out between innings when the opposition was batting and on the next day they had a league meeting and they declared it illegal, immoral, and I stopped."[34]

CHAPTER 5

The Philadelphia Story

BORCHERT FIELD HAD LONG ACTED as a major venue for Negro base-ball teams, both the barnstorming organizations and those associ-ated with the Negro American League. Veeck's predecessor, Henry Bendinger, staged contests there as far back as September 19, 1932, when the Kansas City Monarchs met the bearded and roguish House of David in a night game billed as being between the two leading independent clubs in baseball.[1]

Such contests were all but invisible to *The Sporting News* and the nation's mainstream newspapers, even when white major leaguers faced black teams. Only the African American press reported on a game between the Monarchs and a white barnstorming squad led by major leaguers Dizzy and Paul Dean in late October 1934 at Borchert Field.[2]

By 1937, all but one of the teams in the Negro American League, the Memphis Red Sox, had played in Milwaukee to crowds averaging 2,000 a game. Two games of the Negro American League championship that year—between the Monarchs and the Chicago American Giants—were played at Borchert Field. Bendinger was so enthusiastic about the high quality of play that he offered the league all open dates for 1938, and the crowds con-tinued to grow. A July 1 game between the Monarchs and the Giants drew 3,500, and a game two weeks later between the Giants and the independent Ethiopian Clowns, a nonleague game, drew 4,300.[3]

A year later, on Sunday afternoon, June 4, 1939, the Clowns beat the Madison Blues, a white semipro team that had been the 1938 tri-state league champions, 7–1. Some 4,541 fans turned out at Borchert Field to watch

"Schoolboy" Impo of the Ethiopians pitch against Alvin "Butch" Krueger, a former pitcher for the Brewers and a former state open golf champion who had a large following in the area.[4]

In both 1939 and 1940, the Satchel Paige All-Stars played at Borchert Field, and Paige pitched for the Kansas City Monarchs in a doubleheader there against the Ethiopian Clowns on the eve of Veeck's announcement in June 1941 that he had purchased the Brewers, and twice more in mid-August.[5] Paige had been the subject of a June 1940 feature in *Time* magazine that not only lauded him but also ended with the observation that "many a shepherd of a limping major club has made no secret of his yearning to trade more than a couple of buttsprung outfielders for colored players of the caliber of Satchelfoots Paige."[6] Later that summer *The Saturday Evening Post* ran a feature on Paige, and on June 21, 1941, he was featured in a *Life* magazine pictorial that placed him on a pedestal with fighter Joe Louis and Olympic champion Jesse Owens; the piece quoted Joe DiMaggio calling Paige the greatest pitcher he had ever faced—all the more stunning because it appeared in the midst of DiMaggio's 56-game hitting streak.

Veeck especially appreciated Paige's publicity and drawing power and arranged for him to pitch at Borchert Field on multiple occasions in 1942. At the first of these, on June 28, orchestrated with the help of Abe Saperstein, who was then booking the Negro American League teams out of his Chicago office, the question of Paige's age first became an issue of national significance. Saperstein told the *Milwaukee Journal* that Paige claimed to be thirty-four years old but that he thought Satchel was actually about thirty-eight.[7]

In August, Paige granted an interview to the Associated Press in which he said that he did not think Negroes could be successfully integrated onto white teams because of segregation. "You might as well be honest about it, there would be plenty of problems, not only in the South where the colored boys wouldn't be able to stay and travel with teams in spring training, but in the North where they could not stay or eat with them in many places. All the nice statements in the world from both sides are not going to knock out Jim Crow." His alternative suggestion was that all-Negro teams could operate in each of the major leagues: "That would be something." Paige admitted in the interview that he doubted he would ever be hired by the majors because no team could match the $37,000 he had earned in 1941.[8]

On September 1, 1942, outfielder Hal Peck, in the backyard of his modest home in Genesee Depot, Wisconsin, shot himself in the foot with a shotgun. It was officially reported as a hunting accident, though Charlie Grimm later said that the gun had discharged while Peck was chasing a rat. He lost two toes in the mishap. Grimm later wrote, "When Hal Peck shot off his toe in a hunting accident back in my Milwaukee days, I stayed at the hospital all night with him." Peck had been sold to the Brooklyn Dodgers a few days earlier. "On the day of the accident, we were in the office, and when the phone rang we thought it was Larry MacPhail calling to close the deal for Peck," wrote Grimm in his memoir. "But it was Hal's wife, hysterically reporting the shooting. I thought Veeck had suffered a heart attack when he fell out of his chair. Rudie, who already had marked up the sale in his ledger, lost his voice for about a week." Veeck ultimately persuaded MacPhail to honor the deal, though when MacPhail joined the Army soon after, his replacement, Branch Rickey, tried unsuccessfully to squelch it.[9]

Veeck and Rudie Schaffer arrived at Yankee Stadium on October 2 to watch the three remaining games of the 1942 World Series—all won by the St. Louis Cardinals over the Yankees—before heading back to the Midwest. Veeck denied two rumors, according to Sam Levy of the *Milwaukee Journal*: first, that he was a candidate for Larry MacPhail's vacated post as president and general manager of the Brooklyn Dodgers, and second, that he intended to buy the Philadelphia Phillies. A week later, Veeck acknowledged to Levy that he had in fact gone with Schaffer to confer with Gerry Nugent, president of the Phillies.[10]

Nugent's team was in deep trouble, having lost 111 games in 1941—still the most in franchise history—and drawn only 231,000 fans. The operating losses on the year were $60,000, which added to a note of $55,000 that was due to the bank. Early in 1942 National League president Ford Frick had called a meeting of his Executive Committee to reveal that the team was totally out of cash and unable to even send scouts out to look for new talent. The league, with great reluctance, paid off the loan and extended Nugent additional funds so he could take his team to spring training and open the season on schedule. At the end of the season the league pushed Nugent to sell the team. One strong potential buyer, the Philco Corp., got league approval but lost interest as it concentrated on government war contracts, making radio equipment and fuses for bombs.[11]

"So I called on Nugent and talked about his club," Veeck told Levy. "He quoted some large figures, but that was all." Had he been able to close a deal, Veeck said he would have remained in Milwaukee and sent Grimm to oversee Philadelphia. "The Phils have many potential stars among their younger players who belong in the American Association at least for one season. Those players would win a pennant for us and then be ready for the majors."[12]

What Veeck did not divulge at the time, and what did not become public for some time to come, was his bold plan to buy the Phillies and staff the team with stars from the Negro leagues.

Save for being mentioned in radical papers such as the Communist *Daily Worker*, until 1940 the issue of integrating black players into the major leagues had remained largely dormant since white columnists had first brought it up in 1933. That spring, with both Philadelphia teams faring poorly in the standings and at the box office, the *Philadelphia Record* ran a sensational article headlined "Stars for A's, Pep for Phils—in Negro Ranks," arguing that the time had come to bring Negro leaguers onto the local teams. The previous summer Phils manager Doc Prothro had stated that all his troubles would be over if he could get permission to sign "colored stars." The *Record* quoted a number of managers and players with a "high opinion" of Negro talent and asserted that several managers and owners would sign Negro players in a moment were it not for the "most inflexible unwritten law of the game." The paper agitated for the Jim Crow laws to be broken by the two local teams, adding, "There is even a chance—and a whole lot more—that a few thousand fans that have been staying away from the A's and the Phils might come out to see what Paige and Gibson and a few more like them might do in the major leagues."[13]

Less than a year later, H. G. Salsinger of the *Detroit News* attended a doubleheader in Briggs Stadium between the Homestead Grays and the Baltimore Elite Giants. Not only did he deem the level of play equal or superior to that of the majors, but he said that black players had more verve and a keener spirit of competition. Salsinger also observed that the 27,949 fans, most of them black, who had paid to see the doubleheader were, in his words, "beautifully behaved" and "understood baseball and did not miss a single point of excellence in nineteen innings of play." If there was an unwritten rule keeping blacks off the field, there was also an unwritten fear in the minds of whites about unruly black fans, a fear Salsinger did much to undermine: "For once Briggs Stadium housed customers who refrained from littering the fringe of the outfield with waste paper."[14]

By 1942 Phil Wrigley had decided to host black-versus-white contests and all–Negro league events at Wrigley Field, which added one more roll to the drumbeat for putting blacks and whites on the same field as equals. The stadium had been de facto off-limits to blacks in competition for more than twenty years, since the 1920 championship game of the American Professional Football Association.* On May 24, 1942, the Kansas City Monarchs defeated Dizzy Dean's All-Stars 3–1 before a Wrigley crowd of 29,775 in a game billed as "Zeke Bonura Day," aimed at raising money for the Navy Relief Fund by honoring local favorite Bonura, who had played for both the Cubs and the White Sox and was now in uniform. Members of the Armed Forces were allowed in free if they were in uniform. Dean's team was composed of major and minor leaguers in the service who were on furlough from their respective military bases. Cleveland Indians phenom Bob Feller was supposed to relieve Dean after an inning, but he sent his regrets earlier in the day, as he had been called back to duty by the Navy.

The game's promoter was Abe Saperstein, the star attraction was Satchel Paige, and the event's cheerleader was Fay Young of the *Defender*, who saw it as much more than just another exhibition game, and even as a potential turning point in the racial composition of baseball. The *Defender* noted that Cubs management was going all out to make this game a "tremendous success," and Saperstein employed all of his well-honed promotional skills.[15]

Paige tossed the first six innings for the Monarchs, allowing only two singles and one run. Dean, by then a broadcaster and sometime barnstormer, pitched the first inning, retiring all three batters he faced. But the real story of the game had occurred before it started, as thousands of fans, black and white, had lined up peacefully for hours before game time to get a ticket. Scalpers got several times face value for mere general admission seats. The crowd was the largest the ballpark had seen for the season. Meanwhile, on the other side of town, the White Sox played the Tigers in a doubleheader attended by 10,000 fewer fans. Dean, Paige, and the very popular

---

* Sunday, December 12, 1920, when George Halas's Decatur Staleys (before being renamed the Chicago Bears), champions of the West, played the Akron Steel, the champions of the East, for the championship, Akron was led by their star halfback, Fritz Pollard, the first African American to play in a professional sporting event at Cubs Park. The match-up, billed as "The Game to Decide the Pro Football Championship of the World," was played before 12,000 fans and ended in a scoreless tie. Afterward, George Halas proposed a replay—promising a crowd of at least 15,000 at Cubs Park—but Akron manager Frank Nied declined. Notably, according to Cubs and Wrigley Field historian Al Hartig, Halas "borrowed" Paddy Driscoll from the Chicago Cardinals for the game. A week earlier, Driscoll had played for the Cardinals against the Staleys.

Bonura obliged fans after the game by signing hundreds of scorecards, programs, and scraps of paper.[16]

Apart from its social implications, the other lesson of this game, certainly not lost on Veeck, was that such an event, if properly staged and properly promoted, could attract vast amounts of press attention. The Associated Press in Chicago filed more than a week in advance, and preview articles, as well as coverage of the game, appeared in dozens of papers, including the *New York Times* and the *Washington Post,* which normally paid scant attention to black-versus-white exhibitions, including earlier contests pitting Paige against Dean.[17] Dean and Paige repeated their show in Washington, D.C., on May 30, with Saperstein again promoting the event. It drew 22,000 fans, the biggest crowd ever to watch a non-major-league game in Griffith Stadium.[18]

All of this aggravated Chicago-based Commissioner Landis, a longtime foe of interracial exhibitions, especially those contests in which the major leaguers lost. He was also irked by the fact that exhibitions such as this, which only tangentially provided relief funds for the military, were cutting into major-league contests devoted exclusively to Army and Navy relief. On June 4, Landis ordered the major and minor leagues not to allow the use of their players or facilities for such commercial events and convinced the Army and Navy not to let players in uniform participate.

On June 25, with Paige on loan to the legendary Homestead Grays, Saperstein staged still another event in Washington, drawing about 30,000. The Grays won 2–1 in eleven innings over Dean's team. Landis then banned all future games between the Dean All-Stars and any Negro league team. The game between Paige's and Dean's All-Stars scheduled for July 4 in Indianapolis was cancelled.

Fay Young understood Landis's scrutiny of games played for charity but was livid when the commissioner ruled against Dean and Paige, claiming only one conclusion was possible: "Landis is against Negro ball clubs playing white major league players." Young pointed out that Negro organized baseball had but one park—that of the Memphis Red Sox—and all the other venues were rented from white magnates: "since Judge Landis rules the white ball yard owners, we will have to dance by his music or else."[19] Landis remained determinedly silent. In early July, Ric Roberts, the Washington correspondent for the *Baltimore Afro-American,* wrote that "Landis answers his thousands of hecklers, most of them white, who seek to put colored boys in the white major leagues, with a military tinctured—'No comment!' "[20]

Fay Young reported a rumor that after a heated meeting of baseball executives on the eve of the July 7 All-Star Game, in which the subject of Negro ball players had been raised, the transcription had been ordered destroyed.[21] A few days later Hy Turkin of the New York *Daily News*, then the newspaper with the largest circulation in the country, added fuel to the debate by reviving a charge from the ever outspoken Leo Durocher, manager of the Brooklyn Dodgers, to the effect that Landis and the owners were blocking the signing of Negroes, and that he would sign them if this were not the case. Durocher's comment had appeared in the Communist *Daily Worker* in 1939, but to little effect at the time. Now Turkin brought it front and center: "A casual remark made by Leo Durocher to Lester Rodney, Sports Editor of the *Daily Worker*, now in the Army, may do more for his place in history than all his shortstopping and managing histrionics. He said that he would hire Black players and this is like the tail of the tornado that has overwhelmed Judge Landis with two million signatures and threatens the democratization of our national pastime."[22]

Landis was furious with Durocher and summoned him to Chicago for a closed-door chewing out. He issued a statement on July 17 to the *New York Herald Tribune* that Durocher had recanted his remarks and no such blocking rule existed, "formal or informal, or any understanding, unwritten, subterranean, or sub-anything."[23]

On July 24, J. L. Wilkinson, co-owner of the Kansas City Monarchs, met with Satchel Paige in Chicago and told him the Monarchs would not stand in the way of his joining a major-league team. This Wilkinson-Paige meeting came on the eve of a Wrigley Field doubleheader between the Monarchs and the Memphis Red Sox, which was being promoted as "Satchel Paige Day." As the loudspeakers announced the appearance of Paige on the field, Landis read a prepared statement asserting that "negroes are not barred from organized baseball by the commissioner and never have been during the 21 years I have been commissioner. . . . A manager can have one or 25 negroes if he cares to."[24]

A few days later, Wilkinson asserted that at least twenty-five Negro players were of major-league caliber, led by Paige and Josh Gibson, the latter a catcher for the Homestead Grays who, with his 40 to 70 home runs a season and lifetime batting average of .349, was poised to step into Babe Ruth's shoes. Wilkinson also made public that he had given Paige his blessing to break his Monarchs contract if he could thereby go to the majors.[25]

Negro newspapers were not convinced by Landis's pronouncement. "The statement of Landis is about as empty as the promise of any major league manager to sign a negro ballplayer," Fay Young shot back in an editorial entitled "Judge Landis Decision—Bosh!" "The owners would remove the manager." Young charged that no team had the "nerve or guts" to take Landis at his word and sign a Negro.[26]

In response to the Landis declaration, the *Pittsburgh Courier* contacted the owners and managers of sixteen teams to get their opinions on the ban. Only six replied, and of those, two responded with no opinion; three agreed with Landis but offered no ideas as to how to integrate the game; and one, Clark Griffith of the Washington Senators, suggested that the Negro leagues be developed to the point where they would play the existing teams in a black versus-white World Championship, thus giving the Negro league teams a chance "to really prove their caliber."[27]

Soon after this survey, *The Sporting News* ran an editorial outlining a number of reasons why integration would not work, including "racial overtones," both between players and between fans and players, that would be "damaging to the game." Taking a clear shot at the editors of the *Courier,* the *Defender,* and the other half dozen Negro newspapers that were participating to various degrees in the campaign, the editorial ended with the point that Negro agitators pressing for the integration of organized baseball had the interest of neither the sport nor the race at heart.[28]

AT THE END of July, William Benswanger, president of the Pittsburgh Pirates, offered to give tryouts to Negro ballplayers, admitting to the *Pittsburgh Courier* that he had no idea who would show up for the tryout. A well-meaning racial moderate, he said at the time: "Colored men are American citizens with American rights. I know there are many problems connected with the question, but after all, somebody has to make the first move."[29]

Three players took Benswanger up on his offer: Dave Barnhill of the New York Cubans and Sam Hughes and Roy Campanella of the Baltimore Elite Giants. Campanella later recalled the invitation he got from Pittsburgh: "It began with the attempts made by the *Daily Worker* to get me a tryout but [the offer] contained so many buts that I was discouraged before I had finished reading the letter. 'You must understand that you would have to start at the very bottom . . . you must come up through our minor league farm system in the conventional manner . . . it might take you years to reach the major leagues . . . the pay would be small . . . there is no guarantee that you would

ever make it . . . your years of hard work might be for nothing . . .' The letter
was signed by William Benswanger, president of the club. I didn't let my
feelings stop me from replying to the letter. The prospect of playing in the
big leagues, no matter how remote, was too wonderful to let slip by without
making a try for it. I answered promptly. I wrote that I'd be only too glad to
start in the minors and work my way up. All I wanted was a chance."[30]

Campanella waited and waited but never heard another word from Benswanger, who later claimed that unspecified "pressures had prevented the
tryouts."[31]

With Campanella and the others still in limbo, Benswanger again announced that the Pirates were ready to sign a Negro to play on the team. Several members of the *Courier* staff suggested that Benswanger take his pick of
the players on the local Negro league Homestead Grays, who, along with the
Kansas City Monarchs, were black baseball's most established franchises and
held contracts for catcher Josh Gibson and first baseman Buck Leonard. For
the second time, however, tryouts were never held.

Many years later—on the eve of Jackie Robinson's induction into the Baseball Hall of Fame—Benswanger told Harry Keck, one of the *Courier* reporters at the 1942 meeting, that among the reasons for the trials being cancelled
were that Cumberland Posey, the owner and general manager of the Grays,
had begged him not to go after his players, because if the stars were taken
from the Negro leagues, then it would spell the end of "big time Negro
baseball."[32]

What made Posey's plea especially meaningful to Benswanger was that
the Grays played often at Forbes Field, owned by the Pirates. They also had
a second home in Washington, D.C., at Griffith Stadium. The large revenues
from stadium rentals and concessions that accrued to many owners were a
major factor in keeping the color bar in place—they would be lost if the Negro leagues were drained of stars and eventually folded. Yankee Stadium
and Griffith Stadium were known to net more than $100,000 a season rent-
ing to Negro teams. When the Yankees were on the road, the New York
Black Yankees took over the stadium, and when the Senators left town, the
Homestead Grays rolled in. Larry MacPhail in Brooklyn made no bones
about the fact that this cash payoff—many times Joe DiMaggio's salary—was
paramount in his reasoning. "If I wanted to do it," he said of hiring a Negro,
"I'd just do it. Who the hell would stop me."[33]

Now that Wrigley Field had opened its gates to the black teams, Phil
Wrigley was also among those profiting from baseball's apartheid. During

the remainder of the 1942 season Wrigley hosted five more Negro league events, culminating on September 27 when Paige took the mound for the Monarchs against the Homestead Grays in a Negro World Series game.[34]

WELL APPRISED OF all the arguments regarding integration following the major league World Series in 1942, Veeck made his move to buy the Philadelphia Phillies. His funding was to be from unnamed sources in Chicago, Philly Cigars—"a natural in Philadelphia"—and other backers in Philadelphia. The Congress of Industrial Organizations (CIO), an industrial trade union that would later merge with the American Federation of Labor to become the AFL-CIO in 1955, agreed to help, but as Veeck revealed later, it wanted him to agree that at no time would there be nine whites or nine blacks on the field. "I said I wouldn't tell the manager how to run his club and I certainly wasn't going to let them." But he did accept its backing, although he never publicly revealed the name of his contact within the union.

Having made, he thought, a deal with the Phillies' owner, Gerry Nugent, Veeck headed back to Chicago to make sure his financing was still in place. He made a quick call to his sister, Peg, to let her in on his plan.[35] Then, as he was about to go back to Philadelphia, he ran into John Carmichael, a sports columnist for the *Chicago Daily News* and an old friend.

Carmichael asked Veeck, who was carrying a suitcase, "Where you going?"

"I'm going to Philadelphia."

"What're you going to do in Philadelphia?"

"I'm going to buy the Phillies. And do you know what I'm going to do? I'm going to put a whole black team on the field."[36]

In the hours before the train departed, Veeck decided to alert Commissioner Landis of his intentions. With Saperstein looking on, "we told Judge Landis we wanted to field an entire team of Negroes," Veeck later told Shirley Povich of the *Washington Post*, pointing out that such a move wouldn't have offended anybody. "It wouldn't be integration and it was in line with the old Supreme Court ruling of separate but equal facilities." He figured Landis would not dare say black players were unwelcome, not while blacks were fighting in World War II.[37] Though details of that meeting were never recounted by anyone there, the meeting was no doubt cordial, given Veeck's father's friendship with Landis and their own long association.[38]

Veeck then took the Pennsylvania Railroad's eastbound Broadway Limited, which arrived in North Philadelphia station at 8:03 a.m. the next morning: "I got on the train feeling I had not only a major league ball club but I was almost a virtual cinch to win the pennant next year. And because [black ballplayers were] the only really untapped reservoir of playing talent, it didn't matter to me whether they were pink with blue dots or black. Matter of fact I made arrangements for a strutting band."[39] Before reaching Nugent's office, however, Veeck discovered that the Phillies had been officially taken over by the National League the night before and that a new owner was being sought.[40]

Who scotched the deal has never been revealed. "I have proof," Veeck said in later interviews. "When I was in [Landis's] office, I had them purchased. I always will believe Landis leaked our plans to Frick. Frick wouldn't talk business with us."[41]

"His big mistake in trying to buy the Phillies was going to the Commissioner for permission," said Negro league and major-league player Monte Irvin. "He should have just done it."[42] Veeck realized that an entire team of players from the Negro leagues would still be a form of segregation, but he knew it would not have stayed that way for long. "Other owners would have been forced to sign other Negroes, because the success of my club would have made it a necessity."[43] Veeck would always insist that his attempt to buy and recast the Phillies was a wholly pragmatic decision by a man who was color-blind. "In 1942 I really tried to break the color line and thought I had. It lasted for about 24 hours," he recalled years later.[44] Nonetheless, in its wake the struggle to integrate the game heated up, with the CIO leading the charge.

DURING THE WINTER Meetings in 1942, ten members of the CIO's leadership committee attempted to appear before the assembled major-league executives at the Ambassador East Hotel in Chicago. Nine of the union leaders were white. Landis had ignored their earlier request for an audience, so on December 3, the first day of the meetings, the union leaders told Leslie O'Conner, Landis's secretary, that unless they were admitted to the session, they would bring the issue of baseball's integration before the Fair Employment Practices Committee (FEPC), the agency created by Franklin D. Roosevelt in 1941 to enforce his banning of racial discrimination in any defense industry receiving federal contracts. The order also empowered the FEPC to investigate complaints and take action against any alleged employment discrimination.

The group was rebuffed nevertheless, and they repaired to the press room, where they announced a public campaign to open baseball up to blacks.[45]

Phil Wrigley decided that he would support the union. "When the CIO came to talk to Judge Landis at the meeting of the big leagues, I went down to talk to the committee and invited them to see me," he later told the *Defender*. "I'm an honorary member of the CIO. When they attempted to organize all the stewards on my ships, I paid the initiation fee for all the men." Wrigley encouraged the drive to integrate baseball, acknowledging that a gentlemen's agreement or color bar was indeed in place: "There are men in high places who don't want to see it." The CIO would continue to push for racial integration, but not with the same vigor.[46]

Thwarted in his efforts to buy the Phillies, on December 6, 1942, Veeck teamed up with Rudie Schaffer to announce a deal with Abe Saperstein that would bring the two top Negro basketball teams in the country—the Chicago-based Harlem Globe Trotters and the New York Renaissance—to Milwaukee to play in a basketball doubleheader against Wisconsin's two professional basketball teams, both members of the National Basketball League (NBL), the white Sheboygan Red Skins and the Oshkosh All-Stars.

Fay Young of the *Chicago Defender* was in attendance, and when the time-keeper did not show up, Veeck turned to Young and handed him the controls to the game clock. As Young observed in his column years later: "The Negro fans were somewhat taken off their feet to see a Negro operating a time clock in a game between Negro teams and white teams."[47]

The NBL teams beat the Negro teams by large margins, but the bigger story was that 4,000 fans had paid to see the contest, filling the Milwaukee Auditorium. Even more significant, earlier in the NBL season two of its teams had integrated. The Toledo Jim White Chevrolets and the Chicago Studebakers had between them signed ten black players for the 1942–43 season, including several former Globe Trotters. Veeck staged games with these integrated teams: on January 11, 1943, the Chicago team played the Zollner Pistons of Fort Wayne (later to become the Detroit Pistons), and a few days later opposed Oshkosh in Cicero, Illinois, with five African Americans in the starting lineup.[48] The NBL, a forerunner to the National Basketball Association, became the first major professional league of the modern era to integrate racially.*

ON DECEMBER 30, 1942, Veeck was named minor-league executive of the year by *The Sporting News,* then the official house organ of baseball. He was singled out by editor Edgar G. Brands for his ability to keep the game alive through the fall and winter by making personal appearances on the "mashed potato circuit." But his constant focus on sporting issues took its toll on his young family. A month later, in response to this award, R. G. Lynch of the *Milwaukee Journal* wrote that Eleanor Veeck, not Bill, deserved an award. Lynch's item in *The Sporting News* was entitled "Propose Medal for Mrs. Veeck" and revealed the challenge of being married to Bill.

When Veeck first moved to Milwaukee, he rented a home some ten miles away from Borchert Field. After gasoline rationing was instituted during the war, Bill, perversely, moved some twenty-five miles farther out to a 160-acre farm. According to Lynch, they moved into a summer home on a razor-back ridge overlooking a small lake. There was no place to turn a car on the ridge; the only way out was to back down the hill. "The ridge is so sharp that the Veecks have to be very careful stepping out the back door."

It snowed the day the movers delivered the Veecks' furniture to this outpost, and the road was impassable. A few days later, expected in St. Paul for an old-timers dinner, Veeck had to hike six miles to West Bend in subzero weather to catch a train, then six miles back to get home.

Lynch implored his readers not to feel sorry for "Fuzzy" but to think of his wife. "At first, she had to get two small boys to and from school, but she no longer has that problem. Bill, Jr., has the measles and his brother Pete fell off the ridge the other day and fractured his collarbone. So there is Mrs. Veeck, snowbound on a hilltop about a half mile from the nearest house with the two boys to care for and the fireplace to stoke with maple chunks all day

---

* In "Paving the Way," *Basketball Digest,* February 2001, Douglas Stark wrote, "The reason you may not know about the NBL's pioneering efforts is because integration in the NBL and professional basketball as a whole came with much less fanfare and fewer problems than it did in other sports. Unlike baseball, hockey, and football, basketball was largely an urban game played by a diverse population on every level but the pros." Its integration "came four years before Kenny Washington played football for the NFL's Los Angeles Rams, five years before Jackie Robinson broke Major League Baseball's color barrier, and 16 years before Willie O'Ree skated for the Boston Bruins of the NHL."

because in this zero weather this week, the oil burner Fuzzy installed would not heat the windward side of the house."

Veeck was apparently in residence only when it suited him. "During the winter, Bill invited his baseball friends out to see his wonderful home," recalled Charlie Grimm in his memoir, "... but his main motive was to get help in chopping wood." At one point the pump froze, and for several weeks a farmer hauled water in milk cans to the Veeck home with a team and bobsled. A few weeks later, with the 1943 season drawing nigh, Bill managed to reach Milwaukee. There were big drifts around Borchert Field, but during a snowstorm, he put up a big sign on the front wall. It read: NEXT GAME, MAY 5.*

---

* Some have claimed that the story about Veeck attempting to buy the Philadelphia Phillies is untrue. I believe it to be true based on my own research. A discussion of the matter and a refutation of the charge appears in the Appendix titled *Did Bill Veeck Lie About His Plan to Purchase the '43 Phillies?*

CHAPTER 6

Pvt. Veeck Goes to War

OVER THE WINTER, the U.S. government's Office of Defense Transportation demanded less travel by baseball teams as an austerity measure, and accordingly the Brewers staged spring training in 1943 close to home. Veeck decided his preseason would open April 6 in Wisconsin at Waukesha's Frame Field, the home for Waukesha's entry in the industrial Land O' Lakes League.

In early February, Veeck, Rudie Schaffer, radio announcer and vice president Mickey Heath, and Charlie Grimm went to Waukesha to meet with local officials and make final arrangements for the venue. As the group left a luncheon meeting for an inspection of the frozen, snow-covered field, it was attacked from behind by Veeck, who had circled around them with an armload of well-packed snowballs. Retaliation ensued, and once the snowball fight was over, a photographer from the *Journal* asked the Brewers officials to pose for a picture on the snowy field. They obliged by creating an impromptu baseball scene, with a stick for a bat and a snowball for a baseball.

Just as the shot was about to be taken, Veeck yelled, "Wait a minute—who ever heard of playing baseball in overcoats?" All but Grimm shed theirs. "I just got up from Missouri—do you want me to get pneumonia?" he said. Schaffer at this point had removed his clothes and was standing in his underwear in the snow, prepared to play umpire for the staged show. R. G. Lynch of the *Milwaukee Journal* had previously called Schaffer smart and pleasant but "mousey withal"; now he said the accountant had been transformed. "The metamorphosis was complete; the mouse had become a shameless exhibitionist just like his boss."[1]

Before the month of February was over, Veeck announced that he would schedule morning games during the upcoming season, having listened to fans' concerns during off-season meetings at local factories. The facilities were working at full tilt to accommodate the needs of wartime production, and night-shift workers told him they weren't able to attend games because of their schedules. Veeck therefore changed the start time of certain games to 10:30 a.m., explaining that this would give the workers on both the early and late-night shifts a chance to get to the ballpark. "Those who work from four to midnight will have plenty of sleep before game time, and those on the midnight to eight a.m. shift can have their breakfasts, come out the park, and then go home for their rest."

"Morning baseball? I think it's a pretty darn swell idea," said eighty-year-old Connie Mack, who for all of his reputation as a starched-collar baseball conservative found Veeck's iconoclasm and spirited approach to the game appealing.[2]

The first of these morning games was on May 7. Tickets were sold at local factories, and when fans showed up at the ballpark, they were treated to coffee and donuts and could buy cereal in wax packets at a bargain price. A seven-piece swing band, dressed in nightgowns and stocking caps, entertained the fans, and Veeck doled out Corn Flakes. As it turned out, the train bringing the St. Paul team was late, so the game did not start until noon, and Veeck had to refund the price of 2,000 tickets. The Brewers pounded four St. Paul pitchers for 24 hits and 50 total bases, setting a new American Association record. In posting his 20–0 complete-game three-hitter, Wes Livengood, the Brewers rookie right-hander, hit two doubles and a single.

Veeck's morning game garnered national publicity. *Look* carried an image of Veeck and Schaffer dumping coach Red Smith out of a prop bed that had been placed on the field so that he would be ready for the ten-thirty game. Another photo showed Veeck serving a young boy milk and cereal at the game.[3] A new cadre of fans included "lady riveters." Veeck observed, "Ten of these riveters used to come in as a body, and two of them were among the finest umpire baiters it has been my privilege to meet."[4]

Almost everything Veeck decided to do to promote his club became a national news story. He joked that he was "out for blood" when he announced later in May that every pint of blood given at the Milwaukee Red Cross Procurement Center would win the donor a weekly pass to the ballpark. Other ball clubs were quick to adopt this simple means of promoting their teams while supporting the war effort.

Without Hal Peck in the lineup and with no left-handed pull hitter to replace him, Veeck announced the return of the thirty-seven-foot "spite fence"
atop the right-field wall.[5] People came to see the fence, but just as often they
showed up to see Veeck himself. He had become a drawing card. "It is two
hours before game time at the Milwaukee Brewers baseball park," reported
Arthur Bystrom of the Associated Press on Veeck's oft-repeated public ritual.
"On the mound is a well-built, bare-headed young man, clad in shorts and
sport shirt tossing baseballs to batters for practice. Twenty minutes later, he
quits, dashes to an office beneath the stands, takes a shower, changes into a
pair of slacks, and drinks a 'black cow'—root beer with ice cream. An hour
before game time, a swing band begins 'giving out' from its perch high in the
grandstand and the young man is at the main entrance shaking hands with
fans as they enter."[6]

That summer, Veeck tried in vain to obtain Pete Gray from the Memphis
Chicks. Gray had lost an arm in an automobile accident but was nonetheless batting .300 and was one of the top outfielders in the Southern Association. He was also by any measure the Chicks' biggest drawing card. With an
eye on the box office potential of a player who lacked a limb, Veeck offered a
large sum for Gray. The deal was never made because the Chicks, instead of
money, wanted four of Veeck's top players in exchange.[7] If he could not get
Gray, he did get a damaged Hal Peck back in mid-August. Peck had not
played for Brooklyn since spring training, and Veeck grabbed him on an
option.

On August 2, 1943, Veeck was able to score a publicity coup as well as a
historic first when the Brewers played an exhibition game against the Chicago Cubs at Wrigley Field. It was the first appearance ever of a minor-
league team at a major-league ballpark. Veeck had challenged the Cubs in
spring training, claiming he could beat the Cubs any day of the week. Cubs
officials took him up on the challenge, and Veeck immediately called on
Cubs fans to root for the Brewers.

The game, which the *Milwaukee Sentinel* called "a tribute to Veeck," was
a chance for Chicago to honor the two men that Wrigley had allowed to get
away—Veeck and the ever popular Charlie Grimm, who was making his first
appearance on the Cubs' field since he left the ballpark in 1938. Before the
game Veeck and Grimm performed in their seven-piece pipe band. The Cubs
won 7–6 in the tenth inning on Eddie Stanky's third hit of the day, a long
drive down the right-field line, which scored Lennie Merullo from second,
but Veeck was the ultimate winner.[8]

Before the end of the season, one more stunt garnered still more national publicity. August 28 was Charlie Grimm's forty-fifth birthday, and Veeck engineered a special celebration with various gifts including a $1,000 war bond.* The culmination was the presentation of a twelve-foot-wide birthday cake, out of which came a half dozen dancing girls escorting a newly acquired and somewhat embarrassed pitcher—Julio Acosta, a Cuban hurler with a 17–6 record for Richmond in the Piedmont League. After commenting that he was "floor-strucken," Grimm named Acosta his starting pitcher. Veeck had paid cash for Acosta to preserve the surprise.[9]

On top of all this publicity, the Brewers finished 90–61 during the regular season and set a new attendance record of 332,597. The team lost in the playoffs but did have its first pennant since 1936. In two years the Brewers had gone from last to first, a remarkable feat at any level in baseball.

In the fall of 1943, Veeck became a genuine American celebrity when three of the country's top magazines—*Look*, *The Saturday Evening Post*, and *Esquire*—all published features on him. The *Look* story was illustrated by a pictorial spread on "Baseball's Number 1 Screwball: Bill Veeck of Milwaukee," which included an image of a trim, muscular Veeck stripped to his undershorts to practice fly-casting at the ballpark. It also contained a rare family photo of Bill, Eleanor, and their children, now three in number following the birth of Ellen, and a rare quote from Eleanor: "When I got married, I thought I was all through with circuses. Apparently, I was wrong."[10]

THE SEASON OVER, Veeck tried to accommodate his restlessness with a new career as a boxing promoter. He lined up a partner with boxing experience, and the two went to see the World Series in New York with the collateral mission of making some boxing connections. Veeck had known Barney Ross—a Chicagoan who was the first fighter to hold both the lightweight and welterweight titles simultaneously—for some time, and their dinner at Toots Shor's restaurant was to affect Veeck in a wholly unexpected way. Ross had retired from the ring in 1938 and joined the Marines. As a corporal, he became a hero in the battle for Guadalcanal, protecting wounded fellow Marines over a long, bloody night. He returned to the States suffering from malaria and shock and was awarded the Silver Star for "conspicuous gallantry and intrepidity in

---

* According to Grimm's autobiography, on page 154 : "That bond was deducted from my next paycheck!"

action." He also received the Distinguished Service Cross and the Presidential Unit Citation from President Roosevelt.

When Veeck's plans as a boxing promoter fell through—he and his partner were unable to secure an arena with an exclusive right to stage their matches—he made the stunning announcement that he wanted to become a private in the United States Marine Corps. Ross, he said, was the inspiration for his enlistment and, like Ross, he would demand to go into combat.[11] Until the fall of 1943, Veeck could not have joined the military because of the size of his family and his age, but as the need for manpower increased, the services began to accept fathers and older men.

The officer in charge of his local recruiting office, Capt. Robert Rankin, remembered Veeck's arrival: "My first sergeant came in and told me that Veeck wanted to see me. Many such callers want to become officers. Veeck was different. He told me he did not want a commission, but that he wanted to join as a private and would be very happy to be sent into battle within six weeks." The salary he listed on his application was $150 a week.[12]

The application was approved, on Saturday, November 27, 1943. At the age of twenty-nine, Veeck was sworn in by Capt. Rankin in a public ceremony while Grimm, Schaffer, and others looked on. This was also the first day of the U.S. assault on the Japanese-held island of Tarawa in the South Pacific, during which 1,677 Marines and Navy personnel were killed. Explaining his decision to R. G. Lynch of the *Milwaukee Journal,* who was following Veeck's unexpected enlistment, Veeck reinforced his commitment: "I have to live with myself not only now but after the war is won, and I felt I was in a better position to go than many other fathers who have been drafted. I am satisfied that I have done the right thing by my country, my family, and myself. I am going into the Marine Corps just like any other buck private, and I hope, in time, to earn a promotion from the ranks. Service overseas will be uppermost in my mind."[13]

Whether or not Eleanor approved of this decision—or even knew about it in advance—is a matter for speculation, but Veeck himself believed that his family would not suffer: "Sure, I've got three children, but I can go and know Ellen and the kids will be all right. I mean I'm in a better position to go than a lot of other men who have kids. I couldn't sit back and let the draft get those fellows first, so I volunteered. It's the only way I could feel right about it."[14] The enlistment came as a shock to all but a few of his closest friends; others saw the Marines as an opportunity for Veeck to get a strong dose of discipline. Lynch, both a fan and a critic of Veeck's since they first

met in June 1941, hoped the man he called a "grade A screwball" would return a better person. "He is a little too high pressure now for most people
he deals with. He does just about as he damn pleases, in public and in private, and the devil take anybody that doesn't like it. The Marines will give
him a chance to blow off some of that extra steam."[15]

Because of his celebrity status and his choice of the Marine Corps, later
reports suggested that the Marines had planned to use Veeck for his publicity
value as a recruiter, giving him a stateside position running recreational programs and appearing in newsreel shots. Perhaps a commission would also
have been awarded. But Veeck refused.[16] While some big leaguers—Joe
DiMaggio, Pee Wee Reese, and Johnny Mize among them—spent their military time playing baseball, Veeck joined a cadre of others, including Warren
Spahn, Yogi Berra, and Ted Williams, who would be put in harm's way.

Between the time of the enlistment ceremony and his reporting for basic
training in San Diego, Veeck attended the winter baseball meetings in New
York City, where they were held for the first time in twenty-four years. The
meetings led off with the business of the National Association of Professional
Baseball Leagues—otherwise known as the minors. Veeck was warmly received by his fellow minor-league owners, who wished him good luck in the
service even though he was at loggerheads with many of them. Almost immediately, Veeck's manufactured flap with the city of St. Paul was revisited,
and a rule was enacted to require all teams in the American Association to
stay in a hotel in the city where they were playing. Veeck was the lone dis-
senter, and he fussed and fumed for the cameras and reporters.[17]

The major-league presidents then met behind closed doors. For the second time, an appeal had been made by a group of black publishers and editors to address the winter joint meeting and advocate for the entry of blacks
into baseball. This time the request had been granted, and on December 3,
1943, the journalists presented their case for racial integration to Commissioner Landis and the forty-four assembled owners and officials, including
Branch Rickey, president of the Brooklyn Dodgers. Veeck was not privy to
the meeting, but what transpired behind closed doors would influence what
Rickey and he would later accomplish.

The African American delegation was led by John Herman Henry Sengstacke, publisher of the *Chicago Defender* and president of the Negro Publishers Association, and included the presidents and editors of black newspapers
in New York, Pittsburgh, Baltimore, Cleveland, and Detroit. In addition, top
officials of the Urban League and the black clergy were present. Sengstacke

was an ardent desegregationist working to integrate all elements of American life, including the Post Office and the Armed Forces.*

The star witness was African American actor and former All-American football player Paul Robeson, then drawing raves on Broadway for his portrayal of Othello. Robeson had, in fact, been invited by Landis, who opened the meeting by clearing the room of all reporters and sportswriters save for those in the Negro press. It was to be a closed meeting, and the full transcript was protected as a confidential document for more than sixty years.[18]

Landis introduced Robeson and declared that he had not been taken in by "the propaganda that there is an agreement in this crowd of men to bar negroes from Baseball."[19] Robeson noted that not many years earlier a Negro actor appearing in a white cast would have been considered unthinkable and that he had been told after he had starred in *Othello* in London a few years earlier that he would never be able to take it to Broadway. He considered his role as the Moorish king the outstanding success of his career.[20]

Although known for his activism, Robeson spoke in terms the executives could appreciate. "I played against Frankie Frisch when he was at Fordham and I was a catcher at Rutgers. I was just telling the Judge that. . . . I was a catcher who wound up pretty slowly, and, by the time I drew back, Frisch was practically around second. . . . I later coached at Columbia, when [Lou] Gehrig was playing. I, as you know, was an All-American football player, and played pro football."[21]

The plea Robeson made was a simple one: allow Negroes to enter organized baseball immediately. "I never presumed there was any agreement among you gentlemen to bar Negro ballplayers," Robeson declared, "but merely that you hate to initiate a policy that has not been initiated before. We live in times when the world is changing very fast and when you might be able to make a great contribution to not only the advance of our own country, but the whole world, because a thing like this—Negro ballplayers becoming a part of the great national pastime of America—could make a great difference in what peoples all over the world would feel toward us as a country in a time when we need their help."[22]

Robeson finished and thanked Landis for having invited him.[23] He was followed by Sengstacke and the other editors and publishers, who emphasized that other sports such as track, football, and basketball had integrated,

---

* Ultimately, President Truman named Sengstacke to the commission he formed to racially integrate the U.S. Armed Forces.

that the present world heavyweight boxing champion was Joe Louis, and that baseball was long overdue. When it was suggested that an unwritten rule preventing integration was in effect, Landis interrupted: "I say there is no written rule: never has been. There is no verbal rule: never has been. There is no haymow rule or subterranean rule or understanding, express or implied, between leagues or between any two clubs of any league."*

Ira Lewis, publisher of the *Pittsburgh Courier*, came back at Landis: "But we believe, however that there is a tacit understanding—that there is a gentlemen's agreement—that no Negro players be hired . . . This has become a tradition. Few managers and few owners care to break this precedent. But, gentlemen, precedents are worse than bad laws: Bad laws may be repealed, but precedents, with all their innuendos and implications in a case like this, can be so unfair and so very un-American."

The publishers submitted a four-point resolution, which they asked the joint meeting to approve: (1) that immediate steps be taken to accept qualified Negroes in the framework of organized baseball; (2) that the process by which players were graduated from Classes C, B, A, and AA teams to the majors be applied without prejudice or discrimination; (3) that the same system by which players were selected from school, sandlot, semipro, and other clubs be used in selecting black players; and (4) that a statement be issued by the joint meeting declaring that Negroes were eligible for trials and permanent places on the teams.

There being no questions, Landis ended the session with the Negro press. The delegation left, and without missing a beat, Landis turned immediately to the fact that Ed Barrow, president and general manager of the New York Yankees, was not in attendance. No mention was made of any of the four points, including the last, which the publishers felt would be the easiest for the white owners to agree to. In sum, the delegation was handled with courtesy, but their proposal was dismissed without a moment of reflection.

Branch Rickey, ill at ease with the fact that no position on the proposals had been taken by the owners, broke into a discussion of player contracts a few minutes after the delegation departed. Addressing Landis, he said, "Mr. Commissioner, are we to understand that the report from this meeting, in response to the delegation that came here today, is to be simply that the matter was not considered?"

---

* Landis used "haymow" several times in the discussion as a synonym for a secret or covert decision. The haymow is the portion of a barn in which hay is stored.

Landis retorted: "No, no. The announcement will have to be that it was considered—and my recollection now is that it was considered, and you gentlemen all remember that it was considered: you each participated in the consideration of it—and that no action was taken on it; that the matter is a matter for each club to determine in getting together its baseball team; that no other solution than that, in view of the nature of operations, is possible."[24] Rickey was not satisfied with this fabricated account. Clubs, he pointed out, were now beset with "a great many petitions and a great many visitations" from groups demanding integration. "That they become embarrassing is not the point: they become time-taking, and, from a publicity standpoint, they become important." Rickey then pushed as hard as he could, asking if a club could now state that integration deserved the joint consideration of both leagues. "Is that the position? Is it permissible or advisable for us to make that statement?"

Landis thought not, noting that three major-league managers had stated in Negro newspapers that, but for the bar, there would be a "foot-race run by sixteen Major League managers to sign up Negro players." Landis acknowledged he had "called in these three managers, and, while there was no admission that they had made those statements, I think it is a fair approach to the truth to say that, such was the unconvincing quality of their evasiveness in reply to my questions, they all did make the statement."

Baseball's executives faced the dilemma of how to remove the color bar without admitting it had been in place all along. Landis reiterated the comment he had made at the time Leo Durocher had been pressured into denying his claim about the color bar. Addressing the assembled group of executives, he told them, "If any of you gentlemen want to hire a Negro player, you are as much at liberty to do that as you are to sign up any other player, be he in human form."

The transcript of the meeting reveals that everyone in the room was silent until John Quinn, part owner and president of the Boston Braves, had the last word: "I have been going to these meetings for more than 40 years, and this is the first time I heard as much as I heard in here today."[25] Following the meeting, Landis issued an official statement on behalf of both major leagues: "Each club is entirely free to employ Negro players to any extent it pleases, and the matter is solely for each club's decision without any restrictions whatsoever."[26]

The *Amsterdam News* noted soon after that only two of the ten local New York papers bothered to analyze the integration appeal. Stanley Frank of the *New York Post* interpreted it as a brush-off. "In short," he wrote, "the own-ers continue to evade important social problems behind a smokescreen of words no one believes, least of all those who give them lip service." The other paper, the left-leaning daily *PM* (the initials stood for *Picture Magazine*), was content to withhold comment and wait for the big shots of baseball to answer for themselves.[27]

All but one of the owners were silent on the matter, leaving the impres-sion that nobody wanted to be the first to sign a Negro player to a contract. The lone commentator was Yankees president Ed Barrow, who had been ailing and was unable to attend the meeting. He said he had no objection to hiring Negro players. When asked if the Yankees might hire Negroes for the 1944 season, he replied: "If we find it necessary to hire colored, we will."[28] In the end, no black players were on any roster in organized baseball in 1944, even though some minor leagues came close to disbanding because of the wartime depletion in the supply of players. The one-armed white player Pete Gray and other whites of advanced age and degree of inability made it to the major leagues during World War II, but no black players did.

The Winter Meetings produced one more stunning development that stole some of the thunder away from the Robeson testimony and must have aggravated Bill Veeck to no end. The previous February, the Philadelphia Phillies had been sold to a wealthy, thirty-three-year-old lumber broker named William Cox. Not only had Veeck's bid for the team been thwarted, but Cox had been suspended temporarily during the season on suspicion of betting on a Phillies game. Cox asked for a hearing to clear his name, and the seventy-seven-year-old Landis heard him out. Other evidence was presented at the hearing that convinced Landis of his guilt and earned Cox the distinc-tion of being the first nonplayer ever to be banned from the game.*

SOME FORTY-EIGHT HOURS after the meetings were over, Pfc. Bill Veeck returned to Milwaukee, from where he departed in charge of seventeen other Marine recruits on their way by train to San Diego. Upon arrival, Veeck received a full induction physical that deemed him fit and ready for

---

* Meanwhile, the Phillies were next taken over by Bob Carpenter, whose hostility to blacks would extend up through the moment in 1947 when he told Branch Rickey to bench Jackie Robinson on his first visit to Philadelphia in a Brooklyn Dodgers uniform. Bruce Kuklick, *To Every Thing a Season* (Princeton, NJ: Princeton University Press, 1993), 146.

service. He then endured four weeks of rigorous basic training. The Marine Corps did end up using him in its recruiting efforts, sending out wire photos of him working his way through basic training.

Despite his reluctance to participate in publicity for recruiting, Veeck milked the issue of the Marines' mandatory necktie for all it was worth. He had vowed never to wear one again after prep school, but he was now forced to do so as part of his dress uniform. He joked that he had made the ultimate sartorial sacrifice to keep America safe. "My first tie almost choked me," Veeck lamented. "I kept pulling at my collar as long as I had it on. You can guess how the shoes felt, and I have been wearing a garrison cap almost constantly. I fooled them in one place—the barber couldn't find much hair to cut."

At the end of December, Veeck wrote that he had survived the first ten days of boot camp, expressing rare satisfaction in the experience. He described the obstacle course as a "dandy" and reported that passing his swimming test was easy.[29] "There are some corking nice fellows here, and our drill instructors are all right, one in particular, Stan Green, who played football for Tom Stidham. Yo-Yo Epps [who played for Veeck in Milwaukee] came to see me the other day. He is a sergeant who looks like he is in the top pink of condition and says he has seen a great many really good-looking young ballplayers in his 20 months in the service."*

On another occasion he ran into an old Chicago friend, Jack Brickhouse, who had worked as the announcer for both Cubs and White Sox games on WGN radio in Chicago before entering the service and who would serve as a Cubs broadcaster for decades following the war.[30]

Veeck quickly established himself as a special enlistee. He was featured in a short piece in *Leatherneck* magazine, the official magazine of the Marines, which began: "To the list of well-qualified men who snubbed swivel chair commissions to become enlisted Marines you may add the name of PFC William L. Veeck, Jr." The article reported for the first time that Veeck had been offered commissions in both the Army and Navy but chose to be a private in the Marines instead. *Leatherneck* noted: "In boot camp, Veeck was 'Honor Man' of his platoon, qualified as an expert swimmer and generally had a fine time of it."[31]

However, one aspect of basic training challenged Veeck emotionally: the firing of a gun. Veeck claimed he had never before done so and in fact

---

* Veeck had traded Arnold Moser for Epps in July 1941.

loathed guns because of the accident that had claimed the life of the older brother he never knew. Forced to practice shooting, he overcame his reservations and ended up posting a score of 302 out of a possible 340—enough to officially qualify him as a sharpshooter.[32] Coming out of boot camp, Veeck was sent to a replacement battalion at Camp Elliott, just north of San Diego, where he trained as an antiaircraft gunner. Soon, though, he petitioned to become a Marine Raider and requested a transfer to the Marine Raider Training Camp at Camp Pendleton, near San Diego. The Raiders specialized in amphibious light infantry warfare, particularly landing in rubber boats and operating behind enemy lines.[33] However, his request was denied and Veeck's battalion was shipped overseas to Nouméa, New Caledonia, in March 1944, and then to Guadalcanal.

While there, Veeck continued to trade players for his team through war correspondents, who would convey his ideas back to audiences in Milwaukee. The reporters loved the idea that Veeck was conducting baseball business from a war zone. "A couple of Marines met today beneath the shade of the coconut palm and arranged a player deal probably unprecedented in the history of baseball," began a dispatch on April 14, 1944. "Pfc. Veeck and Capt. Roscoe Conkling 'Torchy' Torrance, vice president of the Seattle Rainiers had conducted a trade." Veeck was reported to have dealt one of his three shortstops for cash.[34]

Torrance, with whom Veeck had done business before, had brought baseball into a war zone. Torrance ran forty teams in the South Pacific. At one undisclosed location, he had established three leagues of ten teams each, involving a total of more than 600 Marines. With the aid of Navy Seabees, he bulldozed jungle to construct twenty-one first-rate diamonds, which had to be trimmed by hand in the absence of lawn-mowing equipment.

Keeping an eye out for talent, Veeck at one point sent word back to Milwaukee that he had signed Homer Chapman, a hot prospect who would start in June 1945 with a Brewers affiliate in Middletown, Ohio, where he would lead the league with 50 stolen bases.

Two days after their war-zone meeting, Veeck told Torrance that he wanted to be reassigned to the Third Division, because he had found out he was being sent to Bougainville as part of the defense battalion while the others were going to invade Guam. "I told him I was a lowly captain and probably couldn't do much about it, but I'd try," remembered Torrance. "I went over to see Col. David M. Shoup at Corps headquarters about the possibilities of getting Veeck reassigned. He asked me if I thought he would make a difference in the landing in Guam, and I told him of course not, but that he was an old baseball friend and was anxious to go."*

The colonel explained that all orders and personnel records had already been cut for the invasion and that there was nothing he could do. But the next day, he called to say that he had worked a deal so that Veeck could change units. Torrance hurried over to Veeck's unit, but it had already been removed to the other end of the island. "I tried all afternoon to get a communication through to his outfit, but with preparations for departure and all the activities going on, I was never able to reach him. The next day, we shipped out, and Bill wasn't in the unit."[35]†

Torrance and his unit left for the invasion of Guam in late summer, after Veeck's Third Defense Battalion was moved on April 27, 1944, to Bougainville Island, then part of the British Solomon Islands, where he would spend some three months. The island had been partially occupied by the Americans in 1943, but it was still mostly controlled by the Japanese when Veeck's unit arrived. The Marines set up a perimeter to protect the U.S. airstrip at Torokina, along the western side of the island.

Bougainville was a tropical hellhole. From the time of the invasion, the impenetrable jungle and relentless rain produced many non-combat-related casualties from filariasis, elephantiasis, diarrhea, and "jungle rot," all of which took their toll. One survivor of the Bougainville campaign described his tropical nightmare: "Your feet began to rot, your clothes were stinking, you would get skin ulcers between your legs to the point where you ran around with Kotex [feminine sanitary pads used to absorb the fluid oozing from the ulcers] on and were downright miserable. . . . Bugs, spiders, an ungodly number of insects [were] biting on you."[36]

Veeck noted later that during his time on Bougainville, he served as an ammunition passer, gunner, and searchlight operator. One or two Japanese planes came over every night heading for the airstrip. "Our battery did get a couple of bombers. They provided the most thrilling moments I can remem-

---

* Shoup would go on to receive the Medal of Honor for his service in the war. He was later appointed commandant of the Marine Corps and after retirement became a severe and highly visible critic of the Vietnam War.

† Torrance tried to get the message to Veeck that he had gotten him the transfer but could not find him. Torchy's position was that not getting Veeck transferred could have saved his life, given the large number who died or were wounded in the invasion of Guam and the subsequent invasion of Iwo Jima.

ber." Veeck's unit got shelled most every night by Japanese artillery. "I was scared plenty," Veeck recalled, "and so was everybody else, but they never did get close enough to our area to do any real damage."[37]

During the early days on the island, the unit was sometimes no more than fifty yards away from enemy snipers. Veeck delighted in shouting insults concerning Japanese prime minister Tojo, which brought angry, heavily accented slurs about Franklin and Eleanor Roosevelt—and the occasional zinging bullet. During much of the deployment, Veeck handled the 90 mm heavy antiaircraft gun shells, which each weighed more than twenty-three pounds and had to be moved with speed and dexterity, as the gun could handle twenty to twenty-five rounds per minute.

"Veeck was a great Marine, gung ho all the way," recalled Don Fordham, who was Veeck's sergeant and immediate commander. "He volunteered for everything he could. At first, I was concerned with getting somebody like him: 'He's going to want special privileges. Why do I get him?' It was just the opposite. He was always the first to volunteer."[38]

Later on, when their portion of the island was well secured, Veeck discovered the unit's lack of baseball equipment. Working through a clandestine network, he got word to a friend in the States, and in a matter of a few weeks, he said, "we had more balls, bats, and gloves than we could handle." Decades later, Fordham still didn't know how Veeck pulled off getting all that baseball equipment into a remote combat zone.

Early in May 1944 Veeck overheard a newscast from the States coming from the recreation tent: ". . . and Charlie Grimm lost his first game as manager of the Cubs." Veeck recalled later that the report continued: "Charlie Grimm, manager of my Milwaukee Brewers, has been signed to replace Jimmy Wilson of the Chicago Cubs. Then the announcer says Casey Stengel is taking over as manager of the Brewers. That's all I hear, but it's enough. I'm stunned."[39]

The Cubs had opened the 1944 season by losing their first thirteen games, occasioning the resignation of manager Jimmy Wilson. Grimm's Brewers, on the other hand, got off to a 10–2 start, after which Phil Wrigley offered Grimm the managership of the Cubs. At two o'clock the next morning, Sam Levy got a call from Grimm.

"I've been asked to come back to the Cubs as manager," said Grimm. "What do you think I ought to do?"

Levy thought he should grab the opportunity.

"But what about my buddy Bill? He's in the South Pacific and I can't get in touch with him. I don't want to leave him at such a time."

Levy reminded Grimm of the day in June 1943 when the Cubs were in deep trouble and Veeck suggested that Grimm be drafted as the new manager, but the Cubs declined.[40]

Grimm immediately called Casey Stengel, asking him to serve as his replacement at the Brewers helm. Stengel had resigned as manager of the Boston Braves the previous winter. He had been hit by a cab in Boston after the 1943 season and, having barely avoided amputation of his leg, had decided not to take a baseball job in 1944. When Grimm first called, he turned down the offer, but Grimm kept calling and Stengel finally agreed, taking the job without a contract so as to help an old friend. Grimm felt that Stengel would protect his as well as Veeck's interests in the team. Indeed, columnist C. M. Gibbs of the *Baltimore Sun* thought the swap of Grimm and Stengel would "ensure a continuation without a break in the hilarious wise-cracking brand of leadership."[41] The *Milwaukee Journal* believed the swap in managers would turn out to be a masterstroke.

"I didn't even know whether we still had a ball club," Veeck later recalled. "It was three weeks before my mail arrived, telling me about [Grimm's] deal with the Cubs."[42] However, the news of Stengel's appointment is what upset Veeck the most. Veeck attacked him professionally and personally in a letter to those running the club, which was reprinted in both Milwaukee newspapers.

"I'd like to have a complete explanation of where Stengel came from," Veeck wrote. "Who hired him? For how much and how long? I don't want anything to do with Stengel nor do I want him to have anything to do with anything I have a voice in. In my humble opinion, he is a very poor manager. . . . I don't believe Stengel is a good judge of players. . . . I have no confidence in his ability and rather than be continuously worried I'd rather dispose of the whole damn thing. . . . If these aren't reasons enough, I don't like him and I want no part of him. If Stengel has an ironclad contract and it will be expensive to break, I guess we'll have to be stuck with him. If not, replace him immediately."[43]

Many years later, Veeck explained his outburst in his introduction to Joseph Durso's 1967 biography of Stengel: "Although I had known Stengel casually since early childhood, I still thought of him as a clown . . . a guy who didn't win. I had bought the then 'public image.' "[44]

After receiving word a few weeks later by return mail of the team's good fortunes—Stengel had extended the Brewers lead in the standings—Veeck eased up on his insistence that Stengel be fired immediately, but he remained steadfast about sending Stengel packing after the season. Veeck never wrote to Stengel, only to the front office staff. In one letter to the Brewers, he wrote: "Possibly you are right, I have misused him. However, I still contend that he is a poor manager."

Milwaukee Journal sports editor R. G. Lynch broke the news to Stengel that the Brewers didn't want him back, and Stengel responded diplomatically. "I took this job to help out my friend, Charlie Grimm, because he said he could not take the job with the Chicago Cubs unless I did. The understanding was that I would just finish up the season, and that would give them time to find a manager for 1945." After Stengel's announcement, Lynch penned an open note to Veeck. "You ought to be ashamed of yourself," he wrote. "Stengel is a swell guy. He did a great job with your ball club, and you have not written him one line all season. Why don't you write the guy?"

The Brewers went on to win the American Association pennant by seven games, though they lost in the playoffs to Louisville, four games to two. Some fans tried to organize a "Bring Back Stengel" campaign, but Stengel declared he would not return as the Brewers skipper in 1945 "under any circumstances."

"Veeck dropped me a note the other day expressing his appreciation for the work I did here this summer," Stengel calmly declared, "and I merely sat down and wrote him about the season. Everything is fine between us."[45]

ALTHOUGH VEECK'S INITIAL account of his time on Bougainville was upbeat and true to his constant urge to put a positive spin on events, his reality was different. A notation in his service records shows that on Bougainville and after his return to Guadalcanal, he had multiple admissions to the sick list for the treatment of abscesses under his arms, on his hands, around his waist, and on his buttocks, legs, and face. While still on the island, an ulcer on his right leg became infected. Much more seriously, Veeck's foot was injured just before his active duty was coming to a close.*

According to Veeck at a much later date, an artillery piece had fired prematurely and recoiled into Veeck's already compromised right foot (originally injured at Kenyon College), cutting a ragged gash to the bone. The

---

* Speculation over the injury was widespread. "No one was ever sure whether Bill got hit by a shell fragment, a sniper's bullet, or one from a Zero's machine gun," Fordham said in an interview at the time of Veeck's death.

injury was patched by Navy medics and Veeck was quickly returned to duty. A short time later, Veeck reported in with a swollen right foot; his arch had collapsed and the foot pointed outward.

He was evacuated on September 19 to a Navy field hospital on Guadalcanal and subsequently transported to San Francisco, where he arrived on October 21. "That Golden Gate coming into view was the most wonderful sight I have ever seen. I've been overseas just nine months, but this was like coming back from another world," he wrote at the time. "The two things I wanted most when I arrived were to talk to my wife Eleanor and to drink as much fresh milk as I could hold." He went directly to the Oak Knoll Navy Hospital in Oakland, where, according to an announcement from the Brewers, he was being sent for treatment of his ankles, which were infected with "jungle fungus."[46] With the aid of a Marine combat correspondent, he penned a small memoir of his experiences overseas, which appeared in *The Sporting News*. The article was remarkably positive given that he was returning injured from a combat zone. He was especially effusive about his fellow servicemen: "I met some really fine boys out there. I went first to New Caledonia, last February, and since then I've come across more good people than I ever knew existed. That's the thing that has impressed me the most." A sidebar accompanying the article, written by a private named E. J. Williams, attested to Veeck's popularity. "I read of his exploits in Milwaukee and expected to run into a prime egoist, but Veeck is a regular guy all the way."

Veeck also praised the Navy doctors who attended to him in medical facilities on Guadalcanal and Espiritu Santo. "They sent me back because my right ankle collapsed, and I couldn't get around very well. I broke it years ago playing football at Kenyon College . . . and it has never been right since. Also, I have a few 'jungle sores' on my legs, which I picked up in Bougainville, but everybody got them there."

A few days after his arrival in San Francisco, a reporter for the *Milwaukee Journal* found Veeck on the hospital grounds moving around with the aid of a cane. He was gregarious and raring to get back to the ballclub, pleased with what the Brewers had achieved in his absence despite (and because of) the signing of Stengel. "I think we set some kind of a record in that of the nine fellows, excluding the pitcher, who opened the season with us all have been sold in the majors. In making these deals, we obtained from 14 to 15 players, giving us something to build around for next season."

He added that while overseas he had signed two pitchers—Tony Jacobs and Lefty Stevens—who would join the team when the war was over and they were discharged. As for baseball after the war, Veeck said: "I believe we will see the biggest boom ever."

Soon thereafter, however, Veeck's injuries necessitated that he be moved to a hospital in Corona, California. There doctors confronted the full range of his maladies: a severely injured ankle and foot, multiple sebaceous cysts on his left ear, an abscess with two draining sinuses, an infected ulcer on the surface of the upper third of his left leg, and a right leg scarred from multiple previous ulcers. Veeck was a mess and an immediate candidate for penicillin, which had come into use with the military only months earlier.

Not surprisingly, he continued to conduct Brewers business from the hospital, signing a new manager in late November. His choice was the popular Nick "Tomato Face" Cullop, who was as enamored of Veeck as Veeck was of him.* Having admired the way Cullop got along with his players as pilot of the Columbus Red Birds in 1943, Veeck considered him a worthy successor to Grimm and Stengel."[47]

Veeck was released from the hospital—in retrospect, prematurely—in late November 1944, just at the time Kenesaw Mountain Landis passed away. His contract as baseball commissioner had recently been extended to January 1953, when he would have been eighty-six.

Clearly ailing and in pain, a pale Veeck showed up at the minor-league meetings in Buffalo from December 5 to 8 with the ever-ruddy Cullop in tow. Cullop observed him in action and told *The Sporting News*: "I've never seen a guy do business like Veeck. I'm not used to seeing a club president spend money so freely. I heard a lot about him while I managed at Columbus, but man, you have to be around Veeck to believe what you've heard and read about him. He's a big leaguer in the double-A circuit."[48]

His deteriorating physical condition notwithstanding, Veeck quickly renewed his public feuding with his fellow American Association owners and club presidents, upbraiding Al Banister, president of the Red Birds, for prematurely leaking news of Cullop's release from the Red Birds to take the Milwaukee job. It was a small matter, perhaps, but one that got him the kind of press coverage he was used to.[49]

---

* Cullop's nickname was inspired from what *The Sporting News* called his "catsup complexion."

Veeck next traveled to New York City for the Major League Winter Meetings beginning on December 12 to see and be seen. Writing about him in the *New York Times*, Arthur Daley described Veeck as easily the "most striking" figure at the gathering. "Young Bill leaned on his cane, his face lined and drawn, but the usual cheery smile on his lips." Veeck joked that due to a pay glitch, he had only received $40 from the Marines so far, so he took the money and blew it at Toots Shor's.[50] Casey Stengel was at the meetings as well, angling for a major-league team to manage, but he settled instead for the Yankees Class AA farm team in Kansas City.

On the night of December 18, a testimonial dinner was held in Veeck's honor back in Milwaukee. Wearing his dress uniform, Veeck, usually a man of many words, was too emotional to talk when called upon to speak. Tears filled his eyes, and after several pauses, he finally had to give up.[51]

After spending Christmas in West Bend, Veeck left for California with his wife and family in tow to see him through his first days of treatment. On New Year's Eve he reentered the Corona hospital, where he would stay until August 15, 1945. His condition had worsened during the thirty-day furlough and was becoming more severe. The bones were now clearly infected, and he was faced with the possible amputation of one or both legs. On January 12, Veeck's right leg was operated on, and three of the bones in his ankle were surgically fused. An ulcer on his left leg was also operated on in January but became progressively worse, and on March 8 he was given a skin graft. He was housed in the amputation ward, being given as many as twenty-four penicillin shots a day for five months while lying in traction—often for both legs at the same time.[52]

One day shortly after the ankle surgery, Casey Stengel, who lived in Glendale, California, dropped by the hospital unannounced to cheer him up and talk baseball. Still limping badly from his injury in Boston, Stengel thought he could help Veeck deal with his injuries. His comic "Ol' Perfessor" act included clowning and conversing with Veeck and others in the mangled form of English that came to be known as "Stengelese." "Here I was feeling sorry for myself as I am sure were a great many of the men in the amputee ward at Corona. Here comes this old man. He was bouncing around that ward doing nips and knee bobs. He did more for morale than all of the psychologists and psychiatrists that the government will ever find," Veeck recalled in a late-1960s radio broadcast, adding, "He is one of my all-time heroes."[53]

The men were pleased with the attention, and Stengel returned periodically over the course of the winter and spring, launching a friendship that would survive even during the years when Stengel managed the Yankees and Veeck was at deep odds with the men who owned that team.

Other than recalling Stengel's visits, Veeck seldom talked about his time in Corona. In a rare 1968 interview with a reporter from the *Cleveland Plain Dealer*, Veeck remembered a moment in the amputation ward in Corona:

"I had both legs in traction and I was staring straight at the ceiling feeling sorry for myself. A fellow comes up to me and says, 'You wanna play rummy?'

"Still looking at the ceiling I said, no thanks.

"The guy says, 'Come on and play some rummy. I'll deal.'

"I look over and he's got two hooks for arms. He starts shuffling and dealing with those hooks across the glass-top table. I remember I started to laugh, because we were in such awful shape. But that's the last time I felt sorry for myself. It was a good lesson."[54]

VEECK CONTINUED TO conduct baseball business from his hospital bed. Among his initiatives was setting up a system of farm clubs for the Brewers. Walter "Dutch" Ruether, who had pitched for the Cincinnati Reds in the World Series against the 1919 Chicago Black Sox, resigned from his scouting job with the Cubs and signed on with the Brewers as Veeck's prime talent scout. In 1943, while employed by the Cubs, Ruether had quietly advised Veeck to buy pitcher Julio Acosta from the Piedmont League. "I'd rather work for a Veeck team than for any other big-league club," Ruether claimed. "Bill's a big leaguer in every respect and a better baseball man than a lot of fellas in the majors."[55]

On July 10, 1945, Veeck was examined by a three-man Medical Survey Board, which recommended that he be given an honorable medical discharge after nineteen and a half months of service. He was still having trouble walking and was deemed unable to perform his military duties; the report noted that he was required to walk very little in civilian life. The discharge report, which Veeck was advised of but was not shown, appears to contain a significant discrepancy. Veeck claimed a shell casing from a .55 mm howitzer had caused his injury, but the board officially determined that his ankle collapse had not occurred in the line of duty but had existed prior to his enlistment and then been aggravated by military service. The report ignored the point that Veeck was now suffering from a war-related bone infection, which threatened both his legs.* The open wound over the ankle had almost certainly led to osteomyelitis with complications from the tropical lesions Veeck called jungle fungus.[56] Veeck later told a friend that a shell casing from a howitzer had caused the wound, complicating the previous Kenyon injury.[57]

VEECK WAS RELEASED from Corona on August 15, 1945, and formally discharged from the Marines on arrival at his West Bend, Wisconsin, home, which took place on the nineteenth. The following night the Brewers held an official welcome-home celebration for Veeck between games of a doubleheader. As the climax to the ceremonies, Bill was treated to a Veeckian surprise: a crate full of pigeons, pigs, and chickens, which were turned loose at home plate. The resulting scramble to recover the livestock was led by manager Nick Cullop, who personally tackled two of the pigs.[58]

The mostly bedridden Veeck had worked with Ruether on the West Coast to create a team that Cullop could win with, and he did. On September 9, Milwaukee beat St. Paul 5–1 in a game at Borchert Field, thereby capturing its third American Association pennant in a row. Though they again lost in the playoffs, Veeck had succeeded to a degree nobody but he—and, perhaps, Charlie Grimm—ever could have imagined.[59]

---

* Reviewing Veeck's medical records, released to the author by the National Archives in June 2010, one is struck by the official assertion that a ten-year-old injury was the cause of a major physical collapse during a military operation. His ankle certainly had been previously compromised, but something else was needed to cause traumatic injury. Veeck had undergone a rigorous induction physical, survived intense basic training, and for months had been handling large munitions as part of a heavy artillery unit. Veeck led an intensely physical life after the 1933 fall and the subsequent football injury. Photos of him prior to his enlistment show him in various situations with all his weight on his right foot. The assertion that Veeck "did not walk much" as a civilian is belied on numerous occasions, including accounts of him walking many miles from his mountain home in Wisconsin in the snow to the train to take him to Milwaukee.

CHAPTER 7

Back in the Game

W HILE VEECK HAD BEEN IN CORONA, a rumor had circulated in late April 1945 that he was putting together a syndicate to buy the Chicago White Sox—further evidence of his involvement in the game while hospitalized. When the rumor appeared in Arch Ward's column in the *Chicago Tribune*, it was denied by Grace Comiskey, president of the team. Reports of dissension within the Comiskey family gave legs to the rumor, which also planted the idea that Veeck was now in the market for a major-league team.[1]

At the 1945 World Series in early October, Veeck told Dan Daniel of the *New York Telegram* that he was ready with a flattering offer for the White Sox, but "she [Grace Comiskey] won't sell." Veeck was also rumored to be in line to replace Harry Grabiner, who had retired, as general manager of the White Sox. Veeck later admitted that he had been offered an important job in the major leagues but had turned it down.[2]

On October 25, as a fresh rumor about Veeck buying the White Sox was beginning to circulate, Branch Rickey matter-of-factly announced that he had signed Jack Roosevelt Robinson, an African American, to play for the Brooklyn Dodgers' Class AA International League team in Montreal. Robinson, who had played for the Kansas City Monarchs, was a former Army lieutenant and UCLA football star. Rickey judged him an "outstanding prospect" and expected him to reach the majors after a period of "orientation."[3]

Bill Bramham, president of the National Association of Professional Baseball Leagues, the minor leagues' governing body, agreed to treat the Robinson contract like any other, but he was clearly unhappy about it. He lashed out at Rickey, branding him the "carpetbagger stripe of the white race" who "under the guise of helping was, in truth, using the Negro for their own selfish interest, who retard the race." He accused Rickey of seeing himself as baseball's Moses, commenting sarcastically: "Father Divine will have to look to his laurels, for we can expect a Rickey temple to be in the course of construction in Harlem soon."[4]

The Sporting News sniffed, "Jackie Robinson at 26 is reported to possess baseball abilities which, if he were white, would make him eligible for a trial with, let us say, the Brooklyn Dodgers Class B farm at Newport News."[5]

A week after the Robinson signing, on November 1, Albert Chandler resigned his seat in the U.S. Senate to officially become commissioner of baseball. The former Democratic governor of Kentucky, Chandler had been elected the previous April after Landis's death in November 1944, but had to finish up his commitments in the Senate. That he was of a different caste and cut than Landis was clear from his oft-used nickname, "Happy."

Anticipating his foray into the major leagues, Veeck decided that his first order of business was to sell the Brewers and realize his profits. His marriage also needed fixing after so much time away, and he was ready to move his base of operations. Having accomplished all his goals in Milwaukee, he knew a good sale of that club would prove that he could make a profit for his investors.

On October 27, 1945, Veeck sold his interest in the club to Chicago attorney Oscar Salenger for an undisclosed sum. The new owner, who had been a batboy for the White Sox in 1923, was admittedly "crazy about baseball." According to his wife, her Russian-born husband was known as "the Encyclopedia of Baseball." Salenger immediately announced that he would keep all of Veeck's staff, including manager Nick Cullop, and that Veeck would remain an honorary vice president of the club.[6]

Later that week in Chicago, in an interview, Veeck acknowledged that he now had the money and backing to go after either the White Sox or the Cubs, and had only been delayed by his own health problems and his wife's "illness." The illness was never specified but was, in effect, a marriage in trouble. Eleanor had visited Bill in the hospital, but his constant absence had alienated her, and she had become increasingly disdainful of his absorption in baseball and all that represented. "She was an animal person, not a people person," remembered Bill's nephew Fred Krehbiel, who knew her when he was a child. "She disliked baseball and baseball people."[7]

Eleanor moved to Arizona alone while Veeck was still hospitalized in

California, leaving their two sons with Bill's mother in Illinois and their daughter, Ellen, in West Bend in the care of a farm woman. The home in West Bend was put on the market and, using some of the money from the sale of the Brewers in a clear attempt to save his marriage, Bill, with the help of Park Parker, former western manager of the National Broadcasting Company and the executor of Bill's father's estate, impulsively purchased the Bar AA ranch, twenty miles southeast of Tucson—a spread with the capacity to comfortably entertain twenty-six guests.

Just before Thanksgiving Veeck reported that his wife was doing well in Arizona and getting better. "Gained five pounds since she went to Arizona," he said, adding, "She weighs 96 pounds now." He also acknowledged that his ankle was acting up inside the cast on his leg and that he was scheduled for more penicillin treatment in Tucson. Veeck spent Thanksgiving in Hinsdale with his mother and two sons, gathered his daughter, and headed for Arizona at the end of the month on a chartered aircraft that landed in an open field near the ranch.[8]

He and Eleanor planned to turn the place into a dude ranch they would call the Double V. Bill wryly said that he was going to Arizona to watch the cacti grow. Interviewed by the *Milwaukee Journal* in December, he sounded wistfully upbeat. "It looks like Ol' Will is about to embark on a new career. I won't say that it replaces the old one, but at least it has kept me busy, and that is something." The ranch was ready for business, and the Veecks expected their first paying guests on January 10, 1946.[9]

Nonetheless, when the Cubs and White Sox came through Tucson on their annual spring training exhibition tour in 1946, Veeck had a joyful reunion with Charlie Grimm. Veeck confided to Grimm that he had discovered cacti didn't grow more than an inch a year, and it was a tedious process sitting there day after day watching them. When the Cubs and White Sox headed back to Chicago, Veeck was not far behind, leaving Arizona in the rearview mirror. As he would later explain, "The Arizona experiment didn't take. Eleanor and I had already grown too far apart. As far as our marriage was concerned the ship had sailed. The fault was mine. It was mine from the beginning."[10]

In 1946, baseball beckoned people who had survived the Great Depression and sacrificed much during the war. Editorialists saw the upcoming season as something special: a reward for winning the war and proof of America's place in the universe. "America and her gallant allies won the war," read an editorial in the *Miami News*, "and so we still have baseball." America was ready to celebrate, and the place to celebrate was the ballpark.[11]

On Opening Day, April 15, President Harry Truman threw out the ceremonial ball at sold-out Griffith Stadium in Washington, D.C. Later that day, Veeck appeared in Milwaukee as Oscar Salenger's guest at an Elks Club baseball dinner, where the speakers included John Bradley of Appleton, one of the five Marines who raised the American flag on Iwo Jima, creating one of the war's most unforgettable images. The next day was Opening Day for the Brewers, and Veeck admitted in an interview at the game that life on a dude ranch was dull, and he hinted that he wanted to get back into baseball.

Perhaps he was also inspired by the exploits of his fellow vets. After three years away from the game serving as a pilot in the Marine Air Corps, Ted Williams had been released on January 12, 1946. On February 26, he hit the first pitch he saw in spring training for a home run. On April 30, Bob Feller, the Cleveland ace just back from active duty in the Navy, threw a no-hitter against the Yankees at Yankee Stadium. A week later, Johnny Pesky of the Red Sox, also lately of the Navy, had eleven straight hits over a two-day period, tying Tris Speaker's major-league record.

In Chicago for the Cubs home opener, Veeck met Harry Grabiner, who, like him, had quickly realized the retired life was not appealing. Veeck was on the prowl for investors and partners with whom to realize his dream of owning a major-league team, but he also needed a good front-office man. While Veeck was with the Cubs, he and Grabiner had worked together on exhibition games between the two Chicago teams and had become friends. Veeck's reaction to Grabiner was sheer amazement.

"Part of my job was checking gates and receipts," Veeck recalled, "and we used to get tangled up with the White Sox in the spring and fall. At Wrigley Field, we had all kinds of adding machines, comptometers, slide rules, and other gadgets to make for the greatest efficiency. We'd make our rounds and get the count started. Grabiner would have a pencil and a piece of paper. I'd have all the modern equipment, and Harry got a kick out of watching me pressing keys and pulling levers. Once in a while, he'd show me the total he had at the bottom of the figures he'd scribbled down on the way around. Darned if he didn't ALWAYS have the correct figure that I'd finally reach by the latest scientific accounting methods."[12]

Veeck's quest for a major-league team surfaced in a mid-May report in the *Pittsburgh Post-Gazette*, recording that he had visited Forbes Field, the home of the National League Pittsburgh Pirates, and was possibly preparing an offer to buy the team. Soon after, the *Milwaukee Journal* reported that Veeck was considering the Pirates or the Cleveland Indians in the American

League. At one point he came within twenty-four hours of making a deal for the Pirates but was stopped by the $2 million price tag. Gradually the scales tipped toward Cleveland, which had a good location and the proper distribution of industry to ensure success (he worried that Pittsburgh was too dependent on the steel industry). It also had an oversized ballpark begging to be filled.[13]

The Indians had had a lackluster 1945 season, finishing in fifth place in the American League, eleven games out of first place. But the value of the team had increased in midseason with the return of hurler Bob Feller from the Navy, who got off to a splendid start in 1946. The team had some promising rookies, including third baseman Bob Lemon and catcher Jim Hegan.

Veeck initially approached attorneys for John Sherwin, the Indians largest stockholder, but not club president Alva Bradley, and his interest was kept secret. Veeck registered in Cleveland hotels under an assumed name. On Sunday, May 28, the Associated Press reported that Veeck was negotiating for the team, and Bradley responded that the Indians were not for sale and that he did not even know Bill Veeck. Bradley opposed the sale, believing the team should be owned locally, but Sherwin had moved too far along and Bradley's opposition was voiced too late. To seal the deal and address the issue of local ownership, Veeck offered to hold $200,000 of stock for the present owners—but none took him up on the offer.[14]

The week before he actually took ownership of the Indians, Veeck roamed around Cleveland in taxicabs and on streetcars, stopping at bars, restaurants, and social clubs such as the VFW and the Knights of Columbus to ask people what they thought of their team. He discovered that they loved the Indians but disliked the syndicate that had owned the team since 1928, as its members seemed aloof and penurious. The promotion-loving Veeck was, for example, shocked to learn that a ball hit into the stands was deemed team property and had to be returned to an usher. He tried to call the ballpark to see if he could reserve a block of seats for an upcoming game and found that to be impossible. He also learned that Indians games were not on the radio and most cab drivers and bartenders were not aware of when the team was in town. To Veeck, this was an opportunity tailor-made for his promotional abilities.

As the sale was moving ahead, Veeck accused the existing group of being more interested in profits than a pennant. The *Cleveland Plain Dealer* conducted a poll that showed that 60 percent of local fans favored a change of ownership.[15]

On June 22, 1946, Veeck bought the Cleveland Indians from Bradley's group for $1,539,000, with a group of partners that included Phil Clarke and Lester Armour (now respectively president and vice president of the City National Bank of Chicago), investment bankers Arthur Allyn and Newton Frye, attorney Sydney K. Schiff, Harry Grabiner, and comedian Bob Hope, who had been born in Britain but raised in Cleveland from infancy. Hope was known in Cleveland sports circles; he had had a brief career as an amateur boxer, fighting under the name Packy East, and would later quip that the locals renamed him Rembrandt because he spent so much time on the canvas. Hope was clearly impressed with Veeck, in whom he had "a world of faith." He was an avid fan of the Indians and now owned about a sixth of the franchise, ensuring the Indians additional national publicity, which pleased Veeck to no end.[16]

Veeck used the moment to make a point: "Nobody in baseball is more aware of the fact that a ball club must sell baseball and win games. There is no substitute for that. But you don't sell your baseball without dressing it up in bright colored paper and red ribbons."[17] Later that day, during the first game played under the new ownership, Veeck took a count of the customers, and the point was made: only 8,526 came to see the Indians beat the league-leading Red Sox.[18]

Veeck's new front office was led by vice president Harry Grabiner. Rudie Schaffer had been summoned from Milwaukee to take over as general manager. Marsh Samuel, Veeck's old schoolmate from Hinsdale, was hired away from the White Sox as his public relations man.

From the outset, rumors indicated that Veeck was not happy with Lou Boudreau as his player-manager and that he planned to replace him as manager with Jimmy Dykes, then managing the Hollywood Stars of the Pacific Coast League, or Charlie Grimm. In June, when Dykes came to Cleveland, it was assumed that he was in town to talk about the job. On June 23, Veeck gave one of many lukewarm endorsements of Boudreau when asked if he would keep him on for the rest of the season: "You can't say just point blank that Boudreau will be the manager for the rest of the year. Something may happen to make a change in managers desirable. But no change is contemplated at present."[19] Rumors followed about Grimm leaving the Cubs to join Veeck in Cleveland. Phil Wrigley denied them.[20] But, as Veeck revealed later, he really had his eye on Casey Stengel, now cooling his heels in the Pacific Coast League in his new position with the Oakland Oaks. In time, Veeck realized he could not afford to lose Boudreau as his shortstop, which might well have happened if he had been sacked as manager.*

His strategy with the public in Cleveland mirrored his approach in Milwaukee: create a good team and make sure the fans left the ballpark happy. After a quick tour of the restrooms, Veeck immediately ordered several dozen mirrors. "Whoever heard of a ladies' room," he asked, "without looking glasses the gals can primp in front of?" Now a ball hit into the stands could be kept, and after most home games, Veeck stationed himself outside one of the gates, where he personally thanked the fans for attending.

When he took over, the team had no radio broadcasts, no Ladies' Day, no posting of National League scores, and no telephone service for fans wishing to reserve tickets. All these things were changed in a matter of weeks. To make it easy to order tickets over the phone, he installed a switchboard with ten lines and hired people to answer them. "If a fan doesn't like his ticket," Veeck told his new employees, "exchange them without any back talk. This is a business in which you must try to please the public. The customer may not always be right, but he thinks he is. We have something to sell, naturally go along with him. I didn't invent this idea, but it works for other businesses, and I don't see why it won't work for us."[21]

The most visible change that Veeck made was with the ushers, whom he dressed in blue coats and trousers with gold stripes, white shirts, and blue neckties. They were to be clean-shaven, with their shoes were brilliantly polished; they were taught courteousness and how to be firm but not tough.[22]

As he had done in Chicago and Milwaukee, Veeck paid personal attention to his stadium's food. Max Axelrod was the concessionaire who worked with Veeck to develop just the right tastes and smells for the ballpark. To Veeck the two most important elements of this mix were the freshly roasted peanuts and the hot dogs. "Veeck took hot dogs very seriously," said Chris Axelrod, Max's grandson.[23] He added that for Veeck the hot dogs had to be

---

* The closest Veeck could get to Stengel was William Stengel, fifty-six, a down-and-outer who claimed to be Casey's cousin and who asked if he could move into the tent in center field that housed the Tribe's fifteen-piece band during games. Veeck found the whole thing deeply amusing and agreed, saying he would charge him no rent (*Montreal Gazette*, July 31, 1946).

just the right flavor and texture to appeal to Cleveland's ethnically diverse audience.*

Continuing the policy he had established in Milwaukee, Veeck made himself available to any group that needed a luncheon or after-dinner speaker. He saw his market as regional rather than local and quickly moved outside Cleveland: "He would go to Buffalo, New York, because we drew quite a bit from Buffalo, which is two hundred miles from Cleveland," recalled catcher Jim Hegan, "and Erie, Pennsylvania, another hundred miles. But he would make all those towns, and just promote the Indians and I think he was very much responsible for our attendance shifts."[24]

On a less formal basis, he worked the nightclubs and bars into the early-morning hours after dinner with local reporters. "In 1946 when Bill first got to Cleveland, I was thirty years old and wanted to get to know him better," Hal Lebovitz of the *Cleveland News* remembered at age eighty-one. "He was always out making speeches, so I offered to drive him so we could talk. I picked him up about 3 p.m., and he fell asleep in the car. He made the speech, and the crowd loved him. On the drive back, he fell asleep again. We got to Cleveland, and I dropped him off at his favorite nightspot, where he was well rested to begin his night rounds."[25]

During one early game, Veeck sat in the bleachers for five innings and discovered that nobody could understand what was being said on the public address system. He quickly installed a new sound system. The fact that an owner would sit in the bleachers hobnobbing with folks in the cheap seats, asking them how to improve their experience, was a startling, radical move that would become one of his trademarks.†

Two weeks after taking over, Veeck arrived in Boston to attend his first American League owners meeting and to attend the thirteenth All-Star

---

* The hot dogs had to be fresh and locally produced, and mustard was all-important. "Every year Veeck and Max would review the mustard to make sure it was just right—a little on the dark side with a touch of horseradish," said Chris Axelrod, who also added that Connie Mack became such a fan of the ballpark franks in Cleveland that he ordered ten pounds of them to take home with him after each visit.

† More than sixty years later, Andy MacPhail, president of baseball operations for the Baltimore Orioles and grandson of Veeck contemporary Larry MacPhail, was asked why the other owners hated Veeck so much. He replied: "For starters, they hated him because he sat in the bleachers. They really hated that. It was a deeply disturbing gesture to these men," who saw themselves as removed from the people who paid to come to their games.

Game on July 9, 1946. This came after a one-day visit with his family in Arizona, which, according to Arch Ward, was his first time home since he'd left in April, intending to be away for only a few weeks. Veeck's unexpected arrival in the American League caught baseball writers by surprise, but as ever, they wrote about him. Ed Rumill of the *Christian Science Monitor* devoted his entire column of July 11 to Veeck. Known for his access at baseball's highest level, Rumill reported that Veeck, having moved his act from Milwaukee to Cleveland, would quickly be reminded that a reasonable amount of dignity was expected in the major leagues. Veeck, however, had already begun his frontal attack on baseball's dignity. The day before, Arch Ward had reported in his column in the *Chicago Tribune* that Veeck had apologized for *not* insulting any of his fellow owners at his first American League meeting. "I've got to get warmed up," he explained.[26]

If Veeck was about to begin tossing barbs at baseball's executives, he also began throwing bouquets to the working-class folks he needed to fill his ballpark. As a first step, he hired Max Patkin as a coach. Patkin was a thin, tall man with a rubber face and a large nose. A below-average pitcher on the Indians Wilkes-Barre farm club, he had been released earlier in 1946 because of a sore arm. But he was a born clown with an ability to contort his body in the most extraordinary manner. He had picked up his clown reputation during the war when, pitching for the Navy against the Seventh Air Force team in Honolulu, Joe DiMaggio nailed him for a home run. Something got into Patkin, who caught up with DiMaggio at first base and followed him around the bases stride for stride. "I weighed 150 pounds, looked like a nose on a lollipop stick," he later told Red Smith of the *New York Times*. "When we got to the plate, the whole team was out there shaking my hand." Smith described him as looking "like a noodle Mrs. Ronzoni left in the box too long."[27]

Just after Veeck bought the club, the Indians were scheduled to play an exhibition game against Wilkes-Barre, and Patkin was brought back to entertain the crowd, which he did as first-base coach. He would pretend to faint over a close or disputed call, falling over backward while remaining as straight as a tree. Boudreau thought Patkin's act was hilarious and reported this to Veeck, who gave Patkin a legitimate coach's contract for $1, but also signed him to a performance agreement for $650 a month. "I want you to work the crowd and then perform for two innings a game in the first base coaching box," he instructed Patkin.[28]

Veeck also knew an oddball shortstop named Jackie Price, who played for the Oakland Oaks of the Pacific Coast League. Price had a broad collection of tricks that he performed either before games or between the games of a doubleheader. These included being able to hit a ball while suspended upside-down from a rack erected over the plate and to catch and throw while standing on his head. He also had a fascination with snakes, which he collected and occasionally brought to the ballpark as part of his pre-game act. During one pre-game sideshow in Oakland in July, he reached for a ball, which somehow ended up inside his shirt, and when he went to retrieve it, he instead pulled out a six-foot-long black snake. Price and his reptile then proceeded to put on a two-creature show in the infield, with Price more than once tossing the snake out at second as it slithered down the base path.[29]

Price was purchased by the Indians on August 2 for the remainder of the 1946 season. The plan was to use him as a pinch hitter, but Veeck added, "He won't hit much, but is the greatest baseball entertainer in the country."

After a few early fan promotions involving free gifts, Veeck hit on a grand scheme for August 1 that recalled his father's Ladies' Day events: give away nylon stockings to the first 20,000 women to arrive at the ballpark. He was reacting to a nearly insane demand for nylon stockings, which had been introduced by DuPont on the eve of World War II but had been taken off the market for the war years, when nylon was needed for parachutes, tires, and other wartime essentials. Not fully recovered from its wartime conversion, DuPont could not keep up with the immediate postwar demand. Women waiting in line to buy the stockings were sometimes disorderly, and police occasionally had to disperse crowds. When stores sold out of the precious hosiery, fights broke out. In Pittsburgh, the mayor arranged for a stocking sale in response to a petition by 400 women. On the day of the sale, 40,000 people lined up to compete for 13,000 pairs.

On August 1, 21,372 women participated in the giveaway in Cleveland, with many of them getting their prize directly from Veeck or Harry Grabiner. Baseball's traditionalists shuddered and cast aspersions. Bob French, in his *Toledo Blade* column the following morning, talked of "terrifying numbers" of the fair sex swarming the stadium. "There probably was more high-pitched cheering on high fouls than ever before in Cleveland." "To this day," Rudie Schaffer recalled five decades later, "I still don't know where he got the nylons."[30]

Veeck next conceived a proper event at which to introduce his two enter-tainers. It had to be a night when a lot of fans would be in the ballpark. One of the most popular people in the Cleveland organization was an ex-prizefighter and paperboy named Max "Lefty" Weisman, who had been the Indians trainer for twenty-five years. Weisman was known for his constant singing, cornball jokes, and memorable quips. Bob Feller, as a rookie, had complained that his cap was too big. Lefty said, "Make sure it stays that way." Weisman was devoted to the team, and Veeck wanted to pay tribute to the man who tended the players' aches and pains. He decided to give Weis-man his own night at the stadium, an honor usually reserved for stars. It was held on Tuesday night, August 13, and featured Price and Patkin, fire-works and fire trucks, singing by Weisman, and, almost secondarily, a game, leading Veeck to boast: "It was a super-duper evening which Abner Double-day of Cooperstown, New York might have had difficulty recognizing as a baseball game." A crowd of 65,765 attended the extravaganza, though on the field the Indians lost the game to the Tigers.

Veeck's clown act, however, did not play as well out of town. In Boston, two fans were taken to the hospital after being hit by a ball that Price fired from a special sling he had brought to Boston and reassembled on the field between games of a doubleheader. Patkin got into the act in the second game. After convulsing the fans for his two innings as first-base coach, he then fol-lowed Red Sox manager Joe Cronin to his preferred post at third base during the Cleveland half of the inning. Cronin bellowed at the Cleveland bench, "I thought this was the big leagues." By the end of the season Patkin's act had become stale. The fact that the Indians were well out of the pennant race allowed him to finish the season in uniform without doing harm to the team's chances.

As the season wound down, Veeck staged an event in sharp contrast to the antics of Patkin and Price, which underscored Veeck's belief that put-ting blacks and whites on the same field was not only acceptable but good box office. In mid-August Indians outfielder George Case and Gil Coan, the speedy Washington Senators rookie, staged a 100-yard footrace in Griffith Stadium for the unofficial title of "fastest man in the American League." Case won in a flat 10 seconds, merely 0.6 second off the 9.4-second world record held by several track stars, including Jesse Owens, known as "the fastest human" after his stunning four Olympic gold medals in 1936. Veeck then announced that he would dress Owens in a baseball uniform and have

him race against Case between the games of the September 8 Indians–
St. Louis Browns doubleheader.* Owens bested Case by a yard.[31]

Meanwhile, Veeck added to his reputation as a shrewd financial man as
word circulated that he had used a debenture–common stock scheme to finance the team. He would remunerate his partners in the syndicate in
nontaxable loan repayments rather than in dividends, which were then tax-
able at rates depending on one's income. Instead of taking their investment
in stock, Veeck's backers got 85 percent in debentures and 15 percent in
stock. As he would later explain, "The attractiveness of my plan was based
entirely upon the opportunity to put as little as possible into the stock and
as much as possible into the debentures." So if the team succeeded, the
loan would be repaid, the investor would have recovered almost all of his
original investment, and that $15,000 worth of stock would actually now be
worth a full $100,000 on the open market. Veeck observed, "Assuming a real
success, it would be worth even more. And if you sold that stock, your
$85,000 profit would be taxed not as regular earnings [but] at a flat 25 percent
rate. This approach was new to baseball. For decades to come, owners in all
professional sports benefitted from it.[32]

OF THE REPORTERS covering the Indians, the ones Veeck became closest to
were Gordon Cobbledick, who had been appointed sports editor of the
Cleveland Plain Dealer eight days before Veeck had taken over the club,
Franklin Gibbons of the *Press*, Ed McAuley of the *News*, and Franklin Lewis
of the *Plain Dealer*. These men and their wives called themselves the "Jolly
Set" and would chronicle Veeck's transformation of a team—and a city.

At the end of August, with the Indians thirty-one and a half games out of
first place, Veeck was on the road with the team in Chicago and told Gibbons that he needed a half dozen solid players to create a winning team in
1947. "All I can say is that it should be a busy winter," said Veeck. "There is
work to be done in the carpenter's shop."

The team had been in constant flux since Veeck took over (forty-eight

---

* Case's son, George W. Case III, addressed himself to the racial significance of the event in
a 2011 personal communication: "I've often thought about that. I don't think at the time
anyone really mentioned it because it was Jesse Owens, the Olympic champion, and he was
not a baseball player. I know that I never heard my dad ever talk about race, although obviously when he played, baseball was all white."

players wore the uniform from that day until the end of the season) and the offense was terrible—the worst in the league. Bob Feller had what many would consider his greatest year (26–15, 2.18 ERA, 348 strikeouts), and manager Lou Boudreau gave Veeck a nice dose of national publicity by creating a novel defense against Red Sox slugger Ted Williams, moving all his infielders to the right side in what later became known as the "Williams Shift."[33]

Having quickly established his big-league skills as a producer of entertainment—Veeck boosted the Indians 1946 attendance above the 1 million mark for the first time in club history despite the sixth-place finish and a record under Veeck of 42–53—he began the process of building his team. "A championship as quickly as possible" was his slogan for Cleveland, as it had been at Milwaukee. Veeck also had another goal in mind, which would be achievable as soon as the team began playing all its home games in cavernous Municipal Stadium, also known as simply Cleveland Stadium. The team was splitting games between two parks, but this would end with the 1946 season. Veeck wanted to beat the Yankees not only on the field but also at the box office. In July 1946, the Yankees had surpassed the long-standing attendance record of 1,485,166 set by the 1929 Chicago Cubs. "I wonder how my dad feels about this Yankee record?" Veeck asked a few days after it was posted. "That turnstile mark was his pride and joy. And now—well, dad must be saying 'It's all for the best and a great thing for baseball.' He had no streak of jealousy in him and he was for everybody in baseball. As for myself, I would feel sore as hell if I piled up an amazing record like that for one season and some guy had come along and kicked it to pieces like [Larry] MacPhail has."[34]

In Boston for the World Series, Veeck chatted with MacPhail, who told the Indians owner that he wanted to trade second baseman Joe Gordon for a pitcher. The Yankees had finished in third place, seventeen games behind the Red Sox, and MacPhail was rebuilding as well. There were also published rumors of a possible Joe DiMaggio–Ted Williams swap, which was neither confirmed nor denied by MacPhail. Gordon had been the American League's Most Valuable Player in 1942, had enlisted in the Navy after the 1943 season, and had rejoined the Yankees in 1946. Although he had made his sixth All-Star appearance, his average plummeted to .210. He had been spiked in the hand during spring training and had tried to play before it healed, and then later he suffered a leg injury that slowed him down.

Gordon's maladies led MacPhail to consider him a malingerer. At one point deep in the season, he called Gordon into his office along with his manager, Bill Dickey. "He accused me of quitting on him," Gordon recalled later. "That's a damn lie. I never quit on anybody in my life. He called me in his office and insulted me all over the place." MacPhail then ordered Dickey to take Gordon out of the lineup. According to Arthur Daley of the *New York Times*, this set off two explosions. "Gordon flared up and came perilously close to punching MacPhail in the nose," and Dickey too erupted. In pointed words, he told MacPhail that no front-office man could tell him how to manage, and that if MacPhail didn't leave him alone, "he could take his managerial portfolio and shove it up the chimney or someplace."[35] Dickey was immediately relieved of his duties.

Veeck, however, had been watching Gordon and said he wanted him, and offered MacPhail a choice of right-handers Allie Reynolds or Red Embree. MacPhail checked with DiMaggio.

"There's no choice," DiMaggio told him. "Get Reynolds."[36]

A few days later, the deal was finalized and applauded in Cleveland.* Cobbledick spoke for many when he opined: "Reynolds is a pitcher and therefore a defensive unit. . . . The Indians were a hopeless team because they could not make runs in sufficient numbers to reward good pitching with victories. Gordon may supply the needed offensive power."[37]

ON OCTOBER 24, 1946, Veeck entered the Cleveland Clinic for treatment of his infected right foot. It was the third hospitalization for the infection since he had bought the Indians in June. A little more than a week later, he realized he might have to submit to amputation. "There's a possibility—a good possibility—that I'll lose the foot before I leave this hospital," he told the *New York Times*. He added, "Right now, the doctors are trying to get all the infection confined to the foot. I'm so full of penicillin that if you were to wring me out, you'd have enough for a dispensary."[38]

For the first time, Veeck was willing to discuss the fact that the injury to his severely damaged right foot had been caused by the recoil of a 90-mm antiaircraft gun while in Bougainville more than two years earlier. Veeck had never mentioned this while in uniform, and his military record con-

---

* Gordon departed New York after precisely 1,000 games and 1,000 hits, holding a deep and abiding contempt for MacPhail and the Yankees front office, not unlike the one Veeck would himself develop. By the time both men had retired, the transaction was regarded as the perfect trade for both teams.

tains no mention of it either. He had osteomyelitis, an acute bone infection common to injuries to extremities, in his foot.

On November 1, Veeck lost not only his right foot but a major portion of his right leg as well, leaving him with a stump below the knee. That afternoon, Frank Gibbons of the *Cleveland Press* got a call at the office and for a moment did not recognize the weak and distant voice.

"Hello, Gibby." There was a long pause. "This is Bill: What's doing?"[39]

When the news got out, Veeck's hospital room was buried in floral tributes and thousands of letters and get-well cards. Soon he was holding an open house in Room 601. An Associated Press wire photo taken on November 2 ran with a caption noting that Veeck's familiar smile was ever present.[40] A week later, Bob Hope visited Veeck in the hospital, which made for a perfect photo opportunity, especially when Hope crawled halfway across the bed and gave Veeck a peck on the cheek. Veeck beamed with delight.

Two weeks after the operation, Veeck was spotted at a Cleveland Browns football game, where he told a reporter he planned to return to the Cleveland Clinic the next day. Veeck would follow this pattern through countless future hospital stays, checking himself out to take in an important sporting event and then returning to the hospital to finish recovering. He was finally released on November 18 and quipped, "My only regret is that I wasted two years before the operation when I could have been mastering the use of an artificial leg."[41]

Veeck went to the Winter Meetings in Los Angeles ready to deal. Shortstop Boudreau had been teamed with second baseman Ray Mack for several seasons, but with Joe Gordon now on the club, there was no place for Mack. Veeck shopped around a bit and then zeroed in on MacPhail once more, bundling Mack and rookie catcher Sherman Lollar to New York in exchange for outfielder Hal Peck, right-hander Al Gettel, and a left-hander named Gene Bearden, whom the Yankees had just acquired from the Oakland Oaks of the Pacific Coast League. Bearden was regarded by many as the "throw-in" to sweeten the trade.

When the deal was completed, much was made of Peck's being reunited with his old Milwaukee boss. Gettel was a known quantity, with a 15–15 record over the previous two seasons with the Yankees. Little was known about Bearden except that he was a knuckleballer about whom Casey Stengel, his manager on the Oakland Oaks, had given Veeck a thumbs-up. On the eve of the trade, the Associated Press distributed a wire photo of Stengel, Veeck, and Grabiner having drinks, clearly underscoring Stengel's role as a talent scout for Veeck.[42]

In mid-January, Veeck announced that he was being fitted for an artificial limb and would soon throw a party in the Vogue Room of the Hollenden House Hotel in Cleveland to celebrate the discarding of his crutches. He fulfilled the promise less than two weeks later. "He was on the dance floor all night," his director of public relations and childhood friend Marsh Samuel later recalled. "The blood soaked his leg and got on the floor. It was not one of his better moves." Foolish or not, to a nation still awed by the sacrifices of members of the Armed Forces, Veeck's determination to dance on his injured leg became a symbol of the American spirit.[43]

On February 2, 1947, the *Chicago Tribune* carried an article on ranches in Tucson where notable Chicagoans were wintering. One ranch featured was the Veecks', which was described as an immense spread, buried in the Rincon Mountains, that featured a main house with five bedrooms, along with a number of outbuildings. "The Bill Veecks, owners of the ranch, are unique in that they cater to parents with children," the article said, adding that a governess and Spanish nursemaids were on hand to attend to the "child colony" at the ranch. A number of people were mentioned as being guests at the ranch that winter, including Eleanor's mother, her sisters (who were assisting in running the ranch), and the Boudreaus, who were spending the winter there with their three children. Another source reported that Hal Peck and his wife, mother, and two children also stayed at the Veeck ranch for several months during the winter of 1946–47.[44]

No mention was made of Veeck himself in the article, and during most of late January his name appeared often in articles with a Cleveland dateline. The day the article ran in the *Tribune*, he was in New York City as a featured speaker at the Baseball Writers' Association of America dinner; two nights later he was in Boston for a similar event.[45]

One of his promotions before the 1947 season was a batboy contest, in which he invited boys ages twelve to sixteen to compete for the position and $1,000 to be set aside for college tuition. Applicants needed to submit an essay explaining why they wanted to be a batboy. Thousands of boys entered the contest, as did one girl, Diane Heidkamp, to whom Veeck sent a regretful letter explaining why she was not eligible.

Veeck's attachment to Patkin and Price remained despite their excesses the previous fall. Early in March 1947, at spring training in Phoenix, Veeck found Max Patkin sitting in the Indians dugout. As Patkin later recalled: "He had on his new wooden leg, and he was just like a kid with a new toy. Then he challenged me to a race. He said, 'I'll bet you $20 I can beat you from here to the outfield fence.' I gave him a head start, but darned if he didn't beat me to that wall. It was amazing. And I had to pay the twenty bucks too."

Later that month, though, Price strained the relationship. The Indians and White Sox were aboard a train from Los Angeles on their way to an exhibition game in San Diego. A group of Indians players shared a Pullman car with women bowlers on their way back from a tournament. Ever the prankster, Price released two of his snakes. Patkin reported that the women began screaming, with "some of them hanging on to the baggage racks, standing on the seats." The panic caused the conductor to halt the train momentarily on the tracks while order was restored.

Boudreau was in another car playing cards, but when the conductor laid into him, Boudreau knew Price was responsible. He ordered him off the team and put him on a train back to Cleveland, wiring Veeck: "I THOUGHT I WAS THE MANAGER OF A BIG LEAGUE BALL CLUB NOT OF A CIRCUS."[46]

Back in Cleveland, Veeck gave Price a good tongue-lashing, but he could not bear to actually fire either him or Patkin, so he sent them on a tour of the club's seventeen farm teams. "That's a worse penalty than even Happy Chandler could devise for that snake escapade," Hugh Fullerton chuckled in his Associated Press column.[47]

CHAPTER 8

Lawrence Doby and the Integration of the American League

A T THE BEGINNING OF 1947 BILL VEECK decided that the time had come to racially integrate the Cleveland Indians. He had long considered breaking the color barrier, and the previous July he had told Cleveland Jackson, a columnist for the Cleveland *Call and Post*, that he had several requirements for such an arrangement. He would purchase the contract of a Negro player only "through regular procedures, not by means of raids similar to Branch Rickey's grabs from the Negro leagues"—an allusion to the fact that Rickey did not pay a Negro league team for Jackie Robinson and several players that followed him. Any player he signed would need the highest "all-around qualifications," including the ability to "take it." And Veeck would bring in such a player only if his presence would mean the difference between a mediocre team and a championship one.[1]

Early in 1947 Veeck called Ray Dandridge in Mexico and invited him to his Arizona ranch for a talk. Dandridge, then thirty-seven, had been an outstanding third baseman in the Negro leagues and had been playing professionally for the previous seven years in the Mexican League under a lucrative $10,000-per-season contract from multimillionaire Jorge Pasquel that included living expenses and a maid. Dandridge had moved his wife and three children to Mexico City and was playing alongside several white former major leaguers who had jumped to the Mexican League in 1946 for guaranteed multiyear contracts, among them pitchers Max Lanier and Sal Maglie and former Pirates and Dodgers outfielder Max Carey, who managed the team in Veracruz.

The previous June, Gordon Cobbledick of the *Plain Dealer* had gone to Mexico to see why so many American players were willing to burn their bridges with their major-league teams by defecting to play for Pasquel. While there, he had seen why Dandridge was regarded as equal to or better than such highly skilled white infielders as Lou Boudreau, Johnny Pesky of the Red Sox, and Marty Marion of the St. Louis Cardinals.

Following Veeck's meeting with Dandridge, Cobbledick revealed how close Dandridge had come to being the first to break the color barrier. Cobbledick watched Dandridge play and then could not hide his admiration for him from his readers or from Veeck.

"[Veeck] said he wanted me to be the first one," Dandridge related. "I even went to the Veeck farm in Arizona and talked to him, but I was playing in Mexico then, making pretty good money." Dandridge asked Veeck about a signing bonus, but Veeck declined and, lacking an option or an offer, Dandridge decided not to sign lest he fail and end up without a job. Dandridge was also doubtlessly aware of other futile "tryouts" that had been granted to some African American players—notably the "don't call us, we'll call you" tryouts with the Boston Red Sox in 1945—and could see no merit in Veeck's offer.

"I thought I would be jeopardizing a whole lot," he later acknowledged, "so I refused. I wouldn't jump."[2] How serious Veeck was about putting Dandrige in an Indians uniform is not known, but if he had made Dandridge an attractive offer, the names Veeck and Dandridge might now be as revered as those of Rickey and Robinson.*

In mid-February 1947, Veeck hired Louis Jones, a black public relations man, to "prepare the black segment of Cleveland for the arrival of a black ballplayer, unnamed." A highly visible force in the community, Jones had been singer Lena Horne's first husband. Veeck then engaged Bill Killefer to "casually scout" for black players, using an updated version of the list he and Abe Saperstein had put together five years earlier. He had heard about a

---

* Dandridge left Mexico in 1949 after the death of his friend and patron Jorge Pasquel, who was killed in an airplane crash, and was signed by the AAA Minneapolis Millers, a farm team of the New York Giants. Despite Dandridge's earning the league's MVP honor in 1950, the parent club deemed him too old to move up. Others insisted it was not that he was "too old" but that there were already "too many"—the Giants had three black players (Monte Irvin, Hank Thompson, and Artie Wilson). Dandridge retired from baseball after the 1955 season. In 1987 he was inducted into the Baseball Hall of Fame at the age of seventy-three.

young war veteran named Larry Doby, who was playing for Effa Manley's Newark Eagles of the Negro National League. On June 13, Cleveland Jackson, who had already tipped Jones to the presence of Doby, wrote to Veeck saying that he was "especially enthused" about Doby as a prospective Indian. Veeck answered that Killefer was already scouting him.[3] Veeck later acknowledged that the strongest influence on his decision came from Wendell Smith, editor of the black weekly the *Pittsburgh Courier*. Veeck believed that Smith, more than anyone, had "influenced Rickey to take Jack Robinson. . . . I had known Wendell since '42. So Wendell and Abe and I met a couple of times and we arrived at Larry Doby as the best young player in the [Negro] league."[4]

Veeck wanted to bring a black player directly to the majors, bypassing the minor leagues. "I'll handle him just like any other rookie," he said, believing Rickey had put too much pressure on Robinson by starting him in the minors. In truth, however, Veeck did not have the option of sending a black player to either of his top farm teams, located in Baltimore and Oklahoma City, because those cities simply would not under any circumstances have accepted a Negro athlete.[5]

Veeck knew that a year earlier, in Baltimore, Jackie Robinson had faced perhaps his toughest harassment while playing for the Montreal Royals. In Robinson's opinion, the taunts and threats of white Baltimoreans were worse than the intentional spikings he received on the field. On one occasion large numbers of whites crowded around the Royals' dressing room after a game, and Baltimore police had to disperse the crowd.[6] Doby had led the Newark Eagles to a championship in 1946. Shy and introverted, he had grown up in a poor but mixed neighborhood of Italian, Irish, Jewish, and black kids in Paterson, New Jersey, where he starred at East Side High School in baseball, basketball, football, and track. Doby ran for the winning touchdown in a game against Montclair High, a team that included astronaut-to-be Buzz Aldrin, which prompted Doby to later quip: "Given the circumstances at the time you could say that I had as much chance of playing in the major leagues as Aldrin did of going to the moon."[7]

Doby could later recall being subjected to a racist insult in high school only once, during a football game. He responded by whirling past the foul-mouthed defensive back to haul in a touchdown pass. "That shut the guy up," said Doby.[8] He then played basketball on a scholarship on the integrated team at Long Island University under legendary coach Clair Bee. In 1943, after three months at LIU, Doby signed a contract with the Newark Eagles of the Negro National League.

The first time Doby encountered Jim Crow was as a Navy draftee in 1943 when he was separated from his white high school friends on a train heading to basic training in Illinois, forced to ride in a separate car with other blacks. The reality of the enforced racial divide in the Armed Forces hit home when he was denied a chance to play for the famous Great Lakes Naval Training Station ball club, managed by Hall of Famer Mickey Cochrane, and had to play instead for the all-black team at an all-black camp. Later in the war he was permitted to play fast-pitch softball with white professionals on the small Pacific island of Mog Mog, part of the Ulithi Atoll, a fog-shrouded speck of a place that one veteran later said reminded him of the "eerie island in the movie *King Kong*." The men he played with included Billy Goodman, who would go on to a career with the Red Sox, and Washington Senators veteran Mickey Vernon, with whom he established a life-long friendship.[9]

Vernon considered Doby the best player in the island's softball and basketball leagues. After Jackie Robinson signed with Montreal in 1945 and while Doby was still in the South Pacific, Vernon wrote a letter to Senators owner Clark Griffith asking him to give Doby a tryout, which never happened. Then, when Doby rejoined the Newark Eagles in 1946, Vernon shipped him a dozen Louisville Slugger bats in a gesture of respect and friendship.

Veeck sent Louis Jones to see Doby play at the start of the 1947 season. "We were playing the Philadelphia Stars in Newark, and he came to the game and he said Mr. Veeck said to talk to me and see how I felt about coming to be a big-league player, and he would come back in a couple of weeks and would take me to see the Yankees play against Cleveland—I guess Cleveland was coming into town." Jones took him to that game and visited with him on several other occasions, including a game in Trenton where he asked Doby if he was ready to play major-league baseball. "I said, 'I don't see any difference in the baseball.' So he said, 'Mr. Veeck is thinking about a contract maybe in a week or two.'"[10]

Meanwhile, Dodger scout Clyde Sukeforth, who had given Rickey a final endorsement of Jackie Robinson, personally scouted every game Doby played in the New York area in the season's opening six weeks. Veeck and his scouts had by then compiled, in Doby's words, "a foot-high notebook that had everything I'd ever done in my life from the time I was born." Rickey was about to sign Doby when Wendell Smith told Sukeforth that he was about to be signed elsewhere. When Rickey found out that it was with the Indians, he relented, passing along the scouting reports and acknowledging that Doby's signing with Cleveland would help the movement and ease some of the pressure on Robinson.

To conclude the deal, Veeck had to formally obtain Doby from Effa Manley, the owner and chief operating officer of the Eagles. Veeck intended to purchase Doby's Newark contract, but when he telephoned on July 1 to say he wanted to sign Doby, Manley asked, "Well, what do you plan to give me for him, Mr. Veeck?" Veeck said $10,000. "Well, I'm not a millionaire," Manley replied, "but I am financially secure, I think, and ten thousand dollars looks like ten cents. I know very well that if he was a white boy and a free agent you'd give him a hundred thousand. But if you feel you're being fair offering me ten, I guess I'll have to take it."* Veeck promised her an additional $5,000 if he kept Doby for at least thirty days. Manley wouldn't give her consent without clearing the deal with her husband, Abe, who thought the price was "ridiculously low." Effa told Abe they had no leverage by which to force Veeck to up the ante, and if they refused the offer, they would be accused by fans and the press of depriving Doby of his shot at the majors. Abe ultimately consented.[11]

Veeck paid the $15,000 even though he probably could have gotten Doby for nothing. Unlike Rickey, who considered the Negro leagues to be "a racket," Veeck's assessment of them was less judgmental: "They were at best marginal. They just scuffled." Veeck knew Rickey had paid nothing for Robinson because Tom Baird, the white owner of the Kansas City Monarchs, couldn't stand in Robinson's way, and Veeck also knew Manley couldn't stand in Doby's way, just as she eventually could not prevent Rickey from taking pitcher Don Newcombe from her. "We could," Veeck said, "just have reached out and said 'Come on.' But we didn't want to do that and we did purchase his contract."[12]

Meager though Veeck's offer seemed to Manley, she knew Veeck was the only major-league official willing to pay for Negro leagues talent. With that in mind, she extended an offer to Veeck: "Take a look at [Monte] Irvin for a thousand dollars and then pay me what you think he's worth."† Veeck de-

---

* In talking with interviewer Bill Marshall about Doby's signing years later, she said, "The whole story has been just one of those kind of things where the strong have taken advantage of the weak. And, of course, that's true of life. I learned that all through life."
† Teammate Frazier Robinson was among those on the Eagles who believed that Irvin would beat Doby to the majors: "I always thought that Monte Irvin would be the first to leave Newark and go to the majors. Monte was just a great ballplayer, but I think the war hurt

clined, acknowledging that he would "have difficulty bringing in one Negro." He would regret not taking Irvin and later told Irvin, who became a close friend, "That was the dumbest deal I never did."[13]

Though improved, the Indians had fallen twelve games behind the Yankees when Veeck told the local writers at an impromptu press conference on July 3 that he had an announcement that might interest them.

"We've signed a new ballplayer named Larry Doby," he said. There was a pause. "He's a Negro."

The room was silent while Veeck let the words sink in.

"He'll be a great ballplayer," Bill went on. "He's a second baseman with the Newark Eagles in the Negro National League."

One reporter then asked when the new phenom was to report.

"In Chicago day after tomorrow," Veeck said.

Doby's last appearance in the Negro National League was to be the next afternoon in a July 4 doubleheader at Newark's Ruppert Stadium. He was batting .415 with a league-leading 14 home runs. At a ceremony at home plate before the first game, his teammates gave him a toilet kit with shaving lotion, soap, a brush, and a comb. His mother and wife accompanied him and Louis Jones to Newark's Pennsylvania Station, where the two men boarded the *Admiral* for the overnight trip west. Doby had been informed that he would be unable to stay at the unintegrated team hotel, so he and Jones checked into the DuSable, the leading hotel for blacks in the city.

Veeck signed the twenty-three-year-old Doby to an Indians contract in the presence of numerous reporters on July 5, 1947—eleven weeks after Robinson had come up with the Dodgers—at the Congress Hotel in Chicago. "I walked into his office," Doby later recalled, "and he got up from the desk and he walked over and he shook my hand and he says, 'Lawrence,' he says, 'I'm Bill Veeck.' And I said, 'Nice to meet you, Mr. Veeck.' So he says, 'You don't have to call me Mr. Veeck. Call me Bill.' And it stuck with me because it's an old Southern tradition, strictly from respect, that those who

---

him. Monte went into the Army at the same time that Larry and I went into the Navy. But Monte came out kind of shook up. They called it combat fatigue, but I've since heard it was some kind of inner ear problem. Whatever it was, he really wasn't himself for a while. So he started back with Newark, and he played there for a while until he got back into the shape he was in before he went in the service. And after that, couldn't nobody get him out. He was such a good hitter. And he played his position well. He was a complete ballplayer." From Robinson's *Catching Dreams: My Life in the Negro Baseball Leagues* (Syracuse, NY: Syracuse University Press, 1999), 127.

are your elders you say 'Mister' to. I had never said 'Mister' to anybody else and got that kind of response. . . . But as I grew older and as I had contact with him, I recognized what he meant and what it was all about."[14]

Following the introduction, Veeck had a heart-to-heart session with Doby to prepare him for the slights and insults he could expect. "He said, 'Lawrence'—he's the only person who called me Lawrence—'you are going to be part of history.' Part of history? I had no notions about that. I just wanted to play baseball. I mean, I was young. I didn't quite realize then what all this meant. I saw it simply as an opportunity to get ahead." Veeck gave Doby a list of dos and don'ts: "No arguing with umpires . . . no dissertations with opposing players . . . no associating with female Caucasians," and above all to act in an appropriate way, as people would be watching." Then Veeck told Doby something he would always remember: "We're in this together, kid." That was enough for Doby. He trusted Veeck immediately and forever.[15]

When Doby was introduced to the Cleveland players that afternoon most of them stood mute, ignoring his existence. "It'd all been arranged before I got there," Doby recalled, "because when I walked in the door they all were lined up by their lockers." Louis Jones introduced Doby to Boudreau, who took him down the line to shake hands. Five players refused to extend their hands. "Name-wise, I'm not going to name the names who did it, but the funny thing about it was it didn't bother me at the moment because I don't think I was thinking too much about it. I was so wrapped up in the game itself in terms of being able to play."[16]

"Sure there was a lot of grumbling and talk behind my back," Veeck later recalled, but he saw it more as an economic threat to fringe players than anything else.[17] "When he went out on the field to warm up along the sidelines, Doby stood alone until second baseman Joe Gordon told him to grab his glove and exchanged throws with him."

The reaction to the Doby signing was varied. Larry MacPhail of the New York Yankees had no comment, but Rickey observed: "If Doby is a good player, and I understand that he is, the Cleveland club is showing signs that it wants to win." But there was more to it than that: Rickey had been vindicated. "I don't think there was a happier day in Mr. Rickey's life than when Veeck brought in Doby," broadcaster Red Barber recalled decades later.[18]

"I got a call from my mother after I signed Doby," Veeck told the *Chicago Defender*'s Doc Young. "She had told me that she had heard that I had hired a Negro and when I confirmed it, she said 'Bill I think that is just awful.' I told her, 'Well, Mother, I don't suppose we agree on some things.'"[19]

Like Jackie Robinson, Doby had to cope without losing his temper.* "I couldn't react to [prejudicial] situations from a physical standpoint. My reaction was to hit the ball as far as I could," he said later. Unlike Robinson, Doby didn't have much preparation. He also got none of the intense and sympathetic media coverage the charismatic Robinson received. "You didn't hear much about what I was going through because the media didn't want to repeat the same story." He told Wendell Smith one night in 1959 while sitting in his living room, "I heard 'nigger' so many times in the outfield that I thought it was my middle name."[20]

While Robinson's struggle was mostly with other players, not the Brooklyn fans, Doby was confronted by players on other teams as well as by the local population, which was not ready for him. One of the reporters who covered the Indians in 1947, Robert Ames Alden of the *Cleveland Press*, years later recalled a city deeply divided along racial lines, which Veeck's hiring of Doby exacerbated. "I was a junior member of the sports staff, one step up from what would now be called an intern, and I was picking up eight to ten calls a night from white people angry about the integration of the team. Some were quite threatening. Both the *News* and the *Plain Dealer* as well as the radio stations decided not to report these calls."[21]

---

* Doby's major-league debut was an event looking for a story, and over time it has spawned several accounts that fall apart under scrutiny. One story circulated for years after Veeck himself repeated the tale on a New York radio station in 1961: "I can remember Doby's first time at bat. He was nervous and hitting against a left-handed pitcher. He swung at three pitches and missed each of them by at least a foot. He walked back to the dugout with his head down. He was so discouraged that he walked right by everyone on the bench and sat in the corner, all alone, with his head in his hands. Joe Gordon was up next and Gordon was having his best year and this particular left-hander was the type that Joe usually murdered. Well, Joe missed each of three pitches by at least two feet and came back to the bench and sat down next to Doby, and put his head in his hands, too. I never asked Gordon then and I wouldn't ask him today if he struck out deliberately. After that, every time that Doby went onto the field he would pick up Gordon's glove and throw it to him. It's as nice a thing as I ever saw or heard of in sports." The radio recollection was reprinted verbatim in *Sports Illustrated* a few days later and was repeated for decades, even appearing in Doby's obituary in the same magazine in 2007. The story does not jibe with the box score or newspaper accounts of the game. The origin of the story appears to have come from *Washington Post* columnist Shirley Povich in a piece on Doby in July 1949. In this version Gordon patted Doby on the back after striking out and said, "We all do that. Watch me"—implying that Gordon was going to strike out on purpose. In reality, Gordon was on third when Doby came in as a pinch hitter.

Veeck later estimated that 20,000 angry letters had come into club head-quarters protesting the Doby signing. He answered many of them himself, and would later acknowledge that he had put Doby in a difficult situation. "Not only being first in the American League but even more difficult was the fact that he himself had never really been exposed to the virulence that racism took once he had donned an Indians uniform."[22] Pitcher Lou Brissie, whose career also began in 1947 with the Philadelphia Athletics, later told his biographer Ira Berkow that he listened in the dugout as his teammates shouted things at Doby like "'Porter, carry my bags,' or 'Shoe-shine boy, shine my shoes' and well, the N-word, too. It was terrible." Brissie, who had been severely wounded in Italy and left for dead, pitched with a large metal brace on his leg and identified with Doby. "He was a kind of under-dog, like me," Brissie told Berkow.[23]

An unnamed New York Yankee, fearing potential discrimination against white players, echoed the feelings of many players in believing that Veeck had brought Doby to the majors "simply because he was a Negro, and the Cleveland club wants to cash in on the Negro trade. I am not opposed to having Negroes in the majors. But let them go through the same rugged preparation as the white players. Send the Negroes into the minors and let them work their way up." He then added a warning, "If there is discrimination against the white youngsters there will be trouble."

His heralded debut aside, Doby was having a hard time finding his swing at the plate. "Larry talked to me one night when he first went to Cleveland," Newark teammate Frazier Robinson later recalled. "He wasn't hitting the ball too well. He was having trouble with breaking pitches. We talked for two or three hours before he went on back to his hotel. He was determined to make good, and it drove him nuts that a Class AAA player named Pendelton was tearing up curve balls. He wondered why he couldn't do that. And I told him, 'You're taking blind cuts.' It looked to me like he was holding his bat too high and when he'd go to swing at it, he'd have to drop his arms, and that was causing him to take his eye off the ball. . . . I also thought it might help Larry if he moved off the plate a little."[24]

Doby's struggles continued, and he spent most of the 1947 season on the bench. Manager Lou Boudreau never explained the decision. He was used as a pinch hitter and could not adjust to the role, batting a mere .156 in 32 at-bats. One highlight for Doby was his August debut at Washington's Griffith Stadium, located in a predominantly black neighborhood. However, black fans were directed to sit together along the right-field line in a section known as the right-field Pavilion.*[25]

Doby felt welcome in D.C., a fact that would be reinforced when he later played in right field. "When people say, 'You played well in Washington,' well, I had a motivation factor there. I had cheerleaders there at Griffith Stadium. I didn't have to worry about name-calling. You got cheers from those people when you walked out onto the field. They'd let you know they appreciated you were there. Give you a little clap when you go out there, and if you hit a home run, they'd acknowledge the fact, tip their hat."[26]

As the players got out of their cabs, they were greeted by a small band of pickets carrying signs, including one that read: CLEVELAND HAS A COLORED BASEBALL PLAYER, WHAT ABOUT WASHINGTON? According to Shirley Povich of the *Washington Post*, Doby turned to Gordon and said, "Gee, Joe, I don't want to be a symbol—I just want to be a big league player."[27]

ON SEPTEMBER 11, with the Indians out of the race, Veeck returned to the ranch to take in the Governor's Cup playoff of the Class C Arizona-Texas League. A week later in Tucson, Veeck's station wagon collided with a car driven by Carl Davis. The next morning Veeck did not contest the police charges that he had failed to yield the right of way to the other car and that he was driving without an operator's license. He paid a $10 fine in police court. Three sisters were in the Davis car: Mrs. H. H. Haas, fifty-six, who had fractured her ribs and possibly her pelvis; Mrs. Ann Anderson, forty-one, who had suffered a minor fracture of the spine; and Rachel Davis, forty-six, the driver's wife, who had a possible back fracture.[28] The Davises sued Veeck for a total of $85,000, alleging he had been driving at "an excessive rate of speed" before running the stop sign.[29]

The lawsuit against Veeck for the traffic accident would be dismissed

---

* Writing in the *Baltimore Afro-American* a year earlier, Richard R. Dier alleged that Jim Crow in the nation's capital was worse than in Dixie: "Washington's baseball fans are more predominantly colored than New York's. Needless to say, Griffith Stadium pursues a jim crow policy in seating customers."

"with prejudice" on August 4, 1948, the matter having been settled out of court.[30]

DURING THE 1947 World Series between the Yankees and Dodgers, Veeck established his social headquarters in Toots Shor's restaurant, as did most of the Cleveland writers.* Shor delighted in insulting his patrons, which pleased Veeck no end.

One evening during the Series Veeck quietly led reporters into a corner one by one to get their reaction, off the record, to the idea of trading Boudreau to the St. Louis Browns. Veeck maintained that he liked Boudreau and considered him one of the two or three best players in the game—he had led the Indians to a fourth-place finish in 1947, their 80–74 record a twelve-game improvement over 1946—but he thought he could improve the team by trading him for three other players who would shore up the Indians weakest positions.

This would have left Veeck without a manager. Al Lopez was in New York for the World Series shopping around for a job as a coach or minor-league manager. The two met and Lopez was offered the job if, as Veeck put it, "things didn't pan out" with Boudreau for the coming season.

For a couple of days the Cleveland reporters mulled the trade privately. Then a one-sentence mention of Boudreau's possible shift to the Browns appeared deep in a Chicago sports column, and the Cleveland writers decided to report the story the next morning. Even though by this time the trade was dead, primarily because Bill DeWitt of the Browns had demanded that the Indians underwrite Boudreau's salary, Veeck chose not to make this fact public, thereby setting off an explosion of emotion in Cleveland.

"To say that the story broke is simply ducking the issue," reported Franklin Lewis of the *Cleveland Press*. "The story broke through every front door in Cleveland. As an observer said at the time, 'It smashed and splintered and shook the community by its civic heels until all hell popped loose.'"[31]

In the sixth inning of the fifth game of the Series, Veeck left his box seat at Ebbets Field and headed for the airport to return to Cleveland. The first fan he talked to in the mob awaiting him at the airport said, "Mr. Veeck, if

---

* The restaurant was, among other things, the subject of one of the great Yogi Berraisms: "Toots Shor's restaurant is so crowded nobody goes there anymore."

you trade Boudreau my two boys will grow up to hate you." Boudreau had been with the club since 1938 and was immensely popular with fans, who felt he could lead the team to a pennant. The Cleveland papers printed ballots on which fans could vote on the trade, and a huge majority rejected it. Letters arrived by the thousands.

To the great relief of the fans, Veeck soon conceded that public opinion had won, and Boudreau remained in place. "This was pure Veeck," Bob August of the Cleveland Press wrote later. "In his playful way, Veeck could make Machiavelli look like a scout leader." Realizing how angry he had made the fans, Veeck spent the rest of the night going from bar to bar apologizing and assuring one and all that Boudreau's job was safe. The non-trade inspired a legendary Veeckism: "The best trades are the ones you don't make."[32]

The Doby signing, however, looked like a blunder after the season ended. His record inspired bigots and skeptics. "If Doby were white," sniffed Rogers Hornsby, looking at Doby's numbers, "he wouldn't be considered good enough to play semi-pro."

After the last game of the season, Doby was sitting at his locker, wondering if that was the end of the experiment, when coach Bill McKechnie came over to him and asked whether he had ever played the outfield. No, Doby said, always infield, in high school, college, the Negro leagues, wherever he played. McKechnie then told him that Joe Gordon was their long-term second baseman. "When you go home this winter get a book and learn how to play the outfield," which Doby dutifully did.[33]

Doby rumors were rife. Bob Hunter of the Los Angeles Examiner reported that Veeck had made efforts to "unload" Doby to the Pacific Coast League but got no takers. The rap was that Doby, as well as the two black players signed by the St. Louis Browns, Hank Thompson and Willard Brown, were nothing but "sandlot performers." Veeck refused to comment.

On New Year's Eve—with his future in baseball in doubt—Doby signed a contract with the Paterson, New Jersey, Crescents of the previously all-white American Basketball League, which allowed the team owner to boast that Doby had integrated two professional sports leagues in the course of six months.[34]

SIGNING DOBY WAS Veeck's first defining moment as a major-league owner. It gave him a voice as a progressive and social critic. He could now portray the sainted Branch Rickey as a cheapskate and castigate the Yankees and the Red Sox for being lily-white and unprepared for an integrated America. The executives in New York and Boston played right into Veeck's hands. Earlier in the year Tom Yawkey, the owner of the Red Sox, had said, "Anyone who says I won't hire blacks is a liar. I have about 100 working on my farm down south."[35]

The acquisition of Doby also put Veeck front and center in the emerging civil rights movement. At the same time Veeck was determined not to be taken too seriously, especially by his friends. Bob August of the *Cleveland Plain Dealer* remembered a story told to him by Spud Goldstein, traveling secretary for the club. Goldstein's family made movies, but Goldstein was so fascinated by Veeck that he gave up Hollywood to go work for him. "On one of the many nights whose adventures sometimes stretched on to dawn, Spud and Bill and companions spent hours arguing whether Bill was a phony. After a lively debate, an agreement finally was reached that he was, but he was a 'sincere phony.' How many high-powered executives would ever have entered such a debate and agreeably accepted such a verdict?"[36]

Veeck's active nightlife had a side effect that was, in all probability, unknown to him for the rest of his life: it served to open up a file under his name at the Federal Bureau of Investigation. On April 10, 1947, a memo was sent to Alex Rosen, a top aide to J. Edgar Hoover, by the head of the Cleveland bureau reporting that Veeck was "constantly associating with known racketeers" at sporting events as well as spending considerable amounts of time at the Theatrical Grill, "a known hangout for Cleveland hoodlums." Memos in the FBI file express concern that Veeck's association with racketeers could make him susceptible to extortion. Nothing more appears to have come of it, but if Veeck had known of the FBI's interest in him, he probably would have bragged about it.[37]*

---

* The final postscript to the season was the fate of Veeck's two clowns. Banishing Price and Patkin to the minors, which had started out as a penalty, turned out well because it was the beginning of careers for both men as pre-game performers. The act that became Price's crowd pleaser was to fire a baseball 700-800 feet into the air from a bazooka which put it out of sight. He was able to field a remarkably high percentage of these balls—catching the ball over his head and then falling down to absorb some of the shock. Price kept performing until he retired in 1959 and lived until 1967 when he took his own life. Patkin, who died in 1999, kept clowning until his retirement in 1995, having given more than 4,000 performances. His crowning achievement came when he played himself in the 1988 romantic-comedy classic *Bull Durham*.

For his part, Veeck was as strongly opposed to gambling at the ballpark as his father had been. During the 1946 season he had had his ushers try to stop the practice, but that had not been effective. In early 1947 he had asked the city to stop gambling at the two ballparks and to make the failure to report a bribe offer a felony. Veeck had told Mayor Thomas Burke, "The gambling element has been disturbing the players." Within a matter of hours the mayor promised to bar gambling and bribery in sporting events in the city.[38]

CHAPTER 9

The Oldest Rookie

On November 24, 1947, Veeck and Lou Boudreau sat down to negotiate a new contract. They met behind closed doors for six and a half hours and came to terms on two contracts: one for two years as a player and one for two years as manager. The player contract was standard, but the manager pact allowed Veeck to fire Boudreau on short notice.

As part of this negotiation Veeck retained the right to hire new coaches. He kept Bill McKechnie, with twenty-five years of National League managerial experience behind him, including four pennants; he hired Muddy Ruel, fresh from a year as the Browns manager; and he converted Mel Harder, the team's ace pitcher for much of the thirties, into a pitching coach at the same salary he had received as a pitcher. He also hired Cleveland immortal Tris Speaker—manager and star of the city's only pennant winner, the 1920 World Champions—as a part-time coach. Veeck had a special role for Speaker that would begin in spring training: to help make Larry Doby a major-league ballplayer.

Veeck even tried to hire Casey Stengel away from the Oakland Oaks. "I wanted Casey because he knows baseball players," he told Ed McAuley of the *Cleveland News*. "He can tell you quickly whether you're wasting your time and money on a rookie." Stengel declined the offer, but not before determining that had he accepted, he would have been made a vice president of the team.[1]

Veeck's first public statement in 1948 came on January 4, after a meeting of his five-man "brain trust," a group that included himself, Boudreau, and three graybeards (Grabiner, Ruel, and McKechnie). After the meeting,

Veeck said that the Indians were ready to trade anybody at any time if it could help the ballclub. He was interested primarily in another starting pitcher and would take any outfield help he could get. A few days later Veeck said that, thanks to "trade engineering and a few other acquisitions," the 1948 team was going to be so tough that "they will surprise even its best friends."[2]

Before the month was out Shirley Povich of the *Washington Post* took a look at Veeck's additions, namely, Wally Judnich from the Browns and Allie Clark from the Yankees, and felt that he could safely declare the Indians to be the "dark horse" of the American League—with a fair share of breaks and one more solid player, they were poised to take it all. "While the Indians don't have much cash to work with compared to the rich clubs, in Veeck they have a smart operator."[3]

Veeck's pitching staff looked solid, though nobody could have predicted the success it would achieve. On January 21 Veeck signed Feller to a new contract, retaining the team's anchor on the mound. Based on his performance in 1947, Bob Lemon appeared ready to join Feller at the top of the Indians' rotation. Lemon had made the switch from infielder to pitcher in 1946 and was nearly claimed by the Senators for his waiver price, but he was reclaimed at the last minute by a petulant Veeck because the news of the trade leaked to the press before he was ready to announce it. Lemon's bags had already been packed when Veeck called off the deal. Lemon then sparkled on the mound, winning eleven games in 1947, his first full year as a pitcher.[4]

In 1947, Gene Bearden had worked only a third of an inning for the Indians, inauspiciously allowing three earned runs. He was to be sent down to the Indians farm team in Baltimore, but instead demanded that he return to the Oakland Oaks and his mentor, Casey Stengel. There he had put together a solid 16–7 season, mastering the knuckleball under Stengel's tutelege. He spent the winter of 1947–48 in the Mexican League and earned a spot in the Indians 1948 rotation in spring training.

Among his hitters, Veeck faced a dilemma on the first day of spring training: Larry Doby did not look ready either on the field or at bat. He knew that if Doby did not make the cut, he could not send him down to either of his top two farm teams in Baltimore or Oklahoma City, and to send him lower in the Indians system would be tantamount to giving up on him. Tentative plans were thus made for him to be sent to a team in the Pacific Coast League if he didn't make the Indians. Doby's lackluster 1947 performance had led to speculation that Veeck had put him on the team merely for public relations purposes—that it was just another stunt.*

Eight outfielders reported to Tucson on March 1, and Doby was assigned to the B squad. Tris Speaker made Doby his special project and worked with him over several weeks. Speaker, who was one of the greatest defensive center fielders in the game's history, helped to convert Doby from a subpar infielder to a superlative center fielder. Speaker had admitted to being a member of the Ku Klux Klan as a young man in Hubbard, a town in central Texas where Jim Crow ruled and where, according to Speaker's biographer Tim Gay, "the Klan operated at a fever pitch. Local KKK leaders were heroes. Lynching was not uncommon." However, Speaker appeared to have overcome his past as he got older.[5]

A significant event occurred during an exhibition game against the St. Louis Browns in Los Angeles in late March. In the fourth inning Doby hurtled into second base, colliding with shortstop Sam Dente. Doby got up safe, but Dente's leg spurted blood. One of the arguments against allowing Negroes into the game had been the fear that if a black man spiked a white player, a riot would break out. As Chris Parry noted in the *Philadelphia Tribune*, a Negro paper, "It was a sort of accident which any two players might have been involved, and to their everlasting credit, that's how everyone in the park regarded it."[6]

With Speaker's and McKechnie's coaching, Doby came out of Arizona batting .354 and playing strong defense. An article in *The Sporting News* claimed that "the No. 1 story" of the spring was the emergence of Larry Doby as a starting outfielder. Boudreau had not yet decided whether he would play the young fielder in center or right, but he was convinced that Doby was the fastest man in the American League.[7] "All through the training season I said that we had eight outfielders fighting for three starting jobs. I wasn't kidding. Doby not only proved himself one of the three best. He was the very best. It would be wrong to keep him out of the starting lineup in view of his great performance."[8]

The team then barnstormed its way back to Cleveland, playing a series of

---

* The Pacific Coast League (PCL) had just signed a Negro player, John Ritchey, who was actually not the first in minor league history. In 1916, an African American named Jimmy Claxton pitched for the Oakland Oaks in the PCL. His time with the team was brief and his departure apparently hastened when it was discovered that he was not an American Indian, as he had claimed, but black.

games with the New York Giants in various cities, including three stops in Texas. The trip was especially harsh on Doby. Since arriving in Tucson he had spent every night away from his white team members because the team hotel barred blacks. The hotels on the road were no better, and Doby was forced to board with local black families and find his own way to the ballpark.

At Lubbock, Texas, he was not allowed into the park by gate attendants until a team official vouched for him. In Texarkana, two taxicabs claimed to be busy and he had to walk several miles to the park in uniform, only to be denied entrance by a new set of gatekeepers. A barrage of bottles and other objects greeted him in center field, and he was taken out of the game for his own protection, to the gratification of those who had attacked him. In Houston, he was greeted with a hostility that was "frightening in its intensity." He was booed until he hit a ball some 500 feet, beyond the center-field fence, after which grudging applause was heard. Doby was not mollified. As he told his biographer Joseph Thomas Moore, "In fact, I resented the cheers."[9] He also told Moore that this was the loneliest time of his life.

Veeck was sensitive to Doby's plight. Claire Smith, the ESPN news executive who traveled and worked with Doby at the end of his life, recalled Doby's observation that from his early days with the Indians, Veeck had the ability to determine when things were getting him down and then "swoop in and grab him and tell him they were going out to a jazz club. Bill was a great jazz fan and he would take Larry to see the great ones—Ella Fitzgerald, Count Basie and all the others. Bill sensed when he needed him and then showed up."[10] Monte Irvin underscored their special relationship. "Larry and Bill became really good friends. They would go to nightclubs together.* Later when Bill would come to New York he would call Larry and me on the phone and say that we were going out."[11]

At the end of March, Veeck's friend Hank Greenberg, then thirty-eight years old, joined the club as an executive, following his retirement the previous year from the Pittsburgh Pirates. He became a vice president along with Harry Grabiner, thus giving Veeck one of the most powerful and visible front offices in baseball. He and Veeck had met at the 1947 World Series and dined into the wee hours at Toots Shor's. "When I first met him he was talking to me about the Indians," Greenberg remembered. "I thought he was

---

* "Doby and Dad would go and listen to music together," Mike Veeck remembered. "Doby liked Miles Davis: it was confrontational, it was in your face. My dad loved Satchmo, who loved everybody. They never did resolve that."

talking about the ball club, but no, he was talking about the American Indians who were treated so badly by the U.S. government. He was very concerned about them and what a shabby deal they had gotten. He loved them."[12]

The two spent further time together at the 1947 Winter Meetings and discussed the possibility of Greenberg buying 10 percent of the team, though Greenberg was never offered the chance to buy the stock.* Nonetheless, Veeck and Greenberg became fast friends, and for the team and its fans, the former Detroit Tigers star became an immediate talisman and a good omen. Greenberg, who was Jewish, could easily identify with what Doby was enduring, having experienced prejudice during his career.

If bringing Greenberg into the management mix would prove to be inspired, so would Veeck's gamble on Russ Christopher, a tall right-handed pitcher with a submarine delivery and a bad heart. A good strikeout pitcher and reliable starter during the war, he had become a fine reliever in 1947 for Connie Mack's Philadelphia Athletics, going 10–7 with 12 saves and a 2.90 ERA. But his health had deteriorated over the winter, and a few weeks before Opening Day he was bedridden with pneumonia, the result of a congenital heart defect that made him vulnerable to respiratory problems. Veeck knew that this would be Christopher's last year in baseball, but when they met in Orlando, Florida, Christopher told Veeck that he understood the severity of his situation and would rather die on the mound than in bed.

Ever willing to take chances on players with physical or emotional flaws, Veeck bought Christopher from Connie Mack for $25,000 on April 3, acquiring him for two reasons. On a personal level, Christopher had two young children at home, and one more year would make him eligible for a higher pension allowance and better death benefits. More important, Veeck foresaw the need for a spot reliever who could pitch a crucial inning here or there. The Christopher deal became the perfect Veeckian bargain: helping another human being while helping himself.

However much Shirley Povich considered the Indians a "dark horse," after a strong preseason the local writers predicted modest success for the 1948 team. Franklin Lewis at the *Cleveland Press* expected them to finish fourth, and Gordon Cobbledick at the *Plain Dealer* had them in third place.

---

* For reasons that are unclear, it was widely reported that Greenberg was an Indians owner when Veeck owned the club, and this error was perpetuated as late as 2011 in Greenberg's Wikipedia biography, among other places. Greenberg did become a 20 percent owner in the club in 1956 under a new ownership group.

Lou Boudreau, after a bit of arm twisting by a reporter, said he thought the Indians would finish in second place behind the Yankees.[13]

The season opened on a good note with eleven wins in the first sixteen games, including a three-game sweep of the Boston Red Sox in Fenway Park. Veeck worked the home crowds during the early days of the season as he had in Milwaukee, this time with Greenberg on his self-appointed rounds, introducing him to fan after fan.[14]

Other good omens emerged in the season's early weeks. Joe Gordon was proving to be exactly what Veeck had hoped for. Veeck relished Gordon's anger—especially when it was directed at the Yankees. In his first appearance at Yankee Stadium in an Indians uniform he walked twice, singled twice, and hit a home run—virtually beating the Bronx Bombers on his own. "I hope Old Liver-Lips was watching that one," Veeck intoned after the game, referring to Yankees general manager Larry MacPhail. Observed Arthur Daley of the *New York Times:* "[Veeck's] eyes twinkled but there was no mistaking the venom which dripped from his words."[15]

AMID THE TEAM'S success, Veeck endured his third amputation on May 5. In the second, during the summer of 1947, his stump had been cut to a point eight inches below the knee, and this new procedure took another critical inch. His doctors at the Cleveland Clinic expected him to be in bed for six weeks, but—fully in character—Veeck used the hospital as a platform for meetings and announcements, and slipped away on occasion.[16] A few days after his surgery he announced that he had appointed Abe Saperstein to be in charge of a nationwide scouting program to find more Negro ballplayers for the Indians farm system. The plan had the backing of his two vice presidents, Grabiner and Greenberg, who had held two days of meetings with Veeck in the hospital.[17]

Wendell Smith of the *Pittsburgh Courier* spotted Veeck a week or so after his surgery on crutches at a meeting of the National Conference of Christians and Jews, and noted that when he left the luncheon, he stowed his crutches in the backseat of his car and headed to Ashtabula to deliver an address on brotherhood and diversity, using the 1948 Indians as his prime example.[18]

On May 8 rookie left-hander Gene Bearden pitched his first game, a magnificent 6–1 three-hit victory over the Washington Senators, his knuckleball dancing to devastating effect. After eight dominant innings, Bearden tired in the ninth, and Russ Christopher came in to gain the final out. Larry Doby also shone, clubbing a home run to dead center that struck the top of the thirty-five-foot wall, hit a speaker, and bounced back onto the field. It made Griffith Stadium history, besting a 1922 homer by Babe Ruth as the longest ever hit there.

After the game, Bearden revealed for the first time that he had been severely wounded in the war. He was a machinist's mate on the cruiser USS *Helena*, one of the few ships in Pearl Harbor that had survived the Japanese attack. On July 6, 1943, the ship was in the South Pacific near the Solomon Islands, part of an American task force battling the Japanese. Bearden was in the engine room when the first torpedo hit; the damage was severe, and the order was given to abandon ship. As he scrambled up the ladder leading out of the engine room, a second torpedo hit, the ladder crumpled, and he was hurled to the deck. His knee was twisted and crushed, his head was split open by flying shards of metal, and he lay unconscious in the pit of a sinking ship. "Someone pulled me out," he recalled. "They told me later that it was an officer. I don't know how he did it. The ship went down in about 17 minutes. All I know is that I came to in the water some time later."

In a semiconscious state, he spent the next two days in a rubber life raft and was finally rescued by a U.S. destroyer and shipped back to the States. He was operated on at the U.S. Naval Hospital in Jacksonville, Florida, in August and told he would never be able to play baseball again. For the better part of the next two years he was in the hospital, where a plate was inserted into his skull and a hinge placed in his damaged knee. He had kept all of this to himself until after his first game "because they might get the idea that I'm not strong enough to pitch."[19]

Bearden's second start, ten days later against the Philadelphia Athletics in the first night game of the season at Municipal Stadium, became known as the "Purple Heart Game." His opponent was Lou Brissie, another tall southpaw who had been awarded a Purple Heart for wounds suffered on December 2, 1944, when a shell exploded, hitting him with fragments that shattered his left shinbone. Army doctors wanted to amputate his leg, but Brissie refused. After two years and twenty-three operations Lou was able to return to baseball with a metal brace on what remained of his leg. Signed by the Athletics in December 1946, he won twenty-five games in the Southern League in 1947. The A's called him up and on September 28 he realized his "life's ambition" of pitching in the major leagues.

Bearden pitched the full nine innings, giving up six hits to defeat the

Athletics 6–1. Brissie faced only ten batters before being relieved by Bob Savage, who had two Purple Hearts himself and a piece of shrapnel still in his shoulder.[20]

The powerful symbolism of the game was quickly forgotten, but Bearden, Brissie, and Savage—and Veeck for that matter—were among many who prevailed over war injuries and disabilities. First baseman Eddie Robinson had been in the Navy when, in 1945, a bone tumor paralyzed his right leg. He was operated on and wore a brace until the first day of spring training in 1946. In August 1947 he fractured an ankle and spent the remainder of the summer on the disabled list. Like Bearden and Brissie, he was told that he would never play baseball again. Other veterans of the Armed Forces were on the field that night as well: Indians Bob Feller, Ken Keltner, and Larry Doby had served in the Navy, as had A's centerfielder Samuel Chapman.

The game underscored a subtle bond that existed between those who had served. Announcer Ernie Harwell, who had served four years in the Marines, recalled "a subliminal feeling that a man who had served was a little bit better than one who hadn't."[21]

Eighty thousand fans jammed into Cleveland Stadium for a double-header against the Yankees on May 25—a sellout by ten-thirty in the morning, with thousands clamoring for standing room. In the fourth inning Veeck, against his physician's orders, arrived in a wheelchair and was rolled into his favorite perch in the press box. Veeck wanted not only to see his team play but also to make sure that the rain that had been forecast for that day would not result in the first game being called off in the fifth or sixth inning, making it a legal game and sending fans home with worthless rain checks. He had a special public address microphone installed in the press box that he planned to use in case the umpires called the game, to assure fans their rain checks would be honored or their money refunded if they preferred. Veeck's spirited generosity—not tested that day, as the rain held off—would have cost him some $90,000, since he would have owed the Yankees their share of the gate. But he believed this was the best way to keep faith with his fans.

In the midst of a tight American League race, the Indians played the Yankees on Old-Timers' Day at Yankee Stadium. Unbeknownst to fans unaware of his illness, this would prove to be the penultimate public appearance of Babe Ruth. Unaccountably, he emerged from the Indians dugout to take his final curtain call, leaning on a bat he had borrowed from Bob Feller. It seemed like a good omen.[22]

With the scouting help of Abe Saperstein, Veeck put other black players into his organization. Three of Saperstein's finds were brought in at the end of June for trials, and one, Fred Thomas, was signed and sent to the Indians farm club in Wilkes-Barre, Pennsylvania. During this same week Josh Gibson Jr. was signed by the Youngstown Colts, a team with a working agreement to develop talent for the Indians.[23]

With Feller flailing at the beginning of the summer, Veeck and Boudreau were looking for pitching help. They made a couple of trades and toyed with moving some of their second-rung pitchers up the ladder; but nothing seemed to be working.

"If only I could find a guy who could strengthen our bullpen," Veeck told Saperstein one night in the press box as the Tigers were making a shambles of the Cleveland pitching staff. "We're desperate for someone who can come in and stop a rally."

"I know just the pitcher you need." said Abe. "If you sign him, you won't have any more bullpen worries."[24]

Saperstein suggested Veeck sign the forty-one-year-old Satchel Paige. Veeck looked at Abe and smiled. The idea was hardly novel. In 1947 Paige had actually wired Veeck and asked when he was going to bring him in. "I wrote him back and said it'll happen but let's just take our time," Veeck explained years later. "I knew that there was going to be a hue and an outcry from the traditionalists, the purists if you will, that I was making even more of a travesty of the game. And I didn't believe that in '46 or '47 I had any chance to win anything. And so I didn't see any sense in causing a great hullabaloo for no particular reason. I felt that in '48 when I brought him in that he could well be the difference between winning a pennant and losing one."[25]

The next day Saperstein was back in Chicago working on his winter basketball schedule for the Harlem Globe Trotters. "I received a long-distance call from Veeck," he recalled. "He wanted to know if I could bring Satchel to Cleveland so that Lou Boudreau . . . and Hank Greenberg could take a look at him." Greenberg was in favor of it, and Feller, who had barnstormed with Paige during the previous two off-seasons, had often talked of his pitching prowess.

Paige was pitching in Seattle. Saperstein told him to get back to Chicago, and left him a plane ticket on to Cleveland with orders to report to Veeck. But Paige stayed in Chicago waiting for Saperstein to return, playing pool every day in a pool hall on the South Side. Finally the date was set for a secret tryout, but meanwhile, Veeck had a fire to put out.[26]

The team returned to Cleveland for a July 5 doubleheader against the Tigers in an atmosphere that was anything but cordial. Days before, an unidentified veteran player had publicly blamed the loss of nine of the previous fifteen home games on the behavior of the fans. "I can speak for just about the whole ball club," he said. "I travel with them and I live with them and I know what they all talk about. We just don't play the same kind of ball at home that we do on the road, simply because of the fan reaction there." He complained of constant booing and said the fans' treatment of the home team was worse in Cleveland than in any other city in the American League. The anonymous indictment also contained an indirect slap at Veeck: "A pitcher throws two or three balls in a row and the crowd hollers: 'What's the matter with him? Get him out of there.' A hitter takes a swing and misses and they holler: 'Sit down, ya bum!' But the payoff is when they start yelling to get the ball game over and start the fireworks when we're behind."[27]

Veeck was incensed at his player's attitude, and felt it was one more reason to expedite Paige's arrival. "We brought him in the dead of night because if I couldn't convince my . . . manager and coaches, I didn't want to shove him down their throats and create disharmony in a club where . . . I thought I could win something."[28]

The morning after Paige reached Cleveland, Veeck phoned Boudreau and said he had a pitcher he wanted him and Hank Greenberg to have a look at. Lou blinked in disbelief when he saw Paige. "Leroy," as Veeck always called Paige, warmed up, slowly jogged about halfway around the park, flipped two balls underhanded, and declared he was ready for his tryout.[29]

"He handed me a folded-up handkerchief," Boudreau remembered, "told me to put it on the plate wherever I liked. He wound up and threw ten pitches—and nine of them were right over the handkerchief. He told me to move the handkerchief to the other side of the plate, and he threw ten more pitches the same as before. Seven or eight of his pitches were right over the handkerchief, and those that missed, didn't miss by much."[30] Veeck described the two pitches Boudreau connected with: "One Boudreau hit sufficiently well that it might with luck have been scored as a base hit and the other was a ground ball which kind of trickled over. . . . So he dropped the bat and Hank was going to take a few swings and Hank walks up to me and he says never mind, I'm convinced. And then he says . . . 'just don't let him get outta here unsigned alive.'" "Now I can believe some of the tall stories they tell about his pitching," Boudreau exulted.

On July 7, his forty-second birthday, Paige was signed in a move that

Veeck termed "pennant insurance" but which nonetheless caused much negative reaction. General manager Billy Evans of the Detroit Tigers tore into Veeck at a meeting of American League club executives before the All-Star break, calling him "a pop-off and a publicity-sensationalist" and Paige's signing "outright exploitation and an affront to major league baseball."[31]

Paradoxically, as various reporters observed, Veeck was taking strong criticism from ball clubs that happily deposited the big visiting-team checks that he provided through his progressive operation of the Indians. "He's making them all rich with the big crowds the Indians are drawing everywhere," wrote Shirley Povich of the *Washington Post*.[32] More than this, club owners feared that Paige's immense following in the black community would bring more blacks to major-league games, thereby diluting their support of the Negro league teams that rented stadiums when the home teams were away. The demise of the Negro leagues would cost owners dearly; rental to Negro teams was worth as much as $100,000 a year to owners such as Calvin Griffith in Washington.

The loudest blast came from J. G. Taylor Spink, publisher of *The Sporting News*, who blistered Veeck for signing the "old man," terming it purely a publicity stunt. "To bring in a pitching 'rookie' of Paige's age casts a reflection on the entire scheme of operations in the major leagues. To sign a hurler of Paige's age is to demean the standards of baseball in the big circuits," Spink ranted, suggesting that American League president William Harridge void the contract. "If Paige were white," Spink went on, "he would not have drawn a second thought from Veeck."[33] To which Veeck responded "If Satch were white, of course, he would have been in the majors twenty-five years earlier."[34]

Ironically, a week after Veeck had signed Larry Doby in 1947, an editorial in *The Sporting News* had proclaimed an end to racial problems in organized baseball. "Just so long as there was a Negro ball player in the National League—Jackie Robinson, with Brooklyn—and none in the American League, there was a Negro question in the majors. Now that the Cleveland club has placed Larry Doby, a first baseman acquired from the Newark team of the Negro National League, on its roster, the race matter no longer is an official perplexity. It no longer exists insofar as Organized Baseball administration is concerned." Now the Spink tirade suggested a new theme—one that argued against the signing of blacks from the excluded generation, as they might prove they should have been playing in the majors all along. Ric Roberts of the *Pittsburgh Courier* wrote an open letter to Spink pointing out that other "old men" had signed such contracts and it was seen as proof of their superiority. Ty Cobb, for example, was signed at forty by Connie Mack, and Cy Young got a fresh start with the Indians at the age of forty-two after leaving Boston. Roberts implored Spink to "give Paige his hour of triumph; let the thronging thousands see him in the plush-lined, gold plated backdrop of the majors."[35]

Lou Boudreau would later put the issue into perspective: "A lot of people complained that Veeck was just up to his old publicity tricks, that he knew Paige was too old to be a winning major league pitcher, and that he was just bent on exploiting Satch's name for a few more dollars at the gate. Such was not the case. Bill signed Paige because we needed another pitcher, preferably one with sharp control who could be of service as a relief man and a spot starter. Satchel was signed for what he could do, not for what he could draw."[36]

Paige's first pitching assignment came on July 9 when he threw two scoreless innings in relief in a loss to the St. Louis Browns. Six days later, on July 15, he was credited with his first major-league victory when he held the Philadelphia Athletics scoreless for three and a third innings after replacing Bob Lemon in the second game of a twi-night doubleheader. The Indians rallied for four runs to win the game.

On August 3 Paige made his first major-league start in Cleveland, pitching seven innings for the win as the Indians beat the Washington Senators 5–3.* The victory moved the Indians into a four-team tie for first place.[37] Images of Veeck and Paige together appeared in newspapers and magazines across the country, and they seemed to be totally at ease with each other. Paige called Veeck "Burrhead" and Veeck called Paige "Leroy," just as he insisted on calling Doby "Lawrence."

IMMEDIATELY AFTER THE controversial signing of Paige, Veeck was embroiled in defending a highly unpopular decision made by Bob Feller. On the eve of the July 13 All-Star Game at Sportsman's Park in St. Louis, Feller, who had not shown up for the All-Star Game in Chicago the year before because of an aching back, again declined the invitation, this time because he had pitched three innings the day before. Veeck promptly accepted the blame,

---

* Veeck later remarked that at least 25,000 of the 72,434 who paid for admission to the game were attracted by the announcement that Paige would start.

pointing out that Feller's first duty was to Cleveland and Cleveland's fans, since from where Veeck sat, it looked as if the Indians were going to be in the championship race all the way. A friend cautioned Veeck that he should not have taken the blame for Feller's "callousness or stupidity or whatever you choose to call it. But back off. What you've heard so far is only the beginning and there is no reason for you to be caught up in the jam."[38]

Bucky Harris, the Yankees manager and the American League's manager for the All-Star Game, denounced Feller and suggested he should be banned from all future All-Star Games. But the real anger came from Feller's fellow players. The Cincinnati Reds held a meeting and asked the commissioner to take disciplinary action against any future player who balked at All-Star participation. Dixie Walker, National League player representative, spoke for many when he said: "I can't see how any player selected for the All-Star game by either the fans or the managers can fail to look on this selection as an honor. I also feel that since the club owners have been good enough to give us this opportunity to raise money for our pension fund, the least we can do is to show our gratitude by making it the best game we possibly can. After all, it's our game and if we don't do our best for it, we don't deserve to have it." When his fellow owners chimed in with their outrage, Veeck quietly admitted his mistake in covering for Feller.[39]

Despite this, Feller remained away from St Louis, while Joe DiMaggio, Ted Williams, and Hal Newhouser, the Tigers great pitcher, all were in uniform, despite being injured.*

The August 8, 1948, doubleheader sweep of the Yankees augured well, and displayed Boudreau's flair for the dramatic. Boudreau had been badly banged up a few days earlier in a collision at second base with Gil Coan of the Senators, damaging his shoulder, knee, ankle, and thumb, and was on the bench as the doubleheader began. In the seventh inning of the first game, Cleveland trailed, 6–4. With the bases loaded and two out, the Yanks

---

* Feller, however, claimed to Bill Gilbert in 1990 that it was actually Veeck who had pulled the plug on the All-Star Game. He claimed Veeck wanted to win the pennant and did not want two of his pitchers in the game. He begged Feller to fake an injury. Feller refused and then, without his knowledge, Veeck told the press that Feller had "withdrawn from the game because of unknown reasons." Feller "blew a gasket" and sought Veeck through a series of phone calls and finally found him in a bar at two in the morning. He demanded a correction, which Veeck issued the next morning. The record supports Feller to the extent that Veeck did take responsibility, stating that he wanted to protect the team and further suggesting that a new rule be adopted that limited All-Star rosters to one pitcher from each team.

brought in their ace reliever, Joe Page. Boudreau called his own number, hobbling to the plate to pinch-hit for Thurman Tucker. On Page's second pitch he drilled a single through the box past the diving shortstop, Phil Rizzuto, to drive in two runs and tie the score. Bob Yonkers of the *Cleveland Press* described the scene as bedlam as Boudreau danced happily on first. The reporter became so choked up he could not cheer while other reporters were "a-whooping and a-clappin and pounding each other on the back." The unwritten rule that there was no cheering in the press box had been ignored, Yonkers explained, because they had just experienced "the thrill of a lifetime." The Indians won both games with the help of three home runs from Eddie Robinson.

On August 13, Paige pitched before a standing-room-only crowd at Comiskey Park. The official attendance was 50,013, but Veeck estimated another 20,000 got in without paying and more than 15,000 more were turned away. "It was an incredible sight. People were coming in around the gates, over them, under them, milling around," wrote Veeck years later. Veeck and his party never made it to their seats, which were occupied by heavyweight champion Joe Louis. According to the *Baltimore Afro-American*, demands for ushers to remove intruders were so numerous that in due course "these uniformed workers resorted to hiding to avoid being bothered."[40]

Before the largest night crowd to that point in the history of baseball, Paige threw a complete game, beating the Chicago White Sox 5–0. After the game, Veeck sent a telegram to Spink that said, "PAIGE PITCHING. NO RUNS. THREE HITS. HE DEFINITELY IS IN LINE FOR THE *SPORTING NEWS* 'ROOKIE OF THE YEAR' AWARD."

CHAPTER 10

Indians Summer

O N AUGUST 20, PAIGE'S START AGAINST the last-place Chicago White Sox attracted 78,382 to Cleveland Stadium, breaking his recent record for the largest night game crowd in major-league history. Satch pitched a 1–0 three-hitter for his second shutout, thereby running his scoreless streak to twenty-three and a third innings. After the win Joe Reichler of the Associated Press declared, "No matter what President Bill Veeck gave Satchel Paige . . . he would be a bargain at twice the price." Reichler pointed out that in his first three starts in the majors Paige had drawn a total of 201,829 paying customers.[1]

The game was also the Tribe's eighth straight win and its fourth straight shutout, tying the American League record set by New York in 1903 and 1932. Despite such dramatic wins during the late summer and the immense fan support, there were those who saw the Indians as a bubble that would soon burst. Al Simmons, the Philadelphia Athletics coach, told anyone who would listen: "Don't worry about the Indians. They'll choke up. They always do."[2] As if on cue, after the Paige game the Indians lost three straight, then won four, and after all the traditional Labor Day doubleheaders had been played, the Indians had fallen four and a half games out of first, though they were still in contention.

The season until then had been filled with melodrama and a sense that it had somehow been scripted by someone with even more imagination than Veeck. September would exceed whatever came before. Rather than the Indians folding, Simmons's Athletics faded out of contention, leaving the race to the Red Sox, Yankees, and Indians.

Off-field drama opened the month. On September 8 Harry Grabiner collapsed in his office, and his condition was deemed serious enough that he was taken to his summer home, a farm in Allegon, Michigan, to recover. It was a terrible blow to Veeck, who so wanted the man he had known and admired since childhood to see this season play to its finale.

Reversing their slide around Labor Day, the Indians started a new streak, and on Sunday the twelfth the team won its seventh game in a row from the hapless St. Louis Browns in the first game of a doubleheader. The second game ended in a 3–3 tie, called because of darkness. The next day was an open date for both clubs, so the Browns stayed in town to play a makeup game.

Journeyman and spot starter Don Black was slated to pitch for the Indians. However, he was even more in the news that day because an article entitled "Don Black's Greatest Victory" had appeared the day before in the *American Weekly*, a Sunday magazine supplement to the Hearst newspapers with a circulation in the millions. Black's reputation as a former alcoholic was well known, but the article focused on his struggle to overcome his addiction and his debt to Alcoholics Anonymous. As Gordon Cobbledick explained in his profile, "Black has voluntarily renounced his anonymity, which is one of the foundation stones of AA, in order to publicize the job that the organization can do for the thousands who are afflicted as he was." The public now knew that Veeck had convinced Black to join AA in 1946, Black's first year with the Indians, when his baseball career appeared to be skidding to a boozy end. When Black's father died in California, Veeck made sure that local AA people were on hand to support Black in a time of sadness. In early 1947, Black lost a game by walking the winning run across the plate. Veeck somehow arranged on short notice to have two of Black's AA buddies in the clubhouse when he came off the field.[3]

Black pitched two strong innings to begin the game on September 13. In the bottom half of the second he batted against Bill "Lefty" Kennedy, who had been an Indian earlier in the season before being traded. Black took a vicious swing at Kennedy's second pitch and fouled it back into the stands. He staggered slightly as he finished the swing, then walked away from the plate and turned in a small circle in back of plate umpire Bill Summers. An odd look crossed his face as he turned to Summers and asked, "My God, Bill, what happened?"

He then sagged and crumpled to a kneeling position. Summers bent over and asked, "What's wrong, Don?"

"It started on that last pitch to Pellagrini."

Eddie Pellagrini, the Browns shortstop, had taken a snapping curveball for a third strike to close out the top of the inning. According to eyewitness Franklin Lewis of the *Cleveland Press*, "The physical effort expended on that pitch, plus the full-bodied swing at the plate a few minutes later, snapped an aneurysm."

A short time later Black lapsed into a coma and was rushed to the hospital. He had suffered a cerebral hemorrhage and his condition was deemed critical—and would be for days to come. His immediate chances for survival were posted at fifty-fifty.[4]

The Indians lost that game to the Browns, which along with a 6–5 loss the next day to the Yankees put them three and a half games out of first place, prompting Harry Jones of the *Cleveland Plain Dealer* to state that the team's pennant prospects were "dimmed to a faint flicker."

The fifteenth was an off day, but on September 16 Veeck announced that he would hold Don Black Night on the twenty-second. He had convinced the American League president and Red Sox executives to switch their afternoon game to the evening. Veeck pledged that the Indians share of the gate would go to the ailing Black. No passes or complimentary tickets would be allowed, and the press corps agreed in advance to pay for their own tickets. "I wanted to do this in the game with the Red Sox," Veeck announced, "This way the fans will be donating to a worthy cause and get the finest attraction we have left."

At this time Veeck boldly reserved a World Series headquarters at a downtown hotel and began making arrangements for the extra press, causing some to wonder if he was not jinxing the team, or, in the parlance of the time, "hanging a whammy around its neck." C. M. Gibbs of the *Baltimore Sun* compared Veeck's early plans for the World Series with those of the 1938 Pirates, who, enjoying a seven-game lead on September 1, brought in carloads of lumber to build field boxes and extra seats for the World Series, only to see the lead evaporate.[5]

The Indians won the game on the sixteenth against the Washington Senators with a first-inning Larry Doby grand slam. "Well, it may only take a minor miracle now," said Veeck after the game. It put the Indians two and a half games behind the Red Sox. They won again on the seventeenth with Feller fanning eleven, and once more on the eighteenth, beating the Senators 10–1 to complete a three-game sweep. The Philadelphia Athletics came to town for a Sunday doubleheader on the nineteenth, and the Indians took both games; Doby won the first with a ninth-inning two-run homer, and Boudreau hit two home runs to complete the double victory. With 75,382 paying fans, the total for home attendance was 2,300,893, eclipsing the record held by the 1946 Yankees. Meanwhile, the Red Sox dropped both games of their doubleheader against the Tigers, and the Indians were now a half game behind the Red Sox.

Don Black Night was held in Cleveland Stadium on the twenty-second with the entire gate going to the stricken pitcher. Black's teammates made a pre-game show of solidarity by paying their way into the game and going through the turnstiles in uniform—providing a unique photo opportunity.

While the Red Sox brass had agreed to the night game, this rankled Red Sox manager Joe McCarthy, who knew they would be facing Feller and much preferred to do so in the daylight. The Red Sox had offered to put up part of their share of the night's take, but Veeck said this was something for the Cleveland fans to do on their own.

On the eve of the Don Black game an article in the *Cleveland Press* featured what it termed the "Whammy Supreme," a manufactured good-luck charm in the shape of a pennant reading "Cleveland Indians—American League Champions, World Series 1948." Ronald Mazur of the State Novelty Co. had come up with the idea and quickly manufactured 50,000 of them, which were available at local stores and on sale at the stadium in time for the big game with Boston.[6]

Feller held the Red Sox hitless through six innings, and the Indians beat Boston 5–2 in a game that had already been nicknamed "the big one." Ken Keltner's first-inning three-run homer was the margin of victory. The fans "simply went nuts . . . delirious is too mild a term to describe them." The gleeful mob was egged on by Veeck, who was in his glory. Effusively he greeted the crowd and thanked them publicly after the game was over. Fireworks were ignited as the fans were leaving the stadium, blazing the words GOOD LUCK DON. The game moved Cleveland into a tie for first place with Boston, with the Yankees just a half game back. Receipts from the great crowd of 76,772 went to Black, netting him more than $40,000.

As if Don Black Night had not already had an effect on the team and its fans, at this critical point in the race Veeck made what Warren Brown of the *Chicago Herald-American* regarded as his "master psychological stroke of the entire season." The White Sox were scheduled to be in town on September 28, and Veeck announced that it would be Good Old Joe Earley Night.

Joe Earley was a thirty-four-year old World War II veteran from Lakewood,

Ohio, and a security guard at a Chevrolet plant who had written a facetious letter to the editor of the *Cleveland Press* complaining that too many special "days" or "nights" honored ballplayers past and present. He argued that athletes got enough attention as it was, and the average fan, who spent his hard-earned money to support those athletes and their teams, deserved more respect. "Now they want a 'Bill Veeck Night,'" wrote Earley. "It's a good idea, but here's another suggestion. Let's have a 'Joe Earley Night.' I pay my rent and my landlord spends it on things that keep business stimulated. I keep the gas station attendant in business by buying gas regularly. I keep the milkman in clover by buying milk. He uses trucks and tires and as a result big industry is kept going. The paper boy delivers the paper, wears out a pair of shoes occasionally and the shoemaker wins. . . . A lot of people depend on me (and you) so let us all get together, and send in your contributions for that new car for 'Good Old Joe Earley Night.'"[7]

The idea was a gift to Veeck, who immediately went to work on what *Life* magazine termed "a night to end all nights." His Indians might have been in a tense pennant race, but the master of ceremonies on Good Old Joe Earley Night was Veeck himself, as zany in this production as he had ever been in Milwaukee. "There in the presence of a near capacity crowd, and his own ball players, Veeck let the world know that the pressure hadn't got him down," Warren Brown wrote. "He was himself. His squad would have had to be dull witted indeed, not to have taken the hint. If the boss saw no reason to show strain of the furious race, why should they?"[8]

As the fans streamed into the big ballpark on the shore of Lake Erie, they were greeted by team officials offering special favors for the female fans in attendance, because in addition to it being Joe Earley Night, Veeck had made it Princess Aloha Orchid Night. Veeck had chartered a plane, equipped with air-conditioning, to fly in 20,000 Princess Aloha orchids from the Hawaiian islands along with the florist who had provided them and a young Hawaiian woman who, dressed in a grass skirt, helped pass out the precious flowers. The florist pointed out a recent survey that showed only two in ten women ever received orchids. The first 20,000 female fans to enter Municipal Stadium that night received one.[9]

After most of the fans had taken their seats, Veeck emerged on the field and grabbed a microphone, and while the puzzled White Sox looked on from their dugout, he picked fans at random and presented them with such thoughtful gifts as fifty-pound blocks of ice, live turkeys, guinea pigs, white rabbits, and bushel baskets of apples, peaches, and tomatoes. One man was presented with three stepladders, another with a sow and her piglets.

Finally, Joe Earley, looking like a Hollywood leading man of his era, was escorted onto the diamond with his wife. The ultimate tribute to the average fan was under way. Veeck built the crowd into frenzy as he spoke of Earley's letter and the inspiration for the special night. He announced that the Indians were rewarding Earley with a brand-new house, built in "early American architecture." With a wave of Veeck's hand, a flatbed truck rolled in from the outfield carrying a dilapidated outhouse. The crowd roared. Then Earley was told that he was being presented with a car, and with that a rickety Model T Ford rolled out onto the diamond. It was a tricked-up circus car filled with young female models who piled out on command. The bumpers fell off the car when the horn was honked. More gifts followed, some of them whimsical, including livestock and a case of Wheaties, and some of them generous—a truck filled with appliances donated by Cleveland business owners, and, most delightful for Mr. Earley, a brand-new 1949 yellow Ford convertible. Veeck gave the Earleys luggage, books, clothes, and a cocker spaniel. Joe, with a wide grin on his face, also received a gold lifetime pass entitling him to entry to any American League ballpark.[10]

After the livestock had been corralled and Joe Earley and everybody else had left the field, the Indians picked up an 11–0 win on Gene Bearden's eighteenth victory. To the delight of Veeck and his faithful, the Red Sox and Yankees both lost, and the Indians pushed their lead to two games, with five games left in the season.*

Working on two days' rest, Feller picked up his nineteenth win pitching the Indians to a 5–2 victory over the White Sox the next day. The Yankees and Red Sox also posted wins. The Indians two-game lead was cut to one with a loss, but on the final Saturday, behind the pitching of Gene Bearden, Cleveland beat the Tigers to clinch at least a tie, and the Red Sox knocked out the Yankees. Cleveland was one game in front of Boston.

"There are two people I want at the World Series, more perhaps than anyone else in the world. One is 'Boots' Weber, and the other is Charlie Grimm,"

---

* The "average fan" had received his night, and the effect was one that many fans would never forget. "My father was one of the 60,405 fans at the Stadium that day," Terry Pluto wrote in *Our Tribe: A Baseball Memoir*. "He didn't receive a gift, but he understood what it was like to be Joe Earley. In 1948 Bill Veeck and the Indians made him feel special."

Veeck told Warren Brown with the pennant not yet secured. When Veeck called Weber, a resident of California since his retirement from the Cubs and baseball, he told Veeck he had already booked a ticket to come east for the World Series.[11]

On Sunday, the last day of the season, Feller was named to pitch against the Tigers. A victory and the Indians were in. It was Veeck Day at the stadium, and the owner accepted congratulations before the game from a committee including Mayor Thomas Burke and the city's newest celebrity, Joe Earley. The Indians share of the gate, $55,000, was to go to the Community Fund, the predecessor of the United Way.[12] Feller, who needed one more victory to join the 20-game ranks once more, was as ready as his tired arm would permit. Before another more-than-capacity crowd, Veeck spoke in the pre-game ceremony, concluding: "I hope everyone will leave the stadium as happy as they are now." But it was not to be. Hal Newhouser of the Tigers bested Feller, who was knocked out of the box in the third inning. The Indians were never in the ball game, losing 7–1 as the scoreboard in center field showed the Red Sox had beaten the Yankees again. As one paper put it, "The gay victory polka slowed down to a dirge."

The American League race thus ended in a flat-footed tie, with Cleveland and Boston posting identical 96–58 records. The pennant would be decided by a one-game playoff the next day, the first time in the league's history overtime had been needed. A flip of the coin determined that it would take place at Boston's Fenway Park.

As the glum Cleveland crowd filed out of the huge stadium, the Indians held an emergency private meeting in their clubhouse to decide who would pitch the next day. Boudreau wanted to share his pitching plans with the team and give them a chance to voice their opinion. "This game we're going to play tomorrow means as much to you men as individuals as it does to me," he said. Then he told them he had decided upon Bearden. "He's the best pitcher we have right now," he said, "better than Feller and better than Bob Lemon and better than Steve Gromek." Finally he told his club that, despite the fact that lefties typically fared poorly in Fenway Park, he didn't think the Red Sox would be able to pull Bearden's knuckleball against the famed left-field wall.[13]

Some discussion ensued, and the records of the various pitchers in Fenway were compared. Then Joe Gordon spoke up. "Lou," he said, "we went along with your choice for 154 ball games and finished in a tie. There's not a man in this room who two weeks ago wouldn't have settled for a tie. I'm sure we can go along with you for another ball game." The decision was kept secret even from Veeck and Greenberg.

On the eve of the playoff Veeck found out that the announcers for the World Series on the Mutual Broadcasting network did not include a Cleveland broadcaster. He threatened to put the broadcast booth far out in right field in retaliation. Jimmy Britt of Boston, who had been picked for the broadcast and was beloved by Red Sox fans, declared, "There won't be any World Series in Cleveland this year."[14]

The overnight train to Boston the team took was delayed by many stops along the way and did not arrive until shortly before game time. The writers and photographers aboard had concluded that the Indians would send Feller or Bob Lemon to the mound, and the secret held until game time. Boudreau warmed up Lemon, Feller, and Bearden (who was working on one day's rest), maintaining the suspense until the end. The likes of Ted Williams, Dom DiMaggio, and Johnny Pesky awaited the rookie knuckleballer.

Even before the game started it was an affair of odd angles and ironies. Columnist Bob Considine wrote that the Boston Braves, who had won their first National League pennant since 1914, were rooting for the Indians, since Cleveland Stadium was much larger than Fenway Park and each Braves player would thereby net an extra thousand dollars or so from the much larger gate receipts in Cleveland.* The number of reporters on hand was believed to be the largest ever for a non–World Series contest, but they had to crawl under police officers mounted on horses to get into the stadium following a rumor that regular season passes would be honored at the press gate, which brought hundreds to jam the narrow entrance.[15]

A crowd of 33,957 shivering fans jammed Fenway Park, and most of them, in the words of John Drebinger of the *New York Times*, "watched the game in glum silence" as Bearden threw a complete-game masterpiece, giving him his 20-win season.[16] Boudreau went four for four with two home runs, Ken Keltner hit a three-run blast, and the Indians won 8–3. As the Indians carried Bearden off the field, Veeck jumped out of his special box and, as one reporter put it, "actually raced" across the field to catch up with the parade. After the game Bearden spotted Veeck, held up a bottle of soda pop, and toasted the boss, pouring its contents on his head.

Veeck, much to his delight, was mocked. "Poor Bill Veeck," wrote Bob Considine. "The Cleveland owner has been trying to fire Boudreau for lo,

---

* At this time the minimum salary for Major League Baseball was $5,500.

these many years."[17] The feeling in Boston was that Veeck had somehow gained an unfair edge over the Red Sox. The *Boston Herald*'s Bill Cunningham suggested that Veeck's ability to get the time of the Don Black benefit game moved into the evening was a "piece of inspired skullduggery." Months later Cunningham wrote: "Black, fortunately, recovered. The Red Sox never did." He asked himself if Veeck's staging of Don Black Night was not altogether charitable but "partly hornswoggling." Cunningham also noted that when the Indians took off to play the Red Sox, they shipped all their spare bats and other paraphernalia directly to Braves Field, not to Fenway, "adding insult to injury."[18]

One ingredient of the game, unknown to all and not revealed until 1967, when Boudreau told the story, was that Bearden had been sipping brandy between innings. The brandy was contained in a hidden compartment in the little black bag carried by trainer Harold Weisman, who kept walking up and down in the dugout during the game. Boudreau kept telling him to sit down. When he did, he sat next to Bearden and surreptitiously slipped him a few sips.

HAVING DEFEATED THE Red Sox, the Indians stayed in Boston to open the 1948 World Series at Braves Field. In a brilliant pitchers' duel, one of Boston's two aces, Johnny Sain, beat Feller 1–0, despite the Braves managing only two hits and being aided by a blown call on a pickoff play. "Sixteen years before," noted Frank Graham, "when Walter Johnson, with whom Feller had frequently been compared, lost his first World Series start after years of waiting—as Feller now has done—millions of fans mourned. But no one seemed to care that Feller had lost. Apparently they thought it served him right."[19]

In the second game in Boston, Bob Lemon beat Warren Spahn 4–1. The contest made television history, as a live broadcast was shown on a passenger train traveling between Washington, D.C., and New York. Bearden returned to the mound in Cleveland to shut out Vern Bickford 2–0 in the third low-scoring game. The next day Larry Doby became the first black man to hit a home run in the World Series, a solo drive off Sain that proved the winning run in the Cleveland victory. "Larry Doby is best remembered for his home run in the fourth game of the 1948 World Series," said Negro league star Buck O'Neil fifty years later. "His home run won the game for the Indians, 2–1. Indians president Bill Veeck told me years later that the Indians received nearly 20,000 pieces of mail in 1947 expressing opposition to Larry's signing. Simply because he was black. But Veeck said that none of the 81,000 fans who were on their feet cheering Larry's World Series home run in 1948 seemed to care about the color of his skin!"[20] The game set a new World Series single-game attendance record, and the Indians were one game away from the championship.

Afterward the clubhouse picture of winning pitcher Steve Gromek hugging Doby went around the world on television screens and in hundreds of newspapers. Doby told his biographer many years later: "The picture was more rewarding and happy for me than actually hitting that home run. It was such a scuffle for me until that picture. The picture finally showed a moment of a man showing his feelings for me. I think enlightenment can come from such a picture."[21]

The night before the fifth game, in the press headquarters at the Hollenden House Hotel, somebody asked Veeck who was going to pitch for his club.

"Feller," Bill said.

The reporter shook his head. "He can't win."

"Why not?" Bill asked.

"It just wouldn't be right, somehow. Things like that All-Star game have to catch up with him."[22]

The crowd of 86,288 for the fifth game eclipsed the previous game's record and was the largest that had ever seen a major-league ball game. The Braves had seemed dispirited over their three straight losses, their pitching strength had been depleted, and manager Billy Southworth had no one to call on as a starter but the veteran Nelson Potter, who figured to be easy prey for the Indians.

Feller seemed to have every chance to win because, despite a rocky first inning in which he gave up three runs, the Indians rallied to knock out Potter, who was relieved by Warren Spahn, and were leading 5–4 going into the sixth inning. But then Bill Salkeld, a .242 hitter during the season, hit a home run to tie, and the Braves scored six runs in the seventh to knock Feller out. As he walked off the mound, the hooting and jeering were deafening. In the press box, Moe Berg said: "They don't feel sorry for him, but I do. He waited all this time to get into a World Series and when he finally made it, he couldn't win." Satchel Paige came in to relieve Feller, becoming the first black pitcher to take the mound in World Series history.[23] Boston won 11–5 to narrow the Indians lead to 3–2. Spahn got the win.

At the end of Sunday's game, a reporter from *Time* magazine found Boudreau in the Cleveland dressing room and asked who would pitch the next day. "It'll be Bob Lemon tomorrow," said Boudreau. When the reporter asked, "How about Tuesday?" Boudreau snapped: "There'll be no game Tuesday."[24]

The sixth game was tight all the way. Twice the Indians took the lead, but the Braves kept coming back. In the last of the eighth, trailing 4–1, Boston rallied again and put the tying run on base. Boudreau was in a difficult spot. Lemon was obviously tiring and had to be relieved, but Feller had worked the day before, and if he put in Bearden and lost, the Braves would have the edge, with Johnny Sain primed for the seventh game. Boudreau took the chance and called on Bearden, who stopped the Braves cold, saving the 4–3 championship victory for Lemon.

That night Veeck held an impromptu victory party, during which someone noticed that Doby and Paige were missing. Practically the entire team went searching for them at their hotel and brought the two men back to the party. Jackie Reemes of the *Amsterdam News* reported this story in his column as evidence that the team had become a model for racial harmony. He added that this was done in Boston, where "numerous signs of Jim Crowism pop up on the horizon and speak well for the guys who comprise the Indian roster."[25]

The party on the train home was memorable. Before the train left South Station, Veeck walked into the dining car and all the players and their wives gave him a standing ovation. As the champagne corks popped, Boudreau proposed a toast to Don Black. Veeck poured milk, water, and champagne on everyone. Bottles of sparkling burgundy were shaken, opened, and aimed like guns. The entire dining car was a shambles, and a worried conductor demanded payment for the damage. Traveling secretary Spud Goldstein told him to send a bill, which came to $3,000.

When the players arrived at the terminal, they were greeted by a howling mob. Fortunately, most of them had topcoats to throw over their burgundy-stained clothes, which Veeck had promised to replace with new tailor-made suits. The victory parade down Euclid Avenue delighted a crowd estimated at more than 300,000 people, who cheered wildly as a caravan of convertibles went by. Oceans of confetti flew out of downtown office buildings, and the police had to struggle to create a path for the cars. Veeck, Boudreau, and Boudreau's wife, Della, occupied the lead car, which was hubcap-deep in confetti by the end of the parade. Inside the rest of the convertibles were the world champion Indians, who, in the words of Hal Lebovitz, "had just taken part in the wildest, wackiest, most dramatic—and melodramatic—season in the history of the American League and, possibly, in the history of all baseball."[26]

Before bidding them goodbye, Veeck told his players they could keep their uniforms and jackets as mementos of the season—a far cry from the pre-Veeck days, when balls hit into the stands were considered property of the club and collected from the fans.

VEECK WATCHED AS the crowd dispersed and his players went their separate ways. "Everybody seemed to have somewhere to go except me. If we had come home at night I would have been all right, but where, I wondered, did people go in the daytime?"

He walked home alone to an empty apartment to savor his moment of triumph and quickly realized triumph has no flavor unless it can be shared. "I sat in my empty apartment, with the sunlight all around me," he recalled years later in *Veeck—as in Wreck*, "and I thought of my son who was something less than proud of me. And I thought of my wrecked marriage and my lost family. And I thought of Harry Grabiner in a deep coma, waiting for death. I'd had it all, everything I'd hoped for when I came to Cleveland. Everything and more." He then wrote perhaps the most moving sentence in *Veeck—as in Wreck:* "I had never been more lonely in my life."[27]

In the days after attaining the World Championship, Veeck continued to display his generosity to his players—or "ath-a-letes," as he called them—with pen and checkbook. Steve Gromek was a case in point. In 1947 the pitcher had hurt his knee and not pitched often, so Veeck had cut his 1948 contract by $2,500, adding that he would make it up to him if he had a good year. He pitched sparingly during spring training and worried that he would not make the twenty-five-man squad, but he ended up with a 9–3 record and won game 4 of the World Series. After the season, Veeck called Gromek at home and told him he had a bonus check for him. "So I asked him what the amount was," Gromek recounted decades later, "and it was $5,000. I told him he was a real Santa Claus. Bill Veeck was a great guy and I just loved him." Gromek was not alone. Batboy Billy Sheriden got his World Series share of $1,693 plus the customary tips from the players, but Veeck tossed in an extra $1,000, sending him home with about $3,000.[28]

Don Black received his World Series share of $6,970 from Veeck on November 8, two weeks after he left Mercy Hospital. The presentation was photographed and put out on the Associated Press wire. Black looked elegant in a jacket, natty tie, and vest. And Veeck smiled as though he knew Black was worth everything he had paid him and then some.

The Indians drew 2,620,627 to the stadium that year, a record that stood until the Los Angeles Dodgers broke it in 1962. What had happened was unprecedented. Veeck had created a "people's team" and a market for that team that not only drew from the immediate area but also attracted fans from Cincinnati, Pittsburgh, and Detroit. Shirley Povich of the *Washington Post* had been in the stadium one Sunday in July and heard the public address announcer say: "The special train for Detroit will leave a half hour after the game"—this on a day when the Tigers were playing at home three hours away.* Povich was so impressed he featured the episode in his column, and the announcement implying that fans from Detroit were chartering trains to get to the game in Cleveland stood as a metaphor for Veeck's drawing power.[29]

Sadness followed the triumph. On October 24 Harry Grabiner died two days after an operation to remove a brain tumor. Veeck had regarded him as his closest friend, his balancing wheel, and "the smartest man I ever met in baseball."[30]

Neither Don Black nor Russ Christopher would ever pitch again. Veeck signed Black for 1949, but Black was unable to make a comeback in spring training and was paid in full for the season. He died at age forty-two in 1959 while watching the Indians on television. Christopher's heart finally gave out in 1954, when he was only thirty-seven.

Gene Bearden would never come close to his magical 1948 performance. Over five more years in the American League he would win only 25 more games and never approach the sparkling 2.43 earned run average of his rookie season.

Joe Earley would fall back into relative obscurity, and more than sixty years later Cleveland fans would still be waiting for a season as satisfying as 1948. For Veeck the satisfaction came at a number of levels, beginning with the World Championship and extending through his deep pleasure in seeing Paige triumph over those who thought he was past his prime. Veeck later summarized Paige's record in 1948: "Six and one. And the one ball game he lost was an unearned run. And he also worked in relief, and

---

* But Ed McAuley of the *News* later revealed that the announcement was bogus and intended for the ears of Frank Lane, GM of the White Sox, who was in the stadium that day. Veeck planned to needle the Tigers brass at the Winter Meetings about how he was stealing their customers and would call on Lane to testify that he had heard the announcement.

saved us a couple ball games. . . . And obviously you can see that he did win the pennant for us. But then I felt I could justify any attack based on the fact that he was going to be the decisive factor and I couldn't find another pitcher of equal ability that was available to me from any other club."[31]

The team harbored a deeper secret that helped it during the season, one that became known only years later: Boudreau and the Indians were involved in an audacious sign-stealing scheme that had, at the least, Veeck's passive blessing and involved three future Hall of Famers: Boudreau, Feller, and Lemon.

To pick up pitch signs from opposing catchers, the Indians employed a telescope that Feller had used as a gunnery officer on the USS *Alabama* during the war. "I used it to pick up enemy aircraft coming in at us," Feller recalled. "It's only about three feet long, maybe a little less, about 2½ feet. I've still got it at my home."[32] The telescope was mounted on a tripod, placed in the Cleveland scoreboard, and operated alternately by Feller or Lemon, the latter recalling that he could see the dirt under the catcher's fingernails. They would call out the next pitch to groundskeepers—brothers Marshall and Harold Bossard or their father, Emil—who would then use another opening in the scoreboard to relay the signs to Cleveland hitters by a variety of changing signals.[33]

The Indians were also involved in what has been euphemistically termed "creative groundskeeping." Groundskeeper Emil Bossard carefully custom-built the diamond for every home game. Other teams did this too, but Bossard was incomparable. The pick-and-shovel artist slanted the foul lines to favor the Indians. And because Keltner, Gordon, and Boudreau were slow, Bossard made the infield soft and slow, giving them time to catch up to hard grounders. This was certainly well known to Veeck, one of whose oft-stated maxims was "A good groundskeeper can be as valuable as a .300 hitter."[34]

The Indians were hardly alone in this skullduggery in the late 1940s and 1950s. "Hey, all's fair in love and war, and when you're trying to win a pennant," said Feller, who admitted that he was "probably" the instigator of the sign-stealing ring, which began a few weeks into the season when the Indians discovered that bullpen spies in Detroit and Boston were keeping them under surveillance. Other teams had a pretty good idea what the Indians were up to; on one occasion, as an Indian home run hit off Joe Page landed in the seats, the whole Yankee bench jumped up and began pointing at the scoreboard.*

Veeck also seemed to have been the beneficiary of plain old-fashioned meteorological good luck, for which he somehow got credit. "At Municipal Stadium. you never knew what would happen next," Red Sox pitcher Mickey McDermott said later. "Mel Parnell, cruising along in the bottom of the fifth inning on a beautiful sunny day, had the Indians beat when, suddenly, a huge black cloud swept in from Lake Erie, blotted out the sun, and dumped tons of water on the field. Mel ran into the dugout cussing. 'That damn Veeck,' he said, 'now the sonovabitch is making it rain!' Game called on account of Veeck."[35]

Veeck could also help deter the effects of Mother Nature when it was called for. "Once we were leading Philadelphia 5–4 and a downpour struck," Boudreau later recounted. "The ground crew had a hard time getting the field covered, so Bill came out and ordered the players to help. Well, he was right with us, too, and later he bought each player a new pair of shoes."[36]

Veeck had done a masterful job of manipulating his players and staff during the 1948 season, making admirers out of people who had reason to be frustrated with him. "I loved Bill Veeck though I probably should have hated him," sometime catcher Ray Murray recounted. In September 1948, Murray was called up from Oklahoma City, the last of several trips up and back during the season. Murray and his wife, Jackie, got into Cleveland at about three in the morning and checked into the Hotel Cleveland, only to be awakened at eight o'clock by Veeck, who told the couple to be in his office in thirty minutes.

"When we got to Veeck's office he said, 'I appreciate the way you people have cooperated with me and I want to do something for you.' He held up a key. 'This is for a new Pontiac car,' he said. 'If you can find it, it's yours,' though he wouldn't tell me where it was, or even where to look. He was laughing, but I knew he wasn't joking."

Murray remembered from an earlier trip to Cleveland that Veeck did business with a Pontiac dealer on the West Side. The couple grabbed a cab and headed for the dealership. "We went in the showroom and there's a new Pontiac sitting over in the corner. I asked the salesman if I could try my key in the

---

* Not all players went along with the plan. Al Rosen, then a rookie, denounced it as "unsportsmanlike," and some chose not to take the purloined signs because they felt it threw their timing off.

ignition, and when I did, VAROOM! The car started. How about that! We drove it out the door. It had to be worth about $4,800 at least. When the season ended, after the World Series, we drove it home and kept that Pontiac for a long time, all because I 'cooperated' with Bill. That means I didn't cuss and raise hell every time they sent me down."

"So, sure, I loved Bill Veeck," Murray said. "Why wouldn't I?"[37]

DURING THE 1948 season, the out-of-town sportswriters had begun to see Veeck as an asset, a unique baseball celebrity always good for a quote or a quip. He attracted photographers wherever he went. There were reports of his leaving Cleveland after a game, flying into New York for a late night at the most visible watering holes such as the Copacabana, and then returning to Cleveland in time for the following day's game. It didn't matter whether this was true or not, because people wanted to believe it.*

In late November, after Thanksgiving, Veeck was in Washington, D.C., and invited to a dinner given by World Bank official Drew Dudley. The two men and their party arrived at the Carlton Hotel, where they were denied admission because of Veeck's open collar.

"Don't you ever let anyone eat here unless he's wearing a tie?" asked Veeck.

"Certainly not!" replied the maître d'.

"What about priests and ministers? Are they refused?"[38]

There was no answer, the reservation was cancelled, and the party moved to the Statler Hotel, where there was no such policy, perhaps because this was where the Indians stayed when in Washington and its management had, to Veeck's surprise, accommodated Doby in 1947, making him the hotel's first Negro guest.

Unremarkable in itself, the incident gained headline status because Veeck was the subject of the story.† It underscored Veeck's ability to get ink for the simplest act of defiance, which pleased him no end.[39]

Writers who had dismissed Veeck as a mere publicity hound were now

---

* Veeck was in fact turned away from the Copacabana in early 1947 because he would not put on a necktie provided by the club.

† It garnered mention in the *Washington Post* ("Bill Veeck, the Cleveland Chief, Remains Unbeaten and Tieless in Brush with Fussy Formality"), the *Plain Dealer* ("Bill Veeck Sticks His Neck Out—and Changes Restaurants in Washington"), and perhaps elsewhere.

warming to him. No such turnaround topped that of Bill Corum of the *New York Journal-American*, who had regarded Veeck's father as the best and most efficient baseball executive of his time but was less than impressed with the son, whom he saw as a "showboat guy without a boat." But then Corum, a veteran of World War I, heard of Veeck's war record and began to see him in action during the 1948 season. The signing of Paige caused him to confess in his column that when he had declared himself to be against Veeck, "I was wronger than I had ever been, which is as wrong as it is possible to be."[40]

While the writers warmed to Veeck, the owners and top executives in the American League were cooling to him. "I've never seen American League President William Harridge happier over a victory in the World Series than he was when the Indians won that last game with the Braves," wrote Ed McAuley in the *News*. "But it saddens me to report that several of his club owners were able to keep from jumping up and down with joy. They were glad the Indians won . . . but they thought it COULD have happened to a nicer guy. Frankly they don't like Bill Veeck." McAuley stated that the opposition to Veeck stemmed from the belief that his methods were "too flamboyant—and too expensive" for the good of the game, adding that some might be "simply jealous."[41]

Veeck had also attracted the attention of the business press, which was given to comparing him to other, less successful owners. *Nation's Business* reported that Veeck had made "a lot of money" in 1948 in spite of such whimsical gestures as spending $90,000 in cash for Sam Zoldak, a pitcher who never had won more games than he lost in most seasons. (Veeck would later admit that Zoldak was probably worth $15,000, but he pointed out that the pitcher had given him nine crucial wins.) The magazine compared Veeck to Tom Yawkey, who in the fifteen years he had owned the Red Sox had paid more than $4 million for ballplayers and gained no profit and only one pennant.[42]

In the aftermath of the 1948 season there were shake-ups in the Red Sox, Yankees, and White Sox organizations, but none so visible as the sacking of manager Bucky Harris by the Yankees. Harris had led New York to its 1947 championship, and he was immediately hired by Veeck as manager of his Pacific Coast League San Diego Padres.[43]

In his last public pronouncement of 1948, from San Diego, Veeck made a series of predictions for the coming year—that Feller would have his greatest season, that Paige was good for another two or three years in the big leagues, and that the Indians would win the 1949 pennant by at least ten games.[44]

In late January 1949 Veeck gave an interview at the *Sport* magazine awards dinner in New York, brashly discussing what he now termed his "knock-their-brains-out" technique of management—a blend of needling, rule bending, and the determined cultivation of enemies. "I make enemies every time I open my mouth and I've been making three after dinner talks a week since the World Series."

He bragged about a moveable fence that he had installed in Cleveland, the mix of sand and dirt he employed on the baselines to make other teams as slow as his own, and the creative use of the stadium's tarpaulin. "We bought an expensive tarpaulin. Really we didn't need it. We got it only so we might save a few ballgames. It takes us 22 minutes to cover the field. And if we happen to be ahead after $4^{1}/_{2}$ innings we drag the tarpaulin around to waste time. When we're behind and want a chance to catch up it takes us two minutes to get the thing down." He added: "So we won a pennant and a world championship. That's why we're here."[45]

CHAPTER 11

Flagpole Sitting

BILL VEECK SPENT A LOT OF TIME going in and out of Manhattan in the late winter of 1949, operating out of a suite at the swank Savoy-Plaza Hotel. When he wasn't at the hotel, he was likely at Toots Shor's on West 51st Street. "Great place, New York, great place, the land of magic," he told Dan Daniel of the *World-Telegram* in the context of parties, dinners, and headline-generating actions, including a casual offer to buy the New York Yankees in late January that was refused with vigor and more headlines.[1] Veeck, a self-described publicity hound, was in his glory in this town of seven daily newspapers, all of which—including the Communist *Daily Worker*—considered him great copy.

The zenith of this pre-spring-training social whirl came on Saturday, February 5, 1949, when professional hostess and society columnist Elsa Maxwell, renowned for her parties for visiting royalty, tossed a celebrity-rich reception and dinner in honor of Veeck at Le Pavillon. If having an Elsa Maxwell–hosted party was the epitome of having arrived socially, having the event at Le Pavillon greatly enhanced the honor. It was simply the finest French restaurant in the United States, and Henri Soule, its proprietor, worked long and hard to ensure that the food was classic, the service impeccable, and the patrons pampered. Soule was the prototype maître d' who relegated those he did not like—or did not know—to a table near the kitchen.

The dress code at the restaurant was all but immutable, and all the men invited to the Veeck dinner wore black tie, with the exception of Veeck himself, who had turned his disdain for neckwear into a sacrament. "I once owned a tie 15 years ago," said Veeck, addressing the issue of why he was not going to wear a tie to the big event, "but I didn't like it. When I joined the Marines, they knew I didn't wear ties, but they suggested that a tie would go nicely with my uniform. I saw their point—quickly." Soule would have to look the other way.

As the guest of honor, Veeck was allowed to invite some of his star players and front-office personnel, among them player-manager Lou Boudreau, who more than any other individual was responsible for the Indians being World Champions; pitching ace Bob Feller; and Hank Greenberg, Veeck's good friend and front-office manager of the Indians. The ruggedly handsome Bronx-born Greenberg, who lived in New York City in the off-season and was married to the department store heiress Carol Gimbel, was probably the only member of the Veeck entourage who could get a prime table at the restaurant on a normal evening, and he and Carol had been instrumental in setting up this affair.

Word had been leaked—and nobody could have possibly guessed the source—that Veeck and Feller were going to come to terms on the pitcher's 1949 contract at the elegant venue. This caused a stampede of photographers, who were denied admission to the restaurant, with the only exceptions being those from *Life* magazine and the fashion magazine *Harper's Bazaar*. It was, in the words of columnist Windsor French, reporting on the event for the *Cleveland Press*, "a gilt-edged diamond-studded coming-out party for Veeck." In terms of diamonds alone, the head of Cartier's was there, as was socialite Rosita Winston. Also attending were circus impresario John Ringling North and British comedienne Beatrice Lillie, who persisted in calling the handsome Indians player-manager Lou Boudreau "Brown Eyes." As an opening for the evening, Jarmila Novotna of the Metropolitan Opera stood by Veeck's table and sang several Czech lullabies in his honor. Veeck danced with his hostess on his latest-model wooden leg. At one point, photographer George Silk of *Life* magazine called for a little action on the dance floor, and Veeck, in the best adagio tradition, hoisted the short, stout Maxwell and swung her around his head.

One of the guests was Salvador Dalí, the surrealist artist with his trademark waxed mustache. When he was introduced to Veeck, he declared: "I know nothing about baseball. Absolutely nothing."

Veeck replied: "Well, that makes us even."

Dalí may have been sincere in his ignorance, but Veeck knew much about many things, including art, and had been a voracious reader about many subjects since childhood.

Leonard Lyons, who had introduced Veeck to Dalí and listened to the original exchange between the two, said: "Dalí must have learned quickly, or else changed his tune. When I introduced him to Lou Boudreau, the artist said: 'I understand we have much in common: There is surrealism in baseball, too—men wearing strange clothes, crouching in moonlight and reaching for objects frequently unattainable.' "[2]

During the course of the evening, the Cleveland owner tried to sign Bob Feller to his 1949 contract. "If I had your talent," Veeck confided, "I'd get $125,000."[3] However, the contract discussion was interrupted by a sobering phone call reporting that Eleanor Veeck, his wife and the mother of his three children, had filed for divorce in Superior Court in Tucson earlier in the day and that the complaint had been served to and accepted by his lawyers.

The divorce itself was based on the claim of desertion, which was asserted to have begun in 1946 and continued to the present, and the petition requested custody of the three children—William L. Veeck III, twelve; Peter Raymond Veeck, seven, and Ellen DeForest Veeck, five—as well as alimony and child support. There are many indications that there was more to the story than was ever made public. According to Fred Krehbiel, his mother had been a friend of Eleanor's when they we growing up yet testified against her in the divorce hearing. Decades later, Eleanor and Bill's daughter, Ellen, chose not to discuss the divorce, saying simply, "I think they were mismatched."[4]

Veeck knew it was coming, but the timing could not have been more melodramatic. This night—when Della Boudreau and other players' wives were very much part of the festivities, hobnobbing with Manhattan's social and artistic elite—underscored the degree to which his family had been edited out of his life. Eleanor's lawyer immediately issued a terse statement: "They're both fine people, but she likes life on the range." A wire service report quoted neighbors who corroborated her fondness for ranch life and called her a "quiet home body."[5]

"Bill," said a friend at the party watching him react to the notice from his lawyers, "I see you have trouble with other contracts too."[6] After the phone call, Veeck and Feller reconvened and came to tentative terms for the 1949

season for a base pay of $72,500, which represented a cut of $10,000—
something Feller referred to as a slice in salary and not an amputation, an
interesting choice of metaphors given Veeck's troubles. But Feller would
still be the third-highest-paid player in the game after Ted Williams ($85,000)
and Joe DiMaggio ($100,000).[7]

Earl Wilson reported in his Monday gossip column that Veeck's new
nickname was "Elsa," bestowed upon him facetiously by Hank Greenberg
after the party because the two got along so famously. Later in her own syndicated column, Maxwell reported that she had received four dozen roses
from "my new friend" Bill Veeck. This tidbit was picked up by other gossip
columnists, including Walter Winchell, the reigning king of the gossips,
whose column was syndicated in more than 2,000 newspapers worldwide,
giving him a readership of 50 million a day.[8] By quadrupling the traditional
top-drawer thank-you gift of a dozen long-stemmed roses, Veeck had gotten
even more favorable publicity. Earl Wilson, Leonard Lyons, Winchell, and
Maxwell populated the Mount Olympus of nationally syndicated gossips,
and Veeck was finding a way into all of their columns with regularity. Even
when he didn't actually do anything, he was there with a ready quip, even at
the expense of his own turbulent personal life. When Earl Wilson asked him
if he was going to remarry after his divorce came through, he wouldn't say
yes, but he did say, "A man has a way of getting out of the frying pan into
matrimony."[9]

During the first half of February, Veeck also dominated the sports pages.
A few days after the party, Veeck flew unannounced to San Juan to sign
shortstop Artie Wilson, who was playing off-season ball for the Mayaguez
Indians of the Puerto Rican Winter League but during the regular season
played for the Birmingham Black Barons of the Negro leagues. He had employed his old friend, promoter Abe Saperstein, to scout for the best African
American ballplayers available. At a league meeting of owners of Negro
American League ball clubs in Chicago the previous day, Saperstein wrote
a check for $15,000 to the Black Barons to acquire Wilson's contract on be-
half of Veeck and the Indians.

Now Veeck had to sign Wilson, but he was unable to find him in Mayaguez, so he returned to San Juan, where he appealed to local radio stations
to put out an all-points bulletin for Wilson, telling him to come to Veeck's
hotel. The two men eventually connected, and Wilson signed a minor-league
contract with the Indians. Upon hearing of the signing, New York Yankees

general manager George Weiss claimed that he had been close to signing Wilson and that Veeck had engaged in "unethical behavior." A verbal duel ensued, culminating in a threat by Veeck to sue over the use of the word *unethical*. "I'm not sure that's not a court word. He'd better be able to prove it." For his part, Weiss twice asked baseball commissioner Happy Chandler to void the contract.[10] Using the shortest month of the year as his canvas, Veeck again made news on the seventeenth, when he was the keynote speaker at the annual meeting of the Urban League of Chicago at the Sherman Hotel. The talk, which was entitled "American Teamwork Works," was about race. It was serious but entertaining, and it was given without script or notes. He said he had first thought about bringing a Negro to a ball club when he was lying wounded in a naval hospital at the end of World War II. He said the first Negro he had ever gotten to know well was a man named Green who was in the bed next to his for eight months. His talks with Green about minority rights brought him to the conclusion that in baseball, just as in other sports, you have to judge players on their ability and nothing else.[11]

Veeck's arrival as a celebrity was helped by a photograph taken by Richard Avedon, the highly talented portrait photographer, who had met Veeck at the party thrown by Maxwell. The photograph appeared in the July 1949 issue of *Harper's Bazaar* in a spread that also included shots of filmmaker Jean Renoir; George Orwell, who had just published *Animal Farm*; and symphony conductor Guido Cantelli, the heir apparent to the great Arturo Toscanini. The caption to Avedon's black-and-white image of Veeck described him as "a young man with a skull cap of kinky pink hair, a wooden leg from the war, and an aversion to neckties even with a dinner coat." Veeck's iconoclastic rejection of neckties had now become somehow fashionable.[12] The *Harper's* spread was entitled "Men to Remember" and was certainly prophetic.

ON MARCH 5, 1949, the World Series champion Cleveland Indians opened their spring training camp in Tucson. Minority owner and comedian-actor Bob Hope was there in uniform reporting to Lou Boudreau as a rookie and engaging with the mainstream press and newsreel cameras. Hope quipped: "Really, I came down here to get Boudreau's trophies. I'm going to melt them down and go into the copper business."

The black press, however, was interested in another story. For the second year in a row the Santa Rita Hotel in Tucson had refused to honor reservations for the Indians Negro players, despite having promised Veeck that it would change its policy in 1949. Nor had the other hotels, and the three who arrived for the first day of spring training, Larry Doby, shortstop Artie Wilson, and outfielder Orestes Miñoso, were forced to stay in a private home, as would Satchel Paige, Luke Easter, and the half dozen other African Americans who would attend spring training in the days to come. Veeck had moved his camp from Florida in part to avoid such situations, and he was still optimistic that the problem would work itself out over time, citing the case of the Biltmore Hotel in Los Angeles, which in 1948 had refused Negro players but this season had given the green light for Doby, Paige, and any others to stay there.[13]

The Bill Veeck portrayed in the leading black newspapers of the time was different from the one-dimensional showman who appeared in the mainstream press. "To my estimation Bill Veeck of the Cleveland Indians did more for the Negro than any other man last year," wrote Jesse Butler in February 1949 in the *Cleveland Call and Post*. "His liberalism and giving Negroes a chance to show their real ability as major leaguers helped spearhead the attack on racial discrimination and segregation in this country."

Veeck had, in fact, joined the National Association for the Advancement of Colored People shortly after arriving in Cleveland and was an eager supporter. He appeared in a recruiting poster with Paige and Doby that was affixed to windows across the country with the catchphrase "The NAACP gets the ball for you."

He had also integrated every level of his ballpark operation—special police, ushers, food vendors, scorecard sellers, grounds crew, and front-office personnel. In May 1949 he hired Olympic sprint champion and world record holder Harrison Dillard to work in the Indians public relations department. New York's *Amsterdam News* dubbed him "the Abe Lincoln of Baseball," which was underscored by the fact that by then he had fourteen Negro ballplayers under contract scattered throughout the Indians organization. *The Sporting News* went one better by running pictures of Veeck and Lincoln side by side with the caption "Lincoln . . . freed the Negroes. Bill Veeck . . . gives 'em baseball jobs."[14]

Veeck had strengthened the Indians on December 14, 1948, with the acquisition of pitcher Early Wynn and first baseman Mickey Vernon from the

Washington Senators, for whom he traded first baseman Eddie Robinson and two pitchers. At the beginning of the season optimism was rampant. Harry Jones of the *Cleveland Plain Dealer* was among those who picked the team to repeat. The oddsmakers made them 8–5 co-favorites with the Boston Red Sox to win the American League pennant.[15]

But the team did not play well at the start. On May 25, after dropping their eighth of ten games on a trip through the East, Veeck announced that he would stage a second Opening Day when the team returned on the twenty-seventh for a long homestand. "We're simply wiping the slate clean. We'll make a fresh start. Everything that happened before will be forgotten." The second Opening Day's ceremonies included a flag raising, bands playing, and a ceremonial first pitch by Mayor Thomas A. Burke. As Red Smith wrote in his column the next day: "The Indians responded by whipping the White Sox 4 to 0, and all was strictly egg-in-the-beer on Lake Erie's shore."[16]

At the end of May, with the team still mired in seventh place, a confectionery owner named Charley Lupica created his own Veeckian stunt, which got him worldwide publicity. On May 30 Lupica and a few friends had stopped for a drink on their way home from work. After overhearing nasty remarks about his beloved Indians from a nearby table, he exchanged words with the offenders, who were fans of the New York Yankees, urging them to move to New York. To this, the other group responded, "If you like the Indians so much, why don't you sit on a flagpole until they get to first place?"

Lupica, a man with a history of publicity stunts and special promotions, accepted the challenge, and a forty-foot pole was erected in the neighborhood the next day, with a platform on top containing a four-by-six-foot enclosed dwelling. He vowed not to come down until the team was back on top of the standings or was eliminated from the pennant race. Word spread instantaneously, newspapers across the country and all around the world covered the story, and sales at his store boomed. Atop his pole he had lights, a telephone, a portable radio, a television, and a public address system—most donated by admirers.

With the team still struggling and Veeck "upset, vexed and jittery," on June 6 he overrode his manager, benching third baseman—and 1948 hero—Ken Keltner and moving Boudreau from shortstop to third. The team gradually came around, and on June 22, 1949, Veeck celebrated his third anniversary with the Indians, deeming these the best three years of his life and predicting that the team would win its second pennant in a row. The ceremony marking the anniversary included a certificate of appreciation from the 10,000 members of the Kiwanis who had come to honor him, along with a huge baseball cake out of which five scantily clad young women popped to sing "Happy Anniversary to You."[17]

Lupica remained on his perch. A question of his violating sanitation regulations arose, almost causing the operation to be shut down, but city lawyers ruled in his favor. When Lupica announced that he was about to become a father for the fourth time, Veeck pledged to have an ambulance ready for the big day. "If Charley can live on a platform," said Mrs. Lupica, "I suppose I shouldn't complain about the ordinary business of having babies."

A strong July put the Indians in second place for a time, and on August 2 they were only two and a half games behind the Yankees. But that would be as close as they would get. With his team on the verge of being mathematically eliminated from the 1949 pennant race, Veeck decided to put on a grand finale. On September 23, before a game with the Detroit Tigers, the 1948 American League championship pennant was hauled down from the center-field flagpole, where it had waved since Opening Day. The flag was tenderly loaded onto a horse-drawn hearse, which had unexpectedly appeared on the field. Veeck, dressed in black with a top hat on his head, climbed into the driver's seat and began a funeral procession, dabbing his eyes frequently with an oversized white handkerchief. Veeck and the two-horse hearse were followed by Boudreau, his coaches, and the beat writers who had witnessed the 1948 season. As 29,646 fans looked on, the cortege moved to a spot just beyond the center-field fence, where a cardboard tombstone read "1948 Champs." As taps played, Boudreau and his coaches shoveled dirt into the shallow grave and final resting place for the flag. Rudie Schaffer read passages from The Sporting News, the "Bible of Baseball." Fittingly, the Indians were shut out in the post-funeral game, 5–0.[18]

The second half of Veeck's season-ending lament came two days later. Before the final home game of the season, Charley Lupica's flagpole home was placed on a hydraulic lift and driven five miles across the city and into Municipal Stadium, where it was positioned at home plate. After 113 days of squatting on a platform above his confectionery store, Charley clambered down from his perch with tears in his eyes and kissed his wife and four children. Although wobbly, he was able to navigate without the aid of the three nurses and the ambulance Veeck had provided. After the reunion he was presented with a souvenir 50-foot flagpole, a bed into which he climbed for the benefit of photographers, a bathtub, bicycles for his children, a gas range, puppies, and a new automobile. The Indians won the game and then went on the road to win their last six games, sweeping the Tigers and the White Sox.[19]

Despite this late spurt and the seven future Hall of Famers on its roster, the club had never been in first place and ended the season in third; perhaps just as galling to Veeck, they were second in the league in attendance to the Yankees. With 89 wins, this was the only Indians team in the period 1948–55 not to win at least 90 games. Looking back on a frustrating season, Hank Greenberg felt that while the team generally performed well, it suffered from a letdown that he saw as "primarily due to Bill Veeck himself." "It seems his imminent divorce had gotten him down. Though he had just come off winning the World Series, he lost enthusiasm for the game, and he wasn't able to instill the same spirit and determination into the entire organization as he had previously. He didn't show up at the ballpark as often or put in as many hours, and while he did a good job, he didn't have the same attitude that he had had in 1948."[20]

As the 1949 season came to an end, a dispute broke out in print between the sports editors of two African American newspapers. Wendell Smith of the *Pittsburgh Courier* penned a column entitled "What's Happening in Cleveland?" It not only asserted that the city had tried to double Veeck's rent and had not provided him enough police protection for his big crowds, but also alleged that "politicians" in the city had led a campaign against him for hiring Negro ballplayers. "Through devious ways they organized a gang of hoodlums who are operating daily at the ball park. Their precise job is to harass Larry Doby, Satchel Paige and Luke Easter." Smith declared that Cleveland did not deserve a man of Veeck's integrity, and he accused the people of Cleveland of being "a sheepish, shiftless and ungrateful lot."[21]

John Fuster of the Cleveland *Call and Post* offered a blistering response, claiming Smith's comments did not appear in the Cleveland edition of the *Courier* because local readers would know that the article's claims were false. "As one of those more than one million Clevelanders whom Mr. Smith has glibly called 'lazy and placid'—and as one of those more than 2,000,000 Clevelanders who last year paid their way into Cleveland Stadium to cheer . . . the Indians on to the 1948 world's championship, I resent Mr. Smith's uncalled for, vicious, and locally untrue statements." Fuster noted that when Larry Doby made a magnificent catch against the Chicago White Sox, he received the greatest ovation Fuster had ever heard at the stadium; that all of the Indians players, white and black, were booed at one point or another, with the single exception of Satchel Paige; and that as far as Smith's hometown was concerned, the Pittsburgh Pirates had still not signed a black player.[22]

RUMORS ABOUT THE impending sale of the Indians had begun to circulate in July 1949; a wealthy Colorado cattleman named Dan Thornton was allegedly buying the Indians. Veeck denied it, saying there was about as much chance of his taking over Thornton's cattle business as there was of Thornton buying the Indians. However, Veeck did not deny that the team was for sale at the right price. Such reports continued through the remainder of the season, including one in late August claiming that Veeck had sold the team to Hank Greenberg, who flatly denied it.[23]

In early October, following the season's last game, Bill met Mary Frances Ackerman, a twenty-eight-year-old onetime drama student who was the press agent for the Ice Capades, then performing in Cleveland. They dated almost daily for two weeks, and then Bill asked her to marry him as soon as his divorce was finalized, which it shortly was. But the new union could not be simple: Mary Frances was a devout Catholic and Bill a divorced man. Her conditions for the marriage were that Bill become a Roman Catholic and immediately begin taking instruction and that they stay apart from each other for a period of six months following his formal divorce.

Years later baseball executive Buzzie Bavasi recounted a call he received from Veeck at the time: "Bill called me at home, about 10:00 p.m. He said, 'Buzzie, I know that you are a good Catholic, and I need a favor. I have asked Mary Frances to marry me. She agreed, provided I take six weeks of instruction in the Catholic Church. I agreed to this, but there is no way I can do it. Being a good Catholic, I am sure you know the Pope. Please call the Pope on my behalf and ask him if I could be excused from doing the six-weeks bit and still become a member of the Catholic Church.' To this day, I think Bill thought it could be done."[24]

His reluctance notwithstanding, Veeck soon found himself taking instruction, albeit with a healthy skepticism. "He had the toughest mind I've ever encountered," recalled the Rev. George Halpin, the priest who ultimately brought Veeck into the Church. "He was a great student of comparative religions. He never asked an ordinary question." When Veeck questioned a footnote in a 600-page volume on Catholicism, Father Halpin spent three days probing through various books in an effort to establish its intellectual validity. Following instruction, Veeck was baptized in the fall.[25]

WITH REMARRIAGE AS an added incentive, Veeck needed money in hand to put in trust for his children as part of his settlement with Eleanor. Because of the income tax rates then in place, the only means of gaining such funds was from a sale of the Indians. He also realized that the team might be near its peak value; despite the falloff from 1948, the Indians were a solid squad.

"The only way a man can make a big chunk of money under the present tax setup is to sell something he has created," Veeck observed. "I could have borrowed the money I needed in any one of several places, but I couldn't have paid it back in less than 20 years because I couldn't make enough money out of salary and dividends—after taxes. I don't know if I will be alive 20 years from now and I don't want my children to be in hock to a creditor."[26] The effective tax rate on the $25,000-to-$50,000 income bracket was 52 percent in 1949; above that, the top rate rose to a maximum of 82.1 percent.[27]

Veeck began getting serious offers as soon as he announced his intention to sell. On Tuesday, November 15, Gordon Cobbledick reported in his *Cleveland Plain Dealer* column that a group that had unsuccessfully attempted to buy the Indians had said it would dispose of the Indians Negro personnel as quickly as it was convenient to do so. The *Call and Post* phoned Cobbledick that afternoon. He said that the statement in his article was absolutely true but that he had pledged not to reveal the names of the men who had made the statement. He admitted it might be possible that this had figured in Veeck's refusal to sell the club to this group. But by the time the article had run in the *Call and Post* on Saturday, prospective new owners had been announced and had assured the newspaper that there would be no change in policy on Negro players.[28]

On November 21, 1949, Bill Veeck sold the Cleveland Indians for $2.2 million to a group of local businessmen led by a forty-five-year-old insurance executive named Ellis W. Ryan. Veeck's delighted investors got a payout that represented close to a two-to-one return on their investment—and this was after having taken out "large profits" in the interim. Veeck left the table with nearly $500,000, which was subject to a 25 percent capital gains tax.[29]

When asked at the signing what major-league city he was planning to invade next, Veeck said: "I'm not even worrying now about getting back into the baseball business."[30] As the new officers and directors were being photographed around Ryan seated at his new desk, somebody puckishly placed one of Veeck's mementos on the desk, a sign reading "Too Many Chiefs, Not Enough Indians."[31]

After lunch with close associates, Veeck said his goodbyes to the staff on his way out of the stadium. "It's been swell," Bill said. "I hope you had as much fun as I did." The women began to cry, and Veeck had a few tears in his own eyes as he hurried out the door into the snow.

"I want to get married. I want to take a good long rest. After that—believe me, I haven't the faintest idea what comes after that," he told his friend Gordon Cobbledick, who had defended him in print over his decision to sell the club.[32]

Time magazine noted upon his departure that Veeck "had turned the crank that gave [Cleveland] its dizziest merry-go-round ride in years. . . . With an expense account of about $100,000 a year, he was the town's most avid check-snatcher and tipper, its most unflagging patron of flower shops and buyer of sparkling burgundy (which he called 'bubble ink')."[33]

But while Cleveland was sorry to see him go, his fellow American League owners were not. Before Veeck joined their ranks, they had been in a "comfortable rut. Veeck blasted them out of that groove, and for that they dislike him," wrote Cobbledick. "They never knew which way he's going to jump next and although his fantastically successful club operation has enriched them all, they wish, on the whole, that he would go back to Milwaukee so that they could resume their naps."[34]

Arthur Daley was a bit more dramatic in his *New York Times* column: "If we are to believe the history books, there once was a fellow named Alexander. He used to wander about in search of new worlds to conquer. Perhaps Bill Veeck is not a lineal descendant of Alexander the Great but he has the same restless conqueror's zeal."

Rumors abounded about his next move. Some wealthy Ohio Democrats tentatively suggested encouraging him to run for the Senate against Robert

Taft in 1950, but Veeck never seriously considered the possibility, feeling politics would be too confining and that Taft—albeit a Republican—was actually doing a good job representing the people of Ohio. (On Taft's death in 1953 Veeck was called in to discuss an interim appointment to the Senate with then Ohio governor. Frank J. Lausche. Veeck left the meeting telling reporters that he was sorry he could not take the job.)[35]

Veeck was anything but apolitical and made no bones about the fact that he was politically left of center and a bona fide supporter of socialist Norman Thomas. "Bill told me he voted for Thomas in every election—even after Thomas had passed away he wrote in his name," reported Mary Frances.[36]

Some wondered if Veeck's absence would mean less pressure to sign black players in the American League. In 1950, other than those playing for the Indians, there were no African Americans in the league. Members of the black press were still barred from certain press boxes, and none had been admitted to the Baseball Writers' Association of America. This was ostensibly because the black papers were weekly newspapers and the BWAA was restricted to those writing for daily papers, but Wendell Smith was turned down when he worked for a daily newspaper, the *Chicago Herald-American*. When Vince Johnson, a white reporter working for the *Pittsburgh Post-Gazette*, made an issue of black exclusion, he was urged to resign from membership in the BWAA by the head of the local chapter.[37] "My opinion," wrote Bob August decades later about Veeck's abrupt departure from the club's ownership, "was that the vast reservoir of great African-American players—including Willie Mays, Roy Campanella, Ernie Banks, Hank Aaron, Frank Robinson, Bob Gibson, Willie McCovey—would be tapped over the next decade or so and almost all the players would go to the National League, swinging the balance of power dramatically in that league's direction." If Veeck had remained with the Indians, August felt certain, he would have signed more than his share and the Indians could have dominated the American League for many years.[38]

VEECK PLANNED TO spend his time away from Mary Frances at his ranch in Arizona. The divorce settlement gave Bill the ranch, while Eleanor and the children moved to a place farther out in the country. Bill then called one of his closest friends in Tucson, Roy Drachman, a local real estate broker who had been among the few outsiders allowed to ride from Boston to

Cleveland on the 1948 victory train, to find someone to serve as caretaker for the ranch until he got there.

Eleanor had taken everything that was not attached by nail, screw, putty, or cement, even the lightbulbs. Drachman hired a couple, Beth and Sam Smith, who needed pasture for their cattle, striking a deal by which the Smiths became the caretakers of the vacant ranch in exchange for allowing them to keep their cattle on the property.

"One morning at 3 AM, a kinky-headed individual knocked on the door," Beth Smith recalled. "This guy looked like he just came out of the gutter. He was wearing shorts in the dead of winter."

"Who are you?" Sam asked.

"I'm Bill Veeck, I live here. Who are you?"

"I'm Sam Smith. I thought I did."[39]

The Smiths moved into one of the smaller houses on the property, while Veeck began the task of making the main house appealing for his bride-to-be. The house had eight bedrooms, and somebody always seemed to be filling them, as a stream of friends arrived: Abe Saperstein, Hank Greenberg and his wife, Phil Wrigley and his family, various baseball scouts and sportswriters, club owners and the occasional celebrity. Even Hopalong Cassidy—in the person of actor William Boyd—came for a visit.

An avid tennis player despite his artificial leg, Veeck built a tennis court on the property and brought Lloyd Budge, brother of tennis great Don Budge, to the ranch to give him lessons.* He stayed for several months and Veeck became a fiercely aggressive tennis player. Responding to the question of his playing tennis and paddleball on an artificial leg, he responded, "Does a man stop smiling because he wears false teeth?"[40]

Veeck's large screened-in front porch came to house some expensive lovebirds, which he named after friends such as Gordon Cobbledick and his wife, Doris, or the Greenbergs. One day Veeck decided that the birds should not be segregated in pairs, so he let them loose on the porch. The birds immediately attacked each other. Beth Smith later recalled that she and Veeck had their hands full catching and re-caging the battling birds. "Then we became aware that someone was watching us." Seven priests

---

* The leg was both a source of amusement and frustration for Veeck. One day when he was convinced that the leg was making too much noise, he pulled a can of sardines from his Marine fatigues, opened the tin, and slathered the fishy oil on the squeaky joint. The artificial leg then smelled so bad that the Smiths made him keep it outside for a week.

had arrived for lunch, having met Veeck during his attendance at mass in Tucson. "They got a kick out of it, watching Bill, who was saying, 'Catch old Hank, catch old Doris.' . . . Bill asked the priests to help us catch the birds and they did."[41]

During his six-month period away from Mary Frances, Veeck was un-characteristically out of the news, though he gave an interview at the end of November in which he predicted his return to the major leagues within six months—perhaps as the owner of the Washington Senators. Clark Griffith, the eighty-year-old owner of the Senators, shot back that his club was not for sale to Veeck or anyone else.[42]

In March 1950, Larry Doby came to Tucson for spring training with his wife, Helyn, and infant daughter, Christina. Not only did they continue to have to room with a black family, but also, according to Doby biographer Joseph Thomas Moore, the situation at the Santa Rita had, if anything, become worse. When Doby's wife took her child into the hotel's lobby to get a drink of water, Moore reports, they were "intercepted there by a vigilant member of the hotel staff . . . [and] instructed to leave the hotel."[43]

Six months to the day after his divorce was finalized, on April 29, 1950, Bill met Mary Frances in Santa Fe, New Mexico, an event he would later call "the most important moment of my life." "The best thing that happened to Veeck was Mary Frances Ackerman," Bob Feller would observe, echoing the sentiments of many of Veeck's friends.

Arriving at the ranch soon thereafter, Mary Frances discovered the Olympic-sized pool Bill had installed as his wedding gift to her. "I told Bill that I like swimming," Mary Frances recalled, "but that didn't mean I wanted to train for the Olympics. That was the first time I learned if I liked something, I would have it the next day—maybe seventeen of it."*

On one notable occasion during their year in Tucson the Veecks returned to Cleveland so that Bill could take on the lead role in the play *The Man Who Came to Dinner*, a three-act comedy by George S. Kaufman and Moss Hart that had debuted in 1939. "Putting me on the stage was like putting Sarah Bernhardt on second base," he remarked at the time. "The theater people would think she was out of place and the baseball people would know it."[44]

From the outset Mary Frances was in charge of her husband's personal

---

* In a 1991 feature on Veeck in the *Arizona Daily Star* on the eve of his induction into the Baseball Hall of Fame it was estimated that the cost of the pool in 1991 dollars was $161,700.

life, including his personal shopping—everything from toothbrushes to the fifty white sport shirts and the half dozen identical blue sports coats and slacks that Bill needed every year. So completely did she manage all of it that on their tenth anniversary Veeck could report, "I haven't bought anything in ten years. Not even a razor blade."[45]

ON MARCH 5, 1951, Mary Frances gave birth to their first child, Michael.

CHAPTER 12

Striking Out with the St. Louis Browns

A T THE END OF MAY 1951 SATCHEL PAIGE, then forty-four and unaffiliated with a major-league team after the Indians new owners did not re-sign him, was in Milwaukee playing at Borchert Field with the Chicago American Giants. In a clubhouse interview he claimed that Veeck had seen him pitch in Chicago the Sunday before and told him that he wasn't "half-through," and that he thought Veeck was just waiting for him to get back into shape before bringing him back to the majors. Paige had actually considered hanging up his spikes over the winter, and this was only his second game of the year.[1]

Not coincidentally, it was Bill Veeck Day in Milwaukee, which was also one of the compelling reasons that had gotten Paige to don his spikes.

The Negro American League presented Veeck with a trophy for aiding "Negro youngsters of sandlot baseball," and Paige threw four solid, scoreless innings. "Every time they crowded the plate I brushed them back and then used my nuthin' ball"—an overpowering fastball with no spin on it.[2]

Veeck was poised to get back in the game. Early in May, Roy Drachman had flown to St. Louis with real estate developer Del Webb to a veterans' hospital Webb's company was constructing. While there, they attended a ball game with Fred Saigh, the owner of the St. Louis Cardinals, who mentioned that the American League St. Louis Browns were having financial problems and that he expected Bill DeWitt and Charley DeWitt, the brothers who owned a controlling interest in the Browns, would probably sell the team in the near future. Drachman reported this to Veeck when he returned to Tucson a few days later. Soon after, Veeck asked if he could use one of his friend's vacant offices and a telephone for a couple of days. "He was there every day for a week, phoning, arguing, selling and doing all kinds of planning. I never bothered him, but I did ask him how it was going, and he said pretty well." At the end of it, Veeck bade Drachman to pack a bag and come with him to San Diego for a breakfast meeting with Mark Seinberg, who held a note for $700,000 from the DeWitt brothers. A deal for the Browns was on the table.

"We got to the Del Coronado Hotel about 2 a.m. and grabbed a few hours sleep," Drachman later recalled. Seinberg asked them to meet him in his box at the Del Mar racetrack that afternoon. "As everyone knows, Bill Veeck was famous for never wearing a tie; in fact, he doesn't even own one. However, the Del Mar absolutely would not allow us to enter the club area without a necktie. They were adamant, and Bill Veeck . . . had to put on a necktie to . . . make it possible to close the deal to buy the St. Louis Browns."[3]

Well before anything could be announced, Jimmy Cannon of the *New York Post* reported that the Browns had been sold to a syndicate headed by Veeck, a story immediately denied by Bill DeWitt.[4] On June 9 DeWitt called an afternoon news conference at which he alluded to the rumors and then introduced a distinguished gentleman from Ohio who had made a great name for himself in baseball, about whom much had been written and from whom he wanted the press to get information firsthand rather than through the rumor mill. Out stepped the Browns best pitcher, Ned Garver, to announce that he was to pitch the next game for the Browns. DeWitt thought more should be written about this so more people would come to the game. Under the headline "Funny Browns at DeWitt's End" the *Globe-Democrat* declared it a joke that had fallen flat.[5]

Finally, on June 21, the announcement was made that Veeck and his investors had obtained an option on the DeWitts' share of the hapless, last-place Browns, pending his ability to gain enough shares in the operation to give him 75 percent ownership. The DeWitts owned 58 percent of the stock, and Veeck was given twelve days to buy at least 17 percent more to give him clear control. Veeck immediately offered $7 a share for the outstanding 114,000 shares in the hands of 1,400 individual investors.

A week later Veeck was 30,000 shares short of his goal and it seemed like the deal might come unraveled, as some were advising Browns stockholders to hold out for $10–$11 a share, and two New York stockbrokers were

acquiring stock at $8.25 a share in an attempt to get the price up.[6] On the
eve of the deadline Veeck was still short 8,500 shares and the deal seemed
all but dead, but at noon on July 3 a Browns board member sold him 8,572
shares and Veeck was over the top. On the Fourth of July, wearing his Browns
cap, Veeck watched his new team lose both games of a seven-hour ordeal in
a doubleheader to the Cleveland Indians, during which he smoked his way
through two packs of cigarettes.[7]

Veeck's financial backers were a familiar group: Lester Armour and Phil
Swift, the Chicago meatpackers; Phil Clarke of City National Bank of Chicago; investment bankers Art Allyn and Newt Frye of Chicago; and attorney
Syd Schiff, all of whom had aided him before with the Indians and some of
whom had backed his purchase of the Milwaukee Brewers. Among the
minority stockholders were entertainer George Jessel and Abe Saperstein,
who would become an "unofficial scout" for the team. Rudie Schaffer would
be Veeck's general manager.[8]

Since the highlight of a 1944 wartime pennant and subsequent loss in
the World Series to the crosstown Cardinals, accomplished with eighteen
players who were labeled as 4-F by their draft boards, the Browns had become an exercise in futility. They performed miserably, finishing in or
close to the cellar the previous five years, and the fans stayed away in droves.
The first twenty-four home games of the 1951 season they drew a total of
only 88,170, an average of 3,674 a game. (Playing in the same ballpark, the
Cardinals brought in 248,083 fans for their first twenty-one games, or 11,813
a game.) Before the sale to Veeck, rumors indicated that the American
League would move the team to Baltimore, which had been crying for a
major-league team since the original Orioles left the city after the 1902 season to become the New York Highlanders (and then the Yankees). Some
suggested the Browns should head for the West Coast, and another proposed shifting the team to Milwaukee.

Veeck's purchase of the doddering Browns was something of a stunner.
"Many critics," sportswriter John Lardner wrote, "were surprised to know
that the Browns could be bought, because they didn't know the Browns were
owned." Veeck himself had said the team was so terrible that "they were
hard to look at," and columnist Arthur Daley of the *New York Times* predicted
failure: "The Brownies have no tradition and no hope." Jim Murray of the
Los Angeles Times called the Browns the most feckless club in the history of
the game. "Every season was one long steady retreat . . . out of the race by
Mother's Day.[9]

Their attendance matched their ineptitude. During the entire decade of the 1930s the Browns drew some 1 million fans, in contrast to some other teams such as the 1935 Detroit Tigers, who were able to draw that many in a single season. The 1940s had not been much better. Ned Garver, the Browns best pitcher, who had come to the team in 1948, remembered, "The crowd didn't boo you, because we had them outnumbered." He also recalled a game in which a foul ball was hit high in the stands; no one bothered to chase it.[10]

Veeck told anyone who would listen that the 1951 Browns might not win, but they would be a lot of fun to watch, and he boasted that he would rather own the Browns than the New York Yankees because "I'd like to show what can be done here, supposedly an American League graveyard."[11]

At Sportsman's Park Veeck was an immediate fan favorite. During a twinight doubleheader soon after he took charge, Veeck surprised the fans with an announcement that drinks were on the house that day. The vendors went into action, and Veeck himself passed out two buckets of cold beer in the bleachers, where he personally promised the fans a winning team and something unexpected every minute. Some 6,041 soft drinks and 7,596 bottles of beer were given away; between games a local band played, and after the game the fans watched fireworks. The fans had never seen anything like this before, and Harry Mitauer of the *Globe-Democrat* wrote the next day: "Happy with it all was Veeck. He was as enthusiastic as a kid with a new toy."[12] The next night he reprised an Indians promotion and gave away free orchids to female fans, then announced that he had upped the ante and signed holdout Frank Saucier, who had batted .343 in the Texas League the previous season.

Veeck's Browns were, however, dropping deeper into the cellar. After a doubleheader loss to the lowly Philadelphia Athletics on July 12 put them seven and a half games into last place, the box score in the *St. Louis Post-Dispatch* was slugged "Double Wreck of Veecks." Veeck persuaded Satchel Paige to leave the Chicago American Giants of the Negro American League and return to the majors. But even he couldn't rekindle the magic from 1948, losing his first game 7–1 to the Washington Senators.

Despite the team's poor standing, Veeck's involvement suggested good things to come. "Bill was like a magnet. As soon as he showed up, players came streaming in to get a tryout. We didn't get any gems, but it did make it more exciting," recalled future executive Hank Peters, who was assistant farm director when Veeck arrived.[13]

Veeck now had a new group of reporters and columnists to deal with and charm. Not only did he have the local papers, but St. Louis was the home of *The Sporting News*. That he would never let anyone else pick up a bar tab was probably the first thing writers learned about Veeck; soon they would also discover how generous he was. "When I was working for *The Sporting News* and Veeck owned the St. Louis Browns, he sent all of the reporters a beautiful portable radio in a green leather case. I still have that radio," recalled baseball historian Cliff Kachline. "It really meant a lot to me when I got it."[14] Finally, reporters would have experienced how incredibly well-informed Veeck was, not only on baseball but also so much else. He consumed four or five books a week; his prime reading time was the several hours he spent soaking his stump each morning to reduce the constant pain, which was exacerbated by the chafing from his prosthesis.

Veeck's goal, suspected by others when he bought the Browns and later confirmed in his autobiography, was to drive the Cardinals out of town. Veeck reasoned that the city could fully support only one team. On July 21, 1951, Veeck touched off the first round in this campaign, challenging the Cardinals to a postseason charity game in support of the Community Chest: "Since it now appears that neither St. Louis team is going to be engaged in the World Series this fall," he wrote Cardinals owner Fred Saigh, "it would seem that there is an opportunity for us to take part in this most important drive." At this point the Cardinals were in third place in the National League while the Browns were mired in sixth.[15]

Saigh's reply was no, but he challenged Veeck to give the charity $10,000, a gift he would match. A quiet traditionalist, Saigh accused Veeck of creating the event to embarrass the Cardinals. If the game came off, Saigh noted, the Browns would take the credit, but if the game was not played, the Cards would be blamed. The day the written challenge to Saigh was published in the St. Louis papers, they also contained a full-page ad with the message "In 25 years the Cardinals have never asked you, the fan, to take a substitute for quality"—an obvious dig at Veeck's sideshows.[16]

It was now Veeck's turn in what the *Post-Dispatch* described as "the Battle of Sportsman's Park." He sent in his check for $10,000, still demanding that the two teams play, which would mean that the charity would have $20,000 in the bank plus the gate from the game. Saigh still refused to play the exhibition game, but Veeck later turned over the proceeds of the final Browns game of the season to the Community Chest.[17]

Mary Frances quickly established herself in St. Louis as a fan favorite and den mother to ballplayers. She was as public as Eleanor had been private. This became evident as the Veecks were settling into their new ten-room apartment in the ballpark. Mary Frances had remodeled the old Browns offices into what she said was a home that was "airy and had the feeling of space. It was also handy for entertaining ball teams, as well as for fans who just got lost and strayed in." Bill and Mary Frances's firstborn, Mike, had the biggest fenced yard in America to play in, except when the Browns were at home.[18]

Mary Frances was quickly becoming an active player in her husband's baseball life—a self-described "second fiddle" who was very much part of the act. For instance, in early 1952 Veeck came up with a scheme to obtain the names of all the baby boys born in St. Louis that year and mail them a faux contract for the 1970 season. The letter that came with the contract was in the form of a poem written by Mary Frances.[19]

By early August Veeck was looking for something to wake up the team and invigorate its dwindling fan base. On August 5, he went on the radio with the then novel idea of a regular pre-game live radio call-in show, willing to give any fan an opportunity to ask him questions about the losing Browns. The host asked him to assess the teams in the American League, which he did with measured cynicism. "Boston? Well, baseball is still a team game. There've been too many guys on the Red Sox club who do a good job of figuring out their batting averages as they trot down to first base after getting hit. . . . The Browns? At least they've been consistent."[20]

On August 10 he went down into a coal mine to talk with 200 miners about his plans to improve the Browns the following year. Also on that day he announced a stunt that would rankle baseball purists. In a game against the Philadelphia Athletics two weeks hence, Veeck promised to allow the crowd to manage the team. They would be led by two onfield managers-for-a-day (selected through an essay contest), who would lead the 1,000 "grandstand managers," who would sit in a special section of the stands and use placards marked YES on one side and NO on the other to decide whether the team bunted, stole a base, changed pitchers, and the like, while manager Zack Taylor would rest in a rocking chair.

As soon as this was announced, Arthur Ehlers, general manager of the Athletics, bitterly denounced the plan as "making a joke out of the game." The stunt had been staged by barnstorming teams and low-level minor-league teams, but never in the majors. At least half a dozen other owners agreed, and *Baltimore Sun* columnist C. M. Gibbs called it an "irresponsible idea, indicating that the foresight of the eminent Veeck is limited to the length of his nose."[21]

Baseball was, for the moment, without a commissioner. Happy Chandler had resigned effective July 15 after a majority of the owners refused to give him another six-year term. Chandler had facilitated the racial integration of the game in 1947, and he became known as "the players' commissioner" for his work on their behalf. During his term, he presided over the establishment of a pension fund for players, largely created from the sale of World Series television and advertising rights through 1956 for $6 million.[22]

The majority of the owners opposed Chandler on one or both of these key issues, but the real reason he was fired may have had more to do with the deep antipathy he had for Cardinals owner Fred Saigh and Del Webb of the Yankees. He would later admit in his memoir that if he had stayed in office, he would have done his best to drive both of them out of the game. Chandler was an authoritarian commissioner who had ruled the game with a strong sense of propriety when it came to things such as conflicts of interest and gambling. On the other hand, Chandler viewed Veeck's antics with a genuine sense of amusement. At a dinner honoring Veeck in 1947 Chandler had labeled him "the type of person baseball needs and is proud of," and their relationship had been cordial during the course of his term as commissioner.[23]

Veeck himself viewed Chandler as a friend of the people and of the players, which in his opinion led to Chandler's undoing. Anticipating by almost two decades the ultimate fight over the reserve clause by which owners controlled their players, he observed: "The owners became a little nervous that he might be going to take some steps to assist the players and to break up the complete iron-clad control the management had over their employees."[24]

The morning after Chandler resigned, it was announced that he was to meet with H. I. Miranda, a manufacturer's representative for a glassmaking firm, about the formation of a players union. Several columnists saw the meeting as a "slap at the fellows who were instrumental in having Chandler ousted." Chandler's job would be to negotiate for the union with the owners. After the meeting he said he would be happy to serve the players if they wanted him.[25] Miranda ultimately got nowhere with his movement, but the concept of unionization was in the headlines for a few days, unnerving all owners save for Veeck.

ABSENT A COMMISSIONER, and with his team languishing, the stage was set for a prime bit of Veeckian anarchy—something far more provocative than drinks on the house or the empowerment of grandstand managers. Attempting to address the most common complaint against the team—that it lacked a leadoff batter who could get on base with regularity—Veeck resolved to find someone sure to get on base, albeit just once. Working with an agency, Veeck sought a perfectly proportioned midget, whose strike zone would be so small that no pitcher could find it, resulting in a walk. After interviewing several candidates he found inappropriate, Veeck signed Eddie Gaedel from Chicago by way of a Cleveland theatrical booking agent named Marty Caine. "When we saw him, there was no question that Eddie was right. He was actually a very attractive guy," Browns official Bob Fishel later recalled on his first seeing the three-foot-seven-inch, sixty-five-pound man.[26]

Two contracts were signed guaranteeing Gaedel $100 for a plate appearance—one for the league and one to be brought to the game in case an objection was made. The contract was not put in the mail to the office of League president Will Harridge until after the last collection of the day, so that it would not appear on his desk before the Monday morning after the game.

Veeck reasoned that this stunt would require a heavy level of secrecy, but it also needed publicity. That night Veeck and Bob Broeg of the *St. Louis Post-Dispatch* were out drinking, and at about midnight, Veeck looked at his watch, established the fact that the last edition of the paper had gone to bed, and then offhandedly told the reporter of his plan to play a midget the next day. "I'm glad you're telling me," Broeg replied. "We don't have many photographers working on Sunday."[27]

The stunt was set for Sunday, August 19, 1951, during a doubleheader at Sportsman's Park with the Detroit Tigers. A celebration was planned to mark the fiftieth anniversary of the American League, and Veeck also unilaterally proclaimed the day to be the fiftieth anniversary of the Browns radio sponsor, Falstaff Brewing, in order to gain publicity for the company—although the actual date of Falstaff's founding was uncertain.

More than 18,000 fans, the largest crowd in more than four years, clicked through the turnstiles on a hot, muggy Sunday. The Tigers took the opener 5–2, setting the stage for the between-games entertainment, which included a parade of 1901 vintage automobiles and a comic performance by Max Patkin. As the finale, a giant papier-mâché birthday cake was brought onto the field. The cake was tapped open by a figure dressed as Sir John Falstaff in honor of the sponsor, and out popped Gaedel, dressed in a miniature Browns baseball uniform and elf shoes with curled toes, to be presented to manager Zack Taylor as a "new Brownie." The fans, who had been given free beer to toast the two anniversaries, cheered approvingly and then settled back for the second game.[28]

The Falstaff executives seated in Veeck's box, however, were unhappy. Promised a memorable event that would gain national publicity for the brewery, unaware of what was to come, they saw nothing extraordinary in the appearance of a large cake containing a midget in a Browns uniform. The second game began with the visiting Tigers going scoreless in the top of the first. In the bottom of the inning, the Browns leadoff hitter was scheduled to be reserve rookie outfielder Frank Saucier. At that point, a public address announcement was made: "For the Browns, number one-eighth, Eddie Gaedel, batting for Saucier."

Brandishing a toy bat, Gaedel stepped up to the plate and immediately crouched so low that his strike zone was only about one and a half inches high. Before the Tigers could protest, the Browns produced a bona fide contract for Gaedel, and the baffled umpire, Ed Hurley, said, "Play ball." Tiger catcher Bob Swift decided to sit down on the ground but was overruled by Hurley, so he positioned himself on his knees. Pitcher Bob Cain, afraid of hitting Gaedel and knowing there was no way to pitch to his strike zone, admitted defeat by deciding to walk him, which was fortunate for Gaedel. "My teammate Dizzy Trout told me that if he'd been pitching, he would have plunked Gaedel right between the eyes," Cain said after the fact. Gaedel skipped to first base, was replaced by pinch runner Jim Delsing, and waved to the roaring crowd as he returned to the dugout. As soon as Gaedel had put on his street clothes, Bob Fishel ushered him to the press box, where he got to boast, "I felt like Babe Ruth out there"—except that in his South Side accent it came out as "Babe Root."

Cain and the Tigers won the game 6–2, but the outcome was overshadowed by Gaedel's unforgettable base on balls. "Pitched as bad as I ever did in my life," said Duane Pillette, the Browns pitcher that day, who had had to contend with a chimpanzee sitting in his lap as part of the between-game festivities. "None of the players knew what was going on."[29] The result was the national publicity Veeck had promised his sponsors, as a photograph of Gaedel at bat appeared in newspapers across the country the next day. Gaedel told reporters he would next like to face Bob Feller and Dizzy Trout.[30]

American League president Will Harridge, in the absence of a commissioner, immediately voided Gaedel's contract and banned "midget" players from the game. Harridge, normally a mild-mannered man, seldom swore, but one of the few exceptions was discussing that "blankety-blank" midget of Veeck's.[31] For his part, Gaedel claimed he was "burned up" because he had been banned in the best interests of baseball. "Where does Harridge get that stuff? What did I do? I didn't talk to no gamblers. There ain't nothing in the rules about my size." On the other hand, he told the Associated Press, "I am happy—I've got a clipping of a box score that shows: 'Gaedel—walked for Saucier in 1st.'"[32]

Veeck had an inkling of what the reaction would be and was not bothered by any of the criticism, justifying the event because the fans loved it and he felt they would come back to the ballpark to see what might happen next. Being contrary, he demanded a ruling on whether New York Yankees shortstop Phil Rizzuto, at five feet six inches, was a short ballplayer or a tall midget. He also protested that six-foot-five-inch Walt Dropo of the Boston Red Sox, who were to follow the Tigers into St. Louis, was "too tall." Alluding to that club's great hitter, he added, "I assume that they feel Gaedel provided unfair competition. I might humbly suggest that Ted Williams also provides unfair competition as far as St. Louis is concerned."[33]

In the weeks that followed, Gaedel's image appeared everywhere and he was paid $17,000 to appear on the Ed Sullivan and Bing Crosby television shows. He got into trouble on a Cincinnati street corner for screaming obscenities while trying to convince a cop he was a major-league ballplayer. He also worked as a Buster Brown shoe man, appeared in the Ringling Brothers Circus, and worked in promotions for Mercury automobiles.*

Responding to speculation as to where Veeck had come up with the idea, the *Toledo Blade* and *The Sporting* News ran columns pointing to James

---

* Gaedel performed an encore with Veeck in 1961 when Veeck, by then owner of the Chicago White Sox, responded to complaints about vendors blocking the view by hiring Gaedel and seven other midgets to service the Comiskey Park boxes on Opening Day.

Thurber as Veeck's inspiration. In his baseball short story entitled "You Could Look It Up," which first appeared in the April 5, 1941, issue of *The Saturday Evening Post*, manager Squawks Magrew, with two out and the bases full, instructs his diminutive batter Pearl du Monville to just hold the bat on his shoulder. "There ain't a man in the world can throw three strikes in there 'fore he throws four balls," Magrew tells him.[34]

A decade later in his own autobiography, however, Veeck dispelled the notion of Thurber's inspiration, explaining that it had instead come from overheard after-dinner conversations between his father and John McGraw at the Veeck home in Hinsdale, Illinois. "McGraw had a little hunchback he kept around the club as a sort of good luck charm. His name, if I remember, was Eddie Morrow. Morrow wasn't a midget, you understand, he was a sort of gnome. By the time McGraw got to the stub of his last cigar, he would always swear to my father that one day before he retired he was going to send his gnome up to bat."[35]

Veeck never denied that he had been informed by the Thurber story, which itself may have been inspired by Eddie Morrow. In an attempt to referee this debate, James Tootle wrote a paper for the scholarly baseball journal *NINE* entitled "Bill Veeck and James Thurber: The Literary Origins of the Midget Pinch Hitter." He points out that Thurber was an avid baseball fan working in New York for the *New Yorker* magazine during McGraw's years with the Giants. "There is a striking similarity in both the names and the irascible personalities of managers John McGraw and Squawks Magrew. In a roundabout way, the germ of the idea of using a mascot in a game could have come to both men from John McGraw."

Tootle also concluded, "The point remains that in hiring Eddie Gaedel in 1951, Veeck owed a debt to Thurber. Thurber gave the idea of a midget pinch hitter shape and substance by showing him how to get the midget in uniform and on the field and by foreseeing the way to get around the objections to his actual participation in the game. Veeck deserves credit for being both an avid reader and a risk taker. But it is clear that the blueprint for actually employing a midget in a game (and for making sure he didn't swing) was drawn in Thurber's whimsical and imaginative story published ten years before three-foot-seven-inch Eddie Gaedel stepped to the plate at Sportsman's Park in 1951."[36]

Two decades later, the incident remained fresh to Veeck. "Were it in my power to turn back the clock," he observed, "I'd never send a midget to bat. No, I'd use nine of the little fellows, including the designated hitter." Veeck speculated that his tombstone would probably read HE SENT A MIDGET UP TO BAT, but he hoped that the epitaph would instead read HE HELPED THE LITTLE MAN.

The Gaedel stunt was received variously by other teams. Ted Williams noted in his autobiography that it worked because it got people interested in the game, but Larry Doby, a great Veeck supporter, told an interviewer many years later there were very few promotions that had not worked for Veeck. "The only thing that I can think of that really worked against him was the midget."[37]

But the greatest impact of the incident came off the field. Despite the hand-wringing reaction of league officials and other team owners who at the time feared losing audience to the new medium of television, Veeck's moment of frivolity had tremendous visual impact and got everyone talking about the game, boosting the idea of baseball as appropriate for the television age.[38]

His next stunt was almost as visually compelling. Making good on Veeck's promise to fans from two weeks earlier, on August 24, 1951, manager Zack Taylor took the field in civilian clothes and bedroom slippers, smoking a curved-stem pipe. He seated himself in a rocking chair near the dugout, picked up a newspaper, and read leisurely as the game proceeded, managed by fans. Two of them had won an essay contest to be manager for a day, but after league president Will Harridge banned them from being on the field, Veeck decided these two would direct everybody who had entered the contest.

Some 1,115 fans—including the newly retired Connie Mack—were given placards marked YES and NO, which they held up to determine what the Browns should do next. The Browns won the game 3–2. The fans had even voted on the starting lineup, opting to replace Taylor's choice of catcher, Matt Batts, with Sherm Lollar.* Clark Mitze, one of the two fan-managers who had won the essay contest, later observed: "We only made one bad call

---

* Bill James in his book *The Bill James Guide to Baseball Managers* noted on page 170: "What strikes me about this is that the fans were obviously smarter than Taylor was, at least in this respect. The Browns had acquired Lollar three years earlier, for nothing, and he had played about half the time, although he was one of the better hitters on the team. After the season the Browns traded him to Chicago, where he played for Paul Richards. Richards made Lollar the regular catcher, and he was the second best catcher in the American League during the 1950s."

which was to tell Hank Arft to steal and he was out by 20 feet." Veeck gave Mitze a trophy, and the two became friendly, with Mitze occasionally dropping by to discuss team matters with Veeck.[39]

In a matter of weeks Veeck had become more fun to watch than his team; as one writer later put it, he was "as hard to ignore in St. Louis as a team of runaway Clydesdales." He was impossible to ignore elsewhere as well: as Arthur Daley archly observed in the *New York Times*, "Bill Veeck not only never lets sleeping dogs lie, he ties tin-cans on every wagging tail he can reach."[40]

AT THIS TIME, all of baseball was slavishly bent on appeasing the U.S. House Antitrust and Monopoly Subcommittee to protect the sport's unique set of privileges, including the reserve clause. Many in Congress felt that baseball, with its networks of farm clubs and its movement of teams, should be subject to the rules regulating interstate commerce. Veeck was a well-established foe of the reserve clause, but he also had little tolerance for those in power who meddled with the game. He said nothing until the chairman of the committee, Rep. Emanuel Celler of Brooklyn, mentioned on television that if not for the reserve clause, pitcher Ned Garver would be making about $90,000 a year instead of the $18,000 he was being paid for the current season by Veeck. "What was Garver's record in 1950?" Veeck shot back, alluding to Garver's 13–18 record. "I've never heard yet of anybody paying $100,000 to a pitcher who lost five more games than he won. I doubt very much if Mr. Celler knows about the intricacies of baseball. I certainly wouldn't assume to tell Mr. Celler about politics. I suggest you reciprocate. Stick to politics, and let the baseball people run baseball." Veeck's fellow owners were not amused by his flippant attitude toward Congress, which held the power to upset their monopoly.

All his promotions aside, the Browns remained a bad team on the field and would end the year with a mere fifty-two wins, forty-six games behind the pennant-winning Yankees. An astonishing twenty of those wins came on the arm of Ned Garver, the lone bright spot on the team, who enjoyed by far the best of his fourteen seasons in the majors. One small consolation occurred on September 11, when the Browns temporarily knocked the Yankees out of first place by taking both games of a doubleheader. Yankee president Dan Topping blamed the twin losses on Max Patkin's clown act at first base. Cleveland executive Hank Greenberg then threatened to trade one of his Indians players for Patkin in order to jinx the Yankees in an upcoming series. Veeck shot back to his former partner and still good friend: "There's no one on the Indians I would take for Patkin."[41]

Heading into 1952, Veeck decided to hire as many ex-Cardinals as he could afford. At the end of the 1951 season, a rumor circulated that Fred Saigh was going to hire Rogers Hornsby as the Cardinals manager. Hornsby had piloted the Seattle Rainiers to the 1951 Pacific Coast League pennant, and while in New York for the World Series, Veeck hired him to replace Zack Taylor as manager of the Browns. A Hall of Fame player, Hornsby's lifetime batting average of .358 was topped only by Ty Cobb's .367. But as a manager, Hornsby had achieved less success. He had been fired as player-manager of the Cardinals despite winning the 1926 World Series. Six years later, Veeck's father had fired him during the Chicago Cubs' pennant-winning 1932 season, and the Browns themselves had axed him during their dismal 1937 season, Hornsby's last as a player. Each time the reason was Hornsby's gambling; he would not stop betting on horses. Veeck thought Hornsby had mellowed after almost sixteen years out of the majors and gave him a three-year contract, the most generous ever accorded to a Browns manager.

At the signing, Veeck declared: "This is the dawn of a new era in Browns history." Hornsby declared it would be a new era of "no midgets, no gimmicks, but good baseball." At Hornsby's insistence, Veeck released all of the Browns 1951 coaches, including Veeck's pal and former Cleveland Indian Johnny Berardino. By the end of the month Hornsby vowed that the Browns would never finish in last place again. When asked what guarantee he had against that eventuality, he answered, "Mel."[42]

Hornsby was, as one columnist put it, "a man apart in baseball." Hardboiled and demonstrably humorless, he eschewed social gatherings, music, books, movies, alcohol, cards, tobacco, and even the company of other ballplayers. He never went to the movies, and when television came along, he avoided it as well, for fear of straining his batting eye.[43] His hiring by Veeck was a surprise given Hornsby's objection at the time to Jackie Robinson's signing. "Negro ball players and white ball players will never get along. It is socially impossible for them to do so. Not only that," he had argued, "but I don't think there are any good enough to make the majors." But Veeck believed he was no longer prejudiced.[44]

After the season Veeck and Fred Saigh, who had hardly spoken to each other other for the previous six months, called off their feud long enough to appear as Romeo and Juliet on a local radio show for the Red Cross blood bank. Picked by the studio audience, Veeck played Romeo to Saigh's Juliet. Said Veeck later, "I congratulated him. He made a dignified Juliet. It was purely platonic."[45]

At the end of November, Saigh fired the very popular former Cardinals shortstop Marty Marion after his first season as the team's manager. Veeck immediately hired him, paying Marion $35,000, which was $10,000 more than he had ever made with the Cardinals, to come out of a retirement as a player, while signing him to a $17,000-a-year contract for three years as a Browns coach.[46]

Aiming to improve on his 1951 squad, Veeck acquired his former Cleveland ace Gene Bearden and dramatically overturned his roster. He tried to attract a name from the list of prominent black players that Abe Saperstein had created for him ten years earlier. Negro league star Buck Leonard got a call from Veeck while playing baseball in Mexico. "He wanted to know would I like to play for his team. I said no thank you," Leonard later recalled. "I was forty-five years old, too old to play major league ball full time. It was all right to play in Mexico where we only had three games a week and the competition was not so rough. But not major league. He said, 'I'm gonna call you back tomorrow evening,' but I still told him no. He even wanted me to come up to L.A. for spring training. I was supposed to ask Bill Veeck for a job, and he was going to give it to me. In that way, he wouldn't be accused of recruiting me for publicity. But I told him no. My *legs* were too old. You know, your legs will always tell your true age. He said, 'You don't have to play the field. We just want you to pinch-hit.' But I didn't want that—to bat just once in a game. Now, if they'd had the DH back then," Leonard added, "I might've gone."[47]

However happy he was to have Hornsby as his manager, Veeck was quickly at odds with him on the issue of Satchel Paige. Hornsby wanted Paige traded, and when Veeck refused, he said that Paige would have to earn a spot on the team as if he were a rookie. Flexing his owner's muscles, in February 1952 Veeck delivered a Brotherhood Week speech at Vashon High School at which he said he had a "firm position" that wherever he operated a baseball team, Paige was going to pitch.[48]

If Veeck had a problem outside the lines, it was at the box office. "Veeck really went into action that winter," says Hank Peters of the winter of 1951–52. "He went anywhere and everywhere he could to sell the team." His problem was that he had so little to sell. But maybe Hornsby could help."[49]

At spring training that year, however, Hornsby insisted on an understanding that he would stand for no tactical interference from Veeck, whose fondness for stunts and promotions went against Hornsby's rough-hewn grain. Early in March two cars pulled up to the practice field and out popped seven midgets led by Billy Curtis, one of the Munchkins in *The Wizard of Oz*, who were there leading the Hollywood Midgets to challenge the Browns to an exhibition game. Hornsby had been tipped off to the publicity stunt and went along with the gag for a few minutes, but then suddenly ordered them to leave. "One of those little old midgets just stared at me," he later wrote in his petulant and aptly titled autobiography *My War with Baseball.* "So I picked him up by the seat of the pants and collar and threw him over the railing. . . . We didn't have any more midgets around after that." When the Browns traveling secretary, Bill Durney, heard about it, he said that Veeck had had nothing to do with it, and he was surprised Hornsby had not greeted them with a shotgun.[50]

All through spring training Hornsby drove his players ruthlessly, trying to instill a little of his own spark into the lackluster group. Impatient with imperfection, he bawled them out repeatedly and publicly. Joe DeMaestri would later talk of the "horror of playing for Hornsby who got on his players for everything. He tried to teach everybody his way. He'd say 'You can't hit that way,' grabbed the bat to show you how he did it like you could have .400 doing it his way, too."[51]

His rules were draconian. Once you were at the ballpark there was to be no talk about anything other than baseball. He banned beer from the clubhouse and enacted a strict ban on smoking, card playing, and any other recreation not associated with the game. Radios were banished for the season. "He was really a tough nut," said Hank Peters, who tried to work with him. "I was working with a new pitcher and he passed by and I asked him how he liked the kid and he looked at me and said, 'That's your job,' and turned away.' He just wouldn't give me the time of day and I was responsible for getting new talent ready for the team. He just didn't like other people."[52] Bill Purdy, a high school student and avid Browns fan, won a contest to become the batboy for the 1952 season and, later in the season, batting practice catcher. Purdy recalled Hornsby as a "a very difficult person" whom he quickly learned to stay clear of: "I was scared to death of him."[53]

If the future of the Browns seemed unsettled, so, suddenly, did that of the Cardinals. In April 1952, as Hornsby was imposing his will on the

Browns, Cardinals owner Fred Saigh was indicted on federal charges of evading $49,260 in income taxes between 1946 and 1949.

Veeck soon attracted attention of his own with a move that seemed to have no greater purpose than to create headlines and perhaps to assert himself over Hornsby in racial matters. With the help of Browns stockholder Abe Saperstein, Veeck signed two farm team players from the Negro American League—third baseman John Britton and pitcher James Newberry—and then loaned them to Japanese teams. Less than two weeks earlier the United States had signed its final peace treaty with Japan, giving the Japanese back their independence and formally ending the war in the Pacific. Veeck proclaimed that the move was his way of celebrating Japan's new status.[54]

Hornsby's drive paid off at the start, as the Browns won seven of their first nine games and led the American League for a few days. But by the end of May they were in seventh place and the team was angry and demoralized under Hornsby's tough hand. Veeck had never seen a team "so tense, so ready to explode," and realized he had to make a change. As the team prepared for a road trip to Washington, New York, and Boston, he alerted Marty Marion to be ready to take over the team on short notice and tipped off several writers as to what was about to happen.[55]

The matter came to a head in Washington on June 3, when second baseman Bobby Young asked permission to visit his wife, who was having a very difficult pregnancy in nearby Baltimore and had been confined to bed for several months. Hornsby denied him. Young was so mad that he positioned himself outside the clubhouse with a bat waiting for Hornsby to emerge. Fortunately, Bill Durney spotted Young and got the bat away from him with the promise that he would be able to go to Baltimore.

When Veeck confronted Hornsby, the manager insisted, "All players are alike to me. I can't have two sets of rules."

"That's just ridiculous," Veeck retorted. "If everybody lived in Baltimore and had a wife who was pregnant and in ill health, and you let some of them go and didn't let others go, then you'd have two sets of rules. You have only one player in that situation, so you let him go and you'll only have one set of rules."

"I don't see it that way," Hornsby said.

"All right, then, I'm informing you, as president of this club, that I am going to call Bill Durney as soon as I hang up and tell him to give Young permission to go home now and for the rest of the series. I'm not going to argue about it with you, I'm just telling you so you won't be able to say I did anything behind your back."

Veeck observed in his memoir, "If Rog had only been the independent character his press agents say he is, he would have quit on the spot and I would have been out of a difficult situation about as cleanly as possible." But Hornsby did not quit, and Veeck let the matter ride for several days. On June 8, however, during the first game of a doubleheader against the Yankees, Browns pitcher Tommy Byrne hit a foul ball near the third-base box seats. A fan interfered with the ball, and the umpire ruled that Byrne was out because infielder Gil McDougald was unable to make the catch. Hornsby complained, but Ned Garver, who was to pitch the second game, disputed the call from the bench and was ejected.

Veeck was listening to the game on the radio in St. Louis and heard the call along with a description of the play, which made it sound as if McDougald had not been close enough to make the catch. Veeck called Hornsby and told him to lodge an official protest. Hornsby claimed it was too late—which it probably was—but Veeck persisted, later lodging his own protest (which was disallowed).

The Browns traveled next to Boston. Veeck met the team there, called Hornsby to his room at the Kenmore Hotel, and fired him without haggling about payment for the remaining years on Hornsby's contract. Hornsby later observed that the $100,000 he netted from his Browns contract was enough to keep him comfortable for the rest of his life.

One of the first calls Veeck received after the firing was from his mother, who reminded him that he should not have thought himself smarter than his father, who had fired Hornsby twenty years earlier in a hotel a quarter of mile from the Kenmore. The Cubs had gone on to win the pennant in 1932 under Charlie Grimm, who was now in Boston managing the Braves.[56]

Veeck then met with reporters. "I blew one by hiring him in the first place. I have known him since I was a child, but I thought he had mellowed. He hasn't. He's grown worse in recent years," Veeck said, maintaining that "he didn't give a damn about his players."[57] As he left for the airport, Hornsby offered a one-line parting shot at Veeck: "When you work for a screwball, you've got to expect screwball tactics."[58]

Veeck replaced Hornsby with Marty Marion, who had been fired by the Cardinals because he did not have enough "drive." The contrast between the two managers, opined Arthur Daley of the *Times*, "borders on the violent."

Back in St. Louis, upon hearing reports that players were happy about his firing, Hornsby insisted that Browns officials "must have put the words in their mouths, I didn't have any trouble with the players." The players disagreed. Earl Rapp, who had been traded to the Senators that week, said, "If Hornsby had stayed, some of the players would have tangled with him. They were getting ready to fight." Shortstop Joe DeMaestri later recalled: "Some guys were ready to strike, just refuse to play for him. But it became a whole team mutiny."[59]

Ned Garver, coming off a 20-win season the previous year, complained that under Hornsby he pitched infrequently and irregularly: "I never knew where I was. I never agitated against him but I didn't like it. We had to stay on the bench when the others were taking batting practice. We had to be on the bench during the first game of a doubleheader even if we pitched the second."[60]

Garver also recalled the dangers involved in playing for Hornsby. "When you pitched batting practice, he wouldn't let you put screens up. Every team when they went to take batting practice and infield practice, the pitcher had a net in front of him, the first baseman had a net in front of him. But he wouldn't let us have that. I don't know why. He just didn't want it. . . . Hank Arft, our first baseman, got hit in the head with a line drive off the bat while he hit ground balls and the infielders were throwing to first. Hank went to catch a ball and about that time a batter hit a line drive. Another time in New York, Gordon Goldsberry got hit with a line drive right in the back. He started limping toward right field, and Hornsby hollered out to him, 'If you're scared, go take your uniform off.'"

Garver was bothered by Hornsby's policy of demanding that his pitchers adhere to his orders. "We'd be on the road, and Hornsby had us go out to the ballpark before the other team did. We'd be sitting on the bench, and we were supposed to watch those guys take batting practice and then decide how to pitch them! Lord have mercy! So we'd be out there sitting while the other pitchers were taking batting practice, and then he'd come up with something like, 'Mickey Vernon is a better high-ball hitter, so you have to pitch him low.' Well, Mickey Vernon was a better low-ball hitter. We'd played in the league for years. He never asked anybody." As if this were not enough, Garver said that for some inexplicable reason Hornsby would not allow his catcher to move his target for his pitchers. "Just put it in the middle of the plate" was his instruction.[61]

Perhaps pointing to a significant reason for Hornsby's firing, Harold Woods in the *St. Louis Argus*, an African American weekly, said that one of the reasons for the dismissal was Hornsby's "sharp resentment against" Satchel Paige. Woods reported that Hornsby had made derogatory remarks about Paige in the presence of other players, and this eventually leaked back to the front office.[62]

"Rogers really hated Satchel," recalled Joe DeMaestri, "and one day tried to set him down for a game and Paige said he wasn't going to do it because all he had to do was to pick up the phone and call Bill Veeck."[63]

Veeck called a team meeting at which he apologized for his mistake and the eight weeks the players had endured. In return, the players presented Veeck with a loving cup inscribed: TO BILL VEECK FOR THE GREATEST PLAY SINCE THE EMANCIPATION PROCLAMATION, JUNE 10, 1952. FROM THE PLAYERS OF THE ST. LOUIS BROWNS.

Even this became a matter for instant controversy. Red Smith termed the players' act a "sorry exhibition of niggling spite, degrading all who participated. The whole affair is redolent of the bush, and Veeck did himself a disfavor by throwing in with the bushers." Smith's disdain for the players was evident in every sentence of his column. As he described the players complaining to Veeck: "They must've come with quivering lips and streaky faces to weep in Bill Veeck's lap. Else how could he know how their little hearts were aching? So Bill dried their eyes and, in effect, told them: There, there the nassy man is gone. Let's see a great big smile, if anybody else pesters you about winning I will take care of him too." Smith's column hit a nerve, and Veeck and his players were assailed for insulting the greatest right-handed hitter the game had ever known.

Although Satchel Paige had made no public comment on Hornsby, he seemed to flourish after Hornsby's departure. Beginning with a relief appearance the night of the firing that saved a game for Garver, Paige pitched ten brilliant innings in relief a few days later in an eighteen-inning win against the Senators, and came back two days later to set down the same club, allowing one hit in two and a third innings. Veeck was so impressed with his work against the Senators that he installed a plush reclining chair with a canopy top in the bullpen for him. Then Casey Stengel picked him for the AL squad for the All-Star Game—the only Browns player to be chosen.

Despite Paige's 12 wins and sparkling 3.07 earned run average, the Browns won just 64 games in 1952, though that was a dozen more than the year before, moving them out of the cellar and into seventh place. Attendance rose by 300,000 during the 1952 season to 518,796 total, second only in team history to the 1944 American League championship season.

By the end of the 1952 season, Veeck had established himself as one of the most player-friendly owners in baseball history. "I thank God for the time with Bill though it be little more than a year," recalled Ned Garver. "He loved baseball and its fans and was always trying to improve his product. You knew he might trade you at any time, but he made you feel ten feet tall when you were with him. He helped me be the best pitcher I could be. Nobody likes a phony, and there was nothing phony about Bill Veeck."

Pitcher Duane Pillette decades later called Veeck "the nicest man I ever met. No matter how badly you did he would come over and try to make you feel good about yourself." Pillette had an extra reason to be thankful. "One evening during the '52 season Bill had us all out for a barbecue and suddenly I looked over and he took off his shoe, dove into the swimming pool and pulled out my son who was unconscious." The boy, eight, was a good swimmer but apparently had hit his head on the side of the narrow pool; Veeck had seen him go in but not come up. A shaken Pillette asked Veeck how he had been the only one to notice, and he answered, "Simple. I like kids."[64]

An even more touching story involved the young outfielder J W Porter. In late July, Veeck made a deal for Porter, who was on the road in Lincoln, Nebraska. At the time, Porter lived in Colorado Springs, and his eighteen-year-old wife did not drive, so Veeck arranged to have her driven to St. Louis by her father, whom he flew in from Oakland, California.

Father and daughter were tragically killed en route in a head-on collision. The job of telling the nineteen-year old Porter fell to Veeck, who told a reporter some years later that it was the hardest thing he had ever had to do in his life. When Porter returned to the team after the funeral, a message was waiting for him at his hotel, inviting him to move in with Bill, Mary Frances, and their young son in their ballpark apartment. Veeck became a father figure to Porter, consoling him and keeping him busy. Porter availed himself of Veeck's gargantuan record collection and the jukebox that allowed him to play Frank Sinatra with the touch of a button. The two men played on the field when the ballpark was empty. "We run with each other and pitch to each other. He'd pitch 20 minutes of batting practice with that artificial leg of his and he'd start to bleed. Then he'd shrug it off," Porter recalled.*

---

* In 1969, when Porter managed the West Palm Beach Expos of the Florida State League, his hitting instructor was Larry Doby and the two men became, as far as they could determine, the first interracial roommates in baseball history. Some nights they would lie in bed and talk about Bill Veeck. As Porter said of Doby: "That man really loved Bill Veeck."

Twice while Porter was living at the stadium, Veeck brought in a big band and a name singer—first Eddie Fisher and then Vic Damone—who entertained between innings. At the end of the game a portable dance floor was put down and dancing commenced until the early hours of the morning. Veeck told Damone what had happened to Porter, and after the festivities were over at the ballpark, Damone took him out for some early morning entertainment. Damone and the young ballplayer became friends and would still see each other occasionally more than fifty years later.[65]

DURING THE IMMEDIATE postseason, Veeck began making moves that would improve the Browns on the field. The most dramatic was the deal he made to acquire shortstop Billy Hunter from the Brooklyn Dodgers for three players and $90,000 in cash—more than the St. Louis Browns had ever paid for a player. The Hunter acquisition represented Veeck's ongoing attempts to turn the Browns into a contender in the American League. Despite his constant ribbing of the team in after-dinner speeches, he was actually trying to develop and trade for players who would make a difference.

In his time with the Browns, Veeck's relationship with the Yankees continued to deteriorate. Veeck genuinely disliked the Yankee brass and they him, but the net effect was to cast him as David fighting the Yankee Goliath. In late April 1952, Yankee public relations director Arthur "Red" Patterson charged Veeck with padding his attendance figures, and claimed that he had also padded his numbers in Cleveland. Veeck offered to open his books to Patterson and suggested that the charge stemmed from the fact that the Browns had outdrawn the Yankees the previous Sunday and that had been an affront to the Yankee ego. "I have never padded my books," declared Veeck. Remarkably—as if to fend off a counterattack from Veeck— Patterson announced that the Yankees had outgrown the practice. "We announce the exact count now. There were times in the past when we padded figures but we no longer do so."[66]

If Bill Veeck was the most constant critic of the New York Yankees brass, he was also one of the strongest supporters of those who wore pinstripes. His friendship with Casey Stengel never wavered even as Veeck's feud with his bosses heated up. In November Rep. Thomas B. Curtis of Montana publicly questioned Mickey Mantle's draft deferment, which had been granted because of his chronic bad knees. The congressman was using Mantle as an example to question why men with more serious disabilities were being declared eligible and a big star like Mantle was seen as unfit. Veeck jumped into the fray in Mantle's defense, saying that Mantle was willing to serve and that Curtis was simply using Mantle and his relationship to military service as a "cheap way of making headlines"—which, of course, now belonged to Veeck.

CHAPTER 13

Baltimore Chop

T HE DEMISE OF THE BROWNS BEGAN off the field after the 1952 season, when Veeck proposed at the league meetings that American League clubs share radio and television revenue with visiting teams. Veeck had several allies, including Fred Saigh, who were prepared to fight for this point. However, at a special American League meeting on television and radio rights on December 4, Veeck was voted down 7–1. The league decided that broadcasting deals should be negotiated separately. Veeck took a "no pay, no television" stance and proclaimed that he would withhold all rights to broadcast games from St. Louis until he got a percentage of the home team television revenue on the road.

Veeck's ongoing feud with the New York Yankees front office escalated to an all-out war during this debate. When he first suggested the revenue-sharing scheme, the Yankee owners were outraged, as were other clubs with a strong presence in the market. "God damn Socialist," Red Sox owner Tom Yawkey was heard to say about him on more than one occasion.[1]

During the first week of 1953, the wealthier clubs—the Yankees, Indians, and Red Sox—expressed their wrath by withholding from Veeck the lucrative night dates on their playing schedules. The Cleveland Indians, showing no loyalty to their former owner, led the group by not booking the Browns for a single night game in 1953 in an "unmasked piece of retaliation." Veeck took his protest to the new baseball commissioner, Ford Frick, on Saturday, January 31.[2]

Veeck argued for a uniform rule giving all clubs equity in night dates. This, he claimed, was the original American League rule passed in 1939 when the league allowed night games for the first time. "If these clubs can throw me out of their night schedule, which will cost our club approximately $30,000, then there will be no limit to what they can do with their money weapon of night baseball." Veeck envisioned a poor club being threatened with the loss of night game revenue if the team did not surrender a desired player at a certain price. "That is the point of equity I present."[3]

The protest was fruitless. As Veeck put it, "Being fond of wasting time, I appealed to Ford Frick. He took the bull by the horns and ruled that it was none of his business."[4] Frick would later allude to this as Veeck's attempt to "take over the American League."[5]

During the previous week, Fred Saigh had been sentenced to fifteen months in jail for multiple charges of income tax evasion. He had pleaded no contest, and as the sentence was handed down, he exclaimed, "Now there is no way I can stay in baseball." Told that he would begin his sentence on May 4, Saigh received an ultimatum from the commissioner's office: sell the club by February 22 or it would be taken over by a group of St. Louis businessmen who would sell it for him.

Two days before the deadline, a deal was reached to sell the team to the deep-pocketed Anheuser-Busch brewery, led by sixty-four-year-old August A. Busch Jr. Veeck knew immediately that he could not outspend a big corporation determined to dominate the market. On meeting Busch for the first time in Fred Saigh's office in Sportsman's Park, across the hall from his own, Veeck welcomed him to the baseball fraternity. "Glad to see you. But I'm afraid you're going to offer us a little difficult competition."

"You're right," said Busch, grinning.

"You know I live right next door, you must come and see me," said Veeck.

"You bet your sweet life I will," Busch promised.[6]

Later in the day, Busch toured the ballpark and was horrified by its decrepit condition, despite the cosmetic changes Veeck had made. It offended his Germanic fastidiousness, and he resolved to build a new stadium.[7]

Veeck now realized with certainty that he had lost the battle for St. Louis and would have to move his franchise, so before February was over, he announced his intention to move the Browns in advance of the regular season, taking advantage of the vague but newly liberalized relocation policy adopted by baseball. No ball club had relocated since 1903, nor had either league added a team. Veeck was poised to force a major change in the geography of baseball.

Knowing that St. Louis could not support two teams, Veeck had begun exploring options after the 1952 season. Although many suitors lined up for the franchise, only Baltimore and Milwaukee, both of which had built pub-licly funded stadiums hoping to lure a big-league team, had adequate facili-ties to host major-league baseball.

With fond memories of Milwaukee, Veeck said that he favored moving there. However, Boston Braves owner Lou Perini now controlled the territo-rial rights to baseball in Milwaukee, and on March 3, 1953, he announced that he would move the Braves there. "I'm sick of pounding my head against a stone wall. This is no sudden thing—I've known for two years it was inevita-ble," Perini said. "Boston simply is not a two club city."[8]

Baltimore had sought a major league team since Mayor Thomas J. D'Alesandro Jr. and lawyer Clarence Miles began a drive in 1951 to return baseball to the city. Older fans could still recall the heyday of the former Ori-oles, who won three straight pennants between 1894 and 1896 and boasted such baseball immortals as third baseman John McGraw, shortstop Hughie Jennings, catcher Wilbert Robinson, and outfielder Wee Willie Keeler. The Orioles had moved to New York after the 1902 season, the last American League franchise to relocate.

Veeck was fully aware of Baltimore's potential as the new home of the Browns, and in the late fall of 1952 he had begun talking with Jack Dunn, the owner of the minor-league Orioles, for the territorial rights to the Balti-more market. These talks were secret—Veeck even had a code name for them, "Ashtray." He and Dunn agreed that if the Browns moved to Baltimore, Dunn would be a part owner and Veeck would buy and dispose of his minor-league team.

D'Alesandro and Miles—the brash, sentimental politician once called a man of "flying-wedge persistence"* and the patrician attorney—were an unlikely pair united by their love of the game and their common desire to get Baltimore a team. In December 1952, D'Alesandro and Miles began dis-cussions with Veeck to bring the Browns to Baltimore before the 1953 sea-son, intending to sell shares of stock in the team to the public, thereby raising enough money to operate the team in a new city. Veeck and the mayor

---

* D'Alesandro passed along his political bent to his son, Thomas D'Alesandro III, who went on to become mayor of Baltimore, and his sister, Nancy D'Alesandro, who married attorney Paul Pelosi in 1963 and became Speaker of the U.S. House of Representatives in 2007.

shook hands on a deal. The Browns went to spring training in 1953 with the expectation that that they would open the season in Baltimore.[9] Veeck and D'Alesandro headed to Tampa for a meeting of the American League own-ers in March, confident that they had six of the eight votes necessary to shift the franchise to Baltimore. On the eve of the meeting, league president Will Harridge indicated that the move had been approved and the vote would be "a mere formality."[10]

But on March 16, with the victory champagne on ice, the American League rejected Veeck's request to move by a vote of 6–2. Charles Comis-key later recalled that he and Veeck were the only two affirmative voters. "All the adjustments had been made for the move," recalled Comiskey, who added, "It would have been a good move financially." Veeck was dumb-founded by what had happened, and he determined to reverse the decision. "I remember working almost three straight days with Bill as he tried to get the decision changed," Comiskey related. "I just about wore out my shoes trying to keep up with Bill." Asked whether he had abandoned the idea of moving to Baltimore, Veeck said he hadn't abandoned anything—but that he had been abandoned.[11]

Harridge hung the rejection on the tight timing of the move, and one unnamed source at the meeting told *Time* magazine that Veeck's plan was "hasty and haphazard," but most understood, as John Carmichael said in the *Chicago Daily News*, that Veeck was the victim of duplicity by "lying own-ers" and that the vote against him was either "silly or malicious."[12] Arthur Daley later summed up what had been done to Veeck: "In a disgraceful dem-onstration of spite and malice, his fellow owners refused that permission in a blatant effort to impoverish him and drive the nettlesome Veeck from baseball."[13]

As if to prove that point, as Veeck, Comiskey, and the Baltimore delega-tion worked in vain for a reversal in Tampa, the National League, meeting across the bay in St. Petersburg, gave unanimous consent for Perini to move the Braves to Milwaukee in time for Opening Day. Milwaukee's minor-league Brewers would move to Toledo. Clearly Perini was as well liked in his league as Veeck was disliked in his.[14]

Undeterred, neither an infuriated Veeck nor the puzzled city of Baltimore would take no for an answer. Baltimore immediately began construction of an upper deck for Memorial Stadium with the goal of having it ready for Opening Day 1954. Veeck, D'Alesandro, and Miles negotiated a new plan for moving the Browns. Baltimore investors would buy 40 percent of the club—half of Veeck's stock—for $1.2 million, with Veeck remaining the principal owner. The deal would be presented to the owners late in the season.

For the city of Baltimore, getting the team had now become a matter of civic pride, all the more so after some called it a bad bet for baseball. "Baltimore is a city of stray dogs, excellent lacrosse players, star-studded experts at the art of the parlay and with a scattering of masterful technicians at pocket billiards," Washington journalist Dick O'Brien of the *Times-Herald* critiqued, insisting that Veeck had gotten a financial break when the transfer was nixed. Nonetheless, Baltimoreans were buying up as many shares of Browns stock as they could.[15]

Fans in St. Louis, however, felt betrayed, and Veeck was chided for his less than frank dealings with the baseball public and the stockholders, whose shares he had bought up with the promise of keeping the team afloat. In the midst of recovering from the Baltimore defeat, on March 23 Veeck threw in the towel and signed the radio and television agreement with the American League regarding night games: "We figured to lose out anyway, just like we lost on everything else." Cleveland restored the Browns night games immediately, with the Yankees and the Red Sox following suit.[16] The Justice Department then decided not to conduct an investigation into the relocation issue despite a call for one from two Maryland congressmen, who called the matter a "grave injustice." Veeck agreed with the Justice Department, stating this was his fight and he didn't want help from anyone.[17]

Just prior to Opening Day, a series of articles highlighted the differing fates of the Browns and Braves. Seven reasons were listed as to why Veeck and Baltimore had been denied, the first of which was personality: Perini was highly regarded by his fellow National League owners, whereas Veeck was disliked by his peers. The other six reasons were motive (Veeck was steamrolling his request), money (Veeck was undercapitalized), minor-league opposition (the American Association opposed the move to Baltimore), schedule (Baltimore did not work in an east-west split), commitments (Veeck was not free of them), and three unresolved lawsuits filed by minority stockholders trying to keep the Browns in St. Louis, which, among other things, accused Veeck of "extravagance" in running the ball club.[18]

On April 10, the Busch brewery bought Sportsman's Park from Veeck for $800,000 plus an additional $300,000 in moving expenses.[19] The place was renamed Budweiser Stadium and the renovations began immediately.*

---

* The league later vetoed the name, and it became Busch Stadium.

Bill, Mary Frances, and Mike went apartment hunting, as they knew they had to move out of the ballpark. The sale was a lifesaver for Veeck, as fans were staying away in droves. After the first twenty-three home games in 1953, the Browns had only drawn some 125,000, barely two-thirds of the previous year's pace, and attendance seemed to be getting worse. (Herb Heft, a reporter for the *Washington Post*, would sit with Veeck one night in June and watch as he counted the crowd from his perch in the press box. "It's a good thing I brought my car along," Veeck would quip. "I can drive all these folks home after the game.")[20] Kansas City, Montreal, Los Angeles, and San Francisco joined in the bidding for the beleaguered team through the summer, and Yankees executive Del Webb, a wealthy builder from Arizona, unexpectedly threw his support behind Los Angeles as the new home for the Browns, observing, "There is too much baseball concentrated in the East."

Underscoring the animosity between Veeck and the Yankees, games between the front-running New Yorkers and the bottom-dwelling Browns took on aspects of warfare. Bespectacled St. Louis catcher Clint Courtney, known for his pugnacity, had declared a personal vendetta against the Yankees ever since they traded him to St. Louis after the 1951 season. Courtney had participated in earlier altercations with the Yankees, including a historic fistfight with Billy Martin in Yankee Stadium in 1952 after the Yankee second baseman had applied a hard tag to Courtney's head as he slid into second base. But this paled beside the mayhem that erupted in St. Louis on April 28 following Courtney's high slide and spiking of Phil Rizzuto. Both benches emptied. Courtney was attacked by three Yankee players, and umpire John Stevens suffered a shoulder dislocation while trying to break up the brawl. The fines imposed were spread over the largest group of players in the history of the league. "I am amazed by the reasoning," Veeck commented after Courtney received the highest fine.

Three days later Veeck was sitting in the press box in St. Louis and, as the night game against the Washington Senators ended with a Browns player striking out with the tying run on third, he stood and kicked a steel chair in anger with his good left foot, breaking a bone. Nothing could stop the slide and the reality that the Browns were on their way out of town.

However, on the cold and drizzly night of May 6, the most unlikely of pitchers provided a brief uplift. In the fourth inning of a game against the Philadelphia Athletics, a feeling of compassion came over Veeck and he announced to the sparse crowd that the game would be on the house—that the fans' rain checks would be good for any later date. To their amazement, the 2,473 in attendance saw one of the most unusual pitching feats in baseball history, as rookie pitcher Alva "Bobo" Holloman pitched a no-hitter in his first start as a major leaguer.* Holloman yielded line drive after line drive, but in every case a Browns player was in the right place to turn them into outs.[21]

Of the eighteen games played following the no-hitter, the team won only three, and after its losing streak reached seven after a May 24 defeat in Cleveland, Veeck decided to throw a party to loosen the team up. The event was held in the Aviation Room at the Carter Hotel, an elegant space decorated with airplane memorabilia from the Cleveland Air Races. The room was dominated by glass-framed picture of World War I ace Eddie Rickenbacker. Veeck insisted the whole ball club be there; he hired a piano player and laid out an enormous spread of food and drink.

"It was a great time; we were singing songs and laughing and telling stories. You'd have thought we had just won the World Series instead of riding [a] . . . losing streak," pitcher Max Lanier recalled, having joined the Browns early in the season, the last of his fourteen-year career. "Around one o'clock in the morning a few of us started getting ready to leave. But Veeck got by the door and said, 'Nobody can leave until I say they can leave.' Then he started opening champagne and squirting it at everybody. Vic Wertz and myself, we caught him and poured a bottle of it right down his back. He was laughing so hard we could hardly hold him. Then there was one bottle of scotch left and Veeck grabbed it and threw it at Eddie Rickenbacker's picture and smashed the glass frame into a thousand pieces. . . . It was a great party. Cost him $1,850." The team went out the next day nice and loose and lost its eighth game in succession, and the day after that the ninth before halting the streak, only to start another.[22]

The Browns limped into Yankee Stadium on June 16 to face a New York team that had won eighteen in a row. Sportswriter Milt Richman found manager Marty Marion in the visitors' clubhouse staring glumly at a blank lineup card. Marion handed the card to Richman.

---

* Holloman won two more games in the majors, beating the Indians and Red Sox, but he was again relegated to the bullpen in July, and he made his final major-league appearance on July 19, after which Veeck sold his services to Toronto of the International League. According to Bill James, Bobo Holloman's no-hitter was the second-least-likely in history. The most unlikely was tossed by Charles "Bumpus" Jones in 1892, also in his first start.

"Here," he said. "You make it out."

Richman protested, but Marion was insistent.

"Pick out any nine you like," he said.

Richman did, and the Browns won 3–1. They then lost the next six games.[23]

The nadir of the season came on July 7, when the Browns lost to the Indians 6–3, setting an unenviable major-league record of twenty losses in a row in their home park, breaking the mark of the 1906 Boston Red Sox.[24]

In August Veeck again began actively looking for other cities in which to place the Browns, starting with Los Angeles and San Francisco but including Kansas City, Minneapolis, Toronto, and, of course, Baltimore. In September Veeck met with officials of the Brooklyn Dodgers to inquire about the cost of acquiring the Dodgers' Montreal farm site, the most valuable minor-league property available. Soon the list of cities being considered had grown to eight with the addition of Houston, although Veeck's preference remained Baltimore.[25]

On the eve of the season-ending American League meeting in New York, at which the future of the Browns would be voted on, the issue of race suddenly entered the picture as the *New York Times* published a telegram to Will Harridge from the National Association for the Advancement of Colored People (NAACP) urging the American League not to approve the transfer of the Browns to Baltimore because the city excluded Negroes from hotels and restaurants. The "racist spirit" of the city was most recently exemplified by the refusal of the Lyric Theatre to book the celebrated African American contralto Marian Anderson.[26] Baltimore-style Jim Crow "wasn't blatant, just thorough"; in the early days of the new Memorial Stadium "black fans testified that anyone buying a seat at the ticket window would then in the stands find himself or herself surrounded by other blacks."[27]

Satchel Paige was already on record as not wanting to go to Baltimore unless it was under Veeck's wing. Earlier in the year he had confided to teammate Gene Bearden: "I never got treated too good in that town, you know I played a couple of exhibitions there. But of course if it's Mr. Bill that goes there, I'll go right along with him. I'd play anywhere for him—even in Afghanistan."[28]

The effect of the NAACP protest on the voting was probably negligible, but it added an unexpected last-minute complication. On Sunday, September 27, Veeck received bad news: he had again lost, this time by a 4–4 vote. "Bill put a lot of work into this and was really hurt by it, and you can understand why," recalled Charles Comiskey. The vote was secret, but one owner told the Associated Press that the opposition had been organized by Webb, a point later confirmed by Detroit Tigers owner Spike Briggs, who sided with Veeck for a number of reasons.[29]

While this vote was being taken in New York, the Browns were in St. Louis before a sparse crowd of 3,174 playing what would be their last game. Fittingly, the Browns lost a twelve-inning struggle with the Chicago White Sox 2–1, suffering their 100th loss of the season. The game ended on a sad and symbolic note. In extra innings, plate umpire Art Passarella called for a fresh supply of baseballs, but was advised there were no more. Rather than call the game on account of lack of baseballs, he went to a box of scuffed balls and pulled out the least damaged. After the game the players changed into street clothes and gave their uniforms to kids who hung around after the game hoping to grab a souvenir.*

The Browns had drawn 311,000 that season—down some 208,000 from the previous season—while the Milwaukee Braves were ending their inaugural season with a record National League attendance mark of 1,826,397.[30]

Baltimore mayor Tom D'Alesandro was furious, complaining to baseball commissioner Ford Frick that Webb was manipulating the owners meetings. D'Alesandro barged into their second session the next day. "He told them he was friendly with presidents and congressmen," D'Alesandro's son recalled, "and vowed he would go to work on baseball's antitrust exemption if they didn't move the Browns to Baltimore. Basically, he threatened the hell out of them. He thought [his chance] was slipping away."[31] This was no idle threat. Emanuel Celler, chairman of the House Judiciary Committee, who was spearheading an investigation of baseball's antitrust exemption, had termed the denial "a damned outrage" and suggested that Congress might want to step into the matter.[32]

At this point in the meeting, Briggs and Comiskey walked out, fearing another negative vote even with the threat. Without them there was no longer a quorum, and the meeting was adjourned. Briggs worked to persuade Webb, who began to relent when the notion of forcing Veeck out of the deal was raised. D'Alesandro and Miles understood quickly that what Webb and his followers really wanted was for Veeck to be pushed out of baseball. The Baltimore group was given forty-eight hours to put together a consortium

---

* Ed Mickelson was one of the few beneficiaries of the game, becoming, as he explained in his 2007 memoir, the answer to one of baseball's toughest trivia questions: "Who drove in the last run for the St. Louis Browns?"

that would buy the team from Veeck. At the same time, Webb remained intrigued by the prospect of a team in Los Angeles and had convinced the Senators' Clark Griffith of this. Griffith, nearing eighty-four, remarked prophetically: "I can't see how we can possibly keep the Browns in St. Louis now. Heck, who is going to come out and see them play? I wouldn't be surprised if we move them to Los Angeles this year and follow-up by moving another club to San Francisco in 1955."[33]*

Miles worked the phones, asking Baltimore investors to raise their stake. They came through, and their pledges, including one from Jerold C. Hoffberger, owner of the National Brewing Company, more than doubled the original offer. With a few hours to spare, Miles arranged to pay $2,475,000 for the 79 percent of the stock still owned by the Chicago holding company controlled by Veeck. There was only one bright spot in the situation: Veeck and his backers had bought the Browns stock at $7 a share and were in a position to sell it two and a half years later for $12, so even after significant operating losses, the transaction netted Veeck and his backers a 38 percent profit.[34]

When the owners met on September 29 for their final session, D'Alesandro and Miles had negotiated a key yes vote from Clark Griffith, who previously had been reluctant to see a team move so close to his Senators but was mollified by Hoffberger's offer that his brewery sponsor the Senators' telecasts, a deal worth a reported $250,000. Meanwhile, the money behind Webb's Los Angeles bid had failed to materialize.[35]

After D'Alesandro and Miles presented their offer, the owners deliberated behind closed doors before calling D'Alesandro back into the room. American League secretary Earl Hilligan addressed reporters in the corridor, and a roar went up when the members of the mayor's contingent heard Hilligan say the word "approved." D'Alesandro then emerged with a huge smile. Baltimore was back in the major leagues. The Browns would become the Baltimore Orioles for the 1954 season and move into Baltimore's rebuilt, 51,000-seat Municipal Stadium, the fourth-biggest ballpark in the majors.[†]

---

* Griffith's vision became a reality three years later when the National League Brooklyn Dodgers and New York Giants moved to Los Angeles and San Francisco, respectively, after the 1957 season.

† Of all the franchise relocations of the 1950s, only the shift from St. Louis to Baltimore resulted in a new name for the team. As soon as the move was approved, Clarence Miles confirmed that the team would be called the Orioles. The other team names are still with us today: Dodgers, Giants, Braves (from Boston to Milwaukee to Atlanta), and Athletics (from Philadelphia to Kansas City to Oakland).

The vote was 8–0, and even the reluctant Webb had voted for Baltimore, receiving in return a concession from his fellow owners to expand to California "if it should become desirable."[36]

Conventional wisdom has it that Veeck was expelled for a long list of issues ranging from the perceived indignity he had caused the game in the Gaedel incident to his verbal baiting of his fellow owners. Mary Frances, among others, has always believed that the owners' dislike of him stemmed from his demands for pooled television and radio income. However, unstated by mainstream media at the time but articulated by Fay Young of the *Chicago Defender* was another viewpoint: that a primary source of the hatred of Veeck by some of the American League owners was his signing of numerous African American players, beginning with Larry Doby in 1947. At the time of the first 6–2 vote in March, five of the teams against him—the Athletics, Senators, Tigers, Red Sox, and Yankees—were still without an African American player.[37]

Veeck himself saw it in intensely personal terms. "I knew they had no regard for me. With all that, it had been a shock to me that Sunday evening to learn that they were out to break me, not just to teach me a lesson. I hadn't thought they hated me that much."[38]

And yet some of the owners still sympathized with him. "Personally I hope Baltimore takes him back," the Tigers' Spike Briggs remarked when he was in Baltimore for an October football game between the Detroit Lions, which he also owned, and the Baltimore Colts. "Veeck's good for baseball. The people who were trying to keep Baltimore out of the American League are not."[39]

CHAPTER 14

Chicago a Go-Go

I DIDN'T LEAVE BASEBALL GRACEFULLY. I was evicted," Veeck declared. The American League had given him the boot and, as his friend the *Cleveland Press* columnist Whitey Lewis put it, "broke his back and his heart." Out of baseball, he vowed to be like the bad penny, fated to turn up again.[1]

Less than two weeks later, he was back in circulation as a $1,000-a-month special assistant to Phil Wrigley, assigned to develop ways of spearheading baseball's move to the West Coast. Veeck was to work closely with Don Stewart of Wrigley's minor-league Los Angeles Angels. Wrigley aimed to put the National League ahead of its rival in moving to the fertile West Coast market. In making the announcement, Wrigley said, "Bill's duties will be to organize the effort so that the great Southern California region may have major league baseball in an orderly and sensible way as soon as possible."[2]

The stakes for Western expansion were huge. Any move would require a joint deal for Los Angeles and San Francisco because, as Arthur Daley explained in the *New York Times*, "each trip to California would cost $10,000 per team and it would be financial suicide for Frisco to be in one league and L.A. in the other."[3]

Veeck was immediately back in the news. "Wait a minute. Give me a chance to catch my breath," he told James Enright of the *Chicago American*, who asked him how long it would take him to accomplish his new task. "I just got the job, and they have been talking about moving teams to the West Coast for years." Apropos of what had happened to him already during the year, he observed: "Don't forget, I'm the only man who ever had a hand in transplanting two major-league teams between March and September of the same year, and then failed to end up with either one of them."[4]

Before the year was over, Veeck had not only proposed a major upgrade of Los Angeles' Wrigley Field to major-league standards but also met with California governor Goodwin Knight to explore the public financing of ballparks in Los Angeles and San Francisco. Veeck told the governor that the publicly owned park in Cleveland was a great success and that California might consider revenue bonds that would be retired from rent paid by teams. Veeck moved his young family to Los Angeles and immediately became the face and voice of western expansion.

If Veeck had an immediate reincarnation, Satchel Paige did not. Although he had led the Browns in saves with eleven in 1953, he still had been 3–9 and was not re-signed by the Orioles, who quietly released him at the end of January, citing his advanced age and high salary as the deciding factors. Veeck had paid Paige $25,000, which meant that under the rules of the time, the Orioles could cut his salary by only 25 percent. He had, in the words of an Associated Press reporter, become more of a character than a pitcher, and had spent many of his final days at ease in the contour chair Veeck had installed for him. "The new bosses told me they were starting a youth movement and they didn't have room for an old man like me" was Paige's interpretation. He was offered up on waivers for $10,000, but nobody wanted him.[5]

BASED IN LOS ANGELES, Veeck attempted deals of all sorts, often for or with friends. One involved the eccentric and reclusive billionaire Howard Hughes, who owned a brewery in Texas that Jerold Hoffberger wanted to buy. Hoffberger asked Veeck to make the approach. As Veeck recalled twenty years later: "With cloak and dagger maneuvering, I got to the Hughes people, and they promised to relay the message to the chief."

A year of silence followed, but then one night at eleven o'clock, the telephone rang and it was Hughes, who instructed Veeck to meet him three hours later at a hamburger joint on one of the main streets of Los Angeles. Veeck kept the appointment, and except for the counterman, Hughes and he were the only people in the place. After asking Veeck if he wanted coffee, Hughes grunted, "I don't want to sell the brewery."

To which Veeck replied, "My friend doesn't want your brewery. He bought one in Detroit eight months ago. Good night!"[6]

In the fall of 1954, Veeck updated an earlier report and sent carefully numbered copies to National League owners. His proprietary study presented the inevitability of expansion, reporting that the demand for baseball was great in both Los Angeles and San Francisco. Voters in San Francisco had already approved a bond issue to build a big-league stadium. Los Angeles was prepared to finance one as well. Veeck concluded that with two National League teams in the West, transportation costs and scheduling for visiting clubs would be reasonable. The game needed to be truly national to retain its financial power and popularity. Adding these two cities would increase baseball's market by 25 percent.

Veeck's report amounted to a business plan for anyone who might want to put a major-league club in either city. It covered political issues, the cost of compensating local minor-league teams, scheduling, transportation logistics, and even summer rainfall figures—essentially zero in Los Angeles and 0.15–0.29 inch per month in San Francisco.

Furthermore, he reported that the American League was secretly planning its own invasion of California. Veeck urged the National League to move quickly: "The plain fact is that the league that gets to the Pacific Coast first will obviously maintain the edge of having a coast-to-coast set up for a long time to come." Veeck had given the National League a road map leading to Los Angeles and San Francisco.[7]

In February 1955, Veeck officially ended his fourteen-month stay in Los Angeles and resigned his post with Wrigley with the understanding that his job was done and the groundwork for moving the National League to California was established. At the final press conference, with Phil Wrigley at his side, he displayed an artist's drawing of how Wrigley Field in Los Angeles could be expanded to seat 50,000 by cutting the grandstand in half and moving it to the outfield.

Veeck also used the press conference to announce that he had bought the 47,000-acre Deep Creek Ranch in New Mexico, fifteen miles north of Glenwood, which now became home for his family. The ranch, he explained, would keep him busy until his return to Los Angeles or San Francisco with a "major role" with a big-league club. Pressed as to which city he would prefer, he said Los Angeles. Years later Mary Frances would recall: "That was a fantastic period in our lives. It was two years of investigating all the possibilities."[8]

Veeck was soon planting and puttering and maintaining a real distance from baseball. So remote was the ranch that he relied on a telephone attached to a weather-scarred utility pole five miles from his house. Twice a day Veeck drove to the pole and called the operator in Glenwood to gather his messages and return his calls. If people really needed to get in touch with Veeck immediately, they would order a messenger sent from Glenwood for a fee.[9]

But Veeck needed some link back to baseball. In March 1955 he signed on as an in-season western scout for the Cleveland Indians. "He belongs in baseball and we don't want him to lose contact with the game to which he has contributed so much," said Hank Greenberg, the Indians general manager, who made occasional trips with Veeck looking at talent west of the Mississippi.[10]

Veeck's remoteness in Glenwood had its dangers. On June 11, 1955, Veeck was painting a shed using a spray gun. "He was supposed to use a quart of paint with the sprayer, but that was too slow for Veeck," recalled Beth Smith, who had moved to Deep Creek Ranch with the Veecks. "So he hooked the sprayer up to a one-gallon jar. The pressure gauge exploded, severing an artery."

Smith somehow got Veeck into a car and rushed him to the hospital. "He was bleeding badly and told me he didn't think he was going to make it. Every time he was nodding off, I'd take another curve at 90 mph that should have been taken at 20." They made it to the hospital in the nick of time, and the bleeding was stopped. He later told her that he willed himself to survive the injury and the wild ride because "I wanted to see how this came out."[11]

Six months later, in December 1955, Veeck reprised his minor-league Milwaukee experience. He and two of his St. Louis friends, former Browns vice president and insurance executive Sidney Salomon Jr. and banker Elliott Stein, bought the Class AAA International League Syracuse ballclub for $100,000 and moved the Philadelphia Phillies farm team to Miami, where it was renamed the Miami Marlins. The group bought the team on the premise that that they could make a lot more money in this new market, but their ultimate goal was to get Miami into the major leagues, a goal Salomon said might materialize in four to five years. They persuaded Veeck to come east and help upgrade Miami to major-league status, giving him the title of vice president.[12]

Veeck's first task was to gain a lease on Miami Stadium. When the hard bargaining stalled, Veeck rolled up his pants leg and began to remove his artificial leg. "Here," said the mock-beleaguered Veeck, "you might as well have this, too." With that one gesture he got the laugh that broke the impasse, secured the lease, and earned his first dose of publicity. His second task was to sign Satchel Paige. He announced his intention at a Kiwanis luncheon in late January and predicted that Paige would do "some pitching" during the season.[13]

Veeck presented his plan to sign Paige for $10,000 to manager Don Osborn, who knew that Paige would have extraordinary privileges and freedoms. He asked his pitchers to vote on the matter, reminding them: "Satch isn't going to do any running to keep his legs in shape. He may not show up till the games are half over—or maybe not at all on some days. But there's not a better relief man in the business, and he'll save a lot of victories for you boys. It's up to you." The staff that season included such future major leaguers as Turk Farrell, Seth Morehead, Don Cardwell, and Jim Owens. There was some reluctance, but they finally voted to take him. But the signing was kept secret even from the local reporters.[14]

On opening night, Veeck arranged for a bubble-top helicopter to deliver Paige to the mound before the game started, but the pilot missed his signal and the landing did not take place until well into the second inning, the helicopter kicking up a miniature storm that blew infield dirt into the stands.

"Welcome to our newest Marlin, Satchel Paige," came the announcement as the lanky pitcher stepped out of the helicopter. The crowd roared.

Outwardly unimpressed, Jimmy Burns of the *Miami Herald* turned to Veeck and said: "You just made your first mistake. People didn't come here to get covered with dirt. They'll never come back." Veeck shook his head and laughed. "In your column tomorrow, tell them to send their dry cleaning bills to me and I'll reimburse them. They'll remember this the rest of their lives." For his part, Paige told reporters, "Veeck better think up something new," and he vowed never again to ride in a helicopter.[15]

Osborn was amused by the stunt but told Veeck that he did not want Paige as a regular pitcher and that he would mostly use him in exhibition games. The next day, Veeck took Osborn to lunch and, insisting Paige had not been hired as a gag, made a deal with the manager. Osborn would line up his nine best hitters, and Veeck agreed to pay $10 to any of them who got a clean hit off Paige. Paige retired all nine, and Osborn agreed to make him a roster player.

In Paige's first game as a Marlins starter, he pitched a complete-game, four-hit shutout. Osborn, a former minor-league pitcher, watched with awe as Paige performed beyond all expectations. In mid-August, with a 10–2 record and a 1.50 ERA under his belt, Paige celebrated his forty-ninth birthday and suggested that he might pitch until he was seventy. He was 11–4 for the season.[16]

While on the sidelines as a minor-league executive commuting between Miami and the ranch, Veeck became increasingly alert to possibilities in the majors. Amounts now being paid for ball clubs were on the rise. In February 1955 the Indians team that Veeck had bought for $1.4 million and sold for $2.2 million was sold again, this time for $3.9 million to a syndicate led by Cleveland industrialist William R. Daley. A share of stock worth $100 when Veeck sold the club was now worth $1,000. One of the owners was Indians general manager Hank Greenberg, delighted to have finally become a major stockholder. Their positions were now reversed—Greenberg an owner and Veeck, when time and inclination permitted, a scout.[17]

But it was an open secret that Veeck was angling to come back to ownership.[18] One of the first rumors was a report in early 1956 that the "former Mr. Big of baseball was assembling Chicago money to buy the Tigers." Veeck knew that Spike Briggs, the heavy-drinking son of the late Walter O. Briggs, who had died in early 1952, was being forced to sell the team by his three sisters, who owned equal shares in the team with Spike. In addition, the bank with the trust for the Briggs grandchildren had gotten a court order demanding the sale.[19]

In early June, Veeck was the front man for one of the eight groups making a bid for the team. The Tigers were regarded as one of baseball's best franchises, and Briggs Stadium was a beautifully appointed venue, seating nearly 53,000 fans, located an easy five-minute walk from the heart of downtown Detroit.[20] But the team's chemistry had recently been upset when, just before the sale was announced, Spike Briggs proclaimed he was "fed up" with those running the team, especially manager Bucky Harris and general manager and former Veeck colleague Muddy Ruel—both venerable baseball men.*

---

* If Spike Briggs was accepted and tolerated by the baseball establishment, he was disliked by many of those who donned the Tigers uniform. Boots Poffenberger, one of the most notorious beer consumers in baseball history, could barely tolerate this man, who, in his words, "wasn't too sharp: He wouldn't know a Pabst Blue Ribbon from a Budweiser." Poffenberger felt that Briggs liked to throw his weight around, and Briggs would yell at him when he would toss balls to kids in the stadium. (*Baseball Digest*, December 1992)

Players Harvey Kuenn and Steve Gromek felt it necessary to demand radio time to defend their manager.[21]

Veeck's group included Hoffberger, president of the National Brewing Company of Baltimore. The other seven groups initially interested included one headed by matinee idol Clark Gable and another involving Cy Block, a onetime Chicago Cubs infielder and now an insurance executive in New York City who specialized in selling life insurance to ballplayers.

Gable and Block dropped out or joined other groups, so the final group that presented sealed bids included Chicago insurance executive Charles O. Finley, backed by the same Chicago men—Philip R. Clarke and Lester Armour—who had helped finance Veeck's purchase of the Indians ten years earlier. Finley, whose office was in the same building as those of Major League Baseball in Chicago, was eager to become a force in baseball, and this was his first attempt to buy in. All groups were told that they should expect to pay at least $5 million for the club and that any deal would require keeping Spike in a top management position for five years.[22]

Detroit News sports editor H. G. Salsinger, the most powerful and persuasive voice in Detroit sports, did not hide the fact that he disliked Veeck. His column on July 11, under the headline "No Veeck Circus," cautioned that if Veeck's bid for the Detroit franchise was accepted, Detroit's fans would have to "view the city's baseball future with apprehension." Recounting Veeck's use of fireworks, clowns, and a midget to get people into his ballparks (Eddie Gaedel had, after all, batted against the Tigers), Salsinger called for the heirs of Walter Briggs to put the future of Detroit baseball in the hands of "those resolved to continue the game with the same affection that he had for it."[23] Veeck asserted that if his bid was accepted by the Briggs family but turned down by the rest of the American League because of owners who did not like him, he would go to court.[24]

A few nights before the bids had to be in, Veeck met with Briggs at the Statler Hotel bar in Detroit and said he would make him chairman of the board but would not let him operate the club. Briggs said that the group headed by Fred Knorr was promising to let him run the team. A close friend, Knorr headed Dearborn-based Knorr Broadcasting, of which Briggs was a stockholder and a member of its board of directors. "All right," Veeck replied. "But watch out. These guys are going to get the club and then throw you out."[25]

On July 16, 1956, an eleven-man syndicate including singer Bing Crosby and headed by Knorr and radio and television executive John Fetzer bought the Detroit Tigers and Briggs Stadium for a record $5.5 million, nearly $1 million higher than any previous transaction in baseball. Veeck attempted to up his bid of $5.25 million by $500,000 to make it the best offer, but it was disallowed. Spike had the control he wanted over the club, and the announcement declared that the sale meant the Tigers would remain a "dignified" operation: "no midgets, no farm nights, no roving musicians, nothing to distract the keen interest of the tie and jacket folk in the audience."[26]

To some, dignity also meant keeping the team safe from racial integration. Nine years after Jackie Robinson and Larry Doby broke the color barrier, the Tigers still had not signed a black player. This had first become an issue before the 1952 season, when Tigers manager Red Rolfe said the club had faltered because it had not maintained a strong farm system and had determined not to sign players from the Negro leagues.[27]

At the time of the sale, the Tigers still had no Negro players and had been taken to task a few days earlier by the National Negro Labor Council for maintaining a "lily-white" organization. Veeck, needless to say, had the strong backing of Detroit's large black population.*

Veeck no doubt would have signed African American players upon taking over. Veeck believed strongly that Satchel Paige was the best two-inning pitcher in baseball and would have signed him, which to some would have been an affront to the much-touted "dignity" of the club. The African American press insisted Veeck was still paying a price for signing Doby in 1947, Paige in 1948, and the other players he had brought to Cleveland in 1949: As Leslie Matthews wrote in the *Daily Defender*, "The reason why Bill Veeck did not latch onto the Tigers is because the AL moguls never forgave him for ending the loop's racial bar."[28]

As the Detroit deal was crashing, Veeck, wanting to show that Miami was a major-league city, hit on the notion of setting a new all-time attendance record for a minor-league game, which he aimed to accomplish with Satchel Paige pitching on August 7, 1956, in the Orange Bowl, never before used for baseball. Paige's agreement with the Marlins required them to get his permission before he would start a game, and he would agree to start in the Orange Bowl only if the team paid off a $500 bill he had incurred in

---

* Two years later, in 1958, the Tigers became the next-to-last club to integrate (the Red Sox would be the last) when they signed Ozzie Virgil Sr., who has the distinction of being the first Dominican to play in major-league baseball. By then the new owners had finally lost patience with Spike Briggs and—as Veeck had predicted—fired him.

Memphis. It was promptly paid. Thanks in part to pre-game festivities that included jazz and blues legend Cab Calloway and TV personality Merv Griffin, a crowd of 57,713 filled the stadium. Paige wandered about taking pictures of the celebrities and regular folks who had come to see him pitch. As the crowd sang "Hi-de-ho!" along with Calloway, Osborn implored Paige to take some warm-up pitches. Three minutes before the game was to start, Paige finally put his camera down, flicked a half dozen pitches, and declared himself ready to go.

The right-field foul pole was only 200 feet from home plate, and the Columbus Jets had loaded their lineup with left-handed batters eager to show Paige up.* But only one hit went to right as Paige kept nipping the outside corner, forcing the batters to hit to left. In the 6–2 victory, Paige not only pitched into the eighth inning but also drove in three runs with a 330-foot double to left center. Osborn later called it "one of the greatest pitching exhibitions I ever saw."[29] The game raised more than $30,000 for charity, and to Veeck's satisfaction, the crowd was officially acknowledged as the largest ever to attend a minor-league game. A week later, Paige pitched a complete-game one-hitter against Rochester that earned him a standing ovation.[†]

In October 1956, it was widely reported that a deal was brewing between Veeck and John Ringling North to keep the big top operating by buying North's Ringling Brothers and Barnum & Bailey Circus. Veeck's group, which included his old pal Abe Saperstein, reportedly offered $21 million for performers, tents, and animals, but North wanted more, and the deal went cold quickly. Veeck and Saperstein had come up with the notion of creating a circus tent that could be inflated by water, and this would have been their moment to test the idea.[30]

By the end of 1956, Veeck had tired of the commute between the ranch and Florida and become dispirited by the generally poor attendance in Miami (the Orange Bowl game aside) and the realization that the team would not reach the majors. He helped his fellow owners sell the team—remarkably, with a handsome profit. Before leaving Miami he managed to find a secure berth for Paige, who remained on the Marlins' roster for two more years.[31]

With the sale of the Miami franchise, Veeck was, in the words of Frank-

---

* Being a football stadium, the Orange Bowl could not offer a normal baseball configuration.
[†] During his three seasons with the Marlins, Paige would compile a record of 31–22 and an ERA of 2.73, two numbers that Paige's biographer Larry Tye would later write were "impressive for a pitcher of any age."

lin Lewis, a "vagrant, wholly without roots," though no less desirous of returning to baseball.[32] During 1957 Veeck did some public relations work for
the Cleveland Indians, whose attendance was falling steadily, to a decade
low of 663,805 in 1958; there were rumors that the team would soon move
to Minneapolis.

Veeck's leg was a constant source of pain, and he still had to soak his
stump for several hours every morning to mitigate the discomfort of the
prosthesis he would wear for the rest of the day. Lou Brissie, now working
for American Legion Baseball, ran into Veeck at the 1957 World Series and
they talked about their mutual affliction of osteomyelitis. Veeck put it directly to Brissie: "If they want to cut it off, let them cut it off and you will
save yourself a lot of pain."[33]

During the 1957–58 off-season, Veeck enjoyed the satisfaction of seeing
his West Coast planning come to fruition as Walter O'Malley moved his
Brooklyn Dodgers to Los Angeles and Horace Stoneham's New York Giants
remained their rivals by relocating to San Francisco. Other chickens were
coming home to roost. When Veeck had been given the job of preparing the
West Coast for major-league baseball, he had told anyone who would listen
that revenge was at least partially on his mind. His prime target was almost
certainly Del Webb, who had been promised first shot at the West Coast by
the American League in return for his vote to send the Browns to Baltimore. When the National League upstaged the junior circuit by claiming
Los Angeles and San Francisco, the American League would have to wait
and settle for Anaheim and Oakland.[34]

In midsummer 1958 Veeck penned a widely syndicated series of five articles entitled "I Know Who's Killing Baseball." Concerned that the game
was on a "toboggan slide" downhill, Veeck argued it could only be saved by
a series of reforms—most notably an unrestricted player draft, a scouting
pool, and shared television revenues. Predictably, Veeck pointed to the existing group of owners as those who were "killing" the game. The series pro-
voked its share of negative response, including op-ed columns in some of
the newspapers that ran the Veeck series, but gained a surprising adherent
in no less a figure than J. Edgar Hoover, the director of the FBI, who was a
well-known baseball fan.

George Davis, sports editor of the *Los Angeles Herald Express*, ran into
Hoover at the Del Mar racetrack in California and chronicled their conversation, during which Hoover told him of his appreciation for Veeck's ideas, especially those relating to a common pool for drafting players. "This could

work out like they have in professional football, and would give the weaker clubs a chance to build, instead of the wealthy ones skimming off the cream." Sounding almost like Veeck himself, Hoover said: "Competition—fair, open and vigorous—is the backbone of our American system. It's what we call free enterprise, and there should be no place for monopoly in sports, any more than any other business." He then added: "Baseball is our national pastime and I'm glad to see people like Bill Veeck doing their part in maintaining it as the great institution it is on the American scene."[35]

MANY PEOPLE AGREED with Veeck's opinion that the American League was in especially bad shape. Red Smith of the *New York Herald Tribune* called it "sickly," stemming in part from the unchallenged dominance of the New York Yankees. Smith believed that what the league needed most was a challenger to the Yankees and a spark to "the bile-green depths where the Senators lie feebly twitching."[36]

As 1958 drew to a close, Dorothy Comiskey Rigney, who was granddaughter of the original Charles Comiskey and who was married to former White Sox pitcher John Rigney, grew tired of a protracted legal battle with her brother, Charles, over control of the Chicago White Sox and decided to sell her 54 percent interest in the club, which she had inherited from their mother, Grace. Charles fought bitterly to gain control of the team, which he felt should have belonged to him.[37]

Veeck let it be known that he was putting together an offer for her shares and thereby a controlling interest in the club, which would, in the words of Red Smith in his Christmas column, be the brightest holiday news the American League had had in years. "It might be like a crackling log on to the whole dreamy organization. They don't deserve to have him back in the lodge, probably don't want him, and will be shot with luck if they get him."[38]

Veeck moved quickly with seven backers and snapped up her stock for $2.7 million. Veeck's associates included both Arthur C. Allyn Sr. and Arthur C. Allyn Jr., Newton Frye, Abe Saperstein, and Hank Greenberg, who had sold his stock in the Cleveland Indians the previous November and was eager to get back into baseball, especially with Veeck as a partner. The team had been in the Comiskey family since 1901, and as a concession to its heritage, Veeck allowed minority stockholder and part owner Charles Comiskey to retain his luxurious, memorabilia-festooned president's office. Veeck was content to run the team from an open area just behind the team's switchboard.[39]

VEECK HAD TAKEN control of a team with a winning record from 1951 through 1958, though perennially behind the Yankees and Indians. Its fan base was declining and its stadium, Comiskey Park, was what Veeck termed "a dun-colored roach pit." His first priority, as usual, was to improve the stadium. "If you remember, it was dark and dank when you came in; it was like going into a dungeon, so we painted everything under the grandstand white, tore down a few useless pillars, and ripped out everything that hung overhead, that loomed over you. We wanted to get away from that dungeon-like atmosphere to one of cleanliness and airiness." He put cloth towels in the restrooms, eradicated the smell of rancid butter around popcorn stands ("We tried 15 chemical sprays before we found one that worked"), and set up a radar system to detect approaching rainstorms so that ushers could distribute free plastic rain capes before patrons got wet.[40]

Veeck attacked what he termed the historic and determined dislike women had for Comiskey Park. He stationed ushers just inside the gates to look for women who appeared to be on their first visit to the stadium and then escort them personally to their seats. He redecorated the once-nauseating powder rooms, tearing out the harsh fluorescent lights and installing flattering lighting as well as full-length mirrors and vanity tables. The men's rooms were magnets for graffiti, so, as he had done in Milwaukee, he installed blackboards, observing, "People write on walls, so why not let them write on a blackboard."[41]

Veeck needed a place to entertain the press and his friends in baseball, so he appropriated the Bards Room, a room with a grill, a working fireplace, and rustic pre–World War I decor. It took its name from the Woodland Bards, a group of wealthy Chicago power brokers and reporters organized in 1912 whose members had included Bill's father.

Few predicted Veeck's new team would finish above third or fourth place. As usual, the Yankees were the preseason favorites, which caused a young Red Sox fan named Frederick W. Byron Jr. to lament in the *Harvard Crimson*: "It is always somewhat distressing, as the opening of the baseball season rolls around, to see writers all over the country scurry to their typewriters and proudly name the New York Yankees as their carefully considered choice to win the American League pennant. Such action on the part of loyal New York sportswriters is, of course, understandable, but to have this prediction spread to every corner of the United States is quite another matter."[42]

Veeck had inherited a team that lacked power but was strong up the middle, with Sherman Lollar catching, Luis Aparicio as shortstop, and Nellie Fox at second, and a solid pitching staff led by Early Wynn, who had become a star in Cleveland after Veeck had departed and would soon celebrate his 250th win. Veeck now had the perfect setup for his dream of taking on the Yankees. Like a pool hustler denying his ability with the cue stick, he acknowledged the wisdom of the scribes and admitted he had little chance of beating the Yankees. This little game was to play on well into the season, including in a profile in the June 6, 1959, issue of *The Saturday Evening Post* entitled "A Visit with Bill Veeck": " 'I hate to admit this,' says the new boss of the White Sox, 'but we cannot beat the Yankees.' " Veeck went on to say in the article that he would need two distance hitters to take the pennant.[43]

On Opening Day in Detroit, April 10, 1959, second baseman Nellie Fox, who had had nary a home run the previous season, hit one of his only two that year with a runner on base in the fourteenth inning to beat the Tigers 9–7. Fox also had three singles and a double, driving home three runs. The White Sox took the next two from Detroit and returned for the home opener on April 14 against Kansas City.

Veeck loved Opening Day, as it was the perfect promotion opportunity. He gave his leadoff hitters, Fox and Aparicio, the "world's longest loaf of bread" to give them carbohydrates to "sustain their pep and energy as home run hitters." A silver tray loaded with 250 silver dollars was given to Early Wynn for his 250th major-league victory, achieved in the season's first week.

Just before game time, a battery of aerial bombs woke up the crowd, followed by a public address announcement: "We wish to announce another Chicago battery—Bill Veeck and Chuck Comiskey." Veeck took to the mound and threw three southpaw pitches to Comiskey, who never got the bat off his shoulder because Veeck's pitches were wild. But their appearance together was symbolic, as Veeck put it, of their partnership in the goal of winning the 1959 American League pennant.

As the fans stood for the seventh-inning stretch, all 19,303 were offered a drink on the house from Veeck. As one press report noted, "Beer vendors were swamped in the rush." The White Sox won the opener 2–0 behind Billy Pierce.[44]

As he had as a young man with the Cubs, and then in Milwaukee and

Cleveland, Veeck understood that attendance could be improved if tickets were more readily available. He hired Dick Hackett to set up an operation that anticipated the computerized ticket systems to come. "We set up a boiler-room-type operation at the downtown Mazer Sporting Goods store," Hackett remembered. "Mazer had thirteen stores scattered around the Chicago area, and he felt this would provide a service to fans by making it easier for them to purchase tickets. We had direct lines into each of the stores. They were provided with blank tickets and would call the central office to get seat locations. We would provide them the locations over the phone and the clerk would write them in. Each ticket had two carbon copies. The store kept one and we received one for auditing purposes. We sold thousands of tickets that way and never dreamed that some day with the use of computers this would become the only way to buy tickets for many events."[45]

Veeck forever courted female fans, and two of his biggest promotions were geared to getting women to come to the ballpark. Free admission and an orchid for each child were offered to any woman who brought a picture of her children on Mother's Day; 3,947 women took home some 10,000 miniature orchids. Some had never been to a ballgame in their life. One of the first-timers was quoted in the *Chicago Daily News* on her fellow rookie fans: "This is one way to get them out in the fresh air and maybe make them want to come back again." At the height of the stamp fad, in which stamps could be traded for goods at special redemption centers, Veeck gave away 3.75 million S&H Green Stamps to women attending a July doubleheader and then repeated the promotion several times later in the season.*

The range of Veeck's promotional ideas had only grown in his years out of the game. Between the games of a doubleheader with the Yankees on June 28, he staged a full-blown circus, complete with prancing stallions, midgets, giants, clowns, snake charmers, sword swallowers, acrobats, and nine elephants. The White Sox won both games. Two weeks later, he staged a cricket match between the games of a doubleheader with Kansas City. The cricket players were imported, but Sox catcher Sherman Lollar and shortstop Luis Aparicio got to take at-bats. As they took baseball-style chops at the ball, the crowd chanted: "That's not cricket."[46]

Veeck outdid himself when, during a single July game, he gave away

---

* This would have given each woman something on the order of 10,000 green stamps. The system is still in operation and in current stamps (now known as points) 7,000 would buy a $5 Starbucks gift card.

items in large quantities, including 1,000 pickles to one fan, 1,000 bottles of beer to another, and 1,000 cans of chow mein noodles to still another. Veeck then gave a fan 1,000 silver dollars embedded in a large block of ice. The trick, of course, was getting the ice to melt so that the lucky winner could get the money home. As the game progressed, the prizes became more outrageous—500 tins of smoked grasshoppers, 10,000 tickets to a minor-league baseball game—until the final gift, when one fan got the free rental of 500 tuxedos.[47]

Quick to align himself with any group that could help bring him publicity and goodwill, Veeck immediately announced a Steel Worker Night at the ball park when the steelworkers union went on strike, and more than 7,000 steelworkers were given free tickets. "Bill was a real hero, not only to the strikers but to the working class and union members," said Hackett. Veeck also scheduled special nights for teachers, cab drivers, and transit workers, and following complaints from neighbors about noise, he held a Good Neighbor Night, sending tickets to everyone who lived in the area around the ballpark.[48]

Amidst all this promotion, the White Sox were holding their own. By the end of June, as the team took a day off to prepare for a seven-day road trip, Veeck acknowledged that he was "almost sold" on his club. They had just swept a Sunday doubleheader from the Yankees, giving them a 39–32 record overall. "If we keep dazzlin' 'em with footwork to get those runners on base, like we've been doing all season and then get the occasional run . . . who knows, maybe I can change my mind about this ballclub."[49]

Fans were coming back in large numbers, and those in the park on July 24 witnessed a moment that was as entertaining for Veeck as it was for fans. Knuckleballer Hoyt Wilhelm was pitching for the Orioles when, in the first inning, he was suddenly attacked by a large swarm of small insects. Wilhelm began swiping at the gnats with his arms and hands, but fans in the stands couldn't see what was bothering him and they began to snicker. Then out of the dugout came White Sox trainer Eddie "Doc" Froelich, who waved a towel at the gnats, to no avail. He soon returned with a handheld insecticide pump, and umpire Hank Soar sprayed the mound and Wilhelm with aerosol bug repellant, but the gnats persisted. Finally Veeck ordered a fireworks crew to erect a crude brace and set off smoke bombs. When the smoke cleared, the gnats were gone.

John Kuenster of *Baseball Digest* was sitting next to Veeck in the press box. "If I didn't know better," he chuckled, "I'd suspect you had spread something around the mound to attract the gnats."

"I wish I had thought of it," Veeck impishly replied.

After the game, Veeck explained the gnats to the press, puckishly framing it as a planned event: "It takes all winter to train them and now . . . pouf. One lousy bomb and they're all blown up."[50]

Playing brilliantly in July and August, the "Go-Go" White Sox won 41 of 57 games, largely on defense, speed, singles, and the pitching of Wynn and Bob Shaw. Many writers and fans acknowledged that their league-leading team had what seemed to be an inferior roster, however much Veeck praised them as a crew that would "connive, scrounge, and hustle just to get one measly run."

Veteran catcher Sherm Lollar led the team in home runs and RBIs, but they needed more power for the pennant push, so Veeck acquired massive first baseman Ted Kluszewski for $20,000 off waivers from the Pittsburgh Pirates. An affable muscleman, "Big Klu," as he was known, tore the sleeves off his jerseys to further intimidate pitchers and ably complemented incumbent Earl Torgeson at first base. He hit nearly .300 for the Sox in the final month of the season.

Not all Veeck's attempts to improve the lot of the team were successful, but they kept his players loose and smiling and the baseball writers engaged. In early September, with the hard-hitting Cleveland Indians coming to town, Veeck announced Project Indian Wall, which would have entailed erecting a wire fence along the left-field wall to the bullpen. Veeck claimed its purpose was "to keep our over exuberant fans from falling out on the playing field." The fence was to be erected by Friday and torn down on Sunday. Not surprisingly, the American League rejected Veeck's request, insisting that the real reason for the wall was to keep Cleveland fly balls in the park.[51]

The White Sox sewed up the 1959 American League pennant on September 22 with a 4–2 defeat of the second-place Indians in Cleveland, paced by home runs from Al Smith and Jim Rivera and the twenty-first victory by Early Wynn, the old man that Cleveland had not wanted. It would be the first postseason appearance for the franchise since the notorious 1919 Black Sox series.

Back in Chicago, fire commissioner and civil defense coordinator Robert Quinn ordered a celebratory five-minute sounding of the city's air-raid sirens that set many Chicago residents rushing down into their cellars or out into the streets anticipating a possible Soviet missile attack. "Them were just Cubs fans," a Sox fan told a reporter. "Everyone else knew why those sirens were blasting."[52] Quinn apologized, but also maintained that he had usefully tested the city's civil defense readiness, which he found lacking. Major Richard Daley claimed that Quinn had acted in accordance with a little-known City Council proclamation that "there shall be whistles and sirens blowing and there shall be great happiness when the White Sox win the pennant."[53]

A crowd estimated at 100,000 greeted the team at Midway airport when it returned to Chicago at one-thirty in the morning. A day later a ticker-tape parade attracted 700,000. Mayor Daley rejoiced, "A Chicago pennant! Now for the World Series. We will win it in four straight."[54]

Before the series, manager Al Lopez was signed for another year. Veeck staged a signing in front of a contract blown up to a height of seven feet and a width of ten feet, his way of saying that it was the largest contract in the history of the team (reportedly ranging from $50,000 to $60,000). Veeck had hoped to sign Lopez for more than one season, but the manager wanted to work on a year-to-year basis. "I think maybe the reason he didn't want a longer contract is that he enjoys this flurry each fall," said Veeck at the ceremony. "I've never seen as fine a job of managing as Lopez has given us."[55]

Veeck held a press conference during which he said winning the pennant was the greatest thrill of his life and marked his triumphant return to the game. He said that this pennant meant more to him than the one in Cleveland, which had come to him when he was cocky and assumed that winning was in the natural order of things. "But then I became an outcast after I sold my share in the Cleveland club and later relieved of my stock in the St. Louis Browns I took quite a kicking around from a lot of people in baseball. I feel I've made a comeback now and I think it's always more exciting to make a comeback than to win the first time."

"You remember last year when we had dinner at Toots Shor's in New York during the World Series?" he asked Bob Addie of the *Washington Post*. "I couldn't even get an extra ticket. The parade had passed me by."[56]

The White Sox had finished a satisfying fifteen games ahead of the Yankees, who also ended up ten games behind Cleveland. Veeck's friend Casey Stengel would miss only his second World Series as Yankees manager since taking the reins in 1949, so dominant had the Yankees been—and Al Lopez had a hand in that both times, having led Cleveland to the 1954 World Series, making him the only manager to interrupt the Yankees pennant run between 1949 and 1964. In the postseason Stengel was hired as a reporter for *Life* magazine, reportedly paid $5,000 to cover the contest between the White Sox and the Los Angeles Dodgers.

The Dodgers, who had had a disastrous first season on the West Coast in 1958, were a surprise team, having survived a thrilling three-team pennant race and a two-game playoff against the Milwaukee Braves. The 1959 Dodgers were seen as underdogs, much as the White Sox were. Led by manager Walter Alston, the team drew more than 2 million fans to Los Angeles Memorial Coliseum, validating the optimistic projections Veeck had made in his report that had paved the way for the National League move west.

Game 1 of the World Series was held at Comiskey Park. Veeck brought in crooner Tony Martin to sing the national anthem, sprang for 20,000 red roses for ladies in attendance, and attired the White Sox in actual white stockings for the first time anyone could remember. Veeck also decided not to festoon Comiskey Park with the traditional red, white, and blue World Series bunting, as he wanted the world to have an unadorned view of the well-scrubbed and freshly painted ballpark.[57]

Paced by a pair of two-run homers and five RBIs by Ted Kluszewski and strong pitching from Early Wynn, Chicago won the opener in a rout, 11–0. The second game was much closer. Chicago jumped on top with two runs in the first, but two home runs by Dodger second baseman Charlie Neal and one by pinch hitter Chuck Essegian bested Bob Shaw, 4–3. The teams moved to Los Angeles for the next three games. Don Drysdale gave the White Sox eleven hits but only one run in a 3–1 Dodger victory, followed by a pulsating game 4 in which Early Wynn was knocked out in a four-run third inning but the White Sox clawed back to tie the game on Sherm Lollar's three-run homer in the seventh; Gil Hodges sealed the 5–4 Dodger win with a homer in the eighth.

Bob Shaw threw a brilliant 1–0 shutout for the White Sox in game 5, before a record World Series crowd of 92,706 in the Coliseum, and Veeck's squad returned home down 3–2. Working on two days of rest, Early Wynn was routed in the fourth inning of the game, and despite Kluszewski's third home run of the Series, the White Sox fell 9–3. The Dodgers were the champions in only their second year in Los Angeles.

The disappointment of losing the Series aside, Veeck's first year of owning the White Sox was an unqualified success. The 1959 club drew 1,423,144 fans to Comiskey Park, double the attendance of 1958. The number of women attending games tripled, to about 420,000. The gross income at the gate alone—excluding the radio-TV rights and concession sales—soared to

$3,587,400. The other great satisfaction afforded Veeck was that Early Wynn won the Cy Young Award—this at a time when one award was given for both leagues.

During the season Veeck had become interested in unlocking the dynamics of the game by testing its conventional wisdom with hard numbers—a precursor to the kind of analysis that later would be embraced by Bill James and the Society for American Baseball Research. "Sent a fellow to the public library in Chicago for the summer to find out about what happened to left-handed hitters against right-handed pitching and vice versa," Veeck revealed on his syndicated radio show in 1968. "We found that a batter with better than a .300 average lost less than a half a percentage point, [those between] .276 and .300 lost 17 percentage points, [those between] .250 and .275 lost 34 percentage points, and below that, they just collapsed. In other words the good hitters weren't affected."[58]

Veeck also pioneered regarding the tax benefits of owning a team. When he bought the White Sox in 1959, he asserted that ballplayers "waste away" over time, and claimed depreciation of their contracts on the club's taxes. The Internal Revenue Service, remarkably, bought it. Since then, owners of pro sports teams have been able to use the so-called roster depreciation allowance to offset profits.

Veeck had become beloved by the South Side fans. Stan Isaacs, then a columnist with *Newsday* in town to cover a Yankees game earlier in the season, recalled an evening during Veeck's first year with the Sox: "When we rode out to the ballpark on the South Side, people recognized him all the way. When we were stopped for a light, people called to him, shouted at him that his Sox would beat the Yankees. He smiled and laughed with them. He was a pied piper of joy," said Isaacs. "He owned the city."

Veeck also addressed the issue of neighborhood safety head-on. Before he took over the Sox, the area surrounding Comiskey Park was considered dangerous, especially after games. Veeck installed lights around the park to brighten up the streets, but he pointed out that the danger was overblown. "Take a look at the police blotter and see what the crime is," he told Isaacs. "I did and saw that almost all of it was people who had thrown beer on the field or been argumentative with each other. No knife fights, robberies, or worse, as was the scuttlebutt."[59]

His penchant for charitable causes and kindnesses to those he knew were on full display. John Kuenster, staff writer and columnist with the *Chicago Daily News*, often accompanied Veeck to speaking engagements. "One time," he recalled, "we drove to Highland Park, a suburb north of Chicago, to talk about baseball to a group of kids. It was late by the time we finished, and as we headed back south to his apartment in Hyde Park, he said, 'Let's stop at the ballpark.'

"I said, 'What for, Bill? It's past midnight.'

"'That's all right,' he responded. 'It won't take long. I just want to pick something up.'

"We pulled alongside Comiskey Park on 35th Street, parked the car, and after being let in by a security guard, we climbed the stairs to the kitchen of the Bards Room. Veeck walked over to the refrigerators and extracted six raw steaks, each almost the size of a catcher's mitt. He said, 'You've got a big family, take three of these.'

"We then went back to my car, and as we pulled away from the curb, Veeck hungrily began devouring one of the raw steaks. He finished most of it, which rather astonished me."[60]

At the end of the year Veeck announced that the red-brick exterior of Comiskey Park would be painted white for the 1960 season and that a picnic area under the left-field stands would be erected for pre-game festivities. It would become a sort of "Veeckskeller" for fans.[61]

Then Veeck headed to the Winter Meetings in Florida, from which he returned in, as his friend Wendell Smith put it in the *Courier*, "a fluffy cloud of joy" because he had acquired Orestes "Minnie" Miñoso from the Cleveland Indians. Veeck brushed aside the notion that the thirty-seven-year-old Cuban was too old: "They don't ask a fellow how old he is before he hits a home run."[62]*

That winter, John Callahan recalled, Veeck "signed on to a once-a-week baseball show for WBBM radio, where I was employed as a young writer/reporter. Every time Bill Veeck walked into the WBBM newsroom he carried a book with him. One week it might be a historical treatise, another week a book of essays, the next week the latest serious examination of current affairs." Callahan went on, "Veeck was a warm and gregarious man, but imposing in his own way. I felt shy around him. But one day I asked him about what he was reading and from that moment on we forged a relationship based on a mutual love of books."[63]

---

* Miñoso was actually younger than listed officially, as he had lied about his age to qualify for service in the Cuban Army. This fact was not revealed until he published his autobiography in 1994 when the world thought he was seventy-one but he was actually sixty-eight.

Also over the winter, inspired by Mary Frances, who attended many of the White Sox home games, Veeck built a room she could use to entertain players' wives and other women. The White Sox and most other ball clubs had club rooms for the team officials and the press, in which women were not welcome. The Bards Room at Comiskey Park was, for all intents and purposes, an all-male retreat. Mary Frances wanted a new room, and she and Bill decided to hold a naming contest in the room on Valentine's Day. Carol Scott Carlson, who worked on a local magazine, was invited by William Barry Furlong of the *Chicago Daily News* to attend the event as a guest.

Carlson was recovering from minor surgery at the time: "I had a tiny bump beside my nose removed that week by a Michigan Avenue plastic surgeon and had three stitches and a small Band-Aid covering the spot," but she felt well enough to take the Elevated to Comiskey Park, where Veeck met her at the door.

"He escorted me to a large comfortably furnished room where already many people were drinking, talking, and laughing. I recognized his special guest, Ted Williams, but the rest (executives of the club) were new to me. But I was most impressed by Mary Frances Veeck. She lit up the room and made everyone feel welcome. She had a great laugh. She was tall, had shoulder-length dark hair, and was wearing a navy blue coat dress with a wide skirt, also pearl earrings, blue pumps, and short white gloves.

"The party extended, dinner was served (pheasant under glass, would you believe), and lots of champagne. It was announced that the reason for the party was to kick off the use of the room and to give it a name. . . . Ballots were distributed for the contest. I had recently read about choosing inductees for the Hall of Fame, and it struck me that this contest was set up the same way—Hall of Fame, hmmm, and it hit me: Hall of Femme.

"Sometime later the winner was announced: Hall of Femme—me. I started laughing and whoosh, the stitches split and blood was running down my chin. I raced to the bathroom, Mary Frances behind me. She put ice on the spot and the blood stopped. She also put on a large Band-Aid and we chatted and became acquainted.

"An hour or so later after more champagne the wound started bleeding again and I took up residence in the bathroom with both Veecks. Bill Veeck was smoking and I was surprised to see him pull up a pants leg and pull out an ash tray from his cork leg and tamp out the cigarette. He had fallen or bumped into something and his nose was bleeding also. This time they could not stop my bleeding and hauled me off to the nearest hospital. A bunch of the guests accompanied us. You can imagine my mortification. The original surgeon was called, I was restitched, and a huge bandage covering most of my head was applied. A bevy of cabs headed north took me home. I was pretty much out of it by then and it was at least 2 a.m. All the ladies at the party had been given a heart-shaped box of chocolates and I left mine where my roommates could see it with a note not to worry about me and not to wake me up.

"I missed work the next day but on Tuesday I was in my office with just a tiny bandage. Midmorning a messenger arrived and presented me with a mammoth twenty-pound box of chocolates—the prize for naming the Hall of Femme.

"Sometime that week there was a short piece in the sports section of the *Sun-Times* about the new room, me the winner, and, jokingly, that Furlong had punched Veeck in the nose."[64]

CHAPTER 15

Bells and Whistles

L EGENDARY PUBLIC RELATIONS MAN Aaron Cushman, who was a
co-owner and publicity director of the White Sox, recalled the night
Veeck dreamed up what became his legendary exploding scoreboard:
"Over a steak dinner and a few beers, he told me he was watching a 1939
play by William Saroyan, *The Time of Your Life*, in which a pinball machine
played a key role. An actor in the production had been playing the machine
through most of the play, and, just before the final curtain, the guy hit the
jackpot and the machine exploded with all types of visual effects and loud
music. It hit Bill right then, and he transposed the idea to the scoreboard
and wrapped it around home runs."[1]

What became a signature device for Veeck, his exploding scoreboard,
debuted in April 1960, featuring a dazzling array of flashing strobe lights,
fireworks, and explosions after every White Sox home run. Loaded with ten
mortars that fired Roman candles, it was a theatrical set piece lasting thirty-
two seconds with sounds galore—foghorns, fire engine sirens, a cavalry-
charge bugle, crashing trains, a steam calliope, the *William Tell* overture, and
a woman screaming, "Fireman, save my child." The board promised an element of surprise, as the tape controlling all the sights and sounds was designed never to repeat itself.

The scoreboard was Veeck's brainchild, but he was aided and abetted by
Abe Saperstein, who shared Veeck's unwavering love of fireworks. "They
would talk about it on the phone and laugh until tears came to their eyes.
They were like two little boys," recalled Abe's daughter Eloise.[2] Built by

Charlie Gibbs of Spencer Advertising at a cost of $350,000, it actually paid for itself through the advertising space Spencer built into it.

The fans and the press loved the scoreboard. The reaction from other teams varied. The first time the New York Yankees faced the White Sox, Bob Fishel smuggled sparklers into the Yankee dugout. These were lit every time a Yankee hit a home run and a small celebratory parade led by Casey Stengel was held in front of the Yankee dugout. Watching from the press box, Veeck chortled and deemed it "brilliant satire."[3]

Another Veeck innovation, for which fans have been grateful ever since, was the labeling of players' uniforms. As the season got under way, White Sox players' last names were sewn onto the backs of their jerseys in sizable black letters—a radical departure from tradition that had been sparked by nothing more than Veeck's noting that the increasing numbers of women coming to the ballpark wanted to know who the players were. Veeck had gotten the idea at a basketball game in Minneapolis, where he noticed that players had their names emblazoned on their warm-up jackets. When the newly labeled Sox played the Yankees in New York in early May, the spectators seemed amused that Ted Kluszewski's name appeared with the letter Z sewed on backward.* Overall the fans were quite taken with Veeck's novel idea.[4]

Veeck got an immediate call from an official of the emerging American Football League (AFL) who had seen a newspaper photo of the Kluszewski jersey and wanted Veeck's blessing to make player nameplates an AFL rule, believing they and other innovations such as the two-point conversion would give the nascent league an edge over the National Football League, especially as it tailored itself to television.[5] Veeck was toying with the notion of attracting an AFL team of his own to play at Comiskey Park and said the idea was fine with him.

In addition to adding Miñoso, Veeck had addressed the White Sox' glaring need for power by trading with the Senators for slugging first baseman Roy Sievers and trading young Johnny Callison to the Phillies for first baseman Gene Freese. And in a poignant move, with the prodding of Al Lopez,

---

* Though it's impossible to prove absolutely, it is almost certain that Veeck, a man with the eye of a newspaper copyeditor, was behind the misspelled jersey as a way of getting extra publicity for the practice of labeling players. The UPI photo of Kluszewski's back appeared in the *New York Times* and many other newspapers.

he acquired lefty Herb Score from Cleveland, giving him another chance after his terrible injury—he had been hit in the eye with a line drive early in 1957, almost losing his right eye, and had struggled to regain the brilliance he had displayed in 1956.

On June 25, 1960, his leg having deteriorated further, Veeck was back in the hospital for another amputation, his seventh, and his twelfth major hospitalization. This time his right leg was amputated to a point three inches above the knee, causing him to need to relearn using an artificial leg. Though he tossed this off as "vexing," he was in considerable pain.[6]

On August 6 Veeck held a midseason party for reporters and their wives. Bob Addie of the *Washington Post* noted that "a woman came to the table with her husband and Veeck gallantly rose to his foot." The right leg of Veeck's blue pants was neatly creased, folded in half above the knee, and pinned to the waist. Addie said that Veeck looked gaunt from his recent ordeal but that his energy and indefatigable curiosity "brooked no time for minor tragedies." He was back on the job attending to the Chicago White Sox franchise, which Addie said "could well become the richest in baseball."[7]

However strong Veeck's own spirit was, and despite their improved power, the White Sox in 1960 lacked the spark that had propelled them the year before. On August 10, they lost a game at home to the Yankees, 6–0, putting the team two and a half games out of first place. That same day, a threatening letter addressed to Veeck arrived at the ballpark. Printed crudely in block letters, it read:

FOR THE SAKE OF YOUR BALL PARK ONE WEEK FROM TODAY I WANT YOU SEND ME $10,000 . . . IF YOU THINK THIS IS A JOKE AND IF YOU DON'T DO LIKE I COMMAND YOU TO DO WE THE UNTOUCHABLES WILL BLOW THAT PARK AND SCOREBOARD UP IF YOU GO TO THE POLICE OR HER. WE WILL TAKE CARE OF YOU BOTH IN THE MEANTIME BE GETTING MONEY TOGETHER—NO BILLS JUST CHANGE . . . YOU WILL BE NOTIFIED IN A FEW DAYS WERE TO LEAVE THE MONEY OUT. PLEASE DON'T THINK YOU CAN CATCH US. REALLY IT IS IMPOSSIBLE. WE KNOW YOU'RE EVER MOVE AND EVEN HAVE A FEW OF US ON YOUR PAY ROLL.

The note went on to say that the explosion would take place during a game, and it demanded that Veeck put a personal ad in the *Chicago Tribune* saying "Poor people will do as you ask. Bill V." if he was willing to go along with the extortion.

Veeck took the matter to the Chicago office of the FBI, which tried to lift fingerprints off the letter and compared it to other ransom notes. He put the ad in the paper saying he was willing to go along, but heard nothing more, and the FBI closed the case in September.[8]

As the season ended, Veeck admitted that he had hoped for more. In August he had predicted the White Sox would win the pennant by five games, but a late-season surge never materialized and the Yankees ended on a fifteen-game winning streak, eight games ahead of the Orioles and ten ahead of the 87–67 White Sox.[9] The acquisition of Miñoso somewhat offset the disappointment of a third-place finish: he slugged 20 homers, drove in 105 runs, hit .311, appeared in the All-Star Game, was awarded a Gold Glove, and ranked fourth in the MVP voting. Herb Score (5–10) was not able to reach his old form and the team had fared poorly on the road.

The scoreboard, too, was a great satisfaction: Veeck claimed it drew an extra 5,000 fans to Comiskey Park for each game, helping him beat the 1959 attendance record by attracting 1.6 million fans. "The Monster," as it was known, was way ahead of its time. Veeck termed it "a prefabricated fresh-air theater, built for rainy-day entertainment. All you have to do is set up a closed-circuit television screen and you can entertain your fans with anything from a follow-the-bouncing-baseball community sing to the pictures of last year's World Series. You can even run interviews from the dressing room or press box. You are bound by nothing except taste and imagination."* Veeck also perfected the idea of corporate sponsorships for his giveaways. He stockpiled plastic rain capes, emblazoned with the Pepsi-Cola logo, to pass out to White Sox customers when it rained, while the bats given away on Bat Day had the Coca Cola logo on them.[10]

Veeck remained closely involved with the Chicago community and with bigger social issues in the off-season. On January 18, 1961, nine Chicago firemen were killed in what became infamously known as the Hubbard Street fire—the largest loss of firefighters in modern Chicago history. No

---

* For the 1982 season, the original exploding scoreboard was torn down to make room for a second version that included a giant Diamond Vision screen. It still shot off fireworks after a home run, but most of the zany touches of the original were lost. That version was torn down when Comiskey Park was demolished to make way for U.S. Cellular Field across the street. The new scoreboard still fires off fireworks after a home run, although now from only one side because of safety concerns. The original exploding scoreboard lives on in various incarnations, including its own Facebook page, which includes great photographs of the scoreboard in operation.

sooner had the news reached the public than Veeck was on the phone to *Chicago Sun-Times* columnist Irv Kupcinet to say that something had to be done for the dead men's families. The phone call started a chain reaction, and a fund and committee were established by the two men. Contributions totaled $90,000, and it was decided that the money would be used solely for the education of the firemen's children.*

During the last week of March 1961, as the White Sox were completing spring training, Veeck met in Chicago with Robert Paul, an official with the U.S. Department of the Interior, to discuss the refusal of Washington Redskins owner George Preston Marshall to racially integrate his National Foootball League (NFL) team. Such public bigotry in the nation's capital had forced the hand of Secretary of the Interior Stewart Udall, whose department ran the stadium in which the Redskins played. Veeck felt the only way to force Marshall to sign Negro players was for the other NFL owners to exert pressure on him, and that to secure this commitment from Commissioner Pete Rozelle, the threat of an American Football League team coming to Washington was needed. Veeck confirmed that he was working toward this end with a group in Washington headed by attorney Edward Bennett Williams, and suggested that Paul share this information with Rozelle in order to force Marshall to change his policy.[11]

Closer to home, Veeck's insistence had compelled Andy Frain, head of the nationwide ushering service—the same group that years earlier provided an honor guard at William Veeck Sr.'s funeral—to racially integrate his ushering operation, starting with Comiskey Park, where fourteen black ushers would serve patrons beginning with the 1961 season.[12]

As the 1961 season approached, however, Veeck's health failed him because of his war injuries and his habit of smoking four to five packs of cigarettes a day. On Opening Day, as he put it, he "just ran out of gas." Though Veeck's health had begun to decline sharply during his tenure as owner of the White Sox, his concern for his own well-being seemed nonexistent, and he reveled in shocking others with his own excesses. "One morning I was working in Bill's office when he and Dizzy Trout came in after being out all night," recalled Dick Hackett. "Bill took off his trademark open collar short sleeve white shirt and threw it in the waste basket. He then opened a file cabinet drawer where he kept clean shirts. He took one out and put it on

---

* It would become one of Veeck's favorite charities, and he would live to see thirteen children educated.

and said to Dizzy, 'OK, let's open the board room for breakfast,' pulling out a beer and a cigarette for each of them.[13]

In addition to the trauma of his leg, severe coughing fits had started to plague him, as did frequent headaches. He would at times suddenly lose control of the right side of his body, and occasionally he would black out. His weight was also dropping at an alarming rate. He stopped driving, afraid he would be a menace on the road, and Trout became his driver beginning in late 1960.

On April 21, 1961, Veeck entered the Mayo Clinic to undergo what was announced as a "routine checkup" but which extended into a stay of more than two weeks. Veeck would later admit: "When I walked into the clinic, I literally did not expect to walk out again." Veeck's doctors suspected he had lung cancer that had spread to his brain—a diagnosis that Veeck also believed. Tests, however, ruled out cancer, and Veeck prevailed on his doctors to be allowed to return to Chicago, under strict orders to avoid anything that might precipitate new attacks. He could not leave the apartment, and he cut down to one pack of cigarettes a day.

In the course of a few months he had become what he had always hated, an absentee owner, and this precipitated the drastic decision to sell his interest in the White Sox to Arthur Allyn Jr., the son of his old benefactor and friend and the brother of John Allyn, who would also be in the ownership group. On June 10, 1961, United Press International reported that Veeck would get $1.1 million and Hank Greenberg, who had more stock than Veeck, would receive $1.4 million. Greenberg would continue to run the club as he had been doing since Opening Day. The sale went through on the thirteenth, two days before Veeck was scheduled to go back to the Mayo Clinic.

Greenberg had the opportunity to increase his stock ownership and become a majority owner of the club. "After a lot of thought," he later recalled, "I finally decided against it. What tipped the scales against buying was the other owners: I recognized then that there was a lot of prejudice against me. I'd have had my life savings tied up in the club, and I realized that if I ever needed any help, I sure wouldn't get it from my fellow owners. It would be closed ranks against me. Strangely enough, that was the first time anti-Semitism really affected me adversely in baseball."[14]

In a scene worthy of a Frank Capra film, more than a hundred Chicago cabbies lined up in their vehicles in front of the Tribune Tower, where the White Sox sale was being finalized, and flashed their lights in tribute to Veeck as he limped from the building. "It was completely spontaneous," Mary

Frances Veeck recalled fifty years later, "and a reminder of a simpler and kinder time."[15]

White Sox ace Early Wynn, almost at the end of his Hall of Fame career, wrote a public letter to Veeck that appeared in the *Chicago Sun-Times* and summed up the loyalty that legions of players felt: "I've never written a letter like this before, especially to my boss—I've had quite a few of them. Probably the others were a little stiff-necked, but whatever the reason, I know I speak for all of us when I say that you have been a helluva lot more than just the boss. You have been a wonderful friend. All of us will always cherish your Friendship."

He told Veeck that, like the fans, the players enjoyed the exploding scoreboard. "I suppose it's because it's like having July 4 everyday, but it affects us, too. Even when we're losing 10 to 0 and Lollar, or Smitty or Sievers hits one, the scoreboard blastoff is like starting a new day." Wynn also praised Veeck for putting players' names on the backs of their jerseys, and for entertaining the players with his stunts and giveaways, and for the way he treated everyone who played for him.* "We've all had a lot of fun, Bill, and we're hoping that you'll be back with us soon. One other thing, and that is when you come back, if you don't return as a club owner, a lot of us are hoping you might consider being a Player's Representative and represent all of us in both leagues. That's how highly we think of you."[16]

In a poignant counterpoint to these encomiums, five days after the White Sox were sold, Eddie Gaedel was mugged and beaten on a Chicago street corner for $11. He somehow made his way home and died in bed three days later of a heart attack caused by the beating. He was thirty-six years old. He and Veeck had remained close—Gaedel had recently and briefly served as an usher in the box seats at Comiskey Park—but Veeck was back in his doctors' care at the Mayo Clinic and unable to attend the funeral. Bob Cain, the Detroit pitcher who had faced Gaedel on that fateful day in 1951, heard about Gaedel's death in the news and "felt obligated to go" to his funeral even

---

* One battle that Veeck had been unable to win was integrated housing during spring training. The first question that Wendell Smith of the *Courier* asked Arthur Allyn was what was he going to do about this problem. Allyn told him that if he couldn't integrate Sarasota, he would move the White Sox to a new site. When Allyn was told by the Sarasota Terrace that it would not allow black players for 1962, he bought the hotel, which housed *all* of the White Sox for 1962 as well as the Cardinals, Mets, Yankees, and Pirates. Charles Fountain, *Under the March Sun: The Story of Spring Training* (New York: Oxford, University Press, 2009).

though he had never actually been introduced to him.* No other baseball people attended. "When we got out of the car," Cain recalled, "Mrs. Gaedel, who was not a midget, ran over and hugged and kissed me. It meant something to her to see us there. I remember how small the coffin was."[17]

The day after Gaedel's death, Milton Gross dedicated his *New York Post* column to Veeck. A rumor had cropped up that Veeck had sold the White Sox so he could buy the Washington Senators. "Would that it were true!" wrote Gross. "It is not. Veeck is disposing of everything he owns because he is a very sick man."

Gross had many other things to say about Veeck, alternately negative and positive, in the column, which at times had the tone of an obituary. He ended with a story he felt was typical of Veeck, one that took place during one of the years he was out of baseball. Veeck had appeared at the Yankees spring training camp in Florida, where he was not particularly welcome. He joined the writers that evening in the press room, where he entertained those who had never before seen him flick his cigarette ashes into a hollowed-out portion of his artificial leg. The next day, he showed up in the press box for an exhibition game. Wanting something to drink but finding nothing available, he went down into the stands and returned followed by a string of soda, hot dog, ice cream, and sandwich vendors. Refreshments for everyone in the press box were on him. The Yankee brass exploded, assuming he had deliberately made them look cheap.

"Such big people," Veeck scoffed, "and they're disturbed by such little things."[18]

---

* Cain would honor Gaedel until his own death in 1997. Each year Cain mailed out hundreds of personalized Christmas cards to family and friends. Each one bore the famous photo of Gaedel watching a Cain pitch sail over his head. Printed inside was his special message: "Hope your target in the future is better than mine was in 1951."

CHAPTER 16

Peachblossom Creek

A T THE END OF JUNE 1961 THE American League paid tribute to Veeck in a statement signed by league president Joe Cronin. It was with "deep regret that the owners noted his departure and wished for his speedy recovery and return to good health and personal vibrancy." No mention, however, was made by his fellow owners of his return to baseball, which was neither welcomed nor anticipated.[1]

On July 22, 1961, the Veeck family left their home in Chicago in a station wagon emblazoned with the White Sox logo. Veeck was in the front seat with his driver and Mary Frances, who was holding their three-week-old daughter, Juliana (the scoreboard at Comiskey Park had been fired off to celebrate her birth). In the backseat were Mike, ten (nicknamed "McGillicuddy" after Connie Mack); Marya, six; Greg, five; Lisa, two; and their nurse, Patricia O'Brian.[2]

The Veecks were on their way to a nineteen-room brown shingle home on a seventeen-acre wooded estate in Easton, Maryland, on the Eastern Shore of Chesapeake Bay. The property sloped toward the banks of Peachblossom Creek and sat on a circular driveway. The estate, which the Veecks immediately dubbed "Tranquility," included a five-room guesthouse and a series of outbuildings, including a greenhouse.

The move had been instigated by Veeck's friend Jerold C. Hoffberger, brewer of National Bohemian, a local Maryland beer that Veeck avidly consumed. The beer cans sported a label alluding to Maryland as "the land of pleasant living." Thereby drawn east, Veeck asked Hoffberger to look for a place in Maryland where he and his large family could enjoy the promised tranquility. Hoffberger came up with several possible properties.[3]

"I hadn't ever been to the Eastern Shore and the doctors gave me a day off, and so we came here and looked at three houses. This was the first one," Veeck later said, also explaining that he picked the Eastern Shore over returning to the ranch in New Mexico because it was closer to a major city and to the Mayo Clinic in Rochester, Minnesota, where he knew he would return with some regularity.[4] Ever impulsive, he bought the house after only one walk-through and without Mary Frances's having seen it—"courageous of me, maybe a little foolhardy."[5]

Veeck remained ill during their early days in Easton, and two weeks after arriving he returned to the Mayo Clinic, accompanied by Mary Frances. Hank Greenberg came from Chicago to be with them, because it looked as though Veeck, whose headaches were insistent, would be slated for brain surgery. On August 19, new tests revealed that Veeck did not have a brain tumor, but he was kept at the Mayo Clinic so doctors could determine why he had lost fifty pounds and seemed to tire so quickly. Veeck was still in considerable pain, and when a rumor attributed to a "family friend" circulated that Veeck was about to get back into baseball, Mary Frances was furious: "We'll have enough trouble with him on this rest routine without something like this. Somebody seems to know a lot more about Bill than the doctors, God, and us. This report supposedly came from a friend of the family, but apparently, it's some friend we don't know about."[6]

On September 1, a spokesman for the clinic announced that Veeck's illness had been diagnosed: "slight concussions caused by violent coughing spells resulting from excessive smoking." When Veeck finally checked out of the clinic and arrived back in Maryland, he was still experiencing headaches and weighed a mere 136 pounds.[7]

The Veecks had had all of their heavy oak furniture and Navajo and Pueblo Indian art trucked in from the New Mexico ranch. A reporter visiting the estate after the Veecks had settled in wrote: "The walls of the house are covered by paintings of Indian scenes, warlike ones dominating. The mantels and shelves are adorned with massive Indian pottery and giant size katchinas, or tribal emblem figures. Those walls which are not occupied by art are lined with tanks of tropical fish."[8]

Within weeks of his return from Minnesota, and despite orders to rest, Veeck began supervising the construction of a brick pathway on his Easton property and the planting of a new field of boxwood trees to augment the existing stands. Veeck called his patch of young boxwoods "the farm club." Having given away thousands of orchids to female fans, Veeck saw his greenhouse as an opportunity to start raising them. By the end of November 1961, his health gradually improving, he could boast that "two orchids bloomed today in my hothouse."[9]

"The place was not in very good shape when the family arrived," nephew Fred Krehbiel, a frequent visitor, observed. "Over time it was transformed into a showcase. Bill was like a very good English gardener who lined his property with strong lines of boxwood and filled the inside with color."[10]

Late that year, during a telephone interview, Veeck's dislike for the Yankees surfaced anew. New York had won the 1961 World Series, and during the season Roger Maris and Mickey Mantle had chased Babe Ruth's single-season home run record, with Maris hitting a record-breaking sixty-first at season's end. Veeck lambasted the Yankees for, in his mind, marginalizing Maris's quest, claiming that the Yankees had actually sided against Maris in an effort to protect Ruth's record, and with it the sacred reputation of Yankee Stadium as the "House That Ruth Built." Far from capitalizing on what he regarded as a "once-in-a-lifetime event," he felt the Yankees had encouraged such a negative image of Maris that it brought down attendance at Yankee Stadium in the final days of his drive for the record.

The following May a profile of Veeck in the *Baltimore Sun* detailed how much his life had been transformed. For the first time, his children were the center of his life. Alluding to those from both marriages, Veeck said he had kids ranging from less than a year to twenty-five years. "You select an age, I've got a child." Pets, too, proliferated. The first thing one encountered when pulling into the circular driveway was a sign that read BEWARE OF PUPPIES. "You saw that," reporter Myra MacPherson recalled, "and you didn't stop smiling until you were on your way home."[11]

With strong encouragement by Mary Frances, Veeck was reunited with the children from his first marriage, William, Peter, and Ellen. "The only recollection I had of him was seeing his leg behind the door," said Ellen, who had not seen him since the time of his divorce from Eleanor in 1949, when she was five, until she went to Easton to see him at age eighteen.[12]

Veeck's rituals often amused his children. Greg recalled that every summer his father would take out a can of copper boat paint and paint the wooden leg so that it would match his tan. Veeck would tuck the leg around the back of his head and spin on one leg to delight his children and their friends.[13]

Mary Frances was a big proponent of holidays, which Veeck had largely ignored before marrying her. Easter egg hunts became a ritual—Veeck would always hide exactly 144 eggs, twelve dozen. Even Arbor Day was celebrated. And New Year's festivities were treasured. "There would be other New Year's Eve parties in the area," recalled Lisa, "but it always seemed like everybody from all the other parties ended up at our house." Bill and Mary Frances developed a tradition they practiced every New Year's Day of forgiving any debts owed to them by others.[14]

Given his liberal inclinations, some of Veeck's friends were puzzled by his decision to move to a locale known for its deep conservatism. "They lived in the midst of the landed gentry, most of them fiercely opposed to integration," recalled writer Jerome Holtzman. Not surprisingly, they quickly established their own ground rules. Early on, Veeck and Mary Frances decided to have a dinner party for their neighbors. By coincidence, Minnie Miñoso arrived for a visit. As cocktails were being served, Veeck announced, "An old friend of mind from Chicago will be joining us for dinner." In walked Miñoso, a coal-black Cuban. "What was really wonderful," Veeck said later, "was that Orestes had them enthralled. He was the star of the evening."[15]

A center for the family was the pool at the Talbot Country Club, less than a mile from the house. When Veeck applied for membership, the two issues that concerned the committee were that he was Jewish, albeit a convert to Catholicism, and that he was too close to African Americans and might propose one as a member. He was, ultimately, admitted, and often came to the pool late in the day to do laps before it closed, taking his prosthesis off and hopping from one end of the pool to the other on one leg.[16] "He could swim the length of the pool three times underwater and then pop out and light up a cigarette," recalled Roger Clark, then a lifeguard at the club.[17]

Over time, as his health continued to improve, Veeck entertained a steady stream of writers and reporters. "I thought they were all coming down to see him die and everyone wanted to get the last shot in," recalled his son Mike. "I would judge [the visitors were split] between those who had a great passion for having conversations with him versus those who were coming down to see if he would click out during the interview."[18]

Writer Roger Kahn visited him often during his Maryland years. "He and Mary Frances had contributed enthusiastically to the population explosion, and there were always Veeck children about for mine to play with. Plus swings, Frisbees, a trampoline, and a broad, calm estuary called Peachblossom Creek that was a gentle place until the jellyfish moved in. On arriving at Chateau Veeck, I usually saw something like this: Veeck was sitting on a couch in shorts and a polo shirt, baring what he called his 'wooden leg.' He was reading a novel, but in case he wanted a change of pace, a biography sat open on the cocktail table. Some sort of talk show barked from the television set. Above that sound, Veeck was explaining to one of the children that certainly, he would drive to the Washington airport to pick up the new pet armadillo, but the animal would not arrive until tomorrow."*

Then he would acknowledge the Kahn family: "And, oh, yes, hi, to all of us and did I know that if the establishment kept barring him from baseball, he might open a bookshop or run for the Senate or even pass the bar exam and sue them all. He was drinking beer. He was always drinking beer. And smoking mentholated cigarettes. No one ever accused Bill Veeck of running a health club."[19]

"I spent an afternoon with him at his home in Maryland," remembered writer John Holway. "He read a book a day and drank a beer a minute and he could talk on any subject, from Aquinas to Steinbeck." Writer Stan Issacs believed that "Veeck had a way of turning moderation on its ear, even in others. I spent a night with Bill at his place on the Eastern Shore of Maryland. I don't smoke and I usually don't stay up late, but he had me up all night smoking Dutch Schimmelpenninck cigars and talking baseball and life. I loved it."[20]

THE MOVE TO Maryland and finally getting a treatable diagnosis opened a new chapter in Veeck's life: that of a writer and raconteur. Hank Greenberg brought a New York writer whose work he liked, Ed Linn, to Easton for a short lunch. Greenberg wanted Veeck to tell his life story and was convinced that Linn could make it happen.[21] Veeck agreed, a contract between them was signed, and Mary Frances suggested the title, *Veeck—as in Wreck*. The two would meet intermittently as Linn commuted from his home in New

---

* One of Veeck's friends from Cleveland asked Greg, then about ten, what he wanted for a pet, and he said he wanted an armadillo. The first one arrived, and he drove with his father to the Baltimore-Washington International Airport and put the wooden crate containing the animal in a greyhound cage. It was dead when they got home, but it was insured. When the second one arrived it clawed its way through the package and the greyhound cage.

York. Linn would prove to be the perfect voice and foil for Veeck. Both men were veterans of World War II, eschewed neckties, and seemed to lack a surrender response. Linn helped Veeck find his voice. "Part of Ed's job was to tone it down to keep Dad out of court," quipped Greg Veeck, who recalled that the two men and their families became very close friends.[22]

Veeck, who had started the book with the hope of getting it all on tape before he shuffled off, now held the final product in his hands.[23] On the eve of publication, Veeck told a *Washington Post* reporter, "I only hope we sell as many copies as we get libel suits."

The book became an instant best seller in 1962, loved by fans but hated by the owners for its belligerence toward them. Red Smith said that it purported to be an autobiography but was better described as "380 pages of aggravated assault."[24] Columnist Milt Gross said Veeck "has bared his teeth and is chewing with obvious relish at the baseball hands which slapped him down." Gross observed that Veeck had dropped the needle and picked up a hatchet to do a job on Ford Frick, depicting him as a man who never used his power to help the game. Gross ended his column on the book with a caveat: "This is a book that should be marked 'for adults only.' It would be a shame if the kids, who take so much pleasure in what transpires on the field, should learn so early in life what goes on off it."[25]

The book closed on what Arthur Daley of the *New York Times* termed "a bright, defiant note" that would be quoted for years to come: "Sometime, somewhere, there will be a club no one really wants. And then Ole Will will come wandering along to laugh some more. *Look for me under the arc-lights, boys. I'll be back.*"[26]

At the time of Veeck's death, Ed Linn wrote in the *New York Times* that after going over the manuscript for the presumed final time, the pair had had what Linn termed "the only real argument we were ever going to have. That late in the game, Veeck had decided that he had given Rogers Hornsby a worse pummeling than an old guy, long out of baseball, was worth. I accused Bill—if you can believe this—of running scared, and he informed me that it didn't matter what I thought. 'It's my book, and those two pages are out.'

"He was, of course, right on both counts. In order to explain away my temper tantrum before I left the next day, I said, 'You have to understand, Bill, that by this time, I think I made you up.'

" 'Don't worry about it,' Bill said. 'You have to understand that by this time, I think I wrote the book.'

"It was the perfect response. From that day on, we understood each other completely. Meaning that when Veeck got blacklisted from baseball for turning out such an honest, hard-hitting book, I could decide whether I wanted to be ashamed of myself."[27]

On June 19, 1962, while Bill was at the Mayo Clinic for a checkup, Mary Frances delivered their third son, Christopher, Veeck's ninth child in all. Veeck returned to Chicago in July 1962 to promote his book and put in an appearance at a White Sox game, where the exploding scoreboard was detonated as the organist, recalling Veeck's father's pen name, played "Bill Bailey Won't You Please Come Home." Veeck was immediately besieged by reporters, and he told them he was in town to push the book and "shop for a new wooden leg." Pointing to the leg he'd come with, he said: "This one is being held together by nuts, bolts, and baling wire—like an old Model-T."[28]

Back in Chicago in September for a quick job promoting a music festival, Veeck was accompanied for a day by William Braden of the *Chicago Sun-Times*, who was amazed by his manic ability to talk about anything and everything. "Between bites of a double corned-beef sandwich," he wrote, "Veeck discusses the nature of disasters, the geometry of baseball, the Milwaukee Braves, democracy, *Treasure Island*, Herman Melville, the development of the Ford Trimotor, friendliness, the sea literature, luck, freewill, telephone numbers, jazz, and Medicare, among other things."

Melville? he was asked. "Ahab is a great character, but the rest of *Moby-Dick* is not very special," Veeck replied.

Everywhere Veeck went, people approached him, and he responded with glee and a kind word. While in an elevator on his way to an appointment, a woman craned her neck and addressed Veeck. "Hope you will remember me," she said. "It was twenty years ago, and—"

"Knox, Indiana," said Veeck.

The woman beamed.[29]

Among the friends and writers visiting him in Maryland were occasional newcomers seeking mentorship. Among these was Pat Williams, then twenty-two, who made the first of many visits to see Veeck in September 1962. Then a minor-league catcher, Williams believed his future lay in the front office of a professional team. Having read *Veeck—as in Wreck* on its publication, he wanted in-person inspiration from its author.

"I approached him on the porch. He shut the book and smiled a broad and unassuming smile." Williams quickly realized this was how Veeck rested—that he and other visitors were part of Veeck's recovery, as were "reading with his wooden leg propped next to him, gardening, refinishing early American furniture, raising his six children, along with a dozen dogs, a horse, multiple fish tanks, gerbils, guinea pigs, and an armadillo. He had a guesthouse that held a dozen people, had a beer tap connected to a keg in the wall, had a game room in an adjacent building, and had a massive Seeburg automatic jukebox."

Veeck immediately befriended Williams, and the two had a number of tutorial sessions as Williams worked his way into front offices in baseball and basketball.* The visits were intense and informative: "Once I came in and Veeck ignored me for a half hour. Didn't say anything to me. Didn't even look up. He was in the dining room, helping one of his daughters fashion a papier-mâché re-creation of Teddy Roosevelt and the Rough Riders storming San Juan Hill. He was gluing. He was cutting. He was irretrievably lost in the moment. When he was finished, he stood. 'Pat,' he said, 'let's talk. I'm ready now.'

"And then it was about me."[30]

The trips to Chicago had convinced his doctors to give Veeck a green light to go back to working full-time. He started talking about his "next team," admitting what others had surmised—that Easton was a perfect perch from which he could attempt to gain control of either of the two ball clubs he most wanted, the Washington Senators or the Baltimore Orioles. He regarded Washington as a great untapped baseball market ready to be developed, and saw Baltimore as the team that was rightfully his.[31]

In October 1962, Veeck made an attempt to buy the expansion Washington Senators as the leader of a group that also included Hank Greenberg, Rudie Schaffer, and Nate Dolin, who had been an associate in his days with the Indians. When baseball expanded at the end of the 1960 season, Minneapolis–St. Paul was granted a franchise. Calvin Griffith, who had inherited the Washington Senators from his uncle Clark, had persuaded his fellow owners to let him move his troubled club there, thereby granting Washington the expansion instead. The new Senators were owned at the time by a group headed by Elwood "Pete" Quesada, but the team had lost money in its first two seasons, coming in last both times. Veeck and a group had tried to acquire the club when it was first created in 1960. Now Quesada quickly denied that the team was for sale, but Veeck had clearly identified himself as a potential buyer.[32]

---

* Up to and including senior vice president of the National Basketball Association's Orlando Magic, a position Williams held as this was written in 2011.

Three months later, in late January 1963, Veeck was again reported to be headed back into baseball in partnership with Nate Dolin, who confirmed that he had placed a deposit of $500,000 for the Washington Senators, hoping to buy them for $5 million. But almost as soon as their intentions were made known, the club was snapped up by investment broker James Johnston and his partner James H. Lemon, who quickly acquired 80 percent of the stock.

If baseball was shutting Veeck out, there seemed to be no limit to what Veeck was willing to involve himself with during his early years on the Eastern Shore. In 1963, Maryland's governor, J. Millard Tawes, was ready to veto the state's costly plan for a pavilion at the 1964 New York World's Fair. The pavilion was to feature an elegant restaurant. The head of the fair committee, a friend of Veeck's, called Veeck for help.

"He was in Annapolis and I told him to drive right over," Veeck recalled. "When he arrived, I drew a picture of the wharf—that was to be the exhibit. They could sell Maryland seafood and beer. The former cost had been something like $1.2 million. I told him this would cost exactly $856,421.19.

"My friend asked how I knew what the cost would be.

"I told him: 'Never mind that, just talk to Tawes.'

"So later if the cost turned out to be $1.6 million, what could Tawes do once he had put up $856,421.19."[33]

Veeck then presented the proposal to a meeting of the Maryland World's Fair Commission, embellishing the idea that the wharf would be over water, allowing for real fishing and crabbing. A board member suggested that perhaps a waterman carving duck decoys or a fisherman mending nets could be featured.

"Exactly," Veeck replied, "there must be action."[34]

Veeck's vision prevailed, and the pavilion was a success.

Veeck was also active in the burgeoning civil rights movement. When he discovered that Negroes were allowed only in the balcony of the local Easton movie house, he initially sat in the balcony with them.[35] He then decided to set up his own impromptu movie theater. Contacting Harold "Spud" Goldstein and other friends in Hollywood, he arranged to have films flown in that would be shown in his guesthouse for all the kids in the area.[36] The movies became a prime attraction for the children who accompanied their parents to the estate. Larry Doby Jr. recalls annual summer visits with his family, cherished memories of his childhood and of the friendship he, like his father, developed with Veeck.[37]

Nearby Cambridge, Maryland, was a hotbed of the civil rights struggle, and during their time in Easton, the Veecks hosted movement leaders at their home. Veeck also offered his estate as a place where both sides in the struggle could come together to talk—and often argue. At a May 1964 dinner, black and white factions shared the table. "Bill had decided he might as well clear up their misunderstandings," journalist Morris Siegel reported. "When I left, a police chief and several others were hollering real loud, and Bill was playing it cool."[38] Whether the local commander of the Maryland National Guard, Jesse Jackson, or Dick Gregory, visitors found the house a place of compromise and conciliation.[39] Indeed, many of those who visited Veeck in Easton found that he was most interested in talking about human rights, athletes in revolt, or the plight of the left-handed individual, such as himself, in a right-handed world.

Others of his ideas bordered on the quixotic. Beginning with a new syndicated column in 1963 and going forward at least into 1965, Veeck became a lone advocate for a return to the baseball employed in the dead ball era, when the game was allegedly played with a much less lively baseball.* Veeck was asking baseball to consciously deaden the baseball to cut down on the number of home runs. "The fans wouldn't mind—they don't like cheap home runs anyhow," he explained in a speech at the National Press Club in Washington. But even Veeck supporter Jim Murray, a columnist with the *Los Angeles Times*, disagreed with his friend: "To me, if they make the ball dead, the game will soon follow. Lilies will be growing in the infield."

Veeck persisted, reasoning that the dead ball would make pitchers work faster and throw fewer pitches. He told an audience in Cleveland: "The lively ball forces the pitcher to work on every batter. If he makes one mistake the ball is gone—and often the game as well. I've got it figured out that 40 percent more pitches are made in today's game than the good old days."

---

* The term is a misnomer, as most baseball historians agree that the era ended in 1920 with rule changes (banning the spitball and other trick pitches and freak deliveries, replacing discolored and scuffed balls with shiny new ones) and use of better-quality materials, not with the change in the ball. The era was characterized by the use of the hit-and-run, the stolen base, the sacrifice, and the bunt; batters choked up on the bat and were loath to take hard swings; runs were at a premium; and ballparks had huge dimensions. The era ended when Babe Ruth began swinging for the fences.

The dead ball campaign went nowhere, though it did underscore Veeck's ongoing ability to get publicity on the thinnest of premises.[40]

VEECK HAD TRADED in his artificial leg and now walked, like Long John Silver, on a peg.[41] In Cleveland in June 1963 to promote the paperback edition of his book, he read about a young girl going through the trauma he had faced. "Dear Christina," he wrote to Christina Simco, an eleven-year-old East Cleveland girl recovering from surgery that removed her right leg because of cancer of the hip, "I have been reading about you in the *Plain Dealer* and decided to write because there is such a great similarity between our experiences. You see, I have but one leg, and I had to have mine removed in Cleveland. I didn't want them to remove my leg. I had 10 or 11 operations performed in a vain attempt to keep it. I know exactly the thoughts passing through your mind." Veeck then advised her that in reality, she could do anything she wanted to do, and do it just about as well. He concluded by telling her not to hesitate to call: "You see, those of us whose feet can only get half as cold have to stick together."[42]

There were constants that Veeck displayed in dealing with the pain and suffering that afflicted him. He not only made light of it ("Suffering is overrated, it doesn't teach you anything" was a line he often used when asked about pain) but also hid it. As best he could, Veeck even shielded his children from his constant ordeal. "I walked in one day and he had this look on his face of extreme pain," Greg remembered. "I said, 'Dad?' and he turned around blushing. I was never supposed to see it, but he wore five or six wool stump socks to keep his blisters under control. He had blisters half as large as his butt." Greg watched as his father's left leg took more and more punishment. "Eventually the good knee was so big that you couldn't look at it," he said.[43]

Veeck had become a source of inspiration for many with disabilities and, save for those times during which he was too ill himself, always had time for others in the same boat. He could also inspire indirectly, as John Herd Thompson, professor of history at Duke University, could attest. "My father, Joe Thompson, was a Canadian World War II amputee—a lieutenant in the Canadian Army who lost his right leg in late September '44. He was active in (and the president of for some years) the Winnipeg branch of the War Amputations of Canada. He and his mates in the War Amps of Canada greatly admired Bill Veeck—they tried to do in Canada what Veeck was doing in the

USA, to help Korean War and civilian amputees deal with the shock of losing a limb and cope with their disabilities. I can't *prove* that Veeck inspired the Canadian War Amps programs for visiting amputees and helping them to adjust, but I'm certain that Veeck was an influence and an inspiration to them. We had a copy of *Veeck—as in Wreck* in our house, and my father (who rarely or never read a book) devoured it."[44]

AT THE END of the 1963 baseball season, a strong and vocal minority, mostly in the press, wanted Veeck back in baseball in some form or another. Most articulate was Jim Murray. If Veeck had been just a gadfly, Murray said, he could have been dismissed, which baseball had tried, but "the compelling national interest of the American League is that it defeats the Yankees once in a while." Murray pointedly remarked that since 1946, the Yankees had lost only three pennants, and teams created by Bill Veeck had won two of them.

Noting that Ford Frick was making retirement plans, David Condon suggested in the *Chicago Tribune* that Veeck might make an ideal commissioner, the one person who could put baseball back in competition with pro football and regain the confidence of the fans. But he knew most of the owners didn't want Veeck back in any capacity. "They don't want him as an owner. They don't want him as a general manager. Some I know don't even want him as a paying customer, although it is an unwritten baseball rule that an owner never passes up a dollar from any source."[45]

Veeck immediately called Condon and proposed what he would do as commissioner. First and foremost, he would base his commissionership on that of the late Bert Bell of the National Football League, who equalized the distribution of talent. "Baseball owners must come to realize that if we are to sell the game on its merits, the talent must be sufficiently distributed to equalize competition." He pointed out that this was the main reason the Green Bay Packers could exist in the NFL. "You know how long Green Bay would last in pro baseball? 30 min, I'd say."[46]

But the year ended sadly for Veeck with the assassination of John F. Kennedy, a man he and Mary Frances deeply admired. Following the assassination, Veeck flew from Easton to Washington with his son Mike to pay his respects in person. His nephew Fred Krehbiel joined them, and the three took their place in line to pass by the closed coffin. Veeck's war service in the Marine Corps was well known and his disability obvious, and members of the Marine Corps guard encouraged the three of them to take a place at the front of the line. A request then came from a representative of the Kennedy family to move forward, but Veeck declined, insisting that he was just an ordinary citizen standing in line with his son and his nephew. "We stood in line for fifteen hours," remembered Mike. His father's pants were soaked in blood from the standing, but they held their positions in the cold.[47]

Veeck's plan for the Maryland Pavilion at the 1964 World's Fair had been adopted and was under construction when *Popular Science Monthly* asked him to design "The Perfect Ball Park," which was depicted in the March 1964 issue of the magazine: a 50,000-seat single-use baseball stadium with a retractable roof, removable sod, foam rubber seat pads, and moving walkways. Human vendors would be replaced by roaming robots. It gave Veeck another chance to take a poke at the stodgy baseball establishment. "Baseball has never been accused of being progressive" was his lead to the article, which continued, "In the words of one ballpark operator, 'If it wasn't done in 1901, it can't amount to much.' "[48]

On August 19, 1964, Bill's mother, Grace DeForest Veeck, died at her home in Hinsdale and was buried under a marker that did not list the year of her birth—a final attempt to obscure the fact that she had married a man who was younger than she was. She had lived a comfortable life in good measure because of the sale of her shares in the Cubs.[49]

In 1964 Veeck became a commentator on ABC's *Wide World of Sports*, which—wisely—taped his pieces to guard against libel. Being on the show put Veeck on the road to major-league cities, where he generated considerable press attention beyond the broadcasts themselves. He was anywhere and everywhere during the mid-1960s, including Harlem Globetrotter events and fund-raisers. Just showing up somewhere often yielded ink. "Bill Veeck was sitting in the manager's office at the White Sox ball park yesterday," commented David Condon in the *Chicago Tribune*, "[and] looked more at home than Whistler's Mother in the rocker."[50]

Veeck continued to let others know that he still wanted to get hold of the Senators or, as he told several writers, the Cubs. "Either of those two would be great fun. The potential with both of them is tremendous," he said at a moment in the 1965 season when the Cubs were in ninth place and had lost ten of their last thirteen games, adding, "Both have more or less fallen into evil ways."[51]

He lobbied constantly to have Hank Greenberg made commissioner. He also gave a steady stream of interviews to reporters who never seemed to get enough of his fresh and/or irreverent take on baseball and the world beyond it. It was as if the writers now needed Veeck as much as he had needed them in the past. The game was becoming blander and more corporate, and Veeck was, as one of the Cleveland papers called him, "baseball's vitamin pill."

His interviews became more and more far-ranging and increasingly political. "Uncle Ho [Chi Min] is a mystic," he told Scott Smith of the *Washington Star* while discussing the Vietnam war in 1966. "I don't think his people are fighting for a cause. They're fighting, I think, because we bomb them. You drop bombs on some guy's rice paddy and he gets mad at you."[52]

At the end of 1966, Veeck published another book written with Ed Linn, *The Hustler's Handbook*, a series of caustic essays on various aspects of baseball. It had been preceded by excerpts in *Look* and *Sports Illustrated* and had one constant refrain—that baseball owners were not to be trusted to do the right thing. A wistful chapter entitled "Where Are the Drunks of Yesteryear?" contained the observation: "Deplore it if you will, but Grover Cleveland Alexander drunk was a better pitcher than Grover Cleveland Alexander sober." Another chapter addressed the issue of race, which Veeck discussed with an edge: "The National League is superior to the American League these days because . . . the National League stocked up on Negro players while the American League was sitting back and admiring how nicely the Yankees were getting along without them."

The big surprise was the fifty pages devoted to the 1919 Black Sox and the scandal that had ensued after that year's World Series. When Veeck had taken over the White Sox in 1959, he had sent his nephew Fred Krehbiel down to clean out three adjacent storerooms underneath Comiskey Park. Krehbiel recalled, "I spent days down there getting rid of junk. In the third room in the back there were shelves with a door behind which was this notebook," which Veeck identified as belonging to Harry Grabiner.[53]

An official for the White Sox during the Black Sox scandal, Grabiner had kept the notes that a private detective had prepared about corruption on the team. Veeck revealed the notes in his book, with this observation: "Looking back at the Black Sox scandal from this comfortable distance it becomes easy to take another drag on your cigarette and sneer that everybody did their best to cover up everybody. Everybody from the Commissioner on down. *Everybody.* From the Commissioner on down."[54]

The most interesting detail in the notebook, on page 27, was the name

Eugene Milo Packard attached to the chilling words "1918 Series fixer."* "Oh Boy," wrote Veeck. "That was the Series where the players struck before the start of the fifth game for a higher share of the receipts." This was, he well knew, also the Series involving the Chicago Cubs that his father had covered and criticized as a journalist just before being hired by the team. Packard had pitched for the Cubs in 1916 and for two games in 1917 before being traded to the St. Louis Cardinals, for whom he pitched in 1918.[55]

This section of *The Hustler's Handbook* succeeded in making the worst scandal in the history of the game look even worse, even more widespread, and perhaps like it was still lurking: "Anyone who thinks the moral climate of the United States today is higher than it was in 1919 hasn't looked out the window lately." The critics loved *The Hustler's Handbook*, some calling it one of the best baseball books ever written.[56]

EARLIER IN 1966 Veeck had launched *The Bill Veeck Show*, a five-minute radio show that aired daily on eighty commercial stations and worldwide on Armed Forces Radio. Veeck was introduced by announcer Bill Cunningham as "That outspoken friend of the fans," or "Now, the explosive man, Bill Veeck."

Unscripted, Veeck spoke in his own distinctive vernacular. He was formal with names: There was Lawrence Doby and Leroy Paige, of course, and he referred to Stan Musial as Stanislaw, Boudreau as Louis (pronounced as if he were a French king), and Aaron and Greenberg as Henry. In hours of broadcasting, he never used the word *woman*, instead always referring to "the female of the species." A notoriously slow infielder became "no gazelle of the greensward"; spring training was simply "spring," as if nothing else was going on; sports were called "ath-a-letics." As always, he called his father "my daddy." His declarations were memorable: "A ballclub is no better than its scouts," or "Beware of pitchers who think. They can get you killed."

On these broadcasts Veeck loved to talk about Satchel Paige, whom he termed the ninth, tenth, and eleventh wonders of the world. "He could still pitch in the majors because he is better than half the relief pitchers in the

---

* Packard is mainly known today for his value in baseball trivia contests. On August 3, 1918, while with the Cardinals, he gave up 12 earned runs in a game and did not take the loss. That feat was never matched.

big leagues." Paige, he stated, had more ways to cheat legitimately than anyone else he knew. Veeck added with discernable glee, "Larceny is a part of
this great old game."

The show was spontaneous and likely to strike out in any direction at any
point. Veeck would never miss an opportunity to refresh his reputation as the
burr under the saddle of the New York Yankees. On one show, the subject of
what city produced the best hecklers came up. Veeck responded: "There was
a guy in Philadelphia who was so good that I finally paid him to root against
the Yankees." When Cunningham told him on a fall 1966 broadcast that one
of his Yankee nemeses, George Weiss, had retired from the position he had
taken with the expansion New York Mets, Veeck said: "Happiness is not a
thing called George. He was a good operator, but he could have been a front
man for a string of mortuaries. He could have sold everyone in Vermont a
tombstone. The great triumvirate of murder, manslaughter, and mayhem are
all gone—Topping, Webb, and Weiss. I'll miss them like the seven-year itch."

Veeck reveled in the Yankees disastrous 1966 season as they finished in
last place, twenty-six and a half games behind the Baltimore Orioles and
"playing like a tenth-place club." Veeck remembered: "They used to beat
you with espirit de corps; now they are losing because they lack it." Toward
season's end, on September 21, 1966, the Yankees drew only 413 fans to a
home game, which Veeck likened to "going to a nightclub and being the
only person there." He mentioned gleefully that this was the smallest crowd
in the majors that year and the lowest at the stadium since World War II.
Allegedly, the fact that Yankee announcer Red Barber mentioned the attendance on the air was enough to get him fired. Veeck defended Barber with
relish, caustically remarking that the Yankees were starting their rebuilding process by firing the announcer.

But after crowing that he had "waited twenty-five years to see them ab-
jectly humiliated" and that he had "enjoyed every second" of their fall into
the cellar, Veeck admitted in a later show that watching the Yankees crum-
ble was not as much fun as he had thought it would be. "It is not good for
baseball to let them languish. Their farm system is depleted. . . . Let them
sneak out of the cellar."

On the air, Veeck took deep umbrage at the maltreatment of people with
physical disabilities. In Veeck's opinion, a ruling by the National Federation
of High Schools prohibiting amputees from playing football set an "all-time
track record for stupidity." As a result of the ruling, Dave Bartlett of North
Chicago found he was banned because his leg was amputated below the knee

and he wore an artificial leg. The federation reasoned that the 220-pound, six-foot-four lineman might hurt himself if he played any more games. What really irked Veeck was that the federation had the backing of the American Medical Association, which he insisted "hasn't been right since 1906. They have a worse win-and-loss record than the Chicago Cubs." He concluded, "Point here is that the kid, his parents, his doctor, and his coaches all want him to play. He was second-team all-conference in his prior year, and this will cost him his senior year and presumably a scholarship."[57]

One of Veeck's prime targets on the radio and elsewhere was the new commissioner, William Dole "Spike" Eckert, a former three-star general who had been selected in November 1965 from a field of more than 150, after a fifteen-month search, to replace Ford Frick. Recommended by Air Force Gen. Curtis LeMay, who had turned down the job himself, Eckert was a poor choice but an ideal foil for Veeck—the personification of all that he thought was wrong with baseball in the mid-1960s.*

Veeck's relentless disdain for the sitting commissioner was based on Eckert's stodginess, his timidity, and the fact that his baseball knowledge was extremely limited. "His baseball background is shallower than the premier of Japan's. The Japanese premier has seen more games."[58] On one broadcast Veeck noted that when Eckert attended the All-Star Game, "people came to see if there was such a person."

In contrast, he was effusive when discussing those he admired, such as Marvin Miller, the new executive director of the Major League Baseball Players Association. "I talked with him a few days ago," Veeck related. "Miller is a professional negotiator. The tougher they make it for him, the tougher he'll make it for them." Veeck was delighted to see someone represent the players.

His protégé Pat Williams, having successfully entered management, had been setting attendance records with the Class A Spartanburg Phillies in South Carolina. Veeck noted that during the 1966 season Williams had staged an Impress Bill Veeck Night—replete with a strong man who pulled loaded automobiles around the bases with his teeth. But what really impressed him was one particular feature of the park: "It has the finest ladies'

---

* Eckert inherited a legal mess in that the same causes that had brought the Braves to Milwaukee from Boston in 1953 took the team away again. In the early 1960s, the team's performance tailed off, as did their remarkable attendance. Eyeing greener pastures in the South, new owners jilted Milwaukee and moved the team to Atlanta after the 1965 season.

rooms I have ever seen in any minor league. This is second only to a winning team in importance." Praising Williams, he concluded, "Minor-league
baseball isn't dead, but too often the guys who run it are."[59]

In early 1967, Veeck's health hit a bump, and he was uncharacteristically
out of the news, spending much of his time in Easton. At this time, months
after his old friend Abe Saperstein had died in the spring of 1966, Saperstein's daughter Eloise asked him to take over management of the Harlem
Globetrotters, but the call came at one of those not uncommon moments
when Veeck felt too sick to tackle a new responsibility. "It would have been
like a hand in glove—can you imagine Bill Veeck running the Globetrotters?" Eloise said many years after the fact.[60]

A GREAT ADMIRER of Martin Luther King Jr., Veeck was able to march in
the slain civil rights leader's funeral procession in Atlanta in April 1968.
Photos of the event in *Ebony* suggest that Veeck, Sammy Davis Jr., and
Stokely Carmichael were the only tieless men in the procession.[61]

In the wake of the assassination came the riots. Opening day in Washington saw District of Columbia Stadium used as a bivouac for the National
Guard, including Pfc. Eddie Brinkman, the Senators shortstop, who was
photographed in his National Guard uniform standing outside the stadium.
But neither these urban disturbances nor the assassination of Robert F. Kennedy that summer deterred Veeck from taking a third swing at getting the
Washington Senators. Owner James Johnston was ill and Veeck knew the
team would soon come on the market; he had a standing offer in place to
buy the club. If he was successful, he wanted to employ former Yankees star
catcher Elston Howard, who had retired after the 1968 season, as his manager. Howard would then become the first black manager in the game.

"We were in St. Louis for the World Series when Elston got a phone call
from Veeck, who at the time was trying to buy the Washington Senators,"
Howard's wife, Arlene, recalled. "We agreed to have breakfast at the Jefferson
Hotel. I came along and heard the whole thing. . . . As we talked over breakfast, I couldn't believe my ears. Veeck wanted Elston to manage his baseball
team. When he asked Elston if he would like to try managing, Elston laughed
and said, 'Would I like to finish this breakfast and go on breathing?' Elston
was so excited. He and Veeck shook hands and agreed that Elston would be
his manager starting in 1969. The only catch was that Elston would have to
wait until the deal went down before he could tell anyone."[62]

Johnston died in October and the team was now officially for sale. Veeck and his old partner from Cleveland, Nate Dolin, offered $6 million, which they could have increased to $6.5 million. Bob Short, an entrepreneur who had earlier owned the Minneapolis Lakers in basketball and moved them to Los Angeles, seemed to come out of nowhere with an offer of $9 million, which was matched by Veeck's old partner Bob Hope, but was then topped by Short.

"Of course," Arlene Howard lamented after Veeck's bid failed, "Elston never got to manage the Senators, or any other major-league team." Short promptly hired Ted Williams as his manager.[63]

If Veeck had failed to help Howard, the same could not be said of Satchel Paige. Frazier Robinson, who had caught for Paige and played with many other legendary Negro leaguers, noted in his autobiography: "I remember when Satchel wasn't eligible for his pension. He didn't have enough time in the majors so in 1968 Bill Veeck convinced Billy Bartholomay, the owner of the Braves, to hire Satchel on as a coach and keep him until he was eligible for his pension." When the story of Paige's hiring by Atlanta was announced, a common headline was "Baseball Displays a Heart."[64]

A month after Paige was hired by Atlanta, guaranteeing his $250-a-month pension, and after Veeck had met with the Howards, Dave Condon noted in his column that it had been ten years since Veeck had taken over the White Sox. In Easton, restless and looking for a source of income and an outlet for his energies now that he was out of the running for the Senators, Veeck said he was eager to have a "piece of the real action."[65]

Two weeks later, rumors were rampant that Veeck was about to get that action. "Look for Bill Veeck, the onetime Chicago White Sox boss, to emerge from his Easton, Md., country home to announce a new venture far removed from Chicago and the baseball that he loves so much," wrote Robert Wiedrich in the *Chicago Tribune*. "It will be an East Coast–based venture, but still in the area of sports."[66]

CHAPTER 17

Off to the Races

A T AGE FIFTY-FOUR, VEECK TURNED to another sport: horse racing. On November 20, 1968, he became president and chief operating officer of Suffolk Downs, a racetrack in East Boston, Massachusetts, a stone's throw from Logan Airport.

"Don't misunderstand me though," he told the Associated Press. "I still think baseball is the greatest game there is. It has to be because of all that we've done to it." He insisted that he was totally committed to his new position, vowing to build a home on the track grounds. "I don't believe in absentee ownership. I'm going to stay with it. I figured this is the last go-around for me. They're going to cart me out of here."[1]

The collapse of the Washington Senators deal had left him feeling at loose ends, and he and his old partner Nate Dolin had been looking at this deal for more than a year. He was to be paid a salary of $50,000 a year plus an unlimited expense account from Realty Equity Corp., the conglomerate that held the track as part of its portfolio of real estate holdings. The media described Veeck as a part owner in the track. Actually, he and Dolin would get 10 percent of the profits over $1 million and were given a five-year option to buy 15 percent of the operation. Veeck and Dolin reasoned that they could use the 10 percent override to purchase the options.

At the time Veeck took over, the track hosted both thoroughbred and harness races. It was an ill-kept 200-acre property commonly known as "Sucker Downs" or "Suffering Downs." Red Smith said it had "the stately charm of an abandoned noodle factory," while Larry Merchant called it "an outdoor roulette wheel with all the warmth of an Alaskan oil field, all barbed wire and pay toilets."[2]

Before the first season, Veeck told Red Smith that he intended to learn the business from "the hooves up" and intended to improve the physical plant and hike the stakes in order to bring in the better stables and attract young people. "Unlike most people who buy into baseball, I'm not going to become a 20-minute expert. There could be several things I don't know about racing, but if people go to the track to have fun, there's something I do understand."[3]

During the winter of 1968–69, as Veeck prepared for a new kind of Opening Day, a search was in progress to replace baseball commissioner William Eckert, who had been let go in December, three years before his contract was up. Eckert lacked experience, charisma, public image, and personality, all of which added up to an inability to use showmanship to sell the game— the very thing that, as many writers were quick to point out, Veeck had been preaching for years.

Once more Veeck plumped hard for the appointment of Hank Greenberg, whom he called "the most qualified man in the country." However, Greenberg took himself out of the running, insisting that the only thing that would get him back into baseball would be another co-ownership with Veeck. With tongue firmly in cheek, Veeck brought up the possibility of himself being made commissioner but then ruled it out, noting that his confirmation vote would be the first time both leagues were unanimous on anything: 24–0 against him.[4]

On February 4, 1969, Bowie Kuhn, an attorney for the law firm that represented the National League, was named commissioner. His strongest credential was that he had won a 1966 antitrust court battle clearing the way for the Braves' move from Milwaukee to Atlanta. Veeck was quick to toss a grenade in Kuhn's direction two weeks into the new season, charging baseball with having juiced up the ball to manufacture home runs. "Since wild William knows a great deal more about baseball than he does about horse racing," wrote Arthur Daley in the *New York Times*, "he can command fancier headlines by jabbing his mischievous needle into the diamond sport than he can for a not-so-learned opinion on the turf." Kuhn was charged with proving Veeck wrong, a difficult task since two spring training games had, in fact, been played that year using a livelier ball. The experiment went no further, but it had put the term "rabbit ball" back in the news.[5]

In April 1969, on the eve of his first sixty-day series of race meetings,

Veeck brought his old friend and business partner Rudie Schaffer aboard to bolster his new track operation. Two hours before the April 19 opening, Veeck noticed 150 horseplayers waiting in the rain outside the locked front gate, waiting to get in.

"What's the trouble?" he asked.

"The armored car with the change hasn't arrived," said an attendant.

"Let 'em in anyway," Veeck roared so that all could hear.

The doors swung open, and 150 fans saved themselves the new bargain admission of $1.50 that Veeck had initiated.

A cry went up: "Thank you, Mr. Veeck."

"It's Bill," he bellowed back, announcing his return to the game—albeit a new one.[6]

For this Opening Day, the fans were treated to $1 million in track improvements that had been engineered with dispatch when Veeck took over. The barbed-wire fence that encircled the track was gone. "Was it supposed to keep people in or out?" Veeck asked. With malice aforethought, Veeck himself yanked artificial plastic flowers from their beds, to be replaced with the real thing. The class distinction between clubhouse and grandstand seating was erased with a flat admission to all parts of the track. The restrooms sparkled, and fresh red and gold paint was everywhere.

"I remember when I went to Suffolk Downs that I think the most important improvement made was that we knocked all the locks off the pay toilets. It seemed somehow indecent to charge people to get in, to charge them to eat and drink, and then to charge them again," Veeck later told a Senate hearing on stadiums, echoing his history in Milwaukee, Cleveland, and Chicago. "We spent $300,000 or $400,000 in toilet improvements. Ladies' rooms specifically."[7]

The opener began with two special races—the Paul Revere for three-year-olds, and the Lady Godiva, a $10,000 race featuring eight fillies ridden by eight female jockeys brought in from as far away as Gulfstream Park in Florida and Santa Anita in California. Veeckian touches abounded. Pink sinks and white curtains were installed in the female jockeys' dressing room. Reasoning that the male jocks had a pool table in theirs, he jokingly put an old-fashioned spinning wheel in the distaff dressing area. The Godiva trophy was presented by Annie Guay, ninety-one, a racetrack regular.

At the end of the second race came the "Veeck Special," celebrated as workmen ran into the infield to plant two dozen crabapple trees in holes that had already been dug. It was Veeck's way of saying that even more improvements were forthcoming. The motto on pasteboard signs around the park read: THINGS ARE LOOKING UP AT SUFFOLK DOWNS.[8]

On Joe Fan Day, he gave away a three-year-old filly named Buck's Delight to a South Boston water department worker named Bob Morgan. The horse would run four times at Suffolk Downs before the season was over, finishing second on her final run of the meeting. On Flag Day, June 14, 3,600 American flags were given out, and anyone named John, Alden, or Priscilla (for Pilgrim John Alden and his wife, the former Priscilla Mullins) got free admission to see that day's John Alden Handicap.

On the day of the Beef Stake Handicap, he entertained 2,500 "beefs" from the track's long-suffering fans. John Savage won first prize, a steer and a calf, for his winning "beef," which was that he wanted to know why the horses could not be saddled up in full view of the fans. Henceforth, the saddling ritual would be a public one. Unable to get the livestock home on the subway, he sold the steer and calf back to Veeck for $100. Later, Veeck answered all the complaints, personally enclosing a coupon with each entitling the recipient to a free McDonald's hamburger.

On June 28, 1969, Veeck posted a purse of $254,750 for the Yankee Gold Cup, the most ever for a race run on a grass track in America. The two-mile race was flawed by too many horses, fifteen, on too narrow a track, but Veeck had made his mark on the big time and endeared himself to the local fans when he refused to move the time of the race to a later hour to accommodate ABC television. Veeck had promised his fans they would get home earlier, and he wanted to keep the promise.[9]

As his 1969 spring meeting drew to a close, Veeck had met with limited success but was making more money at the turnstiles even with a lower admission, having revoked the free passes that had traditionally gone to almost every politician in the Commonwealth. Much to the delight of his fan base, the politicians howled. "For a while, 90 per cent of our mail and phone calls were complaints about the end of free passes," Veeck told Pete Axthelm of *Newsweek*.[10]

Revoking the free passes was Veeck's first salvo in taking on the Bay State political establishment. He went to Superior Court and got a judge to overturn a Massachusetts ban on minors at the track. Veeck's claim was that he wanted to start them off young. One of his early promotions following the decision was to give away 2,000 coloring books. But when Veeck applied to add twenty-four racing dates to his calendar, he was turned down;

he immediately sued the state attorney general, which he would do on several more occasions while running the track.

During his first year in Boston, Veeck also weighed in on other aspects of Boston's sports scene, such as the new multipurpose stadium for football and baseball being contemplated by the Massachusetts legislature. The AFL Boston Patriots were playing in Fenway Park, which could then seat 32,000 for baseball and 37,000 for football. Veeck agreed that the Patriots needed a new stadium but was adamant that the Red Sox resist moving, passionately observing, "In a new stadium, the Red Sox would lose one of the most tremendous assets a ball club could have—that feeling of closeness and intimacy Fenway Park provides."[11]

Veeck became one of Fenway's great defenders, articulating its appeal at a time when momentum was on the side of multiuse stadiums. "I have never seen a stadium built for both baseball and football that did not take something away from both," he stated. "I love the intimacy of Fenway Park. I love the feeling of involvement. You feel as though you are part of the game."[12]

Veeck's third and last meeting of the 1969 season ended in late November with a series of harness races and another personal close call. At about 5:00 a.m. on November 24, Veeck, who was living at the track during the week in a small apartment, smelled smoke. His normal escape routes to an inside stairwell and an elevator were both blocked by billowing smoke, so he climbed out a window, worked his way across a ledge, and escaped via an outside stairway. The fire was put out after Veeck called the fire department. "It does pay to live on the premises," he quipped.[13]

The final accounting done in early December showed that the track had thrived under Veeck's leadership. The Commonwealth's share of wagers and licenses for the three meetings at Suffolk was a record $8,219,120. The holding company was thrilled with the profits it was taking from the track.[14]

As 1969 ended, Veeck got in one final jab at the Establishment—this time it was Harvard University. In early December, John Yovicsin, the popular Harvard football coach who had permission from the university to take an off-season job, was hired by Veeck to help with group sales. When the news became public, Harvard officials and influential alumni were outraged, and the coach was forced to state, "I have completely given up any plans for working at Suffolk Downs." Harvard was so embarrassed by the incident that it withheld the announcement until just before the December 18 wedding of falsetto-voiced singer Tiny Tim on Johnny Carson's *Tonight* show (an event that drew 40 million viewers). But it still made news and attracted comments that were not kind to the Crimson. "I prefer the University for environment, but for company, I'll take the track," said Nathan Perlmutter, vice president for development at nearby Brandeis University.[15]

Veeck came out ranting, filling columns in newspapers from coast to coast with inspired invective. "The Harvard people are being stuffy. One of their people at the race track, perish the thought! It was like attacking the Virgin Mary. . . . It's all right for their faculty to work on lend-lease for the government on atomic bombs and germ warfare. But it's not all right to work at a race track." One of his favorite anti-Harvard punch lines reminded everyone of its nonprofit status: "Those bums haven't paid taxes in 320 years." Harvard now had something in common with the New York Yankees—both were in Veeck's crosshairs.[16]

Early in the new year, Veeck returned to Chicago to celebrate the ascendency of his protégé Pat Williams as the general manager of the surging National Basketball Association Chicago Bulls. In turn, Williams staged "Pack the Joint for Bill Veeck Night" on January 10, 1970. In early February, Veeck also threw himself directly into the problems of the Boston Patriots football team, which found itself within weeks of being forced to leave New England for lack of a stadium in which to play. The AFL Patriots had played their first two seasons in Fenway Park, then moved to Boston College's stadium for a season, but neither venue was large enough to meet National Football League standards that were applied as the two leagues merged. The only remaining option was to play at Harvard Stadium, which had turned down the team initially and again in early February.

The National Football League was scheduled to meet on March 15 in Hawaii, and any team without a stadium with seating for 50,000 would have to move its franchise to a city that did. With no other solution in sight, it appeared that the Patriots would end up in one of several southern cities that wanted a pro team and had an acceptable playing venue. Out of the blue Veeck offered a solution: he would get twelve extra racing dates, which would net the Bay State an additional $1.2 million a year, over time providing the $16 million needed to build a new stadium. The beauty of the plan was that the money would come not from taxes but from betting, which was voluntary.

Veeck then went on the offensive at a packed Chamber of Commerce luncheon at the Sheraton Plaza Hotel, pointing out that Boston had lost one baseball team (the National League Braves) and two football teams (the 1936–37 Boston Shamrocks of the former AFL and the NFL Boston Redskins, driven to Washington in 1937 because of the popularity of the Shamrocks, which moved away shortly thereafter). "If we lose the Patriots now, we may be losing the Red Sox and Celtics one of these days." Veeck was now using the pronoun *we* in talking about the dilemma facing *his* city. He wound up his Chamber of Commerce talk by saying that Boston was unfairly regarded as a cold city, supposedly unfriendly toward strangers. "I have worked and lived at various times in virtually every large city from coast to coast. I tell you Boston is the most abused of cities. In my ten months here, you people couldn't have been more wonderful to me and my associates. It is to show my appreciation that I made the offer to contribute something to make the stadium possible."[17]

Veeck also went on the offensive in the media: "I can't understand why more important people haven't come out in favor of the plan. I for one don't want to see the Patriots leave Boston, but I guess most people just don't care enough about this," he told Tony Romano, a writer for the *St. Petersburg Evening Independent*. Romano added his own comment: "Bill Veeck, a man with only one leg, and the Boston Patriots, on its last leg, may well be fighting a losing battle in efforts to convince the people and the legislators of Massachusetts that pro football in this day and age is no liability, regardless of the problems that may be involved."

Veeck's plan to save the Patriots was ultimately rejected by the Commonwealth, but it was instrumental in getting the NFL to give the team an extension on its deadline; ultimately, the team landed in Foxboro after playing at Harvard Stadium for one season.* Columnists around the nation were aghast that Veeck's solution was not accepted. Wrote Red Smith: "The state government contributes nothing and takes about $7 million a year from

---

* On moving to Foxboro in 1971, the team petitioned to change its name to the Bay State Patriots, which was rejected. The next choice—New England Patriots—stuck. While Veeck had given the Patriots and its owner, Billy Sullivan, enough of a patchwork solution to make it through the owners meeting, he also gave a voice to Boston's professional sports teams, which were on the ropes at the time. His defense of Fenway Park when there were thoughts of replacing it and his assist in keeping the Patriots in New England would later be recalled when he was given the Judge Emil Fuchs Memorial Award in 1981, presented by the Boston sportswriters for long and meritorious service. Fuchs was president of the Boston Braves from 1927 to 1935.

Suffolk; Veeck had the naïve notion that nobody would mind seeing the stadium project helped."[18]

DURING THE EARLY months of 1970, Veeck had become attracted to the case of a thirty-two-year-old African American outfielder named Curt Flood, whom Veeck, in his normal manner, insisted on calling Curtis. Flood had enjoyed a twelve-year stay with the St. Louis Cardinals and saw himself as one of the team's leaders. On October 7, 1969, the Cardinals announced an off-season trade, sending Flood, Tim McCarver, Byron Browne, and Joe Hoerner to the Philadelphia Phillies for slugger Richie Allen, Cookie Rojas, and Jerry Johnson. Flood termed the move "impersonal" and loudly protested being traded to a club that had just had a terrible season and played its games in an old, drab stadium before notoriously belligerent fans. Flood decided he would challenge the trade through the reserve clause. He first asked Commissioner Bowie Kuhn to declare him a free agent, and was of course denied. On January 16, 1970, stating that baseball had violated the nation's antitrust laws, Flood filed suit to have the reserve clause overturned, demanding treble damages amounting to $3 million. Former Supreme Court Justice Arthur Goldberg, who coincidentally was running for governor of New York state, agreed to take Flood's case for expenses and assembled a team of lawyers.

Veeck had been a decades-long foe of the long-established reserve clause in baseball, which bound a player to a club in perpetuity and allowed the player to be traded against his will. Players were generally given new contracts each year, but the clause required a player to stay with whatever team first signed him as long as that team wanted him. Team owners, however, could trade a player whenever they desired. At the core of the reserve clause was baseball's exemption from the antitrust laws, which had been granted by the Supreme Court in 1922 and later reaffirmed by Congress. As Bill Gleason of the *Chicago Sun-Times* observed, Veeck had been warning baseball owners for years: "You'd better give them free agency or the courts will give it to them for you."[19]

Even though Flood was making $90,000 at the time, he likened "being owned" to being "a well-paid slave," an assessment with which Veeck agreed. Veeck had made the same point in a phone conversation with Marvin Miller of the Major League Baseball Players Association shortly after Flood's suit was filed. Miller and two of the attorneys who were working for Flood persuaded Veeck to testify against Commissioner Bowie Kuhn and Major League Baseball.[20]

Veeck suspected—and was reminded by others—that his testimony in support of Flood might be another nail in the coffin regarding his chances of getting back into baseball, but he was willing and eager to speak out for Flood and against Kuhn, whom he disliked intensely.

Although Veeck stayed at the racetrack during most of each race season, the family was still living in Easton, Maryland, where writers were still attracted to him as friends but with less frequency for profiles or baseball stories. Dick Victory, thirty-five, was a veteran newspaper and magazine writer who covered sports for the *Evening Star*. In the spring of 1970, on the advice of his editor, Morris Siegel, Victory drove to Easton to spend a few hours with Veeck, believing him always a good subject for a feature.

The two men spoke for several hours on a wide range of matters. The subject of Eddie Gaedel was broached and quickly discharged; to Veeck it was a stunt he once pulled off on a dull day for a duller team but not his preferred legacy. Victory noticed, as so many others did, that Veeck was in pain, but nonetheless he was not given to cursing or complaining. The men talked mainly about politics and the state of the world and also about the furniture in the room and its restoration, all done by Veeck by hand. Victory, whose father was a carpenter, was fascinated.

As Victory drove away, he felt a sense of melancholy, thinking that Veeck's baseball time had passed, that he was now a purely historical figure, and that his might be one of the last interviews that anyone would have with Veeck

One of the opening lines in the first part of Victory's profile captured Veeck's sense of isolation: "His detractors . . . think of him as a berserk showman who threatened the dignity of the game and accordingly still keep a wary eye on his Eastern Shore retreat, as European heads-of-state once nervously contemplated [Napoleon on] Elba."[21]

Victory's fear that his interview with Veeck might be one of the last was premature. The Flood trial got under way on May 19, 1970, and was accorded national attention by the press and the public, not only because of its potential impact on baseball but also because it had such star witnesses as Jackie Robinson and Hank Greenberg.* Three weeks into the trial, Veeck

---

* The trial opened on a light note when a nervous Flood was asked to reel off his season-by-season batting averages. He was unable to recall them until one of his lawyers handed him his bubble gum baseball card that had the exact statistics.

arrived in Manhattan late in the evening on June 9. The next morning, he met with Flood's lawyers, one of whom, Bill Iverson, was concerned that during cross-examination, the owners' legal team would conjure up images of midgets and moveable outfield fences to make Veeck appear to be a crackpot. Veeck brought out the embossed tribute that had been given to him on his retirement from the game in 1961, and Iverson planned to bring the tribute into Veeck's testimony, emphasizing the words "many valuable contributions to baseball" and the fact that it was signed by the American League.

On June 10, the sixteenth day of testimony, Veeck was to be the last witness for Flood. Sitting in an adjacent courtroom waiting to be called to the witness stand, Veeck ignored the No Smoking signs and lit up a cigarette, much to the horror of Miller and Goldberg, who told him to extinguish it immediately. Without comment, Veeck pulled up his right pants leg and put out the cigarette in the ashtray carved into his wooden leg.

On the stand for more than two hours, Veeck was serious, polite, and forthright: "The argument that a change in the reserve clause will destroy baseball is absurd." Alluding to the letter he had sent to Commissioner Landis in 1941 on the subject, he pointed out that he had long been on record as saying that the reserve clause was both illegal and immoral, and he had never wavered in that conviction. Veeck also emphasized his belief that all individuals should enjoy at least one point in their lifetime when they could determine their own future and not be held in perpetuity by a single firm or entity (and he noted that this moment of self-determination should apply to "every person, every human being," including attorneys).

Again and again, he came back to the immorality of the existing reserve clause and the principle of free choice. Asked how a change would benefit the players and the game of baseball, he responded: "Well, I think that it would certainly help the players and the game itself to no longer be one of the few places in which there is human bondage. I think it would be to the benefit of the reputation of the game of baseball, and I would like to mention just for the record, I happen to think of baseball as the greatest team game there is. I don't happen to agree with all they do, and often I am very unkind about my statements, but I still think it is a game that deserves to be perpetuated and to be restored to the position of honor it once held, and I think this would be a step in that direction. At least it would be fair."[22]

Veeck, however, was no absolutist, arguing that the reserve clause should be modified rather than repealed: the immediate and total elimination of

Maurice Veeck, the older brother Bill Veeck never knew. On September 30, 1909, at the age of seven, he was killed in a gun accident.

Bill at the wheel with his older sister, Peg.

A youthful Bill with his parents in the late 1920s.

Chicago White Sox owner Charles "The Old Roman" Comiskey (left) seated with Chicago Cubs president William Veeck Sr. on September 20, 1920, during the formal hearings into the infamous "Black Sox" scandal.

President William Veeck of the Cubs and his family in their box at the opening game of the 1932 World Series at Yankee Stadium. Left to right: Mrs. Veeck, family friend Mrs. Park Parker, daughter Margaret Ann (Peg) Veeck, and Veeck Sr.

Young Bill Veeck gets batting instruction from Chicago Cubs manager Joe McCarthy at spring training on Catalina Island off the coast of California.

Bill and Eleanor soon after their wedding in 1935.

Milwaukee Brewers business manager Rudie Schaffer (left) and manager Charlie Grimm, with Bill Veeck in the middle, entertaining their fans before a 1943 game.

Coach Red Smith is dumped out of bed during one of the Milwaukee Brewers wartime "breakfast games," staged to allow workers coming off the overnight shift to watch baseball.

Veeck mingles with the fans in Milwaukee, a practice he continued throughout his life.

"Veeck has opinions on everything—even on painting the outfield fence," was how this photograph was captioned when it appeared in a 1943 issue of Look magazine. The caption added: "Note: like almost every celebrated sports screwball, he is left-handed."

Private Bill Veeck, United States Marine Corps.

Veeck soon after his return to Milwaukee, August 1945. The cane on his desk is the only evidence of his leg injury.

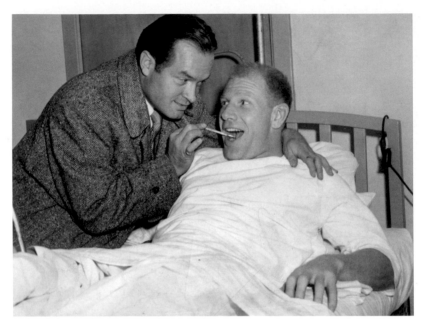

Veeck with Bob Hope on November 8, 1946, in the hospital a week after his first amputation. Hope, an investor in the Indians, and Veeck created a perfect photo opportunity as they mugged for the camera.

Casey Stengel, Veeck, and Harry Grabiner at baseball's Winter Meetings in Los Angeles in December 1946, during which Stengel, then manager of the Oakland Oaks, tipped Veeck to the potential of pitcher Gene Bearden.

Larry Doby signing with the Cleveland Indians on July 5, 1947. The signing took place in Chicago, where the Indians were playing the White Sox.

Cleveland Indians owner and general manager Bill Veeck places a jersey on new Indians executive Hank Greenberg in March 1948. Greenberg joined Harry Grabiner as vice president, giving Veeck one of the most powerful and visible front offices in baseball. Veeck and Greenberg were close friends ever after.

Veeck with Satchel Paige on July 10, 1948, three days after Veeck signed him to a contract with the Cleveland Indians and a day after he had pitched two scoreless innings in relief in a loss to the Browns.

Larry Doby with Satchel Paige after Paige's complete-game shutout of the Chicago White Sox, August 13, 1948.

14 Negro Players Give Tribe Corner on Colored Talent

Doby, Paige Head List of 14 Performers Inked by Veeck

By EDGAR MUNZEL
Of the Chicago Sun-Times

CHICAGO, Ill.

Branch Rickey broke down the racial barrier in baseball by introducing Jackie Robinson to the majors in 1947. But before long Bill Veeck probably will be recognized as the real Abe Lincoln of the game.

The Cleveland impresario has cornered the best Negro talent in baseball. The Indians looked over six Negro players in their spring camp and have a total of 14 scattered through the entire Cleveland organization.

And they aren't a lot of "Joes."

There are some among them who would be regulars on any other club except the World Champion Indians.

The six in the Cleveland camp were Outfielder Larry Doby and Orestes Minoso and Pitchers Satchel Paige, Jose Santiago and Roy Welmaker. Wilson, Santiago and Welmaker were optioned shortly before the Tribe left Tucson.

Doby and Paige probably will be the only ones retained on the Cleveland varsity this season. But Minoso, a third sacker from Cuba, could make almost every other team in the majors as a regular and Wilson could qualify at least as a utility man.

"I wish I had that Minoso," said Manager Leo Durocher of the Giants. "He can hit, run, field and throw. What else is there to this game?"

Speaks Only Spanish, But—

Charlie Grimm, Jack Onslow and every other top baseball man who has had a look at Minoso has said the same thing. Incidentally, he can speak only Spanish. But, brother, you'll hear from him.

Amazingly enough, however, there's another Negro player still down in the minors who may turn out to be even greater than Minoso. That's a first sacker of superman proportions named Luscious (Luke) Easter.

Luke, who is with the San Diego club of the Coast league, stands a mere six feet, four inches and weighs 230 pounds. His shoulders are so tremendous that in his civvies he looks like he forgot to remove the coat hanger.

This is only Easter's fourth year in pro ball, though he's 27. He's pretty fancy around that first sack, as fancy as the suits he wears, the car he drives and the big headlight diamond he flashes. And his hitting is brutal.

In 1946 he hit .415 for the Cincinnati Crescents, in 1947, .336 for the Homestead Grays and in 1948, .396. Last winter in the Puerto Rican League he bashed the ball at a mere .402.

"He's the greatest power hitter I've seen around first base since Lou Gehrig," said Earl Sheely, the old White Sox first baseman.

"He's ready for the majors right now," said Bucky Harris, San Diego manager and former major league pilot.

"I wish they'd get him out of here before he kills every infielder in the Coast league," said Manager Fred Haney of Hollywood.

Verily, it's going to be a happy Easter some day in the majors—for Luke and the Indians.

Emancipators

ABRAHAM LINCOLN
. . . freed the Negroes.

BILL VEECK
. . . gives 'em baseball jobs.

THE SPORTING NEWS, APRIL 13, 1949

April 13, 1949, headline in *The Sporting News*—the newspaper that had chided Veeck a year earlier for signing Satchel Paige.

After elimination from the pennant race on September 24, 1949, Veeck and company bury the championship pennant won in 1948. Reading from *The Sporting News* (baseball's "bible") is Rudie Schaffer, while Veeck dabs at his crocodile tears. From left to right: Marsh Samuel, Schaffer, Veeck, Bill McKechnie, Spud Goldstein, Hank Greenberg, and Steve O'Neill.

Publicity photograph used by Mary Frances Ackerman in her career as press agent for the Ice Capades. She and Veeck met when she was in Cleveland with the show.

Veeck in the 1949 feature film *The Kid from Cleveland*, speaking with actor George Brent. Lou Boudreau is in the foreground. Larry Doby has his hand on Bob Feller's shoulder.

Reunited in St. Louis, Bill Veeck and Satchel Paige.

Eddie Gaedel approaching the plate for his sole at bat, August 19, 1951.

Veeck proudly showing off his prosthesis at a swimming pool, August 30, 1951. His love of swimming lasted a lifetime; he once declared it to be the greatest sport of all.

Veeck and his son Mike, in the bleachers at Comiskey Park in 1959, soon after acquiring the Chicago White Sox.

Veeck with White Sox manager Al Lopez, 1959.

Veeck working the phone in his makeshift office at Comiskey Park.

Bill and Mary Frances at home in Chicago, 1959.

Hank Greenberg and Veeck united again with the Chicago White Sox.

Bill and Mary Frances co-hosted a television show that debuted in Chicago in 1959. The telegenic couple had been radio partners beginning in St. Louis.

Veeck in his new incarnation as a racetrack operator, at Suffolk Downs in Boston, 1970.

Veeck holding his model of the exploding tote board with which he replaced the traditional board at Suffolk Downs, 1970.

An immense poster of W. C. Fields graced Veeck's office at Suffolk Downs.

Veeck among the $2 bettors at Suffolk Downs. He listened closely to these bettors and tried to give them what they wanted.

Veeck in his second incarnation as White Sox owner.

Joe Earley, whom Veeck had made famous years earlier by giving him his own honorific day in Cleveland, presents Veeck with his necktie, July 15, 1976.

Opening Day, 1976: Veeck marches on a wooden peg leg in a "Spirit of '76" reenactment to celebrate the nation's bicentennial. Joining him are White Sox manager Paul Richards, carrying the flag, and business manager Rudie Schaffer on the drum.

The Veeck family in August 1976. Back row: Marya, Mike, Lisa, Julie; middle row: Mary Frances, Bill, Greg; front row: Christopher.

CHICAGO WHITE SOX
COMISKEY PARK

FANS SALUTE
TO
BILL VEECK

Sponsored by
CHICAGO'S BASEBALL FANS
George Langford, Chicago Tribune,
Marty Kaiser, Chicago Sun-Times,
co-chairmen.

TUES., SEPT. 30, 1980
SOX vs. **OAKLAND**
RAIN DATE: OCTOBER 1

№ 1869

ENTER ALL GATES

GENERAL ADMISSION
ADMIT ONE
NO REFUND OR CASH VALUE

FANS SALUTE TO
BILL VEECK

TUES., SEPT. 30, 1980
GOOD THIS DATE ONLY

GAME TIME 7:30 P. M.
ON THE FIELD CEREMONIES
WILL BEGIN AT 6:00 P. M.

№ 1869

Ticket to the Fans Salute to Bill Veeck celebration, in Chicago, September 30, 1980.

the reserve clause would be detrimental to the game, but the clause needed a major overhaul. Veeck then outlined three possible solutions to the problem: (1) a contract like that used in the motion picture industry, in which a player would be held for a specified time, with the contract calling for scheduled raises during the contract period; (2) a variation on the pro football option clause, in which a player could become a free agent by playing out the option year of a contract; or (3) a combination contract under which a team could control a player for a specified length of time in the minors and a separate and specified period in the majors. This would prevent a team from stockpiling players in the minors.[23]

The cross-examination was lackluster and petty, attempting at one point to uncover contradictory opinions on free agency in Veeck's two books, *Veeck—as in Wreck* and *The Hustler's Handbook*. Pressed again and again on statements he had made in the books, Veeck candidly admitted that he was entirely capable of contradictory statements and shrugged off the charge with a smile.

"One of the best witnesses imaginable. Absolutely," said Marvin Miller years later of Veeck's testimony. But if it pleased Flood's team, it made Veeck even more of a pariah with owners, who thought he was trying to destroy the game by freeing players to negotiate with other teams each time their contract ended. Flood, Veeck, and others had gone out on an unpopular limb. Very few active players supported the case; Frank Howard and Harmon Killebrew were among those who expressed public disapproval in the lawsuit. Many in the media feared that Flood and allies such as Veeck would spell doomsday for baseball. A back-page headline in the New York *Daily News* warned, "Curt Win Kills Baseball."[24]

The court found against Flood and in favor of Kuhn and organized baseball, a decision that was upheld by the Court of Appeals. Flood's lawyers petitioned to have the case heard by the Supreme Court.

AT SUFFOLK DOWNS in the spring of 1970, Veeck unleashed a psychedelic tote board that exploded in phantasmagorical colors when a payoff of $100 or more was made. It was coordinated with a 100-foot fountain and was featured in a piece in *Look* magazine, with the accompanying headline "He Convinces the Bettor He's Having a Fine Time Blowing the Rent."[25]

Late in 1970s first race meeting, Veeck bought chariots from the MGM movie *Ben Hur* to stage a chariot race that he dubbed the Ben Hur Handicap. The vehicles were piloted by local disc jockeys aided by professional drivers. Veeck had also turned the track into a venue for all sorts of outside activities, which improved cash flow considerably. "We had one advantage," he logically observed, "and that is that the track represented the largest display area in New England. We scheduled folk music shows, and automobile shows. We scheduled the New England Industrial Show and the Flower Show. We had a great many things that we used the rest of our stadium for. . . . We did have some concerts and we had anticipated some more. My tenure unfortunately was briefer than I had planned on."[26]

By late 1970, Suffolk's parent company, Realty Equity Corp., was in deep financial trouble and was delisted from the New York Stock Exchange, so Veeck's job ended officially in January 1971 with a loss of his 15 percent ownership option in the operation. For all of its success at the gate and the fact that it had returned a record $8.5 million to the state for the year just ended, the track itself was $14.5 million in debt. The parent company had created the debt by siphoning off capital from the track, a move that was devastating to the future of Suffolk Downs. As Veeck put it, "A voracious conglomerate gobbled up the track's operating money," thereby forcing him out of the business and back to the Eastern Shore, where by year's end he was at work on his third collaboration with Ed Linn. It would be called *Thirty Tons a Day*, a memoir of his days at Suffolk Downs. The title alluded to the amount of horse manure produced daily at the track by the 1,600 horses on hand on peak racing days.*

Veeck had genuinely enjoyed Boston and had become an adored public speaker, as likely to show up at a luncheon for the mothers of twins as at the Saugus Lions Club. The sportswriters loved him, an affair whose passion deepened when he worked to save the Patriots. Veeck conquered Boston for a number of reasons, not the least of which was that he was genuinely at home in a place whose residents thought of their city as the hub of the universe—a conceit worthy of Veeck himself. "Boston is one of my favorite towns, and the people are wonderful," he would write in *Thirty Tons*. "I don't understand how they keep electing such creepy politicians. They were just dull and greedy. But, except for them, I had a wonderful time."

Back in Maryland, Veeck reiterated his interest in acquiring the Washington Senators, "a franchise that has never reached its potential." Veeck loved the team with its "personalities"—Denny McLain and now Curt

---

* Mike Veeck, who served as paddock manager for a short period, realized that he was the one to shovel the thirty tons, but he admitted that the tonnage was "slightly exaggerated."

Flood, who had sat out the 1970 season but signed with the Senators in 1971 for $110,000 as he awaited a hearing of his case in the Supreme Court.* Veeck suggested the Senators add pitcher Jim Bouton, the recently retired author of the highly candid memoir *Ball Four*. "They would have an author in residence and Bowie Kuhn would have all his problems in one place," he cheekily observed, including himself in the count.[27] That said, he added, "the Senators are worth maybe $6–7 million. Anything higher than that and I'm not interested."[28] A small item in *The Sporting News* in June quoted Veeck as stating he had four offers pending to get back into baseball, but the writer noted that he had been reading that same story for ten years and it was time for Veeck to make his move. Veeck was indeed prepared to move on the Senators, but not at the asking price of $12 million.[29]

In early September 1970, Senators owner Bob Short announced that the team had to be sold and that he was entertaining offers from various parties who would either keep it in Washington or move it to the Dallas–Fort Worth area. On September 15, Veeck and Hank Greenberg met with Short and on behalf of their proposed group offered him $7.5 million, then met again the following day to up the offering price to an undisclosed amount. A meeting was scheduled for September 21 in Boston to which Veeck and Greenberg were not invited, but which included Joseph Danzansky, president of the Giant Food supermarket chain in the Washington area.

The night before the Boston meeting, Short called Veeck and told him that if he did not get permission to move the Senators to Texas, he would get back to Veeck and his ownership group, as they had made the highest bid among those who would keep the team in Washington.[30] What happened at the meeting remained a mystery for some time, but based on later recollections, Danzansky appears to have made a higher offer of $8.5 million. Danzansky's offer was seen as "soft" in that he claimed two other men were in his group and that they would put up $2.4 million in cash and arrange a loan of $7 million. From the loan they would pay the balance of the purchase price, meet obligations, and have cash for operating expenses. But as Kansas City owner Ewing Kauffman told *Sports Illustrated*, "Danzansky did not have a commitment for a loan. He wanted the league to guarantee the loan first, and then he proposed to go out and negotiate it. In effect, the other teams in the league would be underwriting Danzansky's investment, and few were in a financial position to do so. So they turned Danzansky down."[31]

---

* Curt Flood played 13 games for Washington in 1971, hit a paltry .200, and retired in April.

Veeck, it seems, had been rejected by Short, who never brought Veeck's offer to the table and really preferred to move his team. He was looking at a sweetheart deal in Texas, which ensured him an advance of $7.5 million against television rights. The move was approved and Short retained his ownership until 1974, when he finally sold the team to a group headed by Brad Corbett for $9 million.

Veeck was both "shocked and saddened" by the move to Dallas and wondered aloud why the government could bail out a big corporation such as Lockheed but stand idly by when a little federal aid could have kept a team in Washington. He was alluding to the congressional loan guarantee of $250 million to the nation's largest defense contractor. Veeck said that he understood the team might not compare to an institution such as the Kennedy Center: "Don't get me wrong, I think there is room for Bernstein's 'Mass' and baseball. But no one [in Congress] thinks this [baseball] is a kind of culture too. It's sad."[32]

Veeck also predicted that the transfer of the Senators would tip the balance in the legal challenge by Curt Flood to baseball's reserve clause. His lawyers, he said, would ask the Supreme Court what chances one small individual player has against an industry that "has illustrated its complete lack of candor and interest in the millions of people who surround Washington."[33]

"Ten days after the execution was ordered and carried out in Boston, the body of the Washington Senators was finally laid to rest last night at RFK Stadium." That was how Morris Siegel opened his column on October 1, 1971, the day after the Senators lost to the Yankees in their final game of the season. Out in deep right field in section 110, row 10, seat 9, sat Bill Veeck, who had driven from Easton to pay $5 to attend the burial. Siegel noted: "Had Veeck been sitting in the box of the owner, which he tried to occupy twice, there never would have been the tragedy of last night."

Veeck was still infatuated with the notion of a team in Washington, which would now have to be an expansion club. In mid-December 1971, Congress opened hearings on getting baseball back to D.C. to fill the stadium taxpayers had bought to house the Senators and the Washington Redskins. One faction felt that the proper lure for a new team would be the installation of artificial turf. With great anticipation, Veeck was invited to address the Senate Committee on the District of Columbia on December 15, 1971. "We should learn something about promotions from Veeck," said Senator Thomas Eagleton on the eve of the hearings.[34]

Veeck gave a full account of his knowledge of stadium operations for all sports, sharing details on ideas that had and had not worked over the years. These included, he admitted, a failed plan in his early days with the Cubs to introduce winter sports to Wrigley Field, which would have featured a ski jump affixed to the main scoreboard. Commenting on his desire to bring baseball back to Washington, Veeck wryly observed, "I think I have one rather dubious claim to fame—I have made more unsuccessful offers for the Washington Senators than anyone in history. I live just across the creek, and I think of it as our stadium rather than Baltimore, strange enough."[35]

The spring of 1972 brought a baseball strike and a chance for Veeck to lash out at the power struggle that caused the "crime of the century"—the theft of spring. "You see," he opined in a bylined piece in the *Baltimore Sun*, "Marvin Miller and his 600 hearties, aided and abetted by Bowie Kuhn and his two dozen stalwarts, have peddled spring down the river for a few lousy bucks. It doesn't matter who's right (no one) nor who's wrong (everyone). It's the fans, the guys who pay the freight, that got the shaft."[36]

Despite his vituperations in print, Veeck remained close to Miller. Later in 1972, Miller's son Peter, whose lower leg had been severely damaged in an accident, was about to go in for a second round of surgery. Just before the second operation Miller ran into Veeck in Washington. "He had read about Peter's accident in the paper," Miller recalled. "When I mentioned the second surgery, his face turned solemn. Veeck had injured his leg in the Marine Corps, and despite all medical advice refused for more than two years to have it amputated. In the interim, he endured a dozen operations. He said, 'I'm not a doctor, and it's none of my business, but if I had to do it all over again, I wouldn't go through the poisonous process of one surgery after the other. I would have had an amputation. I wouldn't say this if the amputation had to be above the knee, but below the knee there's almost nothing you can't do with an artificial leg." Miller admitted, "I was struck by the sincerity and power of his speech. And in all the years that I knew Veeck, it was the first and only time he ever mentioned his leg. I never told Peter this because it wasn't necessary. He made a remarkable recovery."[37]

Veeck channeled some of his rants into syndicated op-ed pieces. In one, he listed all of baseball's catastrophes—the strike, the Senators' move, the failure of an expansion team in Seattle, the Braves' move from Milwaukee to Atlanta, the move of the A's from Kansas City to Oakland—and blamed it all on the Yankees, specifically Weiss, Webb, and Topping. His logic may have been faulty, but his anger was real. In his mind, Yankee success had caused others to fail and the American League to be weak.[38]

Among his other reasons to be angry was the delay he had encountered with the publication of his new book, *Thirty Tons a Day*, which had been held up for seven months to give his publisher's lawyers a chance to vet the manuscript, which contained accounts of numerous lawsuits, including eight Veeck had lodged against the attorney general of Massachusetts. Veeck complained that said lawyers had identified 138 to 140 potentially libelous items that he was refusing to change.[39]

Veeck was scheduled to be one of the keynote speakers at the seventy-second annual convention of the American Booksellers Association at the Sheraton Park Hotel in Washington in early June 1972. Despite the book's delay, Veeck won over his audience, acknowledging he read five to six books a week, revealing that he had read almost all of Shakespeare and that he loved to buy and give away books, and describing his increasing role as a book reviewer for such papers as the *Baltimore Sun* and the *Chicago Tribune*. When Alvin Beam, the book editor of the *Cleveland Plain Dealer*, asked him if he might someday return to own the Indians, Veeck replied that he probably would not because—quoting Robert Browning—he felt he could never recapture that "first fine careless rapture." Veeck quoted other bits from English poets, much to the delight of those assembled. Appropriately, another luncheon speaker was Jackie Robinson, who was there to promote his own book. "I happened to fall in behind the two men as they left the hall," Beam reported in his column. "It was good to watch them."[40]

On June 19, 1972, the Supreme Court, by a 5-to-3 margin in the matter of *Flood v. Kuhn*, upheld the antitrust exemption granted Major League Baseball, denying Curt Flood damages and relief from the reserve clause. However, even though the court had ruled in baseball's favor, the ruling admitted that the original grounds for the antitrust exemption were tenuous at best, that baseball was indeed engaged in interstate commerce for purposes of the act, and that its exemption was an anomaly. The contradictory nature of the decision invited a closer look at the sport's status and set the stage for new attempts to achieve free agency.

VEECK RETURNED TO Easton following the collapse of Suffolk Downs. All the while the Veecks lived in Maryland, he maintained a large wooden idea box into which hundreds of promotional ideas were stuffed, some of them written on cocktail napkins. Mike Veeck recalled that because of the nature of the house, periodic fire drills were staged, and "my job was to carry the box in case of fire." The box was maintained in preparation for Veeck's eventual return to the game.[41]

Veeck was still a baseball man at heart and always had an eye out for talent. In 1972 Bob Boinski, a local waterman and friend who was also Veeck's house painter, reported that he had spotted a thirteen-year-old player named Harold Baines who was worth a look. "I recommended him to Bill," said Boinski. "In a small area like this, you get to see all the local kids. Everybody was talking about him. Everybody had heard of him. You could already see that he had all the tools." Veeck was impressed with his flowing swing and told his lifeguard friend Roger Clark, "This guy's got it." He befriended Baines and vowed to maintain contact with him.[42]

Thirty Tons a Day was finally released in late November 1972, allowing Veeck a press conference in Manhattan, where his comments, as usual, made the wires: "Baseball and horse racing are similar sports—both are moribund," he said at one point. Addressing the issue of owners and general managers who insisted on baseball's mystique, he scolded them: "What mystique? Remember Little Leaguers play it."[43]

By early 1974 he was far enough out of the public eye that the *Cleveland Plain Dealer* could run a feature entitled "Whatever Happened to Bill Veeck?" He told the reporter assigned to the story, "I'm a bum living on the Eastern Shore who will occasionally foray into the outside world. The last six weeks I've been carting wood because I can't move around. I recently had another operation, number five on my good leg." The good leg was in a cast, and he told the reporter that he was facing knee replacement surgery in the fall.[44]

Later in 1974, Veeck attempted once again to buy the Baltimore Orioles. Though his offer was initially accepted, negotiations fell apart in June 1975 for reasons that were never made clear. Veeck said that Jerold Hoffberger had given no explanation other than the fact that his problems had nothing to do with Veeck.

"The most bitterly disappointed man on the Eastern Seaboard today is Bill Veeck of Easton, Md.," wrote Red Smith in his column on June 11. "After investing more than a year of his life in an effort to buy the Baltimore Orioles, he was told yesterday that the deal was off—seven months to the day after one offer was accepted." Veeck lamented: "This means the loss of a friend, the loss of a ball club, the loss of a year and a lot of dollars—and for me at the age of 61, the loss of innocence."[45]

Veeck seriously considered a lawsuit and never spoke to Hoffberger again, nor did he ever again consume a can of Hoffberger's beer. He had desperately wanted to get back into baseball and had seen Baltimore, a city he had a genuine affection for, as the place where he would make his final mark on the game, but it was not to be. "I can't hear, can't see, can't walk, and yet I want to get involved in the last hurrah," Veeck, commenting on his deteriorating condition, told Bob Maisel of the *Baltimore Sun*.[46]

CHAPTER 18

The Last Hurrah

A WEEK AFTER THE BALTIMORE deal soured, word reached Veeck that John Allyn, who had bought the White Sox from him with his brother and had subsequently bought his brother out, was having trouble making payroll and that the team would soon be on the block. The other owners wanted to move it to Seattle, which was suing baseball for allowing the expansion Pilots to leave at the end of the 1969 season to become the Milwaukee Brewers the following April.

On July 31, 1975, a Chicago businessman and good friend of Veeck's, Andy McKenna, arrived in Easton to ask him to come back to Chicago and lead a group, including McKenna, that wanted to purchase the team from Allyn.[1] Throughout the summer and into the fall, Veeck, McKenna, and Allyn continued to talk and negotiate. Then on October 1, Dave Condon of the *Chicago Tribune* published a report saying that Veeck was about to spend $10 million to buy the White Sox. Veeck coyly insisted that he had made no offer and wasn't even certain he was interested. But three days later he announced a complicated financial transaction by which he would purchase control of the Artnell Company, of which the White Sox were a division, with Allyn remaining a minority stockholder.[2]

Veeck got some of the best press of his life in the next week. He accepted invitations to speak at prayer breakfasts and other charity events and waxed rhapsodic about the pending deal.[3] "My acquiring the White Sox can be summed up in the titles of two books: *The Return of the Native* and *The Last Hurrah*," he said on one of those occasions.[4] The deal to buy the team was tentative, however, because it would ultimately depend on the approval of the other American League owners. In fact, on the day it was announced, the *Chicago Sun-Times* reported that it was doubtful the American League would approve a sale to Veeck. One unnamed owner was quoted as saying that there was "no chance" the sale would go through.[5]

The owners were to have an answer by November 15, 1975. "I don't expect any problems," Veeck said optimistically, "but I've been wandering too long to know a sure bet is not always a sure bet." Early comments by other owners were generally favorable, but with some genuine reservations. Calvin Griffith of the Minnesota Twins told the *Chicago Tribune*, "He did give us a couple of black eyes when he called baseball owners generally 'stupid,' but my mind is always flexible." Brewers owner Bud Selig was among the most positive, pointing out that he had been weaned on Veeck's Brewers at the old Borchert Field and that he had a lot of respect and admiration for him.[6]

Sportswriters were adamantly in favor of giving Veeck his last hurrah. "When a man is in his 60s, has one wooden leg, has had major surgery on his so-called good leg, with the implanting of a metal-knee hinge next on the schedule, and he still wants to get back into baseball as much as Bill Veeck, he gets my vote," wrote Bob Maisel in the *Baltimore Sun*.[7]

November 15 came and went without a decision. The league had not had enough time to review the paperwork for the deal, which now involved thirty investors, of whom at least twenty-five were from Chicago, and of those, one was an unnamed African American. The ownership group included such baseball notables as former Reds owner William O. DeWitt, Hank Greenberg, and former Orioles manager Paul Richards. The American League owners agreed to meet on December 3 in Cleveland.

The day of the meeting, the *Washington Post* revealed that the black individual in the ownership group was none other than John Harold Johnson, the owner of *Ebony*, *Jet*, and other magazines. If approved, he would be the first of his race with an ownership position in baseball. "There are those who say Johnson was a token black," wrote William Barry Furlong, "but so was Jackie Robinson."[8]

The meeting was held, and after six hours behind closed doors, Veeck was turned down, 8–3, with one abstention. The stated reason was that the package contained too much debt and not enough equity, but three factors were involved, one of them Veeck himself. "He knocked the game and he now wants to re-enter it," said Gene Autry, owner of the California Angels. "I can't bring myself to vote for a man like that." The Seattle lawsuit also intruded. On the day of the vote, Dave Nightingale of the *Chicago Daily News* reported that Veeck would have had the team a week earlier if it were not for "one little item"—a $20 million treble-damages lawsuit cranked up for the courts for January 12, 1976. The White Sox were, in Nightingale's view, a settlement and "payment for an impending legal fee." Lastly, Charles O. Finley wanted the White Sox out of Chicago so that he could move his Oakland A's back to his hometown. Some believed that the owners welcomed Veeck's coming up short as an opportunity to send a team to Seattle, move Finley out of Oakland, and leave the San Francisco Bay area open for the Giants, whose owners had borrowed $500,000 from the National League and were on the verge of bankruptcy.[9]

At the end of the meeting and by unanimous consent, Veeck was given another chance and a new deadline—a week later, on December 10, at the beginning of the Winter Meetings in Hollywood, Florida. By then the Veeck group needed to raise an additional $1.2 million in cash and convert the rest of the purchase price to preferred stock, not debentures. Reporters speculated that Veeck was being asked to jump through an impossible hoop in an impossibly short amount of time so that the league would look good in exploring his offer before moving the team to Seattle.[10]

Veeck scrambled and pulled every string he could. Powerful Chicago Mayor Richard Daley said he would do everything he could to help, and Veeck got a vague pledge of help from multimillionaire philanthropist and motivational speaker W. Clement Stone. To make the deal work, Veeck gave up his 15 percent commission on the sale and pledged his home in Easton as collateral.* At the last minute, Patrick O'Malley, a confidant of Mayor Daley and chairman of the Canteen Corp., came up with $250,000 that put the offer over the top.[11]

When the Winter Meetings convened in Florida, an odd mix of baseball people and celebrities presented their proposals. Entertainer Danny Kaye headed a group that wanted to buy the White Sox and move them to Seattle,

---

* One burden he could not get rid of was a requirement to pay Allyn a $50,000-a-year consulting fee for the next ten years. Wags suggested that given Allyn's poor stewardship of the Sox, the club would be better off if Veeck were to pay him $50,000 a year to stay clear of Comiskey Park.

and comedian Milton Berle fronted for a consortium that wanted to either build a new stadium for the Atlanta Braves, suffering at the box office since moving from Milwaukee, or move the team for the third time since it had left Boston.[12]

The first vote was 8–3 in Veeck's favor with one abstention—one vote short of approval.[13] A shocked Lee MacPhail, president of the American League, then spoke up and insisted that the owners reconsider out of simple fairness, because Veeck had met all the requirements that they had set for him. The credibility of all those who opposed Veeck was now at stake. John Fetzer, owner of the Detroit Tigers and no friend of Veeck's, nonetheless made an impassioned plea that the owners make good on their promise. "We have to be men about this, I don't like the idea of letting a guy back in here who's called me a son of a bitch over and over again, but, gentlemen, we've got to take another vote." He later explained: "I felt that the integrity of baseball was at stake in that decision. If you set up a set of conditions and ask a guy to comply, and he complies, then you are duly obligated to make good on your word."[14]

This time, Veeck's offer received ten votes, with Gene Autry and one other owner holding out—almost certainly Finley, who had linked himself to the Angels' owner. (Finley had at one point put his arm around Autry and parodied the singing cowboy's signature song, "Back in the Saddle Again," as "Back in Seattle Again.") Traditionally, a final ceremonial vote would be taken to make the vote unanimous, but it was not to happen that night. Happiness was in short supply. Calvin Griffith of the Minnesota Twins, who had changed his vote to support Veeck, stumbled out of the meeting, saying, "I just gave eight pints of blood." Haywood Sullivan, representing the Boston Red Sox, was presumably alluding to the Seattle situation when he commented, "We've got a mess now and we'll have a bigger one with Veeck."[15]

Following the vote, Veeck strode back into baseball. Escorted by MacPhail, he entered the owners meeting and put on the charm: "I have not always led an exemplary life. I am not Galahad riding in on a shining white steed. I rather think of myself more as Merlin."[16] The Veeck family was delighted by his return to baseball, and his youngest children, Chris, Juliana, and Lisa, got on separate telephones and sang in unison, "Ta-ra-ra-boom-de-ay, we got the Sox today."[17]

Finally Bill Veeck was back under the arc lights. Speaking for others in the press, Bill Gleason of the *Sun-Times* said, "I was simply amazed that they let him back for a third time."[18]

At the reins of a team of investors, Veeck took control of the sinking club on December 10, 1975. He was an owner again, albeit more in name than on paper because he had given up so much of his ownership to win the vote.* Asked by the *New York Times* what percentage of the Sox he now owned, he replied: "That's nobody's business, if you forgive me for saying so. And if you won't forgive me, it's still nobody's business."[19]

Veeck's group bought the White Sox a day before the trading deadline. The Sox had made no trades because of the uncertain ownership and, coming off a next-to-last divisional finish, had many holes to fill. Within two hours of the final vote, Veeck traded 20-game winner Jim Kaat and minor-league infielder Mike Buskey to the Philadelphia Phillies for two right-handed pitchers, Dick Ruthven and Roy Thomas, and shortstop/center fielder Alan Bannister. General manager Roland Hemond had been working behind the scenes on the deal for several days.

Expediency and the sense that a great publicity opportunity beckoned inspired Veeck to set up a "trading post" in the middle of the lobby of the Diplomat Hotel during the Winter Meetings. It was manned by Veeck and Hemond, who had liberated a sign from the hotel dining room that read OPEN FOR BUSINESS to which Veeck added ANYTIME.

The trading post was in a corner of the lobby, and the two men sat in high-back leather chairs in a sunken seating area. At a glass table were five additional chairs that were constantly filled with other owners, general managers, and reporters. The pit was surrounded by a brass rail. "In the closing hours, dozens of players were traded. One player, pitcher Dick Ruthven, remained with the Sox for like 20 minutes. It was great theater. There was Veeck, sitting at a huge table ringed with phones, answering calls in rapid succession. The lobby quickly filled with guests trying to get a peek at the master at work."[20]

Guests surrounded the trading post two and three deep. Men in their new leisure suits and Qiana shirts and women in their Florida resort finery looked on openmouthed as a master showman let them peak into baseball's sanctum sanctorum.

---

* He became, at once, the man who was an owner in four different decades and the last person to engineer the purchase of a baseball franchise without an independent fortune.

"What are they doing?" a woman asked.

"They're trading players," her escort explained with less astonishment than the scandalized functionaries of the other teams. Commissioner Kuhn called it "gauche," and Brewers owner Selig termed it a "meat market."*

When the dust had settled and the trading deadline had passed, Veeck and Hemond had overseen the exchange of twentyone-players—eleven coming and eleven going, with two players traded twice—and had a new team that Veeck claimed was now 25 percent improved. In the words of Joe Durso of the *New York Times*, the trading pit had been in large part responsible for setting off one of "the fastest trading sprees in history."[21]

Veeck immediately announced that imposing reliever Goose Gossage would be a starting pitcher, in part replacing Kaat. Recognizing his team's power vacuum, he also said that his first order of business back in Chicago would be to tear down the center-field fence at Comiskey Park to create the deepest center field in the American League.[22] Veeck then repaired to the hotel dance floor with Mary Frances, where they proceeded to dance the night away.

In Chicago, the weekend papers reported every move made by Veeck and his party, noting with some irony that the Chicago Cubs, who like the White Sox had won just 75 games in 1975 and had tied for last place in the National League East, had come back from the Winter Meetings without having made a single trade. The *Chicago Tribune* accused Veeck and the White Sox of stealing the town right out from under the noses of the Cubs. "This is White Sox country now, and the Cubs surrendered it without firing a shot."[23]

Veeck made the payments to finalize the sale and thanked all the new owners who had helped him overcome the "almost impossible obstacles" the American League had put in his way. He allowed Sox manager Chuck Tanner to go to Finley's Athletics, and brought back sixty-seven-year-old Paul Richards to manage his team. Veeck said he had chosen Richards, a close personal friend and co-owner, to manage because "this coming season is so important, I feel I have to go with people I know do well."[24]

On December 23, 1975, two weeks after the Winter Meetings, a seventy-

---

* Not until after Veeck's death did Roland Hemond reveal a trick employed during these Winter Meetings. Veeck had given Hemond several rolls of dimes and said, "Go to a pay phone as soon as there's a lull and start calling me." Excited by the hullabaloo, teams started making their own calls.

year-old arbitrator and former fan of the Brooklyn Dodgers, Peter Seitz, ruled that baseball's reserve clause was invalid. In one unexpected moment, the game of baseball at the major-league level was turned upside down. Two players, Andy Messersmith and Dave McNally, had rejected the option years of their contracts, playing without a contract in 1975 in the hope that they would become free agents and able to sign with any team they chose. Their teams' owners had disagreed, insisting that in the absence of a new contract, the earlier contracts were still binding. The players submitted their case to Major League Baseball (MLB) for arbitration, and at the end of the season the case was assigned to Seitz, who had been retained by baseball for such matters. Seitz ruled in favor of Messersmith and McNally. In practical terms, what the decision meant was that any player who did not sign a contract in 1975 yet played under his 1974 terms would become a free agent in 1976.

When Seitz issued his ruling in favor of the players, he was fired on the spot. "Every arbitrator is terminated," Seitz said later at his own press conference. "It's expected because somebody wins and somebody loses. But I've never been terminated this way—two minutes after the order, I'm gone."

Christmas Day was dominated by news of the decision, with Seitz placed in the role of Santa or Scrooge, depending on which side of a paycheck one sat. A few writers sided with the owners, most notably Dick Young of the New York *Daily News*; he called Seitz a man with a Napoleon complex who had challenged the Supreme Court, which had upheld baseball's monopoly. Red Smith of the *New York Times*, however, hailed the decision, noting that Seitz had long before warned MLB that it needed to negotiate working conditions with the players, including the reserve clause.

The path blazed by Curt Flood that had started in 1969 with strong support from Bill Veeck had finally reached its end thanks to Messersmith and McNally. Veeck's initial reaction to the Seitz decision was measured. He felt it was presumptuous on Seitz's part to change the entire structure of the game, but since it had happened, he hoped both sides could sit down and find a permanent solution. He did not think the ruling would cause a mass exodus of players to greener pastures. Veeck's muted response may have had less to do with his true feelings than with the reality of the situation in which he found himself at the time: attempting to build a new team with some players whose contracts would lapse within a week. The team was undercapitalized and he was dependent on his salary of $65,000 a year, so

Veeck was ill prepared for the bidding wars that he knew were likely in the offing.[25]

To Veeck, baseball at that moment became a game "for men with unbridled egos, exceedingly wealthy men who do not want to endure the whips and lashes of outraged vanity at the tennis club and the bathhouse."[26]

Commissioner Bowie Kuhn took a week to weigh in, predicting the ruination of baseball through bankruptcies, sharp retrenchment of franchises, and "great dissatisfaction among the players themselves as the money gravitates to the top—to the superstars at the expense of the majority of players." He warned that the minor leagues—140 clubs that had provided entertainment for 12 million fans during the 1975 season—might soon be a casualty of the decision. Without the reserve clause, baseball could become chaotic and lose its position as a major sport.[27]

Kuhn had "not been thrilled" when Veeck appeared as a witness for Curt Flood against the reserve system, and ironically saw Seitz's decision as a "a kind of justice," with Veeck now inheriting free agency as an owner. Nobody had done better under the old system than Veeck. "I don't think anybody's ever been dissatisfied coming out of the office after talking contract with Bill Veeck," said former Cleveland Indian Bob Lemon, looking back to the era before free agency, pointing out that with Veeck the lesson was simple: "I make money, you make money."[28] The free agency era he had helped instigate had the potential to overturn that rational attitude.

Baseball challenged the Seitz decision in the courts, though its case was weakened by having agreed to binding arbitration conducted by a man of its own choosing. The first court immediately threw out the challenge, and while the appeal continued, the only feasible option appeared to be negotiating with Marvin Miller and the players union. The long-feared new day had dawned.

At the January 10, 1976, meeting of the Chicago chapter of the Baseball Writers' Association of America, Veeck introduced a "mystery guest," who turned out to be his new coach—Minnie Miñoso, returning to the White Sox for the third time. Soon after, with a blizzard swirling outside, Veeck announced at a luncheon that he had rehired Harry Caray as the team's announcer.* Veeck brushed aside Caray's vilification of almost every as-

---

* The contract negotiation in early 1976 between Veeck and Caray was "hilarious, loud, and very public," as reported in the *Chicago Tribune*, January 14, 1976. The two men were scheduled to meet at the restaurant of the Executive House Hotel. Hard of hearing, Veeck shouted

pect of the White Sox' 1975 operation: "We don't need a house dog as our announcer. I think Caray is too great an asset to leave the city, particularly since the White Sox need assets. He is not always kindly, but is never dull."[29]

Veeck then assembled an impromptu touring company, including Caray, that would travel through Illinois and Indiana in late January, drumming up interest and advance ticket sales for the 1976 White Sox. The group included Veeck's son Mike, then twenty-four and experiencing the front office as a young man, as had his father; the team's longtime traveling secretary, Don Unferth; general manager Roland Hemond; and two players, Rich Gossage and the as yet unsigned Ralph Garr, who had come to an unwritten agreement to be the Sox' designated hitter. The two White Sox were "dazzled by the whole thing." The group began in Rockford with radio and television interviews and then moved on to such stops as a combined Optimist and Rotary luncheon in Rock Island, which drew more than 1,000; a father-son sports banquet for 600 in Peoria; a large luncheon in Champaign; a media junket in Joliet; and a tour-ending event in South Bend, Indiana.

Veeck gave much the same presentation in all venues, indulging in the quip "Anytime that we had this many for the Browns, we would play a doubleheader." He also used the tour to take jabs at Oakland Athletics owner Charles Finley: "I can't divulge any of my 1,500 or 1,600 promotion ideas because Finley might use them." He even challenged Finley's claim to be the originator of the orange baseball, saying, "My daddy tried the orange baseball when he was with the Cubs back in 1927 or '28."

But his big guns were trained on the reserve clause, which he deemed "indefensible both legally and morally." At every stop, he invoked the name that still caused his fellow owners to wince: "When I testified five or six years ago on Curt Flood's behalf, the rest of the owners had a pretty good idea of where I stood. And when Mr. [Lee] MacPhail finally got around to reading my testimony the other day, he probably learned that I tried to tell

---

to an approaching Caray and his attorney, Marty Cohn, "Hey, Harry, I want to make you an offer to work for me." Mocking Veeck's thunderous voice, Caray shouted back, with the restaurant patrons suddenly taking notice, "That sounds great, Bill."

Veeck then countered: "How 'bout $100,000 a year, Harry?"

Caray's response: "That sounds great, Bill. When do I start?"

The amazed diners applauded the exchange.

baseball executives to sit down and work on a modified reserve clause rather than to have one shoved down their throat."

There would be a pause and a wink, followed by a line he loved to deliver: "I've always felt that when most owners stick their heads in the sand, their brains are still showing." He felt that a negotiated settlement with the players was the answer, rather than fighting the Seitz decision in court. "I find Marvin Miller a reasonable man, and highly intelligent."[30]

Veeck, who usually shied away from free tickets, made large exceptions to get people going back to the South Side for baseball. In early February, a telethon for cerebral palsy went off the air because of a power failure. Veeck had pledged 10,000 White Sox tickets, but he immediately upped the offer to 12,000 because of the power failure. When he later heard the charity would lose about $250,000, he gave it 25,000 tickets, which he predicted would put about $100,000 in its till.[31]

The same day as the telethon, February 6, 1976, a U.S. District Court judge in Kansas City upheld the Seitz decision, once again pointing out that the courts were not in the business of undermining labor disputes settled by a formal process of arbitration. It was clear even to the most intractable owner that the courts were not going to help, and the only resolution had to come from negotiation with the Players Union.[32]

Reaction to the ruling was varied. Finley was determined to take the case all the way to the Supreme Court, citing the reserve clause as sacred and himself as opposed to modifications that "would wreck the game like basketball and football are being wrecked." Perhaps the most surprising reaction came from Cubs owner Phil Wrigley, who was as unperturbed as Veeck. He "was the only owner who never has worried about the reserve clause," reasoning that he did not want a reserve clause to bind a player to him. "I've always felt that if a man doesn't want to work for you, he isn't going to do a good job."[33]

Because no basic agreement had been signed between the players and the owners, the latter imposed a unilateral lockout during spring training. Veeck threatened to go to court to find a legal way to open the White Sox camp, characterizing the owners as unfair and unreasonable. Morris Siegel of the *Washington Evening Star* wrote that if the other owners had an opportunity to vote again on admitting him to the league, the vote to bar him would be unanimous. Speaking of the owners, Siegel wrote, "In the eyes of the establishment, which has always taken a dim view of Veeck's baseball lifestyle, this was a flagrant case of strike-breaking against their union." Veeck, he said, was against his peers on almost everything they did except inhaling.[34]

The White Sox, Veeck stubbornly insisted, would report to Sarasota on March 1, regardless of what the rest of the league did. But on February 26, Veeck finally backed off because of what he described as intimidation and threats from the league that included "a lot of very unpleasant things, from fines, suspensions and even lifting the franchise." Calvin Griffith proposed a $500,000 fine if Veeck disobeyed. At a hastily called press conference in Chicago, Veeck admitted, "The gun is loaded and pointed at my head. There is actually nothing else we could do—they could have taken away the franchise and kept us in bankruptcy the rest of our lives." He told *Chicago Sun-Times* columnist Tom Fitzpatrick, "Frankly, I quit like a dog."[35]

"I was afraid this kind of thing was going to happen," California Angels owner Gene Autry observed about the affair. "That's why I definitely voted against Veeck when he was about to buy the White Sox."[36] Veeck now felt free to express mock pity for Autry. He told *People* magazine: "I'm sorry for girls in homes for wayward women and for Gene Autry. I say nasty things sometimes, don't I? I mean them."[37]

Veeck decided to open spring training with non-roster players—fifteen minor leaguers and ten former major leaguers hoping to stage a comeback, including former New York Mets star Cleon Jones and the well-traveled Bob Oliver. Lee MacPhail was quick to point out that this was not a violation of anything, and that there was nothing wrong with his bringing players not on his forty-man roster. "Of course I did it to attract attention," Veeck admitted. "Not to us, but to baseball and the fact that it's a game played on the field with a bat and a ball, not in court with writs and pleas. I think it's about time somebody called attention to this." Nonetheless, Veeck predicted the other owners would be furious. As if on cue, Calvin Griffith called Veeck's actions "stupid . . . very narrow-minded . . . self-serving . . . if we thought this was the act of the rational man, we'd worry about it."[38]

As the lockout continued, public interest in the upcoming season seemed to be ebbing. Part of Veeck's plan was to engage the fans in the changes he was making, and on Saturday, March 6, he invited people to come to the ballpark to remove 18,000 square feet of artificial turf that he felt was the blight of the Allyn years. "When you go to the ballpark, you are entitled to the smell of grass freshly cut," he observed. He also knew the players hated artificial turf because it became unbearably hot in the summer and caused injuries. At a time when other owners were crowing about the advantages of artificial turf—even, as in the case of the Cincinnati Reds, building an offense around it—some 1,000 potential White Sox ticket buyers showed up to de-install the carpet, hauling off pieces ranging from ones the size of ceiling tiles to room-sized remnants.

On the heels of the rug removal, Veeck staged a fashion show. He had been talking about putting the White Sox in short pants since February, when he first mentioned it at a press conference, noting that Bucky Dent and Goose Gossage were among those who were keen on the idea, which had sprung from Veeck's what-if imagination. In early March, he announced three possible designs—Hollywood Shorts, Clamdiggers, and Knickerbockers—which he said would be modeled on March 9 in the elegant drawing room of Chicago's Tremont Hotel.

As models, he brought in five large, well-known, knobby-kneed former major leaguers to stage the show in front of about 100 sportswriters and several television crews gathered for the event. Moose Skowron, Moe Drabowsky, Dave Nicholson, and Dan Osinski were the first to come down the runway, and all received polite applause and much laughter as they modeled home and away versions of the two Bermuda-length designs. Then came the Hollywood design, approximating the short, tight "hot pants" of the era. It was modeled by "Jungle Jim" Rivera, who had earned his nickname from a highly aggressive playing style. Rivera sucked in his cheeks, placed his arms akimbo, and did a perfect parody of a twirling, swishing model taking command of a runway. It brought down the house. A small group of women, including Mary Frances and White Sox organist Nancy Faust, were invited to comment while Veeck, who claimed to have designed the three uniforms from scratch, narrated the show: "They're not garish. Like my wife, Mary Frances, said, they have an understated elegance." Dave Condon called it "the most revolutionary fashion event since Adam and Eve introduced the fig leaf."[39]

ON MARCH 17, as Commissioner Kuhn was still debating whether or not to open spring training camps, he took a call from Veeck.

"Do you remember the television special about *The Grinch Who Stole Christmas?*"

"Sure, but what's that got to do with the reserve clause or major league baseball?" Kuhn responded.

"Well, unless we open training camps pretty soon, we're going to be remembered as the ogres who stole spring. You know, to some people, spring is represented by robins and crocuses. But to a lot of people, spring means baseball, and if we steal it, we're going to get into big trouble."

Kuhn laughed and replied, "I don't want to be a Grinch." Within a few hours, he issued the order to take the padlocks off the doors, and the seventeen-day lockout was over.[40]

Veeck was eager to meet his new players as they reported to spring training in Sarasota. Veteran first baseman Jim Spencer recalled how Veeck greeted him. "I had just come over to the Sox in a trade from the Angels for Bill Melton, and he said to me, 'Spence, welcome to the club; you are my first baseman. I want you to go out and play hard, have fun, and always remember, I only fear one thing—*termites*."[41]

Now that the season was ensured, speculation resumed as to how Veeck would launch the home opener on April 9 against the Kansas City Royals. Someone predicted that he would stage a volcano or an earthquake. Replied Veeck, "The earthquake's been done before—in San Francisco—but I will offer something that will astound you."[42]

Dave Condon had been in on the plan since Veeck hatched it late one night: "I'll play the fife, Rudie Schaffer will have the drum, and Paul [Richards] will carry the flag. We'll all wear Revolutionary War garb." The nation was celebrating its bicentennial in 1976, and Veeck latched onto this as his theme, focusing on the famous painting by Archibald MacNeal Willard of three battered Continental Army veterans marching with flag, fife, and drum. The painting, known as *The Spirit of '76*, had a hundred years earlier been the hit of the Centennial Exposition in Philadelphia.

"Would you buy it?" Veeck asked Condon.

A *Chicago Tribune* article described what happened next: "The hour was late—the inevitable hour when . . . all ideas sound like world-beaters. Veeck was assured he'd come up with the greatest idea since stretch pants."

Prior to the first pitch on Opening Day, the three men appeared suddenly and unannounced in white powdered wigs. "When they came out of the dugout, people were spellbound at first. They found it hilarious, and touching," Roland Hemond remembered. "It was quite an interesting moment in the return of Bill Veeck."

The three men stood there with Veeck's wooden leg fully exposed and dour Richards playing his part to the hilt. "It was only Opening Day, with

162 games yet to play," Rick Talley wrote in the *Tribune* the next day, "and there was the distinguished, 67-year-old manager of the Sox wearing a white wig. Actually, he looked pretty good. He did an excellent job, too, in reciting his favorite stanza of 'The Star-Spangled Banner' and he carried the American flag at just the right height." Veeck explained that his favorite stanza was the fourth: "I've tried with every club to get them to sing the 4th verse instead of that first one."[43]

"It combined all the things of great gags," Mike Veeck recalled years later. "It was wonderfully subtle in a lot of ways. It had textures. And it was appropriate. But the fact that it just appeared made it seem magical. It was universally loved. A lot of times, gags were half-and-half. But it was a very literate promotion. Here was a guy who had lost his leg in the war. And here were survivors who represented a couple hundred years in baseball. It had this wonderful delicacy. Fans are very smart and they looked out and they got it. . . . I thought it was wonderful to be raised by a guy who was like Geppetto."[44]

As Veeck stumped triumphantly across the new natural turf, he saw 40,318 fans, double the Opening Day attendance in 1975. With the help of such innovations as toll-free telephone lines, season ticket sales were up some 40 percent. More than 500,000 tickets had been sold before the first ball was pitched, to see a team that had drawn only 750,802 fans at home for all of 1975.

This showing was all the more remarkable because the pre-Opening-Day take on the team was not good. "We'll bunt a lot, steal a lot, and pray a lot," said manager Richards on the eve of the new season. At least two writers used the line "The Sox are a Wreck—as in Veeck," and from the start the team had the unenviable nickname of "Veeck's Wrecks." Although the White Sox won their home opener 4–0, Sox victories were few and far between during the 1976 season, and in June they endured a skid of ten consecutive losses.

Meanwhile, after the school year was over the family moved back to Chicago and into adjoining apartments in the Hyde Park section. Mary Frances said the timing had been perfect. "Our kids are at an age where they can appreciate the city," she said, adding that she loved the house in Easton but was happy to now be "the retired champion of everything that has to do with keeping house."[45]

As always, Veeck listened to the fans. After he had moved the organ played by Nancy Faust from behind home plate for Opening Day to free up space for a dozen box seats, the people who had sat around the organ circulated a petition to have it restored. As Faust recalled, "He did have high regard for the fans' comments, so the second or third series, he moved the organ back down."[46]

He was also listening to fans on Opening Day when he noticed that those who clustered around the broadcast booth were singing along as Harry Caray sang "Take Me Out to the Ball Game" during the seventh-inning stretch, which was his custom. A few days later, unbeknownst to Caray, Veeck snuck a microphone into the broadcast booth attached to the stadium's public address system. When Caray began to sing, his voice carried through the whole stadium, and the fans joined in with discernible gusto. After the game, Caray confronted Veeck in the Bards Room, and Veeck explained, "Harry, I've been looking for a guy to do that for 30 years, but I never could find the right guy before. Well, you're the right guy. Do you know why you're the right guy?"

Then Veeck explained that Caray was perfect because everybody knew that he or she could sing as well or better than him. "Hell, if you had a good singing voice you'd intimidate them and nobody would join in."[47]

Before the end of the 1976 season, the Veecks staged a Harry Caray Appreciation Night, with each fan's complimentary gift bag containing a recording of Harry and organist Nancy Faust performing four variations of the song.[48]

Veeck held promotion on top of promotion. In addition to the usual giveaways, there was a Salute to Mexico Day, complete with caballeros, a parade, and a bullfight in which the bull was spared. There was also a rain-dampened Greek Night with scantily clad belly dancers shimmering in unison. These antics did not sit well with his fellow owners, who criticized his carnival approach as outmoded. Brewers president Bud Selig, a long-standing Veeck admirer, now told a writer for *People* magazine: "What went on in the '40s and '50s is no more germane to baseball today than last winter's snow is to our conversation. Nobody ever paid to see an owner yet, and nobody ever will."[49]

To be sure, people wouldn't pay to see Veeck, but they would go to see what rabbit he would next pull out of his hat. In early August, that proved to be an outdoor shower with an enormous head that Veeck installed in the center-field bleachers, intended to keep the bleacherites cool on hot days and perhaps help them forget that the team was hovering some twenty games out of first place.

"The worst thing we've done is sell the idea that you have to have a winning team. That dooms 20 of our 24 clubs to failure before the season even starts. What we have to create is an atmosphere of enjoyment. Take an example—I put a shower in the bleachers. It had a utilitarian function—it gets hot out there and people like to cool off. But it also attracts a certain number of young girls in bathing suits, and a certain number of young men who like to look at young girls in bathing suits. People in the suburbs aren't going to say, 'Let's go to the game today because there's a shower in the bleachers,' but we create the impression that we are going to have some fun."[50]

On August 8, the White Sox dressed for the first game of a doubleheader against Kansas City in the Bermuda-length navy blue shorts with white pullover tops that had been modeled the previous off-season. The team won the first game so adorned and then rejected the shorts, changing into their regular uniforms before the second game, which they lost. The White Sox played two more games in shorts before the idea was forever shelved, but it had been a publicity bonanza, and Veeck with a wink predicted that the practice would be commonplace within five years.* On the day Veeck introduced the shorts, the White Sox announced that attendance was 200,000 ahead of the previous year's.[51]

Despite the entertainment, the White Sox were plain bad in 1976. No batter hit more than fourteen home runs, no pitcher won more than ten games. And the team's luck was no better. "I've never seen things go as badly for a team as they have for us this year," lamented Veeck. "In every respect—weather, schedule, injuries—we've taken it on the chin." The team had lost Wilbur Wood, the anchor of the pitching staff, when his kneecap was shattered by a line drive in early May, and then lost its top reliever, Clay Carroll, in May when he fell down the stairs at home and broke his right hand. "Let us just say disaster has struck and we are it."[52]

A small glimmer of satisfaction was achieved in September when Veeck reactivated fifty-year-old Minnie Miñoso for eight at-bats so Miñoso could say he had played in four decades. As a DH, he got one hit. The Miñoso moment was especially moving for older Americans who still harbored dreams of baseball glory. Mark Plotkin, an ardent White Sox fan, was managing the 1976 presidential campaign of Senator Eugene McCarthy, who

---

* As Richard Roeper would later write in his book *Sox and the City*, "The short pants will be mentioned forever on every list of the worst sports uniforms of all time."

loved the game as both a spectator and a player, when one night in Florida it occurred to the two men to see if Veeck would activate McCarthy as he had Miñoso.

Plotkin got Veeck on the second ring.

"Is this Bill Veeck?" he asked.

"You've got him."

Plotkin asked if there was any chance Veeck would allow McCarthy to play. Despite scheduled campaign appearances, McCarthy was ready to fly to Chicago on a moment's notice.

"Can he hit?" Veeck asked

McCarthy nodded, and Plotkin said that he could.

There was a long pause, and then Veeck said, "Naaah. Daley would kill me," referring to Chicago mayor Richard Daley.[53]

As the team declined, Veeck was hard-pressed to lure fans to Comiskey Park, and he attempted an array of giveaways—comic books, bats, batting helmets, decals, and more swatches of artificial turf. One night Veeck gave away all sorts of junk and at least one live animal. "I know Bill had an old piano, an old car and a donkey. They were door prizes," organist Nancy Faust recalled. "When nobody claimed the donkey, a few days later I asked Rudie Schaffer if I could take it home. He gave me the OK." Faust brought the 400-pound Rosita to her home in Des Plaines. "I quickly realized how smart they are," she said at the time of her retirement in 2010, after forty-one consecutive years with the team.[54]

Not buying Veeck's efforts, Robert Marcus wryly observed in the *Chicago Tribune*, in a line Veeck would have appreciated, "Marie Antoinette lost her head over only suggesting what Veeck has done. The people are starved for baseball, and he sent them cakes and a circus."[55]

The baseball was, in fact, dull and disappointing, and Paul Richards turned out to be a lackluster leader. "His heart just wasn't in it, concluded Joe Goddard of the *Chicago Sun-Times*." Converting Goose Gossage from a reliever to a starter had been a mistake on several levels, as he had saved 26 games the season before. But the frequent between-innings activity was also a distraction. "It was a three-ring circus, and we were the third act," said Gossage.[56]

The final home game of the season, on September 26, was scheduled to be Bill Veeck Appreciation Night, when the season's attendance was expected to reach 1 million. Anyone who sent in his or her name would be listed in the program as a cosponsor of the honorific game. Bob Feller, Max Patkin, and many others would be on hand for the event, and there would be prizes galore, including a car to be given away by lottery.

Fittingly, it rained on Veeck's big night, and attendance was half what had been hoped for, driving home a point that had become evident a few days earlier—that the million mark in attendance would not be met. "I'd never suggested," Veeck told Roger Kahn after the season, "that promotion by it-self attracts fans. Winning draws fans. Winning plus promotion sets atten-dance records. Promoting with a last-place team, which is what we had to do last year, is only slightly more difficult than running a benefit for Mr. Nixon among people whose names appeared on the enemies list."[57]

To top it all off, the White Sox lost 7–4 that night to the Oakland A's, end-ing the season at 64–97. The last-place Sox had been shut out on twenty-one occasions—not a modern record (the 1963 Mets held that record, thirty) but still indicative of their offensive futility. In all of baseball, only Montreal lost more games in 1976. Pitcher Ken Brett summed it up: "Our season was so bad that by the fifth inning, Bill Veeck was selling hot dogs to go."

Following the game, Veeck apologized to the city of Chicago: "I feel like a thief in the night. I stole their plaudits and gave them nothing in return."[58] But Veeck had, in fact, given himself to the city. He was still the only owner who answered his own phone and listened with real interest to anybody who called. Among the prominent figures in baseball, he alone still made almost daily unpaid speeches to any organization that asked, and he was usually the last person to leave the meeting hall. He didn't watch his team play from a fancy owner's box—which, as he said, put his back to the fans—but ambled around the stadium chatting with fans and asking for their suggestions. Veeck was a reporter's dream, and his craggy face was ideally suited for the television camera.

Now all he needed was a team. In a matter of days after the end of the World Series, he decided he would advertise for one in *The Sporting News*:

UNSIGNED PLAYERS*
For Action and Bucks!
Call BILL VEECK
Collect 312/924-1000
We're building for next year!
* Players who will be free agents at the end of this season or their agents.
                                                      Chicago White Sox

---

Veeck accepted more than 700 collect calls. "Yes, I heard from Joe Rudi and Rollie Fingers. They called me collect—I should say the ALLEGED Joe Rudi and Rollie Fingers called me collect from saloons all across the country." He added that almost all the calls from Rollie Fingers came at 2:00 a.m.[59]

A story then leaked that he was arranging through an Albany, New York, travel agent to go to Cuba to scout players. Veeck had hoped to keep this move secret. Surprisingly, the commissioner had no initial objection. "Ping-pong opened China," Veeck pointed out, predicting that "baseball will open Cuba." Days later, however, Kuhn nixed the plan.[60]

Yet Veeck's off-season would be dominated again by his health. In mid-November 1976, he entered Illinois Masonic Hospital to deal with long-standing spinal problems that had become aggravated and would finally require surgery to remove pressure on his spinal nerves and stabilize his deteriorating neck. Three days before the operation on November 15, Veeck invited an old friend to sneak past the No Visitors signs for a "riotous evening" of watching him take pills. The next morning, Veeck announced from his hospital bed that Paul Richards was stepping aside as manager and would serve the team as a consultant, working with pitchers in the Sox farm system. His new manager was to be his night visitor, trusted friend Bob Lemon, who had been his ace in Cleveland and whose 207 wins had led to his induction into the Hall of Fame earlier in the year. Miñoso would remain on the team as part of the coaching squad, and Larry Doby would join the White Sox as their new hitting coach, further reuniting the miracle Cleveland team of 1948.[61]

Unable to attend the Winter Meetings, Veeck considered a new strategy that could give him an edge in a market increasingly hostile to owners operating on a shoestring. Because of his long-term opposition to the reserve clause, Veeck had become the poster child for the concept of "be careful what you wish for." But one element of the new rules worked in his favor, if only for a season. Veeck invoked the renewal clause with several players who refused to sign, automatically extending their contracts for one more season at a 20 percent reduction in salary, which saved nearly half a million dollars that year.

Veeck conceived a scheme he dubbed "rent-a-player," by which he traded for other clubs' stars in their option years. This allowed him to get Oscar Gamble, plus two pitchers, from the Yankees for the 1977 season in a trade for Bucky Dent, and earlier he sent Gossage and pitcher Terry Forster to the Pittsburgh Pirates for slugger Richie Zisk and a minor-league pitcher. Veeck knew he would have them at bargain prices only until the end of the 1977 season, when they would enter the free agent market, but in a flash he had overcome the team's lack of power.

Interested in the future as well as the present, Veeck was asked what he thought about an eighteen-year-old kid named Harold Baines.

"Greatest rookie I've ever seen," was his response, recalling the first time he had seen Baines play, four years earlier. "I really mean it," he said, adding that he was just a kid and that he may not be ready yet. "But remember the name Baines. Harold Baines."[62]

At the home Opening Day in 1977, all four of Mayor Daley's sons were invited to throw out a first ball. "Not only do we have four first balls," Veeck said with a broad grin, "we have 20,000 more. Everybody wants to throw out a first ball, so I've bought all these harmless Styrofoam baseballs. You can throw one out yourself, if you'd like." After a Styrofoam blizzard, the Sox jumped ahead of the Boston Red Sox, Ken Brett pitched strongly, and Veeck's patchwork heroes won 5–2 before a noisy crowd of almost 34,612.

Veeck was more determined than ever to make his fans happy. His new program contained an unusual personal touch: "If your beer is flat, call Millie Johnson. If the washrooms aren't up to par, call David Schaffer. If you'd like a tryout, give C. V. Davis a call. We don't have a complaint department, but we do have people."

"Attendance remains uncertain," began Roger Kahn's assessment of the 1977 Sox. "Seventeen seasons without a pennant have eroded the old South Side enthusiasm. Compared to what baseball men hold in Los Angeles and New York, Veeck's bank accounts are light. Destructive—possibly planted— rumors are abroad that he may not have the cash to finish this season." Robert Creamer's judgment was no less grim; he felt Veeck had been "blind-sided" by the astonishing surge in salaries brought on by the free agent draft. "The White Sox were not at all competitive in going after free agents, and they had trouble signing their own players."[63]

But the gloomy assessments proved to be unfounded. The club got off to a good start and was at 29–21 on June 7, when Veeck and Roland Hemond picked and signed Harold Baines in the amateur draft. It was a good omen, if for no other reason than it was the first time in the thirteen-year history of the draft that the White Sox had been able to sign their first draft pick. Mike Veeck remembered great internal dissension over the selection of Baines, with Paul Richards and others arguing strongly for Robin Yount and other players with higher rankings. "My dad loved Baines and refused to back off. He said he knew Baines would make it because he had 'great wrists—great roaring wrists.' "[64] When Baines and his parents met with Veeck, he insisted that Baines be represented by a lawyer.[65] Veeck also arranged for Baines to have a financial counselor.*

As summer came, it was obvious that Veeck had transformed the hapless 1976 ball club into a pennant contender, and they had earned a nickname: "the South Side Hit Men." It was an apt allusion to the newly acquired trio of power hitters, Oscar Gamble, Richie Zisk, and Eric Soderholm, who led the team to a franchise-record 192 home runs. Offense overtook pitching and defense, and the team was described as "more like homer-happy 16-inch softball players than a typical White Sox team."[66]

A July 31 doubleheader against the Kansas City Royals drew 50,412 in paid attendance, which was more than 10 percent of the Sox' total attendance for the decade-low season of 1970. Late in the second game, a fight broke out among some fans just outside the press box. A White Sox administrative assistant went outside to break it up, but the brawler began hitting him, which inspired Veeck to charge into the melee. A blow to the face caused his glasses to go flying. Suddenly, the writers were covering the fight while keeping half an eye on the ballgame. One of the brawlers caught Veeck's glasses before they hit the cement, causing one reporter to note that such good reflexes might win him a tryout for the White Sox infield.

The *Milwaukee Journal* noted, "By the time things had broken up Chicago had split a doubleheader and Veeck had split a lip." But, like his team, Veeck didn't go away without some glory: " 'I got one in too,' he said."[67]

Besides an appropriate nickname, the team also got an anthem, which—for better or worse—spread to other stadiums and other sports. "It was in 1977, the 'South Side Hit Men,' and we were vying for first place with Kansas City, so the fans were really charged and they were responding to everything," recalled organist Nancy Faust. When she played "Na Na Hey Hey Kiss Him Goodbye," they all sang. "I'd never heard anything like that, and neither did the writers, evidently, and it just made such an impact that it

---

* Roger Clark, Veeck's old lifeguard friend, who is also a good friend of Baines's, says that this was instrumental in helping Baines manage his money with great skill. Harold Baines's wife, Marla, is an associate in Clark's real estate firm.

was written about. I remember going to the Bards Room and someone asking, 'What song was that?' I said, 'I think it's called "Sha Na Na." ' Well, it isn't.
I just knew it was a good song."[68]

The White Sox ended up finishing third in their division, winning 90
games (including twenty-two in an amazing July), a twenty-six-game improvement over the previous year. Coming out of the All-Star break, both
the Sox and the Cubs led their divisions, giving a whiff of hope for the first
all-Chicago World Series since 1906. The Sox were in and out of first place
in the American League East for most of the summer and in first place as
late as the end of August. Filling the park was a raucous working-class crew
that seldom seemed to sit. "I've never seen anything like it," said Mary
Frances. "They cheer for anything from a home run to a routine play. It's
wonderful."[69]

The 1977 White Sox were a big draw, bringing a record 1,657,135 fans to
Comiskey Park. Veeck, who had had Sox World Series tickets printed up in
advance with permission of the league, chose to send them out to season
ticket holders as keepsakes of the season. Many of the tickets went out with
his autograph under the word "Thanks."[70]

United Press International named Lemon manager of the year and honored Veeck as the baseball executive of the year. Veeck won in a landslide,
with sixteen of the twenty-four participating writers voting for him. Veeck
claimed that he didn't deserve the honor but that his business manager,
Rudie Schaffer, did: "He does the work and I take the bows."[71] But his assessment after the 1977 season reflected his sense of achievement: "There
was such excitement in this ballpark, it's hard to tell whether the fans affected the players or the players affected the fans. But it was the most remarkable year I have ever seen or had in baseball."[72]

As Veeck knew was likely to happen, the demise of the South Side Hit
Men began a few days after the executive-of-the-year honor was bestowed.
In early November, Veeck lost the services of Richie Zisk to the Texas Rang-
ers, who signed him to a ten-year, $2.5 million deal.

Then Oscar Gamble was signed by a fellow Chicagoan. In the late 1930s
when Veeck ran the concession stands at Wrigley Field, the local salesman
of paper cups was Ray Kroc. Now, some forty years later, Kroc owned the
McDonald's restaurant chain and had recently purchased the San Diego
Padres. Gamble was signed as a free agent by the Padres three weeks after
Zisk left. "Gamble went in there with a figure in mind," Veeck related. "Before he could say anything, Kroc offered him twice what he had intended to

ask for and said, 'Take it or leave it.' Did you ever go to an auction? You see how people get when the bidding is on. They don't even care what's up for sale. All they want to do is win the bidding. That's what has happened in baseball."[73]

CHAPTER 19

Demolition

ANTICIPATING THAT HIS "RENTED" PLAYERS would leave at the end of the 1977 season, Veeck began exploring other possibilities during the season. In late May, he ventured to Cuba to see if he could line up a few players for the White Sox. He was accompanied by Frank Mankiewicz, formerly president of National Public Radio and press secretary to the late senator Robert Kennedy. The two men had come together through mutual friends, and Mankiewicz was there to help Veeck but also to gather information for a *Washington Post* column. Veeck had come armed with scouting reports on a group of top prospects, including Bárbaro Garbey, who in 1984 became the first Cuban refugee to make the majors.

Veeck's plan was simple and explained to every Cuban official the two men met, including onetime major-league hopeful Fidel Castro and his brother Raúl. Veeck envisioned a new international alignment of teams in Canada, Mexico, Venezuela, Japan, and Cuba. He wanted to be allowed to sign Cuban players for the White Sox under contracts that would allow them to return to Cuba to play for any valid Cuban team in the majors or the minors once U.S.-Cuban diplomatic relations were restored. He also suggested that the other owners would raise no objections.

Knowing that the Yankees also were making overtures to the island nation, he told the Cubans that the Yankees were "Batistas"—an allusion to the regime the Castros had overthrown—and "capitalistas." He declared, "I am a poor man, a fighter, so you know what side I am on." The Cubans, according to Mankiewicz, would hear none of it, mostly because they did not trust Veeck. "They just couldn't believe that a major capitalist entrepreneur had anyone's welfare at heart but his own and that of his class." Veeck also hurt his own case, according to Mankiewicz, by interrupting his pitch to the Cuban commissioner of baseball with a garbled and erroneous tutorial on the balk rule. "He lost the Commissioner and probably the chance for a major foreign policy breakthrough," Mankiewicz recalled later. "Veeck was always more fan than diplomat."[1]

The trip was a bust, and on his return Veeck stated, "The Cubans aren't interested in exporting the human animal even if would help the economy."[2]

During the winter of 1977–78, Veeck signed Ron Blomberg and Bobby Bonds to plug the gap left by the loss of his heavy hitters. As a Yankee, Blomberg had never lived up to expectations, in large part because he was prone to injuries: he had had only 106 at-bats in 1975, 2 in 1976, and none in 1977.* Despite this, Veeck signed him to a four-year guaranteed deal amounting to $125,000 per year with an $80,000 signing bonus. Gabe Paul, general manager of the New York Mets, who had made a modest offer for Blomberg, could not believe Veeck's: "I don't know if Bill has lost his mind or not."

Veeck told Dick Young of the New York *Daily News* that he hired Blomberg because he liked to hire the handicapped. Wrote Young, "I laughed over the phone when he said it, but then I quickly realized that this is one of the few times in his life Bill Veeck, the carney man, wasn't kidding."

"I'm a believer in guys that want to play ball, and in rehabilitation," Veeck said.

Young and others also believed that Veeck was consumed with the idea of beating the Yankees with one of their own retreads.[3] Also, the fact that Blomberg was Jewish appealed to Veeck, who told him that there were other Jews on the team, including Steve Stone and Ross Baumgarten. "With your personality," Veeck told him, "and all the Jewish people in Chicago, you are going to be a perfect fit."[4]

The slugging Bonds came to the White Sox in a six-player deal from the California Angels, which also involved sending Brian Downing to California. Having played most of his career with the San Francisco Giants, he had been traded to the Yankees in late 1974, then traded by them after the 1975 season to the Angels, for whom he had had a big year in 1977. Soon after the season began, however, Veeck traded Bonds to Texas for Rusty

---

* Blomberg has long been a trivia and *Jeopardy* question because on April 6, 1973, he became the major leagues' first designated hitter.

Torres and Claudell Washington, who took five days to report to the team, explaining, "I overslept."*

With all the changes, the Sox got off to a terrible start in 1978, and as late as May 27 they were at the bottom of the American League West, twelve and a half games out of first place. Then, suddenly, they won fifteen out of seventeen and were only three and a half games off the pace.

But Veeck was not happy. He had become increasingly frustrated by what he perceived to be a lack of coverage from the *Chicago Tribune*, which had supported him for so long. On June 13 Veeck noted that the story about the Sox beating the Cleveland Indians was on page three, while the Cubs, who also won, got front-page treatment. "I've had it up to here," said Veeck, pointing to his neck. "It just isn't fair." He claimed that the Cubs were getting a two-to-one edge in *Tribune* coverage and that he could prove his charge by counting linear inches. Then he dropped a bombshell: "I'm tired of scuffling around. I'd take the franchise out of here if the chance came along." He told Jerome Holtzman of the *Sun-Times*, "The *Tribune* is trying to bury us."[5]

The story was splashed across the top of the sports section in the *Tribune* and was picked up by other reporters in hot pursuit, along with radio and television. "For the first time all season, the smell of TV sportscaster's hair spray wafted through the park," wrote John Schulian of the *Sun-Times*.[6] Veeck's face and voice were everywhere. In a live television interview Veeck explained at great length that the Cubs had received preferred media treatment, even though the Sox had won fifteen of their last seventeen games. Nodding in agreement as he signed off, the interviewer said, "Yes, it's remarkable the way the Cubs have come back in the last 17 games."[7]

But Veeck had picked a fight he could not win. Soon thereafter *Tribune* sports editor George Langford responded in print under the headline "We Like Your Style, Bill, but These Are the Facts."[8] "For those interested," he wrote, "these are the figures: since March 1, when spring-training opened, the *Tribune* sports sections tabulated, there was a total of 1,803 column inches of story type on the White Sox and 1,427 column inches on the Cubs. That figure does not include pictures and outlines during that time. 70

---

* This inspired the fans to hang a sign from the right-field bleachers that read WASHINGTON SLEPT HERE.

White Sox stories appeared on page 1 of sports, compared to 68 Cubs stories on page 1."*

Confronted with this by the *Sun-Times*'s Schulian, Veeck replied: "That's odd."

Then Schulian observed: "A sly smile flickered across the face that looks like it belongs on a woodcarver's doll."[9] Once again, as he had in St. Louis with the Browns, Veeck had become a lot more interesting than the team he put on the field.

On June 30, with the team at 34–40, Veeck removed Bob Lemon and made Larry Doby the second black to manage a big-league club. Once again Veeck had made Doby the second to break the color barrier, and both times it was behind a man named Robinson—this time Frank Robinson, who had been made player-manager of the Cleveland Indians in 1975. When he left, Lemon commented that, absent the offense, this was a team dependent on its pitching, which wasn't very good: "A year ago, we just overpowered people and I was a very smart manager. I guess I wasn't too smart this year." The night after he was fired, Veeck invited him home for drinks and Lemon accepted.[10]

At the same time that Doby was made manager, Veeck replaced Minnie Miñoso as first-base coach with the young manager of the Sox' Knoxville farm club, Tony La Russa. Miñoso was moved into a public relations role in what Veeck termed "a lateral promotion."

When the team began to skid seriously in mid-July with nine straight losses, Veeck made a rare clubhouse appearance to announce that he wanted the players to forget about their mistakes and that, as he had in Cleveland in 1949, he was declaring a new start to the season on July 28. It would be staged with bands and player introductions, just like Opening Day. The Sox lost in the July 28 game, though, and Bobby Bonds, who had been traded to Texas early in the season, was the margin of victory for the Rangers, with a pair of two-run homers, a single, and a stolen base.

As the slide continued, out-of-town writers began calling the team names such as the "Chicago Blight Sox." At one point in August Veeck asked his shortstop, Don Kessinger, to consider taking over for Doby, but Kessinger

---

* After Veeck raised a flap about coverage, *Trib* columnist and Veeck supporter Dave Condon decided to fool Veeck by triple-spacing his copy when he wrote about the Sox so it would look like the team was getting more column inches.

deferred out of fairness to Doby; nor did he want to take over a team he had not led through spring training.[11]

In Cleveland for a late-August series, a local reporter referred to the Sox as "a gimmick that has not gimmicked." He pointed out that Doby, whose dream had turned into a nightmare, was not even calling for the team to take batting or infield practice. After the Sox dropped a 10–1 game to the Indians, Doby admitted, "I have no promises, no contract for next year."[12]

After a September 26 loss to Oakland in the home finale, Veeck advised: "Save the program from tonight's game, because they'll soon be a collector's item. A museum piece. It contains lots of names that never again will appear in a White Sox program. Some probably won't appear in any major-league program again."[13]

Doby's club was 37–50, and the White Sox finished in fifth place in their seven-team division with a 71–90 record. If there was any happy ending for anyone close to Veeck, it was for Bob Lemon, who was made manager of the New York Yankees shortly after being fired by Veeck, after Billy Martin fell out yet again with George Steinbrenner. Lemon went on to win the 1978 pennant after Bucky Dent's famous home run won a one-game playoff with the Boston Red Sox, and then the Yankees took the World Series from the Dodgers.

In October, Veeck named Don Kessinger as his new player-manager to replace Doby, who again became hitting coach. Veeck said, "I took a man away from doing what he does best: instructing hitters. I asked him to manage. It didn't work out." Frank Robinson was not alone in saying that Doby had not been given a decent chance to run the team and was being replaced by a man with no managerial experience.

Doby also felt he had not been given a proper chance. Though he hoped he would get the same kind of redemptive opportunity that had been given to Bob Lemon, he feared it would never happen. "Bill said to me, before he owned the White Sox, when I was with Montreal, that he wanted me to manage some day," Doby recalled years later. "But he said, 'I want to get you a good ball club first.' Yet he gave me an opportunity with a bad ball club. But I just realized now that he knew he was going out of business when he made me manager. And once he goes out of business, there's no chance for me to manage. He wanted to wait, but I think he just ran out of time, because he was running out of money."[14]

Doby seemed to understand why Veeck had made the move, and he had only praise for Veeck for the rest of his life. "Probably one of the best, down-to-earth human beings I've ever met," Doby enthused. "He didn't throw rhetoric around. Dealt with the truth, the facts. I lost my father when I was eight years old. But, he was my father back then. . . . He would never get the accolades that he should get."[15]

Money was looming larger, but Veeck kept on going even as he watched the price of free agents skyrocket, unable to do anything about it other than buy from the lowest rungs of the talent ladder and make quips about the situation. When asked whether free agents leaned toward playing in big cities, he responded: "Not really. They lean towards cash."[16]

The new year brought the tongue-in-check announcement from Veeck that he was adding an additional ladies' restroom to the left-field corner of the park because 36 percent of his paying customers were women, "and they drink beer." Rick Talley wrote a column on the smoke-and-mirrors press conference with the headline "Veeck Gives Smoke a Very Hard Sell." The simple fact was that Veeck had precious little else to announce in terms of the team he would field in the spring.

In February 1979 Veeck turned sixty-five and stood still for several articles profiling him, including one for *Esquire* in which he was described as "surviving despite 32 operations and 4½ years flat on his back in the hospital." Veeck was awaiting the delivery of a new artificial left knee, and noted that he was known to go through two or three wooden legs a year. The Bards Room became the scene for a birthday party staged by Rudie Schaffer. To Veeck, there was nothing special about the occasion; as he said, "You see one birthday, you've seen 'em all."[17]

Throughout the 1978 season and into the early days of the 1979 campaign, Veeck watched as the changes that would end his baseball career took place. The irony that he had advocated for many of them did not escape him. Then Commissioner Bowie Kuhn let the George Steinbrenners and Ted Turners of the world run amok by not forcing them to share the revenues from their massive local television contracts with MLB, a Veeck idea that would have brought parity to baseball even before Pete Rozelle did a similar thing in the National Football League. Steinbrenner proved, with Reggie Jackson and Catfish Hunter and free agency, that you could buy a World Series ring. Veeck couldn't compete with the big boys anymore, and his promotional genius could no longer make up the difference, try as he might. The home opener in 1979—a 10–2 loss to the Toronto Blue Jays— was such a disaster that Veeck invited the fans to come back for the following game without having to pay. "Give us another chance, please!" he pleaded.

The Sox lost the free game as well, putting them at 1–4, an inauspicious omen. Veeck fully realized that he would have to rely increasingly on gimmicks to keep the ballpark filled. Attempting to attract younger fans, he put his son Mike in charge of new ideas, which included some free rock concerts. Bill was harking back to ideas he had used before, including giving an award for the team's greatest performer the previous season to organist Nancy Faust.

In late June, Veeck was admitted to Illinois Masonic Hospital again for tests. On July 2, after the team had run up a 1–10 record, Veeck called a summit to discuss what could be done to salvage the season, officiating from his hospital room. Mike's job was to ratchet up the promotions to keep the fans coming through the turnstiles.

In the popular mind, there are two bookends to the life of Bill Veeck. The first is Eddie Gaedel and the other is Disco Demolition Night. The latter was Mike's idea, but his father agreed to it. Mike had gotten the idea from a Chicago disc jockey named Steve Dahl of WLUP—"The Loop"— who was leading a crusade against disco music. Dahl took the position that disco threatened rock and roll, and this became a rallying point for those with a disdain for the dance music then at the height of its popularity.

Mike invited Dahl to blow up a huge wooden crate full of disco records in center field between games of a twi-night doubleheader against the Detroit Tigers set for July 12, 1979. Dahl's followers were told they could get into the game for 98 cents if they brought a record to be destroyed. Mike was in charge of the event and hired security for an expected crowd of 35,000. On the day of the game, the elder Veeck unexpectedly checked himself out of the hospital and showed up for the event.

"What are you doing here?" Roland Hemond asked.

"I'm worried about this promotion," replied Veeck, who added, "It could be catastrophic."

Some 50,000 fans crowded the stadium, another 5,000 rushed the gates, and others gained admission by climbing ladders they had brought. Approximately 35,000 more were either outside the stadium or stuck on the Dan Ryan Expressway. The smell of marijuana wafted through the grandstand. "This was not a typical baseball crowd," Mike later recalled. "Most of these kids probably didn't know Bill Veeck from Mr. Bill. This is the Woodstock they never had."[18]

As the first game got under way, Mike sent most of his security people to the gates to stem the flow of gate-crashers, which left the playing field unguarded. But thousands more gained entry through gates that had been forced open. By the time the first game ended with a 4–1 Tigers win, probably 60,000 fans were inside the stadium, which had a seating capacity of 41,000.

Suddenly the air was filled with flying LP records. "They would slice around you and stick in the ground," Rusty Staub of the Tigers later recalled. "It wasn't just one, it was many. Oh, God almighty, I've never seen anything so dangerous in my life. I begged the guys to put on their batting helmets." Others reported flying whiskey bottles and firecrackers.[19]

And people continued to arrive. "As soon as I got out of the El stop at Comiskey Park, I was wading nearly ankle deep in broken records," recalled a man who was there that night. "By the time I got to the ballpark, it was already after the first game. Tickets were already sold out at this point, and so I wandered around outside the stadium with hundreds if not thousands of others who could not get into the park either. It was an incredible scene. There were bonfires of burning records on the streets, and records thrown Frisbee-style into the air were slicing down. Cops on horses were charging all over. I still vividly remember how imposing a man mounted on top of a 600-pound block of galloping muscle was. It was a wild scene."[20]

Leading a chant of "Disco sucks," Steve Dahl strode onto the field dressed in military fatigues and a World War II–style battle helmet and blew up the records. All hell then broke loose. Anti-disco forces stormed the field and refused to leave. They ran the bases and then stole them all, including home plate. The batting cage was pulled loose and destroyed, along with other field equipment. People from the upper deck slid down the foul pole to get onto the field.

"It was funny but sort of tragic at the same time," remembered Ernie Harwell, who was announcing the games for his audience in Detroit. "It was quite a scary night because it looked like they were trying to burn the stadium down. There were fires everywhere and nobody was trying to put them out."

Veeck came out and stood where home plate had been with a microphone in his hand, begging the fans to return to their seats. He was completely ignored, as was Harry Caray, who chanted, "People, people, please get off the field!"

Veeck's beloved fans had become a destructive mob of non-fans. "I felt sorry for Bill Veeck last night," Art Hill wrote in his running account of the 1979 season, *I Don't Care if I Never Come Back*. "He was obviously dismayed by the monster he had built, and he spent two hours out on the firing line, first pleading with the revelers to put out their fires and get off the field, and then pleading with the umpires not to forfeit the game." Veeck was even more frustrated when the umpires surveyed the field and deemed it unplayable, causing the Sox to forfeit the second game.[21]

After this announcement, players from both teams had to lock themselves in their clubhouses for hours to protect themselves from rampaging fans. The action spread to the parking lots, where players' wives who had come to pick up their husbands were forced to lock themselves in their cars while fans rocked the cars back and forth. The fans were finally removed by police in full riot gear. Thirty-seven fans were arrested.

If the midget was an idea borrowed from a James Thurber short story, Disco Demolition was right out of Nathanael West's *Day of the Locust*. It seemed emblematic of all that was wrong in the country and in baseball at the end of the 1970s, and it demonstrated that the game—and the times— had passed Veeck by. Veeck's outmoded carnival approach was blamed for causing the riot. Many fans had turned into chemically impaired thugs, and a small operator such as Veeck could not afford the elements of modern crowd control.

"Riot at Comiskey" was the headline in the *Sun-Times*, and the *Tribune* declared the event a "disgrace." Although Veeck was reportedly very unhappy about what had happened, he was at the mercy of those in baseball who saw him as the man who had gone too far and lost control of his own stadium.

The anti-disco movement may have benefited from the night, but there was no benefit to Veeck, the White Sox, or baseball. Forty years later Clarence Page of the *Chicago Tribune* noted: "I think American cultural history will show that Disco Demolition may have killed disco but definitely killed dancing among young white guys."[22]

Mike Veeck blamed himself for the disaster even though his father tried to console him by saying, "The promotion worked too well." But things later got worse, as three rock concerts followed that did further damage to the playing field, exacerbated by some of the heaviest August rains to fall on Chicago in years. Red Sox right fielder Dwight Evans pondered suing Veeck after he suffered a pulled muscle on the chewed-up field in late August; Evans said that, judging by the condition of the field, Veeck had no regard for the safety of players. Three games had to be postponed when umpires ruled the field unplayable. Tons of sand were dumped on the field, and two massive loads of sod were laid down. Veeck took $9,000 out of his own pocket to pay for the sod. He was criticized for having removed the artificial turf from the stadium, and some urged the White Sox to install Astroturf for the 1980 season. Confronted with the issue of a failing playing field, Veeck became philosophical: "We've endured some tough times, but I'm a firm believer things will always get better."[23] Still, at the end of September, Veeck would let it be known that if someone came along with the right offer to buy the club, he might agree to sell the team he had bought four and a half years earlier.

Early in August, in the throes of a seven-game losing streak, manager Don Kessinger resigned. Veeck—with an assist from Roland Hemond—selected Tony La Russa as the new Sox manager. The move was not popular with Sox fans. At thirty-four, La Russa was younger than many of his players, as was his thirty-one-year-old pitching coach, Ron Schueler. Critics laid into Veeck for what were perceived as cost-cutting moves by a begging-poor franchise. Eyes rolled when it was revealed that La Russa had a law degree.

The 1979 White Sox season ended with a 73–87 record, in fifth place in the American League's West Division. But the repercussions of Disco Demolition were still being felt. Mike Veeck stayed with the club for seven months after the event, but for him the fun was gone and he felt blackballed by baseball because of it. As he would confess later in his memoir, he dealt with all this by drinking, which led to the end of his first marriage and caused him to lose custody of his son. He drifted to Florida, where he hung drywall, worked at a jai alai fronton, and, in his words, drank heavily "as I pondered the failure of Disco Demolition Night and my lost baseball career."[24] In his 2006 paean to the team, *Sox and the City*, Richard Roeper called Disco Demolition "the most memorable stunt gone wrong in sports history."[25]

In early November Larry Doby resigned from the White Sox because he no longer played a role with the major-league club. Neither Kessinger earlier nor La Russa had a spot for Doby, and he felt he was no longer needed or wanted. Veeck, in turn, said he owed Doby a debt of gratitude. Several players were disappointed that Doby would not be with the team in spring training, as they claimed he gave the best batting instruction. Among those expressing regret was Chet Lemon, whose 1979 batting average of .318 was the best Sox average since Minnie Miñoso had hit .320 in 1954.[26]

Ending a difficult year on a bad note, Veeck slipped on a wet floor and broke his kneecap in a fall at Tilden High School, where he had gone to speak at an alumni reunion. This required an operation and an estimated six weeks to recuperate. The *Chicago Tribune* nonetheless found him resolute: "It takes more than an operation to insert two pins in his only knee to make White Sox owner Bill Veeck downcast, or even less feisty than he usually is."[27]

DESPITE ALL THAT seemed wrong, Veeck came out of spring training in 1980 in a self-described mood of euphoria. Protégé Harold Baines was now in a major-league starting position along with an infield of eager but little-known players just brought up from the minors. Veeck had a nucleus of young talent, including pitchers Rich Dotson, La Marr Hoyt, and Britt Burns and young outfielder Ron Kittle, signed to minor-league contracts.

Before the 1980 season began, Roland Hemond predicted that the team would come in second in the division, while Veeck predicted no lower than third.[28] After an interview with Veeck during the last week before the season began, John Schulian exclaimed, "There's a school of thought that William Veeck Jr. invented euphoria."

Veeck still had the ability to draw fans, even effecting some rare conversions. On April 20, 1980, Mike Royko, the Pulitzer Prize–winning columnist for the *Chicago Tribune*, played a surprise on the city of Chicago: he became a White Sox fan, claiming he could no longer put up with the Cubs, whose players were making fools of themselves in public. "I don't like these guys. I don't like whiners, I don't like people who go out and cry to the public about their problems when they have no problems. At a time when people at all levels of life are really having a hard time making it, you have a bunch of grown men, not even grown men, young men making these incredible sums of money and just crying and moaning. I don't care how unhappy they are, and what their business dealings are. I don't care how much money they make. I just don't understand people going public with this. . . . These guys are a bunch of jerks. So what am I doing here, wasting my time, cheering for jerks?"[29]

Royko went to Comiskey Park following the article and, accompanied by Veeck, walked out to the pitcher's mound to toss out the first pitch. He said: "It was an uplifting spiritual experience. Veeck bought me a couple of beers; Harry Caray welcomed me and bellowed 'Holy cow' in my left ear, and I went home and learned the words to 'Na, Na, Na Na.'"

Though the game had changed around him, Veeck would not change the way he operated. He was, for example, no less accessible now than he had been in Milwaukee decades earlier. The White Sox had gotten off to a surprisingly good start, recalled Randy Johnson, then managing editor of the *Gadsden Times*, a small daily newspaper in northeast Alabama. "There were rumors the Sox were planning to trade one of their young pitchers for a bat. I had heard of Veeck's open-door policy and how people could call him and immediately be put through to him. As a fan, I called one after-noon and, sure enough, I was put directly through to him. I don't remem-ber the receptionist even asking who was calling. Mr. Veeck put up with a nutty Sox fan from Alabama calling him, and he discussed the pros and cons of a trade with me. I was impressed with that."[30]

Veeck also remained eager to help someone in a jam. Bob Greene of the *Chicago Tribune* devoted one of his columns to the plight of a thirty-five-year-old man with four children whose wife had left him, and who had been out of work for eight months. The gas had been cut off, they had no more hot water, and they were fast running out of food. The man told Greene that although he had never committed a criminal act in his life, he was about to turn to crime to save his children. "It was a story that belonged to another country," Greene wrote, "in another century. But it was happen-ing in the economic environment of the United States in 1980."

The morning the column appeared, the phone didn't stop ringing as people called Greene to offer money. Greene explained that the man was not looking for handouts; what he really wanted was a job. Caller after caller admitted they could not provide one, but around noon the phone rang again.

"This is Bill Veeck," the caller said. The two men had never talked be-fore, and Veeck got right to the point.

"Well, I've got a big old ballpark out here and I could probably use an-other hand to keep things up. It's just manual labor, but if he wants to work why don't you send him out here and let us talk to him."

Greene asked why was he doing this.

"Oh, I went through the Depression. I've seen this before. Sometimes when a fellow is in trouble you want to go out on a limb for him."

About a week later Greene got a call from the *Tribune*'s security that the man was downstairs. He was sent up and said to Greene that he would have been there sooner but that he had been hired on the spot and this was his first time off. The man tried to thank Greene, who said the person he should really thank was Bill Veeck.* The man then began to cry. "I'll never

---

* Veeck asked Greene not to write about this good deed, a request that Greene honored until after Veeck was out of baseball.

forget that somebody was willing to give me a chance. I didn't know that people like Mr. Veeck really existed anymore."[31]

On July 2, White Sox broadcaster and former major leaguer Jimmy Piersall tried to strangle Arlington Heights *Daily Herald* sports reporter Bob Gallas as he conducted interviews in the clubhouse on Piersall's future as a White Sox coach. Piersall was both a television broadcaster and the team's voluntary outfield coach, but he had been going after both Veeck and La Russa on the air and the players had voted to have him removed from his coaching job. He had, in fact, called Mary Frances "a colossal bore" on the radio. Piersall's mental illness and eccentric behavior were well known when he was hired by WMAQ television to cover the White Sox.

Dr. Bruce Kraig, a professor in history and humanities at Chicago's Roosevelt University, had been invited to bring his family to dinner in the Bards Room that night. In the middle of the meal, two security guards suddenly burst into the room dragging a highly agitated and red-faced Piersall behind them. "Veeck jumped up and said, 'I have to go and deal with this,' and that was the last I ever saw of Veeck," recalled Kraig.[32]

Gallas, who according to eyewitnesses turned blue during the altercation, wound up going to work for the White Sox organization. Piersall lost his coaching job and spent four days in Illinois Masonic Hospital for exhaustion, went to Texas for a while, and then, two weeks after the incident, returned to the White Sox broadcasting booth. In his book, Piersall later acknowledged Veeck's role in the incident: "And it was Veeck who took care of me, calmed me down in his office, and got me taken to the hospital."[33]

IN LATE JULY 1980, Veeck traveled to Fort Worth, Texas, in a last-ditch attempt to sign shortstop Turner Gill, the White Sox' second-round pick in June's amateur draft. Gill wanted a quarter of a million dollars, which was well out of the club's price range. "He was the first draft choice I have personally visited that I was unable to sign," Veeck commented. That he could no longer sign prospects was the final sign that keeping the team was no longer an option. Veeck returned to Chicago to tell his board that they could either sell now or watch the club go down the drain in little pieces. The board approved the sale.[34]

However, not only the ballclub was going down the drain; so was Veeck himself. *Chicago Sun-Times* columnist and Veeck confidant Bill Gleason, for one, believed that health was a major reason for the sale: "He was over-stretched, overworked, and totally exhausted."[35]

On August 22, with the team in fifth place in the West Division the White Sox accepted an offer from Edward J. DeBartolo Sr. to purchase the club for $20 million. Described in the press as shy and dapper, DeBartolo was a successful developer of shopping malls from Youngstown, Ohio, who owned several racetracks, the National Hockey League's Pittsburgh Penguins, and the San Francisco 49ers of the National Football League, which he purchased in 1977 and immediately turned over to his son Edward J. DeBartolo Jr. The elder DeBartolo had attempted to purchase the Seattle Mariners and the Oakland A's but failed because of the opposition of Commissioner Bowie Kuhn. Ownership of the White Sox was to be shared with DeBartolo's daughter Rose Denise DeBartolo York.

Two days after the sale was approved, Veeck was hospitalized in Illinois Masonic Hospital with respiratory problems, which landed him in intensive care for several days. The day after being released, Tuesday, September 30, he climbed out of bed to attend the pre-game ceremony at Bill Veeck Appreciation Night, a tribute suggested by Gleason. Veeck, who had a 102-degree fever, was accompanied by Edwin Feldman, a White Sox physician, who remained at his side.

The crowd of 18,903 gave Veeck a roaring two-minute ovation. Veeck, who seemed embarrassed by the attention, told the fans: "This is evidence of what I knew from the first time I was here and what I've known since I've come back. The White Sox have the greatest fans in the world."

He apologized for the club's failure to repeat its 1959 pennant triumph. After that he hesitated, and then, his voice thickening with emotion, he told the fans: "Thank you again for a lovely time and thank you for a delightful night."

"The fans responded with another cheer," reported Jerome Holtzman. "Even the veteran members of the press corps, listening in a jammed press box, joined in the ovation," breaking a set of unwritten rules for the writers never to cheer from the press box, and never to cheer an owner.

Presentations followed, including a telegram from President Jimmy Carter, which read, in part, "You have had a key role in restoring a uniquely American game to its present high level of popularity. Wherever baseball is played, it bears the indelible imprint of your imagination and promotional skill." And Veeck must have chuckled when a woman returned a mannequin that had been awarded to her four years earlier. "I want Mr. Veeck to have his dummy back," she said with a laugh.

Ten minutes before the game began, Dr. Feldman escorted Veeck home, and so he missed the seventh-inning stretch and the chants and rhythmic clapping of "Bill Veeck! Bill Veeck!" that followed the singing of "Take Me Out to the Ball Game."[36] Earlier, on September 9 word came from the hospital that Veeck was so appreciative of his care that he had invited all 2,000 hospital employees and their families to be his guests for two upcoming games with Minnesota.[37]

With the sale of the team still awaiting approval, the Sox under Tony La Russa finished the season with a 70–90 record, in fifth place, twenty-six games out of first place in their division.

On October 24, the American League met in Chicago and owners voted on the transfer of the team to DeBartolo; surprisingly, the plan got only eight of the ten votes needed for approval. DeBartolo seemed like the perfect owner, and he had the right credentials, including having served in World War II. American League president Lee MacPhail cited "absentee ownership" and DeBartolo's interest in thoroughbred horse racing as the probable reasons for the defeat.[38] However, more important was Commissioner Bowie Kuhn's opposition, which was so clear and loud that an Illinois Republican legislator named Henry Hyde called for a congressional investigation into Kuhn's objection, which was allegedly because of DeBartolo's racetrack connections.*

DeBartolo announced that he would sell all three of his racetracks and spend 20 percent of his time in Chicago if that would satisfy Kuhn and the owners. One of DeBartolo's associates posited in an interview that the issues surrounding absentee ownership and the racetracks were a sham and that the real reason Kuhn was so adamant in his opposition was DeBartolo's Italian ancestry. He pointed out that after almost two years of attempting to buy the Oakland A's and discussing the possible purchase of other teams from other owners, it had become obvious that Kuhn's blacklisting of DeBartolo was based on his ethnicity.

Kuhn responded that the charge was "contemptible, irresponsible and false." A small pro-DeBartolo, anti-Kuhn demonstration in Chicago ensued. Kuhn was careful in regard to what he said. He referred to DeBartolo as "not R.P."—not the right people—in cocktail conversations with owners.[39]

At the Winter Meetings in Dallas, the American League met again about

---

* Later in the U.S. House of Representatives, he sponsored the Hyde Amendment, which prohibited federal money being used to fund abortion.

DeBartolo's offer to buy the White Sox. It was defeated again, this time by a vote of 11–3, with only Oakland, Cleveland, and the White Sox standing by DeBartolo. Kuhn had persuaded the Rangers, Angels, Twins, and Yankees to change their votes. Veeck called the turndown capricious, ghastly, and unfair: "I have never been ashamed to be a member of the American League before. Today I am."

DeBartolo, who had cried the first time he was turned down, now felt betrayed and angry. At a press conference he attested to his own character, including three and a half years of honorable service in World War II: "We live in a country where there are still prejudices, where some people create doubts about the viability of free enterprise. I have, and my family has, conducted ourselves in an honorable fashion. . . . And then to have 14 people, as well as a commissioner, to sit in judgment—it's impossible to conceive what has happened."[40]

In DeBartolo's hometown of Youngstown, Ohio, Paul Humes, an official of the company that owned the local newspaper, the *Vindicator,* wrote an open letter to Bowie Kuhn in which he said that it was "inconceivable that the Dallas Debacle of Thursday, December 11, 1980, should have occurred. It is sad for the American way of life, the American League, and baseball in general that a fellow American with 'Hall of Fame' credentials is treated in this manner. May God forgive your part therein."[41]

To those who covered the event, it made no sense. *Dallas Times Herald* writer Blackie Sherrod was not the only one to point out, for example, that the New York Yankees were owned by George Steinbrenner, who lived in Tampa and owned a racetrack. Searching for answers, Sherrod brought up to DeBartolo the unspoken implication that he had something unsavory in his past, such as mob connections. "From the snatches of conversation I have heard and from the innuendos," DeBartolo said to Sherrod, "I have come to the conclusion they didn't think I was 'kosher.' Well, my family has four banks, three racetracks and a pro football club, and we've been checked every way." Sherrod added that the National Football League had a checking system that rivaled the CIA's, and that DeBartolo was clean, a fact verified by NFL commissioner Pete Rozelle himself.[42]

"It was nasty—as nasty as it gets," said Ray Grebey, who at the time headed the Player Relations Committee representing ownership in its dealings with the union. Years after working for Bowie Kuhn, he acknowledged that Kuhn had opposed DeBartolo absolutely and made negative comments about Italians to support that opposition.[43]

Perhaps to take the pressure off Kuhn and get in a shot at Veeck, Yankees owner George Steinbrenner said that the real reason the sale had fallen through was Bill Veeck himself—that the owners were trying to get back at him. Whether this was true or not, the owners now had Veeck in a tough spot. He could not afford to stay in, but he could not get out either. A few days after the meeting Veeck told a columnist that his life had become a little like a soap opera as he tried to get another offer and approval for a sale.[44]

Amidst this turmoil of the sale, White Sox chairman Bill DeWitt gave a series of interviews during which the subject of Bill Veeck came up. "I tell you, Veeck has more things wrong with him than anybody you can think of," he said, ticking them off: quite apart from his leg woes, he was deaf in one ear, his eyes had gone bad, and the many years he had been forced to use crutches had damaged his upper body so that both shoulders, a wrist, and his spine had required operations. "That man has gone through things that normal people would be screaming about all over the world. Never complained, never says a word. And he's one of the most thoughtful persons that you'll ever run into. I can't agree with his philosophy on a lot of things. And I can't agree on his judgment on a lot of things, but he is the most thoughtful person."[45]

Veeck held on to the White Sox through the end of the year. Finally, on January 8, 1981, a $20 million offer to buy the team was made by a local group headed by Jerry Reinsdorf, a real estate investor, and Eddie Einhorn, a television executive. It was essentially the same offer as had been made by DeBartolo, allowing Veeck and his partners to depart with a profit. Three weeks later, the American League owners voted unanimously to allow the sale of the team, and Veeck handed the keys to Comiskey Park to Reinsdorf in a signing ceremony at Sears Tower.

"It was the bitter end, but 66-year-old Bill Veeck was laughing," observed John Schulian, the reporter who had most ably captured Veeck's last White Sox years. "Looking back on the career of baseball's reigning Barnum, with his pinch-hitting midgets and exploding scoreboards, there's really no other way he could leave.

"Sadness was for another time, another place."[46]

CHAPTER 20

Borrowed Time

O N FEBRUARY 2, 1981, BILL VEECK received a lifetime achievement award from *Baseball Magazine at* Gallagher's Steak House in Manhattan. The two other awardees—pitcher Steve Carlton and third baseman George Brett—could not attend, so the show was Veeck's.[1]

Veeck took time to reminisce, complain about the corporate types who had taken over the game, and talk about his retirement. He told the assembled reporters that he thought his departure from baseball was a good thing. His health was failing, and the game had chased away all but one of its dinosaur owners—the sole exception being Calvin Griffith, of the Minnesota Twins. Veeck loved his image as the penultimate example of his species; as newsman John Schulian put it, he "saw himself as a dinosaur nibbling on the last leaves of a dying tree."[2]

Veeck spelled out his latest set of imperatives for improving the game. He thought one set of rules should govern all teams: the designated hitter should exist in both leagues or in neither; one set of umpires should officiate for both leagues, not two sets with different codes; all parks should have either artificial turf or natural grass. On this last point, his opinion had always been clear, he said. "I feel firmly a baseball park should smell like grass, not an extension of the city streets and cigarette smoke and other odors." He thought the leagues should be realigned, with three divisions and a wild card (as in pro football). The emphasis should be on natural rivalries, such as Cubs–White Sox, Yankees-Mets, and Dodgers-Angels. And teams should play more in the same time zone, to save fuel and reduce costs, which in turn would help keep ticket prices low so that family groups wouldn't be priced right out of the park.[3]

Hank Greenberg made a plea for Veeck's election to the National Baseball Hall of Fame, to which Veeck responded: "I would have to refuse it. If there is no room there for Luis Aparicio, Pee Wee Reese, or Phil Rizzuto, then there is surely no room for a scuffler who couldn't hit .001."[4] But perhaps the most memorable story came from Roland Hemond. "I'm sad Bill's leaving," he said. "Let me tell you what kind of a man he is. Last September [1980], he planned a picnic on the playing field at Comiskey Park to thank all of his employees. But a few days before, he was rushed to the hospital and placed in intensive care. The day of the party, we're all concerned about him, and all of a sudden, he shows up. He talked a doctor into letting him out for the party. He stayed for a while, hopped into a cab, and asked the driver to speed up so he could roll down the window and stick his head out for air so that he could breathe. That says what kind of a man he is. He's a genius with compassion."[5] After a talk with his publisher about a possible new book—an indictment of modern baseball leadership—Bill Veeck headed home to Mary Frances in Chicago and their Hyde Park apartment, writing an occasional column and taking writing assignments during the postseason. He still made the newspapers with his comments on the business of baseball and self-deprecating quotes about life. He was, however, as *Chicago Tribune* columnist Bob Verdi put it, "living on broken parts and borrowed time."

His phone number was still listed, however, and he would get occasional crazy calls, as he recounted to a reporter: "Yes . . . about three in the morning, from some fellows at a bar who are bombed and having an argument. One fellow will ask me if Earl Torgeson played for the Sox in '59. I'll answer, yes, he did. Then the caller will say, will you tell this to the guy I've got a bet with? The second guy will ask: Did Earl Torgeson really play for the Sox in '59? I'll say, no, he came three years later. It's my only defense . . . my only way of getting even. I go back to bed with a mental picture of a fight in the bar."[6]

Veeck did put in an appearance at the White Sox spring training facility, where he ran into Marvin Miller. Said Miller, "I was shocked at the change in his appearance. He had been hospitalized with a collapsed lung. He was legally blind; he was deaf in one ear and had a hearing aid in the other. 'The good news is,' Veeck said of the aid, which tended to squeal, 'that with a little deft finger work on the adjustment, I can play a fair approximation of 'Yankee Doodle Dandy.' The bad news is that I can no longer creep up on mine enemies unawares.' That was Bill Veeck, filled with hope and humor."[7]

As the 1981 baseball season got under way, Veeck started to frequent the bleachers at Wrigley Field. The new owners of the White Sox had vowed to create a first-class operation, and Veeck had chosen to react to the perceived insult by embracing the Cubs. "I couldn't be at home in such a class operation as they're operating there," he archly observed about Einhorn and Reinsdorf's White Sox. "The new owner, Fast Eddie—that is his name, isn't it?—is such a professional he doesn't want me and my kind of people spilling beer on the furniture." Veeck was bothered by the fact that the new owners had paid exactly what DeBartolo had offered; he believed that DeBartolo should have been the new owner and that "the wrong people got the team."[8]

Sitting in the Wrigley Field bleachers he had helped construct, below the scoreboard that had undergone only a few simple changes since he had overseen its installation in 1937, Veeck was in a familiar place. The flag signaling system he had installed in 1938 was still in operation, as was the light system that informed elevated train riders of a Cubs win or loss. "I didn't build everything," he told John Schulian of the *Sun-Times*, "but I built enough of it, thank you."

Veeck would help strangers in the bleachers with their crossword puzzles, buy beer for visiting TV anchors, and cut up with erstwhile minor leaguers and football executives alike.[9] When the temperature permitted, he posed shirtless and wearing shapeless Bermuda shorts, bleaching his wooden leg in the afternoon sun. "Dad would sit out there without a shirt with his breasts hanging out. It was his way of saying, 'This is what sixty-eight years looks like,'" his son Greg recalled, adding that an average of a hundred people would come up to him to talk during a game.[10]

He also had clearly lost none of his impishness, as Ray Grebey remembered. "One time I was sitting in the Wrigley Field bleachers with Bill and Dave Condon and an announcement was made over the PA system that Bill Veeck was at the game sitting with Condon and Ray Grebey, who was identified as the man who caused the '81 strike. The booing was intense."[11]

Away from the game, Veeck became increasingly demonstrative in his antiwar pro-gun-control positions. "No Chicago peace march was official if Veeck was not in it. No handgun-control petition was complete if his name was not on it."[12] Not only did he speak out on guns, but on Halloween in 1981 he limped his way through a ten-kilometer walk against handgun violence. He gave speeches, staged press conferences, and lent support to anti-handgun legislation. For the first time, he publicly alluded to the gun death of Maurice, the older brother he had never known.[13]

Drawn by the arrival of spring, the season of hope in baseball, in 1982 Veeck showed up in Phoenix for spring training, catching as many Cubs games as he could muster the energy to attend. He obliged the writers with quotes about how baseball had changed and how it was now all about "agents, the counting house and the lawyers." He also inspired literary allusions. "It was the fourth inning, I guess, before the man of the lined face walked in the ballpark carrying a canvas overnight bag," wrote Tom Fitzgerald in the *Arizona Republic.* "He had a peg leg that he made no effort to camouflage. It was the same type of peg leg that you see Capt. Ahab wearing in the Heritage Illustrated classic version of Melville's great sea story. . . . Bill Veeck, now sixty-eight, but far from bowed, limped through the crowd, looking as proud as a man who could be the sole survivor of the last voyage of the *Pequod.* He might have been the one man who smelled Moby Dick's breath and lived to tell about it."[14]

But later that spring, Veeck, baseball, and America suffered a great loss: on June 8, 1982, Satchel Paige died of a heart attack in Kansas City. Veeck told the *Baltimore Afro-American* that Paige's death was "a tragedy for all of society," and he added, "We need more heroes like him." In the days that followed, Veeck became a willing interpreter of Paige's career for the many reporters who called. He characterized his longtime friend and cohort as "the best pitcher I've ever seen . . . as close to unique as anyone I've ever seen. He had the best fastball and the greatest control, and had he been given the chance, would have compiled the best record of any pitcher ever." Veeck admitted that Paige missed a few airplane flights in his time with the Browns, but that he was always there when they really needed him.[15] Paige's death ended one of baseball's strongest friendships. "Veeck really loved Satch—they would talk on the phone for hours," recalled Monte Irvin, who knew both men well.[16]

As the 1982 postseason approached, Veeck received an assignment he couldn't resist. Reporter Hal Bodley recalled one of Veeck's last jobs. "When we started *USA Today* in 1982," Bodley remembered, "and were preparing for our first World Series, as baseball editor, I suggested we hire Bill Veeck to be a guest columnist. I couldn't think of anyone better suited to help get our fledging publication off the ground. After all, who was better at promoting baseball than Bill? And believe me, we needed all the help we could get in the fall of 1982."

Bodley called Veeck, who accepted before Bodley could get all the words out of his mouth. "We worked out the financial arrangements, and our first celebrity columnist was in the fold." Then a few days after that—about a week before the St. Louis–Milwaukee World Series started—Bill called. "You know, for me to write a column I have to have my ghostwriter, Ed Linn, with me. I'll dictate my thoughts to him, he'll write them and give the column to you," Veeck told Bodley.

"My wheels were turning," Bodley remembered. "How could we make deadlines of 11:30 p.m. and 1:30 a.m. with this arrangement? Well, it was difficult, but we made it work. Neither man understood deadline pressure. They both agonized over each column. But spending nearly two weeks with Bill and Ed was an experience I'll never forget. First, even though I knew Bill fairly well, I had no idea of his popularity in the baseball world. People wanted to interview him and, frankly, got in our way when we wanted him to interview people for the column. And then there were the postgame conversations that lasted until the wee hours. 'Did I tell you about the time . . . ?" he'd start, and the yarn would last an hour."[17]

Veeck thought of himself as just another bleacher bum, and he extolled the virtues of the cheap seats: "An afternoon in the bleachers is the greatest buy in the country. Drinking a few beers and telling a few lies, you can't beat the entertainment." Veeck himself was very much part of the entertainment; among other things, he made a ritual of rubbing suntan lotion on fans' backs.[18]

A year later, Veeck covered the 1983 American League Championship Series (ALCS) playoffs between the White Sox and the Orioles as an analyst for the *Chicago Tribune*. It was a best-of-five affair, and the morning after the second game two in Baltimore, the writers were heading for Chicago, where the series, tied at 1–1, would resume that evening, Friday, October 7. Just prior to the plane's early-morning departure from Baltimore, Veeck was rolled into the plane in a wheelchair.

"Writers knew something was amiss, because Veeck never used his infirmity to gain an advantage," observed Red Foley. "It seems that while walking down the long corridor toward the plane, Veeck's artificial limb became undone. He sprawled on the floor, and though [he was] unhurt, airline personnel loaded him into the wheelchair. As he entered the plane, Veeck was holding the faulty limb on his lap. 'Do you need a doctor?' inquired one of the solicitous airline people. 'No, right now all I need is a carpenter,' Veeck replied, flashing his famous smile."[19]

Upon arrival in Chicago, Veeck had the necessary repairs made, and he was on hand for the third and fourth games, won by the Orioles to capture the American League pennant. The White Sox owners had offered Veeck the opportunity to throw out the opening pitch in Chicago, but he graciously declined, suggesting Roland Hemond as a more appropriate choice.[20] He had reason to be proud of and identify with the 1983 Sox, which still bore his stamp. Hemond had proven to be a skillful team builder, Tony La Russa a first-class manager. The players he had signed were team leaders, including Ron Kittle, who in his first full year clubbed 35 home runs and drove in 100 runs, and Harold Baines, who was fast maturing into one of baseball's best hitters and whom Veeck termed the White Sox' and the American League's most valuable player. "But [Baines] will probably not get the nod," Veeck wrote at the end of September.* "He doesn't pop off. He's too quiet, too dignified, too efficient. He just gets the job done a little better than anyone else."[21]

Veeck also covered the 1983 World Series for the *Tribune*, traveling with the press corps between Philadelphia and Baltimore. "I remember him in the outdoor press box in Philadelphia," wrote Ira Berkow later. "I noticed him at game's end set up his turquoise portable typewriter and begin to hit the keys. He had been forced for financial reasons to sell the White Sox three years before, but his heart was still in the game—it always would be—and now he would write about it. On deadline. He was no phony. This former big-league baseball owner wrote his own stuff. I remember reading one of his pieces afterward and enjoying it very much. He knew the game, had original insights and stuck the adverbs and adjectives in all the right places."[22]

The autumn 1983 deaths of George Halas, then eighty-eight, and Charlie Grimm, eighty-five, underscored his own mortality. Veeck's public eulogy of Halas, whom he had worked for as a young man, captured Halas's enormous impact: "There are very few people who invent a game and see it become national in scope. I don't think there is much more of a tribute to him than every Sunday when 60 million people or so sit down and watch what he achieved." Grimm had been a good friend and mentor for decades,

---

* Baines ended up tenth in the American League MVP voting for 1983, but Hemond was picked as baseball executive of the year, and Kittle won the AL Rookie of the Year Award.

and by special dispensation his ashes were spread over Wrigley Field.* No doubt that pleased Veeck.[23]

The year ended on two happier notes. On December 6 Veeck celebrated the fiftieth anniversary of the repeal of Prohibition, which, in character, he declared a more important holiday than Arbor Day. The next day a show of his mobiles opened in a Chicago gallery. Veeck had been making the intricately balanced sculptures since 1962, when he began constructing them out of pieces of driftwood he found on the banks of Peachblossom Creek in Maryland. He had expanded his craft since then, and his recent work was more colorful and Veeckian. "This one here is my commentary on humankind," he remarked at the opening, pointing to a dozen toy monkeys outfitted with musical instruments suspended at the end of varying lengths of fishing line. "See, they're tooting their own horns and banging their own drums." Dan Brogan of the *Tribune* watched Veeck unpack and hang these mobiles and concluded they were deceptively complex contraptions, dancing precipitously from a series of wooden dowels, sturdy wire, or monofilament line. "Balance is the key," Veeck said. "One thing gets out of whack and the whole thing goes klunk." Greg Veeck observed that very few of his father's mobiles could not be made to work; one such was made of small pots of cacti, which, problematically, had to be watered on occasion.[24]

BY 1984, VEECK's infirmities had taken a firmer grip on him, and he spent fewer days in the Wrigley bleachers. Gravity became his enemy: he was falling more, and the fear of it held him back. On July 2, while grocery shopping, he slipped and fell on the contents of a jar that had fallen from a shelf and broken. "I was sitting in my office when Bill called," said Dr. Sid Shafer. "He said, 'I'm on Roosevelt Road, in a grocery store. I either broke or dislocated my hip. If you're going to be in your office, I'll come right in.' He took a cab, came up to my office. We're on the 17th floor of the Pittsfield Building.

---

* Assisted by the Internet, a "Grimm's ghost" legend has emerged from the spreading of Grimm's ashes, emanating from a Web site hosted by "the Wanna-Be Sports Guy": "Since his burial, many workers who worked at Wrigley recalled seeing his ghost around the front offices late at night. Many security guards have recalled hearing the phone ring in the Cubs dugout in the wee hours of the morning. Many believe that Charlie Grimm's ghost is trying to call up a pitcher from the bullpen."

He had fractured his hip, on the same side as the amputation." He was hospitalized, and two days later, a hospital spokesman described Veeck as "fine," adding, "He's talking on the phone, and he has visitors."[25] Veeck was soon seen prowling the corridors of Illinois Masonic Hospital with a walker, bemoaning the fact that he would have to miss the All-Star Game in San Francisco, where he had planned to link up with his pal Henry Greenberg.

Recalling that day and others like it, Shafer reiterated an oft-stated observation: "Bill Veeck had more physical courage than anyone I've known. And I never heard him complain. Not once."[26]

Veeck came back to Wrigley Field as soon as his good leg could carry him, full of his usual irreverence. "Would you like a lamb chop?" he asked William Nack, who was sitting with him in the bleachers reporting on the Cubs for *Sports Illustrated*. Veeck had brought a large container filled with spiced Greek-style lamb chops to the game, and a friend had a bag of sliced tomatoes. Veeck was holding a beer. "Why are you out here instead of the grandstand?" a spectator yelled from below. "Here the beer is colder, the fans much smarter, and you can see better," he bellowed back. "This is for the people who come to enjoy, to relax!"[27]

When a late-summer rain delay caused him to leave hastily, Veeck told his fellow fans, "There's only two things I live in mortal fear of: rain and termites," the former because it made the walkways slippery. That year Veeck had begun writing a column he titled "Cleanup Man" for a slick magazine called *North Shore*. The themes varied—the Olympics, television and sports, the plight of the left-handed. On several occasions the column was devoted to Veeck's poetry, including one column composed of nine poems all based on Robert Louis Stevenson's *A Child's Garden of Verses*, one of which delightfully emphasized another reason he disliked wet conditions.

"RAIN"
The rain is raining all around,
It falls on mound and plate.
It rains upon the outfield grass
And louses up the gate.[28]

By the fall of 1984, Veeck had yet another physical challenge to overcome. In October, a spot was detected on his lung that had not been there—or, at least, had not been seen—during his July hospitalization. He was scheduled for immediate surgery to have the lung removed.[29] But because he was having trouble breathing, he was put into the intensive care unit instead. By October 11 his condition had improved, and he was scheduled for surgery on the seventeenth, complaining that he felt like "one of the inmates in the monkey house. They keep the monkeys on a short leash, and that's where they've got me. So, I can't have a beer."[30]

Old baseball friend Bing Devine visited Veeck on the thirteenth. "When I got to his room, he was asleep with a bright light on. I walked around his room and noticed on every piece of furniture there were stacks of books . . . must have been 50 of them. The amazing thing was, they all had bookmarks in them. Bill told me later that's how he read. He read six to twelve pages in one book and then moved on to another one. Eventually he'd get through all of them that way."[31]

The surgery was again postponed, and visitors were banned in order to get Veeck ready. His lung was finally removed on October 26. Two weeks later, one Chicago gossip column reported that a rich dessert called a Floating Island had been delivered to him on a silver platter by his favorite chef, Lucien Verge of L'Escargot. Mary Frances reported that it was enough to get Bill out of intensive care.[32]

Veeck called Mike Lupica of the *Daily News* to tell him that his cancerous lung had been removed and that he was now getting better. He told Lupica that he was planning a trip to Miller's Pub at Adams and Wabash to celebrate being "whole" again. He added, "Now you must understand, something whole for me is a little different than whole for everybody else. I now have a lung and an eighth, a leg and a quarter, 40 percent of my hearing, and one legal eye. I figure I've given the rest of the world as much of an edge as I'm going to give." Lupica dedicated his Thanksgiving column to the man who had been blowing "a cool breeze" across baseball for the past half century.[33]

His first major public appearance after he was released from the hospital was in mid-January 1985, at Lino's Restaurant, where a select group of Chicago VIPs was gathering to honor Ed DeBartolo Sr., whose son's San Francisco 49ers were about to play in Super Bowl XIX. DeBartolo had come to Chicago with a batch of Super Bowl tickets for his friends, especially those who had supported his bid for the White Sox years earlier.

Veeck arrived late, hobbled into the room, and moved slowly to the seat that had been held for him at the head of the table. He looked around and said, "Holy smoke, every hustler, con man, and swindler within fifty miles of Chicago is here. The citizenry is safe for twenty-four hours."

"And from there on," said friend and former White Sox board member Nick Kladis, "he completely dominated the proceedings for two straight hours."

ON OPENING DAY 1985, Bill and Mary Frances sat in the bleachers at Wrigley Field surrounded by 200 or so doctors, nurses, and orderlies from Illinois Masonic Hospital. Veeck reasoned that the seats were the best payback he could think of for keeping him alive during lung surgery. During the seventh-inning stretch, Veeck stood on his one leg and sang "Take Me Out to the Ball Game."[34]

Further honors awaited him. On May 8 Veeck was inducted into the Chicagoland Sports Hall of Fame; as Steve Daley of the *Chicago Tribune* put it, "Any hall of fame that carves out a space for Bill Veeck is longer on good sense than the one in Cooperstown, N.Y." At a luncheon announcing his election in mid-April, Veeck was in fine form, mocking the trappings of modern baseball. On Opening Day he had been astonished to see that the time and temperature information posted on the Wrigley Field scoreboard was sponsored. "I've met all sorts of people who wouldn't give me the time of day," he said, laughing. "I never met anybody who wanted to sell it to me."[35]

That September, the local PBS station aired a half-hour documentary entitled *Veeck: Man for Any Season.* The show was the brainchild of producer Jamie Ceaser, who had first met Veeck when she worked on the PBS sports talk show *Time Out,* on which Veeck was a regular guest. Ceaser would occasionally pick Veeck up at his apartment, and during these drives Ceaser listened to the articulate and approachable celebrity. "He was a delicious storyteller," Ceaser later recalled. The more Veeck talked, the more Ceaser wanted to learn. So during her summer vacation—after the *Time Out* show was canceled and before it won an Emmy—Ceaser read *Veeck—as in Wreck.* Out of the reading came the idea for a documentary on Veeck, which he and Mary Frances agreed to.

"We followed Bill around town for the next four or five months, hanging out with him in all his favorite haunts," wrote Ceaser.[36] The show was narrated by Mary Frances, who helped present her husband at his best. At one key moment, he ruminates about old age and the relationship of money to happiness. "How much money can you pay a tulip to bloom?" he asks. The show ends with Veeck in the Wrigley Field bleachers, hoisting a beer and singing "Take Me Out to the Ball Game." "This," he says, "is the epitome of pleasure."

Veeck returned to Comiskey Park that summer as the lesser of two evils, since he had started boycotting the Cubs—Wrigley Field was now selling bleacher tickets in advance, a move he believed had turned his beloved cheap seats into a commodity to be sold by scalpers. He sat with Mary Frances and Otto Denning, who had played for him many years earlier in Milwaukee.

"You oughta buy the club back," a fan yelled to Veeck.

"I've got enough troubles of my own," he shot back.

It was Veeck's last excursion to a ballpark.[37]

A few days later, the Veecks enrolled in a program that would instruct them on how to teach reading to people who could not read. Neither Bill nor Mary Frances could imagine the poverty of a life led without the ability to read.

One final windmill at which Veeck chose to tilt appeared in October 1985: the way players had behaved during and after two cocaine trials conducted in Pittsburgh earlier that fall. They were part of a prosecution against a dealer who had allegedly supplied cocaine to major-league ballplayers. All the players who testified were granted immunity in return for their testimony.

Veeck's diatribe, which appeared in *The Sporting News*, began with a description of the star prosecution witnesses: "They strolled into the courtroom in $500 three-piece suits, $150 custom-made shirts, $200 shoes by Gucci, and a quarter's worth of character." Veeck drilled into them for naming teammates past and present, other ballplayers, and individuals outside the game who had bought cocaine, in order to keep their immunity. Seven well-paid major leaguers had worked in concert to nail a small-time drug dealer named Curtis Strong.

"It's customary to grant immunity to small fry when fishing for sharks. But something smells a mite fishy when the sharks get the immunity," Veeck railed. "There are those who contend that only Curtis Strong was on trial in Pittsburgh, that the spectacle of ballplayers admitting incompetency because of addiction somehow had nothing to do with the game, but with the fans, the owners or the press. There are also those who believe the Easter Bunny lays eggs."

Veeck insisted that ballplayers had come to believe they were a breed apart and no longer subject to the rules the rest of society lived by. Veeck had also been stunned by the matter-of-factness of the confessions. Tim Raines of the Montreal Expos, for example, testified that he routinely stashed a gram of cocaine in the back pocket of his uniform pants during games. Raines, who at the time of the hearing was a four-time National League stolen base champion, testified that he always slid into bases headfirst to ensure that the glass vial wouldn't break. Veeck, who had long sided with problem players and their infirmities, demanded that Commissioner Peter Ueberroth punish the "rat-fink" players immediately and dramatically.[38]

During the Hot Stove season, Veeck hosted and addressed the fifth annual John Fischetti Scholarship Dinner, sponsored by Chicago's Columbia College. His booming voice had been softened to a monotone, but his message was no less sharp. Alluding to Pete Rose's recent September 1985 feat of breaking Ty Cobb's all-time hits record with his 4,192nd hit, Veeck hit his stride when he said of the baseball season just ended: "This should have been the year of the Rose, but instead, it turned out to be the year of the rat fink, as seven wealthy athletes, with seven grants of immunity, banded together to get one poor, fat, black bookie 12 years in the pokey." Then he was off on a grab bag of topics, including college football recruiting violations, cigarette manufacturers, and George Steinbrenner. It would be his last public appearance.[39]

DESPITE HIS PROTESTATION the previous summer, Veeck still dreamed of owning one last team. Just before Christmas, he called Art Modell, then owner of the National Football League's Cleveland Browns, to say that he wanted to get back into baseball, and he asked what his chances were of buying the Cleveland Indians.[40]

Veeck entered Illinois Masonic Hospital on Monday, December 30, complaining of shortness of breath. Hank Greenberg called Veeck at the hospital later in the day and Veeck told him, "You know, I think I can get the Cleveland club."

"You're crazy," was Greenberg's response. "Why don't you go someplace where you have a chance to make some money? Why don't you go into the stock market, or some other business. With your talents you can make a lot of money at anything."

"Wouldn't it be great, Hank, to get the old gang together again?"

"You still want to sell peanuts at the ballpark, don't you?"

"Yeah," said Veeck, "I do."[41]

Bob Fishel, now the executive vice president of the American League, talked to him on New Year's Day, and it seemed like he was getting better. Fishel planned to see him the next day.[42]

However, early the next morning, at 2:55 a.m. Central Standard Time,

Bill Veeck died of cardiac arrest.* "Despite all the time he spent in hospitals," his daughter Lisa recalled, "we were devastated. He was larger than life and none of us ever expected him to die."[43] Lisa later had the task of delivering her father's wooden legs to the group that fit his protheses. "I had three legs to deliver, but I couldn't bear to give them all up, so I kept one of them in the trunk of my Mustang. It made a lot of noise back there, and I was eventually stopped by a policeman who asked me to open the trunk." She had to explain why she had Bill Veeck's leg in her trunk.[44]

Within hours, the tributes began rolling in. One of the first telegrams to arrive was addressed to Mary Frances from Operation PUSH (People United to Serve Humanity, a civil rights group), which was signed by Rev. Willie T. Barrow, national executive director, and Rev. Jesse L. Jackson, founding president. It began: "Mr. Veeck dared to have imagination and he embodied much of what Dr. King described in his dream. He believed this nation could be truly one nation. He rejected every element of bigotry that kept it a patchwork of ethnic rivalries and a hostile camp." Telegrams and letters followed from such notables as the archbishop of Chicago, Senator Paul Simon, and President Ronald Reagan, who wrote a personal note to Mary Frances saying that Bill had brought "joy to the game of baseball and the game of life." As per his final instructions, his remaining organs were harvested and his remains cremated.

Veeck's column appeared one last time in the January 1986 issue of *North Shore* magazine. It contained a ten-stanza Veeck original whose first and last stanzas were:

> *Where did it go? I looked away*
> *And suddenly it seemed*
> *There wasn't any time at all*
> *To do the things I'd dreamed.*
>
> . . .
>
> *So now I sit and ponder long*
> *Who, when and where I'll be.*
> *But when it all is said and done*
> *I'd rather just be me.*[45]

---

* Those who believed that celebrity deaths came in threes noted that Veeck's passing followed the air crash that killed Ricky Nelson and the death of movie producer Sam Spiegel (*The African Queen, On the Waterfront*, etc.), both on New Year's Eve.

Close to a thousand people packed into St. Thomas the Apostle for Veeck's funeral, while thousands more stood in the streets as Veeck's funeral procession came and went. Many of those on the streets told reporters they had known Veeck—most from talking to him and thus befriending him in the bleachers at Comiskey Park, Wrigley Field, or both. Others said they had marched with him in antiwar protests during the Vietnam War or knew him from his days in the gun-control and civil rights movements.

Peter Bavasi, then president of the Cleveland Indians, recalled that the single most important tribute to Veeck occurred as the mourners took their seats. It was "the lone figure of Minnie Miñoso, making his way slowly and a bit haltingly down the aisle to a seat in a pew filled with Bill's former players and other friends. Minnie, in a special tribute to Bill, wore a vintage White Sox uniform, the one with the floppy collar. They say it was Bill's favorite design." Worn by Miñoso when he was reactivated five years earlier by Veeck so that he could say he'd played in four decades, the uniform, with the number 9 on the back, "pierced a sea of mink and camel's hair like Bill Veeck's smile."[46]

The service began with Aaron Copland's *Fanfare for the Common Man* and moved through a series of hymns and readings to Father Thomas J. Fitzgerald's homily, which opened with the words "Bill is loving all of this. Of course, it is worship and prayer. But we're trying to do it with *class*."

He then talked of a man who prayed. "I know some will say, 'Yeah, in the late innings when the score was tied.' But I am referring to something bigger and broader than that. Prayer is not just multiplying words—it is really a state of mind, an acceptance of our littleness before the Lord and our need for His help. I think that Bill had that fundamental posture." He described him as a man totally devoid of pretense, someone who moved as easily in the bleachers as he did in the Pump Room. "He laughed at himself as easily as he laughed at the world around him."

Addressing Veeck directly, Fitzgerald was elegiac: "The word that comes to me about you is the word *prince*. You are a prince in all the good senses of that word, a prince without pretensions, courageous, a Prince Valiant. I just heard from Scripture that you were tried like gold in the furnace. You attacked life with courage and a stout heart. You have overcome the world; and you deserve the victory where every tear will be wiped away. When I heard that you were dead, I could think only of another text: 'Now cracks a noble heart. Good night, sweet prince. And flights of angels sing thee to thy rest.'"[47]

The service ended with Handel's "Hallelujah Chorus" from *The Messiah*, which was, as most worshippers at the service knew, a featured element of the exploding scoreboard that boomed every time one of his South Side Hit Men hit one out.[48]

After the funeral, the media clustered around Miñoso for quotes. Larry Doby, who had sat with Wyonella Smith, Wendell Smith's widow, for the ceremony, attracted no attention. According to Wyonella, none of the reporters paid any attention to Doby as the two passed by the gaggle of reporters surrounding Miñoso. "Larry was delighted. He didn't need the publicity, and neither did Bill. Larry loved Bill, you know"[49]

The tributes expressed in the days and weeks following his death attest to his legacy. Tom Boswell of the *Washington Post* had in 1980 written an anticipatory line about Veeck's passing that was quoted extensively now that he had actually died: "His cause of death should read: Life." Boswell's obituary of Veeck in the *Post* was equally memorable: "The tombstone will say Bill Veeck lived 71 years. Don't believe it. The old rapscallion must have rolled the odometer over a couple of times."[50]

Columnist and good friend Irv Kupcinet of the *Chicago Sun-Times* wrote that his eulogy should read, "He was proof positive that one man with courage constitutes a majority."[51] "Bill Veeck was just as important to me as Branch Rickey was to Jackie Robinson," Larry Doby told Bill Littlefield on his National Public Radio show *Only a Game*. "Veeck told me to curb my temper and to turn the other cheek. The guy really motivated me. There were places my wife, my daughter, and I could not go into. Veeck would say, 'If they can't go in, I won't go in.' Veeck was quite a man, a great man. I think of Veeck as my second father." Hank Greenberg called him the smartest, most innovative baseball executive of all time. Littlefield ended his on-air obituary this way: "If Bill Veeck was a rebel, his most substantial rebellions were against an establishment that was clannish, racist, and smug. His brightest ideas bettered the game, and he brought a pure joy to his work in baseball that most men and women who own ball clubs today will never know."[52]

Stories surfaced at the time of his death that demonstrated the deep regard players and associates had for him. James Loebl, whose friendship with Veeck dated back to 1941 and who was a part owner of the White Sox from 1976 to 1980, revealed for the first time that when Veeck was having financial troubles in St. Louis, Hal Peck, by then a successful automobile dealer, sent Veeck a check for $25,000. It was in repayment for Veeck having given him several second chances after Peck lost part of his foot, including the big chance that allowed him to become part of the 1948 championship team at Cleveland. "He had that kind of hold over everyone he met."[53]

But perhaps the most unexpected was an homage signed by Sig Eisenscher, a self-described Communist activist, in the *People's Daily World*. Eisenscher was not a baseball fan but overtly adored Veeck because of several things that "touched him deeply," beginning with Veeck's record on race and including the fact that he once gave a fistful of Sox passes to a Soviet delegation so that they could sample baseball Chicago-style.[54]

A certain amount of myth building ensued. Mary Frances put an end to one instance: The telegram from Operation PUSH had acknowledged his marching with Dr. King on his momentous march in Selma, Alabama, in 1965, and Veeck's role in the march was also mentioned posthumously in various newspapers. But it was not true. "I think I would have known if he had left me in Maryland with the children to march from Selma to Montgomery," said Mary Frances. "Oh! He was there in spirit all right but not in the flesh."[55]

On January 10, 1986, one week after the death of her beloved younger brother, while she and her husband were watching the evening news, Peggy Veeck Krehbiel gave a quiet sigh and passed away. She had been suffering from a bad heart for years and had had several complicated and debilitating open-heart procedures.[56]

Despite his death, Veeck still seemed to be a factor in the conscience of the game—even, perhaps, in baseball's response to the cocaine trials. Veeck's "rat-fink" op-ed in *The Sporting News* had been widely quoted and formed the basis for other opinions. On February 28, 1986, Peter Ueberroth suspended eleven players for involvement with cocaine, with the harshest penalties going to those with a "prolonged pattern of drug use" and of facilitating the distribution of drugs to others in the sport. Ueberroth suspended them all for one year but said he would hold the suspensions in abeyance if the players agreed to donate 10 percent of their 1986 base salaries to a drug treatment facility or program in the city in which they played, perform a minimum of 100 hours of drug-related community service for each of the next two years, and agree to random drug testing for the rest of their playing careers. All the players accepted.[57]

The 1986 season opener at Comiskey Park featured a tribute to Veeck, which included a three-minute video played on the mammoth scoreboard. The last frame in the presentation focused on a huge banner hanging in

Comiskey. It featured two Chicago giants—on one side was a picture of the Sears Tower, and on the other was a picture of Bill Veeck.[58]

Illinois declared Opening Day Bill Veeck Day, which set off a new wave of editorials demanding his posthumous election to the Hall of Fame. "I will continue to mourn his loss, and I will campaign at every opportunity for his induction into the Hall of Fame at Cooperstown," wrote Rick Talley in *Vineline: The Official Newspaper of the Chicago Cubs*, "Baseball owes him."[59]

"Somehow," wrote William Brashler in *Chicago Magazine* as baseball started up anew, "we will have to muddle through Opening Day without him. And we will have to adjust to a few sad facts: the gross national consumption of beer has diminished, some say measurably. Every day now, one good book goes unread. And marches against handguns and for peace and civil rights have one fewer peg-leg pounding the pavement. . . . But the arc lights must still be turned on, boys. Let us wander over to the ballpark, lift a sign heavenward, and laugh some more."[60]

Epilogue

Bill Veeck had one of the most absorbing and
valuable American lives of the century.
—SCOTT SIMON

ILL VEECK DIED WHILE BOWIE KUHN was writing his autobiography, and the former commissioner toyed with the notion of leaving Veeck out of his book entirely—as had Ford Frick in his 1972 memoir, *Games, Asterisks and People: Memoirs of a Lucky Fan*. But Kuhn decided differently: "Wherever the shade of William Veeck resides, and I have several clear theories as to where that may be, the last thing it would want said of Bill is nothing."

After saying that he could not imagine any two people more unalike than himself and Veeck, he typified Veeck as "equal parts charlatan and rebel," someone who in an earlier age would have been the Music Man, shamelessly "selling elixirs to the unwary." He was "ill at ease with every commissioner he ever knew" and viewed them as an abomination. "I never knew a self-respecting commissioner who failed to return the compliment."[1]

Surely Ford Frick would have agreed with Kuhn's interpretation. Perhaps William Eckert, who Veeck called the "unknown soldier," would have as well, as a result of the constant badgering and baiting he had felt from Veeck during his short time in office. But Happy Chandler disagreed. Two years after Kuhn's book was published, Chandler's autobiography referred to Veeck as "a stand-up fellow," in contrast to many of the other owners he typified as "crybabies." He applauded Veeck's circus razzle-dazzle and praised the fun and excitement he put into the game. "Bill Veeck sometimes broke a rule. I caught him. 'Bill, belly up,' I said. Veeck didn't whimper. He just accepted his punishment. I like that kind of a fella." Chandler concluded that Veeck actually would have made a good baseball commissioner.[2]

Such was the spread of opinion Bill Veeck left in his wake, and such was the polarity on his election to National Baseball Hall of Fame.[3] Although immediately after his death he lacked the votes to get into the Hall of Fame, others saw him in line for other, even higher honors. In June 1988, a newsletter entitled *Initiatives*, published by the National Center for the Laity, contained an article about hidden saints that prompted readers to submit their own nominations for sainthood among those "living saintly lives within ordinary circumstances." The list included Senator Robert Kennedy, Dorothy Day (co-founder of the Catholic Worker movement), and Bill Veeck—which, as the newsletter put it, was not bad for a man who described himself as "a very casual Catholic."[4]

Also while he was in the waiting room for the Hall of Fame, Veeck's name was increasingly invoked by those who appreciated baseball's idiosyncratic past. Chicago architect Philip Bess wrote an article entitled "Bill Veeck Park: A Modest Proposal," in which he designed a traditional 40,000-seat urban ballpark set on a single block, reinforcing the traditional urban pattern of streets and squares. It grew out of the author's disdain for twenty-five years of gargantuan multipurpose stadiums, which he deemed bad for both the sports that use them and the cities that build them. The site for this proposed project was a parcel of land on the South Side of Chicago, which at the time was designated by the city for a multiuse stadium. Next to the south end of the park, Bess wanted to create a public square, complete with a statue of Veeck. While the park was never built, the idea was a perfect honor for the man who had ripped out the artificial turf from Comiskey Park and prized Wrigley Field and Fenway Park above all others.[5]*

By 1990, the inability to gather the votes needed to elect Veeck to the Hall of Fame was becoming a larger issue in the media. Unlike players, who were elected by the sportswriters, executives and umpires were elected by the Veterans Committee, composed of former players and a few writers, a group that Ray Sons of the *Chicago Sun-Times* termed an "establishment committee"

---

* Veeck did not live to see lights in Wrigley Field. Following the Veeck-directed renovation in 1937, the next upgrade of any significance took place in 1988, when the Cubs installed lights after Major League Baseball decreed they could not host any postseason games until they did. Three banks of lights, each on thirty-three-foot steel towers, were added to the left- and right-field rooftops at a cost of $5 million. After playing 5,687 consecutive home day games, the Cubs played their first night game at Wrigley on August 8, 1988, but it was rained out after three innings. The first complete night game was played on August 9.

representing the mind-set of those whom Veeck used to delight in irritating. Sons noted that Veeck would have been voted in immediately had it been the writers voting, but that was not the case, and an "outrageous injustice persists. His matchless contributions to fun and fairness cry for recognition."[6]

There was another problem in that the rules allowed the committee to take only two ballots. Given the minimum number of votes needed for election, with only two rounds the votes might still be split too broadly to elect anyone, which was the case in 1990.

Bill Veeck was finally voted into the National Baseball Hall of Fame in 1991, five years after his death. "It just kind of happened," said broadcaster Ernie Harwell, one of the eighteen members of the Veterans Committee "We just started talking about Veeck and all of a sudden there was a groundswell of support for him. I think we were all a little surprised." Monte Irvin was another member of the committee that selected Veeck and Tony Lazzeri, who played on six championship Yankee teams during the Babe Ruth era, from among thirty nominees who had survived a screening process by the Veterans Committee.[7] They were to be inducted with Rod Carew, Ferguson Jenkins, and Gaylord Perry, who were elected by the Baseball Writers' Association of America. Hank Greenberg's earlier exultation was invoked: "Every innovation in baseball except a couple kookie things that Charlie Finley tried—like orange baseballs and silly uniforms—originated with Veeck. Electric scoreboards, giveaways, fan days, concerts, a pinch-hitting midget."[8]

At the induction ceremony on July 21, 1991, Mary Frances Veeck spoke on Bill's behalf. "Life was not wasted on Bill Veeck. He was born with a great joy of living, tremendous energy, integrity. He was curious, imaginative, creative, spontaneous, stubborn, intelligent, opinionated, witty. He was *such fun* to be around, a pied piper. He was magic. He was a 'pro'! All of these qualities made him the baseball man we remember today."[9]

Mary Frances then concluded with the set of twelve commandments by which Bill Veeck lived, to which he felt anyone in the business of baseball should adhere:

1. Take your work very seriously. Go for broke and give it your all.
2. Never ever take yourself seriously.
3. Find yourself an alter ego and bond with him for the rest of your professional life.*

---

* An allusion to Rudie Schaffer, according to Mary Frances.

4. Surround yourself with similarly dedicated soul mates, free spirits of whom you can ask why and why not. And who can ask the same thing of you.

5. In your hiring, be color-blind, gender-blind, age- and experience-blind. You never work for Bill Veeck. You work with him.

6. If you're a president, owner, or operator, attend every home game, and never leave until the last out.

7. Answer all your mail; you might learn something.

8. Listen and be available to your fans.

9. Enjoy and respect the members of the media, the stimulation and the challenge. The "them against us" mentality should exist only between the two teams on the field.

10. Create an aura in your city. Make people understand that unless they come to the ballpark, they will miss something.

11. If you don't think a promotion is fun, don't do it. Never insult your fans.

12. Don't miss the essence of what is happening at the moment. Let it happen. Cherish the moment and commit it to your memory.

Veeck's Hall of Fame plaque reads:

BILL VEECK
OWNER OF INDIANS, BROWNS AND WHITE SOX.
CREATED HEIGHTENED FAN INTEREST AT EVERY STOP
WITH INGENIOUS PROMOTIONAL SCHEMES, FAN
PARTICIPATION, EXPLODING SCOREBOARD, OUTRAGEOUS
DOOR PRIZES, NAMES ON UNIFORMS. SET M.L.
ATTENDANCE RECORD WITH PENNANT-WINNER AT
CLEVELAND IN 1948; WON AGAIN WITH "GO-GO"
SOX IN 1959. SIGNED A.L.'S FIRST BLACK PLAYER,
LARRY DOBY, IN 1947 AND OLDEST ROOKIE, 42-YEAR-OLD
SATCHEL PAIGE, IN 1948.
A CHAMPION OF THE LITTLE GUY.

"My father would've loved Cooperstown," Mike Veeck observed. "He would've loved to set up a table on Main Street, put a case of beer next to a sawhorse, and sign autographs for free while the other inductees charge $30 a copy."[10]

"Before Bill Veeck, baseball teams simply showed up to play. The decision to come to the ballpark was left up to the fans. . . . Veeck changed all that—he made everybody want to come to the ballpark," said Charlie Brotman, longtime sports announcer and public relations agent.[11] Most who knew Bill Veeck acknowledge that he made his sport more popular. "Times have changed since Veeck's time and the game is more sophisticated now, but you can see Veeck's influence all over the game—the interactive attractions at the ballpark, the promotions and even the design of the ballparks The razzmatazz is different today, but it is in the same spirit," added Stan Kasten, then general manager of the Washington Nationals.[12]

Perhaps Veeck would have appreciated that spirit. And yet, as Jonathan Yardley observed in the *Washington Post*, "no one else has had his combination of ingenuity, intelligence, humor and deep love of the game, so the promotions that now greet fans—over-amped rock music, Jumbotron scoreboards, wildly overpriced concessions—detract from the game rather than enhance it."

Veeck loved to share his passion for the game. "My father [Lee] was American League president," recalled Andy MacPhail. "He loved the late nights with Bill, but he also needed to get some sleep. I was with the Cubs then, and my job was to go with my father and pull him out at a reasonable hour, like one-fifteen or one-thirty in the morning, which of course would upset Veeck, who wondered how I would ever learn anything about baseball if I always had to go home early."[13]

Veeck would have enjoyed the irony of the moment during spring training 2008 when the New York Yankees allowed comedian Billy Crystal to bat during an exhibition game. "Somewhere under the celestial lights," wrote Bill Madden, "the ol' hustler himself, Bill Veeck, is roaring with laughter. Not at the absurdity of 60-year-old Billy Crystal batting leadoff for the Yankees against the Pirates in a spring training game yesterday, but rather at what he would consider the hypocrisy of the lordly Yankees for conceiving such a stunt. After all, who were Veeck's staunchest critics when he held forth as baseball's resident Barnum and establishment-tweaker in four different ownerships stints with the Cleveland Indians, St. Louis Browns and Chicago White Sox from the '40s into the '80s? And who more than the Yankees viewed Veeck, who died in 1986, as a disgrace and embarrassment to baseball for his numerous attendance-boosting gimmicks, most notably sending a 3-foot-7 midget, Eddie Gaedel, to the plate for the Browns against the Detroit Tigers in the second game of an Aug. 19, 1951, doubleheader?"[14]

There are those who still marginalize Veeck as a stuntsman, still re-member him primarily for Eddie Gaedel and Disco Demolition. "If I hear them call him the 'Barnum of Baseball' one more time, I'll gag—that's the image they want to perpetuate," said his son Mike. But he was so much more complex, so much more interesting. Passionate about his business, he also took delight in the rhythms of everyday life—running errands, work-ing with his hands, chatting with doormen, reading books, using his leg as a prop to make kids gasp and laugh.[15]

Greg Veeck captured his father's view of baseball and the world: "It's just a game. Life's hard. Just watch the game."[16]

Following the Family and Close Friends

Mary Frances Veeck
In March 2011 Mary Frances Veeck (born September 1, 1920) finally left the Hyde Park home that she and Bill had bought in 1975. She moved to an independent-living senior citizens' community. Among her closest friends is Wyonella Smith. Greg Veeck said that, like his father, his mother has always been attentive to waiters, waitresses, parking attendants, and so on: "She'll tell the woman who is checking her out at the grocery store that her hair looks especially lovely today."[1]

The Children of Bill Veeck's First Marriage
William Louis Veeck III died on January 30, 1985, at his home in Kauai, Hawaii. He was a teacher and counselor at a community college in Hawaii. He and his wife, Bernice, have two children, Valerie and Raymond. Ellen Veeck Maggs is a retired schoolteacher living in Phoenix; she is very much a part of Bill Veeck's second family, mainly because of Mary Frances, and today she feels lucky to have been his daughter, seeing Bill as a man with a kind heart and a love of people. She finds that she is surprisingly like him as a creative and nonlinear thinker.[2] Ellen and her husband, Chuck, have three children, Lisa, Cynthia, and David. Peter Raymond Veeck lives in Texas and is out of touch with his sister and his father's second family. He and his wife, Ramona, have a daughter, Kimberly.

The Children of Bill Veeck's Second Marriage
Mike Veeck, born on March 5, 1951, is by far the most public of the Veeck children and most like his father in terms of career. He had just turned

sixty when this book was written, and at that time he was co-owner of the St. Paul Saints, the Charleston River Dogs, the Fort Myers Miracle, and the Hudson Valley Renegades, in partnership with comedian Bill Murray and Wall Street lawyer Marv Goldklang. Mike's daughter, Rebecca, who was blinded by retinitis pigmentosa, displays the "same indomitable spirit" as her grandfather, according to Mike. When Rebecca was eight and still partially sighted, Mike took her on a tour of the country to see everything he and her mother, Libby, thought she should see, including her grandfather's marker in the Hall of Fame, a visit she made with Larry Doby. A child from Mike's first marriage, William (known as "Night Train"), lives in Chicago, and works for the Chicago White Sox.[3]

Marya Veeck, born on October 13, 1954, has been an artist and a gallery owner in Chicago since 1987, when her gallery, August House Studio, opened at 2113 West Roscoe Street. She represents a number of other artists and feels that the gift she got from her father was his business sense. Like her father, she has large hands, and she still marvels at the thought of the precision he employed in tying small pieces into mobiles using fishing line. She is married to Scott Smith, who works in film.

Gregory Veeck, born on January 11, 1956, today is a professor of geography at Western Michigan University in Kalamazoo, specializing in economic geography, agriculture, rural development, and rural environmental and ecological issues in the United States and Asia, particularly China. He is married to Ann Veeck, who also teaches at Western Michigan University and is deeply involved in issues of food supply in China. They have two daughters, Sarah and Robin. Greg shares his father's love of baseball and his delight in the rhythms of daily life.[4]

Lisa Veeck, born on August 5, 1958, works today as media communications and publications director for a Chicago-based trade association. She noted that the only time he talked with his children about his experiences in World War II was to say that it had made him appreciate life. And, she noted, "he never had to scream or yell. He just gave you the look."[5] She is married to Don Sanetra.

Dr. Juliana Veeck-Brosnan, whose birth on July 4, 1961, had been celebrated by fireworks from the Comiskey Park scoreboard, died on June 12, 2010, after twenty years of dealing with the cancer that eventually took her life. Her obituary in the *Sun-Times* said, "As a clinical psychologist, Juliana Veeck-Brosnan counseled some of the city's most troubled youth—adolescents others had written off—and helped them find a passage through the chaos of their lives."

"Juliana was probably one of the most gifted psychologists ever," said a close friend and former colleague at Children's Memorial Hospital, psychologist Sharon Berry, "and she worked with the hardest and most difficult situations." Like her father, she had a quirky sense of humor. When she got married in 1989, she brought her black Labrador retriever, Raven, to the church. Raven sat in the back row, wearing a shiny new yellow collar. "It was great," her husband, Tom Brosnan, said. "I thought she was nuts at first, but it really worked well."[6] Juliana and Tom have three children, Christian, Jack, and Olivia.

Christopher Veeck, who was born in Easton on June 19, 1962, died in 1995 at only thirty-two of a heart attack. At the time of his death he ran the concessions for two sports complexes in Houston and lived in Humble, Texas. He is survived by his companion, Ann-Marie Hewitt, and a son, Patrick.[7]

ALTER EGOS AND CLOSE ASSOCIATES

Hank Greenberg died in 1986, the same year that Bill did, on September 4 in Beverly Hills after a thirteen-month bout with cancer. According to Mary Frances, Greenberg used to say to Bill, "If you were as charming to the other owners as you are to cab drivers or doormen, they'd be eating out of your hands."[8]

Ed Linn died on February 7, 2000, at his home in Spring Valley, California, at seventy-seven; the cause was cancer. Linn covered the trial of Jack Ruby for the *Saturday Evening Post* and worked with bank robber Willie Sutton on his autobiography, *Where the Money Was* (1976). But he was best known for sportswriting, having been a contributing editor to *Sport* magazine and co-author with Veeck for *Veeck—as in Wreck* (1962)

Rudie Schaffer died on November 27, 2007, in Menlo Park, California, at the age of ninety-six. "He really was [Bill Veeck]'s alter ego," said Veeck's widow, Mary Frances. "They enjoyed a great relationship. They were the triumvirate—Bill, [Rudie Schaffer], and Roland Hemond. The three ran the Sox."

Larry Doby was at former Brooklyn Dodger pitcher Don Newcombe's home near Los Angeles when he learned in March 1998 that he'd finally made it to the National Baseball Hall of Fame. "It's kind of like a bale of cotton has been on your shoulders and now it's off," he told Hal Bodley of *USA Today*. "I can't tell you my feelings, but they're great." He had waited thirty-six years, during which time he had also lobbied strongly for Veeck's inclusion in the Hall of Fame. Doby died on June 18, 2003, at his home in Montclair, New Jersey. He was seventy-nine.

Acknowledgments

Bill Veeck was afraid for his old friend Casey Stengel in 1967 because a new biography by Joe Durso, a *New York Times* writer, was about to be published. "I was afraid it would be another paint pot glue job in which you read the clippings and put the book together," he confessed on his syndicated radio show. Within this fear was another, deeper one: that Durso would opt to depict Stengel as a clown.

But then Durso, presumably with a wink and a nudge from Stengel, offered Veeck a chance to write the introduction and with it a chance to read the book in the form of uncorrected proof pages. "The real Casey came through," said Veeck. "Durso did him well—magnificent job." He added that in Durso's capable hands Casey's life became a history of our times.

It is in this spirit that I attempt to bring Veeck into focus as neither a clown nor a hero—although he could play either of these roles—but as a remarkable iconoclast and individualist living through a time when conformity and corporate allegiance were valued personal attributes.

If I have achieved this goal and gotten Veeck right or nearly so, then I have many to thank for their help. When I began this project, I could not have imagined how many people would actually contribute to it. The list is a function of Veeck's continuing impact rather than my ability to place phone calls and set up appointments.

Some of those who were interviewed for this book did not end up in the final narrative for the simple reason that their praise for the man became repetitive. From the players who knew Veeck or even those were around during his time, there was a universal response when one asked about him. It typically started with a broad smile followed by a question—"Bill Veeck?"— and a short gleefully delivered comment. "Bill Veeck? He did it up right. He was a real baseball man" was the response of Hall of Fame infielder Brooks

Robinson. Jerry Coleman: "Bill Veeck? The greatest innovator. A lot ballparks could use a Bill Veeck today." Ralph Kiner: "Bill Veeck? He was a fantastic man. I played a lot of tennis with him. Even with that bad leg, he was very competitive."

A—Steve Ackerman, Robert Ames Alden (former sports reporter for the *Cleveland Press* and the *Washington Post*), Carol Alley, Rebecca T. Alpert, Joshua Anderson CHS, Marty Appel, Jon Arakaki (who teaches communications at SUNY Oneonta), Mark L. Armour (SABR Biography Committee), Chris Axelrod.

B—Nina Bahadur, Jack Bales (reference and humanities librarian, University of Mary Washington Library, for his material on Bill's father), Steve Banker (the late oral historian), Ernie Banks, Allen Barra, Monica Pence Barlow (director of public relations for the Baltimore Orioles), Brad Beechen (Cubs usher and former classmate), Myron Belkind, Lea Beresford, Yogi Berra, Hal Bodley, Doug Boyd Jr. (director, Louie B. Nunn Center for Oral History, University of Kentucky Libraries), Lou Brissie, David Broder, Charlie Brotman.

C—Eileen Canepari (membership services manager, Society for American Baseball Research), Terry and Mary Cannon (the Baseball Reliquary), John Carlson (late scholar of the Black Sox), Gene Carney, Jake Carrow (Chicago intern/researcher, Vanderbuilt University), George Case III, Jamie Ceasar, Frank Ceresi, Bill Chastine, Mike Clark, Roger Clark, Jim Clavin, Heather Cogge, Jerry Coleman, Chris Core, Bob Creamer.

D—Ivan R. Dee, Laurina Deliso (Pima County, Arizona, deputy clerk), Joe DeMaestri, Larry Dierker, Larry Doby Jr.

E—Morris Eckhouse, Edmund P. Edmonds (associate dean for library and information technology and professor of law, Kresge Law Library, Notre Dame Law School), Jonathan Eig, the late Gene Ellis, Eric Endess, Jim Evans (of the Jim Evans Academy of Professional Umpiring).

F—Dick Fischman, Donald L. Fordham (Veeck's Sergeant, Headquarters Company, 3rd Special Weapons, 3rd Marine Division, Bougainville), Phil Friedman.

G—Ned Garver, Tim Gay, Bill Gilbert, Mike Gimbel (statistician/organizer and defender of Veeck), Bill Gleason, Patricia Goforth (National Personnel Records Center, St. Louis), Peter Golenbock, Ray Grebey, Deborah Grodinsky (Skokie Public Library, Skokie, Illinois), Steve Grubeck.

H—Ed Hartig (unofficial historian, Chicago Cubs), Ernie Harwell, Dick Heller, Roland Hemond, Katherine Hillenbrand (summer of 2009 intern),

Phil Hochberg (attorney), David Hoekstra, Sam Holt (filmmaker), John Holway, Keith Horvath MD,* Frank Howard.

I—Jeff Idelson (director of the National Baseball Hall of Fame and Museum, who has a copy of Veeck's Twelve Commandments in his office), Monte Irvin (Hall of Famer and World War II vet), Stan Isaacs, David Israel.

J—Bill Jennings, Gary Johnson (Library of Congress, Periodicals Reading Room), Grady Johnson (South Sider and Clarence Page's father-in-law), Randy Johnson, Steve Johnson, Scott Jones.

K—Cliff Kachline, Dave Kaplan, Stan Kasten, Jeff Katz, Dave Kelly, Ralph Kiner (Hall of Famer and World War II vet), Bruce Kraig, Frederick Krehbiel.

L—Joe Lapointe, David Levey, Stephanie M. Lisico, Bob Luke.

M—Andy MacPhail (GM and president of the Baltimore Orioles, son of Lee and grandson of Larry [the only father and son in the Baseball Hall of Fame], Myra MacPherson, Ellen Maggs (Veeck's daughter from his first marriage), Glenn Marcus, Marty Marion, Babe Martin (St. Louis Browns), Lesley A. Martin (Chicago History Museum), Richard Marsh, William Marshall, Skip McAfee, Paul McCardell, Clinton "Butch" McCord, Larry McCray, Jan McKee, Ron Menchine, Bill Mead (friend and Brownie historian), Ed Mickelson (St. Louis Browns), Vick Mickunas, Arthur H. Miller (archivist and librarian for special collections, Donnelley and Lee Library/LIT, Lake Forest College), Marvin Miller, Clark Mitze (Veeck's 1951 grandstand manager), Wally Mlyniec (Georgetown Law School), Willis Monie (bookseller extraordinare, Cooperstown, New York), Joseph Thomas Moore, Russell Mott, Caitlin Mullen.

N—Bill Nack.

O—Andrew O'Toole, Jim Odenkirk.

P—Clarence Page, Ted Patterson, Hank Peters, John Peterson, Duane Pillette, Brian A. Podoll, Murray Polner, Mark Plotkin (political analyst with Veeckian aspirations), Jacob Pomrenke (chairman of the SABR Black Sox

---

* On November 10, 2009, I had open heart surgery to correct a defective aortic valve. Dr. Horvath was my surgeon. Hours after the surgery we talked about this book and he said that as a youngster he had been with his father and, on several occasions, met and shook hands with Bill Veeck. I was not all that coherent at the moment, but I mumbled something to the effect that the hand that had saved my life had also touched the hand of the man I was trying to capture in a biography. It somehow seemed proper to include him in the acknowledgments. He is a White Sox fan.

Committee), Jay Porter (the youngest St. Louis Brown ever), Bill Purdy (St. Louis Browns batboy and batting practice catcher).

R—Tom Randall, Branch Rickey III (president of the Pacific Coast League), James A. Riley, Jacob Roberts (intern summers of 2006 and 2008), Brooks Robinson, Ray Robinson, Lester Rodney, Dan Rodricks, Dick Rosen (vice chair, Philadelphia Athletics Historical Society). George Rugg (Sports and Games Collection, Notre Dame University),

S—Alex Sanders, Eloise Saperstein, Marty Schram, Peter Schilling, Art Schreiber, Fred Schuld (for his help with the 1948 season), Al Silverman (former editor of *Sport* magazine), the late Hubert "Bert" Simmons (the last Elite Giant left in Baltimore and founder of the Negro Leagues Baseball Museum of Maryland), Claire Smith (Major League Baseball writer, currently with ESPN), Curt Smith, Wyonella Smith, Brad Snyder, Michael Spekter, David A. Spenard (Abe Saperstein's nephew), Burt Randolph Sugar.

T—Paul Tenpenny, John Herd Thompson (professor of history at Duke University), Michael Thomas, Erin Tikovitsch (Chicago History Museum), Larry Tye.

V—Gregory Veeck, Lisa Veeck, Mary Frances Veeck, Marya Veeck, Mike Veeck, J. D. Vercett.

W—Willie Weinbaum, Rich Westcott, Pat Williams, Tom Wolf.

X/Y/Z—William Young (of Arlington, Virginia), Bill Young (of Chicago).

The team that created this book also deserves credit, beginning with my agent, Deborah Grosvenor of the Grosvenor Literary Agency. Great thanks to the team at Walker & Company, led by my old friend George Gibson, who edited this book with rare dedication and sublime skill. He was aided by Lea Beresford and Nina Bahadur. Sue Warga copyedited the book, Nathaniel Knaebel led the production team, and Robert "Skip" McAfee was the indexer and final fact checker.

Appendix

Did Bill Veeck Lie About His Plan to Purchase the '43 Phillies?

The narrative you have just read asserts that Bill Veeck attempted to buy the Philadelphia Phillies after the 1942 World Series and turn the team into an all-black or predominantly black team. It points out that the idea of putting a black team or teams in the major leagues had been advanced as early as 1933 to Veeck's father by Syd Pollock, that the notion was current in 1942, and that Veeck was already involved in promoting black-versus-white baseball events in both baseball and basketball with Abe Saperstein, who had scouted financial backers for the 1942 attempt to buy the Phillies.

Today, there are those who think that this is all a lie, a falsehood concocted by Veeck almost twenty years after the fact. This belief stems from a single article, "A Baseball Myth Exploded: Bill Veeck and the 1943 Sale of the Phillies," one of the most influential stories ever published in a Society for American Baseball Research (SABR) publication. This story in the 1998 issue of *The National Pastime* was written by David M. Jordan, Larry R. Gerlach, and John P. Rossi, and it attempts to debunk Veeck's tale about trying to buy the Phillies and stock the club with Negro league players.* The article featured a doctored cover picture of Veeck in a purple and yellow open-collar sports shirt, a clear attempt to make him look clownish and mendacious.

---

* The authors are described in the 2006 SABR *Baseball Research Journal*: David Jordan, the author of three biographies, including one of pitcher Hal Newhouser, is one of the foremost authorities on Philadelphia baseball history; John Rossi is a professor of history at LaSalle University in Philadelphia; and Larry Gerlach, a professor of history at the University of Utah, published the pioneering volume of oral histories *The Men in Blue: Conversations with Umpires*, and, more significant, was the president of SABR in 1998, when the Veeck article was published.

The cover also carried a most unscholarly and intemperate teaser: "The major difficulty with this oft-told story is that it is not true. Veeck did not have a deal to buy the Phillies. He did not work to stock any team with Negro leagues stars. No such deal was quashed by Landis or Frick."[1]

The article was introduced by the magazine's editor, Mark Alvarez, who opined, "The wonder and lesson to researchers is less why Veeck did it than how this story became common baseball currency without ever having been verified."

One of the main arguments advanced by the authors was that Veeck largely invented the story for his 1962 autobiography, *Veeck—as in Wreck*. They could find no reports in the mainstream or Negro press of this story prior to that time (other than an article by Wendell Smith written a few months earlier and based on an interview with Veeck). They note specifically that Doc Young, sports editor of a black paper in Cleveland in the 1940s, never mentioned this incident, and they say, "Young's silence is significant."

The authors made a number of largely speculative points to support their argument and ask why Veeck had not integrated the Milwaukee Brewers. They concluded: "We must face the fact that Bill Veeck falsified the historical record."[2]

Almost immediately members of SABR privately questioned both the tone and accuracy of the article. They especially questioned the assertion that because these researchers could not find confirmation, it did not happen, noting that it is impossible to prove a negative. "I wondered about the piece from the very beginning," said Mark Armour, who is the founder of SABR's Bio-Project, a drive to create short biographies of all major-league ballplayers, and the author of *Joe Cronin: A Life in Baseball*. "Not finding a source is not the same thing as there not being a source."[3]

At least one member wrote a letter of rebuttal. Several days after the magazine was mailed, Mike Gimbel, an avid baseball fan who had held front-office jobs doing statistical analysis for the Expos and Red Sox, wrote to SABR to resign from the group, based on what he called a cover story that was a shameless piece of trash. Gimbel said that when he first got the article with the provocative cover, he was saddened to learn that one of his childhood heroes had not been truthful. But when he actually began reading the piece, he became angry: "I wasn't past the first page before I realized that something was terribly wrong—not with Veeck's 'story'—but with Gerlach's (et al.) research and with the very tone of this shameful article."

Gimbel's points of contention were many, but they centered on the authors' citing evidence that tended to support rather than deny Veeck's original story. For example, they say that the one mention of the attempted purchase before 1961 was Red Smith's writing in the June 25, 1946, *New York Herald Tribune*, "Hardly anyone knows how close Veeck came to buying the Phillies when the National League was forcing Gerry Nugent to sell. He had the backing and the inside track."

The authors said Smith had evidently gotten the tale from "Sportshirt Bill." Gimbel responded: "I guess that makes Red Smith, possibly the most renowned baseball newspaperman of the 20th century, a liar also! I guess that if you're going to tear down one of the great figures in baseball history (Veeck), you might as well throw in the greatest baseball newsman as well!" Gimbel noted in a later communication that Red Smith was a reporter for the *Philadelphia Record* at the time of Veeck's meeting with Nugent in 1942.

Gimbel concluded by lambasting the SABR article with some of the same intemperance that had fueled the original piece: "Shame on SABR for printing this scurrilous article. Shame on SABR for putting it on the cover so that you can get some 'quick response' in terms of sales. Your article belittles Veeck as a hustler, but you are the real, cheap hustlers in this matter. I don't ever remember Veeck taking the low road that SABR has taken. Yes, Veeck was a hustler. He was a damn good hustler, but a hustler with a heart and with the courage to stand up and fight for what he believed in."

Although Gimbel wanted his letter published, it never was.

Gimbel later rejoined SABR, and in 2011 he was profiled on the organization's Web site as one of the group's exemplary members. Yet, twelve years after the fact, he still called the article on Veeck and the Phillies "a vicious, yellow piece of journalism . . . which if you read their own research disproves their case."[4]

An anonymous person sent a copy of the SABR magazine to Marya Veeck, who was upset with the way her father had been portrayed on the cover as well as in the text. She called Ed Linn, who had collaborated with Veeck on *Veeck—as in Wreck*. He assured her that every word of the Philadelphia story was true and not to let it bother her—which, as she pointed out many years later, was easier said than done. Linn told Marya he had not been contacted by the SABR researchers.[5]

The issue lay dormant with the public until March 12, 2005, when an item appeared on the SABR listserve from Jules Tygiel, a professor of history at San Francisco State University and the author of *Baseball's Great Experiment: Jackie Robinson and His Legacy* (1983). Tygiel had spotted an error in the magazine's Veeck story. While browsing through A. S. "Doc" Young's book *Great Negro Baseball Stars*, published in 1953, he said: "I came across the following passage about Veeck when he bought the Indians in 1946: 'Negro writers soon recognized Veeck as a person likely at least to give an ear to the proposition of Negroes playing in the American League. Perhaps they had heard the unsubstantiated story that Veeck once shocked baseball's late commissioner, Judge Kenesaw Mountain Landis, with a proposal to buy a major league club and transform it into an all-colored aggregation.' One of the main points made by the debunkers was that Young's silence was significant, and here was Young discussing it in print under his own byline."[6]

Tygiel, who had interviewed Veeck on the subject in 1980 and had never had any reason to doubt Veeck's word, argued that while Jordan, Gerlach, and Rossi offered many other reasons to be skeptical about Veeck's tale, the Young quote was at least one written reference to it nine years prior to the publication of *Veeck—as in Wreck*. Tygiel concluded, "The story may still be untrue and the source may still ultimately be Veeck himself, but this was not something he created or imagined, as Jordan et al. imply, at the time of the writing of his book."[7]

A SABR member named Chris Hauser then chimed in, "I came across a similar reference that also predates Veeck's autobiography in a story issued by the Associated Negro Press and printed in the August 14, 1954 *Philadelphia Independent*: 'Abe Saperstein of the fabulous Harlem Globetrotters stated this week in a press interview that baseball magnate Bill Veeck had intended to use a baseball trick back in 1942 which would have upset the thinking in the major league, had it materialized. "I'll tell you one thing about Veeck," said Saperstein, "something that few people know. In 1942 the Phillies were for sale and Veeck attempted to buy them. But Bill Cox raised more money and got the club. Do you know what Veeck planned to do? He was going to take the Phils to spring training in Florida and then—on the day the season opened—dispose of the entire team. Meanwhile, with a team composed entirely of Negroes, who would have trained separately, he could have opened the National League season. I don't think there was a team in either league, back in 1943 that could have stopped the team he was going to assemble."'"

On March 14, 2005, Tygiel commented on this and other findings that were spurred by his original posting: "It would appear that the case against Bill Veeck's plan to purchase the Phillies, which was largely based on an absence of supporting evidence, is unraveling and that Veeck's telling of this story was 'remarkably consistent' with the evidence."

Then nine years after the original article by Jordan, Gerlach, and Rossi, Tygiel published a full response in the 2007 *Baseball Research Journal*, entitled "Revisiting Bill Veeck and the 1943 Phillies," in which he amassed all the evidence at hand to conclude that the three authors' "blanket dismissal of Veeck's assertions and confident branding of Veeck as a liar no longer stand uncontested. In their *National Pastime* article, they had correctly chastised earlier historians for accepting Veeck's narrative at face value and injected a dose of skepticism, replacing unwarranted certainty with healthy debate. Their own rush to judgment, however, offers yet another cautionary tale of relying on an absence of evidence and overreaching one's resources in drawing conclusions."[8]

Rob Neyer, who discussed the matter in *Rob Neyer's Big Book of Baseball Legends: The Truth, the Lies, and Everything Else* (2008), noted that Tygiel's rebuttal was shunted to the back of the *Baseball Research Journal*. Neyer hoped that it had not been missed, because if Jordan, Gerlach, and Rossi had "spectacularly debunked Veeck's story, Tygiel spectacularly debunked the debunkers."

Neyer himself sifted through the evidence and concluded that Veeck made preliminary gestures toward buying the Phillies and considered stocking the team with players from the Negro leagues. He then summarized the central point of Tygiel's paper, which he concurred with: "While we don't have a great deal of evidence on what was on Veeck's mind in 1942, we don't have nearly enough evidence to know what was *not* on Veeck's mind."[9]

A problem the original article created was to give many—most notably the SABR faithful—the impression that Veeck lied not only about the 1942 incident but also about other matters. On several occasions I have been told with great confidence that Veeck was a liar and that, as one SABR member put it, there's probably not a single word in *Veeck—as in Wreck* that can be believed. At one informal gathering, I heard a SABR member stand up and suggest that Veeck's claim that he was dealing in players for the Milwaukee Brewers in a combat zone was another example of Veeck making something up out of whole cloth. This led me back to the Pacific edition of *Stars and Stripes*, the newspaper for the Armed Forces during the war, in which it is reported by Marine Corps reporters that Veeck was indeed trading players within a combat zone.

During the three years that I researched this biography, I came to the conclusion that Bill Veeck was telling the truth—not only on the Phillies story but also on other matters of substance. In dozens of interviews conducted for this book, I asked again and again if those who knew him had ever heard Veeck tell a lie or suspected that he was untruthful.

In not one interview I conducted with many who knew him did anyone say that he lied about anything. Again and again I pressed the point because of the SABR allegations, and got virtually the same response—Veeck was a storyteller who could exaggerate, especially in stories of self-deprecation, but never about anything of significance. In fact, Veeck's frankness and truthfulness often got him into hot water. Greg Veeck said that his father was "not capable of a lie" and that while he is not familiar with the details of the debate, he believed that "his rendition of it was accurate."[10]

A few points about Veeck's 1942 attempt to buy the Phillies:

1.   There is no question that it was widely rumored and widely repeated that Veeck was involved in some kind of attempt to buy the Phillies. His name is repeated again and again in the context of taking over the team. It shows up as early as the October 22, 1942, issue of *The Sporting News* (where he was quoted as saying that if the deal had gone through, he would have stayed in Milwaukee and sent Charlie Grimm to Philadelphia to run the team). The rumors and references to Veeck as the failed buyer of the Phils continued into 1943 and beyond. On March 8, "the Old Scout," the pseudonym of Herb Goren of the *New York Sun*, wrote in a profile of Veeck: "He was mentioned as one of the prospective buyers of the Phils, but it is doubtful if his sense of humor could have stood the strain." An article in the September 7, 1947, issue of *Look* by Ray Grody of the *Milwaukee Sentinel* states that Veeck turned down an offer to head the Phillies the previous year because he was "having too much fun in Milwaukee."[11]

2.   At the time of Bill Veeck's death in 1986, Jerome Holtzman of the *Chicago Tribune* interviewed John Carmichael, the former sports columnist for the *Chicago Daily News*, about Veeck. Carmichael, then eighty-three, was an old friend of the elder Veeck and then of his son. He told Holtzman that he had run into Veeck in Chicago trying to raise money to buy the Phils and that Veeck intended to staff the club with Negro leaguers. Both Carmichael and Holtzman were reporters with strong credentials—both received the J. G. Taylor Spink Award for meritorious contributions to baseball writing from the Baseball Writer's Association of America, and Holtzman

served as official historian to Major League Baseball from 1999 until his death in 2008.[12]

3. As Tygiel and others showed, Veeck had discussed the purchase of the Phillies many years before *Veeck—as in Wreck* was published with writers whose reputations were unassailable. As reported earlier, the first mention of the deal by Veeck that appeared in print was in the "Heard in the Press Box" section of the September 1948 issue of *Baseball Digest*, where he is quoted as saying he had not thought about buying the Phillies until he read in the papers that he was rumored to be interested in the ailing franchise and that he was one of the likely buyers. He explained that he had a leading promoter of Negro baseball compile a list of Negro All-Stars, who he had planned to recruit, train, and spring on the world on Opening Day 1943. "What could they have done," Veeck asked. "They would have had to play my team or forfeit the game." The column on the purchase of the Phillies was written by the magazine's editor, Herbert F. Simons, an old Chicago newspaperman who, prior to creating *Baseball Digest* in 1942, had worked for the *Chicago Journal*, *Chicago Tribune*, and *Chicago Times*, for which he had covered baseball. He had been a close associate of the elder Veeck as a reporter and then reported on him as Cubs president. For the SABR researchers, who were so dependent on the written record to make their point, to miss a prominent item in *Baseball Digest* suggests a lack of thoroughness.[13]

4. One of the major points made by the three researchers was that the story had not appeared in print before Veeck's autobiography. Besides the 1948 *Baseball Digest* piece, a search of newspaper databases revealed the following evidence to the contrary:

- The first time the story appeared in print was on July 25, 1947, in the *St. Petersburg Times* in a column by Vernon Gibson, the paper's regular sports columnist: "Bill Veeck, Cleveland Indians owner now in the Cleveland Clinic for another operation . . . revealed recently that he tried to buy the Philadelphia Phillies during the war with an eye to making them an all-Negro club . . . turned down flat."
- In February 1949, at the thirty-third annual meeting of the Urban League of Chicago, Veeck made a startling revelation when he pointed to Young and said that "the gentleman, now sitting at

my right out there, and I talked for several hours about integrating Negroes in major league baseball. At that time I was planning to buy the Philadelphia Nationals"—Nationals being the old-school way that Veeck referred to the Phillies.[14]

- Shirley Povich discussed the plan in detail in the *Washington Post* on May 10, 1953, quoting Veeck: "'Landis stopped me, I think. It was after Gerry Nugent had tossed in the towel with the Philadelphia Phillies and the franchise was back in the lap of the league. Abe Saperstein, an owner in the Negro National League, and I had plans. I don't blame the other club owners. 'We'd have walked away with the pennant.'" The article was part of a groundbreaking thirteen-part series on integration called "No More Shutouts." This article appeared while Ford Frick was baseball commissioner, and again, there was no apparent challenge from Frick or any of the other living individuals mentioned in the context of the article, including Saperstein. Nominated for a Pulitzer Prize by the *Post*, the Povich series was widely read and discussed.[15]

- In August 1954, Abe Saperstein gave an interview to the Associated Negro Press that ran in the Chicago *Defender* and other African American newspapers that discussed the plan in some detail. "I don't think there was a team in the league back in 1943 that could have stopped the team he was going to assemble."[16]

- In April 1956, Jack Mabley of the *Chicago Daily News* published a small paperback as part of a series on economic and social issues from the Public Affairs Committee of New York City. Entitled *Who's on First?*, it was a discussion of baseball and minorities, with an introduction by Lou Boudreau, who was at the time the manager of the Kansas City Athletics. The Philadelphia story was reported in book form six years before *Veeck—as in Wreck.*[17]

5. From 1961 through Veeck's death in 1986 and up to the time of the SABR article, dozens of articles were written that mentioned the attempt to purchase the Phillies, including those by David Israel, David Kindred, Red Smith, Jim Murray, Tracy Ringolsby, and another by Shirley Povich. (Povich again wrote of the incident in 1962 with new details that still depicted Commissioner Landis in an unflattering light.) All these writers knew Veeck—some, like Red

Smith, had known him for decades—and none ever had reason to doubt or question him on this matter. In July 1974, Red Smith ran a column in the *New York Times,* which had large syndication to newspapers around the country, in which Veeck talked about his two greatest regrets—that he did not get to purchase the Phillies in late 1942 and that he was unable to bring Elston Howard aboard as his manager for the Washington Senators.[18]

6. Veeck appeared in public on various occasions during which the incident was reported and never challenged. For instance, he was a participant in a conference on sports and government at the Brookings Institution in 1971, at which time Gerald W. Scully of Southern Illinois University—later of Southern Methodist University—in a scholarly paper on race discussed the 1942 attempt to purchase the Phillies. The story was repeated and accepted as true. Attorney Phil Hochberg, who attended the conference and who had lunch with Veeck that day, attested to the fact that the participants did not dispute the matter.

7. The authors of the SABR piece made no attempt to contact Bill Veeck's family. Mary Frances Veeck said that it was common knowledge in the family. Bill's sister, Peg, got a call from him when he returned to Chicago from Philadelphia, during which the matter was spelled out in some detail. As Mary Frances Veeck expressed it, "Margaret Ann Veeck Krehbiel would never have agreed to saying that it had not happened if it had not. She would never forget how excited she was when he called. We talked about it all the time." Mary Frances also pointed out that the reason that Veeck's name does not appear on Landis's schedule for the day is because Veeck had easy and open access to the commissioner's office. Also, an article in which she discussed the issue was cited by the SABR authors but dismissed in a footnote because her source was "Sportshirt Bill." Bill's son Mike has expressed himself many times on the SABR allegations. "Baseball researchers are constantly screaming that there is no paper trail to prove this," he said to a reporter from the *Baltimore Sun.* "But I never knew my old man to deal in falsehoods. That wasn't his style."[19]

8. Many people who conducted extensive interviews with Veeck attest to the story's veracity. Joseph Thomas Moore, who interviewed Veeck at some length for his biography of Larry Doby, had read the SABR article and said that there is no doubt in his mind that

what Veeck said about the proposed deal actually happened. "Personally, I have in fact no doubt that this actually happened. When I talked with Veeck I had no sense that he was making this up." Stephen Banker, a journalist, conducted a series of interviews, including one with Veeck, for his 1979 audio compilation *Black Diamonds*. Banker was firm in his belief that Veeck had been truthful in the very detailed account of the attempt in the interview. The last time Banker and I discussed it was at a lunch in late 2009, a few months before his death. Banker was a man who suffered neither fools nor liars, and his status as a journalist was unassailable—a point made at the time of his death in a public eulogy written for the *Atlantic* by his friend James Fallows.[20]

9. Those involved in Veeck's account either confirmed (Saperstein) or never denied (Frick) their role in the story, and both were alive when *Veeck—as in Wreck* was published (Saperstein died in 1966, Frick in 1978).

10. The event has always been looked at in isolation, neglecting the general push to put a black team on the field, which had first been proposed to Veeck's father. It is exactly the kind of impetuous move that characterized Veeck's entire life. "For Veeck, it would have been a typical move—rushed, radical, and revolutionary," wrote Jonathan Eig in his book *Opening Day* (2007). "Turning to Negro leaguers to restock the Phillies seemed like just the sort of thing he would do, although no one has ever been able to confirm that version of events."[21]

SINCE THE SABR ARTICLE appeared, it has taken on an even deeper dimension as part of the grand story of the racial integration of baseball. It has been converted into the what-if premise of several novels, including Peter Schilling Jr.'s masterly 2008 work *The End of Baseball*, in which Veeck obtains the Phillies and staffs them with the likes of Satchel Paige and Josh Gibson for the 1944 season.

Veeck's whirlwind attempt to buy and restaff the Phillies has sparked the imagination of both fans and scholars, and engendered no end of conjecture, including that by former commissioner Fay Vincent, who has expressed the opinion that if Veeck had succeeded, he could have delayed the integration of baseball teams, as all-black and all-white teams played one another.

Notes

Prologue

1. Interview with Andy MacPhail, July 1, 2009.
2. Interview with Cliff Kachline, August 1, 2009.
3. Pat Williams interviews: From the transcript of interviews conducted by Pat Williams in 1997–98 for his book, written with Michael Weinreb, *Marketing Your Dreams: Business and Life Lessons from Bill Veeck*. The transcripts are available at the National Baseball Library and are used with permission of both Mr. Williams and the NBL.
4. Interview with Ray Grebey, August 17, 2009.
5. Bill Veeck with Edward Linn, *Thirty Tons a Day: The Rough-Riding Education of a Neophyte Racetrack Operator* (New York: Viking Press, 1972), inside front dust jacket.
6. Interviews with Bert Randolph Sugar, July 9–10, 2009.
7. Interview with Mike Veeck, June 28, 2008.
8. *New York Times*, January 4, 1986, 7B.
9. Bill Veeck with Edward Linn, *Veeck—as in Wreck* (New York: G. P. Putnam's Sons, 1962), 257–258.
10. *Sports Illustrated*, July 4, 1960.
11. Interview with Marty Appel, March 21, 2010.
12. *Sports Illustrated*, July 4, 1960.
13. *Evening Star Sportsweek*, May 10, 1970, S10.
14. Interview with Mary Frances Veeck, June 7, 2010.
15. *Baseball Digest*, September 1972, 34.

Chapter 1: Senior

1. Kenneth M. Stampp, *Indiana Politics During the Civil War* (Indianapolis: Indiana Historical Bureau, 1949), 211; *Chicago American*, October 5, 1933. (The *Chicago American* piece was written two days following Veeck's death by his friend Jim Gallagher and is an invaluable source about Veeck's early days; it was also published in the *Chicago Daily News*, October 5, 1953.) A visit to the Hinsdale cemetery, July 6, 2011, attests to the fact that the two worked to keep their age difference a secret for the rest of their lives and even beyond: his cemetery headstone has the date of birth and death, while hers has none.
2. Louisville experienced twenty-seven 90-degree days and eight 100-degree days (seven of which were consecutive), including a 107-degree day on July 24, which still stands as of 2011 as the highest temperature ever recorded in the city.

3. *Chicago American*, October 6, 1933. Smith also said of this period, "It was Bill's life and did he live! He wouldn't have traded jobs with the President."

4. The *American* was immortalized in Hecht and MacArthur's play and film *The Front Page*.

5. *Chicago Tribune*, September 30, 1909; *Chicago Record Herald*, September 30, 1909. The latter paper played it on page 1, while the *Tribune* put the story on page 3.

6. *Chicago American*, September 30, 1909.

7. James E. Elfers, *The Tour to End All Tours: The Story of Major League Baseball's 1913–1914 World Tour* (Lincoln: University of Nebraska Press, 2003), 15.

8. *Chicago American*, October 5, 1933.

9. Interviews with Fred Krehbiel, June 26 and July 6, 2010.

10. *Baltimore Sun*, March 31, 1953, 19.

11. Discussed by Timothy M. Gay in *USA Today*, June 9, 2005.

12. Sean Deveney, "Did the 1918 Cubs Throw the World Series," *Seattle Times*, April 17, 2008. The Cicotte affidavit sits in a room on the third floor of the Chicago History Museum. In December 2004, the museum won an auction for the rights to a group of documents pertaining to the 1919 White Sox.

13. *Chicago American*, September 4, 1918.

14. Ibid. September 16, 1918.

15. Interview with Jacob Pomrenke, August 11, 2011; online column by Anthony Castrovince at MLB.com, May 18, 2011, http://chicago.cubs.mlb.com/news/article.jsp?ymd=20110517&content_id=19210316&vkey=news_mlb&c_id=chc. Castrovince noted, "The circumstantial evidence, however, lends at least some credence to the claim. Consider that, in 1918, baseball attendance was ravaged by the war. Many top players were drafted, and many fans cut back on their discretionary spending. The game's future—and, with it, the prospect of paychecks for its players—looked uncertain, and it was already assumed that the 1919 season would not take place. The 1918 season was cut short at 140 games, with owners putting a freeze on the salaries of all players not involved in the World Series."

16. *Chicago Daily News*, October 5, 1933; *Chicago American*, October 5, 1933.

17. Warren Brown, *The Chicago Cubs* (New York: G. P. Putnam's Sons, 1946), 80.

18. Interviews with Fred Krehbiel, June 26 and July 6, 2010.

19. *Chicago American*, December 8, 1918; *Chicago Evening Post*, December 10, 1918.

20. *Chicago Tribune*, May 9, 1919, 19; May 10, 1919, 19; *Dubuque Telegraph-Herald*, May 9, 1919, 8.

21. *Fort Worth Star-Telegram*, August 10, 1919, 22.

22. *Chicago Tribune*, August 5, 1919.

23. *Oregonian*, June 3, 1920; *Chicago Tribune*, June 10, 24, 1920; Two Finger Carney, "The Dead Zone," Notes from the Shadows of Cooperstown: Observations from Outside the Lines, no. 335, July 31, 2004, http://baseball1.com/carney/index.php?storyid=247.

24. *Miami Herald*, April 16, 1920.

25. *Idaho Daily Statesman*, September 5, 1920.

26. AP, *Paterson (NJ) Sunday Chronicle*, September 5, 1920, 18.

27. UPI, *Milwaukee Journal*, September 5, 1920, 20.

28. AP, *St. Louis Post-Dispatch*, September 4, 1920, 1.

29. *Cleveland Plain Dealer*, September 10, 1920, 1.

30. Daniel E. Ginsburg, *The Fix Is In: A History of Baseball Gambling and Game Fixing Scandals* (Jefferson, NC: McFarland, 1995), 134; Harold Seymour, *Baseball: The Golden Age* (New York: Oxford University Press, 1989), 298; *Atlanta Constitution*, January 5, 1921, 6; Alexander R. Jones, "It's War to the Finish: Veeck of Cubs Declares There'll Be No Compromise with Gamblers," *Cleveland Plain Dealer*, July 14, 1922, 18.

31. Jeff Davis, *Papa Bear: The Life and Legacy of George Halas* (New York: McGraw-Hill, 2005), 61–62; George Halas, *Halas by Halas* (New York: McGraw-Hill, 1979).

32. *New York Times*, November 9, 1922.

33. Typed notes from the National League Service Bureau, on file in the William Veeck Sr. vertical file at the National Baseball Library.

34. Bill Veeck with Edward Linn, *Veeck—as in Wreck* (New York: G. P. Putnam's Sons, 1962), 24.

35. *New York Times*, February 26, 1929.

36. Brown, *Chicago Cubs*, 110.

37. From an undated five-part series in the *Chicago Daily News* on Veeck obtained from the family but which, from references involved, was clearly written within weeks of his death in 1933. Hereafter Carmichael, *Chicago Daily News* biography, 1933.

38. *Chicago American*, August 16, 1932.

39. *Wisconsin State Journal*, August 2, 1930, 1.

40. Bill Mead interview with Charlie Grimm.

41. An undated clipping from the Veeck vertical file, National Baseball Library.

CHAPTER 2: VEECK ON DECK

1. Joseph Durso, *The Days of Mr. McGraw* (Englewood Cliffs, NJ: Prentice-Hall, 1969), 199.

2. Pat Williams interviews, 1997–98, unnumbered.

3. Scott Jones interview, November 2, 2010.

4. This quote is from an article Jones wrote about their shared childhood in the Hinsdale newspaper, *The Doings*, several days after his Veeck's death. January 9, 1986, 102.

5. Ibid.

6. Pat Williams interviews, 1997–98, unnumbered.

7. Bill Veeck with Edward Linn, *Veeck—as in Wreck* (New York: G. P. Putnam's Sons, 1962), 31.

8. *Chicago Tribune*, May 3, 1959, G16.

9. Scott Jones, *The Doings*, January 9, 1986, 102.

10. Veeck with Linn, *Veeck as in Wreck*, 35.

11. Scott Jones in *The Doings*, January 9, 1986, 102.

12. Ibid.

13. *Chicago American*, October 6, 1933.

14. John Carmichael, *Chicago Daily News* biography, 1933.

15. Warren Brown, *The Chicago Cubs* (New York: G. P. Putnam's Sons, 1946), 109.

16. *San Jose News*, December 8, 1931.

17. *Chicago American*, October 5, 1933.

18. Carmichael, *Chicago Daily News* biography, 1933.

19. Donald Honig, comp., *Baseball When the Grass Was Real: Baseball from the Twenties to the Forties Told by the Men Who Played It* (Lincoln: University of Nebraska Press, 1993), 137.

20. Steve Gietschier, "Joe McCarthy: Architect of the Yankee Dynasty," *Nine* 15 (2006): 132.

21. Newspaper accounts published after the game claimed that Ruth did indeed call his shot: "Ruth Calls Shot as He Puts Homer No. 2 in Side Pocket" (Joe Williams, *New York World-Telegram*); "Babe notified the crowd that the nature of his retaliation would be a wallop right out [of] the confines of the park" (John Drebinger, *New York Times*); "He pointed like a duelist to the spot where he expected to send his rapier home" (Paul Gallico, *New York Daily News*); "Babe Calls His Shot" (Westbrook Pegler, *Chicago Sunday Tribune*). Quin Ryan, the Cubs broadcaster, told his radio audience: "That ball went out to almost the exact spot that Babe

had been pointing to." Perhaps none of these accounts proves that Ruth pointed to center field to say "I'm hitting it there" and then did so, but that was the interpretation of some in the media who covered the game at the time. *Reach Official American League Base Ball Guide* for 1933 and *Spalding's Official Base Ball Guide* for 1933 assumed that Ruth called his shot.

22. This version of the story was actually condensed from the *News* and appeared in *Baseball Digest*, November 1946, 8.

23. *Chicago Tribune*, June 18, 1933; *Sporting News*, June 22, 1933, 8.

24. Veeck with Linn, *Veeck—as in Wreck*, 36.

25. Historian Arthur Schlesinger Jr. noted that Hoover's name became "a prefix charged with hate"—the newspapers the homeless used to cover themselves were "Hoover blankets," farmers called jackrabbits "Hoover hogs," and empty pockets pulled inside out were "Hoover flags." The origin of the term may been a shantytown in Chicago that called itself Hooverville and had streets named Prosperity Road, Hard Times Avenue, and Easy Street. It came to national attention in 1930. "Chicago Jobless Colonize," *New York Times*, November 12, 1930, 12.

26. *Hartford Courant*, February 6, 1933.

27. *New York Times*, February 6, 1933.

28. *Philadelphia Tribune*, February 9, 1933.

29. *Baltimore Afro-American*, February 18, 1933. Heydler's open-mindedness came into question later in the month when he said, "I do not recall one instance where baseball has allowed either race, creed or color to enter into the question of the selection of its players." *Chicago Daily News*, February 25, 1933.

30. *New York Daily News*, February 8, 1933.

31. *Pittsburgh Courier*, March 25, 1933.

32. Jerrold Casway in *The National Pastime* 15 (1995): 120–23.

33. *Washington Post*, May 10, 1953.

34. *Chicago American*, September 20, 1918.

35. Later in this interview Veeck says of Gibson, "He was, at a minimum, two Yogi Berras." Stephen Banker, *Black Diamonds: An Oral History of Negro Baseball* (Westport, CT: Meckler, 1989), cassette 3, side 2.

36. *Baltimore Sun*, March 15, 1933, 10.

37. Jerome Holtzman and George Vass, *Baseball, Chicago Style: A Tale of Two Teams, One City* (Chicago: Bonus Books, 2001), 99.

38. *St. Joseph News-Press*, August 22, 1933, 4.

39. AP, *Miami News*, August 22, 1933; *Chicago American*, August 4, 1933.

40. *Chicago Daily News*, August 22, 1933.

41. AP, *Hartford Courant*, August 24, 1933, 13; *Baltimore Sun*, August 24, 1933, 16.

42. Alan J. Pollock, *Barnstorming to Heaven: Syd Pollock and His Great Black Teams*, ed. James A. Riley (Tuscaloosa: University of Alabama Press, 2006), 81.

43. The *Amsterdam News* published the letter on September 13. It does not seem to have been published in any major non-black newspapers beyond North Tarrytown.

44. Pollock, *Barnstorming to Heaven*, 81.

45. Ibid.

46. *Chicago Defender*, September 16, 1933.

47. *Chicago Tribune*, September 26, 1933.

48. Ibid. September 30, 1933.

49. *Chicago American*, October 5, 1933.

50. Ibid.

51. Edward Linn, *A Great Connection: The Story of Molex* (Chicago: Regnery Gateway, 1988), 63. It almost turned into a circus, according to Mrs. Veeck's friend Jane Ostrum. "People went past his open coffin out into the yard, and all the Cub players were there, and all of Hinsdale still plus all kinds of horrible sightseers and reporters trying to sneak in through the bushes. It was terrible."

52. *Chicago American*, October 6, 1933.

53. AP column by Alan Gould, *Reading (PA) Eagle*, October 17, 1933.

54. Minutes of the National League, December 12–13, 1933, 107–8, National Baseball Library.

CHAPTER 3: A RAMBUNCTIOUS CUB

1. *New York Times*, October 29, 1933. The record of the 1933 team appears in the 2010 Kenyon Media Guide, which is online at http://teamguides.kenyon.edu.

2. Peter Golenbock, *Wrigleyville: A Magical History Tour of the Chicago Cubs* (New York: St. Martin's, 1996), 277.

3. Ibid.

4. Ibid.

5. Roger Angell, *Five Seasons: A Baseball Companion*, (Lincoln, NE : Bison Books, 2004), 315; Bill Veeck with Edward Linn, *Veeck—as in Wreck* (New York: G. P. Putnam's Sons, 1962), 83.

6. Ray Kroc with Robert Anderson, *Grinding It Out: The Making of McDonald's*, 40.

7. *Flood v. Kuhn*, Second Circuit Briefs and Records, Law Library, Library of Congress, Veeck testimony, 1956–57.

8. Interview with Fred Krehbiel, June 3, 2010. Many references to Eleanor appear with an *-e* on the end of her name, especially early in her life, but legal papers she signed end the name with an *-r*.

9. *Chicago Tribune*, August 5, 1935.

10. Mary Margaret McBride column, *Palm Beach Post*, October, 1, 1935; interview with Scott Jones, November 2, 2010.

11. *Chicago Herald-American*, *Chicago American*, and *Chicago Tribune*, all December 6, 1935.

12. Interview with Scott Jones, November 2, 2010.

13. Banker, *Black Diamonds*, cassette 3, side 2.

14. Veeck with Linn, *Veeck—as in Wreck*, 182; "Historical Overview," a handout given to ushers at Wrigley Field for the 2010 season, 115–16.

15. *Baltimore Afro-American*, October 5, 1935, 18; *St. Joseph Gazette*, October 5, 1935, 17.

16. Veeck's relationship with Saperstein is discussed in a number of places, including Banker, *Black Diamonds*, cassette 3, side 2. *The Sporting* News called Saperstein the "Bill Veeck of basketball."

17. Robert W. Peterson, *Cages to Jump Shots: Pro Basketball's Early Years* (Lincoln: University of Nebraska Press, 2002).

18. *Pittsburgh Press*, March 29, 1939.

19. Peterson, *Cages to Jump Shots*, 70.

20. *Sporting News*, undated clipping (annotated 1935), National Baseball Library.

21. *Sporting News*, January 17, 1935.

22. AP, *Anchorage News*, January 14, 1987.

23. Veeck with Linn, *Veeck—as in Wreck*, 37.

24. In his autobiography, Veeck remembered the colors as green for a win and red for a loss, but contemporary newspapers stated that the colors of the lights were blue and white, as they were in 2011.

25. *Chicago Tribune,* September 12, 1937. The article on page B5 entitled "New Wrigley Field Blooms in Scenic Beauty—and Scoffers Rush to Apologize" is the most detailed I could find on Veeck's contribution. Also *Chicago Daily News,* June 26 and July 10, 1937; *Chicago Tribune,* July 10, 1937.

26. *Chicago Tribune, Chicago American, Chicago Daily Times,* and *Chicago Herald-Examiner,* all July 30, 1938.

27. *Pittsburgh Press,* August 4, 1938.

28. *Chicago Tribune,* December 17, 1938.

29. *Chicago Tribune,* April 21, 1940.

30. *Pittsburgh Post-Gazette,* August 17, 1938, 17.

31. AP, *New York Times* and *Chicago Tribune,* November 15, 1940.

32. *Chicago Herald-American,* November 14, 1940.

33. *Dallas Morning News,* November 11, 1943.

34. Harry Grayson in *Pittsburgh Press,* July 14, 1941.

35. Warren Brown, *The Chicago Cubs* (New York: G. P. Putnam's Sons, 1946), 227; Tommy Devine, "Boy from the Bleachers," *Pic: The Magazine for Young Men,* April 1947, 111.

36. Brown, *Chicago Cubs,* 196.

37. Harry Grayson in *Pittsburgh Press,* July 14, 1941.

38. Golenbock, *Wrigleyville,* 278.

CHAPTER 4: BREWERS GOLD

1. Charlie Grimm and Ed Prell, *Jolly Cholly's Story: Grimm's Baseball Tales* (Notre Dame, IN: Diamond Communications, 1983), 141.

2. *Milwaukee Sentinel,* June 17, 1941, 6.

3. These amounts are based on reports in the *Chicago Herald-American* and *Chicago Daily News,* both June 24, 1941; see also Grimm and Prell, *Jolly Cholly's Story,* 141.

4. Warren Brown, *The Chicago Cubs* (New York: G. P. Putnam's Sons, 1946), 195.

5. *Sarasota Herald-Tribune,* June 24, 1941.

6. *Chicago Daily News,* July 24, 1941.

7. *Chicago Herald-American,* July 26, 1941.

8. *Sportsfolio,* April 1949, 9.

9. *Toledo Blade,* June 24, 1941, 18.

10. Bill Veeck with Edward Linn, *Veeck—as in Wreck* (New York: G. P. Putnam's Sons, 1962), 85.

11. Grimm and Prell, *Jolly Cholly's Story,* 143.

12. *Look,* September 7, 1943.

13. *Toledo Blade,* July 21, 1941, 16.

14. *Chicago Defender,* August 23, 1953, 22.

15. *Milwaukee Journal,* August 27, 1941, 3.

16. *Montreal Gazette,* September 13, 1941.

17. *Milwaukee Journal,* September 7, 1941.

18. *Pittsburgh Courier,* March 24, 1962, A29. In this article Wendell Smith asserts that Saperstein stepped in and "probably saved Veeck's baseball career, as well as the Milwaukee franchise", by pulling him out of his financial hole.

19. Ibid; *Toledo Blade,* September 1, 1960, 34.

20. *Washington Post,* November 6, 1941, 26. If Grimm got an offer at this point in his life, he neglected to mention it in his autobiography.

21. *Schenectady Gazette*, January 3, 1942, 9.

22. Peter Golenbock, *Wrigleyville: A Magical History Tour of the Chicago Cubs* (New York: St. Martin's, 1996), 277.

23. *Pittsburgh Post-Gazette*, January 21, 1942, 14.

24. *Time*, December 22, 1941.

25. William B. Mead and Paul Dickson, *Baseball: The Presidents' Game* (New York: Walker, 1997), 76–79. The men behind the scenes were Clark Griffith, longtime owner of the Washington Senators, and Robert E. Hannegan, a crony and confidant of Roosevelt's who held the positions of Internal Revenue Service commissioner and Democratic national chairman during Roosevelt's administration. Griffith had been baseball's unofficial lobbyist for years—a role he carefully kept from Landis. Hannegan hailed from St. Louis and was a close friend of Sam Breadon's, owner of the Cardinals, and Don Barnes's and William DeWitt's, who owned the St. Louis Browns. After the war, Hannegan became part owner of the Cardinals—Stan Musial's boss, so to speak.

26. AP, *Baltimore Sun*, March 10, 1942, 15.

27. *Reading (PA) Eagle*, February 28, 1943, 14.

28. *Look*, September 7, 1943.

29. Grimm and Prell, *Jolly Cholly's Story*, 143.

30. *Milwaukee Journal*, November 28, 1943, 46.

31. Grimm and Prell, *Jolly Cholly's Story*, 144–45.

32. *Reading (PA) Eagle*, February 28, 1943, 14.

33. *Chicago Tribune*, June 3, 1943, 25.

34. *Flood v. Kuhn*, Second Circuit Briefs and Records. Law Library, Library of Congress, Veeck testimony, June 10, 1970, 2035–7.

CHAPTER 5: THE PHILADELPHIA STORY

1. *Chicago Defender*, September 17, 1932.

2. *New York Amsterdam News*, October 27, 1934, 10. "House of David" was a nickname given to several barnstorming or non-league traveling teams whose distinguishing characteristic was that all the players wore long beards. Franklin Huddle (*American Speech*, April 1943) wrote: "These are, quite often, pretty disreputable outfits, since they are likely to be made up of men who have been thrown out of organized baseball. Many of these gentry grow beards and call themselves (in imitation of the real thing) House of David teams. . . . The beards serve the twin purpose of advertising and disguise." The teams were also known as the "Bearded Wonders." "No one seemed to mind that King Ben [Purnell] recruited his wig and false-beard-wearing talent from that category of player which . . . was on extended leave from the major leagues" (Arthur Orrmont, *Love Cults and Faith Healers* [New York: Ballantine, 1961], 105). Grover Cleveland Alexander pitched for a House of David team during the Great Depression; he was the only player granted permission not to wear a beard. A character (Lionel) in William Brashler's 1973 novel *The Bingo Long Traveling All-Stars and Motor Kings* told Bingo: "You got to watch out for the other barnstormers like Max Helverton's Hooley Speedballers and them white teams from Michigan, them House of David boys with the beards." The term is derived from a religious organization founded in 1903 and dedicated to reassembling the twelve tribes of Israel.

3. *Chicago Defender*, April, 16, 1938.

4. Ibid., June 17, 1939.

5. Reference to the two games in August appear in the *Milwaukee Journal*, August 18, 1941, and the *Saturday Evening Post*, July 27, 1940. Also see *Chicago Defender*, June 20, 1942.

6. *Time*, June 3, 1940. The final paragraph of the article is worth noting for several reasons, not least of which is that Pegler was one of the nation's leading conservative voices in 1940: "Columnists Westbrook Pegler, the late Heywood Broun (both onetime baseball writers) and many a sportswriter have protested against color discrimination in big-league baseball. The owners and managers say that their Southern players and their visits to Southern training camps would make trouble if Negroes were on the team. But many a shepherd of a limping major club has made no secret of his yearning to trade more than a couple of buttsprung outfielders for colored players of the calibre of Satchelfoots Paige."

7. *Milwaukee Journal*, August 18, 1941, 13.

8. *Palm Beach Post*, August 7, 1942.

9. Charlie Grimm and Ed Prell, *Jolly Cholly's Story: Grimm's Baseball Tales* (Notre Dame, IN: Diamond Communications, 1983), 153; *Sport Life*, July 1949, 14.

10. *Milwaukee Journal*, October 8, 1942, 36.

11. Transcript of the Special Meeting of the Board of Directors of the National League of Professional Base Ball Clubs, January 17, 1942, 10:45, 30 Rockefeller Plaza, New York.

12. *Milwaukee Journal*, October 18, 1943, 3.

13. *Baltimore Afro-American*, May 25, 1940.

14. *Baltimore Afro-American*, August 5, 1941.

15. *Chicago Defender*, May 16, 1942.

16. A detailed account of this game is in the opening chapter to Tim Gay's *Satch, Dizzy and Rapid Robert* (New York: Simon and Schuster, 2010).

17. *Chicago Tribune*, May 25, 1942.

18. *New York Times*, June 5, 1942.

19. *Chicago Daily News*, June 27, 1942.

20. *Baltimore Afro-American*, July 11, 1942.

21. *Chicago Defender*, August 1, 1942.

22. *New York Daily News*, quoted in Irwin Silber, *Press Box Red: The Story of Lester Rodney, the Communist Who Helped Break the Color Line in American Sports* (Philadelphia: Temple University Press, 2002), 70–76. In a interview with Rodney in 2009.

23. AP, *Deseret News*, July 17, 1942; *Los Angeles Times*, July 18, 1942, 13.

24. *Chicago Defender*, July 25, 1942.

25. AP, *The Day*, July 30, 1942.

26. *Chicago Defender*, July 25, 1942.

27. *Pittsburgh Courier*, July 25, 1942.

28. *Sporting News*, August 2, 1942, 4.

29. *Chicago Defender*, August 1, 1942.

30. *Sporting News*, July 30, 1942, 12.

31. Roy Campanella, *It's Good to Be Alive*, 97–98.

32. *Pittsburgh Courier*, February 24, 1962, A30.

33. *Washington Post*, May 12, 1953.

34. Thanks to Cubs historian Hartig, here are the other games. On June 21 the Cincinnati Ethiopian Clowns, winners of the annual Denver National Semi-Pro Championship in 1941, played the House of David in the first game of a Wrigley Field doubleheader. The Clowns played the Chicago Brown Bombers in an official Negro Major League game in the nightcap. Besides playing baseball, the Clowns also provided in-game entertainment led by the top comedian

and pitcher Peanuts Nyasses. The Clowns beat the House of David 9–8 but lost to the Brown Bombers 1–0. Then on July 26 a crowd of 20,000 attended Satchel Paige Day at Wrigley to watch the Kansas City Monarchs and Memphis Red Sox split a doubleheader. Memphis won the opener 10–4 and dropped the nightcap 4–2 in seven innings. Paige allowed only five hits to win the second game. Between games, Paige received numerous gifts, including a watch, portable radio, suit of clothing, travel bag, and trophy. On September 6 the Birmingham Black Barons and Kansas City Monarchs triumphed in a four-team doubleheader at Wrigley before 8,000. The Black Barons, who tied the game with a homer in the top of the ninth, beat the Memphis Red Sox 7–4 in ten innings with Ted Radcliffe socking a bases-loaded double. Kansas City beat the Cincinnati Ethiopian Clowns 4–3 in the nightcap. The first game was said to be for the Negro Championship for the South, while the second game was billed as the unofficial World's Negro Championship. The Clowns performed their comedy act between games of the doubleheader.

35. Interviews with Fred Krehbiel, June 26 and July 6, 2010. According to Kiehbiel, Veeck conferred with his sister on all major decisions.

36. *Chicago Tribune*, January 6, 1986. Carmichael was interviewed by Jerome Holtzman at the time of Veeck's death. Carmichael was eighty-three, having retired thirteen years earlier. Carmichael later told Holtzman, "I've often wondered what would have happened if he bought the Phillies. But [Veeck] didn't have the money."

37. *Washington Post*, February 4, 1960.

38. It is probable, not provable, that this was a meeting with a certain (if not high) degree of cordiality. Landis was a close friend of Veeck senior's, who had spearheaded the successful drive to make him commissioner. Bill had grown up with Landis often in his father's company. Bill had a natural and easy access to Landis and could see him without an appointment. Veeck's office in Milwaukee featured an oversized portrait of Landis, whom he regarded as the last court of appeal in all baseball matters and a man who had been nothing but loyal to his father, who in turn had been nothing but loyal to Landis. Interview with Fred Krehbiel, June 6, 2010. Krehbiel still has a gift Landis sent for his parents' wedding as one of many hints as to the closeness of the Veecks and Landis.

39. Banker, *Black Diamonds*, cassette 3, side 2. Although he did not mention the racial aspect of the deal, the day that the league took over the team the following February, Veeck reported that he had $500,000 in backing to buy the club but that he had decided to stay in Milwaukee. *Milwaukee Sentinel*, February 10, 1943, 11.

40. Transcript of the Meeting of the Board of Directors of the National League of Professional Base Ball Clubs, November 4, 1942; 10:45 a.m., 30 Rockefeller Plaza, New York, 90–91. On November 4, 1942, a meeting was held at which the sale of the team was again at issue. The team had not yet actually been sold, and Nugent had apparently not been told what had happened—as far as he knew, Veeck was a no-show and he had not a clue as to Veeck's plan. "I had Bill Veeck, young Bill Veeck, stop in and ask me about the ball club. He went back to Milwaukee. He said he had gotten his idea from some Philadelphia newspaper man, who started a rumor, and it just gave him the idea that he would come over and inquire about it. He said that he had some Milwaukee capital that was interested, and so forth, and that he would let me know in a couple of days; but I haven't heard from him and that has been three weeks." The Phillies were eventually sold in February 1943 to wealthy thirty-three-year-old lumber broker William Cox.

41. Jules Tygiel interview with Veeck, August 11, 1980, National Baseball Library; interviews with Shirley Povich, *Washington Post*, May 10, 1953, and February 6, 1960.

42. Interview with Monte Irvin, November 7, 2008.

43. *Pittsburgh Courier,* June 24, 1961. The quote appears in a Wendell Smith column in which the plan is discussed in detail.

44. In 1980 when discussing the incident, he would admonish author Jules Tygiel not to put him "in the guise of sociologist" for what he was attempting to do. Tygiel interview with Veeck, August 11, 1980, National Baseball Library.

45. UPI, *Milwaukee Journal,* December 4, 1942; *Daytona Beach Morning Journal,* December 4, 1942; *Baltimore Afro-American,* December 12, 1942.

46. *Chicago Defender,* December 26, 1942.

47. Ibid., February 26, 1949.

48. Murry R. Nelson, *The National Basketball League: A History, 1935–1949* (Jefferson, NC: McFarland, 2009), 118–19; Douglas Stark, "Paving the Way: History of Integration of African Americans into Professional Basketball League," *Basketball Digest,* February 2001. Roosie Hudson commented on his integrated team in Nelson's book: "The Studebakers played team ball no matter who was on the court. It didn't matter if there were three black players or two white in the game or three whites and two blacks, we played as a team. There was no difference."

CHAPTER 6: PVT. VEECK GOES TO WAR

1. *Milwaukee Journal,* February 3, 1943, 2. R. G. Lynch of the *Milwaukee Journal* had been there for the snowball fight and reported on the transformation of Rudie Schaffer.

2. *Milwaukee Journal,* February 19, 1943.

3. *Look,* September 7, 1943.

4. *Woman's Day,* May 1954.

5. *Sarasota Herald-Tribune,* March 1, 1943, 6.

6. AP, *Prescott Evening Courier,* June 18, 1943.

7. *Milwaukee Journal,* October 14, 1943, 37.

8. *Milwaukee Sentinel,* August 1, 1943; *Chicago Tribune,* August 3, 1943, 19.

9. *Chicago Tribune,* August 29, 1943.

10. *Look,* September 7, 1943.

11. *Sporting News,* December 2, 1943.

12. *Milwaukee Journal,* April 19, 1944, 28.

13. Ibid., November 21, 1943, 97.

14. Ibid., September 28, 1943.

15. Ibid., November 28, 1943, 11.

16. *Chicago Tribune,* January 9, 1945, 15.

17. *Milwaukee Journal,* November 30, 1941.

18. Minutes of the Joint Meeting of the National League of Professional Base Ball Clubs and the American League of Base Ball Clubs, Hotel Roosevelt, December 3, 1943, 10:30 a.m., 3 (hereafter Joint Meeting Minutes). These minutes were made available to the author by Jim Gates at the National Baseball Library and Archives in 2009. This appears to be the first public airing of Robeson's testimony and the reaction to it.

19. Joint Meeting Minutes, December 3, 1943, 3.

20. *New York Times* review of the play by Lewis Nichols, October 20, 1943. "The news, of course, is Mr. Robeson's arrival back home in a part he played a few seasons ago in London and tentatively experimented with in the rural playhouses the summer before last. He looks like the part. He is a huge man, taller by inches than anyone on the stage, his height and breadth accentuated by the costumes he wears. His voice, when he is the general giving orders to stop the street brawl,

reverberates through the house; when he is the lover of Desdemona, he is soft. His final speech about being a man 'who loved not wisely but too well' is magnificent. He passes easily along the various stages of Othello's growing jealousy. He can be alike a commanding figure, accustomed to lead, a lover willing to be led and the insane victim of his own ill judgment."

21. Joint Meeting Minutes, December 3, 1943, 5–6.

22. Ibid.

23. Later secondhand accounts of this meeting put words in Robeson's mouth that are not part of the transcript and are of a significantly stronger nature: "The time has come when you must change your attitude toward Negroes. . . . Because baseball is a national game, it is up to baseball to see that discrimination does not become an American pattern. And it should do this year." *New York Times*, May 2, 1987.

24. Joint Meeting Minutes, December 3, 1943, 84.

25. Ibid., 84–87.

26. *New York Times*, December 4, 1943.

27. Both articles appear in their entirety in the *New York Amsterdam News*, December 11, 1943.

28. *New York Amsterdam News*, December 11, 1943.

29. *Sporting News*, February 17, 1944.

30. Jack Brickhouse, *Thanks for Listening* (South Bend, IN: Diamond Communications, 1996), 11.

31. *Leatherneck*, April 1944, 49.

32. *Milwaukee Sentinel*, February 13, 1944.

33. *Leatherneck*, April 1944, 49.

34. International News Service dispatch on April 14 by John R. Henry. The lowdown came from Staff Sgt. Gordon D. Marston, Marine Corps war correspondent from Stoneham, Massachusetts. The article was carried in many newspapers, including the *Milwaukee Journal*, where it ran with an editor's note appended in italics: *"Charlie Grimm, like you, probably would like to get at least a peek at the two other shortstops he's supposed to have."* Something was lost in the secondhand reporting in *Stars and Stripes* and elsewhere, suggesting that Veeck had acquired shortstops without Grimm's knowledge. *Stars and Stripes*, June 21, 1944.

35. Roscoe C. Torrance, *Torchy* (Mission Hill, SD: Dakota Homestead, 1988), 99–101.

36. Harry A. Gailey, *Bougainville, 1943–1945: The Forgotten Campaign* (Lexington: University Press of Kentucky, 1991), 129.

37. *Sporting News*, November 2, 1944, 11. This article carries Veeck's byline (Pfc. Bill Veeck, USMC) as told to S/Sgt. Dick Hanna, Marine Corp Combat Correspondent, with a dateline "U S Naval Hospital, Oakland, Calif."

38. Interview with Donald L. Fordham, July 13, 2010; *Monterey Peninsula Herald*, January 15, 1986. Fordham and Veeck became lifelong friends.

39. *Milwaukee Journal*, October 3, 1944.

40. *Milwaukee Journal*, July 22, 1945.

41. *Baltimore Sun*, May 7, 1944.

42. *Sporting News*, November 2, 1944.

43. Robert Tanzilo, "Stengel Brewed Up a Title—Brewers Job Was Wrecked by Veeck," *Milwaukee Journal Sentinel*, July 5, 1993.

44. Joseph Durso, *Casey: The Life and Legend of Charles Casey Stengle* (Englewood Cliffs, NJ: Prentice Hall, 1967), viii.

45. *Milwaukee Journal*, September 20, 1944.

46. *Stars and Stripes* (London), October 25, 1944, 3.

47. *Sporting News*, December 21, 1944; *Milwaukee Sentinel*, August 26, 1945.

48. *Sporting News*, December 21, 1944.

49. *Milwaukee Journal*, November 30, 1944.
50. *New York Times*, December 13, 1944, 27.
51. *Sporting News*, December 21, 1944.
52. USMC Personnel Record, Veeck, William L., gathered from several documents in the file; *Sporting News*, January 25, 1945.
53. *Bill Veeck Show*, Recorded Sound Reference Center, Library of Congress, audio file LPA50284.
54. *Cleveland Plain Dealer*, magazine section, October 8, 1978, 13.
55. *Milwaukee Journal*, January 21, 1945.
56. USMC Personnel Record, Veeck, William L., Report of Medical Survey: 10 July, 1945.
57. *Milwaukee Sentinel*, August 22, 1945.
58. *Milwaukee Journal*, September 19, 1945, 30.
59. Roy P. Drachman, *Just Memories* (Tucson, 1979), extracted from online version of the book, http://parentseyes.arizona.edu/drachman/1003.html.

CHAPTER 7: BACK IN THE GAME

1. *Chicago Tribune*, April 29, 1945; May 3, 1945.
2. Ibid., October 3, 1945.
3. AP, *Montreal Gazette*, October 25, 1945, 16.
4. AP, *Ottawa Citizen*, October 26, 1945, 11; *Spalding Guide*, 1946.
5. *Sporting News*, November 1, 1945.
6. *Chicago Tribune*, October 28, 1945.
7. Interview with Fred Krehbiel, June 3, 2010.
8. *Milwaukee Journal*, November 24, 1945; *Sporting News*, November 22, 1945.
9. *Milwaukee Journal*, January 4, 1946, 30.
10. Bill Veeck with Edward Linn, *Veeck—as in Wreck* (New York: G. P. Putnam's Sons, 1962), 81.
11. *Miami News*, April 16, 1946, 21.
12. Warren Brown in *Sportsfolio*, April 1949.
13. *Milwaukee Journal*, May 24, 1946.
14. *Cleveland Plain Dealer*, June 23, 1946, 91; Russell J. Schneider, *The Cleveland Indians Encyclopedia* (Philadelphia: Temple University Press, 1996), 55, 350.
15. *Cleveland Plain Dealer*, June 20, 1946, 1.
16. James Odenkirk, *Plain Dealing: A Biography of Gordon Cobbledick* (Tempe: Spider-Naps Publications, 1990), 142; *Chicago Tribune*, June 21, 1946, 29.
17. Burt Solomon, *Baseball Timeline* (New York: Avon, 1997), 456.
18. *Time*, July 1, 1946.
19. *Miami News*, June 24, 1946.
20. *Milwaukee Journal*, August 27, 1947.
21. Tommy Devine, "Boy from the Bleachers," *Pic: The Magazine for Young Men*, April 1947.
22. *Cleveland Plain Dealer*, July 18, 1946, 15.
23. Interview with Chris Axelrod, January 30, 2009.
24. James Hegan interview with William Marshall, for the University of Kentucky Libraries, A. B. "Happy" Chandler Oral History Project, May 15, 1979.
25. Pat Williams interviews, 1997–98.
26. *Chicago Tribune*, July 10, 1946, 27.
27. *New York Times*, March 14, 1971.
28. Pat Williams interviews, 1997–98, no. 136.

29. *Berkeley Daily Gazette,* July 19, 1946, 6.
30. *Baseball Digest,* October, 1988, p. 78
31. *Baltimore Afro-American,* September 14, 1946; Facebook communication with George W. Case III, March 15, 2011.
32. Veeck with Linn, *Veeck—as in Wreck,* 86.
33. Schneider, *Cleveland Indians Encyclopedia,* 57.
34. *Baseball Magazine,* September 1946, 331.
35. *New York Times,* October 3, 1948, S6.
36. *New York Times,* "Gordon, Overlooked Yankee, Gets His Due," December 13, 2008.
37. *Milwaukee Journal,* February 7, 1955. The AP's Gayle Talbot, writing a few days after Reynolds's retirement, called it the "ideal trade."
38. *New York Times,* October 31, 1936.
39. *Cleveland Press,* July 31, 1969. The call to Gibbons was used more than twenty years later by Bob August of the *Press* to open a profile of Veeck and to comment: "A long list of adjectives can be used to describe Veeck, and one that leaps to mind is 'irrepressible.' Human spirits are not often lighted by such stubborn flames."
40. *Milwaukee Journal,* November 3, 1946.
41. Devine, "Boy from the Bleachers."
42. The picture appeared in the *Miami News,* December 5, 1946, 7.
43. *Cleveland Plain Dealer,* June 28, 1998, A1.
44. *Chicago Tribune,* February 2, 1947; *Sport Life,* July 1949, 14.
45. *New York Times,* February 2, 1947, S2.
46. Pat Williams interviews, 1997–98, no. 137.
47. AP, *Tuscaloosa News,* April 15, 1947.

CHAPTER 8: LAWRENCE DOBY AND THE INTEGRATION OF THE AMERICAN LEAGUE

1. *Call and Post,* July 27, 1946.
2. Dandridge reported on several occasions that Veeck had given him a chance to be first; see Robert Peterson, *Only the Ball Was White* (Englewood Cliffs, NJ: Prentice-Hall, 1970); T. Nicholas Dawidoff, "Big Call from the Hall: Negro Leaguer Ray Dandridge Hears from Cooperstown," *Sports Illustrated,* July 6, 1987; Lyle Spencer interview with Dandridge, *New York Post,* July 11, 1988. The offer from Veeck is also presented in James A. Riley, *Dandy, Day, and the Devil* (Cocoa, FL: TK Publishers, 1987), 8. Riley was with Dandridge during the *Sports Illustrated* interview and attests to Dandridge's veracity in this matter. Interview with Riley. Several online sources claim that Veeck's offer was made after Robinson and Doby came up to the majors, but these are unverified.
3. *Call and Post,* July 5, 1947, 1A; July 12, 1947, 4B.
4. Joseph Thomas Moore, *Pride Against Prejudice: The Biography of Larry Doby* (New York: Greenwood, 1988), 40.
5. Wendell Smith, "The Sports Beat," *Pittsburgh Courier,* July 12, 1947; Al Dunmore, "Cleveland Owner Kept His Word," *Pittsburgh Courier,* July 12, 1947; "Larry Doby, Ace Negro Infielder, Signs Contract with Cleveland," *New York Times,* July 4, 1947.
6. Bob Luke, *The Baltimore Elite Giants: Sport and Society in the Age of Negro League Baseball* (Baltimore: Johns Hopkins University Press, 2009), 138.
7. Cynthia J. Wilber, *For the Love of the Game* (New York: William Morrow, 1992), 350.

8. David Maraniss in the *Washington Post*, July 8, 1997.

9. Joel Zoss and John Stewart Bowman, *Diamonds in the Rough: The Untold History of Baseball* (Lincoln: University of Nebraska Press, 2004), 101.

10. Larry Doby interview with Tom Harris, February 18, 1994.

11. Effa Manley and Leon Herbert Hardwick, *Negro Baseball . . . Before Integration*, ed. Robert Cvornyek (Haworth, NJ: St. Johann, 2006), 74–76.

12. Rickey commented, "There is no negro league as such as far as I am concerned. Negro baseball is in the zone of a racket" (*Palm Beach Post*, October 25, 1945, 10). Larry Doby interview with William J. Marshall for the University of Kentucky Libraries, A. B. "Happy" Chandler Oral History Project, November 15, 1979. Seven weeks later Rickey signed Dan Bankhead of the Memphis Red Sox to a contract but had to pay for the privilege—with the new player contracts containing a reserve clause and the deal coming in the middle of the season, there could be no question but that Bankhead was under contract to the Red Sox, so Rickey paid B. B. Martin, general manager of the Memphis Red Sox, $15,000. The terms were exactly the same as they had been for Doby: $10,000 upon signing the contract on August 23 and another $5,000 if the Dodgers kept Bankhead for more than a month, which they did. Branch Rickey Papers, Box 5, Folder 3, Manuscript Division, Library of Congress.

13. Moore, *Pride Against Prejudice*, 41; interview with Monte Irvin, February 21, 2008.

14. Doby interview with Marshall, November 15, 1979, 3–41.

15. Ira Berkow in the *New York Times*, February 23, 1997.

16. *Washington Post*, July 12, 1947. "Now it sort of dawned on me after the game was over and after I got back to the hotel by myself. When you're sitting there by yourself there's a lot of things go through your mind."

17. Bill Veeck interview with Jules Tygiel, August 11, 1980, National Baseball Library.

18. *New York Times*, July 4, 1947; "Career of Baseball Star Larry Doby, Who Died Yesterday," National Public Radio, *Morning Edition*, June 19, 2003.

19. *Chicago Defender*, December 3, 1949.

20. Interview with Wyonella Smith, March 19, 2011.

21. Interview with Robert Ames Alden, April 28, 2008.

22. Bill Veeck interview with William J. Marshall for the University of Kentucky Libraries, A. B. "Happy" Chandler Oral History Project, February 23, 1977, tape 1, side 2.

23. Ira Berkow in the *New York Times*, February 23, 1997.

24. Frazier Robinson, *Catching Dreams: My Life in the Negro Baseball Leagues*, 127.

25. *Baltimore Afro-American*, August 3, 1946, 8.

26. David Maraniss in the *Washington Post*, July 8, 1997. Doby mentioned this in several interviews, especially later, when he played in right field. He told William Marshall, "So high school, you got cheers. I'd go to Washington, D.C. At that time you couldn't sit . . . you know, behind home plate or third base or first base. Everybody had to sit in the right field bleachers or center field bleachers. And, of course . . . that's close to me."

27. *Baseball Digest*, September 1949, 50.

28. *Tucson Daily Citizen*, September 19, 1947, 2.

29. Superior Court of the State of Arizona in and for the County of Pima, Complaint 29224, October 3, 1947.

30. Stipulation and Order of Dismissal with Prejudice, Superior Court of the State of Arizona in and for the County of Pima, Complaint 29224, August 4, 1948. Bob Feller mentioned in an interview (November 7, 2008) that it was his understanding from conversations with Veeck that he was forced to sell the Cleveland Indians in 1949 not only because of a costly divorce but also because of a settlement he had made for the automobile accident.

31. Franklin Lewis, *The Cleveland Indians* (Kent State, OH: Kent State University Press, 1949), 250.

32. Quotes from a press clipping compiled in *The 1948 Indians Remembered* (Minneapolis: private press, 1988). Presented at the SABR Convention, July 9, 1988, unpaginated.

33. David Maraniss in the *Washington Post*, July 8, 1997.

34. *Cleveland Plain Dealer*, December 31, 1947.

35. *Newark Star-Ledger*, March 4, 1998.

36. Pat Williams interviews, 1997–98, no. 177.

37. A heavily redacted file on Veeck was obtained by Eric E. Enders of the National Baseball Library and Archives in November 1999 under Freedom of Information Act request 909944.

38. *New York Times*, February 9, 1947, S7; February 10, 1947, 23.

CHAPTER 9: THE OLDEST ROOKIE

1. *Baseball Digest*, June 1953.

2. Irving Vaughn in the *Chicago Tribune*, January 9, 1948, 25.

3. Shirley Povich in the *Washington Post*, January 20, 1948, 14.

4. Russell J. Schneider, *The Cleveland Indians Encyclopedia* (Philadelphia: Temple University Press, 1996), 578.

5. Timothy M. Gay, *Tris Speaker: The Rough-and-Tumble Life of a Baseball Legend* (Lincoln: University of Nebraska Press, 2005), 3–4.

6. *Philadelphia Tribune*, April 6, 1948.

7. *Sporting News*, April 14, 1948; *World-Telegram*, April 12, 1948.

8. *Milwaukee Journal*, April 19, 1948, 16.

9. Joseph Thomas Moore, *Pride Against Prejudice: The Biography of Larry Doby* (New York: Greenwood, 1988), 73; *Cleveland Plain Dealer*, April 8, 1960.

10. Interview with Claire Smith, October 2, 2009.

11. Interview with Monte Irvin, November 7, 2008.

12. Pat Williams interviews, 1997–98, no. 76. This interview took place earlier but was folded into the collection when Williams was preparing his book on Veeck's management style. He also said, "He collected Indian artifacts long before anybody thought about collecting things the Indians made."

13. *Indian Highlights of 1948*, 12–13.

14. "After several weeks he probably had introduced Greenberg to several thousand fans. And, more often than not, the introduction would take a number of minutes as Veeck, Greenberg and the fan would share memories of Greenberg's glory days with the Tigers." E-mail from Bob Alden to the author, December 20, 2009.

15. *New York Times*, October 3, 1948.

16. *Washington Post*, April 27, 1948, 19; *Los Angeles Times*, May 4, 1948, A10.

17. *Chicago Defender*, May 8, 1948, 1.

18. *Pittsburgh Courier*, May 15, 1948, 17.

19. George Wiley, *Especially for Cleveland Fans: The 1948 Indians Remembered* (Minneapolis: Society for American Baseball Research, 1988).

20. Ibid. A full interview with Savage appears on the Web site Baseball in Wartime, http://www .baseballinwartime.com/player_biographies/savage_bob.htm.

21. Interview with Ernie Harwell, August 28, 2009.

22. Ruth's final public appearance comes on July 26 at the opening of *The Babe Ruth Story*.

23. *Call and Post*, July 3, 1948, 7B.

24. Stephen Banker, *Black Diamonds: An Oral History of Negro Baseball* (Westport, CT: Meckler, 1989), cassette 3, side 2. A slightly different version of this conversation appears in Franklin Lewis, *The Cleveland Indians* (Kent State, OH: Kent State University Press, 1949), 257. An alternative version in which Grabiner is also in the conversation appears in the *Los Angeles Times*, February 13, 1954, B2.

25. Banker, *Black Diamonds*, cassette 3, side 2.

26. *Pittsburgh Courier*, April 7, 1962, A29.

27. Wiley, *Especially for Cleveland Fans*.

28. Banker, *Black Diamonds*, cassette 3, side 2.

29. Ibid.

30. Lou Boudreau with Russell Schneider, *Covering All the Bases* (Champaign, IL: Sagamore, 1993), 112–13.

31. "This Morning with Shirley Povich," *Washington Post*, July 15, 1948, 18.

32. Ibid.

33. *Sporting News*, July 14, 1948.

34. Bill Veeck with Edward Linn, *Veeck—as in Wreck* (New York: G. P. Putnam's Sons, 1962), 185.

35. *Pittsburgh Courier*, July 24, 1948, 10.

36. Anthony J. Connor, *Voices from Cooperstown: Baseball's Hall of Famers Tell It like It Was* (New York: Collier Books, 1984), 247.

37. *Chicago Defender*, August 14, 1948, 11.

38. Frank Graham, *Baseball Extra* (New York: Barnes, 1954), 141–45.

39. Ibid.

40. *Baltimore Afro-American*, August 21, 1948, 7.

CHAPTER 10: INDIANS SUMMER

1. AP, *Ottawa Citizen*, August 21, 1948, 10.

2. Gordon Cobbledick, "Don Black's Greatest Victory," *American Weekly*, September 12, 1948.

3. *Washington Post*, May 5, 1947. This was Shirley Povich's column and was based on an interview with Black.

4. Franklin Lewis, *The Cleveland Indians* (Kent State, OH: Kent State University Press, 1949), 262–63.

5. *Baltimore Sun*, September 17, 1948, 18.

6. Hal Lebovitz, "The '48 Indians: One Last Hurrah," *Sport*, June 1965.

7. *Cleveland Press*, September 9, 1948.

8. Warren Brown in *Sportsfolio*, April 1949.

9. Douglass Wallop, *Baseball: An Informal History* (New York: W. W. Norton, 1969), 225.

10. AP, *Eugene Register-Guard*, September 28, 1948, 8; Dan Holmes, "Bill Veeck's 'Night to End All Nights,' " Baseballpage.com, July 28, 2008, http://oldsite.thebaseballpage.com/blog.php/108stitches/article/bill_veeck.

11. Brown in *Sportsfolio*, April 1949.

12. David E. Kaiser points out in his book *Epic Season: The 1948 American League Pennant Race* (Amherst: University of Massachusetts Press, 1998), "To match the value of that contribution, a present-day owner would have to contribute about half a million dollars."

13. Lou Boudreau with Ed Fitzgerald, *Player-Manager* (Boston: Little, Brown, 1949), 210–11.

14. "This Morning with Shirley Povich," *Washington Post*, October 4, 1948, 9.

15. *Deseret News*, October 4, 1948, 14.
16. *Boston Herald*, October 4, 1948, 1; *New York Times*, October 5, 1958, 116–17.
17. *Deseret News*, October 4, 1948, 14.
18. Bill Cunningham in *Elks Magazine*, June 1949, 12.
19. Frank Graham, *Baseball Extra* (New York: Barnes, 1954), 145.
20. Pat Williams interviews, 1997–98, no. 210.
21. Joseph Thomas Moore, *Pride Against Prejudice: The Biography of Larry Doby* (New York: Greenwood, 1988), 4.
22. Irving T. Marsh and Edward Ehre, *Best Sports Stories* (New York: Dutton, 1952), 126.
23. Graham, *Baseball Extra*, 146–47.
24. "Pitching Pays," *Time*, October 14, 1948.
25. *New York Amsterdam News*, October 16, 1948.
26. Lebovitz, "The '48 Indians."
27. Bill Veeck with Edward Linn, *Veeck—as in Wreck* (New York: G. P. Putnam's Sons, 1962), 208.
28. *Los Angeles Times*, October 22, 1948, C1.
29. *Baseball Digest*, February 1950, 52.
30. *Sporting News*, November 3, 1948; *Milwaukee Journal*, October 21, 1948.
31. Banker, *Black Diamonds*, cassette 3, side 2.
32. Russell Schneider, *The Boys of the Summer of '48* (Champaign, IL: Sports Publishing, 1998), 38–42.
33. Veeck was at least aware of the scheme, as he mentioned it in passing in Veeck with Linn, *Veeck—as in Wreck*, but Russell Schneider, who covered the Indians for the *Plain Dealer* for fourteen years, revealed the scope of the operation in his 1998 book, *The Boys of the Summer of '48*.
34. *New York Times*, June 21, 1982.
35. Mickey McDermott, *A Funny Thing Happened on the Way to Cooperstown* (Chicago: Triumph Books, 2003), 92.
36. *People*, April 19, 1976.
37. Russell J. Schneider, *Tales from the Tribe Dugout* (Champaign, IL: Sports Publishing, 2001); Pat Williams interviews, 1997–98, no. 165.
38. *Washington Post*, November 21, 1948, S1.
39. *Cleveland Plain Dealer*, November 28, 1948.
40. *New York Journal-American*, July 8, 1948 22.
41. "Veeck Not Fair-Haired Boy of Fellow Owners," *Cleveland News*, undated clipping.
42. *Nation's Business*, November 1948, 36.
43. *Milwaukee Journal*, March 23, 1949, 45.
44. *Cleveland Press*, December 29, 1948.
45. *Milwaukee Journal*, January 39, 1939, 44.

CHAPTER 11: FLAGPOLE SITTING

1. *Sporting News*, February 9, 1949.
2. *Cleveland Press*, February 7, 1949.
3. AP, *Miami News*, February 12, 1949.
4. Decree of Divorce in the Superior Court of the State of Arizona, October 29, 1949, no. 31450; interview with Ellen Maggs, March 15, 2011.
5. *Milwaukee Sentinel*, February 7, 1949, 1; *Reading (PA) Eagle*, February 7, 1949.

6. *Milwaukee Sentinel*, February 6, 1949; Leonard Lyons column in *Miami News*, February 14, 1949.

7. William Marshall, *Baseball's Pivotal Era, 1945–1951* (Lexington: University Press of Kentucky, 1999), 340; "Veeck Won't Amputate Says Bob" was the headline in the *Los Angeles Times*, January 23, 1949.

8. *St. Petersburg Times*, March 19, 1949.

9. *Pewaukee Journal*, October 18, 1949.

10. *St. Petersburg Times*, February 12, 1949.

11. *Los Angeles Sentinel*, February 24, 1949.

12. *Harper's Bazaar*, July 1949, 70.

13. *Pittsburgh Courier*, March 12, 1949; *Tucson Weekly*, February 12, 2009.

14. *New York Amsterdam News*, May 14, 1949; *Sporting News*, April 13, 1949.

15. *Cleveland Plain Dealer*, April 17, 1949, 22; April 18, 1949, 22.

16. *New York Herald Tribune*, May 30, 1949.

17. *Cleveland Press*, June 21 and 24, 1949.

18. *Milwaukee Journal*, September 24, 1949; *Eugene Register-Guard*, September 25, 1949.

19. When Lupica died at age ninety, he was honored with a full sixteen-paragraph obituary in the *New York Times*, November 22, 2002.

20. Hank Greenberg, *The Story of My Life* (New York: Times Books, 1989), 205.

21. *Pittsburgh Courier*, September 10, 1949.

22. *Call and Post*, September 24, 1949, 6B. The exchange was—and is—puzzling shedding more heat than light on the situation. Stephanie M. Lisico, author of *Integrating Cleveland Baseball: Media Activism, the Integration of the Indians and the Demise of the Negro League Buckeyes*, who studied the African American newspapers of the era and read every issue of the *Call and Post* for several years, concluded that the truth may lie somewhere in the middle. Lisico concluded that the *Call and Post* was extremely reserved in its coverage of racial matters and tended to shy away from anything that worked against racial harmony. She added that the *Courier* was much more of a warts-and-all paper. That said, Lisico suggested that there were probably no organized gangs of hoodlums organized by nameless politicians but there were fans who were particularly rough on black players, especially Luke Easter. Telephone interview with Lisico, November 18, 2010.

23. *Daytona Beach Morning Journal*, August 25, 1949; *Pittsburgh Post-Gazette*, July 11, 1949, 14.

24. Pat Williams interviews, 1997–98.

25. *Sports Illustrated*, July 4, 1960.

26. *Cleveland Plain Dealer*, November 21, 1949.

27. After the sale on November 22 the *Cleveland Plain Dealer* ran an editorial entitled "Baseball and Taxes" that agreed Veeck was virtually compelled to sell the Indians because of the tax laws. The paper assumed that he would take away $375,000 after capital gains, but that at an income of $50,000 per year, he would need eleven years to accumulate the same amount.

28. *Call and Post*, November 19, 1949.

29. UPI, *Milwaukee Journal*, November 21, 1949, 38.

30. *Time*, December 5, 1949.

31. *Cleveland Plain Dealer*, November 22, 1949.

32. Ibid., November 17, 1949, 24.

33. *Time*, December 5, 1949.

34. *Baseball Digest*, January 1949.

35. *Washington Post*, October 5, 1949; *Modesto Bee*, September 7, 1953. The thought of Senator Bill Veeck is a delicious notion to consider.

36. Interview with Mary Frances Veeck, April 27, 2010.

37. *Pittsburgh Post-Gazette*, September 25, 1949.

38. Pat Williams interviews, 1997–98, no. 77.

39. Roy Drachman, *Just Memories* (Tucson, 1979). This was extracted from the online version of the book, which can be found at http://parentseyes.arizona.edu/drachman/index.html.

40. *Time*, July 16, 1951.

41. *Arizona Daily Star*, July 14, 1991.

42. *Washington Post*, October 1, 1949. In January Russ Newland of the Associated Press's San Francisco office reported that a reliable but undisclosed source indicated that Veeck was trying to buy the Cubs or the Senators. *Evening Independent*, January 27, 1950.

43. Interview with Joseph Thomas Moore.

44. *Sports Illustrated*, July 4, 1960.

45. Ibid.

Chapter 12: Striking Out with the St. Louis Browns

1. *Milwaukee Journal*, May 29, 1951, 8.

2. *New York Amsterdam News*, July 21, 1951.

3. Roy P. Drachman, *Just Memories* (Tucson, 1979), quoted from the online version found at http://parentseyes.arizona.edu/drachman/1003.html.

4. *St. Louis Post-Dispatch*, May 11, 1951.

5. *St. Louis Globe-Democrat*, June 10, 1951; *Chicago Tribune*, June 10, 1951.

6. *St. Louis Globe-Democrat*, June 29, 1951.

7. *St. Louis Post-Dispatch*, July 5, 1951.

8. Ibid., June 21 and July 6, 1951.

9. "A Very Brave Man," *New York Times*, July 4, 1951

10. *New York Times*, May 1, 1988.

11. *Washington Post*, June 27, 1961.

12. *St. Louis Globe-Democrat*, July 7, 1951.

13. Interview with Hank Peters, August 13, 2009.

14. Interview with Cliff Kachline, August 1, 2009.

15. Bill Veeck with Edward Linn, *Veeck—as in Wreck* (New York: G. P. Putnam's Sons, 1962), TK; *Washington Post*, July 26, 1951, 10.

16. *St. Louis Post-Dispatch*, July 25 and 26 1951; *Washington Post*, July 26, 1951; *St. Louis Globe-Democrat*, July 26, 1951.

17. *St. Louis Post-Dispatch*, July 26, 1951; *Washington Post*, July 28, 1951, 9.

18. *Miami News*, April 19, 1958, 15.

19. *Milwaukee Journal*, February 21, 1952, 22.

20. *St. Louis Post-Dispatch*, August 6, 1951.

21. *Washington Post*, August 16, 1951; *Baltimore Sun*, August 18, 1951.

22. *Sporting News*, July 10, 1951.

23. *Milwaukee Journal*, April 18, 1947.

24. Bill Veeck interview with William J. Marshall for the University of Kentucky Libraries, A. B. "Happy" Chandler Oral History Project, February 23, 1977, tape 1, side 1.

25. *Pittsburgh Press*, July 15, 1951; *Pittsburgh Post-Gazette*, July 19, 1951.

26. Jim Reisler, "Eddie Gaedel: The Sad Life of Baseball's Midget," *National Pastime*, 9. At this time the late Bob Fishel was executive vice president of the American League.

27. Jerome Holtzman quoted Broeg in an article, "Gaedel Stunt Still Tickles Baseball's Funny Bone," published on MLB.com on July 15, 2001. At that time Holtzman was the official historian of MLB.

28. Described in Tristram Potter Coffin, *The Old Ball Game: Baseball in Folklore and Fiction* (New York: Herder and Herder, 1971).

29. Interview with Duane Pillette, August 13, 2009.

30. *St. Louis Globe-Democrat*, August 20, 1951.

31. Jack Brickhouse, *Thanks for Listening* (South Bend, IN: Diamond Communications, 1996), 114.

32. *Eugene Register-Guard*, August 22, 1951; *Ludington Daily News*, August 22, 1951.

33. "AL Puts Ban on Midgets," *Cleveland Plain Dealer*, August 22, 1951.

34. *Toledo Blade*, August 23, 1951. John Thorn discussed the Thurber story on the SABR listserv on September 26, 2010, putting it into a deeper literary and baseball context: "Little known is that the diminutive hero of the story, Pearl du Monville, was named in a sly dig at a writer for whom Thurber had no respect: Zane Grey. The western writer (and author of The Red Headed Outfield, The Young Pitcher and The Short-Stop) was named at birth . . . Pearl Zane Grey, who was named for the city of his birth, Zanesville, Ohio. The son of a dentist, the self-renamed Zane went to Penn to study dentistry, where he also played a great outfield alongside his roommate, Roy Thomas, a 13-year major leaguer and Hall of Fame worthy. . . . But I sense a major digression coming on. Thurber's story opens in the city of his birth, Columbus, Ohio. Pearl du Monville translates as 'the pearl of my city.' " The original Thurber story is available online at http://storyoftheweek.loa.org/2010/09/you-could-look-it-up.html.

35. Veeck with Linn, *Veeck—as in Wreck*, 12.

36. James Tootle, "Bill Veeck and James Thurber: The Literary Origins of the Midget Pinch Hitter," *Nine* 10, no. 2 (2002): 110. Tootle also argued the point that it would have been hard for Veeck to miss the Thurber story: "It was reprinted in *Reader's Digest* in 1943, *My World and Welcome to It* (a collection of his stories) in 1942, *New Stories for Men* in 1941, *Best American Short Stories* in 1942, and *Post Stories of 1941* in 1942. Several of these collections had special armed services editions, just the kind of reading material that would have been readily available in military bases and hospitals. After the war, the story appeared in *American Imagination at Work* in 1947, *Saturday Evening Post Sports Stories* (edited by Red Smith) in 1949, and *The Baseball Reader* in 1951. It was also the subject of a radio broadcast on the *Hallmark Playhouse* in 1947. Veeck's voracious reading habits plus the wide availability of Thurber's short story make it highly likely that he would have encountered it."

37. Ted Williams, *My Turn at Bat: The Story of My Life* (New York: Fireside, 1988), 226; Larry Doby interview with William J. Marshall for the University of Kentucky Libraries, A. B. "Happy" Chandler Oral History Project, November 15, 1979.

38. "I don't think people had any idea at the time how much would be made of it," said Hank Peters in an interview on August 13, 2009. Peters, who was one of the few people in on the secret, added that over the years far more people said they were at the game than were actually there. Mary Frances Veeck, who was also there, said that it is amazing how many people have told her over the years that they watched Gaedel come to the plate "at Comiskey Park."

39. Interview with Clark Mitze, February 22, 2010.

40. Robert Gregory, *Diz: The Story of Dizzy Dean and Baseball During the Great Depression* (New York: Random House Value Publishing, 1994).

41. *Eugene Register-Guard*, September 16, 1951.

42. *St. Louis Post-Dispatch*, October 30, 1951.

43. *New York Times*, October 8, 1951; *New York Telegram*, October 8, 1951.

44. *Pittsburgh Courier*, December 29, 1951.

45. *Time*, November 26, 1951.

46. *St. Louis Globe-Democrat*, November 30, 1951.

47. Anthony J. Connor, *Voices from Cooperstown: Baseball's Hall of Famers Tell It like It Was* (New York: Collier Books, 1984), 247. This offer is also discussed in Robert Smith, *Baseball in the Afternoon: Tales from a Bygone Era* (New York: Simon and Schuster, 1993), 145; and Donald Dewey and Nicholas Acocella, *The Biographical History of Baseball* (Chicago: Triumph Books, 2003), 245.

48. *Baltimore Afro-American*, December 8, 1951; June 21, 1952.

49. Interview with Hank Peters, August 13, 2009.

50. Rogers Hornsby with Bill Surface, *My War with Baseball* (New York: Coward McCann, 1962), 23; *Schenectady Gazette*, February 8, 1952.

51. *Baseball Digest*, September 2003.

52. Interview with Hank Peters, August 13, 2009.

53. Interview with Bill Purdy, June 24, 2009.

54. NNPA, *New Journal and Guide* (Norfolk, VA), May 10, 1952.

55. Veeck with Linn, *Veeck—as in Wreck*, 232.

56. Interview with Mike Veeck, June 28, 2008; *Chicago Tribune*, June 11, 1952, in an article by Gerry Hern republished from the *Boston Post*.

57. *Chicago Tribune*, June 11, 1952.

58. Delivered to Gerry Hern of the *Boston Post*.

59. Interview with Joe DeMaestri, October 10, 2009; *Atlanta Daily World*, June 12, 1952; *Baseball Digest*, September 2003.

60. *Daytona Beach Morning Journal*, June 12, 1952.

61. Ibid.

62. *Baltimore Afro-American*, June 21, 1952.

63. Interview with Joe DeMaestri, October 10, 2009.

64. Interview with Duane Pillette, August 13, 2009; interview with Marty Marion, August 13, 2009.

65. Interview with Jay Porter, September 30, 2009.

66. Fred Down of UPI obtained the quote from Patterson and it appears in the *Sarasota Herald-Tribune*, April 29, 1952, 10.

Chapter 13: Baltimore Chop

1. Curt Gowdy with John Powers, *Seasons to Remember: The Way It Was in American Sports, 1945–1960* (New York: HarperCollins, 1993), 166.

2. *Washington Post*, January 9, 1953.

3. AP, *Milwaukee Journal*, February 1, 1953.

4. Bill Veeck with Edward Linn, *Veeck—as in Wreck* (New York: G. P. Putnam's Sons, 1962), 27.

5. AP, *Miami News*, June 27, 1962, 40.

6. *Baltimore Sun*, February 22, 1953.

7. *St. Louis Post-Dispatch*, February 21, 1993.

8. AP, March 13, 1953.

9. UPI, *Telegraph-Herald*, March 15, 1952.

10. *Baltimore Sun*, March 7, 1958.

11. *The Doings*, January 8, 1986.

12. *Baltimore Sun*, September 28, 2003; *Time*, March 16, 1953.

13. AP, *Daytona Beach Morning Journal*, March 18, 1953; Daley's column syndicated in *Telegraph*, November 10, 1964.

14. *Montreal Gazette*, March 23, 1953.

15. *Baltimore Sun*, March 23, 1953.

16. AP, *St. Joseph Gazette*, March 24, 1953.

17. *Los Angeles Times*, March 23, 1953.

18. *Pittsburgh Press*, April 3, 1953.

19. *St. Louis Post-Dispatch*, February 21, 1993.

20. AP, *Daytona Beach Morning Journal*, April 10, 1953; *Washington Post*, June 7, 1953.

21. Fred Lieb, *The Baltimore Orioles* (New York: G. P. Putnam's Sons, 1955), 219.

22. Donald Honig, *Baseball When the Grass Was Real: Baseball from the Twenties to the Forties Told by the Men Who Played It* (Lincoln: University of Nebraska Press, 1993), 222. In the book, the party is said to have occurred after the eighth game in the losing streak, but the record shows that it was the seventh. The Browns were in Chicago for the eighth loss.

23. *New York Times*, May 1, 1988.

24. *Time*, July 20, 1953.

25. *Los Angeles Times*, September 4, 1953. But almost as soon as he had begun his flirtation with the West Coast, he declared, "Los Angeles and San Francisco were delightful but I don't think they are for us."

26. *New York Times*, September 26, 1953.

27. James Bready, *Baseball in Baltimore: The First 100 Years* (Baltimore: Johns Hopkins University Press, 1998), 214.

28. *Pittsburgh Press*, November 10, 1953. The report alludes to Paige talking to Bearden in March 1953.

29. *The Doings*, January 8, 1986; *Baltimore Sun*, October 4, 1953, 35.

30. Lieb, *Baltimore Orioles*, 221.

31. This recollection was given to John Eisenberg and is an account that has never been made public before. *Baltimore Sun*, September 28, 2003.

32. *Baseball Digest*, June 1953.

33. *Washington Post*, September 29, 1953; *Baltimore Sun*, October 4, 1953, 35.

34. *Sports Illustrated*, July 4, 1960; Gordon Beard, *Birds on the Wing* (Garden City, NY: Doubleday, 1967), 165.

35. *Christian Science Monitor*, October 1, 1953.

36. *Time*, March 23, 1953.

37. *Chicago Defender*, October 10, 1953.

38. Veeck with Linn, *Veeck—as in Wreck*, 305.

39. *Baltimore Sun*, October 4, 1953, 35.

Chapter 14: Chicago a Go-Go

1. *Cleveland Press*, November 7, 1956.

2. *Milwaukee Sentinel*, October 17, 1953.

3. *New York Times*, December 1, 1954.

4. *Chicago American*, October 18, 1953.

5. *Spokesman-Review*, January 27, 1954; Leroy Satchel Paige as told to David Lipman, *Maybe I'll Pitch Forever* (Lincoln: University of Nebraska Press, 1993), 243.

6. *Chicago Tribune*, April 20, 1976. This comes from a David Condon column in which (presumably) Veeck is sitting in the Billy Goat Tavern in Chicago telling stories about his past.

7. The report "Facts on the Coming Expansion of Major League Baseball to the Pacific Coast" is quoted in detail in Michael D'Antonio's *Forever Blue: The True Story of Walter O'Malley, Baseball's Most Controversial Owner, and the Dodgers of Brooklyn and Los Angeles* (New York: Riverhead Books, 2009), which cites the Walter O'Malley archives as the source of the report.

8. *Chicago Tribune*, February 4, 1955, C1; September 5, 1956, D3.

9. AP, *Spokane Chronicle*, December 22, 1955.

10. AP, *Schenectady Gazette*, March 11, 1955.

11. *Arizona Daily Star*, July 14, 1991.

12. Bill Veeck with Edward Linn, *Veeck—as in Wreck* (New York: G. P. Putnam's Sons, 1962), 311; *Ottawa Citizen*, January 4, 1956; *Baseball Digest*, March 1956, 65.

13. *Miami News*, January 28, 1956.

14. *Baseball Digest*, July 1961.

15. *New York Amsterdam News*, December 29, 1956; Pat Williams interviews, 1997–98, no. 138 (interview with Eddie Storin).

16. UP, *Modesto Bee*, August 15, 1956.

17. *Washington Post*, February 15, 1956. Many sources including Wikipedia insist that Greenberg was previously an owner of the Indians, but it is a claim that Greenberg and Veeck both denied. *Washington Post*, February 6, 1955, C1.

18. *Chicago Tribune*, May 28, 1956.

19. Ibid., January 11, 1956.

20. *Washington Post*, July 18, 1956.

21. Ibid.

22. *Washington Post*, July 8, 1956.

23. *Cleveland Press*, July 13, 1956.

24. Bob Addie in *Washington Post*, July 7, 1956.

25. Veeck with Linn, *Veeck—as in Wreck*, 315; *Chicago Defender*, June 11, 1956.

26. *Cleveland Press*, July 19, 1956.

27. Rolfe declared that his Tigers' prospects for the coming season were poor because Detroit had not opted for the ready-made stars who had dominated the pennant races of the past few years. He asked: "Where would the Indians be without Luke Easter and Larry Doby? Or Brooklyn without Jackie Robinson, Don Newcombe and Roy Campanella? Or the Giants without Henry Thompson, Monte Irvin, and Willie Mays?" Rolfe would be replaced during the 1952 season, and the Tigers, for all their dignity, remained a second-division club.

28. *Daily Defender*, July 24, 1956.

29. This whole account appears in Bryson's interview with Osborn in *Baseball Digest*, July 1961. Bryson's son, also writing as Bill Bryson, is a popular journalist and author.

30. *Time*, October 22, 1956. Both Gregory Veeck and Eloise Saperstein mentioned the inflatable tent in separate interviews.

31. *Chicago Defender*, October 16, 1956.

32. *Cleveland Press*, November 7, 1956.

33. Interviews with Lou Brissie, November 7, 2008, and August 13, 2009.

34. *Chicago Tribune*, October 20, 1953.

35. *Los Angeles Herald Express*, August 4, 1958: The article was entitled "Hoover Agrees with Veeck on Baseball, Bonus, Draft." A wire service version of this piece appears in Veeck's FBI file, which would seem to indicate that Hoover was pleased with his declaration of support for Veeck.

36. *New York Herald Tribune*, December 26, 1958.

37. *Chicago Tribune*, January 15, 1956, C1; *Washington Post*, June 3, 1959, A8.

38. *New York Herald Tribune*, December 26, 1958.

39. Interview with Eloise Saperstein, September 27, 2009. Veeck and Abe Saperstein were together again and both a little closer to their mutual pipe dream of owning the Cubs. "They talked of owning the Cubs incessantly," recalled Abe's daughter Eloise, "but at least now they were on the South Side."

40. Edward Linn, *A Great Connection: The Story of Molex* (Chicago: Regnery Gateway, 1988). Interviews with Fred Krehbiel, June 26, 2010, and July 2010.

41. Pat Williams interviews, 1997–98.

42. *Harvard Crimson*, April 10, 1969.

43. *Saturday Evening Post*, June 6, 1959, 31–32, 92–94.

44. UPI, *Cleveland Press*, April 15, 1959.

45. Pat Williams interviews, 1997–98, no. 173.

46. *St. Petersburg Times*, July 13, 1959, 30.

47. Interview with Fred Krehbiel; *Washington Post*, June 29, July 12, and July 27, 1959; *Daily Defender*, July 15, 1959; *Chicago Daily News*, May 11, 1959.

48. Pat Williams interviews, 1997–98, no. 173.

49. *Chicago Tribune*, June 30, 1959.

50. Burt Solomon, *Baseball Timeline* (New York: Avon, 1997), 597.

51. *Chicago Tribune*, September 4, 1959.

52. AP, *Calgary Herald*, September 24, 1959.

53. *Chicago Tribune*, September 22, 1959.

54. Jerome Boltzmann and George Vass, *Baseball Chicago Style: A Tale of Two Teams, One City* (Chicago: Bonus Books, 2001), 115.

55. *Chicago Tribune*, September 30, 1959, C1.

56. *Washington Post*, September 30, 1959, C2.

57. *Chicago Tribune*, October 2, 1959.

58. *Bill Veeck Show*, Recorded Sound Reference Center, Library of Congress, audio file LPA50732.

59. Interview with Stan Isaacs, February 27, 2011.

60. Pat Williams interviews, 1997–98, no. 106. The transcript of this interview includes many more accounts of Veeck's behavior at this point in his life, including this one repeated in its entirely: "In 1959, I asked Veeck if he would address a father-son sports night meeting at my parish. It was on Opening Day in Chicago, and he drew an overflow crowd. Earlier, Veeck and his wife, Mary Frances, had come to our house to socialize and have dinner. Before dinner, Bill sat in the kitchen with a beer in hand, and regaled some of the Kuenster kids with stories, and showed them his wooden leg, which contained a cut-in ashtray. To their amusement, he flicked cigarette ashes into the tray. Following his talk in the parish hall, Veeck stayed on until after midnight, answering questions from his listeners, most of whom were diehard White Sox fans. When we finally returned home, Veeck suggested that Mary Frances, my wife, and I accompany him to the nearby Martinique Restaurant for a few drinks and dancing. 'Dancing?' I said. 'Everybody'll be gone by the time we get there.' Foolish me. When we arrived at the Martinique, everybody was gone but the orchestra. That afternoon, Bill had evidently called Tony DeSantis, the club owner, to tell him he was coming over late in the evening, and DeSantis asked the musicians to stick around after they had finished their regular gig. So, at 1 a.m., there were Bill and Mary Frances dancing gracefully by themselves, later joined by my wife and myself. It was a wonderful way to cap an evening (and early morning) together, and I must say, Bill was a pretty good dancer. He never considered himself as being handicapped despite having only one good leg."

61. *New York Times,* December 18, 1959.
62. *Pittsburgh Chronicle,* December 19, 1959.
63. From the script of "Veeck: A Man for Any Season," WTTW, 1985, http://www.wttw.com/main .taf?p=1,7,1,1,540n.
64. E-mail from Carol Scott Alley, August 10, 2009; interview with Alley, August 13, 2009; *Chicago Sun-Times,* February 16, 1960.

CHAPTER 15: BELLS AND WHISTLES

1. Aaron D. Cushman, *A Passion for Winning: Fifty Years of Promoting Legendary People and Products* (Pittsburgh: Lighthouse Point Press, 2004). Cushman added: "He actually came up with the idea shortly after he sold the Indians. When he pitched it to them, the team turned a deaf ear to the idea. Bill filed it away and unveiled it with the White Sox."
2. Interview with Eloise Saperstein, September 27, 2009.
3. Jack Newfield, *American Rebels* (New York: Nation Books, 2003), 280.
4. *New York Times,* May 9, 1960.
5. Ed Gruver, *The American Football League: A Year-by-Year History, 1960–1969* (Jefferson, NC: McFarland, 1997), 35.
6. *Chicago Tribune,* June 26 and 30, 1960.
7. *Washington Post,* August 6, 1960.
8. The files at the National Baseball Library and Archives in Cooperstown were obtained in 1999 by Eric Enders. A number of pages were withheld from the records, so it is entirely possible that there was more to this story that may never be known. Mary Frances Veeck was unaware of this event based on a discussion with her on February 25, 2011. Her assumption was that Bill did not want to worry her unnecessarily. Veeck never made any comment on this matter, nor was it known to have happened until Veeck's FBI file was opened up under a Freedom of Information Act request in 1999, so one can only speculate what effect it had on him, although it could not have been anything but a great burden and, perhaps, may have lead to the thought that using the word *exploding* for his new scoreboard may have been a bad choice.
9. UPI, *Miami News,* August 11, 1960.
10. *Sports Illustrated,* June 14, 1965.
11. Stewart L. Udall papers, Box 90, University of Arizona, Manuscripts Library. Deepest thanks to Andy O'Toole, at work on a biography of Marshall, for sharing this information with me; also Charles K. Ross, *Outside the Lines: African Americans and the Integration of the National Football League* (New York: New York University Press, 2001), 153.
12. *Washington Afro-American,* May 9, 1961, 10.
13. Pat William interviews, 1997–98, Dick Hackett.
14. Lawrence S. Ritter, *The Glory of Their Times,* enlarged ed. (New York: William Morrow, 1992), 328.
15. Conversation with Mary Frances Veeck, January 25, 2011.
16. *Sporting News,* August 2, 1961. The letter also appears in Bill Veeck with Edward Linn, *Veeck—as in Wreck* (New York: G. P. Putnam's Sons, 1962), 379–80.
17. Danny Peary, *We Played the Game: 65 Players Remember Baseball's Greatest Era, 1947–1964* (New York: Hyperion, 1994), 165.
18. *New York Post,* June 19, 1961.

CHAPTER 16: PEACHBLOSSOM CREEK

1. *Cleveland Plain Dealer,* June 27, 1961.
2. *Sporting News,* August 2, 1961.
3. *Chicago Tribune,* February 11, 1962.
4. *Washington Star,* August 11, 1966.
5. *Baltimore Sun Sunday Magazine,* May 13, 1962, 15–18.
6. *Chicago Tribune,* August 20 and 22, 1961.
7. Ibid., September 2, 1961.
8. Ibid., February 11, 1962.
9. AP, *Chicago Tribune,* November 30, 1961, F1.
10. Interview with Fred Krehbiel, June 26, 2010.
11. *Baltimore Sun Sunday Magazine,* May 13, 1962, 15–18.
12. Interview with Ellen Maggs, March 15, 2011; interview with Lisa Veeck, March 16, 2011; interview with Marya Veeck, March 17, 2011.
13. Interview with Greg Veeck, March 12, 2011.
14. Interview with Lisa Veeck, March 16, 2011.
15. *Chicago Tribune,* January 5, 1986.
16. Interview with Ray Grebey, August 17, 2009.
17. Interview with Roger Clark, September 5, 2009.
18. Interview with Mike Veeck, June 28, 2008.
19. From Roger Kahn's introduction to Pat Williams, *Marketing Your Dreams: Business and Life Lessons from Bill Veeck, Baseball's Marketing Genius* (Champaign, IL: Sports Publications, 2000), viii–ix.
20. Pat Williams interviews, 1997–98.
21. Interview with Mary Frances Veeck, February, 6, 2010.
22. Interview with Mike Veeck, June 28, 2008; interview with Greg Veeck, March 12, 2011.
23. Bill Veeck with Ed Linn, *Thirty Tons a Day* (New York: Viking, 1972), 7.
24. *Washington Post,* February 3, 1963.
25. NANA, *Miami News,* June 27, 1962.
26. Bill Veeck with Edward Linn, *Veeck—as in Wreck* (New York: G. P. Putnam's Sons, 1962), 380.
27. Veeck with Linn, *Thirty Tons a Day,* 7.
28. *Washington Post,* June 20, 1962.
29. William Braden, "A Day with Veeck Wrecked Reporter," *Chicago Sun-Times,* September 4, 1962. The article was reprinted on January 5, 1986, a few days after Veeck's death.
30. Pat Williams interviews, 1997–98.
31. *Washington Post,* September 12, 1962.
32. AP, *Daytona Beach Morning Journal,* October 9, 1962.
33. *Washington Star,* August 11, 1966.
34. *Baltimore Sun,* October 4, 1963, 46.
35. Interview with Greg Veeck, March 12, 2011.
36. *Cleveland Press,* November 15, 1962.
37. Telephone interview with Larry Doby Jr., August 28, 2009.
38. This account appeared in Morris McLemore's column in the *Miami News,* May 22, 1964.
39. Interview with Marya Veeck, March 17, 2011.
40. *Washington Post,* April 28, 1965; *Los Angeles Times,* May 26, 1964; *Sporting News,* June 16, 1963.
41. *Cleveland Press,* June 6, 1963.

42. *Cleveland Plain Dealer*, November 30, 1963. Her amputation was a high-profile incident because she had fled the hospital before finally returning for the amputation.

43. Interview with Lisa Veeck, March 16, 2011; interview with Greg Veeck, March 12, 2011.

44. E-mail from John Herd Thompson, August 5, 2009.

45. *Chicago Tribune*, October 21, 1963.

46. Ibid., October 22, 1963.

47. Interview with Fred Krehbiel, June 3, 2010; interview with Mike Veeck, June 28, 2008.

48. *Popular Science Monthly*, March 1964, 94.

49. *Chicago Tribune*, May 22, 1964.

50. Ibid.

51. *Chicago Daily News*, June 8, 1965, 39.

52. *Washington Star Sunday Magazine*, August 14, 1966, 6.

53. Telephone interview with Fred Krehbiel, June 3, 2010.

54. Bill Veeck with Ed Linn, *The Hustler's Handbook* (New York: G. P. Putnam's Sons, 1965), 298.

55. Ibid., 296.

56. *Reporter*, January 27, 1966, 57–59.

57. *The Bill Veeck Show*, Recorded Sound Reference Center, Library of Congress, Washington, D.C.

58. UPI, December 9, 1968.

59. *Bill Veeck Show*, audio file LPA50104.

60. Interview with Eloise Saperstein, September 27, 2009.

61. *Ebony*, May 1968, 179.

62. Arlene Howard and Ralph Wimbish, *Elston and Me: The Story of the First Black Yankee* (Columbia: University of Missouri Press, 2001), 151. At the beginning of the meeting, Arlene Howard asked Veeck if he remembered her questioning him about the economics of hiring black players, and he said he did. She also recalled: "Mr. Veeck was well loved by the black community in St. Louis. He was very active with black people; he brought baseball to the streets. He knew that black athletes were not treated fairly. I always thought if any owner were to hire a black manager, it would be him. That's just the way he was. He was innovative and fair. Indeed, baseball history would be entirely different had Mr. Veeck named Elston as major-league baseball's first black manager."

63. Ibid.

64. Frazier Robinson, *Catching Dreams: My Life in the Negro Baseball Leagues* (Syracuse, NY: Syracuse University Press, 1999), 207; *Spokane Daily Chronicle*, August 29, 1968.

65. *Chicago Tribune*, October 30, 1968.

66. Ibid., November 15, 1968, 26.

Chapter 17: Off to the Races

1. AP, *Herald Journal*, November 20, 1968, 20.

2. *Look*, June 30, 1970.

3. *Horseman's Journal*, January 1969.

4. *Chicago Tribune*, January 29, 1968.

5. *New York Times*, April 22, 1969.

6. Ibid., April 20, 1969.

7. U.S. Congress, Committee on District of Columbia, Senate, Hearings Held to Consider Future Use of Robert F. Kennedy Memorial Stadium, D.C., and Prospects for Location of Another Major League Baseball Franchise in D.C., December 13, 1971.

8. *New York Times*, April 20, 1969.

9. Ibid., June 28, 1969, 24; *Washington Post*, June 28, 1969 E4, and June 30, 1969 D11.

10. *Newsweek*, July 14, 1969.

11. UPI, *Washington Post*, April 28, 1969, D8.

12. Larry Claffin in the *Record American*, June 5, 1969, 66.

13. AP, *New York Times*, November 20, 1969, 53.

14. UPI, *Cleveland Press*, December 3, 1969.

15. Tim Horgan in the *Boston Herald-Traveler*, December 17–18, 1969.

16. Bob August in the *Cleveland Press*, December 18, 1969.

17. *Boston Record American*, March 18, 1970, 44.

18. U.S. Congress, Committee on the District of Columbia, December 13, 1971, 122.

19. Phone interview with Bill Gleason, August 11, 2009.

20. Brad Snyder, *A Well-Paid Slave: Curt Flood's Fight for Free Agency in Professional Sports* (New York: Viking, 2006), 184.

21. Interview with Dick Victory, August 10, 2009. Victory's pieces appear in the *Evening Star*, May 3 and May 10, 1970.

22. *Flood v. Kuhn*, 407 U.S. 1976.

23. *Washington Post*, June 11, 1970, D1.

24. Marvin Miller, *A Whole Different Ball Game: The Sport and Business of Baseball*, (Secaucus, NJ: Carol, 1991), 368; interview with Marvin Miller, September 1, 2009; *Sports Illustrated*, September 11, 2006.

25. Larry Merchant in *Look*, June 30, 1970, 68–72.

26. U.S. Congress, Committee on the District of Columbia, December 13, 1971, 114.

27. *Washington Post*, February 14, 1971.

28. *Sporting News*, June 21, 1971; *Evening Star*, July 21, 1971.

29. Ibid; Ibid.

30. *Washington Post*, December 16, 1971.

31. *Sporting News*, February 12, 1972; *Lawrence Journal-World*, September 22, 1971; *Sports Illustrated*, October 11, 1971.

32. *Washington Post*, September 22, 1971.

33. *Milwaukee Journal*, November 12, 1971.

34. *Washington Evening Star*, December 15, 1971.

35. U.S. Congress, Committee on the District of Columbia, December 13, 1971, 116.

36. *Baltimore Sun*, April 9, 1972.

37. Miller, *Whole Different Ball Game*, 368; interview with Marvin Miller, September 1, 2009.

38. *Binghamton (NY) Sunday Press*, May 7, 1972.

39. Tim Horgan in the *Boston Herald*, June 5, 1972.

40. *Cleveland Plain Dealer*, June 11, 1972.

41. Interview with Mike Veeck, June 28, 2008.

42. *Baltimore Sun*, January 29, 1993; interview with Roger Clark, September 5, 2009.

43. AP, *Argus-Press*, November 18, 1972.

44. *Cleveland Plain Dealer*, January 29, 1974; *New York Times*, March 24, 1974.

45. *New York Times*, June 11, 1975, 55; November 17, 1975.

46. Peter Richmond, *Ballpark: Camden Yards and the Building of an American Dream* (New York: Fireside, 1995), 57; *Baltimore Sun*, December 18, 1975.

CHAPTER 18: THE LAST HURRAH

1. Pat Williams interviews, 1997–98, no. 122.
2. *New York Times*, October 3, 1975.
3. *Chicago Tribune*, October 10, 75.
4. Ibid., October 5, 6, 7, and 8, 1975.
5. *Washington Evening Star*, October 4, 1975.
6. *Chicago Tribune*, November 4, 1975.
7. *Baltimore Sun*, October 10, 1975.
8. *Washington Post*, December 3, 1975.
9. *Chicago Daily News*, December 4, 1975; Rick Taley in *Chicago Tribune*, December 4, 1975.
10. *Akron Beacon Journal*, December 4, 1975.
11. *Chicago Tribune*, December 11, 1975.
12. *New York Times*, December 10, 1975.
13. *Fort Lauderdale News*, December 11, 1975.
14. This impassioned plea was recalled later in the day to Bill Madden, who reported it through United Press International. *Ellensburg Daily Record*, December 11, 1975. The latter explanation appears in *Sporting News*, February 7, 1976.
15. *Hollywood Journal*, December 12, 1975.
16. Ibid.
17. *Chicago Tribune*, December 12, 1975.
18. Phone interview with Bill Gleason, August 11, 2009.
19. *New York Times*, December 14, 1975.
20. *The Doings*, December 10, 1987.
21. Ibid. *New York Times*, December 14, 1972.
22. *Newsday*, December 14, 1975.
23. Robert Markus in *Chicago Tribune*, December 15, 1976.
24. *New York Times*, December 18, 1975.
25. AP, *Bangor Daily News*, December 25, 1975; *Sporting News*, March 27, 1976; *Chicago Tribune*, March 10, 1976
26. Bill Veeck interview with William J. Marshall, for the University of Kentucky Libraries, A. B. "Happy" Chandler Oral History Project, February 23, 1977.
27. AP, *Bangor Daily News*, December 31, 1975.
28. Bowie Kuhn, *Hardball* (New York: Times Books, 1987), 319; Bob Lemon interview with William Marshall, the University of Kentucky Libraries, A. B. "Happy" Chandler Oral History Project, May 15, 1979.
29. *Chicago Tribune*, January 14, 1976.
30. Ibid., January 22, 1976.
31. Ibid., February 3, 1976.
32. UPI, *Beaver County Times*, February 5, 1976.
33. *Chicago Tribune*, February 5, 1976.
34. *Washington Evening Star*, February 25, 1976.
35. *Sporting News*, March 13, 1976; *Washington Post*, February 27, 1976.
36. *Sporting News*, March 20, 1976.
37. Ralph Novak in *People*, April 19, 1976.
38. *Chicago Tribune*, February 27 and March 1, 1976.
39. *Bangor Daily News*, March 10, 1976.

40. *Chicago Tribune*, March 19, 1976. This appeared in Rick Talley's column, and Talley admits it was a close approximation of the actual conversation.

41. Pat Williams interviews, 1997–98, no. 82. Spencer ended the interview with the words "He enjoyed life and loved the game. I'm glad I played for him."

42. *Chicago Tribune*, February 18, 1976.

43. Ibid., April 10, 1976.

44. The quotes from Condon, Mike Veeck, Talley, and Hemond all come from a piece by Amalie Benjamin in the *Chicago Tribune*, April 14, 2004. Richards's comments on the moment suggest he reverted to character after leaving the field in costume: " 'With Veeck running this team, you got to learn to expect anything,' Richards said afterward, denuded of his wig. 'That outfit is gone now. I put a match to it when I took it off. Would I ever dress up in Revolutionary War gear again? I might for a price.' "

45. *Chicago Tribune*, September 5, 1976, D3.

46. Ibid., December 12, 2010.

47. Harry Caray with Bob Verdi, *Holy Cow!* (New York: Villard, 1989), 210–11.

48. Tim Wiles, "Music of the Sphere," in *Baseball as America: Seeing Ourselves Through Our National Game* (Washington, DC: National Geographic, 2002), 133. Mike Veeck had a different version of how Caray began the custom. According to this version, Caray at first demurred at the request from the Veecks, father and son; they begged for weeks, but Harry did not want to sing it. Finally blackmail was employed: "We told him we had a cassette copy of him singing this song, and we were going to play it whether he wanted us to or not, so he might as well sing live."

49. Ralph Novak in *People*, April 19, 1976.

50. Allen Able, "Baseball Now Game for Unbridled Egos, Veeck One of Dying Breed," *Globe and Mail*, March 17, 1979.

51. *Wilmington Star-News*, August 9, 1976.

52. AP wire copy, August 10, 1976, in Veeck file, National Baseball Library.

53. Interview with Mark Plotkin, July 15, 2009.

54. *Chicago Sun-Times*, September 17, 2010. After Rosita died, Faust bought another donkey, which was six years old when Faust retired in 2010.

55. *Chicago Tribune*, September 2, 1976.

56. Dan Helpingstine and Leo Bauby, *South Side Hit Men: The Story of the 1977 Chicago White Sox* (Charleston, SC: Arcadia, 2005), 24.

57. *Time*, April 25, 1977.

58. *Sporting News*, October 16, 1976.

59. Ibid., October 15 and November 6, 1976.

60. Ibid., October 23, 1976.

61. *Chicago Tribune*, November 24, 1976.

62. *Sporting News*, March 31, 1977.

63. *Time*, April 25, 1977; *Sports Illustrated*, March 28, 1977.

64. Interview with Mike Veeck, June 28, 2008.

65. *Chicago Tribune*, June 8, 1977.

66. Richard Roeper, *Sox and the City: A Fan's Love Affair with the White Sox from the Heartbreak of '67 to the Wizards of Oz* (Chicago: Chicago Review, 2006), 114.

67. *Milwaukee Journal*, August 1, 1977. The article was entitled "As in Wreck: Veeck Joins Fisticuffs in Stands."

68. *Chicago Tribune*, October 2, 2010. The actual name of the song is "Na Na Hey Hey Kiss Him Goodbye."

69. Roeper, *Sox and the City*, 117.
70. *Sporting News*, October 29, 1977.
71. *Chicago Tribune*, November 2, 1977.
72. *Baseball Quarterly* 2, no. 3 (Fall 1978): 17.
73. *Globe and Mail*, March 17, 1979.

Chapter 19: Demolition

1. *Washington Post*, June 1, 1977; January 5, 1986; *Palm Beach Post*, December 5, 1986.
2. *Washington Evening Star*, June 1, 1977.
3. *New York Daily News*, November 19, 1977.
4. Ron Blomberg and Dan Schlossberg, *Designated Hebrew: The Ron Blomberg Story* (Champaign, IL: Sports Publishing, 2006), 138.
5. *Chicago Tribune*, June 14, 1978; *Ocala-Star Banner*, June 14, 1978.
6. *Chicago Sun-Times*, June 16, 1978.
7. Ibid., June 15, 1978.
8. *Chicago Tribune*, June 16, 1978.
9. *Score* (CBS test publication), May 9, 1979.
10. *Milwaukee Journal*, July 1, 1978.
11. Rick Talley, *The Cubs of '69: Recollections of the Team That Should Have Been* (Chicago: McGraw-Hill Contemporary, 1989), 205.
12. Tom Melody in the *Akron Beacon Journal*, August 21, 1978.
13. *Chicago Tribune*, September 29, 1978.
14. Joseph Thomas Moore, *Pride Against Prejudice: The Biography of Larry Doby* (New York: Greenwood, 1988), 164.
15. Larry Doby interview with Tom Harris, February 18, 1994; interview with William Marshall, August 1, 2009.
16. *Los Angeles Times*, January 4, 1986.
17. *Chicago Tribune*, February 10, 1979.
18. Mike Veeck and Pete Williams, *Fun Is Good: How to Create Joy and Passion in Your Workplace and Career* (Emmaus, PA: Rodale, 2005), 147.
19. *New York Times*, July 5, 2009.
20. Eliot Salant, who responded online to the piece on Disco Demolition Night that appeared in the *New York Times*, July 5, 2009.
21. Art Hill, *I Don't Care If I Never Come Back* (New York: Simon and Schuster, 1980), 243.
22. Interview with Clarence Page, October 29, 2009. John-Manuel Andriote, the author of *Hot Stuff: A Brief History of Disco* (New York: HarperCollins, 2001), wrote one of the severest critiques of Disco Demolition in a blog attached to a *New York Times* article on the thirtieth anniversary of the event: "No one wants to admit it—as if all the violence and destruction was somehow just 'innocent fun'—but racism and homophobia were stoking the fire at Comiskey Park as much as those vinyl records. . . . This is why I laugh when I see today's baseball fans doing their silly moves to the Village People's 'YMCA'—one of the gayest songs ever made by a group of men who laughed all the way to the bank with the money they made from people who hated gay men but couldn't (maybe didn't want to) see the stereotyped gay images of the musicians themselves. . . . Disco music was fun dance music. That's all it was ever meant to be. It grew out of the same R&B roots as rock and roll. It was the record companies that drove

it into the ground with overkill (24/7 dance music). Funny that no wedding or bar mitzvah today is much fun without at least some 'retro' disco music!"

23. *Palm Beach Post*, September 16, 1969.

24. Veeck and Williams, *Fun Is Good*, xxiv.

25. Richard Roeper, *Sox and the City: A Fan's Love Affair with the White Sox from the Heartbreak of '67 to the Wizards of Oz* (Chicago: Chicago Review, 2006), 142.

26. *Sporting News*, November 10, 1979.

27. *Chicago Tribune*, December 4, 1979, C3.

28. UPS, *Palm Beach Post*, April 15, 1980.

29. *Chicago Reader*, May 9, 1980

30. E-mail to the author, March 15, 2009.

31. *Chicago Tribune*, August 26, 1980.

32. Interview with Bruce Kraig, October 3, 2009. He added in a follow-up e-mail: "By the way, that night Ross Baumgarten of the White Sox pitched his best game in the bigs, a one-hitter against the Angels (Rod Carew got the only hit or, as Harry Caray used to call him in a guttural voice: Rod Careeeewww)."

33. Jim Piersall, *The Truth Hurts* (Chicago: Contemporary, 1984), 150.

34. AP, *Sarasota Herald-Tribune*, August 24, 1980; *Chicago Sun-Times*, August 24, 1980.

35. Phone interview with Bill Gleason, August 11, 2009.

36. Jerome Holtzman in the *Chicago Sun-Times*, October 1, 1980.

37. *Sarasota Herald-Tribune*, September 9, 1980.

38. *Modesto (CA) Bee*, October 25, 1980.

39. *Palm Beach Post*, December 5, 1980; John Helyar. *The Lords of the Realm* (New York Ballantine, 1995), 242.

40. *Youngstown Vindicator*, December 12, 1980.

41. Ibid.

42. *Dallas Times-Herald*, December 14, 1980. David Israel, then working for the *Chicago Tribune*, called Pete Rozelle of the National Football League and asked him if there was anything at all wrong with DeBartolo. Rozelle had a deep interest in the family, which already owned the 49ers, and he was totally sensitive to the issue of gambling. Rozelle told Israel that DeBartolo was clean; the issue was a matter of not fitting into the club. "Was it bigotry against Italians, the certain generation, or was it disaffection with Veeck?" asked Israel who suspected it was a combination of both. (Interview with David Israel, September 20, 2009.)

43. Interview with Ray Grebey, August 17, 2009.

44. *St. Louis Post-Dispatch*, December 19, 1980.

45. William O. DeWitt interview with William J. Marshall for the University of Kentucky Libraries, A. B. "Happy" Chandler Oral History Project September 29 and October 1, 1980.

46. *Chicago Sun-Times*, February 4, 1981.

CHAPTER 20: BORROWED TIME

1. *Atlanta Journal*, February 9, 1981.

2. *New York Daily News*, February 3, 1981.

3. *Boston Globe*, January 7, 1981.

4. *New York Times*, February 3, 1981.

5. *Newark Star-Ledger*, February 3, 1981; *New York Times*, February 3, 1981.

6. *Chicago Tribune*, May 5, 1981.

7. Marvin Miller, *A Whole Different Ball Game: The Sport and Business of Baseball* (Secaucus, NJ: Carol, 1991), 368.

8. *Chicago Sun-Times*, July 25, 1982; *Los Angeles Sentinel*, October 13, 1983, B2.

9. Usher's manual, Chicago Cubs, 2011; *Chicago Sun-Times*, July 25, 1982.

10. Interview with Greg Veeck, March 12, 2011.

11. Interview with Ray Grebey, August 17, 2009.

12. *Chicago Sun-Times*, January 5, 1986.

13. *Milwaukee Sentinel*, November 12, 1981; *Rock Island Argus*, January 7, 1986.

14. *Arizona Republic*, March 9, 1982.

15. *Baltimore Afro-American*, June 2, 1982; *Tuscaloosa News*, June 9, 1982.

16. Interview with Monte Irvin, November 7, 2008.

17. Pat Williams interviews, 1997–98, no. 1.

18. "It's Been a Wild 50 Years: Wrigley's Famous Cheap Seats Celebrate Silver Anniversary," *St. Petersburg Times*, June 14, 1987; "Pork Chops with Bill," *Sporting News*, December 27, 1999.

19. Pat Williams interviews, 1997–98.

20. *Chicago Tribune*, September 21, 1983.

21. Ibid., September 25, 1983.

22. Ira Berkow, "Sports of the Times: The Pied Piper," *New York Times*, January 4, 1986.

23. *Chicago Tribune*, November 16, 1983; *Bonham Daily Favorite*, November 3, 1983; *St. Joseph Gazette*, November 17, 1983.

24. *Chicago Tribune*, December 7, 1983; interview with Greg Veeck, March 12, 2011.

25. "Veeck's Hip Broken in Fall," *Chicago Tribune*, July 4, 1984.

26. *Chicago Tribune*, January 5, 1986.

27. William Nack, "At Last, the Cubs Are First," *Sports Illustrated*, October 1, 1984.

28. *North Shore*, October 1985, 20.

29. This story is re-told in Father Fitzgerald's homily delivered at Veeck's funeral, Veeck Papers, Chicago History Museum.

30. Bill Granger, "A Get Well Card to Bill Veeck," *Chicago Tribune*, October 17, 1984.

31. Pat Williams interviews, 1997–98, no. 167.

32. *Chicago Tribune*, November 13, 1984, C2.

33. New York *Daily News*, 1985.

34. *Chicago Magazine*, April 1986.

35. *Chicago Tribune*, April 18, 1985.

36. Her recollections appear on the WTTW website, http://www.wttw.com/main.taf?p=1,7,1,1,54. She also wrote in her tribute to Veeck: "I have chauffeured some well-known folks since: from 'Frugal Gourmet' Jeff Smith to Huey Lewis, Steppenwolf's Terry Kinney, and Maya Angelou. But there was no one like Bill Veeck. He was the most approachable and down-to-earth person of any celebrity with whom I worked. He was so instantly recognizable that wherever we were—on the streets of Hyde Park, at a Cubs game, or in down-state Champaign—all types of people crowded around him and wanted to say hello. And he said hello back, and talked. At Wrigley Field, he could only walk a few steps without someone stopping him."

37. *Chicago Tribune*, July 19, 1985.

38. *Sporting News*, October 14, 1985.

39. *Columbia Chronicle*, January 21, 1986.

40. *Dallas Morning News*, January 3, 1986.

41. Conversation recalled by Greenberg on the morning of Veeck's death and reported by Ira Berkow, "Sports of the Times: The Pied Piper," *New York Times*, January 4, 1986.

42. UPI dispatch, January 2, 1986.

43. Interview with Lisa Veeck, March 16, 2011.

44. Ibid.

45. *North Shore*, January 1986, 20.

46. Peter Richmond in *GQ*; Pat Williams interviews, 1997–98, no.

47. Fitzgerald homily, in Veeck Papers.

48. Program, "Mass of the Resurrection for Bill Veeck (1914–1986)," Veeck Papers.

49. Interview with Wyonella Smith, March 19, 2011.

50. *Washington Post*, January 3, 1996, C1.

51. *Chicago Sun-Times*, January 3, 1986.

52. *Chicago Tribune*, January 21, 1986.

53. *Ventura County Star Free Press*, January 11, 1986.

54. *People's Daily World*, January 16, 1986.

55. Veeck Papers. The original telegram is in a collection of letters and news clippings now housed in the National Baseball Library, Cooperstown, New York.

56. Ed Linn, *A Great Connection: The Story of Molex* (Chicago: Regnery Gateway, 1988), 70.

57. The affected players were Joaquín Andújar, Dale Berra, Enos Cabell, Keith Hernandez, Jeffrey Leonard, Dave Parker, and Lonnie Smith.

58. *Chicago Tribune*, April 7, 1986.

59. *Vineline*, March 1986.

60. *Chicago Magazine*, April 1986.

EPILOGUE

1. Bowie Kuhn, *Hardball: The Education of a Baseball Commissioner* (New York: Times Books, 1987), 212.

2. Albert B. Chandler, *Heroes, Plain Folks and Skunks: The Life and Times of Happy Chandler* (Chicago: Bonus Books, 1989), 199.

3. *New York Daily News*, February 3, 1981.

4. *Initiatives* no. 27, July 1988. A copy was sent to Mary Frances Veeck with a note from the editor: "Note our lead story."

5. Philip Bess, "Bill Veeck Park: A Modest Proposal," *National Pastime*, Winter 1987.

6. *Chicago Sun-Times*, January 11, 1990.

7. *Pittsburgh Press*, February 27, 1991, 12.

8. *New York Times*, January 4, 1986.

9. The full text of the speech is available at http://www.wttw.com/main.taf?p=1,7,1,1,54.

10. Interview with Mike Veeck, June 28, 2008.

11. Interview with Charlie Brotman, August 10, 2009.

12. Interview with Stan Kasten, May 12, 2009.

13. Interview with Andy MacPhail, July 1, 2009.

14. "Bill Veeck Is Laughing at Yankees," New York *Daily News*, March 14, 2008.

15. Interview with Mike Veeck, June 28, 2008.

16. Interview with Greg Veeck, March 12, 2011.

FOLLOWING THE FAMILY AND CLOSE FRIENDS

1. Interview with Greg Veeck, March 12, 2011.

2. Interview with Ellen Maggs, March 15, 2011.

3. Interview with Mike Veeck, June 28, 2008.
4. Interview with Greg Veeck, March 12, 2011.
5. Interview with Lisa Veeck, March 16, 2011.
6. *Chicago Sun-Times*, June 17, 2010.
7. *Chicago Tribune*, April 14, 1995.
8. Interview with Mary Frances Veeck, February 6, 2010.

APPENDIX

1. David M. Jordan, Larry R. Gerlach, and John Rossi, "A Baseball Myth Exploded: Bill Veeck and the 1943 Sale of the Phillies," *The National Pastime*, no. 18, 1998, 3–13; Bill Veeck with Ed Linn, *Veeck—as in Wreck* (New York: G. P. Putnam's Sons, 1962), 171–72.
2. Jordan et al., "Baseball Myth Exploded," 13.
3. Interview with Mark Armour, March 12, 2011.
4. Interview with Mike Gimbel, March 15, 2010.
5. Interview with Marya Veeck, March 17, 2011.
6. A. S. "Doc" Young, *Great Negro Baseball Stars and How They Made the Major Leagues* (New York: Barnes, 1953), 52.
7. SABR-L (online mailing list), March 14, 2005.
8. Jules Tygiel, "Revisiting Bill Veeck and the 1943 Phillies," *Baseball Research Journal* 35, 2007, http://research.sabr.org/journals/archive/brj.
9. Rob Neyer, *Rob Neyer's Big Book of Baseball Legends: The Truth, the Lies, and Everything Else* (New York: Fireside, 2008), 29–30.
10. Interview with Greg Veeck, March 12, 2011.
11. *Look*, September 7, 1943.
12. *Chicago Tribune*, January 6, 1986.
13. *Baseball Digest*, September 1948, 53.
14. *Chicago Defender*, February 26, 1949.
15. *Washington Post*, May 10, 1953.
16. *Chicago Defender*, August 14, 1954.
17. Jack Mabley, *Who's on First? Fair Play for All Americans* (New York: Public Affairs Committee, 1956), 8.
18. *New York Times*, July 26, 1974.
19. Interviews with Mary Frances Veeck, October 2009; *Baltimore Sun*, April 18, 2007.
20. Interview with Joseph Thomas Moore, August 20, 2009. Fallows's eulogy can be accessed at http://www.theatlantic.com/national/archive/2010/05/stephen-banker/57386. Banker wrote about the Veeck interview in *Black Collegian*, January–February 1979, 30–32.
21. Jonathan Eig, *Opening Day: The Story of Jackie Robinson's First Season* (New York: Simon and Schuster, 2007), 181.

Select Bibliography

There is a wealth of material available on Veeck. He is one of the most-interviewed and most-quoted figures in baseball history, wrote three books with Ed Linn and hundreds of magazine and newspaper articles, had a syndicated newspaper column, and did hundreds of radio and television broadcasts.

Able, Allen. "Baseball Now Game for Unbridled Egos: Veeck One of Dying Breed." *Globe and Mail*, March 17, 1979.

Adelson, Bruce. *Brushing Back Jim Crow: The Integration of Minor-League Baseball in the South*. Charlottesville: University Press of Virginia, 1999.

Alexander, Charles. *Breaking the Slump: Baseball in the Depression Era*. New York: Columbia University Press, 2002.

Allen, Frederick Lewis. *Only Yesterday: An Informal History of the 1920s*. New York: John Wiley and Sons, 1997.

Allen, Lee. *The Hot Stove League*. New York: A. S. Barnes, 1948.

Ashe, Arthur R., Jr. *A Hard Road to Glory: A History of the African-American Athlete Since 1946*. New York: Warner/Amistad, 1988.

Baldoni, John. *Great Communications Secrets of Great Leaders*. New York: McGraw-Hill, 2003.

Banks, Ernie, and Jim Enright. *Mr. Cub*. Chicago: Follett, 1971.

Banks, Leo W. "An Oasis for Some Pioneers: Lucille and Chester Willis Put Up Black Ballplayers When Tucson's Hotels Wouldn't." *Sports Illustrated*, May 8, 1989: 116–17.

Baraka, Amiri. *The Autobiography of Leroi Jones*. Chicago: Lawrence Hill Books, 1997.

Barber, Red. *1947: When All Hell Broke Loose in Baseball*. New York: Da Capo, 1982.

Barrow, Edward G., with J. M. Kahn. *My Fifty Years in Baseball*. New York: Coward-McCann, 1951.

Barthel, Thomas. *Baseball Brainstorming and Exhibition Games, 1901–1962: A History of Off-Season Major League Play*. Jefferson, NC: McFarland, 2007.

"Baseball: Another Business Facing Change—Interview with Bill Veeck, Former Club Owner." *U.S. News and World Report*, August 12, 1963.

Beck, Peggy. "Working in the Shadows of Rickey and Robinson: Bill Veeck, Larry Doby and the Advancement of Black Players in Baseball." In *The Cooperstown Symposium on Baseball and American Culture*, 1997. Jefferson, NC: McFarland, 2000.

Berkow, Ira. *The Corporal Was a Pitcher*. Chicago: Triumph Books, 2009.

———. "He Crossed Color Barrier, but in Another's Shadow." *New York Times*, February 23, 1997.

———. "Sports of the Times: The Pied Piper." *New York Times*, January 4, 1986.

———. "When Baseball's Circus Came to Town." *New York Times*, October 20, 2005.

Bess, Philip. "Bill Veeck Park: A Modest Proposal." *National Pastime*, Winter 1987.

Boudreau, Lou, with Ed Fitzgerald. *Player-Manager*. Boston: Little, Brown, 1949.

Boynton, Bob. "Ballparks I Have Known." In *Growing Up with Baseball: How We Loved and Played the Game*, ed. Gary Land. Lincoln: University of Nebraska Press, 2004.

Brashler, William. "An April Memory: Facing Opening Day Without Bill Veeck." *Chicago*, April 1986.

———. *Josh Gibson: A Life in the Negro Leagues*. Chicago: Ivan R. Dee, 2000.

———. *The Story of Negro League Baseball*. New York: Ticknor and Fields, 1994.

Bready, James. *Baseball in Baltimore: The First 100 years*. Baltimore: Johns Hopkins University Press, 1998.

Breslin, Jimmy. *Branch Rickey*. Penguin Lives. New York: Viking, 2011.

Brewster, Mike. "Bill Veeck: A Baseball Mastermind." *Business Week*, October 27, 2004.

Broeg, Bob. *Superstars of Baseball*. South Bend, IN: Diamond, 1994.

Brown, Warren. "Bill Veeck: Baseball's Dynamo." *Sportfolio*, April 1949.

Bryant, Howard. *Shut Out: A Story of Race and Baseball in Boston*. New York: Routledge, 2002.

Bullock, Steven R. *Playing for Their Nation: Baseball and the American Military During World War II*. Lincoln: University of Nebraska Press, 2004.

Burk, Robert F. *Much More than a Game: Players, Owners, and American Baseball Since 1921*. Chapel Hill: University of North Carolina Press, 2001.

Caray, Harry. *Holy Cow!* New York: Villard, 1989.

Carroll, Brian. *When to Stop the Cheering? The Black Press, the Black Community, and the Integration of Professional Baseball*. New York: Taylor and Francis, 2006.

Chandler, Albert B. *Heroes, Plain Folks and Skunks: The Life and Times of Happy Chandler*. Chicago: Bonus Books, 1989.

Cleveland, Charles B. *The Great Baseball Managers*. New York: Thomas Y. Crowell, 1950.

Cobbledick, Gordon. "Don Black's Greatest Victory." *American Weekly*, September 12, 1948.

———. "N.L. Has 'In' on West Coast Now: California May Make It by 1956." *Baseball Digest*, March 1954.

Coffin, Tristram Potter. *The Old Ball Game: Baseball in Folklore and Fiction.* New York: Herder and Herder, 1971.

Connor, Anthony J. *Voices from Cooperstown: Baseball's Hall of Famers Tell It like It Was.* New York: Collier, 1984.

Creamer, Robert W. "Bill Veeck 1914–86." *Sports Illustrated*, January 13, 1986.

Cunningham, Bill. "Top Team on a Totem Pole." *Elks Magazine*, June 1949.

D'Antonio, Michael. *Forever Blue: The True Story of Walter O'Malley, Baseball's Most Controversial Owner, and the Dodgers of Brooklyn and Los Angeles.* New York: Penguin, 2010.

Daley, Steve. "'83 Memory: Sharing a Cold One with Veeck." *Chicago Tribune*, September 12, 2003.

Davis, Jack. "Baseball's Reluctant Challenge: Desegregating Major League Spring Training Sites, 1961–1964." *Journal of Sport History* 19, no. 2 (1992): 144–62.

Dawidoff, T. Nicholas. "Big Call from the Hall: Negro Leaguer Ray Dandridge Hears from Cooperstown." *Sports Illustrated*, July 6, 1987.

Debinger, John. "Baseball's Great Target at Frolic." *New York Times*, February 6, 1933.

Devine, Tommy. "Boy from the Bleachers." *Pic: The Magazine for Young Men*, April 1947.

Dixon, Phil. *The Negro Baseball Leagues, 1867–1955: A Photographic History.* Mattituck, NY: Amereon House, 1992.

Drachman, Roy P. *Just Memories.* Tucson, 1979. Also available online at http://parentseyes.arizona.edu/drachman/1003.html.

Durocher, Leo, and Ed Linn. *Nice Guys Finish Last.* New York: Simon and Schuster, 1975.

Durso, Joseph. "Bill Veeck, Baseball Innovator Dies." *New York Times*, January 3, 1986.

———. *Casey and Mr. McGraw.* St. Louis: Sporting News, 1989.

———. *Casey: The Life and Legend of Charles Dillon Stengel.* Introduction by Bill Veeck. New York: Prentice-Hall, 1967.

———. *The Days of Mr. McGraw.* New York: Prentice-Hall, 1969.

———. "Satchel Paige, Black Pitching Star, Is Dead at 75." *New York Times*, June 9, 1982.

Edwards, Bob. *Fridays with Red: A Radio Friendship.* New York: Simon and Schuster, 1993.

Eig, Jonathan. *Opening Day: The Story of Jackie Robinson's First Season.* New York: Simon and Schuster, 2007.

Eisenberg, John. *From 33rd Street to the Camden Yards: An Oral History of the Baltimore Orioles.* New York: McGraw-Hill, 2002.

Elkers, James E. *The Tour to End All Tours: The Story of Major League Baseball's 1913–1914 World Tour.* Lincoln: University of Nebraska Press, 2003.

Eskenazi, Gerald. *Bill Veeck: A Baseball Legend.* New York: McGraw-Hill, 1988.

———. "Fans Recall Bill Veeck Fondly at Service." *New York Times,* January 5, 1986.

Eyman, Scott. "Bill Veeck—He's Seen Better Days but His Mind Still Churns Out Sparkling Ideas." *Cleveland Plain Dealer,* October 8, 1978.

Falkner, David. *Great Time Coming: The Life of Jackie Robinson from Baseball to Birmingham.* New York: Simon and Schuster, 1995.

Fatsis, Stefan. "If Sleuths Are Right, Jackie Robinson Has New Company." *Wall Street Journal,* January 30, 2004.

Feller, Bob. *Bob Feller's Strikeout Story.* New York: Grosset and Dunlap, 1948.

Feller, Bob, with Bill Gilbert. *Now Pitching: Bob Feller.* New York: HarperCollins, 1990.

Fimrite, Ron. "Sam Lacy: Black Crusader." *Sports Illustrated,* October 29, 1994.

Fountain, Charles. *Under the March Sun: The Story of Spring Training.* New York: Oxford University Press, 2009.

Fox, William Price. *Satchel Paige's America.* Tuscaloosa: University of Alabama Press, 2005.

Frank, Stanley. "Fat Cats Don't Win Pennants." *Saturday Evening Post,* April 11, 1953.

Frank, Stanley, and Edgar Munzel. "A Visit with Bill Veeck." *Saturday Evening Post,* June 6, 1959.

Furlong, William Barry. "Master of the Joyful Illusion." *Sports Illustrated,* July 4, 1960.

———. "The Veeck-Yankee Feud Is for Real." *Sport,* April 1960.

Gailey, Harry A. *Bougainville, 1943–1945: The Forgotten Campaign.* Lexington: University Press of Kentucky, 1991.

Gallicho, Grant. "Thanksgiving in October." *Commonweal,* November 18, 2005.

Gardner, Robert, and Dennis Shortelle. *The Forgotten Players: The Story of Black Baseball in America.* New York: Walker, 1993.

Gartner, Michael G. "Remembrance of Baseball Seasons Past." *Wall Street Journal,* October 12, 1977.

Gatto, Tom. "Outside the Box: July 12, 1979: Disco Demolition Night." *Sporting News,* April 21, 2006.

Gay, Timothy M. *Satch, Dizzy and Rapid Robert: The Wild Saga of Interracial Baseball Before Jackie Robinson.* New York: Simon and Schuster, 2010.

———. *Tris Speaker: The Rough-and-Tumble Life of a Baseball Legend.* Lincoln: University of Nebraska Press, 2005.

Gilbert, Thomas. *Baseball and the Color Line: The African-American Experience.* New York: Franklin Watts, 1995.

Gold, Eddie. "My Start in the Newspaper Business." *National Pastime* 20, no. 19 (2000): 33.

———. "The Other Veeck: Reviving the Cubs." *Baseball Research Journal* 25 (1996).

Golenbock, Peter. *The Spirit of St. Louis: A History of the St. Louis Cardinals and Browns.* New York: Avon, 2000.

———. *Wrigleyville: A Magical History Tour of the Chicago Cubs.* New York: St. Martin's, 1996.

Goodman, Mark. "Bill Veeck, 1914–1986." *GQ,* Spring 1986.

———. "If Baseball Is Poetry, Bill Veeck Must Be Shakespeare." *New Times,* April 16, 1976.

Gowdy, Curt. *The Way It Was in American Sports 1945–1960.* New York: Harper-Collins, 1993.

Greenberg, Hank. *The Story of My Life.* Ed. Ira Berkow. New York: Times Books, 1989.

———. "Unforgettable Bill Veeck." *Reader's Digest,* July 1986.

Gregory, Robert. *Diz: The Story of Dizzy Dean and Baseball During the Great Depression.* New York: Random House Value Publishing, 1992.

Grimm, Charlie, and Ed Prell. *Jolly Cholly's Story: Grimm's Baseball Tales.* South Bend, IN: Diamond, 1983.

Grizzard, Lewis. "How Veeck Got Sox." *Chicago Sun-Times,* March 10, 1976.

Heller, Dick. "Veeck's Midget Made Big News for Browns in '51." *Washington Times,* August 21, 2006.

Hill, Art. *I Don't Care If I Never Come Back.* New York: Simon and Schuster, 1980.

Hoffman, John C. "Squirrel Night at the Brewers." *Esquire,* September 1943.

Holtzman, Jerome. *Baseball, Chicago Style.* Rev. ed. Los Angeles: Bonus Books, 2005.

———. *The Commissioners: Baseball's Midlife Crisis.* New York: Total Sports, 1998.

———. *The Jerome Holtzman Baseball Reader.* Chicago: Triumph Books, 2003.

———. "Wendell Smith—a Pioneer for Black Athletes." *Sporting News,* June 22, 1974.

Holway, John. *Black Diamonds: Life in the Negro Leagues from the Men Who Lived It.* Westport, CT: Meckler, 1989.

———. *Blackball Stars: Negro League Pioneers.* New York: Carroll and Graf, 1992.

———. *Josh and Satch: The Life and Times of Josh Gibson and Satchel Paige.* New York: Carroll and Graf, 1991.

———. *Rube Foster: The Father of Black Baseball.* Washington, DC: Pretty Pages, 1982.

———. *Voices from the Great Black Baseball Leagues.* New York: Da Capo, 1992.

Honig, Donald. *Cincinnati Reds.* New York: Simon and Schuster, 1992.

———. *The Man in the Dugout*. Chicago: Follett, 1977.

Hornsby, Rogers. *My Kind of Baseball*. Ed. J. Roy Stockton. New York: David McKay, 1953.

Hornsby, Rogers, with Bill Surface. *My War with Baseball*. New York: Coward-McCann, 1962.

Houk, Ralph, and Robert W. Creamer. *Season of Glory*. New York: Pocket Books, 1988.

Howard, Arlene, and Ralph Wimbish. *Elston and Me: The Story of the First Black Yankee*. Columbia: University of Missouri Press, 2001.

Humphrey, Kathryn Long. *Satchel Paige*. New York: Franklin Watts, 1988.

Jordan, David M., Larry R. Gerlach, and John P. Rossi. "A Baseball Myth Exploded." *National Pastime* 18 (1998).

Kahn, Roger. "The Happy Hustler." *Time*, April 25, 1977.

———. *A Season in the Sun*. Lincoln: University of Nebraska Press, 2000.

Kaiser, David. *Epic Season: The 1948 American League Pennant Race*. Amherst: University of Massachusetts Press, 1998.

Karlen, Neal. *Slouching Toward Fargo: A Two-Year Saga of Sinners and St. Paul Saints at the Bottom of the Bush Leagues with Bill Murray, Darryl Strawberry, Dakota Sadie and Me*. New York: William Morrow, 1999.

Kelley, Brent P. *Voices from the Negro Leagues: Conversations with 52 Baseball Standouts of the Period 1924–1960*. Jefferson, NC: McFarland, 1998.

Kindred, Dave. "She Still Sees Blue Sky." *Sporting News*, November 22, 1999.

Knisley, Michael. "September Song." *Sporting News*, September 7, 1998.

Kubek, Tony, and Terry Pluto. *Sixty-One: The Team, the Record, the Men*. New York: Macmillan, 1987.

Kuhn, Bowie. *Hardball: The Education of a Baseball Commissioner*. New York: Times Books, 1987.

Kuklick, Bruce. *To Every Thing a Season*. Princeton, NJ: Princeton University Press, 1993.

Kurkjian, Tim. "Chip off the Ol' Block." *Sports Illustrated*, July 25, 1994.

———. "Wild Bill." *Sports Illustrated*, July 19, 1993.

Lacy, Sam, and Moses Newson. *Fighting for Fairness: The Life and Story of Hall of Fame Sportswriter Sam Lacy*. Centreville, MD: Tidewater, 1998.

Lamb, Chris. "What's Wrong with Baseball: The *Pittsburgh Courier* and the Beginning of Its Campaign to Integrate the National Pastime." *Western Journal of Black Studies* 26, no. 4 (2002): 189.

Lamb, Chris, and Glen Bleske. "Democracy on the Field." *Journalism History* 24, no. 2 (1998): 51–59.

———. "The Road to October 23, 1945: The Press and the Integration of Baseball." *Nine: A Journal of Baseball and Social Policy* 6 (Fall 1997): 48–68.

———. "Covering the Integration of Baseball—a Look Back." *Editor and Publisher* 27 (January 1996): 48–50.

Lanctot, Neil. *Fair Dealing and Clean Playing: The Hilldale Club and the Development of Black Professional Baseball, 1910–1932.* Jefferson, NC: McFarland, 1994.

———. *Negro League Baseball: The Rise and Ruin of a Black Institution.* Philadelphia: University of Pennsylvania Press, 2004.

Leo, John. "Baseball's Happy Hustler: Bill Veeck, 1914–1986." *Time,* January 13, 1986.

Lester, Larry. *Black Baseball's National Showcase: The East-West All-Star Game, 1933–1953.* Lincoln: University of Nebraska Press, 2001.

Leventhal, Josh. *Take Me Out to the Ballpark.* New York: Black Dog and Leventhal, 2000.

Lewis, Franklin. *The Cleveland Indians.* New York: G. P. Putnam's Sons, 1949.

Lidz, Franz. "The Short End of the Stick." *Sports Illustrated,* June 17, 1985.

Lieb, Fred. *Comedians and Pranksters of Baseball.* St. Louis: Charles C. Spink and Son, 1958.

Linn, Ed. "Veeck . . . as in White Sox." *Sport,* April 1976.

Linn, Ed, and John H. Krehbiel Sr. *A Great Connection.* Chicago: Regnery Gateway, 1988.

Liscio, Stephanie M. *Integrating Cleveland Baseball: Media Activism, the Integration of the Indians and the Demise of the Negro League Buckeyes.* Jefferson, NC: McFarland, 2010.

Lomax, Michael. *Black Baseball Entrepreneurs, 1860–1901: Operating by Any Means Necessary.* Syracuse, NY: Syracuse University Press, 2003.

Luke, Bob. *The Baltimore Elite Giants: Sport and Society in the Age of Negro League Baseball.* Baltimore: Johns Hopkins University Press, 2008.

———. *The Most Famous Woman in Baseball: Effa Manley and the Negro Leagues.* Dulles, VA: Potomac Books, 2011.

Mackay, Harvey. "I'd Like 15,000 Tickets for Tonight's Game, Please." In *Swim with the Sharks Without Being Eaten Alive.* New York: Morrow, 1988.

Maisel, Bob. "In World of Characters, Veeck Was Tough to Top." *Baltimore Sun,* December 9, 1990.

Mandernach, Mark. "Short Hitter, Long Memory." *Sports Illustrated,* September 2, 1996.

Mankiewicz, Frank. "Veeck Balked in Havana, and so Did the Cubans." *Washington Post,* January 5, 1986.

Manley, Effa, and Leon Herbert Hardwick. *Negro Baseball . . . Before Integration.* Chicago: Adams, 1976.

Mann, Arthur. *The Jackie Robinson Story.* New York: Grosset and Dunlap, 1950.

Maraniss, David. "Neither a Myth Nor a Legend—Larry Doby Crossed Baseball's Color Barrier After Robinson." *Washington Post,* July 8, 1997.

Marshall, William. *Baseball's Pivotal Era 1945–1951.* Lexington: University of Kentucky Press, 1999.

McCarthy, Fred. "Veeck as in Wreck?" *Golf World*, January 30, 2004.

McDermott, Mickey, with Howard Eisenberg. *A Funny Thing Happened on the Way to Cooperstown*. Chicago: Triumph Books, 2003.

Mehl, Ernest. "Effort to Put Negro Team in N.L. in 30's Disclosed." *Sporting News*, from an undated clipping in the NBL vertical file marked 1958.

Merchant, Larry. "Bill Veeck Is Off to the Races." *Look*, July 30, 1970.

Metro, Charlie, with Tom Altherr. *Safe by a Mile*. Lincoln: University of Nebraska, 2002.

Miller, Marvin. *A Whole Different Ball Game: The Sport and Business of Baseball*. Secaucus, NJ: Carol, 1991.

Miller, Patrick B. *Sport and the Color Line: Black Athletes and Race Relations in Twentieth-Century America*. New York: Routledge, 2004.

Moe, Doug. "Bill Veeck Made Baseball Fun." *Capital Times and Wisconsin State Journal*, October 20, 2005.

Moffi, Larry. *The Conscience of the Game: Baseball Commissioners from Landis to Selig*.
———. *This Side of Cooperstown*. Iowa City: University of Iowa Press, 1996.

Moore, Joseph Thomas. *Pride Against Prejudice: The Biography of Larry Doby*. New York: Praeger, 1988.

Moore, William. "Bill Veeck's New Life." *Chicago Tribune*, February 11, 1962.

Muret, Don. " 'Turn Back the Clock': One of 49 Events on Chicago White Sox Promo." *Amusement Business*, May 2, 1994.

Murray, Jim. *Jim Murray: An Autobiography*. New York: Macmillan, 1993.

Myslenski, Skip. "Bill Veeck, the People's Maverick." *Chicago Tribune*, September 26, 1980.

Nelson, Murry R. *The National Basketball League: A History, 1935–1949*. Jefferson, NC: McFarland, 2009.

Newfield, Jack. *American Rebels*. New York: Thunder Mountain Press/Nation Books, 2003.

Neyer, Rob. *Rob Neyer's Big Book of Baseball Legends: The Truth, the Lies, and Everything Else*. New York: Fireside, 2008.

Odenkirk, James. *Plain Dealing: A Biography of Gordon Cobbledick*. Tempe, AZ: Spider-Naps, 1990.

O'Neil, Buck. *I Was Right on Time*. New York: Simon and Schuster, 1996.

O'Neil, Buck, with Steve Wulf and David Conrads. *I Had It Made*. New York: Fireside, 1996.

Ottley, Roi. *The Lonely Warrior: The Life and Times of Robert S. Abbott*. Chicago: Regnery, 1955.

Overmyer, James. *Queen of the Negro Leagues: Effa Manley and the Newark Eagles*. Lanham, MD: Scarecrow Trade, 2001.

Paige, Leroy. *Maybe I'll Pitch Forever: A Great Baseball Player Tells the Hilarious Story Behind the Legend*. Lincoln: University of Nebraska Press, 1993.

Paige, Leroy, as told to Hal Lebovitz. *Pitchin' Man: Satchel Paige's Own Story*. Westport, CT: Meckler, 1992.

Parker, Gary H. *Win or Go Home: Sudden Death Baseball*. Jefferson, NC: McFarland, 2002.

Patkin, Max, and Stan Hochman. *The Clown Prince of Baseball*. Waco, TX: WRS, 1994.

Pepe, Phil. "The Hustler Is Always Looking for the Big Score." *Scorebook* (Baseball Writers of America), 1978.

Peterson, Robert. *Cages to Jump Shots: Pro Basketball's Early Years*. Lincoln: University of Nebraska Press, 2002.

———. *Only the Ball Was White: A History of Legendary Black Players and All-Black Professional Teams*. New York: Oxford University Press, 1970.

Peverelly, Charles A. *The Book of American Pastimes, Containing a History of the Principal Base-Ball, Cricket, Rowing, and Yachting Clubs of the United States*. New York: Charles A. Peverelly, 1866.

Piersall, Jimmy, and Dick Whittingham. *The Truth Hurts*. Chicago: Contemporary Books, 1985.

Pluto, Terry. *Our Tribe: A Baseball Memoir*. New York: Simon and Schuster, 1999.

Pollock, Alan J. *Barnstorming to Heaven: Syd Pollock and His Great Black Teams*. Ed. James A Riley. Tuscaloosa: University of Alabama Press, 2006.

Posnanski, Joe. *The Soul of Baseball: A Road Trip Through Buck O'Neil's America*. New York: HarperCollins, 2007.

Povich, Shirley. *All Those Mornings . . . at the Post: The 20th Century in Sports from Famed "Washington Post" Columnist Shirley Povich*. New York: Public Affairs, 2005.

———. "Negro Has Found Real Democracy in Baseball." *Washington Post*, May 10, 1953.

Powers, Jimmy. *Baseball Personalities: Vivid Stories of More than 50 of the Most Colorful Ball Players of All Time*. New York: Rudolph Field, 1949.

Rampersad, Arnold. *Jackie Robinson: A Biography*. New York: Knopf, 1997.

Raphael, Steve, and Terry Brewster. "Bill Veeck: Send in the Clowns." *Friends*, May 1980.

Rapoport, Ron. "Veeck Legacy Glows on for Holiday Fetes." *Chicago Sun-Times*, December 24, 1986.

Ribowsky, Mark. *A Complete History of the Negro Leagues: 1884–1955*. New York: Citadel Press, 2002.

———. *Don't Look Back: Satchel Paige in the Shadows of Baseball*. New York: Simon and Schuster, 1994.

Richmond, Peter. *Ballpark: Camden Yards and the Building of an American Dream*. New York: Fireside, 1995.

Riess, Steven A. *Touching Base: Professional Baseball and American Culture in the Progressive Era*. Urbana: University of Illinois Press, 1999.

Riley, James A. *The Biographical Encyclopedia of the Negro Baseball Leagues*. New York: Carroll and Graf, 1994.

———. *Dandy, Day and the Devil*. Cocoa, FL: TK Publishers, 1987.

Ritter, Lawrence S. *The Glory of Their Times*. New York: Morrow, 1984.

Roberts, Howard. "Bill Veeck . . . Barnum of Baseball." *Modern Man*, June 1952.

Robinson, Frazier. *Catching Dreams: My Life in the Negro Baseball Leagues*. Syracuse, NY: Syracuse University Press, 1999.

Robinson, Jackie. *Baseball Has Done It*. Philadelphia: Lippincott, 1964.

———. "What's Wrong With Negro Baseball." *Ebony* 3, no. 8 (June 1948): 19–25.

Robinson, Jackie, and Alfred Duckett. *I Never Had It Made*. New York: G. P. Putnam's Sons, 1972.

Robinson, Jackie, as told to Wendell Smith. *Jackie Robinson: My Own Story*. New York: Greenburg, 1948.

Rogosin, Donn. *Invisible Men: Life in Baseball's Negro Leagues*. New York: Atheneum, 1983.

Rose, Cynthia. "Veeck—as in Wreck: The Autobiography of Bill Veeck." In *American Decades Primary Sources, vol. 5: 1940–1949*, ed. Cynthia Rose, 590–94. Detroit: Gale, 2004.

Rosebrook, Jeb Stuart. "Integration and the Early Years of Arizona Spring Training." In *Mining Towns to Major Leagues: A History of Arizona Baseball*, ed. Mike Holden. Cleveland: Society for American Baseball Research, 1999.

Rubin, Robert. *Satchel Paige: All-Time Baseball Great*. New York: G. P. Putnam's Sons, 1974.

Ruck, Rob. *Sandlot Seasons: Sport in Black Pittsburgh*. Urbana: University of Illinois Press, 1987.

Rusinack, Kelly, "Baseball on the Radical Agenda: The *Daily Worker* and *Sunday Worker* Journalistic Campaign to Desegregate Major League Baseball, 1933–1947." In *Jackie Robinson: Race, Sports, and the American Dream*, ed. Joseph Dorinson and Joram Warmund, 75–85. Armonk, NY: M. E. Sharpe, 1998.

Sandomir, Richard. "Jackie Robinson: Perspective—the Coverage." *New York Times*, April 13, 1997.

Sanford, David. "Edwards vs. Veeck vs. Edwards." *Skeptic*, September–October 1977.

Sangree, Allen. "Fans and Their Frenzies: The Wholesome Madness of Baseball." *Everybody's Magazine* 17, no. 3 (September 1907).

"Satchel" [editorial]. *New York Times*, June 10, 1982.

Schmuhl, Robert. "Bill Veeck Belongs in Hall of Fame." *Chicago Sun-Times*, July 16, 1996.

Schneider, Russell. *The Boys of the Summer of '48*. Urbana, IL: Sports Publishing, 1998.

Schoor, Gene. *Bob Feller: Hall of Fame Strikeout Star.* New York: Doubleday, 1962.

Schulian, John. *Twilight of the Long-Ball Gods.* Lincoln: University of Nebraska Press, 2005.

Scully, Gerald W. "Discrimination: The Case of Baseball." In *Government and the Sports Business,* ed. Roger G. Noll. Washington, DC: Brookings Institution, 1974.

Seymour, Harold. *Baseball: The People's Game.* New York: Oxford University Press, 1990.

Shane, Ted. "Bill Veeck—Bad Boy of Baseball." *Reader's Digest,* April 1952.

Shea, Stuart, with George Castle. *Wrigley Field: The Unauthorized Biography.* Washington, DC: Brassey's, 2004.

Sherman, Charles. "St. Louis' Iron Man." *St. Louis Globe-Democrat Tempo Magazine,* August 12, 1951, 8–10.

Shoemaker, Robert H. *The Best in Baseball.* New York: Thomas Y. Crowell, 1959.

Sickels, John. *Bob Feller: Ace of the Greatest Generation.* Dulles, VA: Potomac Books, 2004.

Siegel, Morris. "A Way Out." *Baseball Digest,* February 1967.

Silber, Irwin, with Lester Rodney. *Press Box Red: The Story of Lester Rodney, the Communist Who Helped Break the Color Line in American Sports.* Philadelphia: Temple University Press, 2002.

Simon, Scott. *Home and Away: Memoir of a Fan.* New York: Hyperion, 2000.

———. *Jackie Robinson and the Integration of Baseball.* Hoboken, NJ: John Wiley and Sons, 2002.

Smith, Curt. *America's Dizzy Dean.* St. Louis: Bethany Press, 1978.

Smith, Red. *Red Smith on Baseball: The Game's Greatest Writer on the Game's Greatest Years.* Chicago: Ivan R. Dee, 2000.

Smith, Robert. *Baseball in the Afternoon: Tales from a Bygone Era.* New York: Simon and Schuster, 1993.

Smyth, Jeanette. "Shrewd Pitches from the Artful Dodger." *Washington Post,* August 31, 1975.

Snyder, Brad. *Beyond the Shadow of the Senators: The Untold Story of the Homestead Grays and the Integration of Baseball.* New York: McGraw-Hill, 2003.

Solomon, Burt. *The Baseball Timeline: The Day-by-Day History of Baseball from Valley Forge to the Present Day.* New York: Avon Books, 1997.

Spink, J. G. Taylor. *Judge Landis and 25 Years of Baseball.* New York: Thomas Y. Crowell, 1947.

Stark, Douglas. "Paving the Way: History of Integration of African Americans into Professional Basketball League." *Basketball Digest,* February 2001.

Stengel, Casey, as told to Harry T. Paxton. *Casey at the Bat.* New York: Random House, 1962.

Stewart, Mark. "Bill Veeck: The Tucson Years." *Arizona Daily Star,* July 14, 1991.

Sugar, Bert Randolph. *Hit the Sign and Win a Free Suit of Clothes from Harry Finklestein.* Chicago: Contemporary Books, 1978.

Talley, Rick. *The Cubs of '69: Recollections of the Team That Should Have Been.* Chicago: McGraw-Hill Contemporary, 1989.

Terry, Clifford. "Veeck in Boston: Two Years at the Races." *Chicago Tribune,* April 4, 1971.

Tootle, Jim. "Bill Veeck and James Thurber: The Literary Origins of the Midget Pinch Hitter." *Nine* 10, no. 2 (Spring 2002).

Torrance, Roscoe C., and Robert F. Karolevitz. *Torchy!* Mission Hill, SD: Homestead, 1988.

Trouppe, Quincy. *20 Years Too Soon: Prelude to Integrated Baseball.* St. Louis: Missouri Historical Society, 1995.

Tye, Larry. *Satchel Paige: The Life and Times of an American Legend.* New York: Random House, 2009.

Tygiel, Jules. *Baseball's Great Experiment: Jackie Robinson and His Legacy.* New York: Oxford University Press, 1983.

———. *Extra Bases: Reflections on Jackie Robinson, Race, and Baseball History.* Lincoln: University of Nebraska Press, 2002.

———. *Pastime: Baseball as History.* New York: Oxford University Press, 2000.

———. "Revisiting Bill Veeck and the 1943 Phillies." *Baseball Research Journal* 35 (2007).

———. "Those Who Came After." *Sports Illustrated,* June 27, 1983.

United States Congress. *Hearings Held to Consider Future Use of Robert F. Kennedy Memorial Stadium, D.C., and Prospects for Location of Another Major League Baseball Franchise in D.C.* United States Senate, Committee on District of Columbia, December 13, 1971. (Veeck testimony pp. 110–30.)

———. *Organized Baseball, Report of the Subcommittee on Study of Monopoly Power of the Committee on the Judiciary.* United States House of Representatives, 82nd Congress, 2nd Session, report no. 632. Washington, DC: U.S. Government Printing Office, 1952.

Vandenberg, Bob. *'59: Summer of the Sox.* Champaign, IL: Sports Publishing, 1999.

Vass, George. *The Game I'll Never Forget.* Chicago: Bonus Books, 1999.

Veeck, Bill. "The Baseball Establishment." *Esquire,* August 1964.

———. "Dear Bowie: Here's Some Thoughts I've Had on Baseball . . ." *Boston Globe,* March 23, 1989.

———. "The Venerable Satch." *Elks Magazine,* April 1961.

———. "What's Left for the Left-Hander?" *Saturday Evening Post,* March 16, 1963.

———. "What's Wrong with Baseball . . . What Can Be Done About It." *Look,* April 12, 1949.

Veeck, Bill, as told to Gordon Cobbledick. "So You Want to Run a Ball Club?" *Saturday Evening Post,* April 23, 1949.

Veeck, Bill, with Ed Linn. "Back Where I Belong." *Sports Illustrated*, March 15, 1976.

———. *The Hustler's Handbook*. New York: G. P. Putnam's Sons, 1965.

———. *Thirty Tons a Day: The Rough-Riding Education of a Neophyte Racetrack Operator*. New York: Viking Press, 1972.

———. *Veeck—as in Wreck*. New York: G. P. Putnam's Sons, 1962.

Veeck, Bill, as told to Louie Robinson. "Are There Too Many Negroes in Baseball?" *Ebony*, June 1962.

Veeck, Mike. *Fun Is Good: How to Create Joy and Passion in Your Workplace and Career*. Emmaus, PA: Rodale Books, 2005.

Vincent, Fay. *The Only Game in Town: Baseball Stars of the 1930s and 1940s Talk About the Game They Loved*. New York: Simon and Schuster, 2006.

———. *We Would Have Played for Nothing: Baseball Stars of the 1950s and 1960s Talk About the Game They Loved*. New York: Simon and Schuster, 2008.

Voigt, David Q. *American Baseball*. 3 vols. University Park: Pennsylvania State University Press, 1983.

Wallop, Douglass. *Baseball: An Informal History*. New York: W. W. Norton, 1969.

Warfield, Don. *The Roaring Redhead: Larry MacPhail, Baseball's Great Innovator*. South Bend, IN: Diamond, 1987.

Westcott, Rich. *Mickey Vernon: The Gentleman First Baseman*. Philadelphia: Camino Books, 2005.

White, Solomon. *Sol White's Official Base Ball Guide*. Philadelphia, 1907. Reprint: Columbia, SC: Camden House, 1984.

Whitford, David. "Veeck Family Values." *Fortune Small Business*, July 1, 2003.

Wiggins, David. "Wendell Smith, the *Pittsburgh Courier-Journal* and the Campaign to Include Blacks in Organized Baseball, 1933–1945." *Journal of Sport History* 10, no. 2 (1989): 5–29.

Wilber, Cynthia J. *For the Love of the Game: Baseball Memories from the Men Who Were There*. New York: William Morrow, 1992.

Wiley, George. *Especially for Cleveland Fans: The 1948 Indians Remembered*. Minneapolis: Society for American Baseball Research, 1988.

Williams, Pat, with Michael Weinreb. *Marketing Your Dreams: Business and Life Lessons from Bill Veeck*. Champaign, IL: Sports Publishing, 2000.

Wolfe, Rich, and George Castle. *I Remember Harry Caray*. Champaign, IL: Sports Publishing, 1998.

Woodward, Stanley. *Sports Page*. New York: Greenwood Press, 1968.

Yardley, Jonathan. "The Man Who Brought Joy to Mudville." *Washington Post*, September 25, 2006.

Yoder, Robert M., and James S. Kearns. "Boy Magnate." *Saturday Evening Post*, August 28, 1943.

Zang, David W. *Fleet Walker's Divided Heart: The Life of Baseball's First Black Major Leaguer*. Lincoln: University of Nebraska Press, 1995.

Zimbalist, Andrew. *Baseball and Billions: A Probing Look Inside the Big Business of Our National Pastime.* New York: Basic, 1994.

———. *In the Best Interests of Baseball: The Revolutionary Reign of Bud Selig.* New York: Wiley, 2006.

Zimmerman, G. "Veeck . . . A New Bill for the White Sox," *Look,* August 4, 1959.

Zoltak, James. "Legendary Promoter Veeck Shares Tips at Stadium Managers Meet." *Amusement Business* 111, no. 7 (February 15, 1999).

Index

Image Credits

Bill Veeck Collection/The Baseball Reliquary: 4, 5, 7, 12, 15, 22, 41

Cleveland State University Library, *The Cleveland Press* Collection: 14, 16, 17, 18, 19, 21, 26, 38.

Family photos, courtesy of Fred Krehbiel: 1, 2, 3, 6, 32, 40

Jim Hansen, photographer, *LOOK* Magazine Collection, Library of Congress, Prints and Photographs Division, used with permission of Mrs. James T. Hansen: 27, 28, 29, 30, 31, 33, 34, 35, 36

Museum of Modern Art, Film Still Archives: 23

National Baseball Hall of Fame Library, Cooperstown, New York: 20, 25

National Baseball Hall of Fame Library, Cooperstown, New York, *LOOK* photo collection, photographs by Bob Sandberg: 8, 9, 10, 11

Robert Lerner, photographer, *LOOK* Magazine Collection, Library of Congress, Prints and Photographs Division, used with the permission of Mr. Lerner: 24

Paul Tenpenny collection, 13

Washington Star Collection, Washingtoniana Division, Martin Luther King Library, Washington D.C. Public Library: 37, 39.